LEGAL METHOD:
TEXT AND MATERIALS

SECOND EDITION

LEGAL METHOD:
TEXT AND MATERIALS

SECOND EDITION

by

CARL F. STYCHIN, B.A., LL.B., LL.M.
Professor of Law and Social Theory,
The University of Reading

and

LINDA MULCAHY, LL.B., LL.M., Ph.D.
Anniversary Professor of Law and Society,
Birkbeck, The University of London

LONDON
SWEET & MAXWELL
2003

First edition by Carl F. Stychin
Published 1999
Reprinted 2000
Reprinted 2001

This edition published in 2003 by
Sweet & Maxwell Limited of
100 Avenue Road,
London NW3 3PF
www.sweetandmaxwell.co.uk

Typeset by Servis Filmsetting Ltd, Manchester
Printed in Great Britain

No natural forests were destroyed to make this product,
only farmed timber was used and replanted.

A CIP catalogue record for this book is available from the British Library

ISBN 0 421 799 005

PREFACE

The first edition of this text emerged out of course materials developed over several years for the Legal Method module at Keele University. The aim of that course, of which Carl Stychin was course director from 1993–98, was to introduce students, not only to the "traditional" foundations of legal reasoning but also to more socio-legal and theoretical scholarship, including feminist and critical legal theories. This text carries on that approach. We have sought to provide students with a firm grounding in traditional legal methods and ways of understanding legal systems as well as providing them with a range of materials which will encourage them to critique approaches which privilege the statute and case report. We have aimed to create a sourcebook of materials and commentary, along with questions suitable for tutorials and essays, for introductory law courses, covering both "core" doctrinal material, as well as theoretical and empirical perspectives. In our view the best socio-legal and critical scholars are also those that can engage with a range of texts and perspectives.

This second edition offers updates to the original text together with new sections on dispute resolution which draw on course materials used by Linda Mulcahy at Birkbeck. The need for students to be introduced to a broader range of materials on informalism, mediation and negotiation than has traditionally been the case has been necessitated by the wide-ranging reforms introduced in the wake of the reports of Lord Woolf and Middleton. These reforms have done much to broaden our conception of the institutions and methods of dispute resolution which are provided, or sanctioned, by the state. As they have been implemented the need for changes in the way that law students are educated and prepared for academia and practice have also become apparent.

The title of the book is not intended to restrict its usage to "Legal Method" courses *per se*. The selection of topics includes material typically found in "English Legal System" and "Introduction to Law" courses. But our text aims to do more than describe the English legal system and the methods that are employed by lawyers in analysing texts. It also aims to critique and problematise the ideologies behind these systems and techniques. Obviously, the choice of topics and extracts for any casebook is eclectic, and, for an introductory casebook, even more so. While some may claim that the choice of material and the "spin" placed upon it lacks the "neutrality" expected of a casebook, one of the primary goals of this collection is to encourage students to question liberal ideals of "objectivity" and "neutrality", and to encourage critical thinking more generally. The aim is not to indoctrinate, but to stimulate lively debate and scepticism about legal authorities (including the casebook itself!). Too often, in our view, introductory materials fail to stimulate interest in the study of law and its political contexts, encouraging students to memorise facts rather than to think analytically and critically. We have tried to avoid that pitfall.

Each chapter contains sufficient material for a tutorial or seminar and poses a series of questions or exercises and commentaries which aim to guide students in their reading and focus their attention on key points. Each chapter contains sufficient material for one seminar and is self-contained. In selecting extracts and drafting our commentary, our aim has been to familiarise students with the most important work in the field as well as encouraging them to develop their ability to argue a point by use of description, analysis and critique. Because the text seeks to introduce students to theory at an early stage in their legal education, we have attempted to "unpack" the material where necessary. The commentary which accompanies each extract is intended as a "roadmap" through the materials, particularly the more theoretically challenging excerpts. We owe a special debt of gratitude to Martha-Marie Kleinhans, who took responsibility for Chapter 2. We have deferred completely to our colleague and friend's expertise in comparative legal traditions in the editing of this collection, and we thank her for her insightful contribution.

Finally, on a personal note, Carl Stychin would like again to thank his former colleagues at Keele University, where the first edition of this book began. Special thanks to Tony Dugdale, who provided a great deal of assistance, support, and ideas, in the original design of the module. Carl Stychin would also like to thank his colleagues at the University of Reading. Linda Mulcahy's thanks go to her more unconventional tutors over the years and colleagues at Birkbeck. We both owe a debt of gratitude to Marie Selwood without whom the updating and checking of the text would have been much more time consuming and much less fun. Our greatest debt, though, is owed to our legal method students at Keele, Reading and Birkbeck who withstood our attempts at experimentation in the design of our respective courses, and whose enthusiasm we will always appreciate and remember.

Carl F. Stychin and Linda Mulcahy
London
May 2003

ACKNOWLEDGMENTS

Grateful acknowledgment is made to the following authors and publishers for permission to quote from their works:

ABEL-SMITH, B and STEVENS, R.: *In Search of Justice: Society and the Legal System* (Penguin, 1968)

ABRAMCZYK, J.: "The Tyranny of the Majority: Liberalism in Legal Education" (1992) 5 *Canadian Journal of Women and the Law* 442. Reprinted by permission of University of Toronto Press Incorporated

ALDER, J.: *Constitutional and Administrative Law* (3rd ed., Palgrave Macmillan, 1999)

ALTMAN, A.: *Critical Legal Studies: A Liberal Critique* (Princeton University Press, 1993). Copyright © 1993 by PUP. Reprinted by permission of Princeton University Press

ARMSTRONG, N.: "Making Tracks" in *Reform of Civil Procedure: Essays on 'Access to Justice'*, eds. A.A.S. Zuckerman and Ross Cranston (Clarendon Press, 1995). Copyright © The Several Contributors and, in this collection, Adrian Zuckerman and Ross Cranston 1995

ATIYAH, P.S.: *Law and Modern Society* (2nd ed., Oxford University Press, 1995). Copyright © P.S. Atiyah 1983, 1995

BAKER, J.H.: "Statutory Interpretation and Parliamentary Intention" (1993) 52 C.L.J. 353, Cambridge University Press

BALDWIN, J.: "Raising the Small Claims Limit" in *Reform of Civil Procedure: Essays on 'Access to Justice'*, eds. A.A.S. Zuckerman and Ross Cranston (Clarendon Press, 1995). Copyright © The Several Contributors and, in this collection, Adrian Zuckerman and Ross Cranston 1995

BALDWIN, J.: "The adjudication of claims" (June 5, 1992) 142 NLJ 6555, pp.794–996, Butterworths. Copyright © John Baldwin 1992

BALE, C.G.: "Parliamentary Debates and Statutory Interpretation: Switching on the Light or Rummaging in the Ashcans of the Legislative Process" (1995) 74 *Canadian Bar Review* 1, Canadian Bar Association. Copyright © Canadian Bar Review and C.G. Bale

BATES, T. St. J.N.: "The Contemporary Use of Legislative History in the United Kingdom" (1995) 54 C.L.J. 127, Cambridge University Press

BELL, J.: *French Legal Cultures* (Butterworths, 2001)

BELL, J. and ENGLE, SIR G.: *Cross on Statutory Interpretation* (3rd ed., Butterworths, 1995)

BOGDANOR, V.: *Devolution in the United Kingdom* (Oxford University Press, 1999). Reproduced with the permission of A.P Watt Ltd on behalf of Vernon Bogdanor

BOON, A.: "History is Past Politics: A Critique of the Legal Skills Movement in England and Wales" Vol.25(1) *Journal of Law and Society*, Blackwell Publishers

BOON, A., DUFF, L. and SHINER, M.: "Career Paths and Choices in a Highly differentiated profession: the position of newly qualified solicitors" (2001) 64(4) M.L.R. 567, Blackwell Publishers

BRADLEY, A.W.: "The Sovereignty of Parliament—Form or Substance?", in *The Changing Constitution,* eds. Jeffrey Jowell and Dawn Oliver (4th ed., Oxford University Press, 2000)

BROWN, H. and MARRIOT, A.: *ADR Principles and Practice* (Sweet and Maxwell, 1993; 2nd ed., Sweet and Maxwell, 1999)

BUSH, R. and FOLGER, J.: *The Promise of Mediation* (Jossey-Bass, San Francisco, 1994). This material is used by permission of John Wiley & Sons, Inc.

BUTTERWORTHS LAW PUBLISHERS LTD: All England Law Reports; New Law Journal

CANE, P.: *The Anatomy of Tort Law* (Hart Publishing, 1997)

CAPPELLETTI, M.: "Alternative Dispute Resolution Processes within the Framework of the World-Wide Access-to-Justice Movement" (1993) 56 M.L.R. 282. Copyright © Modern Law Review Ltd

COLLINS, H.: *Marxism and Law* (Clarendon Press, 1982). Copyright © Hugh Collins 1982

CONAGHAN, J.: "Feminist Perspectives on the Law of Tort" in *The Critical Lawyers' Handbook 2,* eds. Paddy Ireland and Per Laleng (Pluto Press, 1997)

CONAGHAN, J. and MANSELL, W.: *The Wrongs of Tort* (2nd ed., Pluto Press, 1999)

COTTERRELL, R.: *The Politics of Jurisprudence* (Butterworths, 1989). Copyright © R. Cotterrell 1989. A second edition of this book is now available, published 2003 by LexisNexis UK

—:*The Sociology of Law* (2nd ed., Butterworths, 1992). Copyright © R. Cotterrell 1992

COWNIE, F. and BRADNEY, A.: *English Legal System in Context* (2nd ed., Butterworths, 2000)

CRAIG, P.: "Formal and Substantive Conceptions of the Rule of Law: An Analytical Framework" [1997] *Public Law* 467, Sweet and Maxwell

CRAIG, P. and DE BÚRCA, G.: *EU Law: Text, Cases and Materials* (3rd ed., Oxford University Press, 2002)

CRENSHAW, K., GOTANDA, N., PELLER, G. and THOMAS, K.: *Critical Race Theory: The Key Writings that Formed the Movement* (The New Press, New York, 1995). Copyright © 1995. Reprinted by permission of The New Press (800) 233-4830

CROSS, R. and HARRIS, J.W.: *Precedent in English Law* (4th ed., Clarendon Press, 1991). Copyright © Lady Cross and Jim Harris 1991

DARBYSHIRE, P.: *Eddey on the English Legal System* (7th ed., Sweet and Maxwell, 2001)

DAVIES, M.: *Asking the Law Question* (The Law Book Company, Sydney, 1994). Reproduced with the express permission of © Lawbook Co, part of Thomson Legal & Regulatory Limited, *www.thomson.com.au*

DEHN, QC, C.: "The Woolf Report: Against the Public Interest?" in *Reform of Civil Procedure: Essays on 'Access to Justice',* eds. A.A.S. Zuckerman and Ross Cranston (Clarendon Press, 1995). Copyright © The Several Contributors and, in this collection, Adrian Zuckerman and Ross Cranston 1995

DENNING, LORD.: *The Discipline of Law* (Butterworths, 1979)

DICEY, A.V.: *An Introduction to the Law of the Constitution* (8th ed., Macmillan, 1915). Copyright Albert Venn Dicey 1915

DOWNES, T.A.: *Textbook on Contract* (5th ed., Blackstone Press, 1997)

DWORKIN, R.: *Law's Empire* (HarperCollins, 1986). Reprinted by permission of HarperCollins Publishers Ltd. © Ronald Dworkin 1986

ECLIPSE: *Dawkins v Department of Environment* [1993] I.R.L.R. 284

ELLIOT, C. and QUINN, F.: *English Legal System* (3rd ed., Longman, 2000)

EWING, K.D.: "The Human Rights Act and Parliamentary Democracy" (1999) 62 M.L.R. 79, Blackwell Publishers

FARRAR, J.D. and DUGDALE, A.M.: *Introduction to Legal Method* (3rd ed., Sweet and Maxwell, 1990)

FISS, O.M.: "Against Settlement" (1984) 93 *Yale Law Journal* 1073. Reprinted by permission of The Yale Law Journal Company and William S. Hein Company from <u>The Yale Law Journal</u>, Vol.93, pages <u>1073–1090</u>

FLETCHER, G.P.: *The Basic Concepts of Legal Thought* (Oxford University Press, 1996). Copyright © 1996 by George P. Fletcher. Used by permission of Oxford University Press, Inc.

FRANK, J.: *Law and the Modern Mind* (Peter Smith Publishing, 1970)

GELDART, W.: *Introduction to English Law* (11th ed., Oxford University Press, 1995)

GENN, H.: "Access to Just Settlements: The Case of Medical Negligence" in *Reform of Civil Procedure: Essays on 'Access to Justice'*, eds. A.A.S. Zuckerman and Ross Cranston (Clarendon Press, 1995). Copyright © The Several Contributors and, in this collection, Adrian Zuckerman and Ross Cranston 1995

—:*The Central London County Court Pilot Mediation Scheme Evaluation Report* (1998), *www.lcd.gov.uk/research/1998/598esfr*

—: *Mediation in Action: Resolving Court Disputes without Trial*, published by the Calouste Gulbenkian Foundation (1999) pp.22–25

—: "Tribunals and Informal Justice" (1993) 56 M.L.R. 393, Blackwell Publishers

GLENN, H.P.: *Legal Traditions of the World: Sustainable Diversity in Law* (Oxford University Press, 2000)

GOODRICH, P.: *Reading the Law* (Blackwell Publishers, 1986)

GRAYCAR, R.: "The Gender of Judgments: An Introduction" in *Public and Private*, ed. Margaret Thornton (Oxford University Press, Melbourne, 1995) © Oxford University Press *www.oup.com.au*. Reproduced by permission of Oxford University Press Australia

GRIFFITH, J.A.G.: *The Politics of the Judiciary* (4th ed., Harper Collins, 1991). Reprinted by permission of HarperCollins Publishers Ltd. and J.A.G. Griffith © J.A.G. Griffith 1991

GRILLO, T.: "The Mediation Alternative: Process Dangers for Women" (1991) 100 *Yale Law Journal* 1545. Reprinted by permission of The Yale Law Journal Company

HARDEN, I. and LEWIS, N.: *The Noble Lie: The British constitution and the rule of law* (Hutchinson, 1986)

HARRIS, P.: *An Introduction to Law* (5th ed., Butterworths, 1997; 6th ed., Butterworths, 2002)

HARTLEY, T.C.: "Five Forms of Uncertainty in European Community Law" (1996) 55 C.L.J. 265, Cambridge University Press

HER MAJESTY'S STATIONERY OFFICE: *Human Rights Bill*. Crown copyright material is reproduced with the permission of the Controller of HMSO and the Queen's Printer for Scotland

HIBBITTS, B.J.: "The Politics of Principle: Albert Venn Dicey and the Rule of Law" (1994) 23 *Anglo-American Law Review* 25, Tolley

HOWARTH, D.: *Textbook on Tort* (Butterworths, 1995)

IRVINE OF LAIRG, LORD .: "The Development of Human Rights in Britain under an Incorporated Convention on Human Rights" [1998] *Public Law* 221, Sweet and Maxwell

JACKSON, P. and LEOPOLD, P.: *O. Hood Phillips & Jackson: Constitutional and Administrative Law* (8th ed., Sweet and Maxwell, 2001)

JOWELL, J.: "The Rule of Law Today", in *The Changing Constitution*, eds. Jeffrey Jowell and Dawn Oliver (4th ed., Oxford University Press, 2000)

KAIRYS, D.: *The Politics of Law: A Progressive Critique* (3rd ed., Basic Books, New York, 1998). Copyright 1998 by PERSEUS BOOKS GROUP. Reproduced with permission of PERSEUS BOOKS GROUP in the format Other Book via Copyright Clearance Center

KLUG, F. and O'BRIEN, C.: "The First Two Years of the Human Rights Act" [2002] *Public Law* 649, Sweet and Maxwell

KWAW, E.M.A.: *The Guide to Legal Analysis, Legal Methodology and Legal Writing* (Emond Montgomery Publications, 1992). Reproduced with the express permission of Emond Montgomery Publications

LE SUEUR, A., HERBERG, J. and ENGLISH, R. (eds): *Principles of Public Law* (2nd ed., Cavendish Publishing, London, 1999)

LESTER OF HERNE HILL Q.C., LORD.: "Human rights and the British Constitution", in *The Changing Constitution,* eds. Jeffrey Jowell and Dawn Oliver, (4th ed., Oxford University Press, 2000)

LEWIS, G.: *Lord Atkin* (Butterworths, 1983)

LLEWLLYN, K.N.: *The Bramble Bush* (Oceana Publications, 1996)

LORD CHANCELLOR'S DEPARTMENT: "Lord Chancellor Seeks More Women Judges" (Press Release April 25, 1998); "Lord Chancellor Set to Announce Reforms for Civil Appeal System" (Press Release July 22, 1998). Crown copyright material is reproduced with the permission of the Controller of HMSO and the Queen's Printer for Scotland

MACCORMICK, N.: *Legal Reasoning and Legal Theory* (Clarendon Press, 1978)

MANCHESTER, C., SALTER, D. and MOODIE, P.: *Exploring the Law: The Dynamics of Precedent and Statutory Interpretation* (Sweet and Maxwell, 2000)

MANSELL, W., METEYARD, B. and THOMPSON, A.: *A Critical Introduction to Law* (Cavendish Publishing, London, 1995; 2nd ed., Cavendish Publishing, London, 1999)

MARKESINIS, B. S.: "A Matter of Style" (1994) 110 L.Q.R. 607, Sweet and Maxwell

MARSHALL, G.: "Interpreting Interpretation in the Human Rights Bill" [1998] *Public Law* 167, Sweet and Maxwell

MCLEOD, I.: *Legal Method* (4th ed., Palgrave Macmillan, 2002)

MENSKI, W.: "Race and Law" in *The Critical Lawyers' Handbook 2*, eds. Paddy Ireland and Per Laleng (Pluto Press, 1997)

MIERS, D.: "Taxing Perks and Interpreting Statutes: *Pepper v Hart*" (1993) 56 M.L.R. 695, Blackwell Publishers

MOSSMAN, M.J.: "Feminism and Legal Method: The Difference it Makes". Copyright © 1991 from *At the Boundaries of Law*, eds. Martha Albertson Fineman and Nancy Sweet Thomadsen (Routledge, 1991). Reproduced by permission of Routledge/Taylor & Francis Books, Inc.

MULCAHY, L.: "Can Leopards Change their Spots? An Evaluation of the Role of Lawyers in Medical Negligence Mediation" (2001) Vol.8 No.3 *International Journal of the Legal Profession* pp.203–204. Published by Taylor & Francis Ltd *www.tandf.co.uk/journals*

NICHOLAS, B.: *The French Law of Contract* (2nd ed., Clarendon Press, 1992). Copyright © J.K.B.M. Nicholas 1992

OFFICE FOR OFFICIAL PUBLICATIONS OF THE EUROPEAN COMMUNITIES: *The Queen v Immigration Appeal, ex parte Antonissen* [1991] E.C.R. 1–745. Reproduced with permission from the European Communities. Only European Community's legislation printed in the Official Journal of the European Union is deemed to be authentic. *www.europa.eu.int/eur-lex*

OXFORD UNIVERSITY PRESS Titles; CLARENDON PRESS Titles; BLACKSTONE PRESS Titles: Reprinted by permission of Oxford University Press

PARTINGTON, M.: *An Introduction to the English Legal System* (Oxford University Press, 2000)

PATERSON, A.: "The Racial, Ethnic and Cultural Values Underpinning Current Legal

Education", in *The Critical Lawyers' Handbook 2*, eds. Paddy Ireland and Per Laleng (Pluto Press, 1997)

RIFKIN, J.: "Mediation from a Feminist Perspective: Promise and Problems" (1984) 2.2 *Law & Inequality: A Journal of Theory and Practice* 21, University of Minnesota Law School

SCOTTISH OFFICE: *Scotland's Parliament* (Scottish Office White Paper). Crown copyright material is reproduced with the permission of the Controller of HMSO and the Queen's Printer for Scotland

SHAW, J.: *Law of the European Union* (3rd ed., Palgrave Macmillan, 2000)

SHELDON, S.: *Beyond Control: Medical Power and Abortion Law* (Pluto Press, 1997)

SLAPPER, G. and KELLY, D.: *The English Legal System* (5th ed., Cavendish Publishing, London, 2001)

SMART, C.: *Feminism and the Power of Law* (Routledge, 1989)

STEYN, J.: "*Pepper v Hart*; A Re-examination" (2001) *Oxford Journal of Legal Studies* 59, Oxford University Press

STREET, H.: *Justice in the Welfare State* (2nd ed., Stevens & Sons, 1975)

STYCHIN, C.F.: *Law's Desire: Sexuality and the Limits of Justice* (Routledge, 1995)

SUGARMAN, D.: "'A Hatred of Disorder': Legal Science, Liberalism and Imperialism" in *Dangerous Supplements*, ed. Peter Fitzpatrick (Pluto Press, 1991)

THE INCORPORATED COUNCIL OF LAW REPORTING FOR ENGLAND AND WALES: Weekly Law Reports; Queen's Bench Division; Appeal Cases; King's Bench Law Reports

THOMPSON, E.P.: *Whigs and Hunters* (Penguin Books, 1990)

TOMKINS, A.: "Introduction: on being sceptical about human rights", in Sceptical Essays on Human Rights, eds. Campbell, Ewing and Tomkins (Oxford University Press, Oxford, 2001)

UNITED STATES GOVERNMENT PRINTING OFFICE: *McBoyle v USA* (1930) 293 US 25

VAGO, S.: *Law and Society* (7th ed., Prentice Hall, 2003) © 2003. Reprinted by permission of Pearson Education, Inc., Upper Saddle River, NJ

VANDEVELDE, K.J.: *Thinking Like a Lawyer* (Westview Press, 1996). Copyright © 1996 by Westview Press, Inc., a member of Perseus Books, L.L.C.

WALDRON, J.: *The Law* (Routledge, 1990)

WELSH OFFICE: *National Assembly for Wales* (Welsh Office White Paper). Crown copyright material is reproduced with the permission of the Controller of HMSO and the Queen's Printer for Scotland

WERRO, F.: "Notes on the Purpose and Aims of Comparative Law" (2001) 75 Tul. L. Rev. 1225. Reprinted with the permission of the Tulane Law Review Association, which holds the copyright

WILLIAMS, P.J.: *The Alchemy of Race and Rights* (Harvard University Press, 1991). Copyright © 1991 by the President and Fellows of Harvard College

WOOLF, LORD.: *Access to Justice: Interim report* (June 1995) *www.lcd.gov.uk*

ZANDER, M.: "Are there any clothes for the Emperor to wear?" (February 3, 1995) 145 NLJ 6681, pp.154–156, Butterworths. Copyright © Michael Zander 1995

ZUCKERMAN, A.A.S.: "Lord Woolf's Access to Justice: *Plus ça change . . .*" (1996) 59 M.L.R. 773, Blackwell Publishers

ZWEIGERT, K. and KÖTZ, H.: *Introduction to Comparative Law* (3rd ed., Clarendon Press, 1998)

CONTENTS

PART THREE: INTERPRETING STATUTES

PART FOUR: INTERPRETING CASES

PART FIVE: PEOPLE, SYSTEMS AND METHODS

TABLE OF CASES

Chang's Book/American Civil Engineers #1, for the information of Koh Abe (see S. I.)...

28 n.s.u. see Fri, one Gebrek do die Disziplinen in ein-seine waluerer, (1999) atl. 3768, (1996) H.E. 718 (pp., 364, L. 2049, (pp., 177, v.a.), p.p.(1963) La (1)... 19 c (1999) ...

TABLE OF STATUTES

TABLE OF STATUTORY INSTRUMENTS

PART ONE: KEY IDEAS

1

INTRODUCTION TO LEGAL METHODS: APPROACHES TO LAW AND LEGAL REASONING

In this first chapter, we begin with an introduction to legal reasoning and analysis. As with all the other chapters we have provided you with extracts from important books and articles in the field. Our commentary and questions help to guide you around these writings. The advantage of a cases and materials book over and above a sole-authored text is that it exposes you to a range of different ideas about law which have been espoused by a variety of authors associated with very different schools of thought. The readings in this first chapter are designed to help you to think critically about the basic question "what is law", and to consider a variety of different approaches to answering the question. One of the famous debates over the character of law involves two divergent ways of thinking about law—positivism and natural law—and we consider those schools of thought in this chapter. The debate between positivists and natural lawyers is one of the most famous confrontations in legal theory and continues to have much resonance in contemporary debates about the functions and limits of law. Following on from that debate, the chapter includes a range of readings which inquire into the characteristics of law and legal reasoning from a variety of other perspectives. Many of these readings apply ways of thinking developed in other academic disciplines—such as sociology—to legal analysis. This type of academic work is known as "interdisciplinary", because it involves bringing the ideas and understandings which have been developed in one field of inquiry to the study of law. This material is important because it can provide lawyers (and students of law) with a broader and deeper understanding of the way law operates in practice and the devices which are sometimes used to privilege the interests of some sections of society over others.

These selections might be characterised as critical, because of the ways in which the authors interrogate assumptions about the functions of law and its effectiveness.

The authors argue that the way in which students are taught—and what they are taught—is highly political, but that the politics of law is often disguised and made to appear politically neutral and objective. For example, law students are taught that there is a "method" to legal reasoning but you should also ask yourself, even while you are learning this method, whether there are not other methods of analysing problems which might be preferable to legal reasoning. Thus, one of the aims of this chapter (and, indeed, this book) is to provoke you to think critically about law, legal reasoning, and the way in which law is taught to students in universities.

WHAT IS THE LAW?

If you begin by asking yourself what we mean by the term "law", you will probably assume that it presupposes the existence of a society. Law is often conceived, by lawyers and others alike, as a set of rules which govern a society and create a structure of authority or government to run the social order. In the seventeenth century, the English writer Thomas Hobbes explained and justified the existence of rules and authority in terms of a "social contract". In our original state, Hobbes argued, we lived without rules, which ensured that life was (in his famous phrase) nasty, brutish, and short. In time, people came to realise that an alternative might be preferable, and they entered into agreements with each other; creating rules which governed their relationships. He argued that law might be understood as a social contract, a set of rules and regulations enforced by political institutions, which we refer to as the state or government. In this theory, the idea of law also includes the notion of enforcement of the rules with punishments (or *sanctions*) which follow from the disobedience of rules. Thus, for proponents of social contract theory, law might be said to reflect the values of the population, and this value system, which the legal system advances, might also be called an *ideology*, made up of political, economic, moral and social values. As we will see throughout this book, most of us never *actually* agreed to the laws in force in this society, and the ideology which underpins the legal system may well reflect the interests and beliefs of only some people. But the idea that there is an ideology which underpins the legal order is one to which we shall frequently return. We will also see in this chapter that understanding law simply as a set of rules does not fully answer the question of what constitutes law.

NOTES AND QUESTIONS

- We will begin with an historical consideration of the question of what law is but before doing so we would like you to attempt to define law for yourself. You have probably been asked why you want to study law. Reflecting on the answers you have given, try to analyse what it is that you imagine when you think about law. Does your definition of law involve people, places, things, processes or concepts?

- Where do the ideas that fuel law come from? What is the source of its authority?

In the following extract, Peter Goodrich makes an important distinction between the ideas that shape law and the places it is made.

Peter Goodrich, *Reading the Law* (Blackwell, Oxford, 1986), pp.3–13:

"One of the most longstanding and intractable of the debates surrounding the study of law concerns the nature and definition of the term law itself. At different times and in different cultures the term law may be taken to refer to institutions as radically different as magic, song-contests, vendetta (feuding), trial by ordeal and the rules of war. Even within the relative homogeneity of the western legal tradition, law has taken very diverse forms and has been derived from very distinct sources. At different stages in the development of western law it has been said variously that law 'comes from' God, from nature or the 'natural order of things', from the monarch, from the various forms of commonwealth or sovereignty, from the 'spirit of the people' or from custom and social usage, to name but a few of the more acceptable or prevalent views. Obviously the way in which we define law will, in terms of the examples given, make a considerable difference to the requisite manner of its study; if law comes from God then it would be best to be theologians or priests for the purposes of studying it professionally, whereas if it is really self-help or vendetta then skill with an axe or a gun is more likely to be useful than any knowledge of rules or texts or any ability to argue. The question posed by the difficulty of defining law is a serious practical problem for students and practitioners of the law, and it raises directly important issues of how law is to be differentiated from other social phenomena. Such issues go to the very heart of the professional status of law as a discipline and indeed of lawyers as its interpreters. [Here] we shall outline the traditional modes of defining law by reference to its ideational (conceptual) and institutional (legal) sources and shall then comment more broadly upon the practical meaning of the status law. . . .

To claim that law is a distinct enterprise, that it is independent of other forms of social control and requires institutions and experts, indeed a science, for its proper organization and functioning, is a fairly constant claim within the western legal tradition. Despite the apparent diversity of both the form and the content of law during the course of its lengthy history and of the very different social, political and economic roles played by the law, the legal institution itself has maintained a virtually uninterrupted doctrinal belief in the distinctiveness of law, a belief in its unity and its separation from other phenomena of social control. The two claims, those of unity and of separation, have traditionally been closely linked in legal doctrine; law is kept separate and distinct from other institutions and forms of control precisely by virtue of being a unity, by virtue of having an 'essential' characteristic which distinguishes law from all else. That 'essence' or unifying feature of law has been variable in its content but relatively constant in its form: the formal unity of law has traditionally been based upon its derivation from an absolute source or origin; 'a unitary necessity or cause' is singled out as the basis and origin of all law. Although the content of the ideational source of law has varied within legal doctrine, as we shall see, from being the divine commandments, to the dictates of nature or 'natural law', justice, the commands of the sovereign or even the logical entailments of a basic rule or norm, the conceptual characteristics of the absolute source of law do not greatly alter. The divine origin of law becomes the secular sovereign, the State or even the 'will of the people', but as a source of law it retains its quality as an external and absolute justification for legal regulation, discipline and law. This external, non-legal, legitimation of the legal order provides the law with its ideational unity and renders the wide spectrum of substantive rules into a 'system' of rules. . . . The ideational source of law refers to the 'idea' or 'belief' that lies at the basis of the system of law and provides, either directly or indirectly, an answer to the question of why law is authoritative, the question of why it should be obeyed. The commands and the judgments traditionally obeyed as 'the law' within a given community must 'come from' somewhere or be derived from some acceptable—even if mythical or notional—conceptual source of law. The question of the ideational source of law here invokes the profound and extremely contentious issue of the role of law as the form of communal order: what is it that binds the community, that gives rise to the sense of belonging and the habit of obeying which seem, historically, to be inseparable social functions? We cannot here endeavour to answer directly such questions but we can point to the traditional doctrinal resolutions to the problem of the authority or ideational source and legitimacy of law, and we can also refer to the importance that this definition of law in terms of its source has for legal practice, for the interpretation and application of law. . . .

The assumptions that lawyers make as to the inevitability, the validity and the moral benefit of legal regulation are crucial to their practice and to the maintenance of legal rules, to the ideology of law within the industrialized western nations. Such assumptions as to the conceptual unity of law are, however, increasingly infrequently utilized as explicit sources of law, reference to moral, political and economic factors generally being seen as a function of interpretation and argumentation—of implicit or tacit sources of law—rather than of formally designated legal authority. At the same time as stressing the practical importance of the ideational source of law, we would also rapidly point out that the abstract and external, ideational source of law is neither the most obvious nor the most frequently stated meaning of source of law in contemporary legal cultures. The preferred view is currently one which stresses the institutional sources of law rather than directly or consciously elaborating the myth of an origin or essence of law or indeed the dogmatic status of legal science or legal reason as sources of law. The current legal wisdom views law as a tradition and as a process or practice of regulation. Rather than defining law, legal doctrine is now more content to see it as a series of traditionally established texts and similarly established techniques for the interpretation of those texts . . . The institutional source of law is here seen to be the established practice of the legal institution and of its officials—law is taken to be what lawyers 'recognize' as law."

Our focus in this chapter will be on conceptual or ideational sources for the definition of law. In later chapters, we will shift to institutional sources for understanding what counts as law. The difficulty of defining what "law" is should be readily apparent if we think, for a moment, of the different ways in which the term is used in the English language. It encompasses both scientific laws (such as the law of gravity), and laws created to govern human behaviour. The different ways in which the term is used also lead us to a consideration of the idea of *positivism* as an approach to understanding law.

George P. Fletcher, *Basic Concepts of Legal Thought* (Oxford University Press, New York, 1996), pp.28–38:

"When a legislature enacts a proposed law, the law is called a statute or statutory law. When a scientist validates a hypothesis, he or she confirms a scientific law. This correlation in the use of the word 'law' holds across a large number of languages. This usage of the word 'law' (*Gesetz* in (German), *loi* (French), *zakon* (Russian), *ley* (Spanish) or *hok* (Hebrew)) should make us sit up and take notice. Wherever you go in Europe or the Middle East, you will hear lawyers referring to the work product of their parliaments in the same idiom as physics teachers use to describe the law of gravity or the second law of thermodynamics. This is true, we should note, only for the word used to refer to the law laid down by an authoritative legislature. The notion of 'higher law' as expressed in the terms like *Recht* and *droit* does not fit this pattern. There may, of course, be exceptions, but the correlation between the word for legislated law and scientific law is sufficiently strong that we must wonder about its implications.

Why should one think about human laws as though they were akin to scientific laws? Do we think that when Congress enacts a law, its action will be translated automatically into conforming behavior? Perhaps the question should be put the other way around: Do we expect falling objects to obey the law in the way that humans are expected to obey the criminal law? It seems that either there is some important point underlying the persistent use of the same word for human and scientific laws or, alternatively, we are dreadfully confused.

We are not confused. Nor are we fully conscious of the ways in which the po
of scientific laws, lurking in the background, influences our thinking about l
of law stands, more than anything, for inevitability. When a law applies, thin
otherwise; they conform necessarily to the law. Scientific laws represent more ᴜᴜᴜ ʝ__
observed correlation between cause and effect. As the eighteenth-century German philosopher Immanuel Kant put it in developing his theory of causation, the very fact that we
perceive causal relationships means that we bring to our observations an innate notion of
necessary connection. We see necessity in the spring sun's melting of winter's ice and therefore we describe the relationship as a causal law. To speak about laws, then, is to speak
about necessity.

One thing we know for sure, however, is that human laws are not necessarily obeyed.
Legislatures can pass laws telling people how to behave, but there is no necessary response
from the public at large. Sometimes people conform to changes in the statutory law; sometimes they continue to do what they want to, despite new decrees from the powers that be.
This is particularly the case if the law seeks to change pleasurable habits, such as those connected to smoking, drinking, using drugs, or sex. Yet there is an element of inevitability or
necessity in human laws as well as scientific laws. The necessity arises not in the response
of state officials to violations of the law. Representatives of the state assume that violations
of the law necessitate a response. The most familiar of these responses is criminal condemnation and punishment. But the range of possible responses includes compensation for
injury and judicial injunction to compel compliance with the law.

One assumption unites the phenomena of scientific law, as common people perceive
law in nature, and laws by which society lives. The facts may diverge from the law. When
a divergence of this sort occurs under scientific laws, the appropriate remedy is to reformulate the law. When, for example, the evidence became inescapable that the planets
moved in elliptical orbits rather than in perfect circles, the response was to abandon
Copernicus's model and adopt one that better fit the facts. When a similar divergence
occurs in the realm of human conduct under human laws, we assume that the right thing
to do is to change not the law, but rather to discipline the deviant conduct. This need to
change conduct produces the practices of stigmatization, sanctioning, and punishment
that some philosophers, call positivists, have taken to be the essence of the legal system.
The positivist premise is that a legal system worth its name must use force to close the gap
between norms and actual behavior. The nineteenth-century German philosopher G.W.F.
Hegel wrote in metaphysical terms of the criminal's Wrong displacing Society's Right,
with punishment of the criminal as the only means of reinstating Right over Wrong. We
would not so readily engage in this assumption, were it not for the association in our
thinking between scientific and human laws. The idea of law carries with it the ideal of
full compliance. . . .

Antipositivists deny the proposition that 'all law is enacted law.' They claim that some
principles of law simply exist and are perceived within a particular legal culture. As we have
noted, this second, indwelling conception of law is expressed in the Continental European
languages as *Recht* (German), *droit* (French), *pravo* (Russian), *derecho* (Spanish). English
originally used the term 'Right' as the analogue to *Recht*. This comes through clearly in the
seventeenth-century English decision, Dr Bonham's case, in which the great English judge
Lord Coke (pronounced: Cook) declared a statute of Parliament void as a violation of
'common right and reason.' The assumption guiding Coke's reasoning was that the court
could perceive, without a written source to back it up, what 'common right' requires. If the
will of Parliament was at odds with the court's perception, then so much the worse for
Parliament. . . .

It is hard to know why the term Right has atrophied in English usage. The idea survives
in Continental European languages, but the proper terminology now eludes lawyers in the
common law tradition. It may be that a long line of positivist legal thinkers, extending from
Thomas Hobbes in the seventeenth century to H.L.A. Hart in the twentieth century, has
influenced the language we use in discussing jurisprudence. Admittedly, the notion of
Right survives in the idiom of individual and human rights. . . . Consider the debate
between those who advocate a pregnant woman's right to an abortion and those who insist

upon the fetus's right to life. Both sides of the debate treat these asserted rights as morally true. In this respect debates about personal or human rights fulfill the normative role of the abstract theory of Right in Continental European legal cultures. . . .

The debate between the positivists and the nonpositivists has recurred over the last three hundred years. The issues seem always to be the same—is all law enacted law?—but the political motives change. Positivism is usually associated with the defense of legislative as opposed to judicial authority. The English philosophers Thomas Hobbes (1588–1679) and Jeremy Bentham (1748–1832) sought to vindicate the authority of Parliament to legislate for the common good—without being curtailed by the supposedly given and unchangeable principles of the common law. At the outset of the debate, the antipositivist Sir Edward Coke (1552–1634) led the fight for the power of the courts to limit both legislative and executive authority.

In the mid-twentieth century, the debate took on new contours. Positivism provided a vehicle for de-politicizing legal analysis. Because positivism provides an account of the entire legal system rather than the justice of particular laws, regimes that were stable and predictable qualified as legal systems. It did not matter whether they lacked moral and democratic legitimacy. Nazi Germany, South Africa, and Communist governments in Eastern Europe could meet the supposedly neutral criteria of regular obedience to enacted rules. . . .

Of course, no one expected in the 1960s and 1970s that the most unjust regimes in the world—South Africa, the Soviet Union, the German Democratic Republic—would soon fall. Perhaps a positivist, non-moral approach toward law served the interests of peaceful co-operation in the hostile world of the cold war. After all, one could think that in South Africa under apartheid, all law was enacted law. This meant that regardless of the immorality of the legal system, it was still a legal system. The South African judges even prided themselves on deploying their wits to counteract the worst effects of apartheid. One might say the same for the functioning of the courts under the more or less reformed Communist systems of the 1980s. There is something fundamentally unsatisfying, however, about approaching law in a way that blurs the distinction between legal systems that survive and those that the people overthrow at the first opportunity."

For Fletcher, the definition of law offered by positivism—that any law which satisfies the appropriate technical criteria of enactment "counts" as law—is problematic because of the absence of reference to its *moral* quality. For the positivist, by contrast, the *validity* of a rule—whether it counts as law or not—is determined simply by reference to the question of whether it has been enacted in accordance with the formal requirements set down by the legal system. As we will see in Chapter 3, in the United Kingdom, traditionally that has meant that whatever is enacted by the Queen in Parliament is law. By contrast, an anti-positivist—that is, a proponent of *natural law*—argues that in order to "count" as valid law, positive law must be measured successfully against some standard found outside of the legal system. Under a natural law approach, there must exist some moral code of principles which exists irrespective of positive law, and against which it can be judged. For the proponent of natural law, the "unjust" law, does not count as law properly called and, as a consequence, the individual may be under no moral duty to obey such a "law". This obviously raises interesting political questions about when people are entitled to disobey positive law.

NOTES AND QUESTIONS

- Why do people obey the law?

- Can you think of a law which you have knowingly disobeyed or one which you would be prepared to disobey? If so, how would you set about justifying your behaviour? Are there elements of a positivist or natural law approach in your responses to these questions? If your answer to the first part of this question was "no", can you give a contemporary example where someone in the news attempted to justify their disobedience of the law by claiming that a "higher" natural law ran counter to positive law?

- In your view, is the notion of law interchangeable with the notion of justice? Give reasons for your answer.

The positivist tradition has dominated Anglo-American legal thought, despite the concerns raised by proponents of natural law. As we will see in Chapter 3, the emergence of the principle of Parliamentary supremacy (that Parliament may make or unmake any law no matter what its substantive content) is most easily understandable as an example of positivist reasoning. The basic tenets of the two approaches to legality have been summarised by Cotterrell. First, the positivist tradition.

Roger Cotterrell, *The Sociology of Law* (2nd ed., Butterworths, London, 1992), p.9:

"In essence, positivism is a philosophical position which asserts that scientific knowledge derives from observation of the data of experience and not from speculation that seeks to 'look behind' observed facts for ultimate causes, meanings or essences. What we observe is, therefore, what really exists—and, scientifically speaking, all that exists. Hence judgments of value, of what is good or bad, political or policy questions, questions about the ultimate nature of things which cannot be determined by generalisations from observation—all of these are unscientific. Because these matters are subjective, existing only in the minds of individuals, they are unanalysable by scientific means. In the strongest versions of positivism they do not constitute knowledge at all. Fact and value are thus rigidly separated. Science should be 'value free' in two senses. It should not, itself, make value judgments about what it observes. And it should not seek to inquire into the meaning or ultimate significance of the values held by those it observes. This is not to say that values cannot be studied but they can be studied only as the observable preferences and commitments of actual individuals, not as having significance or reality in their own right.

In the Anglo-American legal world, and indeed to a greater or lesser extent in most modern highly-developed legal systems, a positivist outlook on law is the typical outlook of lawyers and informs much legal scholarship and teaching. Law consists of data—primarily rules—which can be recognised as such by relatively simple tests or 'rules of recognition'. A familiar such simple test is that the rules have passed through certain formal stages of a legislative process, or (less simple) that they can be derived from the *ratio decidendi*—the essential grounds of decision—of a case decided by a court having the jurisdiction and authority to lay down new rules in such a case. According to a positivist conception, these rules of law—possibly with some subsidiary legal phenomena—constitute the law, the data which it is the lawyer's task to analyse and order. In this sense, law is a 'given'—part of the data of experience. If it can be recognised as existing according to certain observational tests it can be analysed. The tests by which legal positivism recognises the existence of law or particular laws are thus analogous to those by which a scientist might recognise the presence of a particular chemical."

In an earlier book the same author summarises the contrasting position of those who have argued that law cannot be separated from values.

Roger Cotterrell, *The Politics of Jurisprudence* (Butterworths, London, 1989), p.120:

"In contrast to legal positivism stands a tradition of thought adopting an apparently diametrically opposed position—that law cannot be properly understood except in moral terms; that it is fundamentally a moral phenomenon; that questions of law's nature and existence cannot be isolated from questions about its moral worth. This tradition is usually termed *natural law theory*. Its history extends through at least 2,500 years of Western philosophy. One of its most powerful themes (though an ambiguous one, as will appear) is expressed in the declaration that *lex iniusta non est lex*—an unjust law is no law at all. It may well be that statements like this in this history of natural law theory have never meant what they seem, at face value, to mean. Nevertheless, they do suggest the persistent claim that questions about the nature of law and the conditions of its existence as an authoritative normative order cannot be treated in isolation from questions about its moral foundations. Thus typically, in many different ways throughout its long history, natural law theory has postulated the existence of moral principles having a validity and authority independent of human enactment, and which can be thought of as a 'higher' or more fundamental law against which the worth or authority of human law can be judged. This fundamental 'natural law' is variously seen as derived from human nature, the natural conditions of existence of humanity, the natural order of the universe, or the eternal law of God. The method of discovering it is usually claimed to be human reason. Natural law thus requires no human legislator. Yet it stands in judgment on the law created by human legislators."

The strength of the positivist tradition as a means of understanding law and the *legitimacy* of law within the English legal tradition has been explored by Atiyah. Of particular interest for us, is the way in which positivism sought to answer claims about the legitimacy of law which were grounded in the idea of a social contract and the consent of the governed to the law.

P.S. Atiyah, *Law and Modern Society* (2nd ed., Oxford University Press, Oxford, 1995), pp.148–151:

"This kind of analytical jurisprudence [the positivist approach] had its origins in the work of Jeremy Bentham (1748–1832) and John Austin (1790–1859). Bentham was a great law reformer and critic of legal and social institutions, and one of the things which he was reacting against was the tendency of lawyers, as he saw it, to assume that law had some legitimacy over and above that given to it by its own creation or observance. Eighteenth-century lawyers often justified particular laws and legal institutions by talking the language of 'natural law' and 'natural rights'. For example, rights of property were seen as 'natural' and the function of property law (and hence the law of trespass, theft, and so on) was therefore to preserve the natural rights of the property owner. Much of this in turn derived from the works of John Locke, whose (second) *Treatise on Civil Government* came to be regarded as an apologia for the Revolution of 1688 and was treated as a sort of political bible by the Whig landowners through most of the eighteenth century. To Locke the only function of government was to preserve and protect the natural rights which men had 'in the state of nature'; it had to be assumed that men in the state of nature had voluntarily consented to the establishment of the State by a 'social contract'; it was this which gave legitimacy to laws and the State, and once the ruler neglected to do his job properly (as of course James II had done) it was right and justifiable for the people to overthrow him by revolution.

But to Bentham, all this talk of natural law and natural rights was just nonsense—'nonsense upon stilts' he called it. The 'state of nature' and the 'social contract' were pure fictions. Property rights did not antedate the existence of society and law; on the contrary, it was only in a society and through law that the very idea of ownership of property had any meaning. So it was impossible to insist that societies existed in order to protect pre-existing property rights. Laws were a human creation, made by humans, for humans; there was nothing sacred or mysterious about them, and bad laws could be and ought to be changed. In propagating this message Bentham was, in the long run, completely successful. None of Bentham's ideas has more powerfully taken root than the notion that laws are mere human creations which can be made and unmade at man's mere pleasure. Indeed, it is permissible to wonder (as previously suggested) whether we are today not too prone to think that modern societies can get along happily without the elements of mystery and majesty and sacredness about law. But to recognize Bentham's triumph in these respects is not to say that the Lockean tradition is completely dead; there is still powerful support for the idea that the State and the laws derive their legitimacy from the consent of the people; and the notion that the function of society and law is to protect pre-existing moral rights is still vigorously defended by some modern theorists.

One of the curious by-products of Bentham's work was the positivist tradition which has had such a profound influence on the development of English law and legal thinking since his time. 'Positivism' is a label which has been used somewhat imprecisely for a variety of theories and ideologies, but, for present purposes, the principal beliefs associated with the positivist tradition can be said to be these: first, laws are commands of human beings addressed to other human beings; secondly, there is no necessary connection between law and morals; thirdly, the analysis of law and legal concepts is a true 'scientific' inquiry which is concerned with the formal requirements of valid law, and not with its content; and fourthly, judges, when deciding new points of law, must confine themselves to 'legal' arguments and not rely upon moral or policy arguments."

QUESTIONS

- Compare "legal positivism" and "natural law". Which do you find more persuasive as a legal theory? Give reasons for your response.

- Do you consider yourself to have natural rights? Are these enshrined in law?

- The various extracts we have examined to date have made references to the citizenry, Parliament and the courts as all having a role to play in ensuring that law has legitimacy. What do you consider to be the appropriate distribution of responsibility between these three groups in the performance of this task?

The underlying beliefs of the positivist tradition have had an enormous impact upon the way in which legal reasoning and decision making is understood in this country and, for that reason, a working familiarity with its basic tenets is important. But many of the legal problems we will focus on in this text should make you sceptical about whether legal reasoning can be separated from moral or political arguments, and whether legal method is, in any sense, a scientific or objective inquiry which is "value free". In the remainder of this chapter, we outline the ideas of the modern proponents of the view that legal reasoning is inextricably intertwined with politics and morality. In particular we introduce you to the ideas of legal realism and its various offshoots.

David Kairys, *The Politics of Law: A Progressive Critique* (3rd ed., Basic Books, USA, 1990) pp.2–4:

"The separation of law from politics is supposedly accomplished and ensured by a number of perceived attributes of the legal decision-making process, including judicial subservience to the Constitution, statutes, and precedent; the quasi-scientific, objective nature of legal analysis; and the technical expertise of judges and lawyers. Together, these attributes constitute an idealized decision-making process in which (1) the law on a particular issue is preexisting, predictable, and available to anyone with reasonable legal skill; (2) the facts relevant to disposition of a case are ascertained by objective hearing and evidentiary rules that reasonably ensure that the truth will emerge; (3) the result in a particular case is determined by a rather routine application of the law to the facts; and (4) except for the occasional bad judge, any reasonably competent and fair judge will reach the 'correct' decision.

Of course, there are significant segments of the bar, trends in legal scholarship, and popularly held beliefs that repudiate this idealized model. The school of jurisprudence known as Legal Realism long ago exposed its falsity. Later jurisprudential developments, such as theories resting the legitimacy of law on the existence of widely shared values, at least implicitly recognize the social and political content of law. Explicit consideration by judges of values in certain forms, such as 'public policy' and 'social utility', is generally acknowledged as appropriate. And it is commonly known that the particular judge assigned to a case has a significant bearing on the outcome. For many, the law's malleability is a matter of common knowledge, not a surprise or a cause for alarm.

But most of this thinking is either limited to law journals or compartmentalized, existing alongside and often presented as part of the idealized process. Despite the various scholarly trends and the open consideration of social policy and utility, legal decisions are expressed and justified in terms of the idealized process. The explicit or implicit theme of almost every judicial opinion is 'the law made me do it'. And this is how the courts as well as their decisions are depicted and discussed throughout society. Even the cynical views one often hears about the law, such as 'the system is fixed' or 'it's all politics', are usually meant to describe departures from, rather than characteristics of, the legal process.

The underlying conception envisions a legal process that, if not perverted by bias, corruption, or stupidity, will produce distinctly legal, fair rules and results untainted by politics or anyone's social values. While this perception is not monolithic or static (at various times substantial segments of society have come to question the idealized model), it has fairly consistently had more currency in the United States than in any other country.

Public debate over judicial decisions usually focuses on whether courts have deviated from the idealized decision-making process rather than on the substance of decisions or the nature and social significance of judicial power. Perceived deviations undermine the legitimacy and power of the courts, and are usually greeted with a variety of institutional and public challenges, including attacks by politicians and the press, proposals for statutory or constitutional change, and, occasionally, threats or attempts to impeach judges.

Dissatisfaction with the courts and their decisions is usually expressed in terms of this notion of deviation from the idealized model. Thus, the conservative criticism that the courts have overstepped their bounds—going beyond or outside legal reasoning and the idealized process—is now commonplace, as is the accompanying plea for judicial restraint and less intrusive government.

[We] reject the idealized model and the notion that a distinctly legal mode of reasoning or analysis determines legal results. The problem is not that courts deviate from legal reasoning. There is no legal methodology or process for reaching particular, correct results. This understanding of the law has been recently most closely associated with Critical Legal Studies and . . . before that with Legal Realism."

Cownie and Bradney build on this understanding of alternative approaches to the study of law by giving us a brief summary of the origins of Legal Realism. Proponents of this approach have provided us with another perspective from which to view the legitimacy of law. Rather than looking to legal texts they have focused on the extent to which legitimacy can be judged by level of compliance with legal rules and the respect in which the law is held. This approach is most simply characterised by the term "law in action".

Fiona Cownie and Anthony Bradney, *English Legal System in Context* (2nd ed., Butterworths, London, 2000) pp.14–15:

"Awareness of the importance of looking at the actual operation of legal systems owes much to studies by a number of American jurists, now know as American Legal Realists, working mainly at Harvard University in the early decades of the twentieth century. In terms of the legal system, the Realists were concerned not primarily with legal rules, *ie* cases and statutes, but with what actually happened when the legal system was at work. A classic statement of the concerns of Legal Realism is that made in a book review by one of the leading Realists, Karl Llewellyn. He wrote:

'The reviewer holds that the time has passed when the study of law could be profitably centred on legal doctrine. At the present juncture, the only serviceable focus of law study is law in action not only in the sense of . . . what the courts and all quasi-judicial bodies actually do; but also [in the sense of] the actual ordering of men's actions.'

American Legal Realism shifted its focus of enquiry firmly away from traditional study of legal rules. This thesis can be illustrated by examining some of the work of Jerome Frank, regarded as one of the more extreme practitioners of Legal Realism. Frank was heavily critical of the work of Christopher Columbus Langdell, the American legal academic who is best known for introducing the 'case method' of teaching law into American law schools. Langdell viewed law as a science, which could be practised very simply by applying legal rules mechanically to specific cases recorded in the law reports. Langdell's method rested heavily on the positivistic notion that law resided solely in the reports of decided cases or in statutes. Jerome Frank criticised this, arguing that Langdellian legal science had very little to do with law, because it overlooked such things as the lawyer-client relationship and the role of the jury. He argued that Langdell's attitude towards law was typical of what he termed 'the basic legal myth'; lawyers promote the myth that legal rules can be applied in a mechanical way because they, like all human beings, are constantly looking for certainty. The purpose of Realism, on the other hand, was to expose this myth. This concern with what Frank saw as law in action, rather than with the 'legal myth' of the law in the books, was typical of the concerns expressed by members of the Legal Realist movement. Given the nature of Frank's work it is not surprising that Legal Realism 'has sometimes been seen as part of a general movement in American social thought called 'the revolt against formalism'.'"

Within the UK, Legal Realism has expressed itself in two different movements; socio-legal studies and critical legal studies. Although distinctions might be drawn between the methodologies employed by these two groups or the extent to which they are motivated by particular political beliefs, they share many of the same concerns about the liberal models of law espoused earlier in this chapter. The socio-legal community represents a 'broad church'. Socio-legal researchers undertake library based theoretical work, empirical work which leads to the development of grounded theory, as well as more policy orientated studies which feed directly into the policy making process. What binds the socio-legal community is an approach to the study of legal phenomena which is multi or inter-disciplinary in its approach. Their theoretical perspectives and methodologies are informed by research undertaken in many other disciplines. Traditionally socio-legal scholars have bridged the divide between law and sociology, social policy, and economics. But there is increasing interest in law and disciplines within the field of humanities. Within the UK socio-legal studies has tended to be characterised by its involvement in undertaking empirical work which focuses on the operation of law in practice. Empirical work involves studying groups who are effected by, or in regular contact with, the law, courts or law enforcers. Much of this work has been influential in encouraging policy makers to reform existing laws so that they are more sensitive to the needs of those using them. Whilst there is increasingly more dialogue between the offspring of legal realism, critical legal scholars have been more vociferous in their criticisms of the ideological foundations of the current legal system. In the following extract, Vago provides us with a rather upbeat analysis of this movement's achievements.

Steven Vago, *Law and Society* (7th ed., Prentice Hall, New Jersey, 2003) pp.65–67:

"Critical Legal Studies (CLS but also referred to as CRITS) is a vibrant, refreshing, controversial and enduring addition to the ongoing jurisprudential debate on law, legal education and the role of lawyers in society. It is widely considered, by critics and followers alike, to comprise some of the most exciting . . . scholarship around, and one sociologist of law described it as being 'where the action is'. The movement began with a group of junior faculty members and law students at Yale in the late 1960s who have since moved to other places. In 1977, the group organized itself into the Conference on Critical Legal Studies, which has over 400 members and holds an annual conference that draws more than 1,000 participants.

The movement has been greatly influenced by Marxist-inspired European theorists and its roots can be traced back to American legal realism. Legal realists in the 1920s and 1930s argued against the nineteenth-century belief that the rule of law was supreme. They contended, because a good lawyer could argue convincingly either side of a given case, there was actually nothing about the law that made any judicial decision inevitable. Rather, they pointed out, the outcome of a case depended largely, if not entirely, on the predilections of the judge who happened to be deciding it. Thus, far from being a science, the realists argued, law was virtually inseparable from politics and economics.

Proponents of the movement reject the idea that there is anything distinctly legal about legal reasoning. As with any other kind of analysis, legal reasoning, they maintain, cannot operate independently of the personal biases of lawyers and judges, or of the social context in which they are acting. Furthermore, law is so contradictory that it allows the context of a case to determine the outcome. That attribute of law—its inability to cover all situations —is called *indeterminacy*. Because law consists of a variety of contradictions and inconsistencies, judicial decisions cannot be self-contained models of reasoning as they claim to be. Decisions rest on grounds outside of formal legal doctrine which are inevitably political.

Critical scholars also reject law as being value-free and above political, economic, and social considerations. Laws only *seem* neutral and independent, even those that reflect the dominant values in society. Therefore, laws legitimate the status quo. They maintain that law is actually part of the system of power in society rather than a protection against it.

Although proponents of the movement insist that their ideas are still tentative and evolving, their attacks on law and legal training have created a good deal of criticism. The movement has been called Marxist, utopian, hostile to rules, and incoherent. Critical legal scholars have been accused of favoring violence over bargaining, of advocating the inculcation of leftist values in legal education, and of being preoccupied with 'illegitimate hierarchies' such as the bar; their approach to law is 'nihilistic', and they teach cynicism to their students, which may result in 'the learning of the skills of corruption'. Nihilist law teachers with a proclivity for revolution are likely to train criminals, and they have, therefore 'an ethical duty to depart from law school'. It is unlikely that the controversy between proponents and opponents of the movement will be settled in the foreseeable future. Further, although the movement has been fairly successful in questioning the validity of the Western legal system, it has failed . . . its major objective of developing and gaining broader support for new legal doctrines that are more representative of class, gender and race differences. So far, the most useful function of the movement is indicating the extent to which politics influences the legal system."

It is clear from this extract that the growth of critical legal studies has been far from uncontroversial. The challenge it poses to liberal jurisprudence is taken up by Andrew Altman.

Andrew Altman, *Critical Legal Studies: A Liberal Critique* **(Princeton University Press, Princeton, New Jersey, 1993) pp.13–15:**

"There are three main prongs to the CLS attack on the liberal embrace of the rule of law, three main elements to the CLS charge that the rule of law, as liberal theory conceptualizes it, is a myth. . . . a preliminary characterization of them is possible at this stage.

The first prong hinges on the claim that the rule of law is not possible in a social situation where the kind of individual freedom endorsed by the liberal view reigns. Such a situation would be characterized by a pluralism of fundamentally incompatible moral and political viewpoints. The establishment of the rule of law under the conditions of pluralism would require some mode of legal reasoning that could be sharply distinguished from moral and political deliberation and choice. There would have to be a sharp distinction, so the argument goes, between law, on one side, and both morals and politics, on the other. Without such a distinction, judges and other individuals who wield public power could impose their own views of the moral or political good on others under the cover of law. Such impositions, however, would destroy the rule of law and the liberal freedom it is meant to protect.

Thus, the liberal view requires that legal reasoning—that is, reasoning about what rights persons have under the law and why—be clearly distinguished from reasoning about political or ethical values. Legal reasoning is not to be confused with deciding which party to a case has the best moral or political argument. Yet it is precisely this kind of legal reasoning that is impossible in a setting of moral and political pluralism, according to CLS. The law-politics distinction collapses, and legal reasoning becomes tantamount to deciding which party has the best moral or political argument. Karl Klare puts the CLS position concisely: 'This [liberal] claim about legal reasoning—that it is autonomous from political and ethical choice—is a falsehood.'

Duncan Kennedy is even more blunt, but the essential point is the same:

'Teachers teach nonsense when they persuade students that legal reasoning is distinct, *as a method for reaching correct results*, from ethical or political discourse in general . . . There is never a "correct legal solution" that is other than the correct ethical or political solution to that legal problem.'

The second prong of the CLS attack on the rule of law revolves around the claim that the legal doctrines of contemporary liberal states are riddled by contradictions. The contradictions consist of the presence of pairs of fundamentally incompatible norms serving as authoritative elements of legal doctrine in virtually all departments of law. These contradictions are thought to defeat the notion that the rule of law actually reigns in those societies that most contemporary liberal philosophers regard as leading examples of political societies operating under the rule of law. Kennedy contends that the contradictions are tied to the fact that legal doctrine does not give us a coherent way to talk about the rights of individuals under the law: 'Rights discourse is internally inconsistent, vacuous, or circular. Legal thought can generate plausible rights justifications for almost any result.' Klare echoes Kennedy's claim: 'Legal reasoning is a texture of openness, indeterminancy, and contradiction.'

As Klare and Kennedy suggest, the CLS view is that the consequence of these doctrinal contradictions is pervasive legal indeterminancy—that is, the widespread inability of the authoritative rules and doctrines to dictate a determinate outcome to legal cases. The contradictions enable lawyers and judges to argue equally well for either side of most legal cases, depending on which of two contradictory legal norms they choose to rely upon. Moreover, the existence of indeterminancy is tied to the collapse of the distinction between law and politics. Judges can and do covertly rely on moral and political considerations in deciding which of two incompatible legal norms they will base their decisions upon. In existing liberal states, we have not the rule of law but the rule of politics. Joseph Singer sums up this phase of the CLS attack on the rule of law nicely:

> 'While traditional legal theorists acknowledge the inevitability and desirability of some indeterminancy, traditional legal theory requires a relatively large amount of determinancy as a fundamental premise of the rule of law. Our legal system, however, has never satisfied this goal.'

Closely associated with the first two prongs of the CLS attack on the rule of law is the thesis that the very idea of the rule of law serves as an instrument of oppression and domination. David Kairys express the general idea in a manner characteristic of much CLS writing:

> 'The law is a major vehicle for the maintenance of existing social and power relations. . . . The law's perceived legitimacy confers a broader legitimacy on a social system . . . characterized by domination. This perceived legitimacy of the law is primarily based . . . on the distorted notion of government by law, not people.'

In the CLS view, then, the idea that our political society operates under the rule of law serves to perpetuate illegitimate relations of power. Exposing the rule of law as a myth is thought of in the CLS movement as an essential part of a strategy designed to undermine those relations of power."

NOTES AND QUESTIONS

- It can be seen from this extract that the critique of Anglo-American models of law provided by critical legal scholars is much more damning of Western ideals of law than other texts included in this chapter. The vision of lawyers as amoral agents choosing between contradictory legal norms is a powerful one. To what extent does this tally with your personal view about the role of lawyers in society? Give reasons for your response.

- In what ways could you argue that the law is capable of serving as an instrument of oppression and domination? Can you think of any examples?

Feminist legal theory has also had an important role to play in questioning the ideals and values which underpin liberal jurisprudence. Like critical legal studies, with which feminists have claimed to have a sympathetic but uneasy relationship, feminist theory also stands in the tradition of legal realism. That is to say that it seeks to expose the false reason behind contemporary claims of traditional legal doctrine. Like critical legal scholars, feminists have worked to question the assumptions which underpin mainstream legal scholarship. In the following extract, Margaret Davies outlines some of the key claims of feminist legal theorists.

Margaret Davies, *Asking the Law Question* (The Law Book Company Limited/Sweet & Maxwell, 1994) pp.167–168:

"The truth of the claim that common law theory or positivism are 'patriarchal' or supported by a 'masculinist ideology' may not be immediately obvious . . . In essence though, to say that Western jurisprudence and law generally are patriarchal or masculinist means several things, which are not unrelated. In the first place, it is empirically true that law and legal theory have been (and still are) the province of men. Very simply, it is men who have written the law and theories about the law. Austin's 'province of jurisprudence' is a terrain dominated by men. (Not all men, of course, but educated white men.) Men have made the legal world.

Secondly, the law, and its resulting jurisprudence, reflect male values. Men have made the legal world in their own image, confusing it, as de Beauvoir says, with the absolute truth. For women, and other marginalised groups, it is not only the over-representation of one group in legal decision-making and theorising which is the problem. A much deeper difficulty lies in the value systems of law and culture, which reinforce in various ways oppressions of gender, race, class, sexuality, and so on. When certain values (such as rationality and reasonableness, independence and autonomy, objectivity and neutrality) are culturally associated with men and masculinity at the same time as they are valued by the law, it is hardly surprising that the law seems to 'speak' to men within this dominant culture in a way in which it does not speak to women or other marginalised groups. This very general ideological form of patriarchy is repeated in the law itself, where substantive legal categories simply overlook or trivialise the concerns of women.

And thirdly, traditional legal theory is patriarchal because it usually purports to present a view of law which is supposed to explain its general characteristics. The idea that such general explanations are possible is not politically innocent, but is rather imposed on us as a way of stifling dissent or different points of view. If there is a 'neutral' or 'objective' way of seeing things, then those of us who do not share it are more likely to accept the characterisation of our own views as distorted or biased, and consequently attempt to fit them into the dominant mould. The fact that the law might look totally different to people whose main experience of it is as an instrument of oppression does not on the whole enter into the consideration of mainstream 'malestream' thinkers. Nor does the complicating fact that many people will in any case have internalised the official message about law and culture, simply because of the power of prevailing ideologies."

In a similar vein, Carol Smart has argued that another of law's functions is to make claims as to the "truth" of things. Law is a form of knowledge which sometimes disqualifies other ways of thinking—namely, those in which someone is not "thinking like a lawyer". According to Smart, legal method is the means through which law (and practitioners of the law) construct law and legal *discourse* as a privileged way of understanding. Smart's analysis should be remembered in those moments in your legal education when you may feel that you are being "indoctrinated" into a particular way of thinking; a way of thinking which seems to run counter to other ways of analysing problems and of viewing society.

Carol Smart, *Feminism and the Power of Law* (Routledge, London, 1989), pp.10–13:

"[L]aw sets itself above other knowledges like psychology, sociology, or common sense. It claims to have the method to establish the truth of events. The main vehicle for this claim is the legal method which is taught in law schools. . . . A more 'public' version of this claim, however, is the criminal trial which, through the adversarial system, is thought to be a secure basis for findings of guilt and innocence. Judges and juries can come to correct legal decisions; the fact that other judges in higher courts may overrule some decisions only goes to prove that the system ultimately divines the correct view.

Law's claim to truth is not manifested so much in its practice, however, but rather in the ideal of law. In this sense it does not matter that practitioners may fall short of the ideal. If we take the analogy of science, the claim to scientificity is a claim to exercise power, it does not matter that experiments do not work or that medicine cannot find a cure for all ills. The point is that we accord so much status to scientific work that its truth outweighs other truths, indeed it denies the possibility of others. We do not give quite such a status to law, although we operate as if the legal system does dispense justice (*i.e.* correct decisions), and we certainly give greater weight to a judge's pronouncement of guilt than a defendant's proclamation of innocence. Indeed there are those who would say that 'law is what the judges say it is'. The judge is held to be a man of wisdom, a man of knowledge, not a mere technician who can ply his trade.

If we accept that law, like science, makes a claim to truth and that this is indivisible from the exercise of power, we can see that law exercises power not simply in its material effects (judgements) but also in its ability to disqualify other knowledges and experiences. Non-legal knowledge is therefore suspect and/or secondary. Everyday experiences are of little interest in terms of their meaning for individuals. Rather these experiences must be translated into another form in order to become 'legal' issues and before they can be processed through the legal system. For the system to run smoothly, whether it is criminal or civil, the ideal is that all parties are legally represented and that the parties say as little as possible (*i.e.* they are mute). The problem for the lawyer is that the litigant may bring in issues which are not, in legal terms, pertinent to the case, or s/he might inadvertently say something that has a legal significance unknown to her/him. So the legal process translates everyday experience into legal relevances, it excludes a great deal that might be relevant to the parties, and it makes its judgements on the scripted or tailored account. . . .

Law sets itself outside the social order, as if through the application of legal method and rigour, it becomes a thing apart which can in turn reflect upon the world from which it is divorced. Consider the following quotation from Lord Denning, written when he was Master of the Rolls (*i.e.* head of the Court of Appeal).

> 'By a series of Acts of Parliament, however, starting in 1870, all the disabilities of wives in regard to property have been swept away. A married woman is now entitled to her own property and earnings, just as her husband is entitled to his. Her stocks and shares remain hers. Her wedding presents are hers. Her earnings are hers. She can deal with all property as fully as any man. . . . No longer is she dependent on her husband. She can, and does, go out to work and earn her own living. Her equality is complete.'

In this conceptualisation it is law that has given women equality (accepting for the moment that they do have formal equality). In this way law is taken to be outside the social body, it transcends it and acts upon it. Indeed the more it is seen as a unified discipline that responds only to its own coherent, internal logic, the more powerful it becomes. It is not simply that in this passage Denning omits to point out how many women chained themselves to railings, demonstrated and lobbied in Parliament to change the law, nor that he ignores the dramatic changes to women's economic position which occurred quite independently of law, it is rather that he constructs law as a kind of sovereign with the power to give or withhold rights. . . . Linked to this idea, law is constructed as a force of linear progress, a beacon to lead us out of darkness. . . .

Lastly in this section on truth and knowledge, I want to consider how law extends itself beyond uttering the truth of law, to making such claims about other areas of social life. What is important about this tendency is that the framework for such utterances remains legal—and hence retains the mantle of legal power. To put it figuratively, the judge does not remove his wig when he passes comment on, for example, issues of sexual morality in rape cases. He retains the authority drawn from legal scholarship and the 'truth' of law, but he applies it to non-legal issues. This is a form of legal imperialism in which the legitimacy law claims in the field of law extends to every issue in social life. Hence Lord Denning states:

'No matter how you may dispute and argue, you cannot alter the fact that women are quite different from men. The principal task in the life of women is to bear and rear children: . . . He is physically the stronger and she the weaker. He is temperamentally the more aggressive and she the more submissive. It is he who takes the initiative and she who responds. These diversities of function and temperament lead to differences of outlook which cannot be ignored. But they are, none of them, any reason for putting women under the subjection of men.'

Here Denning is articulating a Truth about the natural differences between women and men. He combines the Truth claimed by socio-biology (*i.e.* a 'scientific' truth) with the Truth claimed by law. He makes it clear that there is no point in argument; anyone who disagrees is, by definition, a fool. Hence the feminist position is constructed as a form of 'disqualified knowledge', whilst the naturalistic stance on innate gender differences acquires the status of a legal Truth. In this passage both law and biological determinism are affirmed, whilst law accredits itself with doing good."

The realist and critical legal traditions also gave rise to a movement of scholars who became known as critical race theories. In the following extract, it will become clear that, while they share certain values with realists, critical legal scholars and feminists, tensions between these various factions have also emerged.

Kimberlé Crenshaw, Neil Gotanda, Gary Peller and Kendall Thomas, *Critical Race Theory: The Key Writings that Formed the Movement* **(The New Press, New York, 1995) pp.xiii, xxii–xxiii:**

"As we conceive it, Critical Race Theory embraces a movement of left scholars, most of them scholars of color, situated in law schools, whose work challenges the ways in which race and racial power are constructed and represented in . . . legal culture and, more generally, in . . . society as a whole. . . .

[T]here is no canonical set of doctrines or methodologies to which we all subscribe. Although Critical Race scholarship differs in object, argument, accent, and emphasis, it is nevertheless unified by two common interests. The first is to understand how a regime of white supremacy and its subordination of people of color have been created and maintained . . . and, in particular, to examine the relationship between that social structure and professed ideals such as 'the rule of law' and 'equal protection'. The second is a desire not merely to understand the vexed bond between law and racial power but to *change* it. [Critical race theorists] share an ethical commitment to human liberation—even if we reject conventional notions of what such a conception means, and though we often disagree, even amongst ourselves, over its specific direction.

This ethical aspiration finds its most obvious concrete expression in the pursuit of engaged, even adversarial, scholarship. [These] may be read as contributions to what Edward Said has called 'antithetical knowledge', the development of counter-accounts of social reality by subversive and subaltern elements of the reigning order. Critical Race Theory—like the Critical Legal Studies movement with which we are often allied—rejects the prevailing orthodoxy that scholarship should be or could be 'neutral' and 'objective'. We believe that legal scholarship about race . . . can never be written from a distance of detachment or with an attitude of objectivity. To the extent that racial power is exercised legally and ideologically, legal scholarship about race is an important site for the construction of that power, and thus is always a factor, if 'only' ideologically, in the economy of racial power itself. To use a phrase from the existentialist tradition, there is 'no exit'—no scholarly perch outside the social dynamics of racial power form which merely to observe and analyze. Scholarship—the formal production, identification, and organization of what will be called 'knowledge' is inevitably political. Each of the texts in this volume seeks in its own way not simply to explicate but also to intervene in the ideological contestation of race in America, and to create new, oppositionist accounts of race. . . ."

At its inception in the late 70s, Critical Legal Studies (CLS) was basically a white and largely male academic organization. By the mid-eighties, there was a small cadre of scholars of color who frequented CLS conferences and summer camps. Most were generally conversant with Critical Legal Theory and sympathetic to the progressive sensibilities of Critical Legal Studies as a whole. Unlike the law school mainstream, this cadre was far from deterred by CLS critique of liberal legalism. While many in the legal community were, to put it mildly, deeply disturbed by the CLS assault against such ideological mainstays as the rule of the law, to scholars of color who drew on a history of colored communities' struggle against formal and institutional racism, the crits' contention that law was neither apolitical, neutral nor determinate hardly seemed controversial. Indeed, we believed that this critical perspective formed the basic building blocks of any serious attempt to understand the relationship between law and white supremacy. However, while the emerging 'race crits' shared this starting position with CLS, significant differences between us became increasingly apparent during a series of conferences in the mid-eighties.

Our discussions during the conferences revealed that while we shared with crits the belief that legal consciousness functioned to legitimize social power in the United States, race crits also understood that race and racism likewise functioned as central pillars of hegemonic power. Because CLS scholars had not, by and large, developed and incorporated a critique of racial power into their analysis, their practices, politics and theories regarding race tended to be unsatisfying and sometimes indistinguishable from those of the dominant institutions they were otherwise contesting. As race moved from the margins to the center of discourse within Critical Legal Studies—or as some would say Critical Legal Studies took the race turn—institutional and theoretical disjunctures between critical legal studies and the emerging scholarship on race eventually manifested themselves as central themes within Critical Race Theory."

Finally, we turn to one further critical school which has come to be known as "queer legal theory". Whereas feminist legal theory has criticised the positivistic, liberal assumption of traditional legal analysis (which we outlined earlier in this chapter), queer theory has focused on sexuality as the prism through which to critique traditional categories of legal analysis.

**Carl F. Stychin, *Law's Desire: Sexuality and the Limits of Justice* (Routledge, London, 1995)
p.148:**

"Common law legal scholars . . . have been witnesses to and participants in the critique posed by the school of Critical Legal Studies (CLS). In particular, many Critical Legal Scholars challenged the naturalness of the public/private distinction, arguing that it was a social construction which was employed in order to justify the intervention of law in some (but not other) areas. The divide between the public and private justified a *laissez faire* judicial philosophy in the spheres of property law and economic regulation. Like queer theorists, proponents of CLS have sought to denaturalise categories of thought which have been inscribed with a meaning that was made to appear historically and culturally invariant. In the case of CLS, the categories are those of legal analysis. With respect to queer theory, the categories are primarily sexual.

However, in response to the CLS critique of the public/private divide, the importance of a zone of privacy has been defended as important both as a symbolic and practical matter. For example, privacy as a constitutional value has been justified on the basis of its connections to personal (sexual) autonomy. As well, for lesbians and gay men, the private has been a crucial realm of safety from a metaphoric and literal violence that lurks within the public sphere. Although that private sphere has been tenuously protected at the best of times, it has remained an important area of *relative* security.

Of course, the private sphere also serves as the basis of the metaphor of the closet. While privacy has a protective function for lesbians and gay men in allowing some freedom in determining where to position oneself in terms of outness (although this varies from person to person), the public/private distinction has also acted as a regulatory boundary by which sexual minorities are removed from a public dialogic sphere into a realm of 'discretion'. Furthermore, the public/private distinction has a particularly queer function in how it must be utilised by lesbians and gay men seeking a *legally* protected sphere of sexual privacy. In order to achieve a legal guarantee of privacy, it first becomes necessary to come 'out' into the public sphere. The closet can only be protected to the extent that someone has crossed the public/private divide."

NOTES AND QUESTIONS

- Imagine that you have been asked to give a short presentation in your seminar group about major legal schools of thought which have influenced our response to the question "what is law?". Make some brief notes on how you would explain the approaches outlined in the second part of this chapter.

- What do you think these groups are able to tell us about the operation of formal law and its effectiveness?

- Carol Smart and others have sought to analyse the functions of law from a sociological perspective. Is there value in looking at legal methods and legal systems from the perspective of other disciplines? Give reasons for your answer.

- One suggestion made by Crenshaw and colleagues is that scholarship and the "production" of knowledge by academics is political. Is this something that you have noticed in your studies to date?

2

COMPARATIVE LAW AND LEGAL METHOD

By Martha-Marie Kleinhans, Lecturer in Law, The University of Reading

This chapter provides an introduction to the study of comparative law and legal method. Comparative law refers to the comparison of different legal traditions and systems from various parts of the world. The aim is for you to comprehend how the legal tradition of other countries can provide you with a better understanding of English methods and system. We begin with some broad background on the study of comparative law and legal method generally. We also discuss the various ways in which legal systems and traditions have been categorised and how those categories have changed over time. We then proceed to an example of comparative legal scholarship which is particularly pertinent to today's English law student, who needs to be aware of the legal tradition of most member states of the European Union. The legal method of the European Union remains indebted to the civil law (the legal tradition of continental European countries) and, thus, a basic understanding of the civil law tradition is of great importance to the study of English law. Broadening our focus even further, we conclude the chapter with a consideration of the challenges presented by an increasingly globalised legal order.

INTRODUCTION TO COMPARATIVE LAW

The belief that we can compare things rests upon two conflicting but fundamental assumptions. First, we assume that the things compared are the same (*i.e.* that they share something in common). Second, we assume that the things compared are different (*i.e.* that they have some distinguishing features). These are the two assumptions of comparative law, and they are in constant tension.

The aim of this introductory extract is to provide you with a better understanding of the similarity and difference between legal traditions and systems. We begin, therefore, with some material on the meaning of "comparative law" and the establishment of comparative law as a discipline of study.

K. Zweigert and H. Kötz, *Introduction to Comparative Law* (3rd ed., Clarendon Press, Oxford, 1998), pp.2–3, 15–16:

"Before we try to discover the essence, function, and aims of comparative law, let us first say what 'comparative law' means. The words suggest an intellectual activity with law as its object and comparison as its process. Now comparisons can be made between different rules in a single legal system, as, for example, between different paragraphs of the German Civil Code. If this were all that was meant by comparative law, it would be hard to see how it differed from what lawyers normally do: lawyers constantly have to juxtapose and harmonize the rules of their own system, that is, compare them, before they can reach any practical decision or theoretical conclusion. Since this is characteristic of every national system of law, 'comparative law' must mean more than appears on the surface. The extra dimension is that of internationalism. Thus, 'comparative law' is the comparison of the different legal systems of the world.

Comparative law as we know it started in Paris in 1900, the year of the World Exhibition. At this brilliant panorama of human achievement there were naturally innumerable congresses, and the great French Scholars Édouard Lambert and Raymond Saleilles took the opportunity to found an International Congress for Comparative Law. The science of comparative law, or at any rate its method, was greatly advanced by the occurrence of this Congress, and the views expressed at it have led to a wealth of productive research in this branch of legal study, young though it is.

The temper of the Congress was in tune with the times, whose increasing wealth and splendour had given everyone, scholars included, an imperturbable faith in progress. Sure of his existence, certain of its point and convinced of its success, man was trying to break out of his local confines and peaceably to master the world and all that was in it. Naturally enough, lawyers were affected by this spirit; merely to interpret and elaborate their own system no longer satisfied them. This outgoing spirit permeates all the Congress papers; the whole Congress was dominated by disarming belief in progress. What Lambert and Saleilles had in mind was the development of nothing less than a common law of mankind (*droit commun de l'humanité*). A world law must be created—not today, perhaps not even tomorrow—but created it must be, and comparative law must create it. As Lambert put it, comparative law must resolve the accidental and divisive differences in the laws of peoples at similar stages of cultural and economic development, and reduce the number of divergencies in law, attributable not to the political, moral, or social qualities of the different nations but to historical accident or to temporary or contingent circumstances.

Comparative law has developed continuously since then, despite great changes in man's attitude towards existence. The belief in progress, so characteristic of 1900, has died. World wars have weakened, if not destroyed, faith in world law. Yet despite a more sceptical way of looking at the world, the development and enrichment of comparative law has been steady. Comparative lawyers have come to know their field better, they have refined their methods and set their sights a little lower, but they remain convinced that comparative law is both useful and necessary. Scholars are more resistant to fashionable pessimism than people in other walks of life; they have no immediate aim, only the ultimate goal of discovering the truth. This is true also of research in comparative law; it has no immediate aim. But if one did want to adduce arguments of utility, comparative law must be at least as useful as it was, especially as technological developments since 1900 have made the world ever smaller and, to all appearances, national isolationism is on the wane. Furthermore, by the international exchanges which it requires, comparative law procures the gradual approximation of viewpoints, the abandonment of deadly complacency, and the relaxation of fixed dogma. It affords us a glimpse into the form and formation of legal institutions which develop in parallel, possibly in accordance with laws yet to be determined, and permits us to catch sight, through the differences in detail, of the grand similarities and so deepen our belief in the existence of a unitary sense of justice. . . .

It is beyond dispute today that the scholarly pursuit of comparative law has several significant functions. This emerges from a very simple consideration, that no study deserves the name of a science if it limits itself to phenomena arising within its national boundaries. For a long time lawyers were content to be insular in this sense, and to some extent they are so still. But such a position is untenable, and comparative law offers the only way by which law can become international and consequently a science.

In the natural and medical sciences, and in sociology and economics as well, discoveries and opinions are exchanged internationally. This is so familiar a fact that it is easy to forget its significance. There is no such thing as 'German' physics or 'British' microbiology or 'Canadian' geology. These branches of science are international, and the most one can say is that the contributions of the various nations to the different departments of world knowledge have been outstanding, average, or modest. But the position in legal science is astonishingly different. So long as Roman law was the essential source of all law on the Continent of Europe, an international unity of law and legal science did exist, and a similar unity, the unity of Common Law, can still be found, up to a point, in the English-speaking world. On the European continent, however, legal unity began to disappear in the eighteenth century as national codes were put in the place of traditional Roman law. The consequence was that lawyers concentrated exclusively on their own legislation, and stopped looking over the border. At a time of growing nationalism, this legal narcissism led to pride in the national system. Germans thought German law was the ark of the covenant, and the French thought the same of French law: national pride became the hallmark of juristic thought. Comparative law has started to put an end to such narrowmindedness.

The primary aim of comparative law, as of all sciences, is knowledge. If one accepts that legal science includes not only the techniques of interpreting the texts, principles, rules, and standards of a national system, but also the discovery of models for preventing or resolving social conflicts, then it is clear that the method of comparative law can provide a much richer range of model solutions than a legal science devoted to a single nation, simply because the different systems of the world can offer a greater variety of solutions than could be thought up in a lifetime by even the most imaginative jurist who was corralled in his own system. Comparative law is an 'école de vérité' which extends and enriches the 'supply of solutions' and offers the scholar of critical capacity the opportunity of finding the 'better solution' for his time and place.

Like the lively international exchange on legal topics to which it gives rise, comparative law has other functions which can only be mentioned here in the briefest way. It dissolves unconsidered national prejudices, and helps us to fathom the different societies and cultures of the world and to further international understanding; it is extremely useful for law reform in developing countries; and for the development of one's own system the critical attitude it engenders does more than local doctrinal disputes."

NOTES AND QUESTIONS

- According to Zweigert and Kötz, how have the aims of comparative law changed?

- What factors do the authors identify as having influenced the development of the functions of comparative law today? What other factors can you suggest?

- How would you describe what 'comparative law' means?

LEGAL SYSTEMS, CULTURES AND TRADITIONS

The authors of the previous extract referred to comparative law as a science whose aim is knowledge. To achieve this knowledge, however, we must first decide what it is that we are to study. Comparative lawyers have described the object of their inquiry in many different ways: legal systems, legal mentalities, legal traditions and legal cultures. Each of these categories helps bring different aims of comparative law into perspective. In the following extract, you should attempt to understand what the effect for comparative law is for each of these varied ways of identifying the object of comparative legal study.

J. Bell, *French Legal Cultures* (Butterworths, London, 2001), pp.6–7, 11–12, 14–16, 16–17:

"Tradition is an important part of culture, and especially the law. Law is a body of norms and practices which is handed down. The practice of preserving and developing a tradition gives rise to a legal community. Taking part in the tradition is the way one comes to understand the law from the legal point of view. A tradition connects norms, practices and people.

Hazareesingh suggests that 'a tradition is characteristically defined as the transmission of a relatively coherent body of knowledge or thought from one generation to the next'. Legal writers such as Krygier and Gerber concentrate on authoritative texts (statutes, reported cases and key doctrinal writings) as central to the legal tradition. Texts are handed on and become the focus of legal activity. The particular style and influences of the texts and the way these texts are treated and interpreted, are also important features of the legal tradition and make it distinctive. But it is also important to see both procedures and rituals as part of what is handed on. The way lawyers dress and perform legal acts helps to create the law as a way of life. The role of the notary in drawing up wills or marriage contracts in France, the layout of the courtroom and the roles which the different lawyers, advocats, greffiers and judges, perform in court is as much part of the French legal tradition as the Code civil or other received texts. Certainly both a body of principles and a set of practices form the basis for how continuity is preserved within the legal community. Grosso suggests that we should examine the 'experienced tradition', a substantive and continuing body of attitudes and activities which is not only handed on, but is lived out and serves a basis for renewal. This is in contrast to the 'tradition as myth' or the 'sentimental tradition' which is a set of sentiments and attachments to a 'grand past' and aspirations for the future. The focus, as he suggests, is on the experience *from the legal point of view*, which perceives legal activity as a unity and as developing organically.

A tradition has to be transmitted and made accessible to each generation of participants. As a result, there has to be processes of conservation, of authenticating what is handed on and of interpretation. There is also a process of induction is the way by which new participants are formed to be able to make use of the tradition in a way that counts as legitimate. By all means, there is a legitimate activity of external criticism and interpretation. . . . But we are concerned . . . to explain the internal process of making sense of a legal argument. For this purpose, there are established ways in which interpretations can be accepted as valid. There are conventions within the legal community about what are appropriate arguments which support an interpretation—whether cases can be cited and from which courts, whether doctrinal legal writers can be cited as appropriate authorities. Education has an important role in the socialisation of participants into a culture. . . .

Comparative lawyers are agreed that it is not sufficient just to look at legal texts and rules to explain why legal systems are different. Cappelletti, Merryman and Perillo argued:

'. . . a principle source of . . . differences lies quite outside the formal legal order. It is found in the pervading assumptions and attitudes, lay and professional, about law, in the generally accepted view of what law is, of what the legal process in the society should be, of how the legal process should be divided up among various official and unofficial agencies for making and administering the law. In a phrase, what gives the legal order character, individuality, a style of its own, is the prevailing legal outlook in the culture of which that legal order is an integral part.'

Even if there is agreement to go beyond the 'law in the books' for explanation, there is no agreement on how the concept of 'legal culture' can offer an explanatory framework.

In his seminal study, *Law and Society: an introduction*, Friedman distinguishes two different aspects of legal culture:

'. . . legal culture refers to two rather different sets of attitudes and values: that of the general public (we can call this *lay* legal culture) and that of lawyers, judges and other professionals (we can call this *internal* legal culture).'

In his view, comparative lawyers tend to study this internal culture of a legal system, a lawyer's or a jurist's culture, rather than a general or social culture, the culture of the 'living law'. This he considers to be 'the marginal and arcane culture of lawyers in their formal training', the official law, which is the wrong focus of study for legal culture:

'Legal systems are not museums; they are tools, instruments, mechanisms; and those who use them are living people and living entities, grimly determined to float bonds, collect damages for auto accidents, merge with another company, avoid or minimize taxes, avoid or minimize prison, start or end a marriage, vindicate a reputation, go bankrupt, adopt a baby, or do any of the thousand things that people and institutions do by and through the law.'

. . . The concept of 'mentality' as an explanation of differences in cultural practices has become popular, particularly in France since the work of Lévy-Bruhl. It is associated with a pre-logical set of perspectives on the world that shape action. Mentality offers a core explanation for ideas and practices. The concept has been much used by comparative lawyers. Zweigert and Kötz consider that a significant hallmark of a difference in a legal system is 'a distinctive mode of legal thinking' which they also characterise as 'mentality'. The concept has been developed further by Pierre Legrand. For him, a 'mentalité' is the 'collective mental programme' which contains the 'assumptions, attitudes, aspirations and antipathies' which provide the 'deep structures of legal rationality'.

Legrand focuses on the difference between common law and civil law, which he describes as a *primordial cleavage* in ways law is understood. There are radical differences in the nature of legal reasoning, the significance of systematisation, the character of rules, the role of facts, and the meaning of rights. Taken together, these represent a mapping of the world under the sway of culture. Such ideas shape the individual lawyer's mentalité. He considers that a particular mentality is so fundamental to the approach of civilian lawyers to law, that it constitutes a barrier to real harmonisation with common lawyers, even on the basis of common texts. Common lawyers just think differently about law. In this approach, mentalité describes a set of beliefs and interpretative ideas which shape an approach to action:

'I understand the notion of "culture" to mean the framework of intangibles within which an interpretative community operates, which has normative force for this community (even though not completely and coherently instantiated) and which, over the *longue durée*, determines the identity of a community as *community*.'

But there are voices which argue that such a single, macro explanation is unnecessary. Lloyd studied the scientific arguments of ancient Greece and ancient China, their styles of argument, their concepts and their products. He concludes that there are certain features that are common to all societies, such as the pursuit of logic, but there are other features of scientific argument that arise in a specific set of circumstances. Thus within a full set of beliefs, some features of a particular society are held in common with others, and some are specific. Lloyd's concern is how far there is a real difference in beliefs, and how far there are simply differences in the way those beliefs are presented and defended. Presentation depends on the availability of linguistic terms, and defence requires certain paradigms of convincing argument to be used more widely in society. He certainly notes a difference between Greece and China in the presentation of scientific argument. Chinese argument appealed to tradition and used a metaphorical form of language, while Greeks appealed to adversarial and legal forms of proof. But he does not think that the difference in presentation of reasoning demonstrates a difference in the form of scientific thought, since this can be explained by differences in the available and acceptable paradigms of argument and concepts in the two societies. He concludes that differences are best explained not in terms of some grand difference in scientific mentalities, but in the combination of more specific detailed differences of styles of inquiry and interpersonal exchanges. He concludes:

> '. . . the appropriate framework within which we have to tackle the problems of interpretation that such examples [of divers forms of investigation] present is provided by the complex interactions and tensions between a variety of competing ideas and assumptions on the aims, methods and subject-matter of those investigations. It is those ideas and assumptions, together with the contexts of communication in which they are embedded, that define what I have been calling divergent styles of inquiry, and nothing is to be gained from resorting to an appeal to one or more supposed underlying mentalities.'

Lloyd essentially argues that the concept of 'mentality' is too general. It fails to pay adequate attention to the complexity of the diverse individual approaches within a single society and to the way in which the situations of people in one society diverge from another society. His preference is for specific case-studies. Furthermore, he is concerned to explain the environmental conditions which facilitate the development and spread of certain views, rather than just to talk about a shared and global 'mentality' among a group of people.

Lloyd's own reductivist approach to mentality still talks of 'style' of inquiry and reasoning. For Zweigert and Kötz, the notion of 'style' is central to a distinction between legal systems, because it identifies not one single trait, but 'a congeries of particular features which the most divers objects of study may possess' and which mark them out as belonging together. But again, this notion focuses attention on the ideological elements of a legal system — the key factors to be studied are the historical background of the legal system, its predominant mode of legal thought, its distinctive institutions, the kinds of legal sources it acknowledges, and its ideology. In other words, one is looking at a set of ideas and how they are conditioned. 'Style' is used by Markesinis to be essentially about presentation and ways of doing things, a superstructure, rather than something which defines the task in hand, hence his discussion of the style of judgments. I would want to go further and look at mentality and style as ways of describing more deeply rooted activities. The existence of particular styles of presentation may serve as evidence of difference in either a deep level of legal thought, or different traditions about how legal argumentation is presented. It can serve as an indicator that there is a different culture in operation."

NOTES AND QUESTIONS

- How would you describe the difference between a legal tradition and a legal mentality; and between a legal tradition and a legal culture?

- Which term (system, tradition, mentality, culture, style) best describes the set of legal institutions, procedures and rules?

- It has been said that the legal tradition relates the legal system to the culture of which it is an expression. Which aspects of the English legal system are particular expressions of English culture? Can you think of examples of how English attitudes about the nature and role of law are reflected in the English legal system?

In order to compare legal traditions, we must first ask how we are going to "carve up the world's law" and, then, we must choose the particular trait(s) of these carved pieces that we wish to use in order to compare the different legal systems. For example, to compare apples and oranges, we must first have decided to carve up the world of food in such a way that all fruit are grouped together (or perhaps all food that ripens naturally on trees). Once the fruit has been identified as the object of our comparison, we choose to compare particular traits that various fruits may have in common (*e.g.* the presence of vitamin C or an edible skin).

The divisions of the world into legal traditions or families has not remained stable. It has been affected by history and the proliferation of particular legal, political and social theories at specific periods of time. Thus, as we will see in the following extract, the breadth of comparative law today has been increased far beyond previous divisions of the world into the three families of common law, civil law and socialist law.

H.P. Glenn, *Legal Traditions of the World: Sustainable Diversity in Law* (Oxford University Press, Oxford, 2000), pp.319, 320–322, 323–325, 330–331:

"Some very old, long-recognized traditions exists within other (major) traditions. There are endless, particular, chthonic legal traditions, as varied as the means of living harmoniously with the world. They have names, which are the names of chthonic peoples, such as Iroquois, or Aztec, or Masai. Talmudic law knows, among others, sephardic and ashkenazi traditions, and the traditions of orthodox, conservative and reform jewry. The civil law has known traditions of the jus civile, of the jus gentium, of Bartolus, of Cujas, of rhetoric, of constructive rationality, of dissent, of the nation-states which have each given to civil law a particular form of expression. Islamic law has its islams—sunni and shi'ite—and its schools—the Hanafi, Maliki, Shafi and Hanbali, and there are the regional variants, the accommodation—even incorporation—of local, informal, tradition. The common law has had it 'customs', its writs, its now-incorporated Equity, its tradition of judicial restraint (or activism, if you prefer) and now extends in divers national form to many different societies. Hindu law too has its sadachara (the practice of virtue) and its schools—the Mitakshara and the Dayabhaga—and continues to float over, and govern, those who have their particular ways. Asia knows both li and fa, and neither of these places a premium on uniformity of execution; they appear compatible to some extent with both buddhist and taoist attitudes to legal ordering. . . .

You will know, whatever your legal tradition, of other principles and institutions which have earned adherence over time and performed valuable service, for some or many. These too are forms of tradition—of information adhered to over time—and there is no way of limiting the notion of tradition to any definitive list of those which are somehow established. There is no hierarchy and no canon, only hierarchies and canons, and resistance.

There are also, arguably, the 'young traditions', the goslings of the traditional world, those which may (already) have been originated but which lack the accumulated 'pastness' which allows us to verify their staying power. These young, internal traditions seem to appear most often in traditions which value effort, originality or ijtihad, often along with aristotelian forms of logic. So we have the current shi'ite efforts to create a doctrine of the islamic state, or a contemporary legal cadre for islamic banking. The civil law world has known movements of 'libre recherche scientifique', of 'Freirecht' (both perhaps expired), of interest analysis ('Interessenjurisprudenz') and of 'alternative' forms of thinking law and commenting on law. In the effervescent common/civil law world which is the United States of America there are many movements in law, which may be a sign of intellectual strength or a sign of intellectual weakness. There is a movement which would analyse law in terms of its positive and utilitarian characteristics (law and economics); another which would subject it to feminist thought (feminist legal theory); another which would unmask its arbitrary and indeterminate methods (critical legal studies); another which would unearth its empirical assises (law and society); another which would situate it generally in postmodern society (postmodernism and law). Are these traditions *in* law, legal traditions, or do they represent something eventually antithetical to law, at least as it has (traditionally) been thought? We may eventually know. They are in any event presently internal to western law, though there are reflections of them (in varying strengths) in both common and civil law traditions.

There are also further, recognizable traditions which are not particular or internal to any given, larger tradition but which seem to run across many larger traditions. Casuistry is one such tradition, with deep and explicit roots in roman, talmudic, islamic and common laws (and perhaps hindu law, though there is the poetry). Nor would chthonic ways or asian li stand opposed to casuistic thinking, though neither would track its exercise. Analogical reasoning or qyas is also fundamental and explicit in traditions which seek to limit, subtly, judicial creativity (as in talmudic, islamic and common laws). Notions of inter-generational equity are very present in chthonic, hindu and asian law, while contemporaneous notions of equity are explicit in both civil and common law, talmudic law ('acting inside the law') and islamic law. There is a tradition of constructive rationality in law, of ijtihad, most marked in western law (civil and common), the object of passionate debate in islamic law, of incredulity and scepticism elsewhere. Fundamentalism is a lateral tradition, in the name of particular gods, particular texts, particular principles (such as rights). There are also traditions of professional role—those of the adjudicator (*decisor, iudex, judge, qadi*) or, less frequently, of counsel (advocate, barrister, attorney or simple adviser). And there are the undefended, but practised, traditions of racism, of crime, of unthinking and spontaneous antagonism to the other, however defined. . . .

Western theory of tradition teaches that all tradition is normative, that is, that it provides a model, drawn from the past, as to how one should act. Legal traditions, of all traditions, should not depart from this general phenomenon, since law is perhaps the most normative of human endeavours. There are clear differences, however, amongst legal traditions in terms of the extent to which they claim to regulate human conduct. Chthonic law doesn't appear to regulate much, yet in proscribing all conduct incompatible with a recycling cosmos its normativity is unquestionable. Talmudic and islamic law regulate most of life; they are normative in all directions. The civil and common laws are laws of liberty; both have existed as optional, suppletive forms of social regulation, allowing some form of escape from congealed, chthonic patterns. In modern guise, they would both to some extent deny the normativity of their own pasts (reconstructed as fact), both directing attention to a more limited form of present law. Yet underlying notions of intellectual liberty, rights and institutional integrity are inherent and highly normative features of both, however notions of liberty and rights may contribute to present disruption. Hindu law allows a lot of choice, both individually and in terms of multiple informal traditions, yet no one who is hindu would escape some form of law recognized as hindu. Asian tradition rejects much formal law, but does so in favour of another type of normativity, one profoundly anchored, informally, in the past.

So in spite of some confusing signals, normativity is a constant feature of these legal traditions. Even in the western ones, where liberty is most prized, it is often constrained, and where it is not is assumes its own normativity—the obligation to be free and to exercise one's rights. The indecision of relativism is a problem external to these traditions; they do not acknowledge it. Relativism would be a problem, however, where legal traditions meet. It could be avoided by universalism—by insisting on the normativity in all cases of one's own tradition. If one refuses universalism, in the name of some form of tolerance, how does one avoid the indecision of relativism? How is this question dealt with, in the traditions?

Complex traditions

. . . [Legal traditions] nest (like Russian dolls) within one another, such that the largest can even be said to be composed of a series of supporting, complementing, even recalcitrant, sub-traditions. *The largest, major traditions would therefore be large and major because of their complexity.* They succeed in bringing together, in the name of some important principle or being, a number of identifiable other traditions, providing some form of overarching cohesion. . . .

Chthonic tradition allows great diversity within itself, giving quiet approval to all chthonic ways, and even change of them, on condition of ongoing respect for the natural world. Talmudic law knows its principle of 'These and these', which both, though contradictory, represent the word of God, and in the ongoing, often contradictory, talmudic debate, there is constant re-affirmation of the larger synthesis of the Perfect Author. The civil law has always know multiple, and contradictory, versions of itself—from the jus civile and jus gentium of Roman times and the later tension between local, chthonic ways and the ius commune, through emergent then flourishing national legislation, to the 'fuzzy' relations emerging within the European Union. Islam has its ikhtilaf, the doctrine of diversity (the trees and branches, the rivers and seas, the threads and garments) and an entire hadith, that 'Difference of opinion . . . is a sign of the bounty of God'. The common law co-opted local diversity, leaving juries to their own devices, then, as 'chaos with an index', accommodated, then integrated, ecclesiastical, Admiralty and Equity courts and case law, before going on to its present, trans-oceanic diversity. Hindu law gives pride of place to local law, since Brahman infuses all, never dividing, never separating, essentially advita (non-dual) and allowing hinduism to be a 'Commonwealth of all faiths', an illustration of the fundamental unity of the world. Asian normativity knows the 'middle way' of buddhism; the infinite, related, gradations of confucianism; the massive effort of intellectual integration—of individuals and groups, of relations and autonomy, of self-worth and common effort. . . .

The interdependence of complex traditions is evident both from the difficulty in defining the starting points of major legal traditions (even the prophets retain much of previous law, now revealed) and by the ongoing, major forms of communication and debate between complex traditions. Chthonic law is used to criticize civil and common law dealing with the environment. Islamic law criticizes civil and common law jurisdictions for their treatment of the poor and the persecuted; western lawyers criticize islamic criminal sanctions and its limit on human expression and speech. Talmudic law knows that the law of the state is law, and may even incorporate some of it, while itself being cited as a different (and perhaps better) model of law than state law. Civil and common law jurisdictions 'borrow' from one another, or create 'mixed' jurisdictions, and these processes now appear as western and formalized versions of the exchange of information between complex traditions which has always gone in, in a massive way. Hindu and asian law exist as layered traditions, those which have developed indigenously and those which have been developed in some manner from western models. Where is the core of any of these major traditions which could supplant all the law of the rest of them? The answer would appear to be that there is no such universalizable core. This is good news for the sustainability of the major, complex, legal traditions of the world."

NOTES AND QUESTIONS

• Which legal traditions have been identified in the text?

- Can you identify any traditions that have been left out? What does this say about the way in which Glenn has "carved up the world's law"?

COMPARING TWO TRADITIONS: COMMON AND CIVIL LAW

We now turn to a concrete example of the comparison of different legal traditions. In the two extracts which follow, the authors have chosen to use common law (English) and civil law (continental European) traditions as their object of study. Each, however, focuses on different aspects of comparison. In the first text, by Farrar and Dugdale, the authors provide a brief overview of the two traditions with a view to providing some broad conclusions about the differences between them. In the second text, by Nicholas, we look at a particular example of the civil law in practice drawn from a text on the French law of contract. You should attempt to read both these extracts with a view to understanding what the authors identify as the similarities and differences between the common law and civil law traditions, as well as how these similarities and differences are reflected in the English common law and the French civil law systems.

J.D. Farrar and A.M. Dugdale, *Introduction to Legal Method* (3rd ed., Sweet and Maxwell, London, 1990), pp.247–50:

The civilian tradition

"This is the oldest of the surviving traditions and can perhaps be traced to 450 BC, the date of the XII Tables in Rome which were a priestly codification of early Roman law.

It is the tradition of the original six member states of the EEC and Spain and Portugal together with their former colonies. It is the background to much of the early development of the EEC and indeed it has had a strong influence on the development of both public and private international law.

Roman law developed from a priestly system to a highly developed secular system through the influence of jurists (jurisconsults) who did not actually perform the function of a modern lawyer but wrote systematic treatises on particular branches of law. The law itself consisted of the *jus civile*, which only applied to citizens of the Roman empire, and the more flexible *jus gentium* which applied to non citizens. Both systems underwent considerable modification over centuries. In the sixth century AD the emperor Justinian arranged for the production of a Digest and codification of the law which assimilated the laws and doctrinal writings, eliminating conflict. Institutes were also prepared as a primer for law students. This mammoth work of rationalisation enabled Roman law to survive the decline and ultimate destruction of the Roman Empire. The Roman law tradition survived the Dark Ages and was studied in the medieval universities as the basis of rational principles of law.

However, it not only survived as a scholarly tradition, but also as a source of common law of nations at a time when Europe was subject to a multiplicity of local customs and laws. Voltaire reckoned that one changed one's laws as often as one changed one's horse in riding through eighteenth century France. In arriving at a just solution of mercantile disputes Roman law was often resorted to on the Continent. It also influenced the development of the canon law of the Christian Church and the movement towards the early conceptions of international law.

So, therefore, an important ingredient in the civilian tradition is the common inheritance of Roman law. However, a combination of the enlightenment of the eighteenth century and revolution created an impetus to modern codification. This was achieved in the Napoleonic period in France at the beginning of the nineteenth century, although Frederick the Great had attempted a less successful codification of parts of Prussian law in the eighteenth century. The Code Napoléon was a masterly codification of French customary law and Roman law as it stood at 1804. Directly and indirectly it was the blueprint for much European codification. Its basis was simple clear statements of law which left much unsaid. A different approach was adopted in the German codification measures of the end of the nineteenth century. Here the emphasis was on detail and a self contained code—every answer was to be found in the code itself. Most modern Civilian systems opt for one of these two models of codification although each system has areas of law which are not completely codified.

A further characteristic of Civilian systems is the high status accorded to doctrinal writings. While not a source of law as such they rank as high as or of higher status than judicial precedent as a guide to the interpretation of the codes. Where the law is codified the code is the definitive source. The status of judicial precedent is naturally less than in common law systems. It is not that precedent is unimportant in practice but that in theory its validity derives from the words of the code itself. Individual precedents are not binding. A body of precedent is regarded as good evidence of the true meaning of the code. . . .

Last, the Civilian tradition tends to employ more inquisitorial procedures with regard to fact finding than the common law and the whole of its procedure is administered by a career judiciary.

The Common Law tradition

. . . First, the common law, while slightly influenced by the form, did not receive the substance of the Roman law inheritance. It steadfastly resisted it for reasons which were partly political and partly professional. Roman law was linked with Catholicism and later with Stuart autocracy. England, unlike Scotland, developed its own professional structure and tradition from an early date. This was until remarkably recently outside the university framework. English law was not taught at the universities until the eighteenth century, but was the province of the Inns of Court and the profession. The history of legal education in the seventeenth and eighteenth century is rather appalling. Small parts of Roman law did influence some aspects of the common law, but this is mainly as a result of nineteenth century rationalisation.

Secondly, in spite of Bentham and the codification movement in the nineteenth century, the only area of codification has been in commercial law. . . .

Thirdly, as we have seen, although text books by living authors are now cited there is still less status accorded to doctrinal writing in the common law tradition. The status seems to depend *ad hominem* to a greater extent than in the civilian system and reflects perhaps the closed social world of the English judiciary.

Fourthly, the status of judicial precedent is much higher and it is an actual source of law. The standard of the judiciary in the common law world has been high and the process of ratiocination is more obvious in a common law judgment than in the bleak arrested style of a French judgment. As a continuing source, however, with the multiplication of reports the form of the law remains irrational and almost uncontrollable.

Fifthly, the terminology, but not necessarily the practice of interpretation, differs from the civilian tradition as we have seen.

Last, the common law tradition shows a marked preference for adversarial procedure before judges with forensic experience. The emphasis is perhaps more on justice than on truth."

B. Nicholas, *The French Law of Contract* (2nd ed., Clarendon Press, Oxford, 1992), pp.1–23:

"French law belongs to that family of legal systems to which we attach the name of 'Civil law'. This family embraces the systems of continental Europe (or at least western Europe), and also of Latin America and many other countries which derive their legal systems from continental Europe. The name is often criticized, especially by Civil lawyers themselves, because it refers to only one element in the tradition which unites those systems, and also because it ignores the differences which distinguish one from another. (In much the same way in ordinary life a stranger sees the resemblances between members of a family, while they themselves are more aware of their individuality). But the usage is inveterate among Common lawyers, and the name, if properly understood, does point to some important characteristics which the systems have in common and which are foreign to the Common law.

The origin of the name is clear. To the Romans the term *ius civile* had meant, at its widest, the law of a particular state, or more narrowly, the law of Rome herself. It was in accordance with this usage that Justinian's compilation of Roman law came to be known, after its rediscovery in the eleventh century, as the *Corpus Iuris Civilis*. And 'Civil law' thereafter meant the rediscovered Roman law. As this law was 'received' by the emergent states and cities of continental Europe as a *ius commune*, or common law, which was applied in default of, or to a varying extent in substitution for, the local law, it was natural that the English, whose courts had stood apart from this reception, should see in this common factor the identifying mark of the legal systems of the Continent. Nor did they habitually make any distinction between this contemporary Civil law and the historical law of Rome. Blackstone, for example, calls it 'the imperial law'.

During the past two hundred years, however, the justification for thus seeing the law of the Continent as predominantly Roman law in a modern context has diminished. The most important influence in this dwindling of the Roman element has been the movement for codification, the first great achievement of which was the enactment of Napoleon's *Code civil* in 1804. The codes which thereafter spread over Europe were important (in this context) in two ways. First, they cut the law off from its Roman roots, the *Corpus Iuris Civilis* could no long be cited as direct authority. If Roman rules were still applied, this was because they were embodied in the relevant code, and not (except as a matter of history) because they were to be found in the *Corpus Iuris*. Moreover, as Roman law disappeared from the courts, it took on a different appearance in the lecture room. The interest shifted from the task of interpreting the *Corpus Iuris* as a practical system to that of unearthing classical law. For that law lay buried beneath both the editorial work of Justinian and the heavy layer of interpretation and harmonization which had been elaborated by centuries of activity in the universities of Europe. 'Civil law' (or *ius commune*) was now seen to be not the same as Roman law.

This does not mean that there are no common elements in, say, French and German law which justify our still speaking of them as 'Civil law systems', but they are Civil law in a different sense. They belong to the Civil law because their methods of thought, their attitudes to law and its source, derive from the centuries in which the *ius commune*, Romanistic but not Roman, was created out of the materials in the *Corpus Iuris*. And those methods and attitudes were different, as we shall see, from those of the English Common law, which was nurtured in a quite other environment.

The Roman element, therefore, has dwindled since the coming of the codes. Its importance was indeed never as exclusive as the English use of the name 'Civil law' suggested. Apart from Canon law (which was Roman in spirit and, like Roman law, universal), there were everywhere two other elements: customary law and legislation. But these varied from one legal system to another, or even, in the case of customary law, from one local area to another, and it was natural for the Common lawyer to emphasize the universal element. Moreover, the non-Roman elements were mainly to be found in those areas of the law (the law of the family and of inheritance) which are everywhere most likely to be affected by differences of culture and of what one now calls 'policy'. The contribution of Roman law, on the other hand, was strongest in the parts which have, at least until recently, been most exclusively the handiwork of lawyers: the law of obligations (and especially the law of contract, which is the concern of this book), the law of property, and the general conceptual framework of the whole system. The advent of the codes, however (and this was the second way in which they diminished the Roman character of the systems to which they applied), unified and systematized the customary element, while the spirit of the times and the complexity of modern life has everywhere produced an ever-swelling volume of legislation only loosely related to the traditional Roman framework.

It is this framework which provides a link between the Common lawyer's use of 'Civil law' and the meaning which French lawyers give to *droit civil*. In its widest sense this denotes the whole of private law. In practice, however, as a glance at any of the many works published under this title now show, the term refers primarily and usually to the contents of the *Code civil*. And the *Code civil* is concerned with the central and traditional parts of the private law: the law of persons (or family law), the law of property and of succession, and the law of obligations. This is the heart of the private law, the trunk of the tree from which grow the more particular branches. All other parts (and, as has just been said, they are now both extensive and important) pre-suppose the *droit civil*. And the *droit civil* in this sense goes back to Justinian's Institutes, which provide the framework of the *Corpus Iuris* and therefore of the 'Civil law' in the Common lawyer's sense, even though (it must be said again) the substance which is now attached to some parts of this framework is anything but Roman. The framework, however, though it is to be found in varying forms in all 'Civil law' systems, is not, from the point of view of the Common lawyer, the most important of the differentiating characteristics of those systems. We should now look more closely at those differences of method and attitude to which reference has already been made.

Characteristics of French law

The differences of method and attitude which have now to be identified derive, we have said, from the *ius commune*. For though important elements of French law come, as we have seen, from canon law, customary law, and legislation, the Common lawyer finds the principal differentiating characteristics of the system in the inheritance from this *ius commune*.

The heart of the matter is that the *ius commune* is a law of the book, elaborated in the universities, whereas the Common law is a law of the case, created by the courts. The *ius commune*, in theory at least, sprang fully formed from the *Corpus Iuris Civilis*, the function of the universities being that of interpretation. The Common law, on the other hand, is in a state of continuous creation and by its nature is never complete. Again, the *ius commune* was seen as universally valid, regardless of time or place. It was a set of rules for the conduct of life in society—rules which might or might not be applied in any particular court or jurisdiction. (Hence it is still true today that in the universities of the Continent law is studied by large numbers who will never go into practice.) The Common law, by contrast, is concerned to provide solutions to individual disputes, not to propound universal precepts; and it is expressed, in its traditional form, in terms of actions or remedies rather than of substantive rules. Insofar as nowadays it does think in terms of rules, those rules are seen as a generalization from the solutions of individual disputes, whereas for the Civil lawyer the rules logically precede the solutions. In short, for the Common law the beginning is the case, whereas for the *ius commune* the beginning is the book.

With the advent of the codes the character of the book changes, but the conception of law remains the same. The beginning is now the code or codes, not the *Corpus Iuris*, but the primacy of the written law remains. Law is still seen as a system, complete and intellectually coherent, composed of substantive rules. And the creative function is still that of interpretation, a function exercised in the first place by the universities. The decisions of the courts are, in conventional theory, merely an application of the enacted law. Some of these features need further examination in the particular context of French law.

(a) Primacy of legislation

In the conventional French analysis there are only two sources of law: legislation and custom. The latter is only interstitial and in the present context can be ignored. Law is primarily and characteristically a body of rules enacted by the state, to be found in the codes and, in ever-increasing measure, in legislation supplementary to the codes. Indeed, just as a Common lawyer will derive a general principle from particular cases, a French lawyer may, by what has been called 'amplifying induction', find in individual enactments evidence of a wider legislative intent which can be applied outside the area covered by the individual enactments. The Common lawyer's approach is quite different. For him law has characteristically been the unwritten law found in the decisions of the courts. It is true, of course, that legislation is the primary source in the sense that in case of conflict it will prevail, but it has traditionally been regarded as an inroad on or suspension of the Common law, which will revive when the legislation is repealed. Particular enactments will therefore be restrictively interpreted. So far from inferring a more general legislative intent, the Common lawyer will argue that if Parliament had intended to lay down a more general principle, it would have done so expressly.

This difference is reflected in a difference in the approach of the two systems to the interpretation of legislation (and, as a corollary, a difference in the style of drafting). The English courts, seeing legislation as an inroad on the basic unwritten law, interpret it restrictively, so as to minimize the inroad. This attitude would make no sense for the French lawyer for whom the basic law is itself legislation. In the period of the *ius commune*, when lawyers had to adapt the unchanging texts of the *Corpus Iuris* to the changing needs of society and to find a harmony in the rich disordance of these texts, they necessarily adopted a very free and creative method of interpretation. The method remains, and it is indeed in accord with the relatively subordinate position which is allotted to the judiciary by the French version of the separation of powers. Legislation is a manifestation of the will of the state and the function of the judiciary as an organ of the state is to give effect to that will.

This function is pre-supposed by the simplicity and brevity of French legislative drafting. The English draftsman tries to make his text 'judge-proof' by anticipating every eventuality, and he often in consequence produces a complex and technical formulation which only a lawyer can interpret. The French draftsman, by contrast, can rely on the collaboration of the courts, and his text is therefore limited to quite broad propositions. That this is true of the *Code civil* is well known (and it is a source of pride and confidence to the Frenchman that his law is presented in a simple and intelligible form) but even the necessarily more complex legislation of modern times may leave much to be filled in by interpretation.

(b) Character of the codes

If legislation is the characteristic form of law in France and the codes are the characteristic form of legislation, the *Code civil* is the characteristic code. The Napoleonic codification consisted of five codes, but the term *Code Napoléon* was reserved for the *Code civil* alone. And with justice. For the *Code civil* is the centre-piece to which the great influence of the whole codification is attributable.

A code in the strict sense is a systematic and complete statement of a body of law. In this sense the *Corpus Iuris Civilis* of Justinian is not a code. For though it is complete, it is not in any recognizable way systematic. The *Code civil* is systematic, though its system (which echoes, without entirely reproducing, that of the Institutes of Gaius and Justinian) is, as a piece of analysis, easily criticized; and it is a complete statement of the law governing relations between individuals (except insofar as these are governed by the *Code de commerce*) as that law was understood in 1804. We have seen, however, that even then the simplicity and brevity of its drafting left much to be supplied by interpretation, and it is now not complete in any sense. For the increasing complexity of modern life has called forth a large body of additional legislation. Some of this can be said merely to amplify the provisions of the Code, but by far the greater part is concerned with matters quite outside the area of the traditional *droit civil*. Codification, moreover, creates an expectation that all law will be presented in a systematic form, and a good deal of the additional legislation has itself been reduced to the form of subordinate codes. In England, by contrast, even in those areas of the law which are largely the creation of legislation, a systematic statement of the whole body of the law is not undertaken. At most, as in the Companies Act 1985, a consolidation of existing legislation is enacted, but this leaves the essential Common law foundations unstated; and when such a consolidation comes to be amended, as in the Companies Act 1989, no attempt is made to build the new legislation into the old. A codifying statue is a rarity, and the few which have been enacted deal in fact with areas of the law which were almost entirely judge-made.

(c) The courts and the position of the judiciary

Before embarking on the (to an English lawyer) rather elusive subject of the authority of case law, we must look briefly at the French judiciary (*magistrature*) and the court system.

In common with all other Civil countries, France has a career judiciary. Judges (*magistrats*) are normally recruited from among young men and women (the latter having been in recent years in the majority) graduating from the law faculties of the universities. After a competitive examination they are admitted to the *École nationale de la magistrature* (the annual intake to which approached 2,000) for two years of theoretical and practical training. Then, after a further examination, they are appointed to their first judicial post. The more ambitious will hope eventually to reach the *Cour de cassation*.

The court system has three tiers, as in England, but beyond this the similarities are few.

In the lower two tiers the courts, as well as being more numerous than in this country, are markedly decentralized. In the first tier we may ignore the 485 *tribunaux d'instance*, which may be said very roughly to correspond to the English county courts, in that their jurisdiction is limited to relatively minor suits. But there are also 181 *tribunaux de grand instance*, exercising an unlimited jurisdiction. There is nothing to correspond to the concentration of major civil litigation in London: the only cases tried in Paris are those which originate in Paris. Similarly, in the second tier there are 33 *cours d'appel*, each hearing appeals from the *tribunaux* each hearing appeals from one or more *départements* (including those overseas). Each *tribunaux de grand instance* and each *cour d'appel* will be composed of several chambers or divisions.

There is, moreover, a difference between a French *appel* and an English appeal. A *cour d'appel* conducts a re-examination of the whole case, and can substitute its view of either facts or law for that of the original court. It is true that the English Court of Appeal is empowered to do the same, but in practice it will not interfere with the trial court's view of the primary facts (*i.e.* what was said or done), though it may feel free to substitute its own view of the secondary facts (*i.e.* the interpretation to be put on the primary facts). The reason for this difference lies in the difference between the English and the French trial. In England the facts are in principle established by oral evidence elicited by the adversarial process in a single continuous hearing. A repetition of this hearing is impracticable, and for the Court of Appeal to rely on the written record alone would be inconsistent with the firmly held judicial belief in the importance of seeing and hearing the witnesses. In France, on the other hand, the facts are in principle established in a written *dossier* compiled by a predominantly investigatory process by the court itself, and a review of the *dossier* does not present the same difficulty.

The only court with jurisdiction over the whole country is the *Cour de cassation* (composed of five chambers for civil cases and one for criminal). This is a court of error, in the sense that the only basis for recourse to it (*pourvoi en cassation*) is that the judgement of the court below is not in conformity with the law. (The court below must be a court from which there is no appeal. It will usually be a *cour d'appel*, but may be an inferior court if in the particular case no appeal is allowed, *e.g.* because the amount in issue is too small.) If the *Cour de cassation* finds the *pourvoi* justified, it does not substitute its own judgment, as a *cour d'appel* does, but as its name indicates, it merely quashes the decision. The case is them remitted for further consideration, not to the original court but to another court of equal jurisdiction. If this court nevertheless takes the same view of the law as the original court, the matter is referred to the *Assemblée plénière* of the *Cour de cassation*, on which all chambers are represented. The *Assemblée plénière* remits the matter to a third court, which is bound by the view of the law taken by the *Assemblée*. This is the traditional procedure, but recent reforms, designed to save court time, have allowed either the chamber which deals with the first *pourvoi* or the *Assemblée plénière* to enter a final judgment if its decision on the particular point of law in issue leaves nothing further for the court below to consider.

The *Cour de cassation* differs greatly from the House of Lords. Its primary function is to secure a uniform interpretation of the law. In England this unifying function is usually discharged by the Court of Appeal itself, leaving to the House of Lords the function of resolving legal issues of public importance and, in general, guiding the development of the law. This function does indeed also belong to the *Cour de cassation*, but its discharge is hampered by the primacy of the unifying function. For that function requires—or is seen as requiring—that there should be unrestricted access to the *Cour de cassation* for every litigant who wishes to argue a point of law. Any filter such as that provided by the need, before an appeal can be launched in the House of Lords, to obtain leave from the Court of Appeal (or the Appeals Committee of the House of Lords) is ruled out. This absence of a filter, combined with the much larger volume of cases before the French courts, means that the *Cour de cassation* is swamped and cannot find time for the unhurried thought and debate which difficult issues call for. It also means that the court is numerically very large (its established judicial personnel amount to 127) and lacks the unity which a small court like the House of Lords can achieve. The overloading of the court is now acute. The number of cases has tripled in the last ten years and the five civil chambers decide well over 15,000 cases a year, compared with about 70 in the House of Lords, and there is a steadily increasing backlog. It seems likely that some reform will be introduced.

With the exception of the *tribunaux d'instance*, all courts are 'collegial'. By this is meant not only that they consist of a bench of at least three judges (at least seven in the *Cour de cassation*), but also that they act as a body, giving only a single judgment. Dissenting opinions are unknown, and even the existence of dissent is not revealed. Moreover, the laconic form of the judgment (discussed below) offers none of the opportunity for the expression of individual views which is afforded by its discursive English Counterpart. The leading English judges are public figures whose judgments and attitudes are the subject of discussion in the press and elsewhere, but the French judge, even when he has reached the top of the judicial pyramid, is typically anonymous. He is, as Montesquieu puts its, the mouthpiece of the law.

There are two departures from this principle of anonymity: the *rapport* of the member of the court to whom the case is remitted for initial consideration, and the *conclusions* of the representative of the *ministère public*.

The predominantly written character of French procedure makes it possible (and the pressure of business, especially in the *Cour de cassation*, would in any case make it necessary) for the initial consideration of each case to be assigned to only one member of the court (or chamber). He presents a *rapport*, which examines the state of the law, including the case law, and the arguments before the court, and discusses wider considerations of what we would call 'policy'. It reads in fact rather like an English judgment (except that it is directed to convincing the court rather than the parties or their representatives) and it contrasts markedly with the impersonal and unargumentative style of the formal judgment. The *rapport* is then in principle discussed, and the judgment which is proposed is accepted, rejected, or amended, by the full bench, but it is clear that in practice, at least in the *Cour de cassation*, the volume of cases to be dealt with precludes substantial discussion or amendment in all but a small minority of cases.

The *ministère public* has no counterpart in Common law jurisdictions. The judicial profession (*magistrature*) is divided into two branches: the judiciary in the ordinary sense, i.e. those who sit on the bench (*magistrature assise*) and the *ministère public*, whose function is to represent before the court the public interest (*magistrature debout*, since they stand to address the court). There is no rigid division between the two branches: a *magistrat* may pass from one to the other in the course of his career. The *ministère public*, representatives of which are attached to each court from the *tribunaux de grand instance* upwards, has several functions (including the conduct of the prosecution in criminal cases), but we are here concerned with the representations (*conclusions*) made to the civil courts about the cases before them. The representative of the *ministère public* has the right to place before the court his *conclusions* as to how the case before it should be decided. He does so as the representative of the public interest, but this is not to be understood in a broad sense as the interest of society at large, as contrasted with the interests of the individual litigants. The interest which he represents is rather the interest of the state in the correct functioning of the legal system, seen as a public service. (It is for this reason that in cases before the *Cour de cassation* the *ministère public* not only may, but must submit *conclusions*. For every recourse to that court necessarily, as we have seen, alleges that the decision below was not in conformity with the law.) The *conclusions* are therefore similar in content to the *rapport*, though the style may be more rhetorical and more vigorously argued (reflecting the difference in standpoint of the speaker). Both are expressions of the speaker's own views.

The *conclusions* or the *rapport*, or even both, are occasionally published along with the judgment itself. The publication of the *conclusions* is not, of course, a breach of the principle of collegiality, since the author is not a member of the court, but the publication of the *rapport*—especially when, as is sometimes the case, the court has rejected the recommendation made—is tantamount to a breach. But both give an insight into the working of judicial minds and the possible or probable reasoning behind the decision. This, and often the elegance and vigour of their argumentation, make the reader regret that they are not published more often and that such talent is otherwise confined in the strait-jacket of the formal judgment.

(d) Authority of case law

The courts of the *ancien régime* (the *parlements*) were one of the main objects of the hostility of the Revolution, not least because of their pretensions to a law-making function. The Constituent Assembly of 1790 took care that the new courts should be confined to the narrowly judicial function of applying the law in suits between private individuals (or, in criminal matters, between the state and the individual). They were to have no jurisdiction over the administration, and in exercising their proper function they were not to lay down general rules. They were even required to refer any matter of interpretation to the legislature. This was of course quite impracticable and remained a dead letter, but the prohibition against laying down general rules when deciding individual cases was repeated in article 5 of the *Code civil*.

This attempt to prevent the growth of case law was undermined, however, by another requirement laid down by the Assembly. The *parlements* had not given reasons for their decisions, but now, in order to ensure that the courts did not exceed their powers, every decision was to be 'motivated'. The form of judgment which the courts adopted to meet this requirement (and which survives without significant change today) does not set out, as an English judgment does, the process of argument by which the decision was reached—this would have been inconsistent with the ruling mechanistic view of the judicial process; but equally it does not simply state the legislative text upon which the decision was based—the generality of many provisions in the Codes would have defeated the original purpose of the requirement of 'motivation'. Typically the form adopted states the facts, the grounds of the *pourvoi* (in the case of the *Cour de cassation*), and a principle from which, by syllogistic reasoning applied to the facts, the decision can be logically derived. In every case the judgment, however long, is framed as a single sentence, of which the subject ('The Court . . .') is placed at the beginning and the main verb, stating the decision ('quashes', 'rejects', etc.), at the end, everything else being incorporated in subordinate clauses beginning with 'whereas' ('*attendu*' or in some courts *considérant*). The judgments of lower courts are usually fuller than those of the *Cour de cassation* and, since those courts are judges of both fact and law, they state the facts at greater length, but the form is in all essentials the same. The principle is presented as self-evident and is in theory, in the normal case, derived from a text or texts which are cited at the beginning of the judgment. But it is of course in the act of derivation that the creative power of the judiciary resides, and the result of requiring that act to be recorded was inevitably the evolution of what is in substance a vast body of judge-made law.

It was not, however, until late in the nineteenth century that the literature of the law began seriously to take cognizance of this development. This delay reflects the dominance in the though of the period of the positivist view of law as the expression of the will of the state (a view which accords, as we have seen, with the doctrine of the separation of powers and which is still to be found in French textbooks). The persistence of the mechanistic view of the role of the courts was also, however, encouraged by the form of the judgment, which, by making no reference to the arguments which have led the court to adopt the governing principle (even when the court is in fact reversing a previously established principle), conceals the creative process.

No-one, in any event, now disputes that the decisions of the courts (*la jurisprudence*) must play a large part in any attempt to state the law. To go no further, what we should call the law of torts, which is stated in the *Code civil* in only five articles, is very largely a creation of the courts, and the law of unjustified enrichment derives from a decision of the *Cour de cassation* in 1892 which did not even purport to be based on a text. The writers, regularly, and increasingly, take account of *jurisprudence*; no practitioner would fail to deal with it in presenting a case; and though the judgments (with some exceptions in the lower courts) continue to make no reference to it, it is fully examined in the *conclusions* of the representative of the *ministère public* and in the *rapport*.

The constitutional theory that *jurisprudence* cannot be a legal source is, however, normally maintained. Theory and practice may be reconciled by drawing a distinction between a source (in law) and an authority (in fact). It is an obvious and important fact that courts do not follow previous decisions, and statements of what the law is necessarily take account of this fact. But it is nevertheless a fact and not a rule; no court is legally required to follow any previous decision. There is no system of binding precedent, though there is a practice which produces similar results. This may look like splitting hairs to preserve a principle, but the distinction between rule and fact does have practical consequences, and the results, though similar, are not identical. The practical consequences lie partly in the way in which judgments are formulated and partly in the attitude of judges. The former is indeed something of a technicality. A court may not cite as the justification for its decision a previous decision, or line of decisions, even of the *Cour de cassation*. If it does so, the decision will be quashed for lack of legal foundation. Conversely, if the *Cour de cassation* wishes to quash a decision as being in conflict with its own *jurisprudence*, and every lawyer knows that this is what it is doing, it will nonetheless state as the foundation for its decision not the *jurisprudence*, but the text or legal principle of which the *jurisprudence* is ostensibly an interpretation.

As far as the attitude of judges is concerned, the consequences of the distinction between rule and fact are not merely technical. To say that an English judge of first instance is bound by decisions of the Court of Appeal is not merely to say that he will in fact follow these decision, or that even if he does not, his decision will be overturned on appeal; it is an assertion both that the judge accepts that he must follow those decisions and that, if he were not to do so, even on good grounds, he would be subject to criticism by the profession. The French judges accept that they ought usually to follow decisions of the *Cour de cassation*, if only because stability and predictability are important in the law, but their legal duty is to apply the law and if they are convinced that a decision of the *Cour de cassation* does not represent the law, they will ignore it; and they will not incur the same criticism as would an English judge. Resistance of this kind to decisions of the *Cour de cassation* is not very uncommon and may, if maintained, particularly by several *Cours d'appel*, presage a change (*revirement*). For what is true of the lower courts is true also of the *Cour de cassation*, and there has never been any suggestion that the court is bound by its own decisions. It is usually said, however, that there is one court—the *Assemblée plénière*—which has such authority that no other court would think of going against it.

There is, then, no rule of binding precedent, but there is well-established practice that lower courts will normally follow the *jurisprudence* of the *Cour de cassation*. This leaves open, of course, the question of what constitutes a *jurisprudence*. It has often been said that the important difference in practice between the English and the French systems of precedent is that in England a single decision is sufficient, whereas in France authority attaches to what is called a *jurisprudence constante*, *i.e.* to a concordant series of decisions. But it is easy to point to single decisions which marked a new departure—and were immediately recognized as doing so. The significant distinction is rather between an *arrêt de principe* and an *arrêt d'espèce*, i.e. between a judgement which is intended to establish a principle (either because the case law has been uncertain or conflicting or because the court has decided to alter its previous jurisprudence) and one which, as an English lawyer might say, is to be confined to its own facts. This is not to suggest that all decisions are capable of being labelled as one or the other. The great majority of the vast number of *arrêts* rendered every year by the *Cour de cassation* are unremarkable decisions which merely augment an

already well-established *jurisprudence constante* on the matter in issue. It is to the small
residue of cases which do not fit into this category that the distinction applies. It is not, of
course, a distinction which declares itself on the face of the *arrêt*, and its application is a
matter of art as much as of science, but the reader of the French reports will acquire a part
of the skill if he remembers that in a literary form as laconic as that of the French judgment, particularly as it is practised in the *Cour de cassation*, no word is wasted and none is
unconsidered. For example, the formulation of the principle which constitutes the major
premise of the judgment may be repeated unaltered through dozens or hundreds of cases,
while the critical reader wonders at the increasingly forced interpretation of either the principle or the facts which is necessary in order to complete the syllogism, until finally a small
alteration is made which so adjusts the principle that the forced interpretation is no longer
necessary. Again, when the *jurisprudence* is uncertain or in disarray, a categorical statement
of a general principle, particularly if it is placed at the beginning of the *arrêt* as what is
called a *chapeau*, will be seen as the mark of the *arrêt de principe*.

There remains a very considerable difference in the methods by which in the two systems
the principle established by a decision is identified. In the first example given above the alert
reader will notice the change in formulation, but may well be left in doubt as to what it por-
tends. The judgment itself will give him no assistance. If he is fortunate, this may be one of
the rare cases in which the *conclusions* or the *rapport* are published. Otherwise he must
interpret the change in the light of the *doctrine* on the subject, which will have discussed
the difficulties presented by the previous cases. An attempt at such an interpretation will
often be appended as a *note* to the report.

In an English judgment, on the other hand, the principle of the case is not encapsulated in
a single carefully pruned and polished sentence. The decision of the case typically evolves
from an examination of the previous cases and a discussion of how far the pattern set by
those cases needs to be adapted to accommodate the new fact situation. The characteristic
English intellectual device of 'distinguishing' is unknown in France, both because the form
of the judgment provides no opportunity for it and because, at least in the *Cour de cassation*,
the facts play a subordinate role, and may indeed be so elliptically stated as to be unintelligible without a reference to the decision of the court below. The reason for this is in part that
the *Cour de cassation* is, as we have seen, concerned only with an examination of the proposition of law relied on by the court below, and in part that the courts as a whole still think of
the judicial process as one of applying to the facts before them a rule established a priori. The
cases are illustrations of principles rather than the material from which principles are drawn.

This attitude to facts lends considerable importance to the distinction between fact and
law. Findings of fact are within the uncontrolled discretion of the court which tries the case
(and this, on the French view of the nature of an appeal, includes the relevant *cour d'appel*).
The *Cour de cassation* cannot interfere with this *pouvoir souverain du juge du fond* unless
the interpretation of the primary facts is so unreasonable that it can be said to have 'dena-
tured' them. From this it follows that the wider the area of what is categorized as fact, the
more restricted will be the unifying power of the *Cour de cassation*. The view of cases as
illustrations, which is an aspect of the tendency of a 'law of the book' to formulate broad
rules, leaves a large area to fact. In the Common law, by contrast, since the law evolves from
the cases, there is a constant tendency for fact to harden into law. Case-made rules are by
their nature narrow. From time to time an act of judicial generalization, or perhaps the
intervention of the legislature, will produce a broad rule or principle, but the process of
producing small rules out of facts will then resume.

In general therefore the area of fact is wider in French law than in English. This means,
of course, that the operation of the law is less predictable, that the discretion of the court
is more extensive. We shall find instances of this in the law of contract, but two may be
mentioned here. The English law of offer and acceptance embraces a number of detailed
rules evolved from the cases. In French law, by contrast, there is only one broad rule—that
there must be agreement. Whether there is agreement or not, and when and where the
agreement occurred, is a matter of fact. This at least is the position in strict theory, but the
inconvenience of such a lack of certainty and predictability has led, as we shall see, to some
stretching of the area of law.

Again, the *Code civil* lays down the broad rule that a mistake makes an agreement null if it concerns the 'substance' of the object to which the agreement relates. What constitutes 'substance' is a questions of fact outside the control of the *Cour de cassation*, and since the form of the judgment given by the trial court does not require it to justify or explain its interpretation of the word, or to relate that interpretation to the interpretations implicit in other decisions of the same or other courts, there is here a very wide area open to judicial discretion. The French judge, supposedly confined and controlled by a clear written law, often in fact has a much freer hand than the English judge.

To put the matter in another way, in many areas French law is less detailed than English, even though the number of reported decisions is much larger. An English book on contract will be re-edited every four or five years and each new edition will embody many changes. Its French counterpart will probably be re-edited less often and the changes will be much less numerous.

(e) Functions of doctrine

By *doctrine* is meant the whole body of writing about the law by those learned it in. As its name indicates, it originated in the teaching of the universities and it is still to a very large extent the work of academic writers. As we have seen, the *ius commune* was created in the universities out of the material in the *Corpus Iuris*, and it was to the universities that the courts looked for an authoritative interpretation of that law. Any system of law, if it is to be capable of growth and adaptation, must have, in addition to a body of rules, a web of principles from which those rules derive. These principles can never be exhaustively defined or finally fixed. They derive from a continuing debate. In classical Roman law this debate was conducted by the jurists; in medieval England it was to be heard in the courts (and its content was much more technical). In Europe of the *ius commune* the debate was conducted in the universities and in the literature which emanated from them. If one is to find its equivalent in the Common law, at any rate before the beginnings of academic writing in the last two decades of the nineteenth century, one must look in the judgments of the courts. The argumentative form of the English judgment provides, in the hands of the great judges, something of that web of principles to which we have referred. The English judgment fulfils in fact two functions. In its *ratio decidendi* it constitutes a source of law; in its discursive element it provides a part of what is supplied in French law by *doctrine*. The part which it cannot provide is large-scale systematic exposition, and it is only in the course of the last 100 years that this gap has gradually been filled, as it always has been in France, by academic writing. There remains a marked, though diminishing, difference in the authority which is attached to such writing in the two systems. In France *doctrine* has inherited the authority enjoyed by the universities in the period of the *ius commune*, an authority which is augmented by the relatively subordinate position which is, as we have seen, accorded to the judiciary in the constitutional scheme. The positions are reversed in England, though the standing accorded to academic writing by the courts (and its influence on their decisions) has risen considerably in recent decades.

The typical product of French *doctrine* is the large-scale treatise or the student's manual. It is in accord with the French conception of law as a system that these works usually embrace the entire *droit civil*, or the entire *droit commercial*, or at least a large and coherent part of it., such as the law of obligations. The English practice of writing books, such as this one, on the law of contract by itself is unknown, since, as we shall see, the law of contract can only be properly understood as part of the law of obligations. In those areas outside the traditional *droit civil* which constitute appendages to it, the pattern is more like that with which we are familiar.

In addition to the treatises and manuals, there are also specialized monographs (often academic theses) and articles, but the peculiar contribution of French *doctrine* has been the *note* appended to a case and providing an explanation of and commentary on it. This has provided a bridge between traditional *doctrine* and the courts. On the one hand, it has brought into the mainstream of the law the rich contribution of *jurisprudence* which would otherwise have been locked up in the cramped clauses of the judgments, and, on the other hand, it has brought the courts into touch with the critical and creative debate of which we have already spoken.

It should be said that not all *notes* are the work of academic writers. They may also be contributed by practitioners or by judges—even on occasion, as we have already remarked, by a judge who took part in the decision.

(f) Conceptualism and pragmatism

It is sometimes said that the Civil law is excessively conceptual or 'logical' or 'formalist', whereas the Common law is pragmatic and concrete. (A similar contrast is made, within the Common law between English law and American law.) This observation seems to bear two different meanings.

(i) It can mean that the Civil law will apply a given principle or concept 'logically' even though the practical consequences are unjust or inconvenient, whereas the Common law will abandon a principle if its consequences are unacceptable. More precisely this is a contrast not between logic and the lack of it, but between an approach which treats principles as having an immutable meaning (or at least is unwilling to re-examine the established interpretation in the light of its consequences), and one which acknowledges that meanings and interpretations change with circumstances. In other words, it is a contrast between an approach which speculates as to the correct conceptual analysis of a situation or relationship without advertising to the consequences which flow from that analysis (or without considering what policy may account for the attribution of those consequences which flow from that analysis) and an approach which acknowledges that principles and concepts are shorthand for practical consequences. For the realist or antiformalist cannot dispense with concepts without abandoning the element in law which ensures that like is treated alike; he can only insist that concepts be seen in the context of their consequences.

As far as French *jurisprudence* is concerned, this Common lawyer's view is encouraged by the form of the judgment, which gives no place to a consideration of practical consequences or of questions of 'policy'. It appears to treat principles as frozen in a single interpretation, whereas the English judgment makes plain the process by which convenience prevails over 'logic', or, more precisely, by which the previously accepted principle or interpretation is distinguished from one which can accommodate the argument from convenience. We have seen, however, that the form of the judgment does not correctly record the process by which the decision is reached.

As far as *doctrine* is concerned, the criticism was certainly well-founded in the nineteenth century, when the survival of eighteenth century natural law ideas, combined with an exclusive concentration on deriving the law from an examination of the words of the Code, did produce an attitude like that characterized above. Nor was this attitude confined to France. It was to be found even more markedly in German writing. And this in turn dominated the work of the contemporary English analytical jurists and the early English academic textbooks. It probably survived in Italy, where the isolation of doctrinal writing from the decisions of the courts and a general lack of interest in the application of principles to facts is still noticeable.

Present-day *doctrine*, particularly in the most recent works, is much more practically orientated than it used to be and devotes a great deal of attention to the decisions of the *Cour de cassation*, but it can still sometimes appear to the English lawyer to be examining a closed system. To some extent this is a mistaken impression, attributable to the different status of case law. As we have seen, the English lawyer, because he is constantly returning to the cases, is visibly rooting his principles and concepts in practical situations, whereas the French lawyer derives his principles and concepts primarily from the Code and legislation. That these principles and concepts are not reconcilable with *jurisprudence* is not, as it would be in England, a reason for abandoning them outright, though it is one ground for criticizing them. And to say that a principle is not rooted in the cases does not mean that it takes no account of practical considerations. What is true is that the emphasis in doctrinal writings is placed more on rational coherence and less on practical consequences than it is either in Common law writing, or, usually, in the *rapport* or *conclusions* presented to the courts.

(ii) This brings us to the second sense which can be borne by the observation which we are discussing. In this second sense the observation refers to the fact, which we have already noted, that the French *droit civil* is, ostensibly at least, a complete and coherent system, each part of which is capable of being related to every other part. As we can see from the many cross-references which editions of the *Code civil* provide, a French lawyer takes it for granted that one article can be interpreted in the light of another in a quite different part of the Code or in some subsequent legislation. This view of the law as a single, intellectually coherent system is common to all Civil law systems (it is carried to a far higher degree of generality by German law than by French) but it does not come readily to the mind of the Common lawyer. This is not, however, a matter of the presence or absence of logic or concepts, but of the scale on which each system thinks. English law thinks in pigeon-holes and rarely seeks to relate one pigeon-hole to another. This is the reason for its unease when it has to deal, for example, with the borderland between contract and tort. this relative lack of large-scale concepts reflects, of course, the primacy of the judge over the academic lawyer in the development of English law."

QUESTIONS

- According to Farrar and Dugdale, what are the principal points of divergence between the common law and civilian traditions? What are the similarities?

- What do Farrar and Dugdale mean by their statement that, in the common law tradition, "the emphasis is perhaps more on justice than on truth"?

- How would a French judgment differ in style and content from an English judgment?

- What is the role of doctrine in the civil law tradition?

- It is sometimes claimed that common lawyers have a "bottom up" approach to creating law, whereas civilians use a "top down" approach. What does this mean?

COMPARATIVE LAW AND A GLOBALISING LEGAL ORDER

Our story of comparative law began with the romantic hope of a group of jurists for a common law of humanity which would encompass the world. But even at the Paris Congress of 1900 the importance of unification into a single legal system as an aim of comparative law was hotly debated. After more than a century of debate, arguments still focus on the merits of a unified legal system as opposed to a diversity of legal traditions. In a world that is increasingly *globalised*, the issue of legal unification has become all the more important.

The importance placed nowadays on the study of legal *harmonisation* within the European Union makes this a very topical issue. The following two extracts present two opposing viewpoints. The first, by Markesinis, is optimistic about the increasing *convergence* of legal traditions. The author argues that exchange between

English lawyers and their continental European counterparts will help achieve mutual understanding and legal harmonisation in the European Union. The second, by Werro, is pessimistic, arguing that the differences between legal traditions are too great to overcome.

B.S. Markesinis, "A Matter of Style" (1994) 110 L.Q.R. 607 at 625:

"In this lecture a number of differences have been noted between the style and contents of the English and German cases which can, ultimately, be traced to fundamental and inter-related decisions taken by these systems in the distant past. The English ones, of course, are well-known: a preference for procedure over principles of substantive law; a neglect of the academic component of the law; the appointment of judges from a small group of leading practitioners; and the adoption of the jury system with all the consequences this has had on procedure and presentation of legal argument. Known though these are, they may well be repeated here since two new developments are seriously affecting the second of the above-named factors and, indirectly, the law that is handed down by our courts. The developments to which I am referring are the greater interaction between English and con-tinental European universities and the fact that nowadays in England a university training has become an essential ingredient of a legal (including judicial) career. These two devel-opments are, I believe, to determine what we will 'take' in future years from continental systems and, also, what we might be able to 'give' them in exchange. . . .

If this development is now seen in the context of the even newer 'European' perspective —and by that I mean the growing significance for municipal law of the decisions of the European Courts in Luxembourg and Strasbourg and the growing contacts under Erasmus-type programmes—it can lead to the conclusion that it is no longer fanciful to predict a steady growth in the impact that European law and doctrine will have on ours. This may not affect the style of judgments—a main theme of this paper—indeed, I hope it does not! But it is bound to strengthen their doctrinal content—the second theme of this paper—combatting the idea that because the tasks of judge and jurist are (in *some* respects) different *they must also be carried out in complete isolation from each other*. In this sense, too, the tide of European ideas will prove difficult to contain. The student of today, who will be the judge of tomorrow, will be unlikely to resist this influence since it will not be alien to him but, on the contrary, will have played a part in his formation and training.

But will the influence be one-sided? I think not and I hope not. If we do not remain in our shells we, too, can and will influence developments elsewhere. Moreover, I believe our *main* contribution may well be something of a paradox since it will come from our univer-sities (which in historical terms were the junior partners in the development of our law) exporting the teaching techniques they have developed relying on the work of our judges. For, though statutory law is increasing in size and complexity, case law is still at the base of common law education. This and the tutorial system (to varying but, by comparison to continental universities, small numbers of students) are the distinctive features of our legal education. The political tradition of the European universities makes the second feature enviable but totally inimitable. But the first feature, coupled with the emergence of English as the new *lingua franca* of the western world, gives the common law a powerful instrument with which to make its own contribution to the transnational set of legal rules which many refer to as the new *jus commune*. Let me say just a few more words as to how this could come about.

Though certain features of the common law judgment may come to be imitated by foreign judges (and others rightly avoided), it would be foolish to predict any wholesale European importation of the model. But the study of English judgments is growing as more and more young lawyers from the continent of Europe spend short or longer periods of time in common law universities (the Oxford *Magister Juris* being, perhaps, one of the best illustrations). Though particular solutions of our law may often appeal to foreign lawyers, none, I think, return to their countries believing that our doctrinal analyses or theoretical constructions can ever equal theirs. But I do believe that they return to their base impressed by the common law decision, by its grammatical clarity, by the way it has revealed and discussed the issues that in their country are hidden by legal jargon, and—most importantly—by the way it is used as a tool for imparting further legal know-how. Here, I believe, we score heavily over continental models. And, I hope, we will exploit this strength in the context of many current, private and semi-public schemes aiming to draw up a European law curriculum or, even, design a European law school by becoming involved in such projects rather than rejecting them out of hand. For, behind these projects is not utopian idealism but the growing need *somehow* to harmonise teaching materials and interrelate legal cultures for the world of tomorrow in which lawyers will find themselves being as mobile as their clients. (And this is not mentioning the former eastern European countries which are looking westward for ideas for their legal education and for new laws which they need in order to cope with the new kind of economies that they have adopted.)

The English judgment—and the learning of law through studying the judgment—is, in short, along with our language, one of the two major implements at our disposal in the struggle for shaping the European legal culture of the next century. If we wish to have some impact on this new world we must be prepared to use them."

F. Werro "Notes on the Purpose and Aims of Comparative Law" (2001) 75 Tul. L. Rev. 1225 at 1230:

An Evaluation of the Difference between the American and the European approaches

"Beyond the fact that comparative law in the United States was largely shaped by European immigrants and that this fact might be a source of discontent and doubt for contemporary Americans, it seems to me that the difference in attitude can also be explained from a more general point of view. One could venture two explanations. One is contemporary American intellectual leadership, and the other is the very way Americans and Europeans deal with law; this latter explanation explains perhaps in part the former. Let me briefly develop the second explanation.

The opposition between law as a science and law as a practical tool for solving conflicts remains valid in explaining the ways in which Europeans and Americans deal differently with comparative law. The European belief in law as a system, which one is only really able to understand if one is Kant's grandchild, on the one hand, and the American belief in law as a constantly evolving and overtly political method of dispute resolution, accompanied by a suspicion against any attempt of systematization or conceptualization, on the other hand, remains a distinction deeply rooted in lawyers' attitudes toward the law and thus toward comparative law. Another way of explaining this important difference in sensibility between (continental) Europeans and Americans should perhaps focus on the contrast between law as ultimately defined by a parliament after years of broad consultation with all possible interest groups and law as ultimately made in the courtroom with the understanding that majority votes should not restrain the judge's ability to shape fundamental principles. This difference also explains the differences in style in the teaching and training of future lawyers.

These differences should not be seen as absolute, but rather as influencing the varied emphases placed on doctrine versus practice at different levels of the legal edifice. For example, I do not believe that European lawyers have not understood the teachings of legal realism, even if it might look that way in most European classrooms. It is rather that legal realist considerations occur in a different place: not so much in the courts, but rather in the parliaments. In fact, I would think that lawmaking involves a wider range of people and interest groups in Europe than in the United States. Arguably, once the process is finished, there is less need than in the United States to debate the choice made. This explains in part why European studies tend to ignore the forces that shape the law; these forces are taken care of in advance. Thus, law gets taught as a finished and coherent product, rather than an ongoing, context-driven process.

Thus, to go back to our inquiry about the big questions in comparative law today, it is tempting to think that we need to take a differentiated view. We need to define the answer in accordance with our own context. In the United States, arguably, we need to take the concerns raised by the 1998 symposium seriously, and in some ways step out of the European shadow while taking full advantage of 'law and –ism'. In Europe, although regrettably in my view—a bit more 'law and –ism' as well as certain distrust for the pure grammar of the law in education would not hurt—we may want to satisfy ourselves with the idea that comparative law is doing well and serving essentially all the practical and doctrinal purposes it should be serving.

Yet having said this, I wonder if it is not the task of comparativists to try to define a common agenda. In a globalized world, one would think that there is much need for such an objective.

The phenomenon commonly referred to as globalization or other integrative processes triggers two questions that comparativists need more than ever to tackle: the first relates to the way in which one can acknowledge and integrate cultural diversity, and the second relates to the means of avoiding Western hegemony.

There may be many other questions linked to these two. For example, comparativists should study the risks of provincialism and parochialism, both on the part of minorities and on the part of hegemonic majorities. One major question appears to be how to put in place a better understanding amongst lawyers that law within the Western sense of the word is not the only way to define social norms of conduct.

The Need for Understanding Diversity

In a world driven by trends toward global law, the question of diversity has become essential. The need to define diversity and its proper boundaries arises more fundamentally than ever. To the extent that cultural diversity is a reality, law is bound to be defined in diversified terms.

It seems to me, however, that we are even less sure than ever before of what cultural diversity means and to what extent diversity should be reflected in legal choices. We run into this question in relation to World Trade Organization (WTO) issues for example. On a smaller scale, on a European level, we run into this question in relation to the project of unification of private law. Claiming 'the impossibility of legal transplants' is probably too extreme a position and betrays an exaggeration of cultural diversity, at least on the European level.

However, the statement that law and society are not in close relationship is also quite obviously an oversimplification. . . . both approaches need adjustment and corrections. To deny the possibility or the desirability of legal transplants seems to contradict the teachings of history and is at odds with the need for legal integration in certain geographic areas. It also assumes a degree of cultural diversity in Europe, for instance, that I fail to recognize. If diversity exists, it does not, in my view, reach a level of intensity that is necessarily relevant for legal integration, at least in certain areas of the law. Of course insisting on the nomadic or transplantable character of rules of law cannot mean that 'change in the law is independent from the workings of any social, historical, or cultural substratum'.

In other words, it appears that we need to find a middle road. While 'pain' is not 'bread' nor 'Brot', we might want to recognize that 'pain' is not 'pain' either, even in the same place, and that it might nevertheless be useful to treat all "pains" under the law in the same way. I do not wish to argue here the essential ingredients of the middle road. I think, however, that it is a necessity to define them. . . . if we want to make the European single market a reality, we need at least a common law of contracts. This may require an adaptation of legal education. I fail to see, however, why the European Principles of Contract Law would necessarily reduce European cultural diversity—whatever this evolving notion means—even if they were to become common law enacted by the European Parliament. I might use Pierre Legrand's eloquent but exaggerated views as a target. If we were to take his warnings as seriously as he expresses them, not only should we refuse the idea of a European civil code or of a European model law, but we should work toward abolishing all contemporary civil codes: they do not pay enough tribute to local culture.

Questioning Western Hegemony

The most important challenge in a globalized world seems to me related to the necessity to define the tools that will help prevent Western hegemonic thinking. We need to help lawyers acquire the means of nonchauvinistic legal thinking and work toward reducing nationalistic legal tendencies.

In an era of globalized trade and exchanges, it appears to be an absolute necessity to . . . safeguard competition in legal rules. To think that one country or one system has the monopoly of good ideas is not only naive and silly, but quite dangerous. Acknowledging the other as such . . . is a vital necessity. Nobody is entitled to be responsible for the well-being of the world. The North must acknowledge that it has to learn from the South as much as the West has to learn from the East. It might be that the WTO will have an impact on China. It may also very well be that China will change the WTO: we must prepare for that possibility and define mechanisms that help us fight chauvinism.

Comparativists are the first who must learn to change their attitudes so that they can teach their colleagues who deal only on the local level. Comparativists should define the appropriate tools for such an endeavor. I do not see that happening enough, and I think that this will be a problem if there is no improvement in the next century."

NOTES AND QUESTIONS

- What is meant by the term "hegemony"? What does Werro mean when he refers to "western hegemony"?

- What has this chapter on comparative law taught you about the common law tradition and English legal method?

PART TWO: THE LAWMAKERS

3

CONSTITUTIONAL ASPECTS OF LEGAL METHOD: THE RULE OF LAW AND THE SUPREMACY OF PARLIAMENT

In this chapter, we begin examining those key constitutional concepts and doctrines which are relevant to the way in which legal reasoning is carried out. Our primary focus is on two concepts which historically were seen as foundational to legal analysis: the "rule of law" and the supremacy of Parliament. These concepts will be dealt with in far more detail in law courses dealing specifically with constitutional and administrative law. However, a basic understanding of them is also important to an understanding of legal method and reasoning.

THE RULE OF LAW

If you were to conduct a poll on any street in the United Kingdom, and ask the so-called "average person" if he or she was subject to the "rule of law", you would probably get an affirmative response. However, if you also asked what is meant by the phrase "rule of law", you would likely get a great variety of responses. On one level, to claim that a society is subject to the rule of law is simply to make the claim that it is governed by fixed rules set down in law, rather than by the arbitrary force of a despot. But, of course, a society governed by rules will also be governed by individuals who make, amend, and enforce the law. Moreover, the simple fact that a society is governed by rules—even lots of rules—may mean that it is subject to the rule of law, but it certainly does not in itself ensure that the society qualifies as a "just" or fair regime.

Wade Mansell, Belinda Meteyard and Alan Thompson, *A Critical Introduction to Law* (Cavendish, London, 1995), p.136:

"There is, of course, no necessary causal link between the rule of law and the restraint of the powerful. Apartheid South Africa always claimed to be a rule of law state even while 4.5 million white people ruled 28 million disenfranchised black people and also owned 87% of the land. Apartheid South Africa also executed more people than any comparable state (in fact no other state was comparable) and yet, because of the appearance of safeguards for defendants, was able to claim that this practice too was consistent with the rule of law. Certainly in some ways it was the rule of law ideology which provided the clothes with which the state attempted to hide the nakedness of government aggression."

The example of apartheid in South Africa suggests that the rule of law may be a rather empty concept, capable of being deployed to justify the most egregious violations of individual and group dignity and self-determination. In fact, some might argue that given the *types* of laws which characterised apartheid, it is inappropriate to describe that regime as governed by the rule of law. At this point, we can make another observation about the rule of law: it means different things to different people, and the concept is a difficult one to pin down with an easy definition.

George P. Fletcher, *Basic Concepts of Legal Thought* (Oxford University Press, New York, 1996), pp.11–13:

"Of all the dreams that drive men and women into the streets, from Buenos Aires to Budapest, the 'rule of law' is the most puzzling. We have a pretty good idea what we mean by 'free markets' and 'democratic elections'. But legality and the 'rule of law' are ideals that present themselves as opaque even to legal philosophers. Many American jurists treat the rule of law as though it were no more than governance by rules. Thus we find Justice Scalia arguing explicitly that the rule of law is no more than the law of rules. And philosophers, such as Friedrich Hayek and Joseph Raz, make the same assumption that the rule of law means that the government 'is bound by rules fixed and announced beforehand.' Playing by the rules is, in some dubious contexts, a great achievement, but once societies have minimized graft and arbitrary rule, the 'rule of law' seems to promise more than blindly playing the game. After all, the rules of the game might be horribly unjust.

There are in fact two versions of the rule of law, a modest version of adhering to the rules and a more lofty ideal that incorporates criteria of justice. We shuffle back and forth between them because we are unsure of the import of the term 'law' in the expression 'rule of law.' . . . Do we mean rule by the laws laid down—whether the legal rules are good or bad? Or do we mean 'rule by Law,' by the right rules, by the rules that meet the tests of morality and justice? Because we have only one word for law in place of the two commonly found in other legal systems, we suffer and perhaps cultivate this ambiguity."

Ian Harden and Norman Lewis, *The Noble Lie: The British constitution and the rule of law* (Hutchinson, London, 1986), pp.19, 26:

"The rule of law is a highly connotative, value-laden idea and as such must be sharply differentiated from a rule of law, a specific norm or guide to action. It speaks to a belief in the kind of polity which seeks to subordinate naked power and to elevate civic order and rational progress. It implicitly rejects the idea of immunity from criticism, of being above collective institutions rather than facilitating their operation. Legality assumes a shared sphere of legitimate action and has come to be concerned with the procedures for the emergence of policies and rules. As the rule of law it can be regarded as an essential part of the 'moral heritage of the West'. It is the central legitimating feature of organized public life—the supreme constitutional principle. . . .

The rule of law has done service under a number of different regimens and has been the vindication of a number of different claims at different times. This is not to argue that the rule of law is mere rhetoric but rather that it has tended to be shorthand for legitimation claims in widely different sets of circumstances. That a society should be informed by cogent ideals relating to order, rule-governed behaviour, opposition to arbitrariness, looser or stronger versions of accountability—but that such congeries of beliefs should gain expression in different ways and conjure up different expectations at different times—should occasion no surprise."

Paul Craig, "Formal and Substantive Conceptions of the Rule of Law: An Analytical Framework" [1997] P.L. 467 at 467:

"Formal conceptions of the rule of law address the manner in which the law was promulgated (was it by a properly authorised person, in a properly authorised manner, etc.); the clarity of the ensuing norm (was it sufficiently clear to guide an individual's conduct so as to enable a person to plan his or her life, etc.); and the temporal dimension of the enacted norm (was it prospective or retrospective, etc.). Formal conceptions of the rule of law do not however seek to pass judgment upon the actual content of the law itself. They are not concerned with whether the law was in that sense a good law or a bad law, provided that the formal precepts of the rule of law were themselves met. Those who espouse substantive conceptions of the rule of law seek to go beyond this. They accept that the rule of law has the formal attributes mentioned above, but they wish to take the doctrine further. Certain substantive rights are said to be based on, or derived from, the rule of law. The concept is used as the foundation for these rights, which are then used to distinguish between 'good' laws, which comply with such rights, and 'bad' laws which do not."

QUESTION

Explain what is meant by the claim that there are two versions of the rule of law.

The tension between formal and substantive conceptions of the rule of law is central to the confusion over its meaning. Nevertheless, it has long been claimed that the English legal system is characterised by the rule of law, most famously in the late nineteenth century by the law professor Albert Venn Dicey. According to Dicey, the rule of law was a key feature which distinguished the English *constitution* (or fundamental structure of government) from those of continental Europe. While "foreigners" might be subject to the exercise of *arbitrary* power, the English, by contrast, were protected by the rule of law. It is hardly surprising that Dicey is characterised as a thoroughly chauvinistic "anti-European"!

Albert Venn Dicey, *An Introduction to the Law of the Constitution* (8th ed., Macmillan, London, 1915), pp.183–197:

"When we say that the supremacy of the rule of law is a characteristic of the English constitution, we generally include under one expression at least three distinct though kindred conceptions.

We mean, in the first place, that no man is punishable or can be lawfully made to suffer in body or goods except for a distinct breach of law established in the ordinary legal manner before the ordinary Courts of the land. In this sense the rule of law is contrasted with every system of government based on the exercise by persons in authority of wide, arbitrary, or discretionary powers of constraint.

Modern Englishmen may at first feel some surprise that the 'rule of law' (in the sense in which we are now using the term) should be considered as in any way a peculiarity of English institutions, since, at the present day, it may seem to be not so much the property of any one nation as a trait common to every civilised and orderly state. Yet, even if we confine our observation to the existing condition of Europe, we shall soon be convinced that the 'rule of law' even in this narrow sense is peculiar to England, or to those countries which, like the United States of America, have inherited English traditions. In almost every continental community the executive exercises far wider discretionary authority in the manner of arrest, of temporary imprisonment, of expulsion from its territory, and the like, than is either legally claimed or in fact exerted by the government in England; and a study of European politics now and again reminds English readers that wherever there is discretion there is room for arbitrariness, and that in a republic no less than under a monarchy discretionary authority on the part of the government must mean insecurity for legal freedom on the part of its subjects. . . .

We mean in the second place, when we speak of the 'rule of law' as a characteristic of our country, not only that with us no man is above the law, but (what is a different thing) that here every man, whatever be his rank or condition, is subject to the ordinary law of the realm and amenable to the jurisdiction of ordinary tribunals.

In England the idea of legal equality, or of the universal subjection of all classes to one law administered by the ordinary Courts, has been pushed to its utmost limit. With us every official, from the Prime Minister down to a constable or a collector of taxes, is under the same responsibility for every act done without legal justification as any other citizen. The Reports abound with cases in which officials have been brought before the Courts, and made, in their personal capacity, liable to punishment, or to the payment of damages, for acts done in their official character but in excess of their lawful authority. A colonial governor, a secretary of state, a military officer, and all subordinates, though carrying out the commands of their official superiors, are as responsible for any acts which the law does not authorise as is any private and unofficial person. Officials, such for example as soldiers or clergymen of the Established Church, are, it is true, in England as elsewhere, subject to laws which do not affect the rest of the nation, and are in some instances amenable to tribunals which have no jurisdiction over their fellow countrymen; officials, that is to say, are to a certain extent governed under what may be termed official law. But this fact is in no way inconsistent with the principle that all men are in England subject to the law of the realm; for though a soldier or a clergyman incurs from his position legal liabilities from which other men are exempt, he does not (speaking generally) escape thereby from the duties of an ordinary citizen. . . .

There remains yet a third and a different sense in which the 'rule of law' or the predominance of the legal spirit may be described as a special attribute of English institutions. We may say that the constitution is pervaded by the rule of law on the ground that the general principles of the constitution (as for example the right to personal liberty, or the right of public meeting) are with us the result of judicial decisions determining the rights of private persons in particular cases brought before the Courts; whereas under many foreign constitutions the security (such as it is) given to the rights of individuals results, or appears to result, from the general principles of the constitution. . . .

There is in the English constitution an absence of those declarations or definitions of rights so dear to foreign constitutionalists. Such principles, moreover, as you can discover in the English constitution are, like all maxims established by judicial legislation, mere generalisations drawn either from the decisions or dicta of judges, or from statutes which, being passed to meet special grievances, bear a close resemblance to judicial decisions, and are in effect judgments pronounced by the High Court of Parliament. To put what is really the same thing in a somewhat different shape, the relation of the rights of individuals to the principles of the constitution is not quite the same in countries like Belgium, where the constitution is the result of a legislative act, as it is in England, where the constitution itself is based upon legal decisions. In Belgium, which may be taken as a type of countries possessing a constitution formed by a deliberate act of legislation, you may say with truth that the rights of individuals to personal liberty flow from or are secured by the constitution. In England the right to individual liberty is part of the constitution, because it is secured by the decisions of the Courts . . . [I]n Belgium individual rights are deductions drawn from the principles of the constitution, whilst in England the so-called principles of the constitution are inductions or generalisations based upon particular decisions pronounced by the Courts as to the rights of given individuals. . . .

The fact, again, that in many foreign countries the rights of individuals, *e.g.* to personal freedom, depend upon the constitution, whilst in England the law of the constitution is little else than a generalisation of the rights which the Courts secure to individuals, has this important result. The general rights guaranteed by the constitution may be, and in foreign countries constantly are, suspended. They are something extraneous to and independent of the ordinary course of the law. . . . [W]here the right to individual freedom is a result deduced from the principles of the constitution, the idea readily occurs that the right is capable of being suspended or taken away. Where, on the other hand, the right to individual freedom is part of the constitution because it is inherent in the ordinary law of the land, the right is one which can hardly be destroyed without a thorough revolution in the institutions and manners of the nation."

It is essential to recognise that Dicey was writing at a particular historical period, and more importantly, he was writing from a political perspective that saw the maintenance of individual property and freedom to use that property as the paramount value to be protected. He was opposed to any increase in activity by the state. He clearly thought that law should ignore differences that existed between people in terms of wealth and power, and should treat them all the same (*formally* equal), rather than the state taking steps to make people more *substantively* equal. Yet he was also opposed to the movement for women's suffrage (a demand for *formal* equality).

Since Dicey's time, most lawyers have come to realise many inadequacies in his limited (and often incorrect) concept of the rule of law. Today, governments do have fairly wide discretionary powers, and most people would agree that governments do need *discretion* to operate effectively. That is, ensuring that officials of government only act in accordance with strict *rules* may prove too inflexible in the implementation of public policies. Instead, officials need flexibility and discretion in tailoring law and policy to fit individual circumstances. However, while we increasingly have come to recognise the importance of discretion on the part of officials of the state, there are also situations in which clear rules and guidelines—the rule of law—may seem important as a way to limit the power of officials to act in ways which are perceived as *arbitrary* or unfair. Thus, it might be argued that although discretion is not inconsistent with the rule of law, discretion should also be exercised in accordance with general principles of law. The actions of state officials thereby should be constrained by the law so that they do not act arbitrarily. This historical tension between clear rules and administrative discretion has been described by Jowell, along with other criticisms of Dicey's rule of law vision.

Jeffrey Jowell, "The Rule of Law Today", in *The Changing Constitution* (4th ed., Jeffrey Jowell and Dawn Oliver, eds., Oxford University Press, Oxford, 2000), pp.5–11:

"The second and third of Dicey's meanings of the Rule of Law display a concern not to allow the British to go the way of other countries, where a separate system of public law is administered by separate courts dealing with cases between the State and the individual.

In 1928 William Robson wrote his celebrated book *Justice and Administrative Law*, in which he roundly criticized Dicey for his misinterpretation of both the English and French systems on that ground. He pointed out that there were in England 'colossal distinctions' between the rights and duties of private individuals and those of the administrative organs of government even in Dicey's time. Public authorities possessed special rights and special exemptions and immunities, to the extent that the citizen was deprived of a remedy against the State 'in many cases where he most requires it'. Robson also convincingly showed how Dicey had misinterpreted French law, where the *droit administratif* was not intended to exempt public officials from the rigour of private law, but to allow experts in public administration to work out the extent of official liability. Robson also noted the extent of Dicey's misrepresentation that disputes between officials and private individuals in Britain were dealt with by the ordinary courts. He pointed to the growth of special tribunals and inquiries that had grown up to decide these disputes outside the courts, and was in no doubt that a 'vast body of administrative law' existed in England.

The attack on Dicey continued a few years later with W. Ivor Jennings's *The Law and the Constitution*, which appeared in 1933. Repeating many of Robson's criticisms of Dicey's second and third meanings of the Rule of Law, Jennings also delivered a withering, and almost fatal, attack upon Dicey's first meaning—his claim that wide discretionary power had no place under the Rule of Law. It should be remembered here that Dicey was a trenchant critic of notions of 'collectivism'. . . .

Jennings felt that the Rule of Law implicitly promoted Dicey's political views. He equated Dicey's opposition to State regulation with that of the 'manufacturers who formed the backbone of the Whig Party', who 'wanted nothing which interfered with profits, even if profits involved child labour, wholesale factory accidents, the pollution of rivers, of the air, and of the water supply, jerry-built houses, low wages, and other incidents of nineteenth-century industrialism'. . . .

The Second World War then provided compelling reasons to centralize power, an opportunity further built upon by the Labour government of 1945. As Robson wrote in the second edition of his book in 1947, increasingly Parliament had given decision-making powers not to the courts—to Dicey's 'ordinary law'—but to specialized organs of adjudication. This was not 'due to a fit of absentmindedness' but because these bodies would be speedier and cheaper, and would possess greater technical knowledge and have 'fewer prejudices against government' than the courts. Here he may have been echoing the words of Aneurin Bevan, Minister of Health in the 1945 Labour government and architect of the National Health Service, who caused a stir in the House of Commons by establishing tribunals in the Health Service, divorced from 'ordinary courts', because he greatly feared 'judicial sabotage' of socialist legislation.

Despite this onslaught on Dicey's revision of the Rule of Law, its epitaph refused to be written. Two particularly strong supporters wrote in its favour in the 1940s. F.A. Hayek's *The Road to Serfdom* in 1943 graphically described that road as being paved with governmental regulations. C.A. Allen, with less ideological fervour, pleaded for the legal control of executive action. Not much heed was paid however until the late 1950s when the Franks Committee revived interest in Diceyan notions by suggesting judicial protections over the multiplying tribunals and inquiries of the growing State. It was in the 1960s, however, that disparate groups once again started arguing in favour of legal values. Some of these groups were themselves committed to a strong governmental role in providing social welfare, but objected to the manner in which public services were carried out. Recipients of Supplementary (Welfare) Benefit, for example, objected to the fact that benefits were administered by officials in accordance with a secret code (known as the 'A Code') and asked instead for publication of a set of welfare 'rights'. They also objected to the wide discretion allowed their case-workers to determine the level of their benefits. The heirs of Jennings and his followers, such as Professor Richard Titmus, opposed this challenge to the free exercise of official discretion and objected strongly to a 'pathology of legalism' developing in this area.

Just one other example of a plea for the Rule of Law came at about the same time from individuals and groups who were being displaced from their homes by programmes of urban redevelopment. While not asking for a catalogue of 'rights', the claim here was for participation in decisions by which they were affected. The plea of these groups (and others like them) did not primarily concern the substance of the law. The welfare recipients were not simply arguing for higher benefits, but for fair procedures to determine the benefits. They and the local amenity groups directed their demands for the Rule of Law less at the content of the decisions ultimately taken than at the procedures by which they were reached. They were by no means adopting the undiluted Diceyan view that all discretionary power is bad. Nevertheless, they recognized the value of legal techniques to control the exercise of official power. . . .

An official possessed of discretion frequently has a choice about how it should be operated: whether to keep it open-textured, maintaining the option of a variety of responses to a given situation, or to confine it by a rule of standard—a process of legalisation. For example, officials administering welfare benefits could provide them on a case-by-case basis according to their conception of need, or they could announce precise levels of benefit for given situations. Similarly, laws against pollution could be enforced by a variable standard whereby the official must be satisfied that the polluter is achieving the 'best practicable means' of abatement. Alternatively, levels of pollution could be specified in advance, based on the colour of smoke emission, or the precise quantities of sulphur dioxide. A policy of promoting safe driving could, similarly, be legalised by a rule specifying speeds of no more than 30 miles per hour on given streets.

Now for Dicey, and particularly for Hewart and Hayek, who mistrusted the grant of virtually any official discretion, the virtue of rule-bound conduct was principally that it allowed affected persons to know the rules before being subjected to them *ex post facto*. As a principle of justice, it was felt that no person should be condemned without a presumed knowledge of the rule alleged to have been breached. This assumes a penal law or criminal regulation of one form or another, and is understandable in that context where the lack of rules would involve risky guesses with serious consequences for non-compliance. It is fairer to a person prosecuted for a tax offence to have been made aware of the precise tax required than for the levels to be determined at the discretion of an official.

This argument, however, has a somewhat different compulsion when dealing not with penalties but with regulation involving the allocation of scarce resources. Should an applicant for a university place be entitled, out of fairness, to know the precise grades required for entrance? Should the applicant for welfare benefits be entitled to know the rules about allocations of winter coats? In cases such as these the argument in favour of rules over discretion is an argument less from certainty than from *accountability*. This argument has two facets, the first being a concern to provide a published standard against which to measure the legality of official action and thus to allow *individual redress* against official action that does not accord with the rule or standard. Thus, an announced level of resources to qualify for welfare assistance ought to allow redress to a person who qualifies but is refused assistance. The second facet of accountability refers to the fact that the actual process of making rules and their publication generates *public assessment* of the fidelity of the rule to legislative purpose. Many statutes confer powers on officials to further the policy of the Act in accordance with wide discretion. The power may be to allocate council housing, or to provide for the needy, or to diminish unacceptable pollution of the air or water. The process of devising a points system for housing allocation, benefits for the needy, and acceptable emission levels of pollution thus forces the official into producing a formal operational definition of purpose. . . .

The virtues of rules, as we have seen, include their qualities of legality, certainty, consistency, uniformity, congruence to purpose, and accountability loosely so called, all of which play an important part in the control of official discretion and may be seen as concrete manifestations of the Rule of Law. . . .

Officials are well aware of the benefit of rules to their own efficiency. Rules announce or clarify official policies to affected parties, and thus facilitate obedience. They may also allow routine treatment of cases, thus increasing the speed of decision-making. A zoning system in planning, a list of features of 'substandard' housing, and a list of grades for university admission all allow decisions to be taken more quickly than a system that requires constant reappraisal of each case on its merits. Rules therefore reduce the anxiety and conserve the energy needed to reach decisions on a case-by-case basis. . . . Despite the fact that rules may promote criticism, they also, in the short run at least, provide a shield behind which officials may hide, pleading consistent and uniform justice in response to criticism that the individual's case is unique.

So here we have the tension: the virtues of rules—their objective, even-handed features—are opposed to other administrative benefits, especially those of flexibility, individual treatment, and responsiveness. The virtue of rules to the administrator (routine treatment) may be a defect to the client with a special case (such as the brilliant applicant for a university place who failed to obtain the required grades because of a family upset or illness just before the examination). The administrator's shield may be seen as an unjustified protection from the client's sword. Officials themselves may consider that the job itself requires flexibility, or genuinely want to help a particular client, but feel unable to do so: hence the classic bureaucratic response, 'I'd like to help you—but there is this rule.' . . .

Before leaving the relative merits of rule-based official action, we should note that the existence of a rule does not ensure its implementation. Nor is it always desirable that rules be enforced. The existence of a rule outlawing a speed of over 30 miles per hour, for example, will not necessarily mean that people who speed are automatically prosecuted. Sometimes the prosecuting official will lack the resources to prosecute some offenders, or lack the will. Occasions may exist, however, when a policy of full enforcement could, for example, mean that a doctor narrowly exceeding the limit of 30 miles per hour on a deserted street late at night while speeding to the scene of an accident would be prosecuted. The prosecution makes no sense in furthering the goal of preventing unsafe driving. Full enforcement would in this case play no part in the achievement of fidelity to purpose. On other occasions laws may not be enforced in order to further other values in society. For example, studies have shown that assault laws may not be enforced in a situation of marital violence as police will not wish to exacerbate poor relations or cause deprivation for children. The objective of the law prohibiting violence is in these situations considered secondary to a value which seeks to preserve the well-being of the family unit.

This last example shows that even the most clear-cut rule may or should not be enforced. Most law-enforcers assessing prosecution weigh the cost in damages of the prohibited act against the cost of abating the act. An example is the regulation of pollution, where the damage of the polluter to the environment is, according to a number of studies, measured against the costs of abatement: the firm may be forced out of business, or may locate elsewhere, causing damage to the local economy and unemployment. Or the cost of abatement may be passed on to the ultimate consumer of a needed product."

QUESTIONS

- To what extent is the rule of law compatible with the exercise of discretion by officials and agencies of the state? Give examples.

- Should a lecturer's decision whether to grant someone an extension on his or her essay deadline be governed by clear rules or the exercise of a broad discretion tailored to the particular circumstances?

Dicey's "rule of law" vision has been widely criticised for many decades on a range of different grounds. It is important to recognise that, while the "rule of law" as a concept may continue to be useful and important, Dicey's understanding of it obviously does not retain a great deal of relevance.

Andrew Le Sueur, Javan Herberg and Rosalind English, *Principles of Public Law* (2nd ed., Cavendish, London, 1999), pp.108–110:

Jennings' criticisms of Dicey's rule of law

"In Appendix II of his book, Jennings considers Dicey's theory of the rule of law. In relation to Dicey's first meaning (the absence of arbitrary and discretionary powers) Jennings explains that what Dicey really meant was that 'wide administrative or executive powers are likely to be abused *and therefore ought not to be conferred*'. But the discretionary powers of ministers and local authorities were as much part of the 'regular' law of the land as any others. And while, of course, occasional abuse of power might occur, this was no reason for not conferring discretionary powers on officials. These powers, remember, were used to ensure things like minimum standards of health and safety in workplaces and to clear slum housing. This, Jennings said, was of no interest to Dicey:

> 'Dicey . . . was much more concerned with the constitutional relations between Great Britain and Ireland than with the relations between poverty and disease on the one hand, and the new industrial system on the other. In internal politics, therefore, he was concerned not with the clearing up of the nasty industrial sections of towns, but with the liberty of the subject. In terms of powers, he was concerned with police powers, and not with other administrative powers.'

In relation to Dicey's second definition of the rule of law (equality before the law), Jennings flatly denied that there was any equality between the rights and duties of an official and that of an ordinary person. Dicey surely realised this, but had chosen to ignore the public law position of officials—for example, the duty of local authorities to provide education to children and the powers of the tax inspectors to demand information. Dicey was only writing about the position in tort law—not public law. While it was true that, generally, officials could be sued personally by an aggrieved citizen for a tortious act or omission in the course of their duty, Jennings' withering retort was that 'this is a small point upon which to base a doctrine called by the magnificent name of "rule of law", particularly when it is generally used in a different sense'.

Lastly, Jennings questioned Dicey's proposition that the rule of law meant that the 'constitution is *the result* of the ordinary law of the land' rather than a constitutional code. Jennings could not see Dicey's point. 'I do not understand,' wrote Jennings, 'how it is correct to say that the rules are the consequence of the rights of individuals and not their source. The powers of the Crown and of other administrative authorities are limited by the powers of the administration. Both statements are correct; and both powers and rights come from the law—from the rules'.

The rule of law and Parliament

Everyone agrees that an important principle within our constitutional system is that government (that is, all public bodies) carry out their tasks in accordance with the law. The meaning and practical application of this principle, however, continues to be contentious. Most modern writers, as did Jennings, come to the conclusion that Dicey's particular formulation of the concept of the rule of law is an adequate description both of how the principle actually operates, and also what ought to be regarded as important about it.

As we have seen, Dicey's version of the rule of law did not include the placing of legal restraints on the power of Parliament to pass Acts. The implication of Dicey's approach is that, if it were to be enacted that all blue eyed babies be strangled at birth (to use a classic illustration), the court would be under a duty to recognise the validity of such legislation like any other. Dicey's only answer to people who asked whether a court should recognise even a plainly evil enactment duly passed by Parliament was that such legislation was unlikely to be enacted. To a considerable extent, Jennings shared Dicey's confidence in Parliament and so did not disparage him on this ground. More recent critics have not shared this faith. For Ferdinand Mound, 'Dicey's doctrine of the rule of law is inescapably a narrow, shrivelled thing. It applies vigorously enough to the rights of individuals in their dealings with one another and with the State, but it does not really touch the untrammelled quality of parliamentary sovereignty' (*The British Constitution Now*, 1993, London: Mandarin, p. 207). As we have already noted, the Human Rights Act 1998 gives courts the power to declare that Parliament itself has failed to respect civil liberties (including, of course. those like personal liberty and freedom of assembly which Dicey regarded as important) set out in the ECHR. The Act stops short of allowing courts to enforce any such finding by refusing to recognise the validity of the offending statutory provision."

Bernard J. Hibbitts, "The Politics of Principle: Albert Venn Dicey and the Rule of Law" (1994) 23 Anglo-American Law Review at 25–26, 29:

"The first element of the Rule . . . corresponded with Dicey's fears that a socialist-collectivist Parliament would seek to displace the common law and the common courts by the creation of alternative adjudicative standards and bodies, so as to achieve its political ends more conveniently. The second element of the Rule corresponded with his desire to ensure that in legal disputes the state and the individual were equal, and that the state would not be able, at least in the context of the judicial forum, to take advantage of its overwhelming power. The third element of the Rule corresponded with an underlying conviction that fundamental individual rights (such as the right to personal freedom, the right to freedom of discussion and the right of public assembly) had to be put beyond the reach of governments which might seek to curtail them to facilitate broader social and economic goals . . .

At the end of the day there is little about the rule of law that is sacred. . . . the Rule as Dicey formulated it was very much the expression of one man's political, philosophical and professional concerns. To the extent that one shares Dicey's opinions and attitudes the Rule is supportable; to the extent one holds contrary views, it is not."

Although Dicey's understanding of the "rule of law" may have been informed by his nineteenth-century world view, some of the concepts to which he referred, such as "equality before the law", continue to have relevance. With respect to the ideal of equality, it is also worth considering that Dicey was opposed to the extension of the vote to women! Waldron places the rule of law in a contemporary context in which the idea of equality and the rule of law continues to have political and legal importance.

Jeremy Waldron, *The Law* (Routledge, London, 1990) pp.29–42:

PEDRO v. DISS "Late one night in 1979, a man called Ya Ya Pedro was standing by the door of his brother's house in London. Another man, Martin Diss, came up to him, identified himself as a police officer, and asked Pedro what he was doing there. Pedro walked away without answering. When Constable Diss repeated his question, Pedro told him to 'fuck off'. Eventually he allowed himself to be searched, but when the policeman began to question him about some keys that he found in his pockets, Pedro walked away again. Constable Diss grabbed him by the arm and said, 'Do you live here?' Pedro replied with another obscenity and swung backwards, striking the constable in his chest with an elbow. As he did this, the constable took hold of his clothing, and Pedro punched him. He was eventually restrained with the assistance of two other officers, and they arrested Pedro and charged him with assaulting a constable in the execution of his duty.

When Pedro appeared before the Highbury magistrates, he was convicted and fined £50. But he appealed to the High Court, and the Chief Justice, Lord Lane, with one other judge, overturned the conviction and sentence. They said that when Pedro punched Constable Diss, the officer was *not* acting in the lawful execution of his duty. The police, said Lord

Lane, do not have an unlimited power to detain people for questioning: their powers of legitimate detention and arrest are set down and governed by law. If they go beyond those powers, the person they have got hold of is entitled to strike back in self defence, just as he may resist *any* other person who attacks him. Lord Lane went on:

'It is a matter of importance, therefore, to a person at the moment when he is first physically detained by a police officer, to know whether that physical detention is or is not regarded by that officer as a formal arrest or detention. That is one of the reasons why it is a matter of importance that the arresting or detaining officer should make known to the person in question the fact that, and the grounds on which, he is being arrested or detained.'

Constable Diss claimed that he had thought Pedro was a burglar, and that he was authorized by Section 66 of the Metropolitan Police Act 1839 to 'stop, search and detain any person who may be reasonably suspected of having or conveying in any manner anything stolen or unlawfully obtained'. The problem was he didn't tell Pedro that that was what he was doing; he didn't say this was the power he was exercising and these were the grounds of his suspicion. So Pedro had no way of distinguishing the situation from one in which he was being unlawfully attacked. That was why Lord Lane held that he was entitled to defend himself, even against a police officer.

It is tempting to say that Pedro got off on a 'technicality'. In some countries, you are not allowed to resist a police officer even if his attempt to detain you is unjustified; moreover the officer has no obligation to say why you are being detained and you certainly have no entitlement to resist him if he does not. I don't want to argue that the rule in *Pedro v Diss* is necessarily better. But the case illustrates a couple of broader points of principle.

First, it involves a determination to subject members of the police force, as far as possible, to the same basic rules of law as every other citizen. Ordinary members of the public are not normally allowed to detain one another forcibly and they are entitled to resist anyone who tries to do that to them. The police are subject to that basic framework of rules along with everyone else.

Second, it embodies a particular attitude towards any *special* powers that may be thought necessary for the police to be able to do their job. The special powers of the police are to be limited and governed by rules — not just any rules, but rules which are known and publicized rather than hidden away in the Police Training Manual. Indeed, the striking thing about the case is the judges' insistence that Diss ought to have told Pedro the particular rule on which he was relying. Members of the public shouldn't have to submit to a general sense that the police are simply 'special' and can interfere with their lives in ways in which they may not interfere with one another. They are entitled to know what's going on, and to know by what authority the constable is acting in what would otherwise be an objectionable (and resistible) way. Otherwise they will be at the mercy of unpredictable arbitrary power. . . .

One law for all

Think back for a moment to Ya Ya Pedro and Constable Diss. Diss grabs hold of Pedro, and Pedro punches him in the struggle to free himself. The magistrates say he is guilty of assault. On appeal, the High Court says (in effect): 'No. Unless the arrest is lawful, Pedro is entitled to defend himself against Martin Diss just as if he were any other citizen who tried to grab hold of him. Once they go beyond their specified powers, the police have no special privileges. The ordinary rules of self-defence apply. If it's wrong for me to attack Pedro, it's also wrong for Constable Diss to attack Pedro. The law is the same for everyone.'

This requirement of universality — the idea of 'one law for all' — is a prominent feature of the normative ideal of the rule of law. But why is it universality a good thing? Why is it desirable that there should be one law for everyone, irrespective of who they are, or what their official status?

One obvious application of universality is that we don't, on the whole, allow personalized laws; we don't have laws that make exceptions for particular people. In medieval

England, there used to be things called 'Bills of Attainder', announcing that someone in particular (the Earl of Warwick, or the king's brother for example) was thereby banished from the realm and his estates confiscated. The idea of the rule of law is that the state should not use personalized mechanisms of that sort.

Moral philosophers link this requirement of universality with morality and with rationality. They say that if you make a moral judgement about someone or something, your judgement can't be based simply on that person or that incident in particular, or if it is, it's arbitrary. It must be based on some feature of the person or action—something *about* what they did, something that might in principle be true of another person or another situation as well. In other words it must be based on something that can be expressed as a universal proposition. For example, if I want to say, 'It is all right for Diss to defend himself', I must say that because I think self defence is all right in general in that sort of case, not merely because I want to get at Pedro or say something special about Diss. So I must also be prepared to say that it would be all right for Pedro to defend himself in a similar circumstance. Unless I can point to some clearly relevant difference between the two cases, then I must accept that the same reasoning applies to both.

Another way of putting it is that universalizability expresses an important principle of justice: it means dealing even-handedly with people and treating like cases alike. If I am committed to treating like cases alike, then I ought to be able to state my principles in a universal form. If I cannot—that is, if I can't find a way to eliminate references to particular people from my legislation—that is probably a good indication that I am drawing arbitrary distinctions based on bias or self-interest or something of that sort.

As well as these philosophical reasons, there are also pragmatic arguments in favour of universality. We are less likely to get bad laws or oppressive laws, if the burden of any law falls as much on those who make it as on the rest of the population. The king might think twice about banning tobacco, if it means that he can't have a cigarette. An MP may be reluctant to impose heavy penalties on adultery when he remembers what he was doing last week. If our legislators are human in their inclinations and temptations, they may be less likely to enact laws that are inhumanly demanding if they know that the legislation may be applied to their conduct as well.

Now I say you are *less* likely to get oppressive laws. There are no guarantees. An ascetic sovereign may be perfectly willing to subject his own conduct to the same harsh discipline he imposes on his subjects. When the Iranian parliament enacted amputation as a penalty for repeated offences of theft, its members presumably welcomed the possibility that they too should have their hands cut off if they offend against Allah in that way. The idea of the rule of law usefully prohibits legislation which singles somebody out for special treatment. But being singled out is only one way of being oppressed. People may be oppressed as members of a group or because they possess some general characteristic, such as being a black or being a woman, and it is much more difficult to rule out this sort of legislation on the basis of the ideal of the rule of law. As soon as we recognize that, then we recognize that the idea of universality—the idea of 'one law for all'—is not nearly as straightforward as it looks. It rules out one type of discrimination: discrimination against (or in favour of) named individuals. But it doesn't rule out discrimination against (or in favour of) certain *types* of people. It doesn't, for example, rule out the sort of discrimination that we find in the [former] South African Group Areas Act, since that discrimination is stated in terms that make no reference whatever to particular individuals. It is true of course that the Group Areas Act treats different people differently: apartheid applies one set of standards to blacks and another set of standards to whites. But if that *by itself* were enough to rule out apartheid legislation, it would also rule out an awful lot of legislation which we regard as desirable and necessary.

The trouble with the purely formal idea of 'one law for all' is that, if it is interpreted absolutely literally, it becomes really far too simple to capture the requirements of good legislation in a modern state. When you think about it, it seems crazy to say we should apply literally the *same* legal rules to everyone in all circumstances. Do we want to enforce the same standards of cleanliness in a paint-shop as in a restaurant? Is there to be one law to govern children and adults? Must ambulance drivers observe the same speed limits as the rest of us? No-one thinks that ought to be the case. . . . We don't want our commitment to universality to blind us to those distinctions and discriminations that are morally or pragmatically justified.

Special rules for officials?

As a matter of fact, this point has important implications for the way law applies to politics. The simple idea with which we began was that the same rules should apply to officials like Constable Diss as apply to citizens like Ya Ya Pedro. There should be one law for all, and no special law for officials of the state. But now if it is reasonable to apply different standards of hygiene to paint-shops and restaurants, if it is reasonable to allow a higher speed limit for ambulances than for private motorists, why isn't it also reasonable to apply rules of behaviour to police officers that are different from the ones we apply to ordinary citizens? After all, don't the police—like ambulance drivers—have a *special* job to do?

It is amazing what a grip the simple idea of 'one law for all' has had in British law and legal theory. For a long time, it was fashionable to pretend that a police officer was nothing but 'a citizen in uniform'—that his powers to question suspects and arrest felons were no greater than that of the ordinary 'man in the street'. It was simply that he did this for a living, and was trained at it, whereas the ordinary citizen had better things to do. This has long since become a fiction. The police have a whole array of powers to arrest people, to detain them for questioning, to break, enter and search their homes, and so on, which are conferred on them specifically by legislation. And the same is true of many other state officials—from the VAT-man to the social worker. They have a job to do, and Parliament has given them special powers to do it. These special powers may or may not be excessive; the issue is politically controversial. But few deny that state officials need *some* special powers (and also *some* special protections) if they are to be able to do their job.

Equally important, we may also want to say that state officials need to have special *restrictions* on their conduct (that are different from, and additional to, the ones that apply to the rest of us), as well as special powers. I will use a case to illustrate this point.

In a 1979 case, *Malone v Metropolitan Police Commissioner*, an antiques dealer, James Malone, who was suspected of handling stolen property, sued for an injunction [an order to stop someone from doing something] to restrain the London police from tapping his telephone. The judge refused to give an injunction. He held that the police had a perfect right to do it, not because there was any specific legal authorization, but simply because telephone-tapping did not involve any trespass or other unlawful act.

> 'The subscriber speaks into his telephone, and the process of tapping appears to be carried out by Post Office officials making recordings, with Post Office apparatus on Post Office premises, of the electrical impulses on Post Office wires provided by Post Office electricity. There is no question of there being any trespass on [Malone's] premises for the purpose of attaching anything either to the premises themselves or to anything on them: all that is done is done within the Post Office's own domain.'

In other words, since the ordinary law of trespass has not been violated here, the action of the officials does not require any specific authorization. Malone's case, the judge said, rested on the assumption 'that nothing is lawful that is not positively authorized by law'. But England has always been a country where anything not expressly forbidden by the law is permitted: that is the basis of our liberty. It seems to follow that, since there is no law on the matter, the police have the right to tap telephones.

We have already seen the absurdity of holding that the police should have no more powers than the ordinary citizen. Now we are seeing the absurdity of the converse proposition—that the police should not be subject to any special restrictions that don't apply to other people. They should have as much freedom as the rest of us. That proposition is absurd, because the power (both legal and physical) that the police have makes them especially dangerous *as well as* especially useful. Acting within the state apparatus, officials can do things to citizens which are quite different in character from the sort of things citizens can do to one another. It is a mistake for us to think that the laws we use to deal with one another will necessarily be adequate for our dealings with the officials of the state. . . .

In other words, we might talk in terms of a *modified* 'rule of law' doctrine to be applied to the conduct of officials. The simple principle of 'one law for all' holds that state officials should be bound by exactly the same rules as everyone else. That's the version we have to give up. The modified version, however, insists that official conduct should be governed by *the same sort* of legal rules, even if they are not literally the same rules, as the rest of us. We may take the simple version as our default position. State officials (police officers etc) are to be governed by the ordinary law of the land, unless there is a specific legal provision to the contrary. If, however, there is a need for a special provision (because the police, for example, have a special job to do), we should not simply make an exception in the ordinary law of the land; we should lay down *rules* to govern the conduct of the officials."

QUESTIONS

- What is meant by the claim that the rule of law includes a requirement of universality? Does that mean that the law should not be used to draw distinctions between people? When, if ever, are such distinctions justifiable?

- How does the rule of law apply to the conduct of officials? Are state officials governed by the same rules as everyone else?

The rule of law is capable of encompassing a range of ideas. For example, it has been argued that the rule of law requires that laws generally should be prospective and not retrospective. That is, Parliament should not enact laws which seek to regulate (and make illegal) events which have already occurred, and which were permitted at that time. Furthermore, the rule of law sometimes is said to include the idea that laws should be open, published, and reasonably intelligible to those who are required to regulate their conduct in accordance with them. In other words, people need to be able to understand the law. A judiciary which is independent of the other branches of government is also sometimes described as central to the rule of law, as is the accessibility of the courts to the general public. Further elements of the rule of law might be said to include: the fact that new laws should be enacted only after publicity, opportunity for debate and consultation; and that warning should be given to the public before the law is changed (so that behaviour can be changed to meet the altered legal situation).

For some commentators, the range of constraints on the exercise of the power of the state, which are contained within the concept of the rule of law, make it an inherently positive and important ideal. Despite its limitations, such as the way in which equality is defined in a formal rather than substantive way, the rule of law, for them, remains a valuable concept in our constitutional rhetoric.

E.P. Thompson, *Whigs and Hunters* (Penguin Books, London, 1990), p.266:

"I am insisting only upon the obvious point, which some modern Marxists have overlooked, that there is a difference between arbitrary power and the rule of law. We ought to expose the shams and inequities which may be concealed beneath this law. But the rule of law itself, the imposing of effective inhibitions upon power and the defence of the citizen from power's all-intrusive claims, seems to me to be an unqualified human good. To deny or belittle this good is, in this dangerous century when the resources and pretentions of power continue to enlarge, a desperate error of intellectual abstraction."

Other commentators, especially on the political left, argue that the rule of law is not an "unqualified human good", because its limited scope does not advance the cause of social justice or substantive equality. Moreover, the underlying philosophy of the rule of law, especially in the form articulated by Dicey, positively discourages progressive social change because of its conservative focus on rules, formal equality, and rights under law. That is, while the rule of law may constrain the exercise of state power, it does not recognise how the power of the state might be used to create a more just, equal society. Horwitz has made this point in a direct response to Thompson.

Morton Horwitz, "The Rule of Law: An Unqualified Human Good?" (1977) 86 Yale Law Journal 561 at 566:

"I do not see how a man of the left can describe the rule of law as an 'unqualified human good'! It undoubtedly restrains power, but it also prevents power's benevolent exercise. It creates formal equality—a not inconsiderable virtue—but it *promotes* substantive inequality by creating a consciousness that radically separates law from politics, means from ends, processes from outcomes. By promoting procedural justice it enables the shrewd, the calculating, and the wealthy to manipulate its forms to their own advantage. And it ratifies and legitimates an adversarial, competitive and atomistic conception of human relations."

Finally, the rule of law is based upon an assumption about the character of human relationships; namely, that law (and its "rule") is necessary to the maintenance of civilised society. The assumption here is that without the rule of law, society would degenerate into a chaotic and/or authoritarian state. Marxists criticise this idea because, they argue, it accords too much power to law, and it ignores the way in which the rule of law actually serves to legitimate the political and economic status quo.

Hugh Collins, *Marxism and Law* (Clarendon Press, Oxford, 1982), pp.12–13:

"Few would doubt the important role of law in preventing the disintegration of social order or restricting authoritarian governments. Yet Marxists claim that legal fetishism embodies a distorted image of reality which must be unmasked. To begin with, the notion that society rests on law is too simplistic. It is implausible to think that without law everyone would be at each other's throat, or would use superior physical force to take another's possessions. It is much more likely that informal standards of behaviour based on reciprocity would permit an elementary form of stable community to exist. Clearly there is a subtle relationship between the function of laws and informal customs in constituting the normative basis for a peaceful and prosperous society which will not be revealed if an assumption about the necessity and priority of law is adopted. Growing from that insight, Marxists portray the heavy dependence of organizations of power in modern society upon law as the result of a specific historic conjuncture of circumstances, and argue that the important role of law today in maintaining social order is not an immutable feature of human civilization in the future."

We thus have seen how the rule of law for some is an ideal, for others, an illusion which justifies the existing social and political order (and its hierarchies). The concept of the rule of law, then, is not a neutral one, but rather, is politically charged. Your view of the rule of law will depend upon your assessment of its political and ideological underpinnings. Your social, political, and ideological positioning inevitably will impact upon your views of the politics of the rule of law. As a student, the most important point is to think *critically* about any claim to speak the "truth" about the rule of law (or anything else!).

THE SUPREMACY OF PARLIAMENT

Returning again to Dicey's analysis of the English constitution, the rule of law was only one of two fundamental elements; the other was the supremacy of Parliament. The tension between the rule of law and Parliamentary supremacy is particular to the British Parliamentary system of government. According to Dicey, the essence of the law of the constitution was that Parliament has the right to make or unmake any law whatever. Thus, no person or body is recognised as having a right to override or set aside legislation. Parliament is the supreme law making body, its legislative power is substantively unrestricted, and the laws it passes cannot be invalidated by the courts. The role of judges, in relation to statutes enacted by Parliament, is to interpret and apply them, rather than to pass judgment on their merits. This fact distinguishes the British constitutional structure from that found in many other jurisdictions, in which a written constitutional document—such as a Bill of Rights—is the fundamental law which provides the basis for courts to invalidate legislation on constitutional grounds, should it contradict, for example, the rights and freedoms guaranteed in the constitution. In Chapter 5, we will see that this historic principle of British constitutionalism is now altered by virtue of membership in the legal order of the European Union.

Parliamentary supremacy also includes the idea that no Parliament can bind itself or a future Parliament to retain any particular law now on the books, for to do so would mean that the Parliament in the future was not supreme. Thus, any law, no matter how fundamental, in theory can be repealed by ordinary Parliamentary procedure at any time in the future. Parliamentary supremacy, as a constitutional principle, intuitively would seem to have the potential to easily undermine the ideal of the rule of law, which we have already examined. The fact that Parliament conceivably can do just about anything would seem extremely dangerous to the idea of a society governed by law. Dicey sought to answer such concerns, and claimed that the rule of law and Parliamentary supremacy (or sovereignty, as he referred to it) in fact were complementary.

Albert Venn Dicey, *An Introduction to the Law of the Constitution* (8th ed., Macmillan, London, 1915), pp.402–409:

"The sovereignty of Parliament and the supremacy of the law of the land—the two principles which pervade the whole of the English constitution—may appear to stand in opposition to each other, or to be at best only counterbalancing forces. But this appearance is delusive; the sovereignty of Parliament, as contrasted with other forms of sovereign power, favours the supremacy of the law, whilst the predominance of rigid legality throughout our institutions evokes the exercise, and thus increases the authority, of Parliamentary sovereignty.

The sovereignty of Parliament favours the supremacy of the law of the land.

That this should be so arises in the main from two characteristics or peculiarities which distinguish the English Parliament from other sovereign powers.

The first of these characteristics is that the commands of Parliament (consisting as it does of the Crown, the House of Lords, and the House of Commons) can be uttered only through the combined action of its three constituent parts, and must, therefore always take the shape of formal and deliberate legislation. The will of Parliament can be expressed only through an Act of Parliament.

This is no mere matter of form; it has most important practical effects. It prevents those inroads upon the law of the land which a despotic monarch, such as Louis XIV, Napolean I, or Napolean III, might effect by ordinances or decrees, or which the different constituent assemblies of France, and above all the famous Convention, carried out by sudden resolutions. The principle that Parliament speaks only through an Act of Parliament greatly increases the authority of the judges. A Bill which has passed into a statute immediately becomes subject to judicial interpretation, and the English Bench have always refused, in principle at least, to interpret an Act of Parliament otherwise than by reference to the words of the enactment. . . .

The second of these characteristics is that the English Parliament as such has never, except at periods of revolution, exercised direct executive power or appointed the officials of the executive government.

No doubt in modern times the House of Commons has in substance obtained the right to designate for appointment the Prime Minister and the other members of the Cabinet. But this right is, historically speaking, of recent acquisition, and is exercised in a very roundabout manner; its existence does not affect the truth of the assertion that the Houses of Parliament do not directly appoint or dismiss the servants of the State; neither the House of Lords nor the House of Commons, nor both Houses combined, could even now issue a direct order to a military officer, a constable, or a tax-collector; the servants of the State are still in name what they once were in reality—'servants of the Crown'; and, what is worth careful notice, the attitude of Parliament towards government officials was determined originally, and is still regulated, by considerations and feelings belonging to a time when the 'servants of the Crown' were dependent upon the King, that is, upon a power which naturally excited the jealousy and vigilance of Parliament.

Hence several results all indirectly tending to support the supremacy of the law. Parliament, though sovereign, unlike a sovereign monarch who is not only a legislator but a ruler, that is, head of the executive government, has never hitherto been able to use the powers of the government as a means of interfering with the regular course of law; and what is even more important, Parliament has looked with disfavour and jealousy on all exemptions of officials from the ordinary liabilities of citizens or from the jurisdiction of the ordinary Courts; Parliamentary sovereignty has been fatal to the growth of 'administrative law.' The action, lastly, of Parliament has tended as naturally to protect the independence of the judges, as that of other sovereigns to protect the conduct of officials. It is worth notice that Parliamentary care for judicial independence has, in fact, stopped just at that point where on a priori grounds it might be expected to end. The judges are not in strictness irremovable; they can be removed from office on an address of the two Houses; they have been made by Parliament independent of every power in the State except the Houses of Parliament. . . .

The fact that the most arbitrary powers of the English executive must always be exercised under Act of Parliament places the government, even when armed with the widest authority, under the supervision, so to speak, of the Courts. Powers, however, extraordinary, which are conferred or sanctioned by statute, are never really unlimited, for they are confined by the words of the Act itself, and, what is more, by the interpretation put upon the statute by the judges. Parliament is supreme legislator, but from the moment Parliament has uttered its will as lawgiver, that will becomes subject to the interpretation put upon it by the judges of the land, and the judges, who are influenced by the feelings of magistrates no less than by the general spirit of the common law, are disposed to construe statutory exceptions to common law principles in a mode which would not commend itself either to a body of officials, or to the Houses of Parliament, if the Houses were called upon to interpret their own enactments. In foreign countries, and especially in France, administrative ideas—notions derived from the traditions of a despotic monarchy—have restricted the authority and to a certain extent influenced the ideas of the judges. In England judicial notions have modified the action and influenced the ideas of the executive government. By every path we come round to the same conclusion, that Parliamentary sovereignty has favoured the rule of law, and that the supremacy of the law of the land both calls forth the exertion of Parliamentary sovereignty, and leads to its being exercised in a spirit of legality."

According to Dicey, then, the concepts of rule of law and Parliamentary supremacy were actually complementary. Both acted as a control mechanism on officials of the state (the "executive" branch of government). The government of the day always needs the support of Parliament to act, and judges, in their role as interpreters of statutory law, can ensure that the powers of government, as granted by Parliament, have not been exceeded. Finally, the ultimate political supremacy, according to Dicey, rested with the electorate. Once again, Dicey's constitutional vision is informed by a political ideology; one in which government should have a limited role, and where individualism and individual rights to private property are central.

Despite being grounded in a particularly nineteenth century Diceyan view of the world, the idea of Parliamentary supremacy as central to the British constitutional structure has continued to be of central importance.

A.W. Bradley, "The Sovereignty of Parliament—Form or Substance?", in *The Changing Constitution* (4th ed., Jeffrey Jowell and Dawn Oliver, eds., Oxford University Press, Oxford, 2000), pp.26–28:

The essence of parliamentary sovereignty as a legal doctrine

"Nevertheless, not only since the publication in 1885 of A.V. Dicey's *The Law of the Constitution* but also before this, the sovereignty of Parliament has been accepted as one of the fundamental doctrines of constitutional law in the United Kingdom. In 1689, after the overthrow of James II but before the union of the English and Scottish Parliaments in 1707, the Earl of Shaftesbury wrote:

'The Parliament of England is that supreme and absolute power, which gives life and motion to the English Government.'

The significance of Dicey's analysis is that, despite the extensive political and social changes that have occurred since 1885, and despite criticism which his work received from constitutional lawyers such as Sir Ivor Jennings, his statement of the doctrine has retained a remarkable influence on both legal and political thinking about Parliament. Dicey summarized his views in this way:

'The principle of parliamentary sovereignty means neither more nor less than this, namely, that Parliament [defined as the Queen, the House of Lords, and the House of Commons, acting together] . . . has, under the English constitution, the right to make or unmake any law whatever; and, further, that no person or body is recognised by the law as having a right to override or set aside the legislation of Parliament.'

The principle, 'looked at from its positive side', ensures that any Act of Parliament will be obeyed by the courts. The same principle, 'looked at from its negative side', ensures that there is no person or body of persons who can make rules which override or derogate from an Act of Parliament or which, 'to express the same thing in other words', will be enforced by the courts in contravention of an Act of Parliament.

A further implication drawn from the sovereignty of Parliament is that a sovereign Parliament is not bound by the Acts of its predecessors, and thus that no Parliament can bind its successors. This facet of sovereignty has arisen in part because the courts, when faced with two conflicting statutes on the same subject, have applied the rule that the later Act of Parliament prevails. By the doctrine of implied repeal, the later Act repeals the earlier Act. This doctrine has been pressed into service to sustain the proposition that the one rule of the common law that Parliament may not change is the rule that the courts must always apply the latest Act of Parliament on the subject. But this view ought not to be taken as axiomatic and scope for a contrary view is considered below.

The source of legislative sovereignty

It will be evident that discussion of this subject raises fundamental questions about the relationship between courts and Parliament about the source of that relationship. It would be attractive if we could identify the legal source of the doctrine, but this is not an easy task. Could the source of the sovereignty of Parliament be found in an Act of Parliament itself? A well-known, but possibly over-simple, answer to this question was given by the New Zealand jurist, Sir John Salmond:

'No statute can confer this power upon Parliament for this would be to assume and act on the very power that is to be conferred.'

But Parliament might be entitled to make such an assumption if over many years a wide variety of statutes had been enacted without its authority to legislate being questioned. Indeed, this leads directly to the next question, whether the legal source of authority for the doctrine may be found in decisions of the courts. Decisions of the courts are authoritative in determining the common law. Thus the sovereignty of Parliament can be said to be based upon decisions of the courts in apply Acts of Parliament, since, if the courts apply Acts of Parliament and say that they must do so because they are bound by *all* such Acts, then the courts appear to be declaring a fundamental rule, namely that effect must be given to Acts of Parliament, whatever their content.

A third and intermediate possibility, rather than attributing the source of legislative sovereignty to Parliament or to the courts acting separately, is to examine the past and present relationship between the courts, the legislature, and other holders of office in the state, looking at what the courts and the legislature have done in relation to each other, and also at the stance of other key actors in the political system (such as ministers of the Crown). Such an explanation looks at past institutional behaviour and implies that this can be expected to continue. However, if the rule of legislative sovereignty came about from an historical process, rather than as a result of a 'big bang' creation of a fundamental rule, can we be certain that this area of constitutional evolution has come to a full stop? On this basis, future changes in the relationship may occur over time. Indeed, such changes may happen more rapidly where the incentive to change is brought on by an event such as a novel and radical initiative taken by the legislature. Thus the courts might respond to such an initiative in a manner for which there was no direct precedent, and in a manner that the new legislation might not have expressly invited."[1]

This historical relationship between Parliament and the courts, in which Parliament is supposedly supreme, and the courts apply laws enacted by Parliament, is demon-

---

[1] We will examine these inroads in Chapter 4.

strated by a case decided by the House of Lords (the highest court in the United Kingdom). Decisions of the Law Lords generally include five judgments, and portions of three of those judgments (all of which agreed in the result) illustrate how the Lords in this case sought to respect the principle of Parliamentary supremacy.

British Railways Board and another v Pickin [1974] 1 All E.R. 609, HL.

The Bristol and Exeter Railway Co. was incorporated (created) by statute in 1836 to make a railway from Bristol to Exeter with branch lines to Bridgwater and Tiverton. The Act provided that if the line was abandoned, the lands acquired by the company to build the railways would return to the owners of the land on either side of the railway. In the 1960s, the line fell into disuse. The land adjacent was sold to George Pickin. Meanwhile, Parliament, at the behest of the British Railway Board (the successor to the Bristol and Exeter Railway Co), enacted the British Railways Act 1968, which provided that provisions such as the one governing the reversion of the land on either side of the Bristol and Exeter railway, would not apply to land vested in the British Railway Board. Pickin commenced action against the Board claiming, amongst other things, that the Board had misled Parliament in its promotion of the Bill and that the court should declare him owner of the adjacent land. The portions of the judgments in the House of Lords of interest to us concern the claim that Parliament was misled into enacting the statute.

Lord Reid [Lord Reid recited the facts of the case and the issues raised]:
"... The respondent's [Pickin's] alternative ground of action is not easy to state concisely. He appears to allege that in obtaining the enactment of s.18 of the 1968 Act in their favour the board fraudulently concealed certain matters from Parliament and its officers and thereby misled Parliament into granting this right to them. ...

The function of the court is to construe and apply the enactments of Parliament. The court has no concern with the manner in which Parliament or its officers carrying out its standing orders perform these functions. Any attempt to prove that they were misled by fraud or otherwise would necessarily involve an enquiry into the manner in which they had performed their functions in dealing with the bill which became the British Railways Act 1968.

In whatever form the respondent's case is pleaded he must prove not only that the board acted fraudulently but also that their fraud caused damage to him by causing the enactment of s.18. He could not prove that without an examination of the manner in which the officers of Parliament dealt with the matter. So the court would, or at least might, have to adjudicate on that.

For a century or more both Parliament and the courts have been careful not to act so as to cause conflict between them. Any such investigations as the respondent seeks could easily lead to such a conflict, and I would only support it if compelled to do so by clear authority. But it appears to me that the whole trend of authority for over a century is clearly against permitting any such investigation.

The respondent is entitled to argue that s.18 should be construed in a way favourable to him and for that reason I have refrained from pronouncing on that matter. But he is not entitled to go behind the Act to shew that s.18 should not be enforced. Nor is he entitled to examine proceedings in Parliament in order to shew that the board by fraudulently misleading Parliament caused him loss. ..."

Lord Morris of Borth-y-Gest:
"... The question of fundamental importance which arises is whether the court should entertain the proposition that an Act of Parliament can so be assailed in the courts that

matters should proceed as though the Act or some part of it had never been passed. I consider that such doctrine would be dangerous and impermissible. It is the function of the courts to administer the laws which Parliament has enacted. In the processes of Parliament there will be much consideration whether a bill should or should not in one form or another become an enactment. When an enactment is passed there is finality unless and until it is amended or repealed by Parliament. In the courts there may be argument as to the correct interpretation of the enactment: there must be none as to whether it should be on the statute book at all. . . ."

Lord Simon of Glaisdale:
". . . The system by which, in this country, those liable to be affected by general political decisions have some control over the decision-making is parliamentary democracy. Its peculiar feature in constitutional law is the sovereignty of Parliament. This involves that, contrary to what was sometimes asserted before the 18th century, and in contradistinction to some other democratic systems, the courts in this country have no power to declare enacted law to be invalid. . . ."

A NOTE ON THE CONSTITUTION

The Law Lords in several places in their judgments in *Pickin* refer to the constitution and constitutional law. Although law students take at least one course in constitutional and administrative law, a few notes on the constitution are needed now in order for you to understand its implications for legal reasoning and legal method. The term constitution refers to the fundamental rules and limitations under which the power of the state is exercised. The constitution establishes institutions of government and divides powers between them; it limits the power of the state; and sometimes, it sets out rights held by citizens. The constitution is the fundamental framework of the legal and political system. In some countries, such as the United States, that constitutional framework is easy to identify. It is written down in a document called the "Constitution", and it includes a "Bill of Rights". But, in the United Kingdom, the constitution is more elusive. It is sometimes referred to as an "unwritten" constitution, because it is not set down in a single, comprehensive document. Rather, the British constitution consists of a variety of rules, customs, and understandings which empower and limit government. We would say, for example, that the idea of Parliamentary supremacy and the rule of law are elements of our constitution.

The constitutional framework can be "found" in a variety of places: in ordinary statutory law enacted by Parliament, which deals with matters which are considered to be fundamental to the structure of governance; in laws created by judges in the course of deciding cases before them (which is known as the "common law"); and the rules which Parliament has set down to govern its own internal procedures ("the law and custom of Parliament").

It is also of constitutional significance that the United Kingdom is a constitutional monarchy. This means that government is still conducted in the name of the Queen, which signifies the ultimate governing authority. Our governing structure is also characterised by a bicameral Parliament. This means that Parliament is composed of two "houses": a lower house (the House of Commons) chosen through popular election, and an upper house (the House of Lords), which is hereditary and now partly appointed. We also characterise our system as an example of "responsible government", in that the government of the day (the executive) is accountable to the House of Commons (the legislature) and can be defeated on the floor of the House in a vote. We also would describe the United Kingdom as a unitary, rather than a federal state, in that ultimate power rests with a central government in London (although this might be characterised somewhat differently given decentralisation of power to Scotland, Wales, and Northern Ireland through the policy of the devolution of power). Finally, the British constitution might be described as exemplifying the principle of "limited government", to the extent that government can only do what it is empowered under law to perform. This idea was central to Dicey's ideal of the rule of law.

Also of constitutional significance is what Dicey referred to as "conventions of the constitution", which he acknowledged were sometimes more important in constitutional terms than the law itself. These are simply practices or customs which have become so fundamental to our governing structure as to be considered of constitutional significance. They include the fact that the Queen assents to all laws passed by both Houses of Parliament (this is called the "Royal Assent"); the Queen acts only on the advice of her ministers, and ministers exercise the prerogatives (rights) which have been retained by the Crown; ministers are responsible to Parliament; members of the government are collectively responsible to Parliament; and the Prime Minister must be a member of the House of Commons rather than the House of Lords.

These conventions are not written down. They are simply practices of constitutional government which have grown up over time. Most importantly, disobedience of a convention means that it ceases to exist. If the Prime Minister was chosen from the House of Lords (and he or she chose to stay a member of the Lords) then the convention would no longer be a convention. This is what distinguishes convention from law: disobedience of a law does not signal its demise. Moreover, unlike law, there is no *sanction*, other than potentially a political one at the ballot box, for violating a convention. Thus, a convention may be recognised as part of the constitution, but it is not *enforceable* by the courts. It is politically, rather than *legally*, binding.

For Dicey, writing at the end of the nineteenth century, Britain's constitutional structure—the rule of law, supremacy of Parliament, and conventions of the constitution—was a *model* of constitutional government, superior to anything offered in other countries with written constitutions contained in a single document. Central to that balanced constitutional structure was the role of the courts. The courts' job was to uphold the intention of Parliament in the interpretation of legislation, but the role of the courts also was to review the actions of the executive branch of government (the cabinet and civil service) to ensure that its actions were within the lawful authority granted by Parliament. In this way, the courts upheld the rule of law, because they protected the individual against the potential for the arbitrary exercise of power by the executive.

However, in the twentieth century, that model of a balanced and harmonious constitution (if it ever really existed) increasingly has come unstuck. The House of Commons has become dominant, while the role of the House of Lords has been constricted both by legislation and the political environment in which an unelected body is seen an illegitimate. In this way, the upper house becomes less of a "check" on the actions of the Commons. Nor does the Royal Assent act as a "check" on legislation, because of the convention that the Queen acts only on the advice of ministers and does not withhold her consent (which also was the case in Dicey's time). Moreover, because of the development and entrenchment of the system of political parties, the individual Member of Parliament has less and less a role in independently scrutinising legislation proposed by the government (although there are still instances where this effectively occurs).

As a result of these developments, the government of the day dominates the legislative and executive functions of government. Moreover, the principle of Parliamentary supremacy limited the power of the courts to act as a "check" on government in that, as we have seen, they could not invalidate legislation on its merits. This relationship between Parliament, the executive branch of government, and the courts is often referred to as the doctrine of *separation of powers*. This term refers to the three primary functions of government: legislative (the making of laws); executive (the execution of laws, or putting laws into operation); and judicial (the interpretation of laws), and the degree to which those functions are distributed amongst different people. The classic example of a pure separation of powers is found in the United States, where the legislative function is the task of Congress; the executive function is the job of the President and his or her cabinet, who are not members of Congress; and the judicial function is the task of judges. That degree of separation of powers is absent in the United Kingdom. In part, this is because the Prime Minister and his or her cabinet are Members of Parliament; they are part of the legislature as well as being the head of the executive branch. Consequently, we say that the legislative and executive branches are largely fused together.

However, there is a partial separation of powers in the United Kingdom. While the legislative and executive functions are fused, the courts are more or less separate, with some exceptions. The most obvious exception is the House of Lords. The House of Lords is the highest court of appeal in the United Kingdom and, although the Law Lords are not members of the government, they do sit in the House of Lords in its legislative capacity. However, constitutional convention dictates that the Law Lords should not offer opinions to the government on political matters, at least until retirement from the bench. The judiciary has an important function with respect to the executive, in that judges act as a "check" on executive actions. That is, judges can and do assert their power, derived from the rule of law, to *review* actions taken by the executive. We look at the relationship between Parliamentary supremacy, judicial review, and the rule of law in Chapter 4.

THE HUMAN RIGHTS ACT 1998 AND THE SUPREMACY OF PARLIAMENT

We will consider the impact of the Human Rights Act 1998 in connection with the principles of statutory interpretation in Chapter 9, but it is also important with respect to the principle of Parliamentary supremacy. Its importance lies in its attempt to empower the judiciary to uphold certain rights of the individual from being infringed by the state, while also, at the same time, remaining true to the supremacy of Parliament—even if Parliamentary law undermines those fundamental rights. The Act protects a number of rights enshrined in the European Convention on Human Rights, and the relationship between the Act, the Convention, Parliament and the courts is a complex one.[2]

Lord Lester of Herne Hill QC, "Human rights and the British Constitution", in *The Changing Constitution* (Jeffrey Jowell and Dawn Oliver, 4th ed., Oxford University Press, Oxford, 2000), pp.90, 92–96, 100–101, 104, 106:

"The idea of 'fundamental rights', and of a 'fundamental' constitutional law taking precedence over ordinary laws, became eclipsed at the end of the seventeenth century by the concept of absolute parliamentary sovereignty. In the early part of the century, the judges had struggled not only for independence from undue Executive interference but also for the right to withhold effect from laws that they regarded as unconscionable or as contrary to a higher, fundamental natural law. The judges won the struggle for independence against the Crown's claim to rule by prerogative, but the price paid by the common lawyers for their alliance with Parliament against the divine right of kings was that the common law could be changed by Parliament as it pleased. The 'glorious bloodless' revolution of 1688 was won by Parliament, and although the Bill of Rights of 1688–9 and the Act of Settlement of 1700 recognized some important personal rights and liberties, the terms of the constitutional settlement were mainly concerned with the rights and liberties of Parliament. The alliance of Parliament and the common lawyers ensured that the supremacy of the law would mean the supremacy of Parliament; more realistically, it meant, between general elections, the supremacy of the central government in Parliament. The doctrine of the supremacy of Parliament, described by Lord Hailsham of St Marylebone as operating in practice as an 'elected dictatorship', became the keystone of the British Constitution. . . .

Although the ideology of fundamental rights was rejected by successive generations of British governments and constitutional thinkers on the political left and right, it has been a potent force across the world. American and French concepts of human rights and judicial review shaped systems of government subject to binding constitutional codes in Europe and beyond. The conquests of Napoleon's armies spread through the European continent not only the Code Civil but also the public philosophy and public law of the United States and France. These ideas and systems were also spread to other continents. Today, the many countries whose legal systems are based upon the civil law have legally binding constitutional guarantees of fundamental human rights derived from seventeenth-century England and the eighteenth-century enlightenment. In the common law world, as the colonies of the British Empire gained independence, Bills of Rights were introduced giving constitutional protection to human rights.

The human rights-based philosophy also became profoundly influential in creating a new international legal order in the wake of the horrors of the Second World War. In December 1948, the UN General Assembly adopted the Universal Declaration of Human Rights, recognizing certain rights as basic human entitlements: free speech as much as freedom from torture. In 1966, two International Covenants were opened for signature, a Covenant on Civil and Political Rights, and a Covenant on Economic, Social and Cultural Rights. The two Covenants came into force in 1976, and are reinforced by several UN human rights conventions, for example, against torture, race and sex discrimination, and protecting the rights of the child.

Meanwhile, in Western Europe, a second terrible war in half a century and the barbarous atrocities of the Nazi Holocaust convinced European politicians and jurists of the need to forge a new Europe. The need to guard against the rise of new dictatorships, to avoid the

---

[2] The relevant provisions of the Human Rights Act and the European Convention on Human Rights can be found in Chapter 9 at pp. 251–259.

risk of relapse into another disastrous European war, and to provide a beacon of hope for the peoples of Central and Eastern Europe living under Soviet totalitarian regimes, inspired the foundation, in1949, of the Council of Europe. Members of the Council of Europe are obliged to accept the principles of the rule of law and the enjoyment by every-one within their jurisdiction of human rights and fundamental freedoms.

One of the Council of Europe's first tasks was to draft a human rights convention for Europe, conferring enforceable rights upon individuals against sovereign states. It was a revolutionary enterprise. The master builders knew why human rights protection had to transcend national boundaries, nationality, and citizenship. They saw the need to link pos-itive law with ethical values, and to protect individuals and minorities against the misuse of power by elected governments and unelected public officials in periods of emergency and normal times. The inventors of the European Convention were determined never again to permit state sovereignty to shield from international liability the perpetrators of crimes against humanity, never again to allow governments to shelter behind the traditional argu-ment that what a state does to its own citizens or to the stateless is within its exclusive juris-diction and beyond the reach of the international community. So they resolved to create a binding international code of human rights with effective legal safeguards for all victims of violations by contracting states.

For the first time, individuals would be able to exercise personally enforceable rights under international law, before an independent and impartial tribunal—the European Court of Human Rights—against the public authorities of their own states. No matter whether the violation occurred because of an administrative decision by a minister or civil servant, or because of the judgment of a national supreme court, or because of legislation enacted by a national parliament; there would be no privilege or immunity enabling state authorities automatically to shield themselves against supra-national European judicial scrutiny. . . .

The Convention guarantees basic civil and political rights to everyone within the juris-diction of the Contracting States: the right to life (Article 2); the prohibition of torture and inhuman or degrading treatment or punishment (Article 3); the prohibition of slavery and forced labour (Article 4); the right to liberty (Article 5); the right to a fair trial (Article 6); no punishment without law (Article 7); respect for private and family life (Article 8); freedom of thought, conscience, and religion (Article 9); freedom of expression (Article 10); freedom of assembly and association (Article 11); the right to marry and found a family (Article 12); the right to an effective national remedy (Article 13); and non-discrimination in the enjoyment of Convention rights (Article 14).

The United Kingdom ratified the First Protocol to the Convention, on 3 November 1952, which added the right to the protection of property (Article 1); the right to Education (Article 2); and the right to free elections (Article 3). The United Kingdom ratified the Sixth Protocol to the Convention on 27 January 1999, abolishing the death penalty.

In December 1965, the first Wilson Government decided to accept the right of individ-ual petition and the jurisdiction of the European Court of Human Rights to rule on cases brought by individuals against the United Kingdom. It was a momentous decision, for it meant that, in fact if not in a formal sense, political sovereignty was henceforth to be shared with the European institutions created by the Convention. . . .

In all there have been some sixty judgments of the European Court finding breaches by the UK, many of them controversial and far-reaching. They include: the inhuman treat-ment of suspected terrorists in Northern Ireland; inadequate safeguards against telephone tapping by the police; unfair discrimination against British wives of foreign husbands under immigration rules; unjust restrictions upon prisoners' correspondence and visits; corporal punishment in schools; criminal sanctions against private homosexual conduct; the exclusion of homosexuals from the armed services; ineffective judicial protection for detained mental patients, or would-be immigrants, or individuals facing extradition to countries where they risk being exposed to torture or inhuman treatment, or homosexuals whose private life is infringed; the dismissal of workers because of the oppressive opera-tion of the closed shop; interference with free speech by unnecessarily maintaining injunc-tions restraining breaches of confidence, or a jury's award of excessive damages for libel, or punishing a journalist for refusing to disclose his confidential source; the right to have a detention order under the Mental Health Act reviewed; parental access to children; access to child care records; review of the continuing detention of those serving discretionary life sentences; access to legal advice for fine and debt defaulters; court martial procedures; availability of legal aid in criminal cases; access to civil justice. . . .

The Human Rights Act is a first major step towards a full British Bill of Rights. The Act is an essential element in the constitutional re-settlement of the different nations and regions of the United Kingdom, and the recognition of people of the United Kingdom as citizens endowed with basic human rights. Half a century after the European Convention on Human Rights was drafted, it creates a direct link between Convention rights and the laws of the UK, enabling British courts to give direct effect to Convention rights. The Act is no ordinary law. It is a fundamental, constitutional measure of greater contemporary significance to the protection of human rights than any previous constitutional measure. . . .

Section 3 of the Act is pivotal. It imposes a duty on courts and tribunals to strive to avoid incompatibility between domestic legislation and the Convention. Existing and future legislation must, so far as possible, be read and given effect in a way which is compatible with Convention rights. . . .

Although the courts will be required to adopt new interpretive techniques, they will not usurp the legislative powers of Parliament by adopting a construction which it could not be supposed that Parliament had intended by enacting the Human Rights Act and by previously or subsequently enacting the impugned statutory provision. Where only a fanciful or perverse construction is possible to make the statute compatible with Convention rights, or where the problem created by the apparent mismatch between the statute and Convention rights requires extensive redrafting and choice among different legislative options, the courts will make a declaration of incompatibility. By doing so, they will be marking the boundary between the powers of the Judiciary, the Legislature and the Executive in deciding how the constitutional principles contained in the Act are to be applied. . . .

In view of the constitutional importance of a declaration of incompatibility, only specified higher courts may make such a declaration, and the Crown must be notified where a court is considering making such a declaration. The declaration of incompatibility is expressed as a discretionary power, but the courts will inevitably exercise the power if it is impossible to interpret legislation compatibly with Convention rights, unless the government indicates its willingness to resolve the issue without the need for a remedial legislative order. A declaration is not binding on the parties involved, so as to leave open the possibility for the government to argue before the European Court of Human Rights that the measure concerned is compatible with Convention rights.

The declaration of incompatibility is essential in bringing the problem to the attention of the executive and the legislature, and acting as trigger for amending legislation by means of a remedial order. Despite its incompatibility with Convention rights, the offending legislation will remain valid and effect, unless and until legislative amendments are made. Parliamentary sovereignty is maintained and Parliament's legislative powers remain intact in deciding whether to remove the incompatibility. However, failure to make such amendment to remedy the domestic court's declaration of incompatibility will lead to a complaint to the European Court of Human Rights in Strasbourg, with a high probability that the European Court will come to a similar conclusion. This will be a powerful incentive to the government to introduce, and for Parliament to approve, the necessary remedial order.

The fact that courts and tribunals have a duty to act compatibly with the Convention is significant because of the Act's potential 'horizontal effect'. The main focus of the Convention is upon protecting the individual against the abuse of power by the public authorities of the state. However, like other national constitutional charters of human rights, it is necessary to extend protection beyond the state and its agents to 'private governments'—those bodies which are private in form but public in substance. The courts have a duty of acting compatibly with the Convention, not only in cases involving other public authorities in this extended sense, but also in developing the common law when deciding cases between private persons. This will be especially the case where the Convention imposes positive obligations on the state to protect individuals against breaches of their rights."

Some might argue that the Human Rights Act 1998 is an imperfect attempt at protecting individual rights because of its deference to the principle of Parliamentary supremacy. Ewing, by contrast, argues that this is the great strength of the legislation.

K.D. Ewing, "The Human Rights Act and Parliamentary Democracy" (1999) 62 M.L.R. 79 at 79, 98–99:

"The Human Rights Act 1998 is the culmination of an aggressive campaign for the incorporation into domestic law of the European Convention on Human Rights, a campaign in which the judges joined forces with other political activists. Variously described as 'brilliant'; 'a masterly exposition of the parliamentary draftsman's art'; and even 'a thing of intellectual beauty'; the Act has also been greeted as an 'ingenious compromise' between the 'maximalists' and 'minimalists', the former supporting a judicial power to invalidate legislation, as is the case in Canada. But although it is purported to reconcile in 'subtle' form the protection of human rights with the sovereignty of Parliament (a claim even more credible after an important but unsung Commons amendment), the Act also represents an unprecedented transfer of political power from the executive and legislature to the judiciary, and a fundamental re-structuring of our 'political constitution'. As such it is unquestionably the most significant formal redistribution of political power in this county since 1911, and perhaps since 1688 when the Bill of Rights proclaimed loudly that proceedings in Parliament ought not to be questioned or impeached in any court or any other place. In the words of Baroness Williams of Crosby, we have crossed our 'constitutional Rubicon', at least to the extent that the courts may now declare a statute incompatible with Convention rights. . . .

[For] all that, the inevitable incorporation of the Convention has been secured in a manner which subordinates Convention rights to constitutional principle and democratic tradition. We should not diminish the importance of the fact that the Human Rights Act does not give the courts the power to strike down legislation. Nor should we diminish the reasons why the government withheld this power from the courts, grounded as they were in a desire to ensure that 'no court in this land, not even the Judicial Committee of the House of Lords, can place itself in the position of sovereignty over the High Court of the elected Parliament'. The government appeared particularly concerned to preserve 'the fundamental position established in our constitution: the sovereignty of Parliament', said to be 'one of the profound strengths of our system'. This is a refreshing position to have adopted, if only because the sovereignty of Parliament is something which should not really be conceded, acting as it does as a constitutional and legal principle which has metamorphosed in a dynamic constitution, to give effect to one of the first political principles of democratic self-government. This is the principle of popular sovereignty whereby the elected and accountable representatives of the people should be empowered by the authority of a mandate to give effect without restraint to what used to be called the General Will.

This is not to deny that the Human Rights Act confers a significant political power on the courts, or indeed that it enables the courts formally to set the agenda on human rights questions. Nor is it to deny that in the 'overwhelming majority of cases', a declaration of incompatibility will be accepted by the government and Parliament of the day, thereby ensuring that the elected branch will in practice defer to the unelected branch. But the government appears genuinely to anticipate the possibility that this will not always be so, and there may well be cases (such as abortion) where Parliament will assert its political and legal authority over the courts. In this way the sovereignty of Parliament will be preserved both in principle and in practice, even though it is unquestionably the case that Parliament's position would have been stronger politically and constitutionally if incorporation of the ECHR had stopped short of giving the courts the power to challenge primary legislation."

An example of the potential clash between the principle of Parliamentary supremacy and the protection of individual rights already is becoming apparent. After the events of September 11, 2001, Parliament enacted the Anti-terrorism, Crime and Security Act 2001, which includes extended powers to detain individuals by the state which may be inconsistent with Art. 5(1) of the European Convention (the right to liberty and security of the person). This is because the legislation empowers the Home Secretary to order the indefinite detention of a suspected terrorist, without the right to trial. In order to enable this measure, the government 'derogated' from Art. 5(1) of the European Convention in this case. That is, the legislation was enacted even though the Home Secretary did not make a statement to the House of Commons that the provisions of the legislation would be compatible with the European Convention. Thus, the government and Parliament clearly supported this measure *even though* it may infringe the Convention rights, and the Courts are unable to *invalidate* the law on that (or any other basis). That is the essence of the principle of Parliamentary supremacy.

ESSAY QUESTION

"The rule of law is neither a simple ideal nor an easy one to live up to. It expresses a number of principles and requirements, based on various grounds. They look attractive enough when they are expressed as slogans, but they prove to be strikingly difficult to apply in any straightforward way to the governing apparatus of modern society" (Jeremy Waldron, *The Law* (Routledge, London, 1990), p.52).

Discuss with examples.

4

CONSTITUTIONAL ASPECTS OF LEGAL METHOD: JUDICIAL REVIEW

In this chapter, we continue to look at fundamental constitutional doctrines which are of importance to a study of legal method. Our focus now turns to *judicial review*, one of the principal ways in which the judiciary is supposed to "check" (or control) the actions of the executive branch of government, to ensure that the executive acts in accordance with the principle of legality. Judicial review is not concerned with the wisdom or merits of executive action. Rather, it is the judicial function of determining whether the executive has acted under legal authority and has followed proper procedure in its actions. The sorts of questions judges ask in judicial review are: did the government have the power granted to it under law to take this action? Did it follow the procedure set down in legislation? Has it acted unreasonably and, therefore, outside of its powers? Has it acted compatibly with rights protected under the European Convention on Human Rights? This inherent power of the courts to review the executive exemplifies Dicey's rule of law vision; that under our constitutional structure, judges will ensure that executive power is not exercised in an arbitrary fashion. Rather, it must be exercised under lawful authority. In this way, the judiciary is supposed to keep the government in "check". Judicial review raises important questions about the relationship between the judiciary and the executive and legislative branches of government and, in addition, it has given rise to difficult questions about the legitimacy of judges appearing to "override" the intention of Parliament as expressed in legislation.

JUDICIAL REVIEW AND THE RULE OF LAW

The basis for judicial review of executive action can be found in the fundamental tenets of the rule of law, which we examined in Chapter 3. For Dicey, the role of the judiciary was to ensure that power was not exercised by governments in an arbitrary, "lawless" fashion. Judicial review, it is argued, is the means by which judges ensure that power is exercised in conformity with the authority granted by Parliament under statute.

Jeffrey Jowell, "The Rule of Law Today" in *The Changing Constitution* (4th ed., Jeffrey Jowell and Dawn Oliver, eds., Oxford University Press, Oxford, 2000), pp.17–20:

"How does the Rule of Law operate in practice in the United Kingdom? Let us first note that our courts have not, outside of directly effective European Law, felt themselves able to review the validity of primary legislation.[1] This means that a principle like the Rule of Law *can* be expressly overridden by Parliament. As Dicey required, the principle of parliamentary sovereignty prevails. But the absence of judicial review of primary legislation is by no means fatal to the Rule of Law. As a constitutional principle it still serves as a basis for evaluation of laws and a critical focus for public debate. A British government may succeed in introducing detention without trial, or retroactive legislation, but strong justification is needed for such a law to withstand the Rule of Law's moral strictures.

In addition, the Rule of Law is upheld by the courts to this extent: in interpreting the scope of a statutory power, the courts make the implication that Parliament intended to conform to the Rule of Law. If the scope of the power is ambiguous, the principle applies. It is only excluded where clearly stated to the contrary.

The day-to-day practical implementation and enforcement of the Rule of Law is through the judicial review of the actions and decisions of all officials performing public functions. As Dicey contended (although by no means solely through that route) the rule of law is today defined and delineated through our common law. There are three principal 'grounds' of judicial review: review for 'illegality', for 'procedural impropriety', and for 'irrationality' (or unreasonableness). The implementation of each of these grounds involves the courts in applying different aspects of the Rule of Law.

Under the ground of illegality the courts act as guardian of Parliament's purpose, and may strike down official decisions which violate that purpose. Even when wide discretionary power is conferred upon an official the courts are not willing to permit decisions which go outside its 'four corners'. Under the ground of procedural propriety the courts may, even where the statute is silent, supply the 'omission of the legislature' in order to insist that the decision-maker grant a fair hearing to the applicant before depriving him or her of a right, interest or legitimate expectation. The doctrine of legitimate expectation is itself rooted in the notion of legal certainty; the courts require a decision-maker at least to provide the affected person with a hearing before disappointing him of an expectation reasonably induced. At times the promised benefit itself may be required. In either case certainty triumphs over administrative convenience.

It is perhaps more difficult to countenance the application of the Rule of Law in the third ground of judicial review, that of irrationality or unreasonableness, because it raises the question whether the principle governs the substance and not merely the procedure of official action.

To what extent does the Rule of Law touch on the substance, as well as the procedure, of official action? We have seen that laws in practice are not always enforced rigorously, but rather selectively, allowing for personal and other mitigating factors (as with the doctor speeding to the scene of an accident in the early hours of the morning). But suppose the police decide to charge only bearded male drivers with traffic offences and leave the clean-shaven and women drivers alone? Or to charge only drivers of a particular race? Suppose an education authority chose to dismiss all teachers with red hair? Would these decisions infringe the Rule of Law on the ground of their substance? Courts in this country interfere with this kind of decision on the ground of its being an abuse of discretion, the term used being 'unreasonableness' in the sense set out in the celebrated *Wednesbury* case.[2] Is this judicial interference ultimately justified on the ground that the offending decision was a breach of substantive Rule of Law? If so justified, judges lay themselves open to accusations of improper interference with the substance of administration, about which they are reputed to know very little.

---

[1] This has now been made possible under the Human Rights Act 1998 but the courts may only issue a "declaration of incompatibility" and not strike down the legislation.

[2] *Associated Provincial Picture Houses v Wednesbury Corporation* [1948] 1 KB 223.

Those who deny that judges interfere with the substance of decisions contend that what the courts are doing when interfering with arbitrary, capricious, irrational or oppressive decisions is ensuring that the official action is faithful to the law's purpose, thus achieving the containment of the administration in accordance with an implied legislative scheme. Even if a minister has power to act 'as he thinks fit', it is assumed that the statute conferring that power requires standards that are rationally related to purpose, and that the charging of only bearded drivers could not be related to the purpose of preventing unsafe driving. In practice, however, the legislation frequently has no clear 'purpose' itself, and to pretend otherwise is to adopt a fiction. Parliament often delegates enforcement to ministers, other authorities, or officials precisely in order to allow *them* to define and elaborate purpose. Implementation is often a process from the bottom up, rather than from the top down. When the Rule of Law allows judicial interference on grounds of 'unreasonableness', 'irrationality', or 'oppressiveness', it does become a substantive doctrine—one that is less easily accepted than the procedural, particularly in a society without a written constitution. Courts therefore tread warily on substantive Rule of Law and seek to exclude (or disguise) policy considerations from the decision. The 'unreasonableness' doctrine itself carefully avoids judicial second-guessing of the administration on the grounds of mere disagreement, and only permits interference if the official decision verges on the outlandish.

Nevertheless, in certain cases the 'unreasonableness' doctrine does not even attempt to pretend that judicial interference with administrative action is based on lack of fidelity to statutory purpose. Take, for example, the case where a condition attached to a planning permission was held 'unreasonable' because it required the owner to dedicate some of his land to the local authority for a public right of way. The condition here is by no means unrelated to the purpose of the planning legislation (the right of way was necessary for good planning), but it violates the owner's legitimate expectation not to be deprived of his property without compensation. Here the Rule of Law as substantive principle justifies judicial intervention. A local authority which withdrew the licence of a rugby football club because some of its members had visited South Africa also fell foul of the principle in the form of the doctrine that there should be no punishment where there was no law (prohibiting contact with South Africa).

The Rule of Law does, therefore, possess substantive content. It is a principle that promotes the virtues of regularity, rationality, and integrity on the part of officials, and thus protects the legitimate expectations (to both fair procedures and substance) of affected individuals. Because it does not itself provide specific content, it requires elaboration in the light of the practical reason of each generation.

It has therefore provided the background principle justifying much of our developing rules of judicial review. It is broad enough to require laws as enacted by Parliament to be faithfully executed by officials; to require individuals wishing to enforce their rights to have access to the courts, and not to be condemned unheard; to insist that power not be arbitrarily exercised, and that law be certain, that is predictable and not retrospective in its application."

QUESTION

- How does judicial review forward both a procedural and a substantive conception of the rule of law?

Jowell hints at the possibility that judicial review, at times, may appear to involve the judiciary substituting its view of appropriate public policy for that which has been implemented by officials of government. In those situations, the judiciary appears to be exercising a highly *political* function. Moreover, the politics of the judiciary has often appeared to be very conservative. A "classic" example of judicial review which seemed to tread very close to party politics occurred in the early 1980s:

Bromley London Borough Council v Greater London Council and another [1982] 1 All E.R. 129, CA.

[This case was a judicial review of the action of the Greater London Council (GLC) in attempting to reduce fares on London Transport by 25 per cent. Bromley London Borough Council brought the proceedings, asking the courts to stop the implementation of the policy (which required substantial increases in rates) on the grounds that it was beyond the powers of the GLC as defined by the relevant statutes of Parliament or, alternatively, that the policy implementation was an invalid exercise of the GLC's discretion provided under statute. The Divisional Court refused the application, but the Borough Council appealed to the Court of Appeal.]

Lord Denning M.R.:

Introduction in outline

"On 7 May 1981 there was an election for the Greater London Council (the GLC). In advance of the election, the Labour Party issued a manifesto. In it they promised that, if they won, they would within six months cut the fares on London's buses and tubes by 25%. They did win the election. They kept their promise. They told the London Transport Executive (the LTE) to cut the fares by 25%. The travelling public were well pleased with the gift. It meant millions of pounds in their pockets instead of in the ticket machines. But not the ratepayers of London. They were required to contribute £69m to pay for it. In order to enforce payment, the GLC made a supplementary precept. This was an order directed to all the 35 London boroughs commanding them to raise the necessary funds. They were to do it by making a supplementary rate on all the ratepayers. The London boroughs have most reluctantly obeyed. They have made the supplementary rate and have required their ratepayers to pay it. But meanwhile one London borough, Bromley, has challenged the validity of the whole procedure. They apply to the courts for an order of certiorari to quash the supplementary precept.

At the outset I would say that all three members of this court are interested on all sides. We are all fare-paying passengers on the tubes and buses and benefit from the 25% cut in fares. My wife and I also have the benefit of senior citizens to travel free. We are all ratepayers in the area of Greater London and have to pay the increase in rates imposed by the supplementary precept. No objection is taken by any party to our hearing the case. Any Court of Appeal would be likewise placed.

Now for the detail

The manifesto

In March 1981 the Greater London Labour Party issued a manifesto headed 'Socialist Policy for the G.L.C.'. It filled a printed book of some 180 pages containing detailed proposals and promises. At the same time they issued a summarised version headed 'Vote Labour in London May 7th'. It was priced at 30p. It filled a printed booklet of 14 pages of close print. It said in the foreword: 'All candidates are committed to the proposals and pledges contained in the manifesto.' It set out proposals for action on jobs, on housing, on transport, on the environment, on safety and on recreation. On transport it made this pledge:

'*Fares.* Within six months of winning the election, Labour will cut fares on London Transport buses and tubes by an average of 25%. At the same time a much simpler system of fares will be introduced, one which will be easy to understand, will allow faster boarding and will ease the burden on transport workers. There will then be a freeze on fares for four years. The existing system of free travel for senior citizens on London's buses will be extended to the tubes and British Rail services within London.'

There was a paragraph dealing with the cost of all the proposals, taken together. It was headed '*Paying for the Programme*':

'Labour presents this programme in the full knowledge of its financial implications. As more than half of the G.L.C.'s rate revenue comes from the commercial sector, individual householders will only be paying about £1 a week more by 1983/4 for cheaper fares, better public transport services, less congestion, better housing, more jobs, and a safer, cleaner environment. For example, regular users of London Transport will benefit by £1.50 a week.'

The effect of the election

At the election of 7 May 1981 the Labour Party won by a small majority of seats. This was interpreted by their spokesmen on many occasions as giving them a 'clear mandate' from the people of London to cut the fares by 25%. Not only as giving them a mandate but also as a 'promise' and also a 'commitment' by which they promised and committed themselves to implementing a reduction in fares by 25% overall.

The leader of the council gives instructions

The election was on Thursday, 7 May. They lost no time. On Tuesday, 12 May 1981 there was a meeting between Mr Kenneth Livingstone, the leader of the council, and Sir Peter Masefield, the chairman of the LTE. There is no record of what took place, but Dunn LJ inferred, and certainly reasonably inferred, that 'the leader told Sir Peter that the GLC intended to put into immediate effect the policy of overall reduction of fares of 25% and asked him to produce proposals for a new fare structure to implement the policy and a revised budget for 1981'.
This inference is supported by a report of 2 June which recorded that:

'The Leader of the Council has *instructed* London Transport to submit to the Transport Committee at their meeting on 1 July 1981 fares proposals which incorporate a proposal for an *immediate* reduction in London Transport fares of 25%.

That is the very word, 'instructed': 'The Leader of the Council has instructed London Transport . . .'

Those instructions were duly carried out. On 9 June 1981 London Transport submitted a memorandum and issued a press release saying that the GLC had made a '*requirement* of a 25 per cent overall cut' and put forward alternative methods of implementing that requirement. I stress again the words 'requirement of the GLC'.

The block grant

Whilst the LTE was arranging for the 25% cut, the officers of the GLC were looking into the effect on the rates. They then drew to the attention of the GLC that the ratepayers would suffer a heavy penalty. It would lose the block grant which the government gave it. So they would have to pay not only for the cut in fares but also for the loss of the grant. That was pointed out on 23 June 1981 by the comptroller of finance. In a report of that date he said:

'... The Council faces a loss of block grant of £91 million under the block grant system for a decision to finance £110 million revenue costs from rates instead of fares. Therefore, the Council has to decide not only how to finance the operating shortfall in 1981–82 but whether rate payers should pay a heavy penalty ... the Council is faced with the fact that ... the rate payers will pay heavily ...'

This was nothing more nor less than a plea by the officers that the ratepayers should be considered. But it fell on deaf ears. Notwithstanding the clear warning, the GLC decided at a meeting on 7 July 1981 to implement the cut in full regardless of the heavy penalty on the ratepayers. It had before it a report saying that it was necessary to 'implement the *commitment* to reduce fares by an overall 25 per cent'. This meant the levy of a supplementary rate precept. The whole was to take effect by 4 October 1981. That recommendation was approved by a majority of 43 to 33.

The final steps are taken

On 21 July 1981 the GLC did all that was necessary to complete the cut and to issue a supplementary precept. In advance of it, it issued a press release which is most illuminating. It put all the blame on the government. I will quote two sentences from it:

'The bill to ratepayers for the GLC's cutting of bus and Tube fares by 25 per cent and keeping London Transport out of the red will be a 6.1p rate—"as predicted during the GLC election campaign", announced Dr. Tony Hart, Chairman of the Council's Finance and General Purposes Committee, today. But "vindictive" Government policies over local council grants will double the cost to ratepayers without any benefit to Londoners.'

The press release is worth reading in full. All I would say is that it shows that the Labour Party in their manifesto had reckoned only on a 6.1p increase in the rates; but also that in point of fact it would have to be 11.9p in the rates. So their calculations during the course of the election have all been falsified by events since the election in regard to the block grant. Nevertheless they determined to press on with their cut and the precept, regardless of the penal blow it would inflict on the ratepayers. It was carried by 42 to 38 on 21 July 1981.

The supplementary precept is issued

On 22 July 1981 the GLC issued to all the London boroughs a supplementary precept for 1981–82. It said:

'The Greater London Council hereby require you to levy in respect of the current year the rates specified below:

General London Purposes at 6.1 new pence in the pound (chargeable on the whole of Greater London).'

Then there is this significant addition about the loss of the block grant:

'The supplementary precepts issued are gross precepts and therefore take no account of the GLC or ILEA block grant losses consequent on the issue of the supplementary precepts. Authorities are therefore recommended to levy an additional rate for grant loss ....'

The London borough of Bromley received that precept on 28 July. They took legal advice and decided to challenge it. They telephoned the GLC on 10 August and told it so. Then on 11 September they issued proceedings in the courts.

The law

This brings me to the law. It was divided in the argument in two parts. First, the statutory powers of the GLC. Second, the way it exercised its powers.

The statutory powers of the GLC

We have studied in detail the provisions of the Transport (London) Act 1969. I will state the result. The LTE is a statutory corporation, a body corporate. It is entrusted with the task of running the buses and tubes of London. It is its duty to run it on business lines. It must manage its income and expenditure so as to break even so far as practicable. If it cannot pay its way, the GLC can make grants to it to keep it going. The GLC have a degree of control over it, but it is of a limited character. The GLC can give it general directions on matters of policy (see s.11(1)) but it cannot interfere with the day-to-day running of its affairs. But even those matters of policy are not open-ended. They are confined to policies which will 'promote the process of integrated, efficient and economic transport facilities and services for Greater London' (see s.1(1)). This includes the objectives of quick, frequent, reliable services, and reasonable fares. But it does not include the promotion of social or philanthropic or political objectives. It does not include free travel for all. It does not include a reduction in fares which is completely uneconomic. The word 'economic' is significant. It means what we all mean when we say of a financial proposal, 'That is not an economic proposition,' meaning that under it expenditure will exceed the income. It certainly does not warrant the instruction given here to cut fares by 25%.

Apart from this fundamental point, the statute contains specific provisions about fares. The LTE is the charging authority, not the GLC. The LTE has in the first instance to settle the general level and structure of the fares to be charged. These are subject to the approval of the GLC. If the GLC approve, they are to be published. If the GLC disapprove, then there is this important provision in s.11(3):

'. . . the Council may direct the Executive to submit proposals for an alteration in the Executive's fare arrangements to achieve any object of general policy specified by the Council in the direction.'

Any such direction has by s41(3) to be in writing. No such direction was given in this case.

Furthermore, when the LTE is settling the general level and structure of fares, it must consider the position of those parts of its undertaking which fall outside the London area. It must consult the county councils concerned and see if they are prepared to make any contribution to the cost. No such consultation was held in this case.

In view of these considerations, I am of opinion that the GLC had no power whatever to give instructions to the LTE as it purported to do. The leader had no right whatever to go to Sir Peter Masefield and tell him to cut the fares by an overall 25%; nor had Sir Peter any business to accede to it. The GLC itself had no power to make resolutions to enforce a 25% cut. That was a completely uneconomic proposition done for political motives, for which there is no warrant; including the supplementary precept. It was beyond its powers. It is ultra vires and void. It cannot be allowed to stand.

The way it exercised its powers

In case I am wrong on that point, I go on to consider whether the GLC exercised its powers properly.

It appears to me that the GLC owed a duty both to the travelling public and to the ratepayers. Its duty to the travelling public is to provide an integrated, efficient and economic service at reasonable fares. Its duty to the ratepayers is to charge them as much as is reasonable and no more. In carrying out those duties, the members of the GLC have to balance the two conflicting interests: the interest of the travelling public in cheap fares and the interest of the ratepayers in not being overcharged. The members of the GLC have to hold the balance between these conflicting interests. They have to take all relevant considerations into account on either side. They must not be influenced by irrelevant considerations. They must not give undue weight to one consideration over another, lest they upset the balance. They must hold the balance fairly and reasonably. If they come to a decision which is, in all the circumstances, unjust and unreasonable, then the courts can and should interfere. . . .

[T]he majority of the GLC gave altogether undue weight to the following consideration. They had issued a manifesto in which they had promised to cut the fares on London Transport by 25%. They regarded the election result as giving them a *mandate* to fulfil that promise. They regarded themselves as *committed* to the implementation of that promise. They were determined to 'honour' that commitment, come what may. They afterwards discovered that it would injure the ratepayers severely, far more severely than they had realised when they made the promise. It would injure the ratepayers because of the loss of the block grant. This loss has doubled the burden on the ratepayers. But nevertheless the majority of the GLC determined to go ahead with the cut of 25% irrespective of the penalising hardship on the ratepayers.

In giving such weight to the manifesto, I think the majority of the GLC were under a complete misconception. A manifesto issued by a political party, in order to get votes, is not to be taken as gospel. It is not to be regarded as a bond, signed, sealed and delivered. It may contain, and often does contain, promises or proposals that are quite unworkable or impossible of attainment. Very few of the electorate read the manifesto in full. A goodly number only know of it from what they read in the newspapers or hear on television. Many know nothing whatever of what it contains. When they come to the polling booth, none of them vote for the manifesto. Certainly not for every promise or proposal in it. Some may be influenced by one proposal. Others by another. Many are not influenced by it at all. They vote for a party and not for a manifesto. I have no doubt that in this case many ratepayers voted for the Labour Party even though, on this item alone, it was against their interests. And vice versa. It seems to me that no party can or should claim a mandate and commitment for any one item in a long manifesto. When the party gets into power, it should consider any proposal or promise afresh, on its merits, without any feeling of being obliged to honour it or being committed to it. It should then consider what is best to do in the circumstances of the case and to do it if it is practicable and fair.

Another thing is that the figure of 25% was not explained in any way whatever. No councillor has given evidence or has made an affidavit before the courts at all. It is acknowledged by the GLC that the statute does not empower it to abolish fares altogether, or to give free travel for all. But in principle I see no difference between abolishing fares altogether and cutting them by one-half or one-quarter. It is a gift to the travelling public at the expense of the general body of ratepayers. There seems to be no financial reason for choosing 25%. Why not 20% or 30% or even 50%? It seems to me that the figure of 25% was an arbitrary figure clutched from the air in order to be attractive to the electorate.

In the result I hold the GLC did not hold the balance fair. The 25% was more than fair to the travelling public and less than fair to the ratepayers. Millions of passengers on the buses and tubes come from far outside the London area. They come every day. They get the benefit of the 25% cut in fares without paying a penny on their rates at home. That is more than fair to them. It is a gift indeed to them, given without paying a penny for it. Whereas thousands of ratepayers in London who pay the rates never use the buses or tubes at all. Bromley, for instance, has no tubes. It is less than fair to them. It is positively penal. It is not fair to make these ratepayers pay for these gifts to people who come from far afield. The employees of London Transport see the 'cut' as equivalent to a money gift. They get free travel anyway. They each claimed, and got, an extra £50 because the free travel was worth less after the 'cut'. It cost £3m, all to be paid by the ratepayers.

Conclusion

My conclusion is that the actions here of the GLC went beyond its statutory powers and are null and void. Even if they were within their statutory powers, they were distorted by giving undue weight to the manifesto and by the arbitrary and unfair nature of the decision. The supplementary precept must be quashed, and a declaration made accordingly.

I realise that this must cause much consternation to the GLC and the LTE. They will be at their wits end to know what to do. But it is their own fault. They were very foolish not to take legal advice before they embarked on this sequel to their election. Even after legal proceedings were intimated to them in August, they went ahead with their plans and put them into operation on 4 October 1981. They must unscramble the affair as best they can. At any rate, they cannot burden the ratepayers of London with this supplementary precept. I would allow the appeal accordingly."

[Oliver L.J. and Watkins L.J. delivered separate reasons, concurring in the result reached by Lord Denning M.R. The case was appealed by the GLC to the House of Lords, which affirmed, on varied grounds, the result reached by the Court of Appeal.]

The *Bromley* decision was subject to harsh criticism, as an example both of judicial intervention in matters properly left to elected representatives, as well as for the alleged failure of the judiciary properly to recognise either the purpose of the legislation which empowered the GLC in this matter, or the legitimacy of the concerns which gave rise to the fare policy.

J.A.G. Griffith, *The Politics of the Judiciary* (4th ed., Harper Collins, London, 1991), pp.130–131:

"In this case, the Law Lords chose to say that the GLC had not adequately taken into account the interests of the ratepayers and that the interests of the users of public transport had been unduly preferred. Such an argument can logically be applied whenever public authorities spend the ratepayers' (or the taxpayers') money to further some statutory purpose. Particular public expenditure can always be criticized on the ground that it is excessive or wrongly directed, whether on defence or education or the building of motorways or any other public service. The constitutional reply is that public authorities, being directly or indirectly elected, are the representatives of the public interest and that their function is precisely that of making such decisions. The criticism is then seen as being political and if the electors of Greater London disapprove of what is being done in their name by their representatives, the remedy lies in their hands at the next election. Nor is this merely constitutional or political theory, divorced from reality, for without doubt the election in 1985 for the GLC would have turned very largely on this issue and on the view taken of the controversial Labour administration at County Hall during its four years in office. It is surely no more the function of the judiciary to tell the GLC where the public interest lay in its spending of public money than it is the function of the judiciary to make similar arguments about spending by the Departments of the central government."

J.A.G. Griffith, *The Politics of the Judiciary* (4th ed., Harper Collins, London, 1991), pp.302–304:

"The judgments delivered in the Court of Appeal and the House of Lords in *Bromley v GLC* demonstrate how ill-suited is judicial review to the examination of administrative policies. They show how the narrow approach of the courts to the interpretation of statutes leads to a misunderstanding of the purpose of legislation. . . .

The crisis in urban transport received popular recognition in the publication in 1963 of Colin Buchanan's *Traffic in Towns*. This was followed in 1966 by the white paper on *Transport Policy*. This emphasized the 'severe discomforts' brought by the growth of road traffic: congestion, the misery of commuter travel, noise, fumes, danger, casualties and the threat to the environment; and the need to plan, as a whole, for the related needs of industry, housing and transport. The paper drew attention to the mutually contradictory objectives of providing adequate services and self-financing.

In January 1968, the London Transport Joint Review was published and was followed in July by the white paper *Transport in London*. The Review found that the major factor underlying London Transport's recurrent financial deficit was the imbalance between peak and off-peak demand. The Review was somewhat ambiguous about the need for financial viability, but it certainly envisaged some form of grant and emphasized the social benefits of controlling the level of fares while providing proper services. *Transport in London* went further in emphasizing the need of the transport system to take account of 'the social as well as the economic needs of the country'. Subsidization through the local rates was one of the means adopted by the Transport Act 1968 for conurbations outside London and this was intended to enable the transport authorities to achieve, in part, the purpose of developing transport as a social service.

The Transport (London) Act 1969 was seen by ministers as taking this approach further. For the first time in London, the responsibility for transport was given to a directly elected local authority acting through an Executive appointed by itself. Comparison has been made with a nationalized industry operating the day-to-day management under the general directions of a minister. But the control by the GLC over the LTE was much tighter than that of a minister over the coal, gas or electricity authorities. The GLC was not merely empowered but required by section 1 'to develop policies, and to encourage, organize and, where appropriate, carry out measures'. The LTE existed to implement policies of the GLC (section 4(1)) and to act 'in accordance with principles laid down or approved by the GLC' (section 5(1)). Additionally, the GLC might give the LTE general directions in relation to functions which the GLC was under a duty to perform (section 11(1)). There were also other more detailed provisions emphasizing the powers of the GLC. Above all, the GLC's primary duty was to promote 'the provision of integrated, efficient and economic transport facilities and services for Greater London'. Finally, the LTE was required to submit to the GLC for their approval the general level and structure of the fares to be charged and the GLC might 'direct the Executive to submit proposals for an alteration in the Executive's fare arrangements to achieve any object of general policy specified by the Council in the direction' (section 11(3)). . . .

Bromley v GLC raises all the questions about the nature, the function, and the limits of judicial review. The whole method of adjudication as presently adopted by the courts is inappropriate to the consideration of political decisions affecting the distribution of costs between the tax and rate-paying public, on the one hand, and the users of public services, on the other."

Following the decision of the House of Lords in *Bromley v GLC*, fares doubled, and the GLC produced a new scheme, in which it directed the LTE to cut fares by 25 per cent, with an accompanying grant from the Council to the LTE to make up the lost revenues. The LTE objected, and the case was heard by the Divisional Court, which upheld the validity of the scheme, on the ground that the grant allowed the LTE to balance its revenue account, and because the GLC had now considered its statutory duties. Griffith commented:

"The new scheme, upheld by the Divisional Court in the later case, was made under the same statute and did not appreciably hold a different balance between ratepayers and transport users. The decision of the Divisional Court bears the marks of a rescue operation, seeking to save some sanity for transport policy in London and for the right of statutory authorities to exercise statutory powers within the statutory terms given to them."[3]

NOTES AND QUESTIONS

- To the extent that judicial review adopts a substantive conception, can it be constitutionally justified? Use the judgment of Lord Denning MR in *Bromley v GLC* as evidence for your argument.

[3] J.A.G. Griffiths, *The Politics of the Judiciary* (4th ed., Harper Collins, London, 1991) pp.135–136.

- The judgment of Denning MR in *Bromley v GLC* contains numerous assertions about the political process, as well as a number of ideological assumptions about the self-interest of individuals with regard to tax and transport policy. Summarise those assertions and assumptions. Would you describe the judgment as more "political" than "legal"? Could a judgment be written in this case which did not appear to be "political"?

- In 1984 the Conservative government announced its intention to introduce legislation to abolish the GLC, and under the Local Government Act 1985 the abolition took effect on April 1, 1986.

In some cases, by contrast, the judiciary has been highly deferential to the actions of the executive, particularly in those cases where executive action is justified on the basis of "national security".

Council of Civil Service Unions and others v Minister for the Civil Service [1984] 3 All E.R. 935, HL.

Lord Fraser of Tullybelton:

"My Lords, Government Communications Headquarters (GCHQ) is a branch of the public service under the Foreign and Commonwealth Office, the main functions of which are to ensure the security of the United Kingdom military and official communications, and to provide signals intelligence for the government. These functions are of great national importance and they involve handling secret information which is vital to the national security. The main establishment of GCHQ is at Cheltenham, where over 4,000 people are employed. There are also a number of smaller out-stations, one of which is at Bude in Cornwall.

Since 1947, when GCHQ was established in its present form, all the staff employed there have been permitted, and indeed encouraged, to belong to national trade unions, and most of them did so. Six unions were represented at GCHQ. They were all members, though not the only members, of the Council of Civil Service Unions (CCSU), the first appellant. The second appellant is the secretary of CCSU. The other appellants are individuals who are employed at GCHQ and who were members of one or other of the unions represented there. A departmental Whitley Council was set up in 1947 and, until the events with which this appeal is concerned, there was a well-established practice of consultation between the official side and the trade union side about all important alterations in the terms and conditions of employment of the staff.

On 25 January 1984 all that was abruptly changed. The Secretary of State for Foreign and Commonwealth Affairs announced in the House of Commons that the government had decided to introduce with immediate effect new conditions of service for all staff at GCHQ, the effect of which was that they would no longer be permitted to belong to national trade unions but would be permitted to belong only to a departmental staff association approved by the director. The announcement came as a complete surprise to the trade unions and to the employees at GCHQ, as there had been no prior consultation with them. The principal question raised in this appeal is whether the instruction by which the decision received effect, and which was issued orally on 22 December 1983 by the respondent (who is also the Prime Minister), is valid and effective in accordance with art.4 of the Civil Service Order in Council 1982. The respondent maintains that it is. The appellants maintain that it is invalid because there was a procedural obligation on the respondent to act fairly by consulting the persons concerned before exercising her power under art.4 of the Order in Council, and she had failed to do so. Underlying that question, and logically preceding it, is the question whether the courts, and your Lordships' House in its judicial capacity, have power to review the instruction on the ground of a procedural irregularity, having regard peculiarly to the facts (a) that it was made in the exercise of a power conferred under the royal prerogative and not by statute and (b) that it concerned national security.

It is necessary to refer briefly to the events which led up to the decision of 22 December 1983. Between February 1979 and April 1981 industrial action was taken at GCHQ on seven occasions. The action took various forms: one-day strikes, work to rule and overtime bans. The most serious disruption occurred on 9 March 1981, when about 25% of the staff went on one-day strike and, according to Sir Robert Armstrong, the Secretary to the Cabinet, who made an affidavit in these proceedings, parts of the operations at GCHQ were virtually shut down. The appellants do not accept the respondent's view of the seriousness of the effects of industrial action on the work at GCHQ. But clearly it must have had some adverse effect, especially by causing some interruption of the constant day and night monitoring of foreign signals communications. The industrial action was taken mainly in support of national trade unions, when they were in dispute with the government about conditions of service of civil servants generally, and not about local problems at GCHQ. In 1981 especially it was part of a campaign by the national trade unions, designed to do as much damage as possible to government agencies including GCHQ. Sir Robert Armstrong in his affidavit refers to several circular letters and 'campaign reports' issued by CCSU and some of its constituent unions, which show the objectives of the campaign. . . ."

[The first and second appellants obtained leave from Glidewell J. to bring proceedings for judicial review on the basis that the instruction of December 22, 1983 was invalid. Glidewell J. found it to be invalid on the basis of a procedural irregularity in failing to consult before issuing the instruction. The Court of Appeal reversed the judge's decision and dismissed the application for judicial review. Lord Fraser considered the first issue—the reviewability of the exercise of prerogative powers, leaving the question open. He then considered the national security issue, but only after finding that in the absence of a pressing matter of national security, a duty to consult the trade unions would be found on the basis of a legitimate expectation based on prior practice.]

"The question is one of evidence. The decision on whether the requirements of national security outweigh the duty of fairness in any particular case is for the government and not for the courts; the government alone has access to the necessary information, and in any event the judicial process is unsuitable for reaching decisions on national security. . . .

The evidence in support of this part of the respondent's case came from Sir Robert Armstrong in his first affidavit . . . . [I]t does set out the respondent's view that to have entered into prior consultation would have served to bring out the vulnerability of areas of operation to those who had shown themselves ready to organise disruption. That must be read along with the earlier parts of the affidavit in which Sir Robert had dealt in some detail with the attitude of the trade unions which I have referred to earlier in this speech. The affidavit, read as a whole, does in my opinion undoubtedly constitute evidence that the minister did indeed consider that prior consultation would have involved a risk of precipitating disruption at GCHQ. I am accordingly of the opinion that the respondent has shown that her decision was one which not only could reasonably have been based, but was in fact based, on considerations of national security, which outweighed what would otherwise have been the reasonable expectation on the part of the appellants for prior consultation."

[All of the Law Lords dismissed the appeal. Lords Scarman, Diplock and Roskill found that powers exercised directly under the prerogative are not automatically immune from judicial review. Rather, the issue was the justiciability of its subject matter. But the Lords agreed that once a minister produced evidence that her decision was taken for reasons of national security, the question became non-justiciable because the executive alone was sole judge of what national security required.]

QUESTIONS

- In light of the decision of the House of Lords in *CCSU v Minister for the Civil Service*, what advice would you give a government minister as to how to ensure that his or her decisions are immune from judicial review?

- Compare the level of *deference* given to the executive in *Bromley* and *CCSU* by the judiciary. How would you explain the difference?

Another famous example of judicial review was also highly politically charged, and generated much criticism of the judiciary's determination that the local council had misused its power.

Wheeler and others v Leicester City Council [1985] 2 All E.R. 1106, HL.

Lord Roskill:

"My Lords, this is an appeal by members of the Leicester Football club suing on their own behalf and on behalf of all other members of the club. In reality it is an appeal by the club and I shall so treat it. It is brought by leave of the Court of Appeal. That court on 14 March 1985 by a majority (Ackner LJ and Sir George Waller, Browne-Wilkinson LJ dissenting) dismissed an appeal by the club against the refusal of Forbes J on 27 September 1984 to grant the club judicial review of a decision by the respondents, Leicester City Council made on 21 August 1984. That decision is recorded in minute no 46 of the council's policy and resources committed in the following terms:

'RESOLVED: that the Leicester Football Club be suspended from using the Welford Road recreation ground for a period of 12 months and that the situation be reviewed at the end of that period in the light of the club's attitude to sporting links with South Africa.'

As a result of the passing of that resolution, the club applied for a judicial review of the decision for the purpose of quashing it, for a declaration that it was of no effect and for an injunction preventing, inter alia, the implementation of the resolution. On 10 September 1984 Otton J gave the club leave to move for judicial review and, pending the hearing of the motion, granted the injunction sought. As already stated, Forbes J refused the relief sought and since the appeal to the Court of Appeal failed, the club has remained banned from the use of the Welford Road recreation ground save for training purposes, this last by virtue of a concession later made by the council in circumstances to which I will refer in due course.

My Lords, the background to this unfortunate dispute between a rugby football club of renown, now over a century old, and the council is fully stated in the judgments below. I gratefully adopt those statements for in truth the relevant facts are not in dispute. But some reference to the facts is essential for the proper understanding of the issues involved.

The story starts with the announcement of the Rugby Football Union (the RFU) on 30 March 1984 that they had accepted an invitation to take a touring side to South Africa. On 19 April 1984 the membership of this side was announced. The membership included three well-known members of the club. All three were regular England players. It should be mentioned that the club does not have any direct representation of the RFU. It has one representative on the Leicestershire Rugby Union and the latter body has one representative on the main committee of the RFU.

On 1 April 1984, Mr John Allen, the secretary and former captain of the club, was telephoned by the assistant chief executive of the council and asked if representatives of the club would attend a meeting with Mr Soulsby, the leader of the council, in connection with the projected tour and the participation of the club's three members.

That meeting took place on 12 April 1984. Mr Soulsby read out four questions. These four questions have been recorded in writing but no copies were given to the club representatives at the meeting. Since I attach importance to the content of these four questions, both individually and collectively, I record them in full:

'1. Does the Leicester Football Club support the Government opposition to the tour? 2. Does the Leicester Football Club agree that the tour is an insult to the large proportion of the Leicester population? 3. Will the Leicester Football Club press the Rugby Football Union to call off the tour? 4. Will the Leicester Football Club press the players to pull out of the tour?'

Mr Allen told Mr Soulsby he would take the questions back to the committee of the club and would return for a further meeting on 8 May 1984. At that latter meeting it was made plain by Mr Soulsby (Mr Allen's affidavit was not contradicted on this matter) that 'the club's response would only be acceptable if in effect all four questions were answered in the affirmative'.

On 14 May 1984, Mr Allen again wrote to Mr Soulsby and handed him a written statement of the club's response:

'Leicester Football Club have always enjoyed cordial relations with Leicester City Council on a strictly non-political basis and seek to continue that relationship. The club join with the council in condemning apartheid but recognise that there are differences of opinion over the way in which the barriers of apartheid can be broken down. The government have not declared sporting contacts illegal or even applied sanctions against those involved in tours. Their opposition is on an advisory basis, similar to the advice to athletes at the time of the Moscow Olympics, leaving the decision to the individuals concerned. The decision by the Rugby Football Union to approve the tour was taken by a large majority of their committee, but the club had forwarded to the Leicestershire Rugby Union, the club's constituent body, the anti-apartheid case against the tour, which merits serious consideration. Rugby Union players as amateur sportsmen have individual choice as to when and where they play, subject only to the constraints of R.F.U. rules and club loyalty. However, the club, having read the memorandum to the R.F.U. prepared by the anti-apartheid movement, and accepting the serious nature of its contents, have supplied copies to the tour players and asked them to seriously consider the contents before finally reaching a decision whether to tour. The club are and always have been multi-racial and will continue that principle for the benefit of Leicester and rugby football.'

Mr Soulsby said he noted the club's response but added that he did not think 'it would have gone far enough to satisfy the membership of the controlling Labour group on the council'.

This meeting was followed by various statements through the media and elsewhere that the council were considering sanctions against the club for what the council regarded as the club's failure to discourage its members from taking part in the South African tour.

No solution was found during the ensuing weeks. On 21 August 1984 the resolution banning the club from the use of the Welford Road recreation ground was passed in the terms which I have already mentioned. This resolution was subsequently notified to the club. Mr Small, the club's solicitor and also one of its members wrote on 30 August 1984 to ask whether the ban included a ban on using the recreation ground for training. A brief reply, dated 31 August 1984, indicated that the ban was intended to be total. The letter, over the signature of the assistant chief executive, included these sentences:

'It was and is the council's intention to prevent members of the Tigers [*ie* the club] training on the recreation ground in the evenings as well as banning the use of the rugby pitch for the club matches. For the ban on training the council would seek to rely on Byelaw 16 of the Parks Byelaws and would maintain that the use of the recreation ground by the Tigers would per se interfere with other use of the recreation ground.'

Mr Small (whose evidence on this matter was not contradicted) was subsequently told by Mr Stephenson that if the club tried to train on the ground the floodlighting would be discontinued and this would be effective to prevent training.

By the time the matter was before Forbes J it was recognised that this reliance on byelaw 16 was indefensible. I say no more about it save to express regret that the contention should ever have been advanced. Any defence of the council's action based on the Race Relations Act 1976, however well founded, could not possibly have extended to justify a ban on training, as Forbes J pointed out.

The reasons for the imposition of the ban are clearly set out in para 13 of Mr Soulsby's affidavit. I quote that paragraph in full:

'I refute any suggestion that the purported sanction against the club was imposed in response to the actions of their players. I wish to make it clear that the action taken by the council was in response to the attitude taken by the club in failing to condemn the tour and to discourage its members from playing. The council has taken its steps therefore because of what the club did or did not do. It was always recognised that the club were not in the position of employers and could not instruct their players. However, the club is, as the applicants' evidence shows, a premier rugby football club and an influential member of the Rugby Football Union. At no time was the club asked to do anything by the city council which was beyond their powers to do. The steps taken by the city council have not been taken in order to penalise the club for having members who went to South Africa, still less, to penalise the club in order to penalise the players.'

It is important to emphasise that there was nothing illegal in the action of the three members in joining the tour. The government policy recorded in the well-known Gleneagles agreement made in 1977 between the Commonwealth heads of government, has never been given the force of law at the instance of any government, whatever its political complexion, and a person who acts otherwise than in accordance with the principles of the agreement commits no offence even though he may by his action earn the moral disapprobation of his fellow citizens. That the club condemns apartheid, as does the council, admits of no doubt. But the council's actions against the club were not taken, as already pointed out because the club took no action against its three members. They were taken, according to Mr Soulsby, because the club failed to condemn the tour and to discourage its members from playing. The same point was put more succinctly by counsel for the council: 'The club failed to align themselves wholeheartedly with the council on a controversial issue.' The club did not condemn the tour. They did not give specific affirmative answers to the first two questions. Thus, so the argument ran, the council, legitimately bitterly hostile to the policy of apartheid, were justified in exercising their statutory discretion to determine by whom the recreation ground should be used so as to exclude those, such as the club, who would not support the council's policy on the council's terms. The club had, however, circulated to those involved the powerfully reasoned and impressive memorandum which had been sent to the RFU on 12 March 1984 by the anti-apartheid movement. Of the club's own opposition to apartheid as expressed in its memorandum which was given to Mr Soulsby, there is no doubt. But the club recognised that those views, like those of the council, however passionately held by some, were by no means universally held, especially by those who sincerely believed that the evils of apartheid were enhanced rather than diminished by a total prohibition of sporting links with South Africa.

The council's main defence rested on s.71 of the Race Relations Act 1976. That section appears as the first section of Pt X of the Act under the cross-heading 'supplemental'. For ease of reference I will set out the section in full:

'Without prejudice to their obligation to comply with any other provision of this Act, it shall be the duty of every local authority to make appropriate arrangements with a view to securing that their various functions are carried out with due regard to the need—(a) to eliminate unlawful racist discrimination; and (b) to promote equality of opportunity, and good relations, between persons of different racial groups.'

My Lords, it was strenuously argued on behalf of the club that this section should be given what was called a 'narrow' construction. It was suggested that the section was only concerned with the actions of the council as regards its own internal behaviour and was what was described as 'inward looking'. The section had no relevance to the general exercise by the council or indeed of any local authority of their statutory functions, as for example in relation to the control of open spaces or in determining who should be entitled to use a recreation ground and on what terms. It was said that the section was expressed in terms of 'duty'. But it did not impose any duty so as to compel the exercise by a local authority of other statutory functions in order to achieve the objectives of the 1976 Act.

My Lords, in respectful agreement with both courts below, I unhesitatingly reject this argument. I think the whole purpose of this section is to see that in relation to matters other than those specifically dealt with, for example, in Pt II (employment) and in Pt III (education) local authorities must in relation to 'their various functions' make 'appropriate arrangements' to secure that those functions are carried out 'with due regard to the need' mentioned in the section.

It follows that I do not doubt that the council were fully entitled in exercising their statutory discretion under, for example, the Open Spaces Act 1906 and the various Public Health Acts, which are all referred to in the judgments below, to pay regard to what they thought was in the best interests of race relations.

The only question is, therefore, whether the action of the council of which the club complains is susceptible of attack by way of judicial review. It was forcibly argued by counsel on behalf of the council that once it was accepted, as I do accept, that s.71 bears the construction for which the council contended, the matter became one of political judgment only, and that by interfering the courts would be trespassing across that line which divides a proper exercise of statutory discretion based on a political judgment, in relation to which the courts must not and will not interfere, from an improper exercise of such a discretion in relation to which the courts will interfere. . . .

I do not for one moment doubt the great importance which the council attach to the presence in their midst of a 25% population of persons who are either Asian or Afro-Caribbean in origin. Nor do I doubt for one moment the sincerity of the view expressed in Mr Soulsby's affidavit regarding the need for the council to distance itself from bodies who hold important positions and do not actively discourage sporting contacts with South Africa. Persuasion, even powerful persuasion, is always a permissible way of seeking to obtain an objective. But in a field where other views can equally legitimately be held, persuasion, however powerful, must not be allowed to cross that line where it moves into the field of illegitimate pressure coupled with the threat of sanctions. The four questions, coupled with the insistence that only affirmative answers to all four would be acceptable, are suggestive of more than powerful persuasion. The second question is to my mind open to particular criticism. What, in the context, is meant by 'the club'? The committee? The playing members? The 4,300 non-playing members? It by no means follows that the committee would all have agreed on an affirmative answer to the question and still less that a majority of their members, playing or non-playing, would have done so. Nor would any of these groups of members necessarily have known whether 'the large proportion', whatever the phrase may mean in the context, of the Leicester population would have regarded the tour as 'an insult' to them.

None of the judges in the courts below have felt able to hold that the action of the club was unreasonable or perverse in the *Wednesbury* sense. They do not appear to have been invited to consider whether those actions, even if not unreasonable on *Wednesbury* principles, were assailable on the grounds of procedural impropriety or unfairness by the council in the manner in which, in the light of the facts which I have outlined, they took their decision to suspend for 12 months the use by the club of the Welford Road recreation ground. I would greatly hesitate to differ from four learned judges on the *Wednesbury* issue but for myself I would have been disposed respectfully to do this and to say that the actions of the council were unreasonable in the *Wednesbury* sense. But even if I am wrong in this view, I am clearly of the opinion that the manner in which the council took that decision was in all the circumstances unfair within the third of the principles stated in *Council of Civil Service Unions v Minister for Civil Service*. The council formulated those four questions in the manner of which I have spoken and indicated that only such affirmative answers would be acceptable. They received reasoned and reasonable answers which went a long way in support of the policy which the council had accepted and desired to see accepted. The views expressed in these reasoned and reasonable answers were lawful views and the views which, as the evidence shows, many people sincerely hold and believe to be correct. If the club had adopted a different and hostile attitude, different considerations might well have arisen. But the club did not adopt any such attitude.

In my view, therefore, this is a case in which the court should interfere because of the unfair manner in which the council set about obtaining its objective. . . .

Since preparing this speech I have had the advantage of reading in draft the speech of my noble and learned friend Lord Templeman with which I find myself in complete agreement.

I would, therefore, allow the appeal and order certiorari to issue to quash the council's decision of 21 August 1984, the terms of which I have already set out. I do not think that the declaration or the injunction sought is necessary at this juncture, but lest they become so, I would remit the matter to the High Court with liberty to the club to apply for such further relief as may be thought necessary to protect their rights. The council must pay the costs in this House and both courts below."

[Lord Templeman delivered separate reasons in which he agreed with Lord Roskill. Lords Bridge of Harwich, Lord Brightman and Lord Griffiths also agreed.]

QUESTION

• Was the decision of the council a matter of political judgment on which the courts should have intervened? What responsibility did the council have in this situation?

PARLIAMENTARY SUPREMACY AND JUDICIAL REVIEW

The *Bromley v GLC* and *Wheeler v Leicester City Council* cases did not directly raise the issue of Parliamentary supremacy. The councils had limited powers which had been granted pursuant to statutes enacted by Parliament. The issue was whether they had exceeded their powers or exercised their discretion unreasonably. In that sense, the judges saw the cases as directly raising "rule of law" issues about the importance of ensuring that officials of the state exercise only those powers granted to them under statute, and do so in a reasonable, rather than arbitrary, fashion.

However, the principle of Parliamentary supremacy, as we saw in Chapter 3, demands that Parliament, provided its procedural rules are followed, has unlimited scope in terms of the substance of the laws it wishes to enact. For example, Parliament could have specifically and explicitly empowered the GLC to cut fares, had it so wanted. Moreover, Parliament has frequently attempted to prevent the courts from judicially reviewing the exercise of discretionary powers by officials of the state, by including provisions within the empowering statutes, known as *ouster clauses* (designed to "oust" the judiciary from reviewing government actions). An ouster clause is an attempt by the legislature to explicitly exclude review of a decision by judicial review, within the terms of the relevant statute. Given the principle of Parliamentary supremacy, we might think that such clauses—if they are clear and unambiguous in their language—should ensure that judges do not review the decisions made by officials. However, courts in general have interpreted ouster clauses narrowly, and have jealously guarded their ability to judicially review, on the basis of the importance of this supervisory role for the judiciary in ensuring the legality of executive actions. The "classic" case on ouster clauses is *Anisminic*.

Anisminic Ltd v Foreign Compensation Commission and another [1969] 2 A.C. 147, HL.

Lord Reid:
"My Lords, in 1956 the appellants owned a mining property in Egypt which they claim was worth over £4,000,000. On the outbreak of hostilities in the autumn of that year it was occupied by Israeli forces and damaged to the extent of some £500,000. On November 1, 1956, property in Egypt belonging to British subjects was sequestrated by the Egyptian Government and on April 29, 1957, after the Israeli forces had withdrawn, the Egyptian Government authorised a sale of the appellants' property and it was sold to an Egyptian organisation referred to in this case as T.E.D.O.

The appellants' property had included a large quantity of manganese ore and steps were taken by them to dissuade their customers from buying ore from T.E.D.O. This seems to have embarrassed the Egyptian authorities, and on November 23, 1957, an agreement was made between the appellants, T.E.D.O. and the Sequestrator General whereby the appellants purported to sell to T.E.D.O. for a price of £500,000 their whole business in Egypt, but this was not to include any claim which the appellants might 'be entitled to assert against any government authority other than the Egyptian government, as a result of loss suffered by, or of damage to or reduction in the value of' their business or assets during the events of October and November, 1956. . ."

[Lord Reid then described a treaty between the Governments of the United Kingdom and the United Arab Republic whereby £27,500,000 was paid in full and final settlement of any claims arising from properties such as Sinai Mining (the name of which was changed to Anisminic). The Foreign Compensation Commission, which had been established in the United Kingdom with powers contained in the Foreign Compensation Act, 1950, was responsible for the payment of compensation arising out of agreements with foreign governments. The primary claim made by Anisminic was dismissed by the commissioner, on the basis that it had sold its interest to T.E.D.O., which was its "successor in title". Anisminic brought an action in the courts against the commission, seeking a declaration to the effect that this determination was a "nullity" and that they were entitled to participate in the compensation fund, on the basis that the commission had misconstrued the statutory order which defined their jurisdiction (which was the basis for the determination that Anisminic was not eligible for compensation). Of relevance to us is the language of the 1950 legislation.]

"The next argument was that, by reason of the provisions of s.4(4) of the 1950 Act, the courts are precluded from considering whether the respondent's determination was a nullity, and therefore it must be treated as valid whether or not inquiry would disclose that it was a nullity. Section 4(4) is in these terms:

'The determination by the commission of any application made to them under this Act shall not be called in question in any court of law.'

The respondent maintains that these are plain words only capable of having one meaning. Here is a determination which is apparently valid: there is nothing on the face of the document to cast any doubt on its validity. If it is a nullity, that could only be established by raising some kind of proceedings in court. But that would be calling the determination in question, and that is expressly prohibited by the statute. The appellants maintain that that is not the meaning of the words of this provision. They say that 'determination' means a real determination and does not include an apparent or purported determination which in the eyes of the law has no existence because it is a nullity. Or, putting it in another way, if you seek to show that a determination is a nullity you are not questioning the purported determination—you are maintaining that it does not exist as a determination. It is one thing to question a determination which does exist: it is quite another thing to say that there is nothing to be questioned. . . .

But there are many cases where, although the tribunal had jurisdiction to enter on the inquiry, it has done or failed to do something in the course of the inquiry which is of such a nature that its decision is a nullity. It may have given its decision in bad faith. It may have made a decision which it had no power to make. It may have failed in the course of the inquiry to comply with the requirements of natural justice. It may in perfect good faith have misconstrued the provisions giving it power to act so that it failed to deal with the question remitted to it and decided some question which was not remitted to it. It may have refused to take into account something which it was required to take into account. Or it may have based its decision on some matter which, under the provisions setting it up, it had no right to take into account. I do not intend this list to be exhaustive. But if it decides a question remitted to it for decision without committing any of these errors it is as much entitled to decide that question wrongly as it is to decide it rightly."

[Lord Reid then construed the relevant statutory order empowering the commission as not empowering them to inquire into the existence of a "successor in title" (T.E.D.O.) in this case. As a consequence, he found the decision of the Commission to be a nullity, despite the existence of the ouster clause.]

NOTES AND QUESTIONS

- Lord Reid's analysis exemplifies what we might call *legalese*—the use of complicated legal language, difficult to understand, in part to disguise the impact of the decision. What Lord Reid has done, in substance, is to review the decision of the Commission, despite the existence of the ouster clause; and that clause was explicitly designed to keep the courts from reviewing decisions of the Commission! Lord Reid's point is that the kind of mistake made by the Commission in this case—which he argues goes to its very *jurisdiction* (or powers granted under the statute)—could not have been the kind of review which Parliament intended to oust the courts from conducting. Thus, Lord Reid *interprets* the ouster clause narrowly, reading it as not covering this situation. We might ask how such reasoning can be reconciled with the fundamental constitutional concept of Parliament supremacy; that is, that Parliament's wisdom, as enacted into statutory law, should be applied, rather than overridden, by the courts.

- Does the language of the ouster clause seem clear? What does it appear to mean? Does Lord Reid's reasoning persuade you of his interpretation?

- Consider Lord Reid's statement that, subject to the provisos he sets out, an agency of the state is entitled to decide an issue rightly or wrongly. Implicitly, from whose perspective is the "rightness" of a decision to be interpreted? Does this statement confirm the argument that judges assume themselves to be in a position from which they alone can determine "truth"?

DEFINING "THE STATE"

It is important to recognise that the ability of the judiciary to review those actions of officials of the state through judicial review depends, by definition, on those officials being part of the apparatus of *the state*, or *public* officials. For Dicey and his followers, the fear of arbitrary power and the defence of the "rule of law" was exclusively focused upon the dangers that the state posed to the individual. The doctrine of judicial review is the procedural response to those fears. However, that raises the question first whether "the state" is always to be feared or whether it should be seen as largely benign and able to exercise power positively and proactively. Moreover, since the 1980s, many commentators would argue that, in some respects at least, the state has "shrunk", with many of its functions no longer clearly being exercised by "public" officials as a result of government policies such as privatisation of nationalised industries. As a consequence, the line between "public" and "private" is far from bright and clear. Finally, we might question Dicey's premise that it is always the exercise of discretion by *public* officials that we need to fear. Should we not also be concerned (or *more* concerned) about "privately" employed individuals who may have been granted wide discretionary powers that can have a severe impact upon the citizen? The definition of the "public", for the purposes of administrative law, is a very complicated issue, and Allison provides a good introduction to how it has increased in complexity in the last number of years.

John W.F. Allison, **"Theoretical and institutional underpinnings of a separate administrative law"**, in *The Province of Administrative Law* (Michael Taggart, ed., Hart Publishing, Oxford, 1997), pp.82–83:

"Identifying the state and its administration has not been facilitated by the privatisation schemes of the last two decades. . . .

First, statutes, such as the British Aerospace Act 1980 and the Telecommunications Act 1984, sought to roll back the frontiers of the state, but the state's former role, together with its continuing role chiefly through regulation, contributes to the vague sense that a public function is still being performed by the privatised industry. A commentator in *The Economist* observed: '[m]any of the once-nationalised companies do retain much of the feel of state behemoths'. The contraction of the state administration, like its earlier extension, obscures its distinctness.

Secondly, after initially attempting to reduce the number of hybrid institutions, central government increased expenditure on them, created new agencies [institutions related to central government but not part of government] (*e.g.* OFTEL and OFGAS) to regulate the privatised industries, and hived off more executive functions to quasi-governmental agencies (*e.g.*, the Housing Action Trusts) and to the many new semi-autonomous departmental agencies envisaged by the Next Steps Programme.

Thirdly, although central government has preferred regulation as the formal corrective to privatisation, it has nevertheless continued, in fact, to bargain with the privatised industries and has also effectively promoted the 'contracting-out' of numerous service functions. . . .

In short, privatisation has not resulted in a clearly-defined core of government or minimal state administration. Woolf and Jowell rightly conclude that the:[4]

> 'legal relationships that arise out of . . . new forms of service provision (*e.g.* through contracting out and the "hiving off" of central departmental responsibilities to new agencies) are neither wholly "public" or "private".'"

NOTES AND QUESTIONS

- Try to think of examples in which it is unclear whether an official operates as part of the state or should be considered "private".

- If judicial review was unavailable to review the actions of an official—because she was exercising a private function—are there any other areas of law to which a disgruntled individual could turn? HINT: think about the other law subjects you are currently studying.

THE HUMAN RIGHTS ACT 1998 AND JUDICIAL REVIEW

The Human Rights Act 1998 expands the role and scope of judicial review because the state is placed under a legal obligation to act in accordance with European Convention rights. As McLeod explains:

> "Section 6 of the Act makes it unlawful for a public authority (which is defined as *excluding* both Houses of Parliament but as *including* courts and tribunals, as well as 'any person certain of whose functions are functions of a public nature') to act in a way which is incompatible with Convention rights. (The phrase 'functions of a public nature' is likely to import into this area of law the principles which the courts have developed to help them identify the distinction between public and private law for the purposes of judicial review generally.) . . . The effect of s.7 of the Act is that a person who wishes to establish that there has been a breach of the duty under s.6, may do so proactively by claiming judicial review, or reactively by way of defence to proceedings brought by, or at the instigation of, the public authority." (Ian McLeod, *Legal Method*, 4th ed., Palgrave, Basingstoke, 2002, pp.95–96.)

This brings us back to the difficult question—one which courts will be forced to grapple with—of what exactly are "functions of a public nature", as opposed to private acts. Although the public/private distinction appears central to the Human Rights Act 1998, this may be somewhat misleading. The relationship between individual and the state (the "public function") is often described as the *vertical* effect

---

[4] S.A. Smith, Lord Woolf and J. Jowell, *Judicial Review of Administrative Action* (Sweet and Maxwell, London, 5th ed. 1995) p.165.

of the Act (the state being conceived as *above* the individual). By contrast, the legal relationship of private individuals to each other (conceived as being side-by-side), is the *horizontal* effect of the Act, which remains a very contentious issue, as McLeod explains.

Ian McLeod, *Legal Method* (4th ed., Palgrave, Basingstoke, 2002) pp.97–98:

"The fact that the Human Rights Act places a duty on public authorities to act in a way which is compatible with Convention rights, without imposing a similar duty on anyone else, might seem to make the Act enforceable only against the state and its emanations, or . . . *vertically* but *not horizontally*. Furthermore, this view might appear to be supported by a contribution which the Lord Chancellor made to the Committee stage in the House of Lords, when he said that 'the Convention had its origins in a desire to protect people from the misuse of power by the state, rather than from the actions of individuals' and therefore s.6 of the Act 'does not impose a liability on organizations which have no public functions al all.' (HL Deb, November 13, 1997, cols 1231–1232.)

However, some eleven days later, he said:

'We . . . believe that it is right as a matter of principle for the courts to have the duty of acting compatibly with the Convention not only in cases involving other public authorities but also in developing the common law in deciding cases between individuals.' (HL Deb, November 24, 1997, col.783.) . . .

In short, therefore, the courts now have a duty to develop the common law in accordance with Convention rights, but any developments made on this basis must apparently stop short of creating new rights of action against private individuals and organizations. Of course, as time goes on, some judges may acquire a taste for the kind of creativity which they are now required to exercise. In other words, whatever the expectation may have been at the time the Act was drafted, debated and passed, it remains possible that the common law's potential for development will be boosted by the Act."

QUESTIONS

- Explain the importance of the concepts of the 'public and 'private' in judicial review. Why do those concepts prove so difficult to apply?

- What impact has the Human Rights Act 1998 had on the role and scope of judicial review?

5

CONSTITUTIONAL ASPECTS OF LEGAL METHOD: THE IMPACT OF MEMBERSHIP IN THE EUROPEAN UNION

In this chapter, we examine the most significant change to English legal method in recent years, which continues to unfold: the impact of our membership in the European Union (EU). Although you will study the EU in much greater depth in law school courses devoted exclusively to it, a rudimentary knowledge of the impact of membership in the EU is essential for a complete picture of the constitutional context within which our legal method operates. We begin with a brief overview of the institutional framework of the EU, followed by a consideration of its impact on the supremacy of Parliament and, finally, we examine the increasing role and impact of European individual rights on our constitutional structure.

THE INSTITUTIONAL STRUCTURE OF THE EU

When the United Kingdom joined the EU in 1972, it signed up to a political and economic union of nation states, with a wide ranging institutional structure by which this community (and now 'union') was governed.

Phil Harris, *An Introduction to Law* (6th ed., Butterworths, London, 2002), pp.223–231:

"Over the years the European Union has expanded both its membership and its agenda. In terms of its member states, the original European Economic Community, created through the Treaty of Rome in 1957, consisted of six members—Germany, France, Italy, Belgium, the Netherlands and Luxembourg—who came together with the purpose of creating closer economic relationships. In 2002, the European Union comprises 15 member states, including Britain, and with applications currently under consideration from many other European countries, membership is set to reach 27 members states by 2004. Arrangements were put into place in the Treaty of Nice to accommodate this enlarged membership, which will involve European states of a much more disparate nature, in terms of size, population, relative economic development and wealth, than has been the case up to now. Several applications, for example, are from what used to be known as 'eastern bloc' countries during the long period in the twentieth century of Russian domination of eastern Europe: countries such as Hungary, Romania, Poland and the Czech Republic.

As regards the objectives and aspirations of the European Union, the Treaty of Rome, together with the Single European Act 1986, provided for, among other things, the harmonisation of the legal codes of member states to the extent required for the proper functioning of the common market. What was originally an *economic* community, however, has increasingly moved towards both monetary and political union; the Treaty on European Union (the Maastricht Treaty) of 1992 established the European Union, and contains provision for closer ties on matters including foreign policy, national security and defence. . . . [M]onetary union has been achieved for most member states, although the issue remains highly controversial for those member states—including Britain—who are currently outside the 'euro zone'. There is little doubt that Britain's membership of the still-developing European Union will generate domestic political upheavals for some time to come, especially given the controversy which still surrounds the question of Britain's adoption of the euro, which will involve not only the satisfaction of the government's economic tests, but also a referendum which will sound out the views of the electorate.

The Maastricht Treaty was important, too, for creating the current structure of the European Union, which is said to comprise the three 'pillars' of the Economic Community, the common Foreign and Security Policy, and co-operation in justice and home affairs. The latter 'pillar' was re-designated 'police and judicial co-operation in criminal matters' by the Treaty of Amsterdam in 1997. The first 'pillar' actually refers to three European 'communities'—the European Community (originally the economic community), the European Coal and Steel Community and the European Atomic Energy Community. Given the three 'pillars', the general aim of the European Union. as originally set out in the Treaty of Rome and amended by Article 2 of the Maastricht Treaty[1] is as follows:

'. . . by establishing a common market and an economic and monetary union . . . to promote throughout the Community a harmonious and balanced development of economic activities, sustainable and non-inflationary growth respecting the environment, a high degree of convergence of economic performance, a high level of employment and of social protection, the raising of the standard of living and quality of life, and economic and social cohesion and solidarity among the Member States.'

The Maastricht Treaty signified the broadening-out of the European agenda to include, in particular, social policy as well as economic. The Treaty originally included the 'social chapter' which covered, among other things, extended legal protection of workers' rights. The government of the United Kingdom was opposed to these provisions, and refused to endorse them, with the result that they were removed from the Treaty and contained within a Protocol to the Treaty, signed by all the other member states. It was not until the New Labour government came to power in 1997 that the United Kingdom signed up to the social chapter, which became fully part of the EC Treaty in 1999 by means of the Treaty of Amsterdam.

This 'opting out' by Britain is another example of the way in which the European Union allows the 'twin tracking' referred to above. Another more recent illustration of this is in relation to the Treaty of Amsterdam in 1997. This Treaty incorporated what are known as the Schengen Agreement arrangements whereby member states of the European Union agreed on the removal of border controls in order to implement fully the policy of free movement of individuals within the European Community. The United Kingdom and the Republic of Ireland both opted out of these arrangements, insisting on the importance of retaining border controls and passport checks. . . .

In the Treaty of Nice 2000, provision is made for the expansion of the membership of the European Union, by means of changes to the arrangements regarding individual members states' voting power, and this will increase the voting strength of the larger states. This Treaty also made provision, in the context of the second pillar of foreign and security policy, for the European 'rapid reaction force', a military unit comprising 60,000 personnel to be deployed mainly for peace-keeping missions. This is another example of the extent to which the policies of the European Union have moved well beyond the strictly 'economic'.

Britain's membership of the European Union means that the legal provisions contained in the Treaties are part of the law of the United Kingdom, and there is also provision for

---

[1] Originally Article B. This was amended by the Treaty of Amsterdam: see below.

the output of the European legislative bodies, discussed below, to be incorporated into English law. There are various kinds of European Community legislation in addition to the Treaties, the most important of which are the Regulation and the Directive.

Principal institutions of the European Community

Before we discuss in more detail the forms which European Community law-making may take, and the implications for domestic law in Britain, it is important to appreciate the principal institutions of the European Community. It is by means of these institutions that the political representatives of member states are able to register the positions taken and views adopted by the governments of the Community countries.

The Council of the European Union, created by Article 204 of the EEC Treaty, comprises one representative of the government of each member state. The Council, which prior to the Maastricht Treaty was known as the Council of Ministers, is essentially a co-ordinating body with regard to general European Community economic policies. It should not be thought that Britain's representative on the Council is always the same person: exactly which government minister represents Britain's interests will depend on the issue under discussion—if it is transport policy, for example, then it will be the British Minister for Transport who represents the country. The Council is presided over by the representatives of member states, each holding office for six months, and rotating in a strict cycle.

The Council is distinguishable form the *European Council*, which refers to the meetings of the heads of government of all the member states—in fact, what we would normally understand by the term 'summit meetings'. These essentially political and rather more high-powered meetings date back only as far as 1974, when the heads of government first agreed to meet regularly three times a year. The Maastricht Treaty now provides, rather more formally, that the European Council 'shall bring together the Heads of State . . . of the Member States and the President of the Commission . . . assisted by the Minster of Foreign Affairs of the Member States and by a Member of the Commission' (Article 4). The council is to meet at least twice a year. The European Council, according to Lasok and Bridge,

'(i) provides a forum for free and informal exchange of views between the Heads of Government; (ii) it can range over matters of Treaty competence, of political co-operation and of common concern to the member states; and (iii) it can generate an impetus for the progressive development of the Community.'

Although the Council can initiate European Community legislation, it is common for such initiatives to originate with the *Commission*. This body comprises 20 Commissioners who, though citizens of member states, are chosen for their known competence, and independence. It is not their function simply to represent the interest of their own country; and member states must respect their independence and not try to influence them. A member state must have one Commissioner, but may not have more than two, and at present the larger states—France, the United Kingdom, Germany, Spain and Italy—have two Commissioners (in practice, one from the party in government and one from the opposition parties) while the remaining states have one. The Treaty of Nice provides that—taking into account the anticipated enlarged European Union by 2004—after 2005 the Commission will include one person from each member state, which will effectively reduce the membership of each of the five largest states to one.

The Commissioners' period of office is five years, though this period is renewable. Although individual Commissioners may well undertake special responsibilities within the Commission (rather like ministers of the government), responsibility for the acts of the Commission is collective, not individual. The Commission is divided into 24 sections known as *Directorates General*, each one headed by a Director General who is responsible to the relevant Commissioner for the work of that section. The Commission has considerable administrative support: it is backed up by some 14,000 staff, including a large body of interpreters and, in addition, each Commissioner has a private staff.

The functions of the Commission, in essence, are to initiate and co-ordinate European Community policy and to act as the executive body of the Community. In the process of initiating and formulating policies, the Commission engages in consultation with interested parties from across the whole Community, including industry, trade unions and the civil service equivalents of each member state: it is clear that such consultation should ensure that the positions taken on any given matter by member states' governments are brought to the Commission's attention. The Commission's role includes the specification of detailed practical aspects of policy, and the final policy statements of the Commission go to the Council for deliberation.

The executive powers of the Commission include both the making and the enforcement of rules of European Community law, these powers deriving either from the general terms of the Treaty, or in some instances through specific delegation by the Council to the Commission of law-making powers with regard to specific areas, such as the common agricultural policy. The Single European Act 1986 has strengthened this law-making role as delegate of the Council. As to general law-making powers, Article 249 of the EC Treaty provides that:

> 'In order to carry out their task . . . the European Parliament acting jointly with the Council and the Commission shall make regulations and issue directives, take decisions, make recommendations or deliver opinions.'

. . . With regard to the enforcement of European Community rules, the Commission has a major role in investigating alleged breaches of European Community law, and notifying the defaulting member state of the breach. In practice, it is usually the case that the member state concerned takes steps to remedy the problem well before the completion of an investigation. The Commission's enforcement powers extend to individuals (such as companies) who are in breach of, for example, community competition law, and it has powers to bring legal action against such individuals which may result, in the case of breaches of competition law, in substantial fines.

In addition to these important functions, the Commission also prepares the preliminary draft budget, which then goes to the Council and duly becomes the draft budget, which in turn is placed before the European Parliament. The latter, as we will see, has considerable powers to require amendments or modifications to the draft budget, and ultimately has the power to reject it: the draft budget was in fact rejected by the European Parliament in 1979 and 1984. Finally, the Commission is also the body which acts as negotiator in the process of making treaties.

At this point it will be clear that a considerable amount of output from the Commission must be referred for further deliberation and/or action to the Council. Given the fluctuating composition of the latter body, and its relatively infrequent meetings, there was established a body sitting, so to speak, between the Council and the Commission: this is a Committee of Permanent Representatives of the member states, normally known as COREPER (an acronym derived from the French term for this committee). COREPER is a permanent, full-time committee whose function is to sift and filter proposals coming from the Commission to the Council. Through this filtering process, only issues involving major problems or controversies actually come before the Council: the unproblematic and uncontentious proposals are effectively dealt with by COREPER, though the Council always has the final say.

Originally known as the European Assembly, an unelected body with few powers and certainly never meant to be a law-making body, the *European Parliament* (so called since the Single European Act 1986) has undergone significant change and since 1979 has comprised members democratically elected by the electorate of each member state.

Over the years, the role and powers of the European Parliament have been considerably extended, and those powers have been extended further by the provisions of the Maastricht Treaty which came into force in 1993. There are 626 Members of the European Parliament (MEPs) elected from the member states and each serving for five years. Germany elects 99; France, the United Kingdom and Italy each elect 87; Spain 64; the Netherlands 31; Belgium, Portugal and Greece 25; Sweden 22; Austria 21; Denmark and Finland 16;

Ireland 15; and Luxembourg 6. The Treaty of Nice provides for a total of 732 MEPs, to allow for representation by new member states, though this will entail a reduction in the numbers allocated to all of the above states except for Germany, which, because of the size of its population, will retain its 99 members. MEPs are not mandated by their home governments but, rather, operate on a personally independent basis. Not surprisingly for a political body, however, MEPs make political alliances, though these are political groupings which reflect European, as opposed to domestic, political stances. The essential and original function of the European Parliament is to act as a consultative body; however, since the introduction of elections for MEPs in 1979, the Parliament has sought and won wider powers with regard to the legislative functions of the European Community. On some issues, the European Parliament must be consulted as part of the Community's specific procedural requirements, and it has been known for legal rules made by the Council to be annulled on the grounds that the latter failed to consult the European Parliament on the matter.

If the European Parliament, having duly considered and discussed a proposal, rejects it, or wishes to propose amendments, then the Council will normally reconsider its proposal in light of the reasons for the rejection or proposed amendments. Clearly, the Council may accept and implement the amendments, but should it not wish to do so, or if it considers that the proposal should take effect despite rejection by the European Parliament, then it may pass its original proposal, provided that it does so unanimously and (in the case of a rejection) within three months (Single European Act 1986). There are other procedures whereby the European Parliament participates in the legislative function, the most recent of which is the 'co-decision' procedure. This was created by the Treaty of European Union and is a mechanism whereby, with regard to certain specified European Community matters, the Parliament may veto Council proposals—this is the first time such a power has been vested in the European Parliament, and arguably increases the degree of democratic representation within Community institutions, which according to some critics had hitherto been overly dominated by the Council of Ministers. However, on the other side of this 'democratic deficit' argument, it might be said that democratic control of the Community, and in particular of the members of the Council, ultimately lies with the electorate of each member state through the national election procedures of each member state.

One of the most important powers of the European Parliament is that of political control over the Commission. It discusses the reports of the Commission; it may question individual Commissioners, who must answer either orally or by a written response; and it has power, ultimately, to dismiss the entire Commission by a vote of censure. This power, though threatened on occasion, has never been used. The European Parliament has no direct powers of control over the Council, although it has been held by the European Court that the European Parliament may bring an action against either the Council or the Commission if either of these bodies fails to act in circumstances where it should have done so. In 1999, following criticism by the European Parliament, the Community's Court of Auditors reported that the Commission had been responsible for fraud and mismanagement. The entire Commission resigned—indeed, if it had not done so, the Parliament would have exercised its powers to remove Commission members. Following the re-establishment of the Commission by mid-1999, the new Vice-President, Neil Kinnock, took on the responsibility for reforming the Commission, and the proposals put forward to achieve this were adopted by the Commission in 2000.

The *European Court of Justice*, comprising 15 judges (one from each member state) and the President, has as its main task the responsibility of 'ensuring that in the interpretation and application of this Treaty the law is observed' (Article 220). The role and functions of the court have been concisely summarised thus:

> 'It is the supreme authority on all matters of Community law, and in this capacity may be required to decide matters of constitutional law, administrative law, social law and economic law in matters brought directly before it or on application from national courts . . . In its practices and procedures the ECJ draws on Continental models; in developing the substantive law it draws on principles and traditions from all the Member States.'

The judges are assisted by eight Advocates-General, chosen for their personal and guaranteed independence, whose primary function is to prepare analyses of cases coming before the court and make recommendations to the court on matters arising from those cases. The court differs from English courts of law in a number of respects, not least being the fact that the European Court is not bound by a doctrine of precedent, and that the general outlook taken by the court is far more creative and proactive in its interpretations of the general provisions of the Treaties than that of its English counterparts.

The Single European Act 1986 created a new court—the Court of First Instance—which is intended to relieve the European Court of some of its very heavy workload, and which presently deals with a limited number of disputes, including those arising between the European Community and its staff. There is provision for appeal from the Court of First Instance to the European Court, and, because there are very many such appeals, the creation of the Court of First Instance has had little effect on the case load of the European Court. Article 234 provides that:

'The Court of Justice shall have jurisdiction to give preliminary rulings concerning:

(a)   the interpretation of this Treaty;
(b)   the validity and interpretation of acts of the institutions of the Community;
(c)   the interpretation of the statutes of bodies established by an act of the council, where those statutes so provide.'

Article 234 also provides that, where such a question arises in any case before a court or tribunal within any member state, that court or tribunal may refer the question to the European Court for a ruling. This jurisdiction is essentially one of preliminary rulings on matters of interpretation of European law (not the domestic law of member states). The European Court hears and decides disputes concerning matters of Community law arising from Article 234 references from domestic courts, and so has an important function regarding matters of interpretation of the Articles of the Treaty."

The mission of the EU, which is important to an understanding of the way in which the EU legal order is evolving, has been described by Shaw.

Jo Shaw, *Law of the European Union* (3rd ed., Macmillan, Basingstoke, 2000), pp.11–14:

"Broad statements of the aims, goals and values of the European Community and the European Union are to be found in the Preambles and introductory sections of the founding Treaties. Article 1 TEU [Treaty on European Union] recalls the long-standing commitment in the Preamble to the EEC Treaty to the creation of an ever closer union among the peoples of Europe, and identifies the creation of the Union as a new stage in this process, one 'in which decisions are taken as openly as possible and as closely as possible to the citizen'. The task is 'to organise, in a manner demonstrating consistency and solidarity, relations between the Member States and between their peoples'. The Union has the following objectives (Article 2 TEU):

'—to promote economic and social progress and a high level of employment and to achieve balanced and sustainable development, in particular through the creation of an area without internal frontiers, through the strengthening of economic and social cohesion and through the establishment of economic and monetary union, ultimately including a single currency . . .;

—to assert its identity on the international scene, in particular through the implementation of a common foreign and security policy including the progressive framing of a common defence policy, which might in time lead to a common defence . . .;

—to strengthen the protection of the rights and interests of the nationals of its Member States through the introduction of a citizenship of the Union;

—to maintain and develop the Union as an area of freedom, security and justice, in which the free movement of persons is assured in conjunction with appropriate measures with respect to external border controls, asylum, immigration and the prevention and combating of crime;

—to maintain in full the *acquis communautaire* and build on it with a view to considering to what extent the policies and forms of cooperation introduced by this Treaty may need to be revised with the aim of ensuring the effectiveness of the mechanisms and the institutions of the Community.'

The specifically socio-economic aspects of these aims are further elaborated in Articles 2, 3, 4 and 6 EC. Article 2 sets the European Community the task of achieving the promotion of harmonious, balanced and sustainable development of economic activities, a high level of employment and social protection, equality between men and women, sustainable and non-inflationary growth, a high degree of competitiveness and convergence of economic performance, a high level of protection and improvement of the quality of the environment, the raising of the standard of living and quality of life, and of economic and social cohesion and solidarity among Member States. The twin means for attaining this task are the creation of a common market and an economic and monetary union, including the creation of a single currency. Article 6 strengthens the provisions of Article 2 and 3 relating to the environment by requiring that environmental protection 'must be integrated into the definition and implementation of the Community policies and activities referred to in Article 3, in particular with a view to promoting sustainable development'. The reference to gender equality in Article 2 is picked up by another mainstreaming provision. Article 3(2) requires that 'in all the activities referred to in this Article, the Community shall aim to eliminate inequalities, and to promote equality, between men and women.'

In the earlier stages of the EU's development, the substantive law has comprised, above all, the law of the common market, which has been developing steadily since 1958. For present purposes, we can take the common market referred to in Article 2 as practically identical to the 'internal market' defined in Article 14 EC, the achievement of which was the official central objective of the old European Economic Community between 1986 and the end of 1992. This provides that:

'The internal market shall comprise an area without internal frontiers in which the free movement of goods, persons, services and capital is ensured in accordance with the provisions of this Treaty.'

The goal appears, therefore, to be a free market ideal that, as far as possible, the territory of the fifteen Member States should resemble a single national market, where there is a level competitive playing field for all economic actors and where distortions of competition based on artificial legal barriers such as differences in consumer protection or environmental regulation will be eliminated.

Article 3(1) EC in turn gives more details on the activities that are to be pursued with a view to attaining this goal. These include the creation of a customs union, involving the abolition of internal customs duties on trade in goods and the erection of a common external tariff and a complementary common policy on external trade, the abolition of other obstacles to trade in goods, measures to achieve the free movement of services, persons and capital between the Member States and measures concerned with the entry and movement of persons. These are essentially negative measures, in that they promote integration by removing existing barriers. Positive integration measures include the establishment of common policies, in fields such as agriculture and transport; the creation of these policies also reveals a certain *dirigiste* element in the thinking of the founders of the Treaty, alongside the commitment to the free market principles inherent in the four freedoms. The commitment to a policy on the harmonisation of national legislation also demonstrates a recognition that deregulated markets alone will not bring about the creation of a single internal market which respects the interests of consumers and the environment, to name but two interests which may be sacrificed in unfettered free market competition. In addition, although subsequent amendments to the original Treaty have brought regional policy goals of social and economic cohesion and solidarity within the remit of the EU's pre-scribed activities, there is no clear commitment in Article 3(1) (EC) to a general social policy, as a complement to the economic policies described above. However, particularly with the effective conclusion of the substantial legislative programme to complete the inter-nal market by the end of 1992, the focus of law making has shifted more into the fields of social policy, consumer policy and environmental policy. Article 3(1) also refers to a number of flanking policies where the EU is to make 'a contribution' or to 'promote' or 'encourage' policy, highlighting its secondary role in policy making. These include research and technological development, education and training and the 'flowering of the cultures of the Member States'."

THE EUROPEAN UNION AND PARLIAMENTARY SUPREMACY

Harris states the issue succinctly:

"Now, given that European law takes precedence over the domestic law of the member states, it can happen that a legal rule of the EC is in direct conflict with a rule of domestic law. What is the consequence of this for English law, and the constitutional doctrine of the supremacy of Parliament? Can we still, in Britain, speak of the constitutional 'sovereignty' of our own Parliament, given the relationships between our law and legislation and those of the European Community?"[2]

That question—the impact of membership in the EU on the supremacy of Parliament—has been explored by Bradley.

AW Bradley, "The Sovereignty of Parliament—Form or Substance" in *The Changing Constitution* (4th ed., Jeffrey Jowell and Dawn Oliver, eds., Oxford University Press, Oxford, 2000), pp.39–43:

"The European Union, of which the European Community forms part, is a unique, supra-national grouping of states created in 1993 by the Maastricht Treaty. The European Economic Community (the precursor of the present Community) was created by the Treaty of Rome in 1957. The United Kingdom acceded to the EEC by the Treaty of Brussels 1972, which was implemented in the United Kingdom by the European Communities Act 1972. What is distinctive about the Community compared with other international organizations is that broad executive, legislative, and fiscal powers are vested in organs of the Community. The European Court of Justice at Luxembourg (together with the Court of First Instance) exercises judicial powers in applying and enforcing Community law. Regulations made by the Council of Ministers are directly applicable in all Member States as soon as they have been promulgated by the Council. Treaty provisions and other Community measures may have direct effect in Member States, i.e. they may create rights that are directly enforceable by individuals in national courts, without needing to be implemented by national legisla-tion. As was said by the Court of Justice in 1963:

'the Community constitutes a new legal order of international law, for the benefit of which the states have limited their sovereign rights, albeit within limited fields, and the subjects of which comprise not only Member States but also their nationals.'

---

[2] Phil Harris, *Introduction to Law* (6th ed., Butterworths, London, 2002), p.231.

From the perspective of the Court of Justice, it is essential that the main rules of Community law should have direct effect in the legal systems of the Member States:

> 'The binding force of the Treaty [of Rome] and of measures taken in application of it must not differ from one state to another as a result of internal measures, lest the functioning of the Community system should be impeded and the achievement of the aims of the Treaty placed in peril.'

Community law cannot be overridden by domestic legal provisions 'without being deprived of its character as Community law and without the legal basis of the Community being called into question'. Community law thus creates obligations upon Member States, and also individual rights enforceable in national courts.

The Community legal order is plainly inconsistent with the sovereignty of Parliament. Dicey asserted that 'no person or body is recognised by the law of England as having a right to override or set aside the legislation of Parliament'. In fact, United Kingdom law now recognizes that Community organs have the right to make decisions and issue regulations which may override legislation by Parliament. The supremacy or primacy of Community law within the economic and social areas with which it deals was already a significant aspect of the Community system during the 1960s, but it does not stand comfortably beside structures of constitutional law based on national frontiers. While the problem takes a special form in the United Kingdom, other Member States have experienced comparable difficulties in adjusting their systems of constitutional law to take account of Community law. The Court of Justice has repeatedly emphasized that the application of Community law may not be delayed by obstacles in national law, even where these arise from constitutional consideration, such as concern for the protection of fundamental rights. As the court said in 1978:

> 'A national court which is called on within the limits of its jurisdiction, to apply provisions of Community law is under a duty to give full effect to these provisions, if necessary refusing of its own motion to apply any conflicting provisions of national legislation, even if adopted subsequently, and it is not necessary for the court to request or await the prior setting aside of such provisions by legislative or other constitutional means.'

When Denmark, the Republic of Ireland, and the United Kingdom acceded to the European Community together in 1973, they were each required to take steps to accommodate Community law within their legal systems. In Denmark and Ireland, formal constitutional amendments were necessary. This course of action was not open to the United Kingdom, but it was essential that Parliament should authorize the reception of Community law. Legal effect had to be given not only to existing but also to future rules of Community law.

Given this necessity, the sovereignty of Parliament was 'at once an advantage and a source of difficulty'. The advantage was that no constitutional amendment was necessary. It took only a few lines in an Act of Parliament to give effect to a massive body of Community law and to equip the British government with additional powers to handle Community affairs. The difficulty came so far as the future was concerned: could a guarantee be given or an undertaking entrenched that Parliament would in the future neither legislate to leave the Community nor (whether by accident or design) legislate in a manner which conflicted with Community law?

The view of the government in 1972 was that no absolute legislative undertaking by Parliament could or should be given, since a future Parliament could disregard such an undertaking. Instead, the European Communities Act 1972 went so far as was thought possible in instructing British courts how to apply Community law in the future. Section 2(1) of the 1972 Act gave effect in the United Kingdom to all rules of Community law that have direct application or direct effect within Member States. This applied both to existing and to future Community rules. By section 2(4), it was *inter alia* provided that 'any enactment passed or to be passed, other than one contained in this part of the Act, shall be construed and shall have effect subject to the foregoing provisions if this section'—subject, in other words, to the comprehensive reception of existing and future Community law made by section 2(1). By section 3, questions of Community law were to be decided by the European Court of Justice or in accordance with the decisions of that Court, and all national courts were in future to take judicial note of such decisions. It was, however, section 2(4) that was the subject of most discussion, both in 1972 and subsequently. In form a new rule of construction, it appeared to require all legislation, both existing and future, to have effect subject to the rules of Community law that operated in national law under section 2(1). Arguably, the rule went far beyond being a rule of construction by declaring that, within the post-accession 'hierarchy of norms', Community law would be superior to any Act of Parliament, whenever enacted.

When these provisions were debated in Parliament, it was widely agreed that they did not exclude the possibility that Parliament might one day wish to repeal the Act and thus prevent the continued operation of Community law within the United Kingdom. The ultimate sovereignty of Westminster was thus not affected, as ministers admitted, though they refused to allow a statement to this effect to be included in the Act.[3] But there was for many years uncertainty about a less extreme situation, namely what the position would be if an Act passed after 1972 were found to contain a provision that was impossible to reconcile with a rule of Community law. In this situation, we have already seen that the European Court would insist that Community law must prevail. Should the British courts adopt the same position, as sections 2 and 3 of the 1972 Act might indicate was their duty, or does the later Act of Parliament override these sections of the 1972 Act, to the extent or requiring the later Act to prevail?

In 1972, since it was impossible to undertake that no such conflict would arise in future, the government accepted that a later Act might prevail over the European Communities Act 1972 to the extent of the conflict. A senior law lord, Lord Diplock, advised Parliament that, in the event of a conflict between Community law and a later Act that could not be resolved by construction, the British courts would be bound to give effect to the later Act.[4]

Not surprisingly, the response of British judges to the questions posed by the 1972 Act showed a preference for resolving potential clashes and inconsistencies by interpretation, and they were reluctant to reach the sovereignty question. Thus in 1974 in a much quoted dictum, Lord Denning MR said that the incoming tide of Community law could not be held back. 'Parliament has decreed that the Treaty is henceforward to be part of our law. It is equal in force to any statute.'[5] The crucial question, however, was not whether Community law has the same force as any statute, but whether it has greater force than a statute by prevailing over subsequent Acts which conflict with it.

Some of the most important instances of actual or potential conflict arose in relation to sex discrimination and employment law. Article 119 (now Article 141) of the EC Treaty, requiring Member States to maintain the principle that men and women should receive equal pay, was in 1976 held at Luxembourg to be directly effective. This enabled employees to enforce rights against employers that went further than the Equal Pay Act 1970 and the Sex Discrimination Act 1975; thus questions as to the application of those Acts necessarily arose. Similar questions arose in relation to the Equal Treatment Directive, with the difference that in Community law a directive has 'vertical' effect against the State and bodies that are emanations of the state, but does not have 'horizontal' effect between all public and private persons; in a leading case, vertical effect enabled a female employee dismissed at the age of 62 (when a male employee would have been dismissed only at 65) to sue a health authority (an emanation of the state) for sex discrimination at a time when matters relating to retirement age were not covered by British legislation."

As Bradley suggests, British courts have faced a number of claims by female workers seeking to enforce their rights to equal pay under European law. These cases under-

---

[3] HC Debs July 5, 1972, cols. 556–644.

[4] HL Debs Aug 8, 1972, col. 1029.

[5] *H.P. Bulmer v J. Bollinger SA* [1974] Ch. 401, 418. *cf. Felixstowe Dock and Railway Co. v British Transport Docks Board* [1976] Lloyd's Rep. 656, 663.

score how the principle of Parliamentary supremacy by necessity has had to be modified by the judiciary to reflect the new European legal order.

Garland v British Rail Engineering Ltd [1982] 2 All E.R. 402, ECJ and HL.

[The appellant, a married woman, complained to an industrial tribunal that her employer, British Rail, was discriminating against her because of sex contrary to s.6(2) of the Sex Discrimination Act 1975 by continuing to provide male employees after they retired with non-contractual concessionary travel facilities for themselves and their wives and dependent children. When female employees retired the provision of such facilities for their families was withdrawn. The industrial tribunal dismissed the complaint on the ground that s.6(4) of the Act exempts "a provision in relation to . . . retirement" (*i.e.* such provisions are outside of the purview of the Sex Discrimination Act) and, therefore, the discrimination was not unlawful. An appeal to the Employment Appeal Tribunal was upheld on the basis that the continuation of the privilege after retirement was not "a provision in relation to . . . retirement". The Court of Appeal then restored the decision of the industrial tribunal on the grounds that the statutory phrase "a provision in relation to . . . retirement" included any provision about retirement. The appellant then appealed to the House of Lords, which referred to the European Court of Justice the question whether the discrimination was contrary to Art.119 of the EEC (now EC) Treaty (which reads "each Member State shall . . . maintain the application of the principle that men and women should receive equal pay for equal work"), and if so, whether the article conferred enforceable Community rights on individuals.]

"European Court of Justice [After reviewing the facts and questions raised, the Court ruled]:
    "It follows from those considerations that rail travel facilities such as those referred to by the House of Lords fulfil the criteria enabling them to be treated as pay within the meaning of article 119 of the EEC Treaty.
    The argument that the facilities are not related to a contractual obligation is immaterial. The legal nature of the facilities is not important for the purposes of the application of article 119 provided that they are granted in respect of the employment.
    It follows that where an employer (although not bound to do so by contract) provides special travel facilities for former male employees to enjoy after their retirement this constitutes discrimination within the meaning of article 119 against former female employees who do not receive the same facilities. . . ."

[Following receipt by the House of Lords of the judgment of the European Court of Justice, the matter was reconsidered:]

Lord Diplock [Lord Diplock reviewed the facts, legislation, and the ruling of the Court of Justice]:
    ". . . My Lords, even if the obligation to observe the provisions of article 119 were an obligation assumed by the United Kingdom under an ordinary international treaty or convention and there were no question of the treaty obligation being directly applicable as part of the law to be applied by the courts in this country without need for any further enactment, it is a principle of construction of United Kingdom statutes, now too well established to call for citation of authority, that the words of a statute passed after the treaty has been signed and dealing with the subject matter of the international obligation of the United Kingdom, are to be construed, if they are reasonably capable of bearing such a meaning,

as intended to carry out the obligation and not to be inconsistent with it. A fortiori is this the case where the treaty obligation arises under one of the Community treaties to which s.2 of the European Communities Act 1972 applies."

[The other Law Lords concurred, and the appeal was allowed.]

The *Garland* case stands for the proposition that the judiciary should interpret, if possible, domestic legislation in such a way as to be consistent with obligations entered into by the United Kingdom government under international treaties. This is especially true with respect to the treaties of the European Union, which are part of United Kingdom law. Given that this principle deals only with the *interpretation* of domestic legislation (*i.e.* how broadly or narrowly it is read), it can be argued that it does not directly undermine the principle of Parliamentary supremacy. Lord Diplock undoubtedly would say that we must *assume* that Parliament intended to abide by its international obligations, and judges must interpret legislation accordingly. This has proven to be an important principle in widening the scope of sex discrimination provisions in British law.

Although EU law has been important in widening the scope of employment protection, particularly for women, it was not perceived as directly challenging the historic, constitutional precept of the supremacy of Parliament. Rather, the impact of the European legal order on Parliamentary supremacy was demonstrated by a different legal struggle, known simply as the *Factortame* decisions. Atiyah sets the scene.

P.S. Atiyah, *Law and Modern Society* (2nd ed., Oxford University Press, Oxford, 1995), pp.96–97:

"The profound effects of membership of the Community on the sovereignty of Parliament were not fully demonstrated until the dramatic *Factortame* case, when it first became apparent that English courts now had the power to declare Acts of Parliament to be void or invalid because they contravened European Community law. In this case the Community had allocated fishery quotas to its members, but a number of Spanish fishermen attempted to evade the effect of the quotas by registering companies in England, and then transferring their trawlers into the names of these companies, which were thus English companies. Their trawlers fished in British waters, but continued to land their catch in Spain. Not surprisingly, the British government thought that this was an evasion of the whole system of quotas and they introduced into Parliament a Bill which was in due course enacted as the Merchant Shipping Act 1988. Under this Act the companies, though registered in England, were to be treated as Spanish companies because their owners were Spanish. This Act of Parliament was then challenged as invalid on the ground that it contravened one of the basic corner-stones of European Community law, namely, that member states were not allowed to *discriminate* against nationals of other states. In this particular case the non-discrimination principle was invoked in a highly technical way, and because the fishery quotas had actually been agreed by the Community, it was obviously somewhat unfair that the Spanish fishermen were able to invoke it. But that is not really relevant to the crucial importance of the case. What happened when the case first reached the House of Lords was that it was held that as a matter of English law it was impossible to challenge the validity of the Merchant Shipping Act, and it was not even possible to suspend the operation of the Act while the case was referred to the European Court. But the matter was referred to the European Court, which decided that since European Community rights were at stake (the right not to be discriminated against) the English courts *had* to have the power to suspend the operation of the Act pending a full hearing of the issue at the European Court."

Factortame Ltd and others v Secretary of State for Transport (No. 2) [1991] 1 All E.R. 70, ECJ and HL.

European Court of Justice:

". . . In accordance with the case law of the court, it is for the national courts, in application of the principle of co-operation laid down in article 5 of the EEC Treaty, to ensure the legal protection which persons derive from the direct effect of provisions of Community law. . . .

The court has also held that any provision of a national legal system and any legislative, administrative or judicial practice which might impair the effectiveness of Community law by withholding from the national court having jurisdiction to apply such law the power to do everything necessary at the moment of its application to set aside national legislative provisions which might prevent, even temporarily, Community rules from having full force and effect are incompatible with those requirements, which are the very essence of Community law . . . .

It must be added that the full effectiveness of Community law would be just as much impaired if a rule of national law could prevent a court seised of a dispute governed by Community law from granting interim relief in order to ensure the full effectiveness of the judgment to be given on the existence of the rights claimed under Community law. It follows that a court which in those circumstances would grant interim relief, if it were not for a rule of national law, is obliged to set aside that rule. . . .

Consequently, the reply to the question raised should be that Community law must be interpreted as meaning that a national court which, in a case before it concerning Community law, considers that the sole obstacle which precludes it from granting interim relief is a rule of national law must set aside that rule."

[Upon receipt of the opinion of the Court of Justice, the House of Lords granted an interim injunction restraining the enforcement of legislation pending a decision in the case. In so doing, Lord Bridge commented on the relationship between EC law and Parliamentary supremacy:]

Lord Bridge of Harwich:

". . . Some public comments on the decision of the Court of Justice, affirming the jurisdiction of the courts of member states to override national legislation if necessary to enable interim relief to be granted in protection of rights under Community law, have suggested that this was a novel and dangerous invasion by a Community institution of the sovereignty of the United Kingdom Parliament. But such comments are based on a misconception. If the supremacy within the European Community of Community law over the national law of member states was not always inherent in the EEC Treaty it was certainly well established in the jurisprudence of the Court of Justice long before the United Kingdom joined the Community. Thus, whatever limitation of its sovereignty Parliament accepted when it enacted the European Communities Act 1972 was entirely voluntary. Under the terms of the 1972 Act it has always been clear that it was the duty of a United Kingdom court, when delivering final judgment, to override any rule of national law found to be in conflict with any directly enforceable rule of Community law. Similarly, when decisions of the Court of Justice have exposed areas of United Kingdom statute law which failed to implement Council directives, Parliament has always loyally accepted the obligation to make appropriate and prompt amendments. Thus there is nothing in any way novel in according supremacy to rules of Community law in those areas to which they apply and to insist that, in the protection of rights under Community law, national courts must not be inhibited by rules of national law from granting interim relief in appropriate cases is no more than a logical recognition of that supremacy."

A full hearing of the European Court of Justice subsequently declared that the Merchant Shipping Act did indeed violate Community law, and it was eventually invalidated by the High Court. The offending sections were removed by Parliament through amending legislation. The significance of the decision is considered by Atiyah.

P.S. Atiyah, *Law and Modern Society* **(2nd ed., Oxford University Press, Oxford, 1995), pp.97–100:**

"In one sense this decision was little more than a practical necessity. If national courts could not declare their own national law to be invalid when it conflicted with European Community law, the practical working of the European Community legal system would be immensely cumbersome. It would mean that any conflict of this kind would have to be decided in defiance of Community law, the government would then be obliged to introduce amending legislation, and in the meantime, anyone whose rights had been adversely affected would be entitled to compensation, but there would be no machinery by which that compensation could be secured in an English court. So it would take years to enforce rights accorded by Community law, and if governments dragged their heels, the whole system would collapse into chaos. In this connection, it must be appreciated that conflicts between our national law and Community law are potentially very common, far more common than conflicts with international law or ordinary treaties. Even though the UK government has one of the best records among members of the Community in giving effect to Community Directives and other decisions, it has become increasingly apparent that many conflicts arise because our ministers and their advisers have not fully appreciated the way in which the European Court was likely to interpret Community law. So, in a practical sense it is really imperative that national courts should recognize the precedence of Community law over national laws, and the courts of all other member states in the Community in fact do recognize this. It must also be said that this is an absolute prerequisite of a federal state, and although the Community is not yet a federal state, it may eventually evolve into one. Without the *Factortame* decision it is doubtful if that could be done.

So the *Factortame* decision was a practical necessity. But at the same time it was, in a legal sense, a revolutionary decision. It was the first time for more than 300 years that an English Court had declared an Act of Parliament to be unenforceable in law. What this means, therefore, is that English law is now subject to European Community law. If there is a conflict between them, the English law may, and sometimes *must*, be declared invalid by English courts. In a sense, therefore, we have now acquired a written constitution—consisting of the various European Treaties—and laws contrary to the constitution will in future be invalid. So the sovereignty of Parliament seems to have been dethroned from its pivotal point at the centre of English constitutional law with very little appreciation of that fact by Parliament, politicians, or the public.

How has this happened? Many lawyers thought that the sovereignty of Parliament was the centre-piece of our unwritten constitution, and was something which simply could not be surrendered or abandoned. Every Parliament was traditionally thought to be legally sovereign and so capable of altering any previous law simply by passing a new Act. Why therefore was the Merchant Shipping Act of 1988 not treated simply as altering all previous law and, if necessary, the European Communities Act itself? If this had been done, the UK government would have been in breach of the Treaties and would have been under an obligation to amend or repeal the Merchant Shipping Act, but at least the traditional doctrine of Parliamentary sovereignty would have been preserved. In fact, the judges in the House of Lords did not deny that this *could have been done*. Parliament could have phrased the Merchant Shipping Act to make it quite clear that it was to be applied whether or not it was in conformity with European law. In that case, said the judges in the House of Lords, they would have obeyed the Act, and so the sovereignty of Parliament would have been respected. But of course the government and Parliament did not *want* to pass an Act which violated European law. They thought that the Act they passed was good in law, but it turned out that they were mistaken. So the judges in the House of Lords thought that they should look at the Merchant Shipping Act as though Parliament had said at the beginning of the Act:

'The following Act is passed on the assumption that it is not in violation of European Community law; if it is contrary to Community law, do not enforce it.'

In this way the traditional respect for Parliamentary sovereignty was to some degree reconciled with the practical need to recognize the supremacy of European Community law.

In one sense this reconciliation may seem pretty empty. It now seems quite clear that we shall see many Acts of Parliament challenged in future as contrary to European law, and some of these challenges will be upheld. Moreover, it will not, of course, be open to Parliament to overrule these decisions by passing another Act, unless Parliament chooses openly to defy the Community Treaties—which could only provoke a political crisis of the first order. So, to a limited extent, we shall have what many politicians (and perhaps the public and the press) intensely dislike, 'government by judges'. On the other hand, there is also reality in the way the House of Lords approached this problem, because it is very unlikely that Parliament will ever pass an Act which is clearly and plainly invalid as contrary to European law. Where it happens at all, it will nearly always happen by accident or mistake, and it may well accord with Parliament's intent that if the Act is found to conflict with Community law, it should not be enforced.

It must not be thought that all this means that English law can be challenged as invalid because (for instance) it is contrary to French or German law. It is only invalid if it is contrary to European Community law, which is the central law of the Community. In this respect the Community increasingly resembles a federal system of law, like that of the USA or Canada or Australia, where there is a federal government and a federal legislature, on the one hand, and state governments and state legislatures on the other. There are two sets of laws, each perfectly valid within its own sphere, but state laws which conflict with (valid) federal laws are invalid. In a strict legal sense, the situation in the European Community is thus similar to that of a federal state."

NOTES AND QUESTIONS

- How does membership in the European Union directly impact upon the constitutional principle of the supremacy of Parliament?

- Given our membership in the European Union, is Parliament supreme as either a political or legal matter? Does a "legal" versus a "political" perspective lead to a different answer?

- Explain the legal and political significance of the *Factortame* case.

THE IMPACT OF EUROPE ON THE PROTECTION OF INDIVIDUAL RIGHTS

The constitutional structure of the United Kingdom, with its historical focus on the supremacy of Parliament, has often been contrasted against those systems of government in which a fundamental, constitutional Bill of Rights serves as a means for the judiciary to limit the exercise of power by the state. The merits and demerits of constitutionally entrenched rights is a complex subject, and one which you will undoubtedly consider in more detail in your constitutional law course. For our purposes, of particular interest is the way in which political and legal developments have altered the principle of Parliamentary supremacy with respect to the judicial recognition (and enforcement) of rights, particularly those of *individuals*. We have already considered the role of rights in the context of the Human Rights Act 1998 and the European Convention on Human Rights. The Convention should not be confused with those obligations which arise by virtue of our membership in the European Community and European Union.

The law of the European Union legal order also increasingly is proving a source of legally enforceable rights for individuals. The *Garland* case, which we have already examined, exemplifies how European rights of equal pay and equal treatment in employment and social security, on the basis of sex, will be enforced by the judiciary. The *Factortame* case exemplifies the enforcement of rights of free movement of nationals within the European Union, which again was enforced by the courts directly against the British government. Moreover, the European Court of Justice has recognised that European law confers rights on individuals which can be enforced against other *individuals*, rather than the state. This is a complex area of European law, and one which you will look at in much greater detail in courses on the law of the European Union. For our purposes, these developments highlight the extent to which important social and economic rights are no longer solely the prerogative of Parliament to grant. Instead, the sources of these rights are the Treaties, regulations, and directives of the European Union, and will be enforced by the European Court of Justice as well as by domestic courts.

The recognition of rights cannot be separated from broader social and political questions; issues with which Parliament might not be prepared to deal. Thus, it might be argued that the recognition of European rights (and the derogation from the principle of Parliamentary supremacy) is an important means for the furtherance of social change—for altering the norms and values of society as a whole. The relationship between legal and social change is complex, but the following case illustrates that there have been limits on the extent to which the European Court of Justice has been prepared to go in its furtherance of the "equal pay" principle.

Grant v South-West Trains Ltd [1998] All E.R. 193, ECJ.

European Court of Justice:
"1. By decision of 19 July 1996, received at the Court of Justice of the European Communities on 22 July 1996, the Industrial Tribunal, Southampton, referred to the Court of Justice for a preliminary ruling under art.177 of the EC Treaty six questions on the interpretation of art.119 of that Treaty, Council Directive (EEC) 75/117 on the approximation of the laws of the member states relating to the application of the principle of equal pay for men and women (OJ 1975 L45 p 19), and Council Directive (EEC) 76/207 on the implementation of the principle of equal treatment for men and women as regards access to employment, vocational training and promotion, and working conditions (OJ 1976 L39 p.40).
2. Those questions were raised in proceedings between Ms Grant and her employer South-West Trains Ltd (SWT) concerning the refusal by SWT of travel concessions for Ms Grant's female partner.
3. Ms Grant is employed by SWT, a company which operates railways in the Southampton region.
4. Clause 18 of her contract of employment, entitled 'Travel facilities', states:

'You will be granted such free and reduced rate travel concessions as are applicable to a member of your grade. Your spouse and depend[a]nts will also be granted travel concessions. Travel concessions are granted at the discretion of [the employer] and will be withdrawn in the event of their misuse.'

5. At the material time, the regulations adopted by the employer for the application of those provisions, the Staff Travel Facilities Privilege Ticket Regulations, provided in cl 8 ('Spouses') that:

'Privilege tickets are granted to a married member of staff . . . for one legal spouse but not for a spouse legally separated from the employee . . . Privilege tickets are granted for one common law opposite sex spouse of staff . . . subject to a statutory declaration being made that a meaningful relationship has existed for a period of two years or more.'

6. The regulations also defined the conditions under which travel concessions could be granted to current employees (cls 1 to 4), employees having provisionally or definitively ceased working (cls 5 to 7), surviving spouses of employees (cl 9), children of employees (cls 10 and 11) and dependent members of employees' families (cl 12).

7. On the basis of those provisions Ms Grant applied on 9 January 1995 for travel concessions for her female partner, with whom she declared she had had a 'meaningful relationship' for over two years.

8. SWT refused to allow the benefit sought, on the ground that for unmarried persons travel concessions could be granted only for a partner of the opposite sex.

9. Ms Grant thereupon made an application against SWT to the Industrial Tribunal, Southampton, arguing that that refusal constituted discrimination based on sex, contrary to the Equal Pay Act 1970, art.119 of the EC Treaty and/or Directive 76/207. She submitted in particular that her predecessor in the post, a man who had declared that he had had a meaningful relationship with a woman for over two years, had enjoyed the benefit which had been refused her. . . .

13. As a preliminary point, it should be observed that the court has already held that travel concessions granted by an employer to former employees, their spouses and dependents, in respect of their employment are pay within the meaning of art.119 of the Treaty (see, to that effect the judgment in *Garland v. British Rail Engineering Ltd* 12/81 [1982] 2 All ER 402). . . .

15. In view of the wording of the other questions and the grounds of the decision making the reference, the essential point raised by the national tribunal is whether an employer's refusal to grant travel concessions to the person of the same sex with whom an employee has a stable relationship constitutes discrimination prohibited by art.119 of the Treaty and Directive 75/117, where such concessions are granted to an employee's spouse or the person of the opposite sex with whom an employee has a stable relationship outside marriage.

16. Ms Grant submits, first, that such a refusal constitutes discrimination directly based on sex. She submits that her employer's decision would have been different if the benefits in issue in the main proceedings had been claimed by a man living with a woman, and not by a woman living with a woman.

17. Ms Grant argues that the mere fact that the male worker who previously occupied her post had obtained travel concessions for his female partner, without being married to her, is enough to identify direct discrimination based on sex. In her submission, if a female worker does not receive the same benefits as a male worker, all other things being equal, she is the victim of discrimination based on sex (the 'but for' test).

18. Ms Grant contends, next, that such a refusal constitutes discrimination based on sexual orientation, which is included in the concept of 'discrimination based on sex' in art.119 of the Treaty. In her opinion, differences in treatment based on sexual orientation originate in prejudices regarding the sexual and emotional behaviour of persons of a particular sex, and are in fact based on those persons' sex. . . .

19. Ms Grant claims, finally, that the refusal to allow her the benefit is not objectively justified. . . .

26. The refusal to allow Ms Grant the concessions is based on the fact that she does not satisfy the conditions prescribed in those regulations, more particularly on the fact that she does not live with a 'spouse' or a person of the opposite sex with whom she has had a 'meaningful' relationship for at least two years.

27. That condition, the effect of which is that the worker must live in a stable relationship with a person of the opposite sex in order to benefit from the travel concessions, is, like the other alternative conditions prescribed in the undertaking's regulations, applied regardless of the sex of the worker concerned. Thus travel concessions are refused to a male worker if he is living with a person of the same sex, just as they are to a female worker if she is living with a person of the same sex.

28. Since the condition imposed by the undertaking's regulations applies in the same way to female and male workers, it cannot be regarded as constituting discrimination directly based on sex.

29. Second, the court must consider whether, with respect to the application of a condition such as that in issue in the main proceedings, persons who have a stable relationship with a partner of the same sex are in the same situation as those who are married or have a stable relationship outside marriage with a partner of the opposite sex.

30. Ms Grant submits in particular that the laws of the member states, as well as those of the Community and other international organisations, increasingly treat the two situations as equivalent.

31. While the European Parliament, as Ms Grant observes, has indeed declared that it deplores all forms of discrimination based on an individual's sexual orientation, it is nevertheless the case that the Community has not as yet adopted rules providing for such equivalence.

32. As for the laws of the member states, while in some of them cohabitation by two persons of the same sex is treated as equivalent to marriage, although not completely, in most of them it is treated as equivalent to a stable heterosexual relationship outside marriage only with respect to a limited number of rights, or else is not recognised in any particular way. . . .

35. It follows that, in the present state of the law within the Community, stable relationships between two persons of the same sex are not regarded as equivalent to marriages or stable relationships outside marriage between persons of opposite sex. Consequently, an employer is not required by Community law to treat the situation of a person who has a stable relationship with a partner of the same sex as equivalent to that of a person who is married to or has a stable relationship outside marriage with a partner of the opposite sex.

36. In those circumstances, it is for the legislature alone to adopt, if appropriate, measures which may affect that position. . . .

50. Accordingly, the answer to the national tribunal must be that the refusal by an employer to allow travel concessions to the person of the same sex with whom a worker has a stable relationship, where such concessions are allowed to a worker's spouse or to the person of the opposite sex with whom a worker has a stable relationship outside marriage, does not constitute discrimination prohibited by art.119 of the Treaty or Directive 75/117."

NOTES AND QUESTIONS

- The ECJ in *Grant* adopts a posture which might be described as judicial restraint, in that it explicitly throws the issue over to the legislatures, and the political institutions of the European Union. Do you think that such an approach to rights is justifiable? Why do you think the Court did not adopt a more *activist* stance, as it had done in other cases, such as *Garland*?

- Should "spouses" of employees (or "partners" or *whatever*) be entitled to benefits such as these? Why?

- Do you think that the ECJ might have been worried that a result in favour of Lisa Grant would have been out of step with current thinking in some EU countries? Is that concern justifiable? How should the judiciary approach the relationship between progressive law reform through claims to individual rights, and more socially conservative attitudes which may be present in the general population? Is there only one perspective on these issues across the EU?

Although the European Court of Justice adopted an approach in *Grant* that might be described as *deferential* to the member states, subsequent developments have demonstrated the entrenchment of human rights in EC law through the collective actions of the member states. Craig and de Búrca explore this deepening of human rights in the European Union.

Paul Craig and Gránne de Búrca, *EU Law: Text, Cases and Materials* (3rd ed., Oxford University Press, Oxford, 2003), pp.355–357:

"Undoubtedly the main 'hard' source of EC competence in the field of human rights protection within the EU . . . has been that introduced by the Amsterdam Treaty into Article 13 of the EC Treaty, supplementing the existing range of EU gender equality policies. Article 13 provides that the Community legislature may, within the limits of the Community's powers, take 'appropriate action to combat discrimination based on sex, racial or ethnic origin, religion or belief, disability, age or sexual orientation'. Hitherto, discrimination on grounds of sex and nationality was expressly prohibited by Community law, even though the basis for adopting general legislation in these fields was unclear. And while the case of *P* v *S* appeared to suggest that a more general prohibition on discrimination extending beyond sex and nationality to embrace transsexuality and other grounds were already part of the 'great value of equality' and one of the fundamental principles underlying EC law, the ECJ in *Grant* v *South West Trains* beat a hasty retreat from that position. In *Grant* the Court ruled, in a case concerning an employee who had been refused travel benefits for her same-sex partner, that EC law did not currently cover discrimination on the basis of sexual orientation. The Court confined its ruling in *P* v *S* to discrimination based essentially on the sex of the person, which did not, in its view, apply to discrimination on the grounds of sexual orientation which was not yet in force at that time, the ECJ argued that it was not for it to extend Community law beyond the scope provided for in the Treaty. . . .

Article 13 EC is not in itself a prohibition on discrimination on grounds of race, disability, sexual orientation, etc., and, unlike the equal pay provision in Article 141 EC on sex discrimination, it is not directly effective. Rather it enables the Community to adopt measures to combat discrimination on the grounds listed within the scope of the policies and powers otherwise granted in the Treaty. Prior to the coming into force of Article 13, the European Monitoring Centre for Racism and Xenophobia had been established by a regulation based on Articles 284 and 308 (ex Articles 213 and 235) EC, but, Article 13 has since facilitated stronger law-making in this field. Two directives were adopted in 2000, the first being a directive to prohibit discrimination on grounds of race and ethnic origin, and the second being the so-called framework employment directive, covering discrimination in the field of employment on the grounds listed in Article 13 (other than race, ethnic origin, or sex, which are already covered by other legislation): religion, belief, disability, age, and sexual orientation. While the jurisdictional limitation in Article 13 specifies that the EC can act only within the limits of the Community's powers, Article 3 of the anti-racism directive gives it an apparently wide scope, including a prohibition on discrimination in relation to social protection, health care, housing, and education. An action plan to combat racism had been adopted in 1998, and in 2000 a broader action programme to combat discrimination on all the grounds listed in Article 13 (other than sex, which is already covered by an action programme) was adopted. Further, the Commission has begun to promote 'mainstreaming' policies in the areas of gender, race, and disability in particular, to integrate anti-discrimination considerations into other areas of EC policy formation. Finally, Article 13 was amended by the Nice Treaty, which added a power for the Council to adopt non-harmonizing 'incentive measures' under the co-decision legislative procedure."

NOTES AND QUESTIONS

- Do you think that the decision in *Grant* may be partly responsible for the subsequent developments described by Craig and de Búrca?

- Are there reasons why the collective actions by member state governments may be preferable to decisions of the European Court of Justice in advancing human rights in the European Union?

Finally, you should be aware that the EU has developed another important rights document, the Charter of Fundamental Rights which contains a number of fundamental human rights. The legal status of the Charter remains ambiguous, as Criag and de Búrca explain.

Paul Craig and Gránne de Búrca, *EU Law: Text, Cases and Materials* (3rd ed., Oxford University Press, Oxford, 2003), pp.43–44:

"The European Council at Cologne in 1999 had launched another initiative of major constitutional significance, in establishing a 'body' which included national parliamentarians, European parliamentarians, and national government representatives to draft a Charter of fundamental rights for the EU. This body, which renamed itself a 'Convention', began work early in 2000 and drew up a Charter before the end of the same year. The Convention worked in an unusually open and transparent way, posting all of its documents and all of the materials submitted to it and the drafts discussed by it on a specially dedicated website, and holding its meetings openly. The Charter was 'solemnly proclaimed' by the Commission, Parliament and Council and received the political approval of the Member States at the European Council meeting in Nice in December 2000, but a decision on its legal status and specifically the question of its possible integration into the Treaties was placed on the so-called 'post-Nice agenda' and postponed until the 2004 IGC. The Charter was a significant development for the EU in a number of ways. In the first place, despite criticisms of its content—for example, of the ambiguity and weakness of many of its provisions, the rights which were not included, the relationship with other constitutional and international human rights instruments, and the numerous questions left unresolved—the document was largely well received and welcomed as a step forward for the legitimacy, identity, and human rights commitment of the EU. Secondly, the process by which it was adopted also attracted positive comment as a considerable improvement on the typically secretive and intransparent process—including Intergovernmental Conferences—by which treaties and other agreements have traditionally been negotiated and drawn up at EU level. So much so that, without actually agreeing to abandon the government-dominated IGC process, the European Council at Laeken in 2001 established a similar Convention (including the participation of members from the candidate countries) to 'prepare' for the 2004 IGC, alongside a Forum to structure a public debate on the constitutional future of Europe."

"There is little reason to trust judges as arbiters of controversial political issues. They will generally interpret law and facts from the standpoint of dominant groups in society."

Discuss, with particular reference to the decisions in *Grant v South West Trains, Garland, CCSU, GLC v Bromley* and *Wheeler*.

6

CONSTITUTIONAL ASPECTS OF LEGAL METHOD: THE DEVOLUTION OF POWERS

In this chapter, our focus turns briefly to new constitutional arrangements in the United Kingdom and Northern Ireland which have resulted in a substantial *devolution* of governmental powers. That is, power has been turned over from direct exercise by Parliament to created assemblies in Scotland, Wales, and Northern Ireland. These assemblies are responsible for areas of particular relevance to each jurisdiction. The devolution of powers raises issues of constitutional importance, and thus we examine these arrangements as an aspect of our legal method. The relationship between the devolution of powers and the supremacy of Parliament is an important issue but, as we will see, Parliamentary supremacy is less affected by the way in which power is devolved, than it is by membership in the European Union.

DEFINING DEVOLUTION

A definition of devolution, which underscores its theoretical consistency with the principle of Parliamentary supremacy, has been provided by Hood Phillips, Jackson and Leopold.

Paul Jackson and Patricia Leopold, *O. Hood Phillips & Jackson: Constitutional and Administrative Law* (8th ed., Sweet and Maxwell, London, 2001), para 5-002:

"The term devolution refers to the delegation of central government powers without the relinquishment of supremacy by the central legislature. Devolution may be legislative or administrative or both, and in its more advanced forms involves the exercise of powers by persons or bodies who, although acting on authority delegated by the Westminster Parliament, are not directly answerable to it or to the central government. Devolution is said not to affect the unity of the United Kingdom or the power of Westminster to legislate (even in devolved matters) for all or any part of the United Kingdom, or to repeal or amend the devolution arrangements themselves. It should be distinguished from 'decentralisation', which is a method whereby some central government powers of decision-making are exercised by officials of the central government located in various regions, and federalism. In a federal system supremacy is *divided* between the federal legislature and government on the one hand and the legislatures and governments of the constituent units on the other, and the basic terms of a federal constitution (notably the distribution of

powers) are *entrenched* so that they cannot be amended at the sole discretion of the federation or of any province or combination of provinces."

The history and structure of the devolution of powers—and a comparison to other
constitutional arrangements—has been provided by Alder.

**John Alder, *Constitutional and Administrative Law* (3rd ed., Macmillan, Basingstoke, 1999),
pp 112–127:**

Federal and Unitary Constitutions

"In a federal state such as the USA, the constitution divides power between a central
federal government and separate state units in such a way that each is independent within
its own sphere and neither can override the other. Federalism is therefore a way of giving
effect to communitarian values by allowing diverse units to retain their distinctive identity
while at the same time providing for unity where there is a common interest. Federalism
also serves to reduce the risk of tyranny. A unitary state such as the UK has an overriding
supreme lawmaker which can devolve power to subordinate units but is free to take the
power back and to interfere with the smaller units.

Federalism is practicable where the component units have sufficient in common economically and culturally, for example a shared history or language, to enable them to co-
operate, while at the same time each unit is sufficiently distinctive to constitute a
community in its own right. Thus a delicate balance must be struck. The United States and
Australia are relatively successful federations whereas Canada, with its split between
English-speaking and French-speaking regions, is less stable. Yugoslavia, with its many
ethnic tensions, has been unsuccessful. It cannot be seriously suggested that federalism is
the best way of achieving efficient government but efficiency cannot be the overriding
purpose of a liberal society. Federalism is a mechanism for giving political rights to a wider
range of group interests than is possible in a unitary system and therefore a means of
resolving conflicting loyalties.

The relationship between federal government and the state governments within it, is not,
in law, one of superior and inferior, but of partnership. Each has its own sphere of activity and its own constitution and courts and it may be unlawful for one to trespass upon the
other. There is a single federal citizenship and free movement within the federation. The
central government typically represents the country on the international level and exercises
defined functions—typically, defence and foreign affairs, currency, postal services and
important commercial activities—while leaving the residual power with the states. Some
versions allocate particular matters to the states leaving the federal level as the residuary
power.

Where responsibilities overlap, doctrines such as 'pre-emption' or the supremacy clause
of the United States Constitution provide resolving mechanisms usually policed by the
courts. Representatives of the states may sit in the federal legislature. In the USA the states
are equally represented in the Senate, the upper House of the legislature, so as not to disadvantage the smaller states. The lower House is elected in proportion to the population
of the states. In the European Union the more powerful states have greater voting power
in relation to certain issues. As with any constitution, the actual disposition of power in
reality depends on political and economic as well as legal factors. Thus the real balance
between centre and state may not be apparent from reading the constitution.

As with many political ideas, it is probably best to regard terms such as 'federal' or
'unitary' not as precise definitions, but as convenient points upon a political spectrum

ranging from loose associations of countries for particular purposes to simple one-government states. On this spectrum the UK Constitution is close to the latter extreme and is therefore called a 'unitary' constitution. The whole country is subject to the over-riding power of the central government and to parliamentary supremacy. Within the UK certain powers have very recently and in varying degrees been devolved to elected assemblies in Scotland and Wales but without in any way limiting the powers of Parliament. Northern Ireland has enjoyed devolved powers in the past and legislation is in force to enable it to do so again. There are also local authorities within the UK based upon cities, counties and units within the county. Although elected and having certain tax-raising power, local authorities obtain their powers exclusively from statute, are closely regulated by central government and depend upon the central government for most of their funding. Variations in the level of local services is discouraged.

Dicey strongly opposed federalism in the United Kingdom, a factor which influenced his attitude to parliamentary supremacy. He thought that 'federal government means weak government' although he qualified this by recognising that federalism might make it possible to unite communities that otherwise could not be united at all. He also thought that federalism tends to conservatism, creates divided loyalties and that it elevates legalism to a primary value, making the courts the pivot on which the constitution turns and perhaps threatening their independence.

During the late nineteenth century there were some advocates of a federal UK as a way of avoiding home rule for Ireland and also proposals for a federation of the UK and some of its overseas territories. However, on the whole, federalism has not been a serious element of UK politics. The Kilbrandon Report (1973) argued against a federal constitution for the UK on the following grounds. Firstly the units are widely different in economic terms, with England being the dominant member. Any federation is therefore likely to be unbalanced. Secondly, a federal regime would be contrary to our constitutional traditions in that it would elevate the courts over political machinery. Thirdly the UK was thought to require central and flexible economic management since its resources are unevenly distributed geographically. Fourthly, apart from Northern Ireland, regional issues were not high on the agenda of the main parties, which suggested that there was little public desire for federalism.

The Structure of the United Kingdom

Devolution

The United Kingdom is a union of what were originally four separate countries united partly by violent conquest and partly by commercial self-interest. Before devolution, the internal affairs of Scotland and Wales were governed by the UK central executive with what has been described as overtones of colonialism, an echo of which survives in the present devolution arrangements. The informal and secretive nature of government in Britain makes it difficult to assess the influence of the Scottish and Welsh Offices upon policy. Such matters as personal status, relationships between departments, party politics and tradition are as important as the statutory allocation of power. Scotland and Northern Ireland have separate courts but the House of Lords and Privy Council are final courts of appeal for all the UK jurisdictions.

Devolution not only creates separate governmental mechanisms in each region *vis à vis* the UK government but also enables the devolved regions to increase their influence in dealings at international level, notably with the EU. Moreover the Belfast Agreement (1998) contemplates a 'Council of the Isles' with representation from the various units of the UK.

Despite its opposition to a federal solution the Kilbrandon Report in 1973 asserted that government in the UK was over-centralised and recommended devolved government. Referendums were subsequently held in Scotland and Wales which foundered because they failed to obtain the required two-thirds majorities in favour of change. Nothing further was done until the present Labour government took office in 1997. There was considerable public support for devolution in Scotland, and significant support for complete independence. In

Wales there was substantial support for some form of devolution. Following referendums in Scotland and Wales, legislation was introduced to give both legislative and executive power to a Scottish Parliament and executive power to a Welsh Assembly. At the same time the peace process in Northern Ireland included proposals to restore legislative and executive power to the province which had been directly governed by the UK government since 1972. These proposals were also approved by a referendum.

The devolution arrangements are asymmetrical in four ways. Firstly, the powers of the three devolved bodies are very different. Secondly, England, which comprises 85 per cent of the population of the UK has no democratic political institutions of its own nor indeed a legal identity. Thirdly, Scottish, Welsh and Northern Ireland members of the UK Parliament are entitled to vote in debates affecting exclusively English matters (the 'West Lothian' question, so-called after the constituency of Tam Dalziel, one of the more vociferous pursuers of the matter). Fourthly, Scottish, Welsh and Northern Ireland voters are represented in the UK Parliament roughly in proportion to their population. This means that the UK Parliament, which retains unlimited power to legislate in relation to Scotland, Wales and Northern Ireland and provides most of the funding for the regional governments, is dominated by English MPs.

An equitable solution to the West Lothian problem would be devolution to the English regions or to England as a whole and perhaps equal regional representation in a reformed House of Lords. In the USA for example the states are represented in the lower House in proportion to their population but have equal representation in the upper House. There seems to be little public support for devolution within England. The Kilbrandon Report (1972) was divided. Experience of devolution in Northern Ireland from 1920 to 1972 suggests that without greater economic equality a devolved power cannot function properly nor be accountable to its people. There is considerable inequality between the English regions.

England has Regional Development Agencies wholly appointed by the Secretary of State and charged only with one group of purposes, that of advancing economic development including related matters of education and training. They are accountable only to the Secretary of State (Regional Development Agencies Act 1998). The Secretary of State can give Directions and Guidance to the Regional Development Agencies. The Agencies will exercise powers delegated to them by ministers and, subject to the consent of the Secretary of State, can provide funds and acquire land.

Devolution might have a de-stabilising effect on the UK as a whole. This is firstly because it generates pressure for Scottish and Welsh independence; secondly the electoral system and the timing of elections to the Scottish Parliament differ from that in the UK as a whole; and thirdly because the resolution of demarcation disputes relating to devolution falls to local and UK courts in Scotland and to UK courts in Wales, in both cases with the Privy Council as a final court. The introduction of a genuine federal system might have alleviated these problems.

Northern Ireland

The history of Ireland is complex and raises fundamental constitutional issues. These centre upon religious divisions and upon a history of imposed settlement from England and Scotland. The correlation between religion, national identity and voting preference in Northern Ireland has been said to be the highest in the liberal democratic world. The Protestant community is today the majority in Northern Ireland. Every election since 1921 has returned a Protestant majority and without proportional representation it is unlikely that the Catholic minority (about 38 per cent) would gain political power.

Ireland had been formally subject to the English Crown since the tenth century, although in practice England originally controlled only an area around Dublin called the Pale. Elizabeth I attempted to extend English government to the whole of Ireland, precipitating rebellion followed by confiscation of land belonging to the Catholic population and extensive settlement by the English and Scots. Cromwell's regime during the 1650s consolidated this policy with large-scale massacres, thus sowing the seeds of current problems. There was a formal union of Scotland and Ireland with England in 1654. However, this was never acknowledged by the Irish which retained its own Parliament until 1800. After the 1688 revolution a Protestant supremacy was imposed which denied Catholics full participation in public life and imposed disadvantages upon them in property law. The conquest of Ireland was completed in 1690 when William III, supported by the Pope, defeated the deposed Catholic king of England, James II, at the Battle of the Boyne.

After a series of violent rebellions, the Act of Union of 1800 joined Britain and Ireland into the United Kingdom thus creating the UK parliament. The separate Irish parliament was abolished in favour of Irish representation in the UK parliament. The Act of Union declared that the Union was to last 'for ever'. The Act of Union also protected the United Church of England and Ireland but the repeal of this provision by the Irish Church Act 1879 has been upheld (*Ex parte Canon Selwyn* (1872)). Unrest continued throughout the nineteenth and early twentieth centuries. There were problems about discrimination against Catholics particularly in relation to landholding, these being compounded by the apparent indifference of the United Kingdom government to economic disasters of the 1840s which decimated the Irish population. From 1870 to 1920 the question of 'Irish Home Rule' was the most important question in United Kingdom politics. It weakened the personal authority of the monarchy which unwisely took sides in the dispute and gave rise to debate about the most fundamental principles of the constitution including the balance of representation in the UK parliament, a matter that has not yet been resolved. No agreement was reached but the notion of parliamentary supremacy became a powerful symbol. Dicey in particular was a strong supporter of the Union and thought that home rule would be possible only by abolishing Parliament.

In 1906 Sinn Fein was formed as a political party dedicated to the cause of Irish unity and both sides generated armed factions. Between the Easter Rising of 1916 and 1922, Sinn Fein clashed with loyalist groups in violent uprisings and campaigns of terrorism. The Government of Ireland Act 1920 partitioned Ireland. It established a devolved government in Northern Ireland and created a parliament with a larger degree of autonomy in the south. The Irish Free State (Constitution) Act 1922 gave the southern states a status similar to what were then the dominions of Australia, Canada, New Zealand and South Africa. These measures were ignored in Southern Ireland which created its own constitution based upon the sovereignty of the people. This constitution created the present Republic of Ireland in which the constitution claimed to include the whole of Ireland. However, according to UK law, the status of Ireland still depended upon the Act of Union and on the Irish Free State (Constitution) Act 1922. There were therefore conflicting legal orders, each being valid from its internal viewpoint.

From 1922 until 1972, Northern Ireland which was predominantly Protestant had devolved government together with representation in the UK Parliament. s.75 of the 1920 Act provided that 'notwithstanding the establishment of the Parliament of Northern Ireland *or* anything contained in this Act, the supreme authority of the Parliament of the United Kingdom shall remain unaffected and undiminished over all persons, matters and things in (Northern Ireland) and every part thereof' (italics repealed). The Ireland Act 1949 recognised the independence of the republic but provided in s.1(2) that 'Northern Ireland remains part of . . . the United Kingdom and . . . in no event will Northern Ireland cease to be part of . . . the United Kingdom without the consent of the Parliament of Northern Ireland'. Originally there was proportional representation, thus giving a voice to the Catholic minority, but this was abolished in 1929, allowing Protestant majority rule until 1972.

However, the Northern Ireland government was unable to raise sufficient finance to provide equivalent social and public services to those on the mainland. These problems led to increasing intervention by the United Kingdom. Rising living standards made the problem of discrimination against the poorer Catholic community more acute. There was a lack of confidence in the impartiality of the judiciary and the police, and Catholics had little access to political power. From 1968 increased terrorist activity on both sides led to the introduction of emergency laws restricting civil rights and empowering the army to support the police. In 1972 the Northern Ireland Parliament was prorogued and direct rule from Westminster imposed. The Ireland Act 1949 was repealed by the Northern Ireland Constitution (Amendment) Act 1973 and a new Assembly with proportional representation was created (Northern Ireland Assembly Act 1973). The entrenchment of the Union in the 1949 Act was replaced by a provision requiring a referendum of the people. However, the 1973 Act was opposed by unionist politicians and never fully implemented. The concept of power-sharing led to strikes and disturbances and stringent emergency legislation was imposed on Northern Ireland. . . .

Throughout the following two decades discussions continued as to how to accommodate the unionist and nationalist interests in Northern Ireland, the goal of the nationalists being union with the Republic of Ireland. Terrorism persisted throughout this period on both sides. The Northern Ireland Act 1982 provided machinery for discussing proposals for future devolved government but the parties were too polarised for these provisions to be of practical use.

More recently there has been a series of agreements which attempted to reconcile the conflict or at least engineer a compromise. In 1985 a new approach was taken which recognised the international dimension of the problem. This took the form of the Anglo-Irish Agreement between the United Kingdom and the Irish Republic now superseded by the Belfast Agreement (below) which retains many of the same principles. The Anglo-Irish Agreement provided for political co-operation between the two countries on matters of security, human rights, elections, prisons, the courts and extradition. It affirmed that devolution is desirable and recognises that the status of Northern Ireland should not be changed without popular consent. The Agreement also set up an Intergovernmental Conference aimed at tackling discrimination and combating terrorism. The 'Downing Street Declaration' (1994, cm 2422) created machinery for inter-party negotiations.

This led to the Belfast Agreement ('Good Friday Agreement'), made in 1998 between the two governments and the main political parties in Northern Ireland. The agreement provides for the restoration of devolved government, the amendment of the Irish Constitution so as to accept that Northern Ireland is currently part of the UK, the creation of a 'British Island Council' as a consultative forum representing the interests of Ireland and the various parts of the UK and the Channel Islands, and for an extension of cross border co-operation in the form of a North-South Ministerial Council. The Good Friday Agreement was endorsed by 71 per cent of voters in Northern Ireland and 94 per cent in the Republic of Ireland in referendums.

These agreements have led to the current attempt to create devolved government in Northern Ireland. The Northern Ireland Act 1998 repeals the 1920 Act and the 1973 legislation. It makes new provision for devolved government in Northern Ireland with power shared between the political parties. . . .

The 1998 Act (s. 1) includes the principle that Northern Ireland remains part of the UK and that the status of Northern Ireland will be altered only with the consent of a majority of its electorate. If a referendum favours a united Ireland, the Secretary of State is required to 'make proposals' to implement this by agreement with the Irish government. This less than absolute commitment can be interpreted as reducing the UK's claim to Northern Ireland to the 'one hinge' of the will of the majority, although it can be argued that because the Irish Constitution now renounces territorial claim to Northern Ireland the Union is thereby reinforced. The 1998 Act is ambivalent on the question of the Act of Union with Ireland 1800 which purported to make the union permanent. Unlike its Scottish counterpart, the 1998 Act does not expressly override the Act of Union but leaves the position arguable.

The Act is designed to reduce the impact of sectarianism and to encourage power-sharing between the political communities. The existing power of Parliament to make law for Northern Ireland is not affected (s. 5(6)). Eighteen Northern Ireland members sit in the Westminster Parliament. . . .

Scotland

Scotland was a separate nation state from 1010 until 1706. It has never been conquered by the English and possesses a separate legal system which has stronger links with civil law systems than is the case with England. In 1603, as result of inheritance, the Crowns of

England and Scotland were united in James I (England), James VI (Scotland). This led to economic and social integration including free trade and common citizenship. In 1689 Scotland offered its Crown to William and Mary on the same terms, the supremacy of Parliament, as in England.

After quarrels between the two Parliaments the Treaty of Union 1707 abolished the separate Scottish and English Parliaments and created a new Parliament of Great Britain. The treaty was confirmed by separate Acts of each Parliament. The Acts of Union are still in force. They preserve the separate Scottish legal system and Church and safeguard the private rights of Scottish subjects. The Union was unpopular but was brought about by economic interest on the part of Scotland and fear of invasion on the part of England. Since the sixteenth-century Reformation there had been cultural assimilation between the two countries, but also religious warfare between Catholics and Protestants. There were violent uprisings and government oppression throughout the eighteenth century followed by governmental attempts to instil a distinctive Scottish culture during the nineteenth century. Much land in the highland region was expropriated by the government during the eighteenth century, which remains a source of grievance.

There are special committees in Parliament to examine Scottish Affairs. In particular the 'Scottish Grand Committee' deals with bills exclusively relating to Scotland. Before the Scotland Act 1998, Scotland was entitled to at least 71 seats in the UK Parliament, thus, as in the case of Wales, making it over-represented in terms of its population. Section 86(1) of the 1998 Act abolishes this entitlement and places Scotland under the same regime as England in terms of the criteria of defining constituencies. This is likely to reduce the number of Scottish MPs in the UK Parliament.

The Scotland Act 1998 creates a Scottish Parliament elected by the first-past-the-post system, topped up by a regional party list elected by the additional-member version of proportional representation. There are eight regions each having seven seats and currently 73 single member constituencies. The Scottish Parliament has a general power, subject to restrictions, to legislate by means of Acts which will receive the Royal Assent. The Parliament elects a Presiding Officer and two Deputies (s. 19).

The Scottish Parliament can legislate generally subject to the restrictions in the Act (s. 28, s.29 sched. 4). These are substantial and make it clear that, in law at any rate, this is devolution rather than federalism. The Scottish Parliament cannot, except in minor respects (sched. 4 para 4), amend the Scotland Act itself nor alter basic constitutional provisions nor the Act of Union's free trade provisions. It cannot override European law, nor the ECHR rights binding in UK law under the Human Rights Act 1998. It has a limited tax-raising power to vary income tax by up to 3 pence in the pound, so that the government will depend on supply from Westminster. There is also a list of 'reserved matters' on which only UK Parliament can legislate (sched. 5). They include the main economic levers, foreign policy, defence and national security, border controls security, transport safety and regulation, employment and the regulation of key professions and social security (see Cm 3658 (1997) and s.30 sched. 5). By virtue of s.29(3) the questions whether a matter is a reserved matter must be decided by reference to its purpose having regard among other things to its effect in all the circumstances. Legislation will not therefore be invalidated if it incidently effects matters outside its field. There is a variation applicable to Scots criminal law and private law whereby a provision which would otherwise not relate to a reserved matter but does so because it alters these areas of law is treated as a reserved matter unless its purpose is to secure consistency between reserved matters and others (s. 29(4)). This allows the Scottish Parliament to make general reforms to Scots law. The purposive approach is capable of giving rise to considerable difficulty. However, s.101(2) requires laws to be interpreted narrowly in favour of their competence.

The Scotland Act 1998 (s. 27(7)) expressly confirms the power of the UK Parliament to legislate for Scotland and s.37 empowers the UK Parliament to override the Act of Union. However, if the argument that the UK Parliament cannot override the entrenched provisions of the Acts of Union is correct, this would be unlawful and there would be a federal relationship between Scotland and the UK.

Despite the royal assent, Acts of the Scottish Parliament are subordinate legislation owing their validity only to the Scotland Act 1998. They can be set aside by the courts and be overridden by inconsistent UK legislation. The validity of proceedings leading to an enactment does not affect its validity (s. 28 (5)), but otherwise Acts of the Scottish Parliament which are outside its competence 'are not law' (s. 28). Indeed it is arguable that, as in the case of other delegated legislation, for example local by-laws, the courts might set aside an Act of the Scottish Parliament on the grounds of unreasonableness or unfairness (see *Kruse* v. *Johnson* (1898)). The same argument applies to legislation made by the Northern Ireland and the Welsh Assemblies. Indeed laws made by the Welsh Assembly are ordinary subordinate legislation made under particular statutes and not underpinned by tax-raising power. However, the democratic character of the devolved law-making process provisions suggests that the court will be reluctant to interfere on these grounds. The parliament has no immunity from legal proceedings but has absolute privilege in defamation and protection in relation to contempt of court (ss. 40–42).

There are mechanisms for ensuring that the Scottish Parliament keeps within its powers. 'Devolution issues' concerning whether legislation is within the powers of the parliament can be raised in any court and can ultimately be decided by the Privy Council either on appeal or by way of a reference from a lower court similar to the reference procedure in EC law (sched. 6). Where a devolution issue arises before the House of Lords it must be referred to the Privy Council unless the House in all the circumstances thinks that it is more appropriate to decide it itself. The Advocate General, the Lord Advocate or the UK Attorney General can bring proceedings or require to be made a party to any litigation. The court can protect people who may have relied on invalid laws passed by the Scottish Parliament by removing the retrospective effect of the invalidity or suspending the invalidity to allow the effect to be corrected (s. 102). . . .

The Scottish Parliament is stronger in relation to the executive than is the case with the UK Parliament. The Parliament lasts for a fixed term of four years, so that, unlike the case with the UK Prime Minister, the First Minister cannot request a dissolution. A first minister can resign at any time and must do so if the Scottish Executive is defeated on a vote of confidence (s. 45). The First Minister ceases to hold office if a person is appointed in his place, as where a new Parliament is formed after a general election (s. 46). Other ministers must also resign if the executive is defeated on a vote of no confidence, and automatically lose office on ceasing to be a member of Parliament except in the case of a dissolution where they retain office until removed by the incoming administration.

Suppose an administration finds itself deadlocked because of tensions within a coalition. Under the Scotland Act the Parliament can resolve that it be dissolved. The resolution must be supported by at least two-thirds of the total number of seats. The Presiding Officer must then propose an election and the Queen 'may' dissolve Parliament and call an election (s. 3). It is not clear what advice, if any, the Queen should take or whether she must automatically dissolve Parliament on a request by the Presiding Officer. The same procedure applies if the Parliament cannot agree on a choice of First Minister. This procedure seems to mean that a minority can hold a government to ransom. Bagehot's claim for the Westminster system that Parliament can easily get rid of a struggling government would not therefore seem to apply to Scotland.

Wales

Wales has strong cultural traditions, but unlike Scotland and Northern Ireland has never had its own government or legal system. Wales was relatively little affected by the invasions and occupations of Britain that started with the Romans in AD 55 and ended with the Norman Conquest of 1066. Wales was never a separate state but consisted of a number of principalities. The largest of these passed into English rule in 1084 (Statute of Wales) and the others were subdued by England by the sixteenth century (see Act of Union with Wales 1536). A separate Welsh Assembly was abolished in 1689. English law applied throughout Wales and a single court system was introduced in 1830. Within Wales there are markedly different areas both economically and culturally, so that it is more difficult than in the case of Scotland to regard Wales as a country or a nation. Earlier proposals for Welsh devolution in the Wales

Act 1978 were defeated by a referendum and the current proposals were only narrowly approved. . . .

The Government of Wales Act 1998 has given Wales less power than the other regions and with a weaker element of proportional representation. The Act creates an elected Welsh Assembly of 60 members, small compared with the eighty envisaged by the 1978 Act. The Assembly is elected by a combination of first-past-the-post and the 'additional member' system similar to that in Scotland. The Welsh electoral system is less proportional than the Scottish system, having a greater proportion of first-past-the-post seats (40/20 compared with 73/56). This gives greater power to the majority party which in Wales is likely to be the Labour Party.

The Assembly is a combination of executive body and a method of scrutinising the executive. Significantly it is a corporate body and a crown servant. It can exercise only such legislative or executive powers as are transferred to it by Order in Council from UK ministers. There are restrictions requiring compliance with European law and the ECHR as far as it is applied to domestic law by the Human Rights Act 1998. The subordinate nature of the Assembly and the complexities of the distribution of functions within Wales may well encourage legal challenge as a weapon in the political power play.

The Assembly exercises the functions that were previously exercised by the Welsh Office. These include agriculture, forestry, fisheries and food, environmental and cultural matters, economic and industrial development, education and training, health, housing, local government, social services, sport and tourism, town and country planning, transport, water and flood defences, and the Welsh language. There is particular concern with economic development, and the Assembly is required to prepare schemes dealing with sustainable development, the sustaining and promotion of local government and the promotion of relevant voluntary organisations.

The Assembly also has certain powers of control over Welsh QUANGOs, these being various specialised non-elected bodies that have been established in Wales in recent years. These powers include in some cases the power of abolition or to transfer functions to the Assembly or a local authority. This is designed to meet widespread concerns about the lack of democratic accountability in Wales. An expanded Welsh Development Agency takes over the functions of the Development Board for Rural Wales and the Land Authority for Wales, both of which are abolished. . . .

There are no separate Welsh courts nor a separate Attorney General for Wales, the UK Attorney General having responsibility also for Wales. It seems that any court can invalidate decisions and legislation made by the Assembly. Nevertheless there are provisions similar to those in Scotland and Northern Ireland, for the Privy Council to deal with challenges to the powers of the Assembly and other Welsh bodies by way of appeal or by a reference from the Assembly or the Attorney General."

Whether devolution will strengthen or weaken the "national unity" of the United Kingdom (if, indeed, one believes it to be "one" nation) is a highly contentious issue. Bogdanor outlines the arguments and draws some tentative conclusions.

Vernon Bogdanor, *Devolution in the United Kingdom* (Oxford University Press, Oxford, 1999), pp.294–298:

"Dicey believed that a federal system, in order to be successful, requires 'a very peculiar state of sentiment among the inhabitants of the countries which it is proposed to unite. They must desire union, and must not desire unity. If there be no desire to unite, there is clearly no basis for federalism.' This 'peculiar state of sentiment' will also be needed if the quasi-federal arrangement established by the Scotland Act is to prove workable. The sense of common feeling will have to prevail over the sentiment of states' rights. Indeed, because it creates governmental relationships of some complexity, quasi-federalism probably requires a *greater* sense of loyalty to the whole, to the United Kingdom, than is necessary in a unitary state.

Will the new constitutional settlement preserve the unity of the United Kingdom; or will it prove a springboard for separatism? In the debate on the White Paper on Wales in the House of Commons, a senior Welsh Labour back-bencher, Donald Anderson, declared that devolution was the beginning of a 'mystery tour' whose final destination was unclear. 'I recall', Anderson went on, 'the fine story of a Welsh mystery tour by bus from Cwmrhydyceirw in my constituency. There was a sweep about where the tour would end, and it is said that the driver won. The people of Wales are driving this mystery tour. They will decide the pace and the direction'. The same is true in Scotland. It will be the people of Scotland who will decide whether devolution yields a stable settlement, or whether it proves but a staging-post on the way either to federalism or separatism.

Some of the demands which have fuelled support for devolution in Scotland and Wales have been economic in nature. Resentment against London stems from a feeling that Westminster and Whitehall have ignored Scotland's economic problems. Yet few economic powers are being devolved. This could lead to disillusion when the exaggerated claims made by supporters of devolution are contrasted with the realities. Critics would then argue that devolution had given Scotland the power to deal with matters on which there was comparatively little discontent, while denying them the power to deal with matters on which there was a great deal of discontent. If there is no rapid improvement in public services in Scotland, the Scottish Parliament could become a focus for discontent. Then, devolution would weaken the Union. The contrast between the powerful electoral base and legitimacy of the Scottish Parliament and its comparatively limited powers could thus fuel separatism.

Devolution to Scotland, where nationalism is stronger than it is in Wales, may thus, by providing legitimacy for Scottish national claims, stimulate the demand for independence. It is sometimes, however, suggested that devolution will, in these circumstances, have *caused* separatism—the slippery-slope argument—but that is misleading. For it implies that the Scots will somehow find themselves independent without having sought to do so.

The constitutional hurdle to be overcome before Scotland becomes independent remains the same after devolution as it was before. Independence requires the Scots return a majority of SNP MPs to Westminster. Parliament would not, as it did with the Irish, resist the wish of the Scottish people for independence, but it would ensure that independence was in fact Scotland's settled demand by holding a referendum. Separation, therefore, could come about with minimal disturbance, but it would hardly be possible to occur through inadvertence on the part of the Scottish people. It is unlikely to happen by accident.

It may be seen . . . that an independent Scotland would be worse off economically than it is today. Indeed, Ian Lang, the then Secretary of State for Scotland, declared in 1995 that an independent Scotland would have to raise income tax by 19p in the pound to maintain public services at their current level. Yet a country seeking independence tends to find that it is economically feasible. Nations struggling to be free have rarely been deterred by the constraints of economics.

It does not follow, however, that devolution will in fact lead to break-up. A more benign scenario is possible. In Spain, Belgium, Italy, and France, devolution has led not to break-up but to power-sharing. In Catalonia and the Basque country, it has weakened the demand for independence, not strengthened it. The main nationalist parties there no longer seek independence, while electoral support for parties campaigning for separation has declined. Devolution in Britain could well have the same effect, defusing the demand for independence, isolating extremists, and strengthening rather than weakening those powerful forces holding the United Kingdom together. The leitmotif of the twentieth century has, admittedly, been nationalism. But that of the twenty-first century could well prove to be power-sharing.

Separatism, then, is by no means the necessary or even the most likely outcome of devolution to Scotland. The nationalist parties may find that they have achieved not independence, but rather a dispersal of power to Scotland and Wales, the greatest reversal of the trend to centralization in government for many years. Many of the supporters of the nationalist parties indeed have sought not separation, but the humanization of the state through a reduction in the scale of government. If they succeed, then the economic and technological developments whose tendency has been to make men and women more and more alike will have found themselves checked by political pressures—the search for identity and the urge to participate. It was Rousseau who was the first to understand that these emotional needs demand satisfaction if men and women are to lead truly fulfilling lives. 'Mankind has lost its home,' Franz Kafka told his friend Gustav Janouch. 'Men always strive for what they do not have. The technical advances which are common to all nations strip them more and more of their national characteristics. Therefore they become nationalist. Modern nationalism is a defensive movement against the crude encroachments of civilisation.' The demand that government be made more responsive and less remote, that its scale be smaller, may be seen as the reassertion of a human imperative against the dominant economic and technological forces of the age.

If there are these powerful centrifugal forces at work in Britain today, it might well be that the best way to strengthen national unity is to give way to them a little, the better to disarm them. Then those deep underlying causes which make for unity can be allowed to operate without arousing antagonism or disenchantment.

Political science has been much concerned with the key question of how political societies are held together. To that question, the traditional British answer has been to concentrate responsibility and political authority in one undivided central parliament. But the case that centralization makes for national unity is something that needs to be argued for and not simply asserted. This book has attempted to show that an alternative answer is possible—that society may be held together through what Gladstone called a 'recognition of the distinctive qualities of the separate parts of great countries'. If that answer is correct, then devolution will strengthen the United Kingdom, not weaken it."

NOTES AND QUESTIONS

- The Scotland Act makes provision in s.32 for the determination of any question concerning whether a Scottish bill is within the legislative competence of the Scottish Parliament. Such questions can be referred to the Judicial Committee of the Privy Council—a judicial body made up of members of the House of Lords—for decision. The decision to refer can be made by the Advocate General for Scotland (a new law officer for Scotland), the Lord Advocate (the principal law officer to the Scottish administration), or the Attorney General for the United Kingdom. Thus, there is the potential for a new field of judicial review of legislation, so as to ensure that the jurisdiction of the devolved Parliament has not been exceeded. This is clearly of constitutional significance.

- To what extent is the devolution of power to a Scottish Parliament compatible with a system of Parliamentary supremacy? What sorts of disputes between Parliaments can you envision arising?

- Should Scottish members of the United Kingdom Parliament be allowed to vote on matters solely affecting England? Explain your position.

- In what ways can the more limited devolution of powers to Wales, as compared with Scotland, be justified? Can there be a principled basis for the difference?

- The Good Friday Agreement, of course, is of historical significance. From a constitutional perspective, it is of interest how an ongoing relationship between two national governments—of the United Kingdom and the Republic of Ireland—has become somewhat constitutionalised. To what extent do traditional notions of Parliamentary supremacy make sense in an era of increasingly entrenched international relationships—such as the Good Friday agreement or, indeed, membership of the European Union?

• Should further steps towards the devolution of powers be taken within England? Should assemblies be established within the regions, with a devolution of power to them?

• What is the impact of the new constitutional arrangements discussed in this chapter on (i) Parliamentary supremacy; and (ii) judicial review?

PART THREE: INTERPRETING STATUTES

7

STATUTORY INTERPRETATION: INTRODUCTION TO LEGISLATION

In this chapter, our focus shifts to the interpretation of legislation—statute law—by the judiciary. We begin with an examination of the historical relationship between the common law and legislation and then proceed to a brief introduction to the legislative process itself. Next, we look at the role of judges in interpreting legislation through some examples. We then turn to the "rules" of interpretation and the extent to which they constrain judicial decision making. Finally, we examine a case study on interpretation, involving the Race Relations Act.

THE RELATIONSHIP BETWEEN LEGISLATION AND COMMON LAW

Although our legal system is referred to as based on judge made "common law", we will see in this chapter that it is statutory law—the law enacted by Parliament—which is increasingly at the centre of our legal world. The historical relationship between these two pillars of the legal order provides a starting point for understanding the way in which statutes are dealt with by the judiciary.

Peter Goodrich, *Reading the Law* (Blackwell, Oxford, 1986), pp.40–44:

"In historical terms the primary source of law within the English legal system is unwritten law. Whilst in this respect it does not differ significantly from the early history of vernacular local legal systems in the rest of Europe, it does differ from those legal systems in that the unwritten law has retained its position as a significant source of law. Unwritten law (common law) is defined as custom derived from time immemorial. Written law is seen as a subsequent development. It has since medieval times been seen as a technique used to strengthen, interpret, regulate or amend the common law. This image of the relationship

between written and unwritten law has persisted even through the economic transforma-
tions of the eighteenth and nineteenth centuries, and Blackstone in the mid-eighteenth
century refers to legislation as fulfilling a variety of roles, 'either declaratory of the
common law, or remedial of some defects therein'. Remnants of this position can still be
seen in operation contemporarily in that many of the presumptions brought to bear upon
the interpretation of legislation have their basis in presuppositions as to the historical relationship between the common law and legislation. For example, there is the presumption
against the alteration of the law, that Parliament knows the law and only consciously
changes the law. More substantively, we would cite the presumption that, following the
common law principles of culpability, liability may not be imposed without fault. The presumptions, too numerous to be here detailed, collectively suggest that there already exists
a seamless web of law, the common law, which may be changed but only as a result of a
conscious act which will be interpreted accordingly as an interference with pre-existing law
and principle and will be interpreted restrictively in its effects. . . .

In effect, legislation is frequently ascribed a secondary role not only because it is seen to
post-date the common law but also because it is not infrequently seen by the judiciary as a
substantively inferior source of law. The common law is historically often represented as a
statement of human reason that has been refined and perfected to such a degree that it is
superior to other forms of law in its content, a view classically expressed by Lord Coke in
Dr Bonham's Case (1610) 8 Co Rep 106. Blackstone, to take a later example, considered the
common law to be the concentrated wisdom of the various peoples who had invaded and
settled in Britain. They had brought with them their own legal system, imposing certain features upon the native system and refining parts of it. The resulting common law represented
a body of law of superior quality. Legislation was therefore to be treated as a technique for
the improvement of this body of law and confined to the extent that it improved the wisdom
of ages rather than abrogating or ignoring that time-hallowed legal wisdom. . . .

The history of the English State machine is important in so far as it represents one of the
oldest and most stable institutional orders in the western world. Its embryonic base is found
to be in operation at least as early as the Norman Conquest of 1066. The administrative
skill of the later Norman and Angevin monarchs created an administrative and adjudicative structure which effectively pervaded all parts of the kingdom and was controlled by a
small elite of centrally based royal administrators. The court system itself was composed of
central courts located at Westminster together with travelling judges who regularly visited
the rest of the kingdom which was for legal purposes divided into assize circuits. This system
was fully operational by the end of the thirteenth century and remained largely intact until
the middle of the nineteenth century. It provided an effective bureaucratic structure which
was capable of producing a coherent body of law based upon the custom of the realm—
common law. Secondly, it provided a system whereby that law could be brought to effect
upon the kingdom as a whole. The small number of royal judges who presided over both
the central courts and the assize courts could effectively control the development of the substantive law, generally claiming to foster the doctrinal values of consistency and coherence
which contributed significantly to the status of the common law. Common law was seen to
represent a rational ordering of the rules governing human behaviour and it was the claim
of the developing class of lawyers to provide a seamless web of regulation. All of these
factors contributed to the ability of the common law to withstand the threat of codification
and to provide an effective resistance to the incursion of piecemeal legislation.

A second important feature of the institutional history is the development of the dichotomy between the legislative and the judicial functions of the sovereign power. The separation of these two functions is a relatively modern and sophisticated development.
Originally the king was the ultimate source of law, be it divine law, the custom of the realm
or the creation of new law. The scale of the operation in practice demanded the delegation
of tasks. In addition, changes in the structure of political power led to the transfer of power
to a variety of administrative institutions. The capacity of the sovereign to declare what
the law was represented the embryonic development of legislation. When the monarch was
the sole source of knowledge as to both common law and new law (legislation), the likelihood of conflict between the two was minimal. Nor did the early delegation of the adjudi-

cative function and the development of the role of the judiciary as the source of knowledge about the content of common law lead to problems, in so far as the judiciary was often intimately involved in the drafting of the new law and retained a close connection with the monarch which facilitated the relationship between legislation and the common law. A final factor in the early relationship was the infrequency of the use of legislation.

With the separation of the judicial and legislative roles of the sovereign the problem of the relative status of the two sources arises. From the time of the Tudor monarchs legislation begins to develop as a major source of new law. For example, in the reign of Henry VIII over 600 statutes were enacted, a number which probably exceeds the total number of statutes passed from the time of the Magna Carta of 1215. The importance of legislation and its incursion upon the field of interest of the common law and the activities of the judiciary at this time is also reflected in case law. For example, in *Dr Bonham's Case* (1610), Lord Coke provides one of the earliest reflections upon the nature of the distinction between the common law and legislation and it is also from this period that one of the earliest rules of statutory interpretation was formulated, the rule in *Heydon's Case* (1584), suggesting the growing importance of statutory law. The importance of legislation and the development of the power of the House of Commons continues throughout the Restoration until the crisis which culminated with the 'Glorious Revolution' of 1688 and led to the enactment of the Bill of Rights which provides a formal statement of the new balance of power within the State, establishing the supremacy of the two Houses of Parliament over the monarch.

The importance of Parliament and the primary status of its legislative statements was consolidated in the political and jurisprudential traditions arising from the seventeenth century through to the nineteenth century in the work of Hobbes, Bentham, Austin and Dicey, works which may generally be characterized as emphasizing the written law of the sovereign institution, Parliament, as the supreme source of law. The impact of the concept of the 'supremacy' of Parliament is to be found increasingly acknowledged in the contemporary decisions of the common-law courts, as for example, in *Edinburgh and Dalkeith Railway v. Wauchope* [1842] 8 Cl & F 710, and in *Lee v. Bude and Torrington Railway* [1971] LR CP 577, 582, where it was acknowledged that although natural equity represented the 'law of laws' or the 'immutable law of nature', the substantive principles of such law stand 'as a warning, rather than [as] authority to be followed. We sit here as servants of the Queen and the legislature. Are we to act as regents over what is done by Parliament with the consent of the Queen, Lords and Commons? I deny that any such authority exists. . . . The proceedings here are judicial not autocratic'; and the judiciary are correspondingly the servants and not the judges of the content of legislation. The effect of this ideological tradition is that in the last instance legislation must supersede all previous law, be it previous enactments or the established common law."

The excerpt from Goodrich illustrates the development of the principle of Parliamentary supremacy, as legislation enacted by Parliament came to have priority both over the common law and earlier inconsistent statutes. The role of the judges, in relation to legislation, thus became *interpretive*, as they applied statute law to cases brought before them. Before we further consider the precise role of judges in relation to statutes, however, it may be useful to review the legislative process itself.

THE LEGISLATIVE PROCESS

Gary Slapper and David Kelly, *The English Legal System* (5th ed., Cavendish, London, 2001), pp.49–62:

"If the institutions of the European Community are sovereign within its boundaries, then within the more limited boundaries of the United Kingdom the sovereign power to make law lies with Parliament. Under United Kingdom constitutional law, it is recognised that Parliament has the power to enact, revoke or alter such, and any, law as it sees fit. Even the Human Rights Act 1998 reaffirms this fact in its recognition of the power of Parliament to make primary legislation that is incompatible with the rights provided under the European Convention on Human Rights. Whether this will remain the case in the future is, however, a moot point. Coupled to this wide power is the convention that no one Parliament can bind its successors in such a way as to limit their absolute legislative powers.

The absolute power is a consequence of the historical struggle between Parliament and the Stuart monarchy in the 17th century. In its struggle with the Crown, Parliament claimed the power of making law as its sole right. In so doing, Parliament curtailed the royal prerogative and limited the monarchy to a purely formal role in the legislative procedure. Prerogative powers still exist and remain important, but are now exercised by the government in the name of the Crown, rather than by the Crown itself. In this struggle for ultimate power, the courts sided with Parliament and, in return, Parliament recognised the independence of the courts from its control.

Although we still refer to our legal system as a common law one and although the courts still have an important role to play in the interpretation of statutes, it has to be recognised that legislation is the predominant method of law-making in contemporary times. It is necessary, therefore, to have a knowledge of the workings of the legislative process.

The pre-parliamentary process

Any consideration of the legislative process must be placed in the context of the political nature of Parliament. Most statutes are the outcome of the policy decisions taken by government and the actual policies pursued will of course depend upon the political persuasion and imperatives of the government of the day. Thus, a great deal of law creation and reform can be seen as the implementation of party political policies. Examples of this type of legal reform are the changes in trade union law, or education law, or the financing of local services introduced by the previous Conservative administrations.

It also has to be recognised that the previous Labour Government, elected in May 1977, introduced considerable constitutional reform as proposed in its manifesto. Thus, the Scottish Parliament and the Welsh Assembly have been instituted and many hereditary peers have been removed from the House of Lords.

As, by convention, the government is drawn from the party controlling a majority in the House of Commons, it can effectively decide what policies it wished to implement and trust to its majority to ensure that its proposals become law. Accusations have been made that, when governments have substantial majorities, they are able to operate without taking into account the consideration of their own party members, let alone the views of opposition members. It is claimed that their control over the day to day procedure of the House of Commons, backed with their majority voting power, effectively reduces the role of Parliament to that of merely rubber-stamping their proposals.

It is certainly true, as the experience of the previous Conservative administration in the United Kingdom demonstrated, that governments with small majorities, if not actually in a minority, have to be circumspect in the policies they pursue through Parliament. The fact that the May 1997 parliamentary elections returned the Labour Party to power, with a much larger majority than even they expected, has raised, once again, the prospect of an over powerful executive forcing its will through a politically quiescent Parliament.

The government generates most of the legislation that finds its way into the statute book, but individual members of Parliament may also propose legislation in the form of Private Members' Bills.

There are in fact three ways in which an individual member of Parliament can propose legislation:

- through the ballot procedure by means of which 20 back-bench members get the right to propose legislation on the 10 or so Fridays in each parliamentary session specifically set aside to consider such proposals;

- under Standing Order 39, which permits any member to present a Bill after the 20 balloted Bills have been presented;

- under Standing Rule 13, the 10-minute rule procedure, which allows a member to make a speech of up to 10 minutes in length in favour of introducing a particular piece of legislation.

Of these procedures, however, only the first has any real chance of success and even then, success will depend on securing a high place in the ballot and on the actual proposal not being too contentious. As examples of this can be cited the Abortion Act 1967, which was introduced as a Private Members' Bill to liberalise the provision of abortion; and the various attempts that have subsequently been made by Private Members' Bills to restrict the original provision. In relation to particular reforms, external pressure groups or interested parties may very often be the original moving force behind them; and, when individual members of Parliament are fortunate enough to find themselves at the top of the ballot for Private Members' Bills, they may well find themselves the focus of attention from such pressure groups proffering pre-packaged law reform proposals in their own particular areas of interest.

The decision as to which Government Bills are to be placed before Parliament in any session is under the effective control of two cabinet committees:

- the *Future Legislation Committee* determines which Bills will be presented to Parliament in the *following* parliamentary session;

- the *Legislation Committee* is responsible for the legislative programme conducted in the *immediate* parliamentary session. It is the responsibility of this committee to draw up the legislative programme announced in the Queen's Speech delivered at the opening of the parliamentary session.

Green Papers are consultation documents issued by the government which set out and invite comments from interested parties on particular proposals for legislation. After considering any response, the government may publish a second document in the form of a White Paper in which it sets out its firm proposals for legislation.

The legislative process

Parliament consists of three distinct elements; the House of Commons, the House of Lords and the Monarch. Before any legislative proposal, known at that stage as a Bill, can become an Act of Parliament it must proceed through and be approved by both Houses of Parliament and must receive the Royal Assent. The ultimate location of power, however, is the House of Commons which has the authority of being a democratically elected institution.

A Bill must be given three readings in both the House of Commons and the House of Lords before it can be presented for the Royal Assent. It is possible to commence the procedure in either House, although Money Bills must be placed before the Commons in the first instance.

When a Bill is introduced in the Commons, it undergoes five distinct procedures:

- *First reading*. This is purely a formal procedure in which its title is read and a date set for its second reading.

- *Second reading*. At this stage, the general principles of the Bill are subject to extensive debate. The second reading is the critical point in the process of a Bill. At the end, a vote may be taken on its merits and, if it is approved, it is likely that it will eventually find a place in the statute book.

- *Committee stage*. After its second reading, the Bill is passed to a standing committee whose job it is to consider the provisions of the Bill in detail, clause by clause. The committee has the power to amend it in such a way as to ensure that it conforms with the general approval given by the House at its second reading.

- *Report stage*. At this point, the standing committee reports the Bill back to the House for consideration of any amendments made during the committee stage.

- *Third reading*. Further debate may take place during this stage, but it is restricted to matters relating to the content of the Bill and questions relating to the general principles of the Bill cannot be raised.

When a Bill has passed all these stages, it is passed to the *House of Lords* for its consideration. After consideration by the Lords, the Bill is passed back to the Commons which must then consider any amendments to the Bill that might have been introduced by the Lords. Where one House refuses to agree to the amendments made by the other, Bills can be repeatedly passed between them but, as Bills must complete their process within the life of a particular parliamentary session, a failure to reach agreement within that period might lead to the total loss of the Bill.

Since the Parliament Acts of 1911 and 1949, the blocking power of the House of Lords has been restricted as follows:

- a 'Money Bill', that is, one containing only financial provisions, can be enacted without the approval of the House of Lords after a delay of one month;

- any other Bill can be delayed by one year by the House of Lords.

The House of Lords, no doubt, has used its reforming and delaying powers to good effect, but its inbuilt Conservative/conservative majority has also been deployed for less than totally praiseworthy campaigns. The latest of these involves the procedure of equalising the age of sexual consent between homosexuals at 16, as it is with heterosexuals. In 1998, the House of Lords managed to avoid an equalisation of the age of consent by threatening the government's major Criminal Justice Bill, subsequently, the Crime and Disorder Act 1998. In order to get the Bill through Parliament before the end of the session, the Home Secretary removed the provision. The Lords maintained its resistance, but gave way when the government stated that it would use the Parliament Acts to ensure that the necessary legislation would be passed, The age of consent was equalised by the Sexual Offences (Amendment) Act 2000. However, the House of Lords was not finished with resisting liberalisation of homosexual rights and forced the government to drop its promise to remove s.28 of the Local Government Act 1988. That section had introduced the requirement that local authorities shall not:

    (a)   intentionally promote homosexuality or publish material with the intention of promoting homosexuality;

(b) promote the teaching in any maintained school of the acceptability of homosexuality as a pretended family relationship.

The section was much resented within the gay and lesbian community and was seen by many as signally illiberal. That it remains on the statute book is due to the efforts of the newly reformed House of Lords.

The Royal Assent is required before any Bill can become law. There is no constitutional rule requiring the monarch to assent to any Act passed by Parliament. There is, however, a convention to that effect; and refusal to grant the Royal Assent to legislation passed by Parliament would place the constitutional position of the monarchy in jeopardy. The procedural nature of the Royal Assent was highlighted by the Royal Assent Act 1967 which reduced the process of acquiring Royal Assent to a formal reading out of the short title of any Act in both Houses of Parliament.

An Act of Parliament comes into effect on the date of the Royal Assent, unless there is any provision to the contrary in the Act itself. It is quite common either for the Act to contain a commencement date for some time in the future, of for it to give the appropriate Secretary of State the power to give effect to its provisions at some future time by issuing statutory instruments. The Secretary of State is not required to bring the provisions into effect and it is not uncommon for some parts of Acts to be repealed before they are ever in force.

The drafting of legislation

In 1975, in response to criticism of the language and style of legislation, the Renton Committee on the Preparation of Legislation examined the form in which legislation was presented. Representations were made to the Committee by a variety of people ranging from the judiciary to the lay public. The Committee divided complaints about statutes into four main headings relating to:

* obscurity of language used;

* over-elaboration of provisions;

* illogicality of structure;

* confusion arising from the amendment of existing provisions.

It was suggested that the drafters of legislation tended to adopt a stylised archaic legalism in their language and employed a grammatical structure that was too complex and convoluted to be clear, certainly to the layperson and even, on occasion, to legal experts. These criticisms, however, have to be considered in the context of the whole process of drafting legislation and weighed against the various other purposes to be achieved by statutes.

The actual drafting of legislation is the work of parliamentary counsel to the Treasury who specialise in this task. The first duty of the drafters must be to give effect to the intention of the department instructing them, and do so in as clear and precise a manner as is possible. These aims, however, have to be achieved under pressure, and sometimes extreme pressure, of time. An insight into the various difficulties faced in drafting legislation was provided by a former parliamentary draftsman, Francis Bennon in an article entitled 'Statute law obscurity and drafting parameters' ((1978) British JLS 235). He listed nine specific parameters which the drafter of legislation had to take into account. These parameters are:

* *Legal effectiveness.* This is the need for the drafters to translate the political wishes of those instructing them into appropriate legal language and form.

- *Procedural legitimacy*. This refers to the fact that the legislation must conform with certain formal requirements if it is to be enacted. For example, it is a requirement that Acts be divided into clauses and Bills not assuming this form would not be considered by Parliament.

- *Timeliness*. This refers the requirement for legislation to be drawn up within particularly pressing time constraints. The effect of such pressure can be poorly drafted and defective provisions.

- *Certainty*. It is of the utmost importance that the law be clearly set down so that individuals can know its scope and effect and can guide their actions within its provisions. The very nature of language, however, tends to act against this desire for certainty. In pursuit of certainty, the temptation is for the person drafting the legislation to produce extremely long and complex sentences, consisting of a series of limiting and refining subclauses. This process, in turn, however, tends merely to increase the obscurity of meaning.

- *Comprehensibility*. Ideally, legislation should be comprehensible to the lay person, but given the complex nature of the situation that the legislature is dealing with such an ideal is probably beyond attainment in practice. Nonetheless, legislative provisions certainly should be open to the comprehension of the members of Parliament who are asked to vote on it and they certainly should not be beyond the comprehension of the legal profession who have to construe it for their clients. Unfortunately, some legislation fails on both these counts.

- *Acceptability*. This refers to the fact that legislation is expected to be couched in uncontentious language and using a traditional prose style.

- *Brevity*. This refers to the fact that legislative provisions should be as short as is compatible with the attainment of the legislative purpose. The search for brevity in legislation can run counter to the wish for certainty in, and acceptability of, the language used.

- *Debatability*. This refers to the fact that legislation is supposed to be structured in such a way as to permit it and the policies that lie behind it to be debated in Parliament.

- *Legal compatibility*. This refers to the need for any new provision to fit in with already existing provisions. Where the new provision alters or repeals existing provisions, it is expected that such effect should be clearly indicated.

A consideration of these various desired characteristics shows that they are not necessarily compatible and indeed some of them, such as the desire for clarity and brevity, may well be contradictory. The point remains that those people charged with the responsibility for drafting legislation should always bear the above factors in mind when producing draft legislation but if one principle is to be pursued above others it is surely the need for clarity of expression and meaning.

Types of legislation

Legislation can be categorised in a number of ways. For example, distinctions can be drawn between:

Public Acts which relate to matters affecting the general public. These can be further subdivided into either government Bills or Private Members' Bills.

Private Acts, on the other hand, relate to the powers and interests of particular individuals or institutions, although the provision of statutory powers to particular institutions can have a major effect on the general public. For example, companies may be given the power to appropriate private property through compulsory purchase orders.

Enabling legislation gives power to a particular person or body to oversee the production of the specific details required for the implementation of the general purposes stated in the parent Act. These specifics are achieved through the enactment of statutory instruments.

Acts of Parliament can also be distinguished on the basis of the function they are designed to carry out. Some are unprecedented and cover new areas of activity previously not governed by legal rules, but other Acts are aimed at rationalising or amending existing legislative provisions.

Consolidating legislation is designed to bring together provisions previously contained in a number of different Acts, without actually altering them, The Companies Act of 1985 is an example of a consolidation Act. It brought together provisions contained in numerous amending Acts which had been introduced since the previous Consolidation Act of 1948.

Codifying legislation seeks not just to bring existing statutory provisions under one Act, but also looks to give statutory expression to common law rules. The classic examples of such legislation are the Partnership Act of 1890 and the Sale of Goods Act 1893, now 1979.

Amending legislation is designed to alter some existing legal provision. Amendment of an existing legislative provision can take two forms:

- a *textual amendment* is one where the new provision substitutes new words for existing ones in a legislative text or introduces completely new words into that text. Altering legislation by means of textual amendment has one major drawback in that the new provisions make very little sense on their own without the contextual reference of the original provision it is designed to alter;

- *non-textual amendments* do not alter the actual wording of the existing text but alter the operation or effect of these words. Non-textual amendments may have more immediate meaning than textual alterations but they too suffer from the problem that because they do not alter the original provisions the two provisions have to be read together to establish the legislative intention.

Neither method of amendment is completely satisfactory, but the Renton Committee on the Preparation of Legislation favoured textual amendments over non-textual amendments.

Delegated legislation

Delegated legislation is of particular importance. Generally speaking, delegated legislation is law made by some person or body to whom Parliament has delegated its general law making power. A validly enacted piece of delegated legislation has the same legal force and effect as the Act of Parliament under which it is enacted but, equally, it only has effect to the extent that its enabling Act authorises it.

The Deregulation and Contracting Out Act (DCOA) 1994 is an example of the wide ranging power that enabling legislation can extend to ministers. The Act gives ministers the authority to amend legislation by means of statutory instruments, where they consider such legislation to impose unnecessary burdens on any trade, business, or profession. Although the DCOA 1994 imposes the requirement that ministers should consult with interested parties to any proposed alteration, it nonetheless gives them extremely wide powers to alter primary legislation without the necessity of having to follow the same procedure as was required to enact that legislation in the first place. For this reason, deregulation orders are subject to a far more rigorous procedure (sometimes referred to as 'super-affirmative') than ordinary statutory instruments.

Apart from the public consultation, they are subject to a two-stage scrutiny by the Deregulation Committee in the House of Commons and the Delegated Powers and Deregulation Committee in the House of Lords. First the minister lays the deregulation proposal before Parliament in the form of a draft order. After 60 days, the Parliamentary Deregulation Committees in both Houses make their first reports. If the reports are favourable, the next stage is for the minister formally to lay a draft order in each House, along with an explanation of any changes made compared to the original proposal. The ability to make changes to the draft order while it is being scrutinised is a major difference between deregulation and ordinary statutory instruments, where no such procedure exists.

The two Deregulation Committees then produce second reports on the draft and both Houses vote on the relevant Committee report. The procedure leading up to the final vote on the order differs in the two Houses. In the Commons, the way in which the draft order is dealt with depends on how the Committee reported. If Committee members voted unanimously to approve the draft order, the motion to approve it is put to the House without debate. If the Committee was divided on the proposal, then there is a debate on the Committee's report before the draft order is voted on. If the Committee recommended against the order, but the minister still wished to pursue it, then he either agrees to amend it or he may table a motion to disagree with the Committee report and then vote on the order itself. This has never happened in practice. In the Lords, following the publication of the Committee's second report, the minister tables a Motion that the House should approve the draft order. There is also the opportunity for a debate if any peer wishes it.

The current order-making power is limited in its scope and has mostly been used for small items. The previous and present government intends extending deregulation and to replace the DCOA with a new Regulatory Reform Act (RRA). There are a number of differences between the proposed new order-making power and the power under the DCOA. Orders under the new power, which are expected to be called regulatory reform orders, will be capable of:

- making and re-enacting statutory provision;

- imposing additional burdens where necessary, provided they are proportionate and they strike a fair balance between the public interest and the interests of those affected by the new burden;

- removing inconsistencies and anomalies in legislation;

- dealing with burdensome situations caused by a lack of statutory provision to do something;

- applying to legislation passed after the Bill if it is at least two years old when the order is made and has not been amended in substance during the last two years;

- relieving burdens from anyone, including ministers and government departments, but not where only they would benefit; and

- allowing administrative and minor detail to be further amended by subordinate provisions orders, subject to negative resolution procedure.

The super-affirmative procedure of the DCOA is maintained and supplemented by an additional test that no order should prevent anyone from exercising an existing right or freedom which they might reasonably expect to continue to exercise (the 'reasonable exceptions' test). Two further stringent tests, proportionality and fair balance, will be applied if an order would impose or increase a burden. Finally, ministers bringing forward regulatory reform orders will be required to present more explanatory information to Parliament than they did with deregulation orders, to reflect the wider powers provided under the proposed RRA.

An example of the effect of the DCOA 1994 may be seen in the Deregulation (Resolutions of Private Companies) Order 1996, which simplifies the procedures which private companies have to comply with in passing resolutions. The effect of this statutory instrument was to introduce new sections into the Companies Act 1985 relaxing the previous provisions in the area in question. A second example is the Deregulation (Model Appeal Provisions) Order 1996, which set out a model structure for appeals against enforcement actions in business disputes.

The output of delegated legislation in any year greatly exceeds the output of Acts of Parliament as may be seen from the 2000 statistics which reveal that although just over 48 general public Acts were passed, no less than 3,499 statutory instruments were made.

In statistical terms, therefore, it is at least arguable that delegated legislation is actually more significant than primary Acts of Parliament.

There are various types of delegated legislation:

- *Orders in Council* permit the government through the Privy Council to make law. The Privy Council is nominally a non-party-political body of eminent parliamentarians but in effect it is simply a means through which the government, in the form of a committee of ministers, can introduce legislation without the need to go through the full parliamentary process. Although it is usual to cite situations of State emergency as exemplifying occasions when the government will resort to the use of Orders in Council, in actual fact, a great number of Acts are brought into operation through Orders in Council. Perhaps the widest scope for Orders in Council is to be found in relation to European Community law, for, under s.2(2) of the European Communities Act 1972, ministers can give effect to provisions of the Community which do not have direct effect.

- *Statutory instruments* are the means through which government ministers introduce particular regulations under powers delegated to them by Parliament in enabling legislation. Examples have already been considered in relation to the DCOA 1994.

- *Bye-laws* are the means through which local authorities and other public bodies can make legally binding rules. Bye-laws may be made by local authorities under such enabling legislation as the Local Government Act 1872.

- *Court Rule Committees* are empowered to make the rules which govern procedure in the particular courts over which they have delegated authority under such Acts as the Supreme Court Act 1981, the County Courts Act 1984 and the Magistrates' Court Act 1980.

- *Professional regulations* governing particular occupations may be given the force of law under provisions delegating legislative authority to certain professional bodies who are empowered to regulate the conduct of their members. An example is the power given to The Law Society, under the Solicitors' Act 1974, to control the conduct of practising solicitors.

Advantages in the use of delegated legislation

The advantages of delegated legislation include:

- *Time saving*
  Delegated legislation can be introduced quickly where necessary in particular cases and permits rules to be changed in response to emergencies or unforeseen problems.
  The use of delegated legislation, however, also saves parliamentary time generally. Given the pressure on debating time in Parliament and the highly detailed nature of typical delegated legislation, not to mention its sheer volume, Parliament would not have time to consider each individual piece of law that is enacted in the form of delegated legislation. It is considered of more benefit for Parliament to spend its time in a thorough consideration of the principles of the enabling Act, leaving the appropriate minister or body to establish the working detail under its authority.

- *Access to particular expertise*
  Related to the first advantage is the fact that the majority of members of Parliament simply do not have sufficient expertise to consider such provisions effectively. Given the highly specialised and extremely technical nature of many of the regulations that are introduced through delegated legislation, it is necessary that those authorised to introduce the legislation should have access to the necessary external expertise required to formulate such regulations. With regard to bye-laws, it practically goes without saying that local and specialist knowledge should give rise to more appropriate rules than reliance on the general enactments of Parliament.

- *Flexibility*
  The use of delegated legislation permits ministers to respond on an *ad hoc* basis to particular problems as and when they arise and provides greater flexibility in the regulation of activity subject to the minister's overview.

Disadvantages in the prevalence of delegated legislation

The disadvantages in the use of delegated legislation include:

- *Accountability*
  A key issue involved in the use of delegated legislation concerns the question of accountability and erosion of the constitutional role of Parliament.
  Parliament is presumed to be the source of legislation, but with respect to delegated legislation, the individual members are not the source of the law. Certain people, notably government ministers and the civil servants who work under them to produce the detailed provisions of delegated legislation, are the real source of such regulations. Even allowing for the fact that they are, in effect, operating on

powers delegated to them from Parliament, it is not beyond questioning whether this procedure does not give them more power than might be thought appropriate, or indeed constitutionally correct, whilst at the same time disempowering and discrediting Parliament as a body.

- *Scrutiny*
  The question of general accountability raises the need for effective scrutiny, but the very form of delegated legislation makes it extremely difficult for ordinary members of Parliament to fully understand what is being enacted and to monitor it effectively. This difficulty arises in part from the tendency for such regulations to be highly specific, detailed and technical. This problem of comprehension and control is compounded by the fact that regulations appear outside the context of their enabling legislation but only have any real meaning in that context.

- *Bulk*
  The problems faced by ordinary members of Parliament in effectively keeping abreast of delegated legislation is further increased by the sheer mass of such legislation. And, if parliamentarians cannot keep up with the flow of delegated legislation, how can the general public be expected to do so?

  These difficulties and potential shortcomings in the use of delegated legislation are, at least to a degree, mitigated by the fact that specific controls have been established to oversee it.

- *Parliamentary control over delegated legislation*
  Power to make delegated legislation is ultimately dependent upon the authority of Parliament and Parliament retains general control of the procedure for enacting such law.

  New regulations in the form of delegated legislation are required to be laid before Parliament. This procedure takes two forms depending on the provision of the enabling legislation. Some regulations require a positive resolution of one or both of the House of Parliament before they become law. Most Acts, however, simply require that regulations made under their auspices be placed before Parliament. They automatically become law after a period of 40 days unless a resolution to annul them is passed.

  The problem with the negative resolution procedure is that it relies on members of Parliament being sufficiently aware of the content, meaning, and effect of the detailed provisions laid before them. Given the nature of such statutory legislation, such reliance is unlikely to prove secure.

  Since 1973, there has been a *Joint Select Committee on Statutory Instruments* whose function it is to consider statutory instruments. This Committee scrutinises statutory instruments from a technical point of view as regards drafting and has no power to question the substantive content or the policy implications of the regulation. Its effectiveness as a general control is therefore limited. European Community legislation is overseen by a specific committee and local authority bye-laws are usually subject to the approval of the Department of the Environment.

- *Judicial control of delegated legislation*
  It is possible for delegated legislation to be challenged, through the procedure of judicial review, on the basis that the person or body to whom Parliament has delegated its authority has acted in a way that exceeds the limited powers delegated to them. Any provision outside this authority is *ultra vires* and is void. Additionally, there is a presumption that any power delegated by Parliament is to be used in a reasonable manner and the courts may on occasion hold particular delegated legislation to be void on the basis that it is unreasonable. . . . an interesting example of this procedure may illuminate the point. In January 1997, the Lord Chancellor raised court fees and, at the same time, restricted the circumstances in which a litigant can be exempted from paying such fees. In March, a Mr John Witham, who previously would have been exempted from paying court fees, successfully challenged the Lord

Chancellor's action. In a judicial review, it was held that Lord Mackay had exceeded the statutory powers given to him by Parliament. One of the judges, Rose LJ, stated that there was nothing to suggest that Parliament ever intended 'a power for the Lord Chancellor to prescribe fees so as to preclude the poor from access to the courts'."

AN INTRODUCTION TO INTERPRETATION

Our primary focus in this chapter is on the *interpretation* of legislation by judges. After a statute successfully completes the Parliamentary process, it enters the statute book and will be implemented by the machinery of the state. However, questions about the scope, meaning, and applicability of legislation to particular factual situations may arise. This is where the judiciary may be called upon, within a legal dispute, to *interpret* the meaning of a statute. This is what we mean by the phrase statutory interpretation. We will see that while it is commonplace to say that the creation of law is the role of Parliament, the function of interpretation leaves the judiciary, in some cases, with a considerable degree of latitude in determining what that legislation *means*. This task often involves highly controversial *choices* which the judiciary is forced to make. Good examples of the problems faced by judges in interpretation are provided by Dworkin.

Ronald Dworkin, *Law's Empire* (Harper Collins, London, 1986), pp.15–23:

Elmer's case

"Elmer murdered his grandfather—he poisoned him—in New York in 1882. He knew that his grandfather's existing will left him the bulk of the estate, and he suspected that the old man, who had recently remarried, would change the will and leave him nothing. Elmer's crime was discovered; he was convicted and sentenced to a term of years in jail. Was he legally entitled to the inheritance his grandfather's last will provided? The residuary legatees under the will, those entitled to inherit if Elmer had died before his grandfather, were the grandfather's daughters. Their first names are not reported, so I will call them Goneril and Regan. They sued the administrator of the will, demanding that the property now go to them instead of Elmer. They argued that since Elmer had murdered the testator, their father, the law entitled Elmer to nothing.

The law pertaining to wills is for the most part set out in special statutes, often called statutes of wills, which stipulate the form a will must take to be considered valid in law: how many and what kinds of witnesses must sign, what the mental state of the testator must be, how a valid will, once executed, may be revoked or changed by the testator, and so forth. The New York statute of wills, like most others in force at that time, said nothing explicit about whether someone named in a will could inherit according to its terms if he had murdered the testator. Elmer's lawyer argued that since the will violated none of the explicit provisions of the statute it was valid, and since Elmer was named in a valid will he must inherit. He said that if the court held for Goneril and Regan, it would be changing the will and substituting its own moral convictions for the law. The judges of the highest court of New York all agreed that their decision must be in accordance with the law. None denied that if the statute of wills, properly interpreted, gave the inheritance to Elmer, they must order the administrator to give it to him. None said that in that case the law must be reformed in the interests of justice. They disagreed about the correct result in the case, but their disagreement—or so it seems from reading the opinions they wrote—was about what the law actually was, about what the statute required when properly read.

How can people who have read the text of a statute in front of them disagree about what it actually means, about what law it has made? We must draw a distinction between two senses of the word 'statute.' It can describe a physical entity of a certain type, a document with words printed on it, the very words congressmen or members of Parliament had in front of them when they voted to enact that document. But it can also be used to describe the law created by enacting that document, which may be a much more complex matter. Consider the difference between a poem conceived as a series of words that can be spoken or written and a poem conceived as the expression of a particular metaphysical theory or point of view. Literary critics all agree about what the poem 'Sailing to Byzantium' is in the first sense. They agree it is the series of words designated as that poem by W.B. Yeats. But they nevertheless disagree about what the poem is in the second sense, about what the poem really says or means. They disagree about how to construct the 'real' poem, the poem in the second sense, from the text, the poem in the first sense.

In much the same way, judges before whom a statute is laid need to construct the 'real' statute—a statement of what difference the statute makes to the legal rights of various people—from the text in the statute book. Just as literary critics need a working theory, or at least a style of interpretation, in order to construct the poem behind the text, so judges need something like a theory of legislation to do this for statutes. This may seem evident when the words in the statute book suffer from some semantic defect; when they are ambiguous or vague, for example. But a theory of legislation is also necessary when these words are, from the linguistic point of view, impeccable. The words of the statute of wills that figured in Elmer's case were neither vague nor ambiguous. The judges disagreed about the impact of these words on the legal rights of Elmer, Goneril, and Regan because they disagreed about how to construct the real statute in the special circumstances of that case.

The dissenting opinion, written by Judge Gray, argued for a theory of legislation more popular then than it is now. This is sometimes called a theory of 'literal' interpretation, though that is not a particularly illuminating description. It proposes that the words of a statute be given what we might better call their acontextual meaning, that is, the meaning we would assign them if we had no special information about the context of their use or the intentions of their author. This method of interpretation requires that no context-dependent and unexpressed qualifications be made to general language, so Judge Gray insisted that the real statute, constructed in the proper way, contained no exceptions for murderers. He voted for Elmer.

Law students reading his opinion now are mostly contemptuous of that way of constructing a statute from a text; they say it is an example of mechanical jurisprudence. But there was nothing mechanical about Judge Gray's argument. There is much to be said (some of which he did say) for his method of constructing a statute, at least in the case of a statute of wills. Testators should know how their wills will be treated when they are no longer alive to offer fresh instructions. Perhaps Elmer's grandfather would have preferred his property to go to Goneril and Regan in the event that Elmer poisoned him. But perhaps not: he might have thought that Elmer, even with murder on his hands, was still a better object for his generosity than his daughters. It might be wiser in the long run for judges to assure testators that the statute of wills will be interpreted in the so-called literal way, so that testators can make any arrangements they wish, confident that their dispositions, however amusing, will be respected. Besides, if Elmer loses his inheritance just because he is a murderer, then that is a further punishment, beyond his term in jail, for his crime. It is an important principle of justice that the punishment for a particular crime must be set out in advance by the legislature and not increased by judges after the crime has been committed. All this (and more) can be said on behalf of Judge Gray's theory about how to read a statute of wills.

Judge Earl, however, writing for the majority, used a very different theory of legislation, which gives the legislators' *intentions* an important influence over the real statute. 'It is a familiar canon of construction,' Earl wrote, 'that a thing which is within the intention of the makers of a statute is as much within the statute as if it were within the letter; and a thing which is within the letter of the statute is not within the statute, unless it be within the intention of the makers.' (Notice how he relies on the distinction between the text, which he calls the 'letter' of the statute, and the real statute, which he calls the 'statute' itself.) It would be absurd, he thought, to suppose that the New York legislators who originally enacted the statute of wills intended murderers to inherit, and for that reason the real statute they enacted did not have that consequence.

We must take some care in stating what Judge Earl meant about the role intention should play in constructing statutes. He did not mean that a statute can have no consequence the legislators did not have in mind. This is plainly too strong as a general rule: no legislator can have in mind all the consequences of any statute he votes for. The New York legislators could not have contemplated that people might bequeath computers, but it would be absurd to conclude that the statute does not cover such bequests. Nor did he mean only that a statute can contain nothing that the legislators intended that it not contain. This seems more plausible, but it is too weak to be of any use in Elmer's case. For it seems likely that the New York legislators did not have the case of murderers in mind at all. They did not intend that murderers inherit, but neither did they intend that they should not. They had no active intention either way. Earl meant to rely on a principle we might call intermediate between these excessively strong and weak principles: he meant that a statute does not have any consequence the legislators would have rejected if they had contemplated it.

Judge Earl did not rely only on this principle about legislative intention; his theory of legislation contained another relevant principle. He said that statutes should be constructed from texts not in historical isolation but against the background of what he called general principles of law: he meant that judges should construct a statute so as to make it conform as closely as possible to principles of justice assumed elsewhere in the law. He offered two reasons. First, it is sensible to assume that legislators have a general and diffuse intention to respect traditional principles of justice unless they clearly indicate the contrary. Second, since a statute forms part of a larger intellectual system, the law as a whole, it should be constructed so as to make that larger system coherent in principle. Earl argued that the law elsewhere respects the principle that no one should profit from his own wrong, so the statute of wills should be read to deny inheritance to someone who has murdered to obtain it.

Judge Earl's views prevailed. They attracted four other judges to his side, while Judge Gray was able to find only one ally. So Elmer did not receive his inheritance. . . .[T]he dispute about Elmer was not about whether judges should follow the law or adjust it in the interests of justice. At least it was not if we take the opinions I described at face value and (as I shall argue later) we have no justification for taking them any other way. It was a dispute about what the law was, about what the real statute the legislators enacted really said.

The Snail Darter case

I now describe a much more recent case, though more briefly, in order to show that this kind of dispute continues to occupy judges. In 1973, during a period of great national concern about conservation, the United States Congress enacted the Endangered Species Act. It empowers the secretary of the interior to designate species that would be endangered, in his opinion, by the destruction of some habitat he considers crucial to its survival and then requires all agencies and departments of the government to take 'such action necessary to insure that actions authorized, funded, or carried out by them do not jeopardize the continued existence of such endangered species.'

A group of conservationists based in Tennessee had been opposing dam construction projects of the Tennessee Valley Authority, not because of any threat to species but because these projects were altering the geography of the area by converting free-flowing streams into narrow, ugly ditches to produce an unneeded increase (or so the conservationists believed) in hydroelectric power. The conservationists discovered that one almost finished TVA dam, costing over one hundred million dollars, would be likely to destroy the only habitat of the snail darter, a three-inch fish of no particular beauty or biological interest or general ecological importance. They persuaded the secretary to designate the snail darter as endangered and brought proceedings to stop the dam from being completed and used.

The authority argued that the statute should not be construed to prevent the completion or operation of any project substantially completed when the secretary made his order. It said the phrase 'actions authorized, funded, or carried out' should be taken to refer to beginning a project, not completing projects begun earlier. It supported its claim by pointing to various acts of Congress, all taken after the secretary had declared that completing the dam would destroy the snail darter, which suggested that Congress wished the dam to be completed notwithstanding that declaration. Congress had specifically authorized funds for continuing the project after the secretary's designation, and various of its committees had specifically and repeatedly declared that they disagreed with the secretary, accepted the authority's interpretation of the statute, and wished the project to continue.

The Supreme Court nevertheless ordered that the dam be halted, in spite of the great waste of public funds. (Congress then enacted a further statute establishing a general procedure for exemption from the act, based on findings by a review board). Chief Justice Warren Burger wrote an opinion for the majority of the justices. He said, in words that recall Judge Gray's opinion in Elmer's case, that when the text is clear the Court has no right to refuse to apply it just because it believes the results silly. Times change, however, and the chief justice's opinion was in one respect very different from Judge Gray's. Burger recognized the relevance of congressional intention to the decision what statute Congress had made. But he did not accept Earl's principle about the *way* in which congressional intention is relevant. He refused to consider the counterfactual test that Earl's analysis made decisive. 'It is not for us,' he said, 'to speculate, much less act, on whether Congress would have altered its stance had the specific events of this case been anticipated.'

Instead he adopted what I called, in discussing Earl's opinion, the excessively weak version of the idea that judges constructing a statute must respect the legislature's intentions. That version comes to this: if the acontextual meaning of the words in the text is clear—if the words 'carry out' would normally include continuing as well as beginning a project—then the Court must assign those words that meaning unless it can be shown that the legislature actually intended the opposite result. The legislative history leading up to the enactment of the Endangered Species Act did not warrant that conclusion, he said, because Congress plainly wanted to give endangered species a high order of protection even at great cost to other social goals, and it is certainly possible, even if not probable, that legislators with that general aim would want the snail darter saved even at the amazing expense of a wasted dam. He rejected the evidence of the later committee reports and the actions of Congress in approving funding for the continuation of the dam, which might have been thought to indicate an actual intention not to sacrifice the dam to this particular species. The committees that had reported in favor of the dam were not the same as the committees that had sponsored the act in the first place, he said, and congressmen often vote on appropriations without fully considering whether the proposed expenditures are legal under past congressional decisions.

Justice Lewis Powell wrote a dissent for himself and one other justice. He said that the majority's decision constructed an absurd real statute from the text of the Endangered Species Act. 'It is not our province,' he said, 'to rectify policy or political judgments by the Legislative Branch, however egregiously they may disserve the public interest. But where the statutory and legislative history, as in this case, need not be construed to reach such a result, I view it as the duty of this Court to adopt a permissible construction that accords with some modicum of common sense and the public weal.' This states yet another theory of legislation, another theory of how the legislature's intentions affect the statute behind the text, and it is very different from Burger's theory. Burger said that the acontextual meaning of the text should be enforced, no matter how odd or absurd the consequences, unless the court discovered strong evidence that Congress actually intended the opposite. Powell said that the courts should accept an absurd result only if they find compelling evidence that it was intended. Burger's theory is Gray's, though in a less rigid form that gives some role to legislative intention. Powell's theory is like Earl's, though in this case it substitutes common sense for the principles of justice found elsewhere in the law.

Once again, if we take the opinions of these two justices at face value, they did not disagree about any historical matters of fact. They did not disagree about the state of mind of the various congressmen who joined in enacting the Endangered Species Act. Both justices assumed that most congressmen had never considered whether the act might be used to halt an expensive dam almost completed. Nor did they disagree over the question of fidelity. Both accepted that the Court should follow the law. They disagreed about the question of law; they disagreed about how judges should decide what law is made by a particular text enacted by Congress when the congressmen had the kind of beliefs and intentions both justices agreed they had in this instance."[1]

The examples outlined by Dworkin raise issues central to statutory interpretation, including whether words can have a "literal" meaning, how the purpose of a statute should be determined, and how the intention of the legislature in enacting statutory language should be discovered. These inquiries are important, for students, lawyers, legal academics and judges spend a good deal of their time determining what statutes mean in particular factual settings. And the first rule for engaging in that task is a simple one: START WITH THE WORDS OF THE STATUTE! After all, statutes operate in a *mandatory* fashion. That is, if the words of a statute clearly do apply to a factual situation, then courts cannot disregard the operation of a statute, given the fundamental principle of the supremacy of Parliament. So too, if the facts do not fall within the terms of the statute, then the statute does not apply. Otherwise, the will of Parliament would again be undermined by an overbroad application by the judiciary. The problem of statutory interpretation arises in the case where the facts are neither clearly within or outside the parameters of the statute. Generally speaking, that uncertainty is a product of the language of the statute—either it is found to be uncertain or vague in its scope and impact.

However, sometimes statutory language may give rise to contested issues of interpretation even when that language *appears* to be perfectly clear, as the following cases demonstrate.

Fisher v Bell [1960] 3 All E.R. 731, QBD.

Lord Parker C.J.:

"This is an appeal by way of Case State by justices for the City and County of Bristol, before whom an information was preferred by the appellant, a chief inspector of police, against the respondent that he on a certain day in a shop unlawfully did offer for sale a knife which was to use ordinary terms, a flick knife, contrary to s.1 of the Restriction of Offensive Weapons Act, 1959. Section 1(1) of the Act provides:

'Any person who manufactures, sells or hires or offers for sale or hire or lends or gives to any other person—(a) any knife which has a blade which opens automatically by hand pressure applied to a button, spring or other device in or attached to the handle of the knife, sometimes known as a "flick knife". . . . shall be guilty of an offence. . . .'

The justices, without deciding whether the knife in question was a knife of the kind described in the statute, decided that the information must be dismissed on the ground that there had not been an offer for sale.

The short facts are these. The respondent keeps a retail shop in Bristol and, in October, 1959, a police constable, walking past the shop, saw in the window, amongst other articles, one of the knives. Behind the knife in the window was a ticket with the words 'Ejector knife —4s.' The police officer went in and informed the respondent that he would be reported for offering for a sale such knife, and the respondent replied: 'Fair enough'.

---

[1] For further reading on *Riggs v Palmer*, see Kenneth S. Abraham, "Statutory Interpretation and Literary Theory: Some Common Concerns of an Unlikely Pair" (1979) 32 *Rutgers Law Review* 676.

The sole question is whether the exhibition of that knife in the window with the ticket constituted an offer for sale within the statute. I think that most lay people would be inclined to the view (as, indeed, I was myself when I first read these papers), that if a knife were displayed in a window like that with a price attached to it, it was nonsense to say that that was not offering it for sale. The knife is there inviting people to buy it, and in ordinary language it is for sale; but any statute must be looked at in the light of the general law of the country, for Parliament must be taken to know the general law. It is clear that, according to the ordinary law of contract, the display of an article with a price on it in a shop window is merely an invitation to treat. It is in no sense an offer for sale the acceptance of which constitutes a contract. That is clearly the general law of the country. Not only is that so, but it is to be observed that, in many statutes and orders which prohibit selling and offering for sale of goods, it is very common, when it is so desired, to insert the words 'offering or exposing for sale', 'exposing for sale' being clearly the words which would cover the display of goods in a shop window. Not, only that, but it appears that under several statutes—we have been referred in particular to the Prices of Goods Act, 1939, and the Goods and Services (Price Control) Act, 1941—Parliament, when it desires to enlarge the ordinary meaning of those words, has a definition section enlarging the ordinary meaning of 'offer for sale' to cover other matters including, be it observed, exposure of goods for sale with the price attached.

In those circumstances I, for my part, though I confess reluctantly, am driven to the conclusion that no offence was here committed. At first sight it appears absurd that knives of this sort may not be manufactured, they may not be sold, they may not be hired, they may not be lent, they may not be given, but apparently they may be displayed in shop windows; but even if this is a *casus omissus*—and I am by no means saying that it is—it is not for this court to supply the omission. . . .

For my part, approaching this matter apart from authority, I find it quite impossible to say that an exhibition of goods in a shop window is itself an offer for sale. We were, however, referred to several cases, one of which is *Keating v Horwood*, a decision of this court. There, a baker's van was being driven on its rounds. There was bread in it that had been ordered and bread in it that was for sale, and it was found that that bread was under weight, contrary to the Sale of Food Order, 1921. That order was an order of the sort to which I have referred already and which prohibited the offering or exposing for sale. In giving his judgment, Lord Hewart, C.J., said:

'The question is whether, on the facts, there were (i) an offering, and (ii) an exposure, for sale. In my opinion there were both.'

Avory, J., agreed. Shearman, J., however, said:

'I am of the same opinion. I am quite clear that this bread was exposed for sale, but have had some doubt whether it can be said to have been offered for sale until a particular loaf was tendered to a particular customer.'

There are three matters to observe on that case. The first is that the order plainly contained the words 'expose for sale', and, on any view, there was in that case an exposing for sale. Therefore, the question whether there was an offer for sale was unnecessary for decision. Secondly, the principles of general contract law were referred to; and thirdly, albeit all part of the second ground, the respondents were not represented and there was, in fact, no argument. For my part, I cannot take that as an authority for the proposition that the display here in a shop window was an offer for sale. . . .

Accordingly, I have come to the conclusion in this case that the justices were right, and this appeal must be dismissed.

Ashworth, J.: I agree.

Elwes, J.: I also agree.

Appeal dismissed."

Smith v Hughes [1960] 1 W.L.R. 830, QBD.

Lord Parker C.J.:
"These are six appeals by way of case stated by one of the stipendiary magistrates sitting at Bow Street, before whom informations were preferred by police officers against the defendants, in each case that she 'being a common prostitute, did solicit in a street for the purposes of prostitution, contrary to section 1(1) of the Street Offences Act, 1959.' The magistrate in each case found that the defendant was a common prostitute, that she had solicited and that the solicitation was in a street, and in each case fined the defendant.

The facts, to all intents and purposes, raise the same point in each case; there are minute differences. The defendants in each case were not themselves physically in the street but were in a house adjoining the street. In one case the defendant was on a balcony and she attracted the attention of men in the street by tapping and calling down to them. In other cases the defendants were in ground-floor windows, either closed or half open, and in another case in a first-floor window.

The sole question here is whether in those circumstances each defendant was soliciting in a street or public place. The words of section 1(1) of the Act of 1959 are in this form: 'It shall be an offence for a common prostitute to loiter or solicit in a street or public place for the purpose of prostitution.' Observe that it does not say there specifically that the person who is doing the soliciting must be in the street. Equally, it does not say that it is enough if the person who receives the solicitation or to whom it is addressed is in the street. For my part, I approach the matter by considering what is the mischief aimed at by this Act. Everybody knows that this was an Act intended to clean up the streets, to enable people to walk along the streets without being molested or solicited by common prostitutes. Viewed in that way, it can matter little whether the prostitute is soliciting while in the street or is standing in a doorway or on a balcony, or at a window, or whether the window is shut or open or half open; in each case her solicitation is projected to and addressed to somebody walking in the street. For my part, I am content to base my decision on that ground and that ground alone. I think the magistrate came to a correct conclusion in each case, and that these appeals should be dismissed."

[Hilbery J. and Donovan J. agreed].

NOTES AND QUESTIONS

- In *Smith v Hughes*, Lord Parker, having found the language of the statute to be ambiguous, turned to a consideration of the statute's purpose in order to determine whether it applied to the conduct of the defendants. But can one criticise Lord Parker on the basis that, even though that may have been the intention of the legislature, it is not what the legislature actually wrote in the statutory provision? Should a defendant be found guilty of a criminal offence on the basis that an ambiguity in a statute is resolved against her? As we will see shortly, the judiciary often claims that "penal statutes" (those which punish the individual for his or her acts) should be construed "narrowly". This means that ambiguities are resolved in favour of the individual. Why do you think that "rule" of interpretation was not applied in *Smith v Hughes*?

- Why does it appear that the rule *was* applied in *Fisher v Bell*? Why does one defendant get the benefit of the presumption while the other does not?

The issue of prostitution in the criminal law has given rise to other questions of statutory interpretation, one of which involved the meaning of "common prostitute".

R. v McFarlane [1994] 2 All E.R. 283, CA.

Lord Taylor of Gosforth C.J.:
"Delivered the following judgment of the court. On December 16, 1991 in the Crown Court at Knightsbridge, the appellant was convicted of living on the earnings of prostitution. He was sentenced to four months' imprisonment. This appeal involves a point of law as to the meaning of prostitution which surprisingly has not been the subject of judicial decision with any finality prior to this.

The appellant lived as man and wife with Miss Josephs who, on the judge's ruling, was a prostitute. She maintained she was not a prostitute but a clipper—one who offers sexual services for reward and pockets the reward in advance never intending to provide the service. She said that she engaged in this occupation four or five nights a month, earning up to £400 on a good night. There was evidence, and it was accepted by the appellant and Miss Josephs, that he lived at least partly on her earnings in that they shared their living expenses. The main issue in the case was whether he was thus living on the earnings of prostitution knowingly. The prosecution pointed to the fact that he had lived with her for eleven years, the past five of which she had on her own account been engaged on this business. It was pointed out that he must have been aware of the pattern of her life, the fact that she had more money than could be accounted for by the £50 a week job as a cloakroom attendant which she said she told him she did.

Further, on 16 January 1990 the appellant was seen taking Miss Josephs and her sister into the court at Bow Street where they both appeared on charges of loitering for the purposes of prostitution. There was also evidence from two police officers who kept observation on the appellant between 29 January and 6 February 1991. Those observations tended to show that he assisted her in her occupation. At 10 pm on 30 January he drove Miss Josephs in his car to the West End of London. Later that night, in the same area, Miss Josephs offered one of the police officers sexual intercourse for £40 (which of course was not accepted). On 4 February the appellant drove Miss Josephs to Rupert Street and left her there. In Wardour Street she offered the other officer in the case sexual intercourse for £40. He too did not accept it. At 11.30 pm on 5 February the appellant drove Miss Josephs to the top end of Rupert Street and left her there. He met her an hour later in Shaftesbury Avenue. She took something from her shoe which she gave to the appellant. At 10.15 pm on 6 February the appellant again drove Miss Josephs to the same area and waited in the car in Rupert Street. At 10.40 pm she went off with someone in a taxi, returning to the appellant an hour later. Whether or not that was an occasion of 'clipping' or the real thing is a matter which we need not consider in any depth.

The defence case was that the appellant knew nothing of Miss Joseph's activities. She gave evidence that she told him she worked as a cloakroom girl and also behind the bar at a club. She kept her real occupation secret from him. She used to go out to make it look as if she was at the job which she told him she did. She told him the money for items she bought for the home came from her mother. As regards the attendance at Bow Street Magistrates' Court, the appellant said that he had not stayed for the hearing, and Miss Josephs told him that it concerned a deception charge of which she was acquitted. As regards the observation evidence, essentially the appellant and Miss Josephs, together with her sister, challenged the evidence of observations, maintaining that it was all lies.

A submission was made to the learned judge that acting as a clipper did not amount to acting as a prostitute. Although at that stage counsel both for the prosecution and the defence supported that view, the learned judge rejected it. When the appeal came on before another constitution of this court, counsel then appearing for the Crown (not counsel who has appeared for the Crown today) again supported the appellant's submission that the learned judge's ruling was wrong. However, the court itself took the view that the matter should be fully argued, saying: 'There was a substantial argument in favour of the view taken by the trial judge.' It is most convenient therefore to deal first with what the learned judge said both in giving his ruling and in directing the jury. In his ruling he said:

> 'The question of whether someone offering themselves, but intending—and it has to be intending—firmly never, ever to make good that offer—it has to go that far—it has never, so far as I can see, been adjudicated upon. My view is that the indications in the textbooks—and I have looked at *Blackstone's Criminal Practice* and it is not so obvious, but again it speaks of offering—the dictionary, and decided cases say that as soon as you are offering yourself for lewdness for reward, you are indulging in prostitution and that is how I propose to direct the jury.'

When it came to the summing up, the learned judge said this to the jury:

> 'She has told you she is not a prostitute, she is a clipper. But, a prostitute is a person who offers her body for lewdness for reward. Put in slightly more 'with it' words, such as Sarah Tuckey [that is the sister] used, 'offers sexual services'. I am bound to say that I prefer the directness of the old Anglo-Saxon, but there it is. Miss Josephs said, 'Yes, I do offer sexual services, but I do not mean to make that offer good.' And she suggests to you that for that reason she is not a prostitute. But, members of the jury, she has made the offer. It is at that point that she is a prostitute. The fact that the offer is bogus, rather than genuine, if it was, is neither here nor there. There are not two categories—a clipper and a prostitute. There are prostitutes who are honest and prostitutes who are dishonest. Miss Josephs tells you that she is a dishonest prostitute. But she is a prostitute, members of the jury.'

The issue on this appeal is whether, as a matter of law, the judge was correct to rule and direct the jury that a woman who offers herself for sexual services, takes the money and fails to provide the services, is engaging in prostitution within the meaning of s.30 of the Sexual Offences Act 1956. Section 30, so far as is relevant, provides as follows:

> '(1) It is an offence for a man knowingly to live wholly or in part on the earnings of prostitution . . .'

Mr Carne for the appellant submits that to be a prostitute a woman must not only offer sexual services, but must provide them, or be prepared to do so. For the Crown, Mr Carter-Manning Q.C. submits the essence of the offence is the offer of the sexual services in return for reward.

The word 'prostitute' and 'prostitution' are not defined in any statute. Our attention was drawn to dictionary definitions and to three decided cases. *The Concise Oxford Dictionary* defines a prostitute as: 'A woman who offers her body to promiscuous sexual intercourse esp. For payment . . .'. *The Shorter Oxford English Dictionary* defines a prostitute as: 'A woman who is devoted, or (usu.) [who] offers her body to indiscriminate sexual intercourse, esp. for hire; a common harlot . . .'. Mr Carne points to the definition of 'offer' in *The Shorter Oxford English Dictionary*, and to one meaning given there: 'To give, make presentation of . . . To tender for acceptance or refusal . . .'. However, another meaning within the same dictionary is: 'To make the proposal, suggest . . . To propose, or express one's willingness (to do something), conditionally on the assent of the person addressed.' . . ."

[Lord Taylor then considered the relevant case law on the definition of prostitution, and concluded:]

> "In our judgment both the dictionary definitions and the cases show that the crucial feature in defining prostitution is the making of an offer of sexual services for reward. Mr Carne submits that the true offence here was not one of living off immoral earnings, and that the woman in question, Miss Josephs, was not acting by way of prostitution. She was acting dishonestly and she could have been proceeded against, he submits, for obtaining money by false pretences. It may be that the appellant could have been proceeded against for conspiring with

her to do so, or of aiding and abetting her. But it is submitted that the offence of living off immoral earnings is not made out. Mr Carne also submits that the mischief against which s.30 of the Sexual Offences Act 1956 is directed is the exploitation of women. Here, the appellant was not exploiting Miss Josephs sexually, only dishonestly. . . .

We have no doubt that the ruling of the learned judge was both robust and correct (to adopt the phrase used by Mr Carter-Manning in his submission). For a man to live off the earnings of a woman who offers sexual services, takes the money and then reneges on the offer, if she does, is in our view to live off the earnings of prostitution, or, as it used to be termed, immoral earnings. Indeed, most people would consider such earnings doubly immoral. This appeal is dismissed."

NOTES AND QUESTIONS

- Does the Court of Appeal's definition of prostitution accord with a "common sense" understanding of the term? Would most people agree that the essence of prostitution is the offer of sexual services for compensation? The accused was convicted of the offence which is commonly known as being a "pimp". What evidence was there that he was a pimp? Is living with someone who sells sexual services sufficient to constitute living off the earnings of prostitution?

- The appellant in this case argued that he should have been charged with a different offence, namely, aiding and abetting the offence of obtaining money by false pretences, or conspiracy to do so. Why do you think the appellant was not charged with that offence? Finally, this case also involves a "penal statute", again raising the question why an apparent ambiguity was not resolved in favour of an accused, in accordance with the "rule" that penal statutes should be strictly construed.

- There are numerous cases which have considered the statutory language of the Street Offences Act 1959. For a good overview and discussion of the way in which the judiciary has developed a gendered interpretation of the law, see Alison Diduck and William Wilson, "Prostitutes and Persons" (1997) 24 Journal of Law and Society 504.

- Can a man be a "common prostitute"? For the answer, see *DPP v Bull* [1994] 4 All E.R. 411, QB.

Although judges will rarely admit that the process of statutory interpretation is "political", in the sense of involving important *choices* concerning social issues of widespread concern, judges are sometimes required to make such decisions. Moreover, the language which judges use is often itself highly politically charged. A "classic" example is the judgment of Lord Denning M.R. in *Royal College of Nursing v DHSS*. The case concerned the interpretation of the Abortion Act 1967. Pay close attention to the language which Lord Denning uses to describe the termination of a pregnancy.

Royal College of Nursing of the United Kingdom v Department of Health and Social Security [1981] 1 All E.R. 545, QBD, CA & HL.

Lord Denning M.R.:

"Abortion is a controversial subject. The question for us today is this: when a pregnancy is terminated by medical induction, who should do the actual act of termination? Should it be done by a doctor? Or can he leave it to the nurses? The Royal College of Nursing say that the doctor should do the actual act himself and not leave it to the nurses. The Department of Health take a different view. They say that a doctor can initiate the process and then go off and do other things, so long as he is 'on call'. The controversy is so acute that it has come before us for decision.

Throughout the discussion I am going to speak of the unborn child. The old common lawyers spoke of a child *en ventre sa mère*. Doctors speak of it as the fetus. In simple English it is an unborn child inside the mother's womb. Such a child was protected by the criminal law almost to the same extent as a new-born baby. If anyone terminated the pregnancy, and thus destroyed the unborn child, he or she was guilty of a felony and was liable to be kept in penal servitude for life (see the Offences against the Person Act 1861), unless it was done to save the life of the mother. Likewise anyone who assisted or participated in the abortion was guilty, including the mother herself. I have tried several cases of 'back-street abortions', where the mother died or was made seriously ill. I have passed severe sentences of imprisonment for the offence.

The Abortion Act 1967

The approach to the subject was revolutionised by the Abortion Act 1967. It legalised abortion if it was done so as to avoid risk to the mother's health, physical or mental. This has been interpreted by some medical practitioners so loosely that abortion has become obtainable virtually on demand. Whenever a woman has an unwanted pregnancy, there are doctors who will say it involves a risk to her mental health. But the Act contains some safeguards. It provided that, in order for the abortion to be lawful, it was subject to three conditions. (1) The woman had to get two doctors to give a certificate. (2) The abortion had to be done in hospital. (3) The pregnancy had to be 'terminated by a registered medical practitioner'. It is this last condition which comes up for consideration today. It arises because of the advance in medical science.

The material words of the 1967 Act, in s.1(1), are that '. . . a person shall not be guilty of an offence under the law relating to abortion when a pregnancy is terminated by a registered medical practitioner . . .'

At the time that the Act was passed, and for five years afterwards, there was no difficulty of interpretation. All abortions then, at any rate when the mother was three months pregnant or more, were done by surgical methods. The knife with the cutting edge was operated by a registered medical practitioner. He used it to remove the unborn child. The knife was never handled by a nurse. She was not a registered medical practitioner.

Medical induction

Since 1972 a new method has been used. It is called medical induction. It does not involve a knife. It started quite simply in ordinary full-time births, so as to induce labour a few hours early, to save the mother the stress of waiting, or for the convenience of doctors and staff. But it is now becoming much used to effect abortions, when the mother is pregnant for three months or more. It is done by pumping a chemical fluid into the mother's womb. It is called prostaglandin. This fluid so affects the muscles and shape of the mother's inside that it forces her into labour prematurely, so that the unborn child is expelled from the body, usually dead, but sometimes at the point of death.

There are two distinct stages in this process. The first stage is done by a doctor, a registered medical practitioner. The mother is taken from the ward to the operating theatre. She is given a general anaesthetic. The doctor inserts a fine catheter into her body so as to reach a particular part of her womb. But no fluid is pumped into her at that stage. She is then taken back to the ward. She is left there until she recovers from the anaesthetic. The doctor writes out a few notes telling the nurse what to do. He then goes off, saying, 'Give me a call if there is any difficulty'.

The second stage is done by the nurses. When the mother comes round from the anaesthetic, they get a flexible tube and connect up the catheter to a pump which is electrically driven; or to a dripping device. They then get the special fluid called prostaglandin. They have to see that it is of the right concentration. They have it in a bottle, and pump the fluid into the woman's body. They have to regulate the dose and control the intake, by speed and amount, as occasion requires. If need be, they have to get another bottle. They have to watch the woman and note her reactions; and take such steps as occasion requires. Labour is induced. The unborn child is expelled from the woman's body. The process make take 18 hours, or even up to 30 hours. If the unborn child is not expelled by that time, the process is stopped. The child is allowed to live on, to await normal delivery later.

Here I would stop for a moment to point out that the first stage (done by the doctor) does nothing to terminate the pregnancy. The insertion of the catheter is only a preparatory act. It is the second stage (done by the nurses) which terminates the pregnancy. There is an agreed statement of facts which shows that the causative factor is the administration of prostaglandin. . . .

The Royal College's objection

I can quite understand that many nurses dislike having anything to do with these abortions. It is a soul-destroying task. The nurses are young women who are dedicated by their profession and training to do all they can to preserve life. Yet here they are called on to destroy it. It is true that the statute gives them an escape clause. They can refuse to participate in any treatment to which they have a 'conscientious objection': see s.4 of the 1967 Act. But the report of Dame Elizabeth Lane and her colleagues (Report of the Committee on the Working of the Abortion Act) shows that many nurses do not take advantage of this 'escape clause': because it means that other nurses will have to do this heart-rending task; and they feel it may be held against them by their superiors. So they take part in it, much against their will.

It is against this background that the Royal College of Nursing ask the question: is it lawful for nurses to be called on to terminate pregnancy in this way? The Royal College say No, it is not lawful; it is not a nurse's job to terminate a pregnancy. The Department of Health and Social Security say Yes, it is lawful. They have issued a circular in which they presume to lay down the law for the whole of the medical profession. They say that it is no offence if the pregnancy is terminated by a suitably qualified person in accordance with the written instructions of a registered medical practitioner. This is the wording of the circular:

> 'However, the Secretary of State is advised that the termination can properly be said to have been terminated by the registered medical practitioner provided it is decided upon by him, initiated by him, and that he remains throughout responsible for its overall conduct and control in the sense that any actions needed to bring it to conclusion are done by appropriately skilled staff acting on his specific instructions but *not necessarily in his presence.*'

Note those words 'not necessarily in his presence'. They are crucial.

The interpretation of the 1967 Act

The lawfulness depends on the true interpretation of the statute; but, before going into it, I would say a word or two about the approach to it.

(i)   Abortion is a subject on which many people feel strongly. In both directions. Many are for it. Many against it. Some object to it as the destruction of life. Others favour it as the right of the woman. Emotions run so high on both sides that I feel that we as judges must go by the very words of the statute, without stretching it one way or the other, and writing nothing in which is not there.

(ii) Another thing to remember is that the statute is directed to the medical profession, to the doctors and nurses who have to implement it. It is they who have to read it and to act on it. They will read it, not as lawyers, but as laymen. So we should interpret it as they would.

(iii) If there should ever be a case in the courts, the decision would ultimately be that of a jury. Suppose that during the process the mother died or became seriously ill, owing to the nurse's negligence in administering the wrong chemical fluid, and the nurse was prosecuted under the 1861 Act for unlawfully administering to her a noxious thing or using other means with intent to procure her miscarriage. The nurse would have no defence unless the pregnancy was 'terminated by a registered medical practitioner'. Those are simple English words which should be left to a jury to apply, without the judge attempting to put his own gloss on them. I should expect the jury to say that the pregnancy was not terminated by a registered medical practitioner but by a nurse.

(iv) If in such a case there were a claim for damages, the nurse might not be covered by insurance because she would not be engaged in 'nursing professional services acceptable to the Royal College of Nursing'.

(v)   Statutes can be divided into two categories. In the first category Parliament has expressly said 'by a registered medical practitioner or by a person acting in accordance with the directions of any such practitioner', or words to that effect. In the second category Parliament has deliberately confined it: '*by* a fully registered medical practitioner' omitting any such words as 'or by his direction'. This statute is in the second category.

(vi) Woolf J. tested the statute by supposing that a registered medical practitioner performed an abortion operated on a woman whom he believed to be pregnant but who was not so in fact. The 1967 Act would give him no defence to a charge under the 1861 Act.[2] That is such a fanciful instance that I do not think it throws any light on the true construction of this statute.

(vii) The Solicitor General emphasised the word 'treatment' in ss.1(3), 3(1)(a) and (c) and 4(1). He suggested that s.1(1) should be read as if it said that a person should not be guilty of an offence 'when the treatment (for termination of a pregnancy) is by a registered medical practitioner'. He submitted that, whenever the registered medical practitioner did what the Department of Health advised, it satisfied the statute, because the treatment, being initiated by him and done under his instructions, was 'by' him. I cannot accept this interpretation. I think the word 'treatment' in those sections means 'the actual act of terminating the pregnancy'. When the medical induction method is used, this means the continuous act of administering prostaglandin from the moment it is started until the unborn child is expelled from the mother's body. This continuous act must be done by the doctor personally. It is not sufficient that it is done by a nurse when he is not present.

Conclusion

Stress was laid by the Solicitor General on the effect of this ruling. The process of medical induction can take from 18 to 30 hours. No doctor can be expected to be present all that time. He must leave it to the nurses: or not use the method at all. If he is not allowed to

---

[2] Woolf J., the trial judge in this case, was making the point that this anomaly would result from a narrow interpretation of the 1967 Act, from which he concluded that overly narrow interpretations should be eschewed.

leave it to the nurses, the result will be either that there will be fewer abortions or that the doctor will have to use the surgical method with its extra hazards. This may be so. But I do not think this warrants us departing from the statute. The Royal College of Nursing have advised their nurses that under the statute they should not themselves terminate a pregnancy. If the doctor advises it, he should do it himself, and not call on the nurses to do it.

I think that the Royal College are quite right. If the Department of Health want the nurses to terminate a pregnancy, the Minister should go to Parliament and get the statute altered. He should ask them to amend it by adding the words 'or by a suitably qualified person in accordance with the written instructions of a registered medical practitioner'. I doubt whether Parliament would accept the amendment. It is too controversial. At any rate, that is the way to amend the law and not by means of a departmental circular.

I would allow the appeal accordingly."

[Brightman L.J. and Sir George Baker delivered separate reasons, allowing the appeal].

The case was then appealed to the House of Lords. The Law Lords divided 3:2, and the majority allowed the appeal from the Court of Appeal, restoring the original judgment of Woolf J. The analysis offered by Lord Diplock is in sharp contrast with that of Lord Denning.

Lord Diplock:
". . . Subsection (1) although it is expressed to apply only 'when a pregnancy is terminated by a registered medical practitioner' . . . also appears to contemplate treatment that is in the nature of a team effort and to extend its protection to all those who play a part in it. The exoneration from guilt is not confined to the registered medical practitioner by whom a pregnancy is terminated, it extends to any person who takes part in the treatment for its termination.

What limitation on this exoneration is imposed by the qualifying phrase, 'when a pregnancy is terminated by a registered medical practitioner'? In my opinion, in the context of the Act, what it requires is that a registered medical practitioner, whom I will refer to as a doctor, should accept responsibility for all stages of the treatment for the termination of the pregnancy. The particular method to be used should be decided by the doctor in charge of the treatment for termination of the pregnancy; he should carry out any physical acts, forming part of the treatment, that in accordance with accepted medical practice are done only by qualified medical practitioners, and should give specific instructions as to the carrying out of such parts of the treatment as in accordance with accepted medical practice are carried out by nurses or other members of the hospital staff without medical qualifications. To each of them, the doctor, or his substitute, should be available to be consulted or called on for assistance from beginning to end of the treatment. In other words, the doctor need not do everything with his own hands; the requirements of the subsection are satisfied when the treatment for termination of a pregnancy is one prescribed by a registered medical practitioner carried out in accordance with his directions and of which a registered medical practitioner remains in charge throughout."

NOTES AND QUESTIONS

- Give examples, drawn from Lord Denning's judgment, where the language which he uses to describe abortion mirrors that which is often used by anti-abortion campaigners. What alternative phrases and sentences could have been employed to convey the ideas which he expressed, but which would be less inflammatory?

- What evidence does Lord Denning provide for his assertion that abortion "on demand" is now available in the United Kingdom because of the willingness of doctors to certify that a woman's health is endangered by the continuation of her pregnancy? Is this part of the judgment relevant to the issue before the Court?

- In his judgment at trial, Woolf J. made clear that the position of the Royal College of Nursing was "neutral" towards the issue in this case, but that they merely sought clarification of the law. Does Lord Denning portray their position in that way?

- Is Lord Diplock's analysis of the termination procedure as the work of a team of medical personnel more convincing than Lord Denning's analysis of the potential liability of nurses for carrying out their duties?

The decision of the House of Lords in *Royal College of Nursing v DHSS* might seem a victory for the right of women to have safe, medical abortions. However, the decision can be read as more complex in its political meanings.

Sally Sheldon, *Beyond Control: Medical Power and Abortion Law* (Pluto Press, London, 1997), pp.97–98:

"This case is notable for several reasons. Perhaps its most striking feature is the extent to which those judges who found for the DHSS are prepared to stretch an interpretation of the terms of the Abortion Act in order to reach an acceptable decision. The decision which the House of Lords eventually comes to is the common-sense verdict and no doubt accords with 'the obvious intention of the Act', yet it is one that is squared with the actual wording of the statute only with great difficulty. When the doctor's actual involvement in the termination is limited to the insertion of the catheter—an act preparatory to the administration of the postaglandins which cause the uterus to contract and expel the foetus—it involves a rather creative interpretation to see the doctor as terminating the pregnancy rather than the nursing staff who do everything else. Explicitly underlying this decision is a refusal to interfere with 'good medical practice'.

. . . Whilst nurses are hereby authorised to carry out certain actions in this kind of termination, they can still do so only under the control of the doctor who retains the ultimate responsibility for the operation. This strict hierarchy of the relationship between doctors and nurses is thus reproduced in the legal assessment and the doctors' monopoly over the performance of abortions is reasserted. . . .

The *RCN* case demonstrates again how the reluctance of law to interfere with medical discretion and good medical practice can benefit women by protecting the provision of abortion services. It also emphasises, however, how this goes hand in hand with an entrenchment of doctors' control over such services."

METHODS OF STATUTORY INTERPRETATION

No consideration of statutory analysis would be complete without some mention of the so-called "rules" of statutory interpretation: the literal rule; the golden rule; and the mischief rule. Most lawyers today would readily concede that these approaches to interpretation have been misnamed as "rules", for they provide at best guidance to different judicial approaches. Alternatively, they are merely justifications for decisions which have been reached by judges on other, unarticulated grounds. As Goodrich explains, the rules of interpretation also reflect different approaches to the judicial process itself.

Peter Goodrich, *Reading the Law* (Blackwell, Oxford, 1986), pp.54–57:

"On numerous occasions judges, during the course of giving judgment in a dispute, have taken the opportunity to make statements as to how they approach the task of interpretation, not only to justify their own conclusions as to the meaning of statutory provisions under consideration, but also to provide models of behaviour for others to follow. The content and the taxonomy of the techniques is a reflection of many of the matters relating to the relationship between the legislature and the judiciary and the distinction between the written law and unwritten law discussed earlier. The methods of interpretation embody a vast collection of frequently overlapping and on occasion conflicting rules, principles and presumptions which have accumulated over several centuries.

The general approach which is said to be the primary method of common-law statutory interpretation is usually referred to as the literal approach. The classic statement of this technique is found in *The Queen v Judge of the City of London Court* [1892] 1 QB 273: 'If the words of an Act are clear, you must follow them, even though they lead to a manifest absurdity. The Court has nothing to do with the question whether the legislature has committed an absurdity.' The literal approach demands that the court apply the ordinary, natural meaning of the words used . . . .

An adaptation of this first approach is often referred to as the Golden Rule. Its concern is to provide an alternative approach in the face of an absurdity resulting from the literal interpretation. The rule, however, is inadequate in that it provides little guidance as to how interpretation is to proceed beyond the conclusion of absurdity. The classic exposition of the rule is to be found in *River Wear Commissioners v Adamson* [1877] 2 AC 743, where Lord Blackburn stated:

'But it is to be borne in mind that the office of the Judge is not to legislate, but to declare the expressed intention of the legislature even if that expressed intention appeared to the court to be injudicious; and I believe that it is not disputed that what Lord Wensleydale used to call the Golden rule is right viz. That we are to take the whole statute together and construe it all together, giving the words their ordinary significance unless when so applied they produce an inconsistency or an absurdity or inconvenience so great as to convince the court that the intention could not have been to use them in their ordinary signification and to justify the court in putting on them some other significance which though less proper is one which the court thinks the words will bear.' (763)

The third and oldest statement relating to techniques of interpretation is found in the rule known as the Mischief Rule or the Rule in *Heydon's Case* [1584] 3 Co Rep 7. This rule emphasizes the interrelationship between the status quo prior to the legislation and the objectives of the new law: 'four things are to be discussed and considered: 1. What was the common law before the making of the Act; 2. What was the mischief and defect for which the common law did not provide; 3. What remedy the Parliament hath resolved and appointed to cure the disease of the commonwealth; and 4. The true reason for the remedy.' In following this line of approach the ultimate objective is to interpret the law in such a fashion that the objectives of the enactment are realized.

Finally, a technique which is reminiscent of the rule in *Heydon's Case* is referred to as the *purposive approach*. It embodies the general ethos of the previous method in that it stresses the need to interpret the enactment in such a way that the objectives (purposes) of the statute are realized. It differs from Heydon's formulation in that it does not locate the approach purely in the context of the common law, nor does it confine objectives to their historical origin though this may be one source of information about the objectives. In *Royal College of Nursing v DHSS* [1981] AC 800, Lord Diplock discusses the interrelationship of approaches with respect to the interpretation of the Abortion Act 1967: 'whatever may be the technical imperfections of its draftsmanship, however, its purpose in my view becomes clear if one starts by considering what was the state of the law relating to abortion before the passing of the Act, what was the mischief that required amendment, and in what respect was the existing law unclear'. The historical, social and economic aspects to abortion were then examined as well as the more obvious features of its moral and legal history to the conclusion that 'the wording and the structure of the section are far from elegant, but the policy of the Act, it seems to me, is clear. There are two aspects to it: the first is to broaden the grounds upon which abortions may be lawfully obtained; the second is to ensure that the abortion is carried out with all proper skill and in hygienic conditions.'

The relative importance of these styles of interpretation is itself a source of considerable controversy which raises the theoretical and substantive issues about the role of the judge, the law-making dimension of interpretation and the threat this poses to the abstract supremacy of written law. The controversy can be reduced, for present purposes, to two positions which have both a descriptive and a prescriptive quality. The first represents the judge as a passive actor in the process of interpretation, merely giving the words of the Act their natural meaning and applying that meaning to the situation in the dispute. It stresses a mechanical representation of interpretation, emphasizing the impartiality involved in adjudication. The model is most sympathetic to the adoption of the literalist style of interpretation. The second model rejects the notion that this can be the only role-model for a judge. This model represents the judge as a party who necessarily undertakes an active role in the task of interpretation. Whilst the judge is not a completely free agent, this model stresses the role of the judge as an active participant in the process of creating legal meaning and the need for the judge to resort to the whole range of resources within the legal culture which may lead variously to references to social policy, economics, and other broad-ranging administrative and political considerations of the 'consequences' of the rules to be applied. This model suggests a dynamic role for the judiciary. It is most sympathetic to those techniques of interpretation which seek to realize the purpose and objectives of legislation, the Mischief Rule and the purposive style of interpretation in particular. The first model, on the other hand, provides no threat to the law-making role of the legislature, as the judge is the passive servant merely reading the written law and applying it. The second model potentially threatens the superiority of the written law in that the judge may be seen as a law-maker with the capacity to change or even to undermine the supremacy of the written law by resorting to sources and materials outside the statutory provision, and thereby threatening its status.

Judicial observations on the merits and demerits of the various styles of role-model are numerous. One of the most quoted examples is found in a confrontation between Lord Denning when in the Court of Appeal and Viscount Simonds in the House of Lords in the case of *Magor and St Mellons Rural District Council v Newport District Council* [1952] AC 189. A more recent example of the controversy, and one which provides a clearer expression of the political considerations which underpin the debate is to be found in the judgment of Lord Diplock in *Duport Steels Ltd v Sirs and Others* [1980] 1 WLR 142:

> 'When Parliament legislates to remedy what the majority of its members at the time perceive to be a defect or a lacuna in the law (whether it be written law enacted by existing statutes or the unwritten common law as it has been expounded by the judges in decided cases), the role of the judiciary is confined to ascertaining from the words that Parliament has approved as expressing its intention, what the intention was, and to giving effect to it. Where the meaning of the statutory words is plain and unambiguous it is not for the judge to invent fancied ambiguities as an excuse for failing to give effect to its plain meaning because they themselves consider that the consequences of doing so would be inexpedient or even unjust or immoral.'

A statute passed to remedy what is perceived by Parliament to be a defect in the existing law may in actual operation turn out to have injurious consequences that Parliament did not anticipate at the time the statute was passed. . . . [I]t is for Parliament, not for the judiciary, to decide whether any changes should be made to the law as stated in the Acts . . .

It endangers continued public confidence in the political impartiality of the judiciary, which is essential to the continuance of the rule of law, if judges, under the guise of interpretation, provide their own preferred amendments to statutes which experience of their operation has shown to have had consequences that members of the court before whom the matter comes consider to be injurious to the public interest."

First year law students frequently assume that the three "rules" of statutory interpretation are just that; and that courts mechanically choose between them to resolve issues of statutory interpretation. This is not the way in which courts approach their task. As Lord Reid explained: "They are not rules in the ordinary sense of having some binding force. They are our servants not our masters. They are aids to construction, presumptions or pointers. Not infrequently one 'rule' points in one direction, another in a different direction. In each case we must look at all relevant circumstances and decide as a matter of judgment what weight to attach to any particular 'rule.'"[3] In that same case, Lord Simon of Glaisdale outlined an approach to interpretation which sought to synthesise the various rules, and which provides a useful description of the way in which courts go about the task of statutory interpretation:

"It is sometimes put that, in statutes dealing with ordinary people in their everyday lives, the language is presumed to be used in its primary ordinary sense, unless this stultifies the purpose of the statute, or otherwise produces some injustice, absurdity, anomaly or contradiction, in which case some secondary ordinary sense may be preferred, so as to obviate the injustice, absurdity, anomaly or contradiction, or fulfil the purpose of the statute: while, in statutes dealing with technical matters, words which are capable of both bearing an ordinary meaning and being terms of art.in the technical matter of the legislation will presumptively bear their primary meaning as such terms of art.(or, if they must necessarily be modified, some secondary meaning as terms of art). . . .

But, in fact, these two statutory situations—dealing with ordinary people in their everyday lives, on the one hand, and dealing with technical branches of the law, on the other—are only two extreme situations. Statutory language, like all language, is capable of an almost infinite gradation of 'register'—*i.e.* it will be used at the semantic level appropriate to the subject-matter and to the audience addressed (the man in the street, lawyers, merchants, etc). It is the duty of a court of construction to tune in to such register and so to interpret the statutory language as to give to it the primary meaning which is appropriate in that register (unless it is clear that some other meaning must be given in order to carry out the statutory purpose or to avoid injustice, anomaly, absurdity or contradiction). In other words, statutory language must always be given presumptively the most natural and ordinary meaning which is appropriate in the circumstances.

It is essential that this 'golden' rule is adhered to. An English court of construction must put itself in the place of the draftsman, and ascertain the meaning of the words used in the light of all the circumstances known by the draftsman—especially the 'mischief' which is the subject-matter of the statutory remedy."[4]

The determination of the "natural and ordinary meaning" of legislation may be a controversial task.[5] Note, for example, the contrasting views with respect to what constitutes "using" personal data.

---

[3] *Maunsell v Olins* [1975] 1 All E.R. 16 at 18, HL.
[4] *ibid.* at 25–26.
[5] For further reading on "ordinary meaning", see Robert S. Summers and Geoffrey Marshall, "The Argument from Ordinary Meaning in Statutory Interpretation" (1992) 42 N.I.L.Q. 213.

R. v Brown [1996] 1 All E.R. 545, HL.

Lord Goff of Chieveley:

"My Lords, the defendant, Gregory Michael Brown, was charged with offences under the Data Protection Act 1984, *viz.* that on two occasions he used personal data held within the memory of the police national computer for a purpose other than the purpose described in the relevant entry in the register, contrary to s.5(2)(b), (3) and (5) of the Act. In the case of the first offence (count 1) he was convicted of an attempt. In the case of the second (count 2) he was convicted of the full offence. His convictions were quashed on appeal, and the prosecution now appeal to your Lordships' House. The appeals raises the question of the meaning of the word 'use' in s.5(2)(b). To explain how the question has arisen, it is necessary first to set out briefly the simple facts of the case, and the outcome of the trial; and then to examine the relevant provisions of the Act in order to ascertain the meaning of the word 'use' in its statutory context.

The facts of the cases

The defendant was formerly a police constable in the Kent Constabulary. The Chief Constable of Kent is a registered data user for the purposes of the Act. His agents, of which the defendant was one, were entitled to make use of the data stored in the database of the police national computer for the registered purpose of policing.

The defendant was friendly with a Mr English, who set up a debt collection business under the name of Capital Investigations Ltd. On two occasions the defendant made use of the police national computer to check the registration numbers of vehicles owned by debtors of clients of Capital Investigations. These checks were effected by him through other officers who operated the computer on his behalf.

In the case of the first vehicle (the subject of count 1) the search did not reveal any personal data as defined by the Act, because the vehicle was owned by a company. In the case of the second vehicle (the subject of count 2) the search did reveal personal data; but there was no evidence that the defendant, or indeed any person, subsequently made any use of the information so obtained. The judge directed the jury that, in the case of count 1, the defendant could only be guilty of an attempt. The essence of the defendant's defence was that he made his inquiries legitimately for the purposes of policing, and that it was a coincidence that the vehicles were also of interest to Capital Investigations. The jury convicted the defendant of an attempt under count 1, and of the full offence under count 2. It is therefore plain that they rejected his defence. The defendant was fined £500 on each count, and ordered to pay £1,750 towards the prosecution costs.

The 1984 Act

The Act is a substantial and elaborate statute, but for present purposes the essential provisions are the following. At the centre of the Act is Pt II, which provides for the registration and supervision of data users. A data user is a person who holds data (s 1(5)). 'Data' is defined in s.1(2) as—

'information recorded in a form in which it can be processed by equipment operating automatically in response to instructions given for that purpose.'

In other words, data may be broadly described as information recorded in computer readable form. 'Personal data' is 'data consisting of information which relates to a living individual who can be identified from that information' (s.1(3)). A data user must not hold personal data unless there is an entry in respect of him in the register (s.5(1)). Certain restrictions are placed upon such a person; these are set out in s.5(2). By s.5(3), a servant or agent of a person so registered is subject to the same restrictions as that person. By s.5(5) any person who knowingly or recklessly contravenes any of the provisions of s.5(2) shall be guilty of an offence.

The restrictions under s.5(2) are:

'A person in respect of whom such an entry is contained in the register shall not—(a) hold personal data of any description other than that specified in the entry; (b) hold any such data, or use any such data held by him, for any purpose other than the purpose or purposes described in the entry; (c) obtain such data, or information to be contained in such data, to be held by him from any source which is not described in the entry; (d) disclose such data held by him to any person who is not described in the entry; or (e) directly or indirectly transfer such data held by him in any country or territory outside the United Kingdom other than one named or described in the entry.'

The defendant, as the servant or agent of the Chief Constable of Kent (who was a data user so registered), was charged with two offences of using personal data for an improper purpose contrary to s.5(2)(b).

The question in the case

Now the only action taken by the defendant in relation to the relevant data was that he caused another police officer to operate the computer and so caused the information which constituted the data to be displayed on a screen. The defendant then read the information so displayed, and observed what it consisted of, but took no other action in relation to it. The question is whether by so acting he used the data, contrary to s.5(2)(b). . . .

The true construction of the Act

I approach the matter as follows. I accept that, since the word 'use' is not defined in the Act, it must be given its natural and ordinary meaning. Synonyms of the verb 'use' are to 'make use of' or to 'employ for a purpose'. Here the word is used in relation to 'data', and data means information recorded in a computer-readable form. I must confess that at first sight I would not have thought that simply retrieving such information from the database in which it is stored, so that it appeared on a screen or a print out and could therefore be read by a human being, could properly be described as 'using' the information so recorded. Of course, the computer would be used to retrieve it; but the retrieval of the information would not of itself be 'using' the information so retrieved. It would simply be transferring the information into a different form. This to my mind underlines the fact that the definition of data as information in a computer-readable form does not mean that such information is only data while it is so recorded. It means rather that, if information is so recorded, it becomes data for the purposes of the Act; and if such information from that source is thereafter made use of it is used within the meaning of the Act. So if for example a police constable with the Kent Constabulary operates the police computer to retrieve personal data from the database so that he becomes aware of its contents, and then proceeds to make use of that information, he uses the personal data within the meaning of the statute. In such a case, the retrieval is not the use; it is simply a prerequisite of the use. Moreover, if the police officer, who is the servant or agent of the data user (the chief constable) knowingly or recklessly puts the information to an improper use, he will be guilty of an offence under the Act. This may occur not only where the police officer retrieves the personal data from the database and then puts the information to an improper use, but also where, for example, he improperly makes use of personal data which has come to his knowledge when he operated the police computer innocently on a previous occasion, or where the data has been communicated to him by a colleague who had innocently operated the computer. . . .

It seems to me that the above reading of the statute accords not only with the natural and ordinary meaning of the word 'use' in its statutory context, but also with the statutory purpose of protecting personal data from improper use (or disclosure). It is a startling fact that, if the construction urged upon your Lordships by the prosecution were correct, a police officer who idly operated the police computer, retrieving personal data onto the screen without putting it to any use, would not merely be subject to disciplinary action (where appropriate) but would be guilty of a criminal offence; whereas another police officer who learned from a colleague of certain information constituting personal data stored in the database of the police computer and then, knowing of its source, used the information for business purposes, would not. This surely cannot be the statutory intention; indeed if it were so, it could give rise to justifiable concern on the part of individuals who are the subject of personal data. Strange results such as these would, in my opinion, be avoided if the relevant words in the statute were given their natural and ordinary meaning. If that had been done in the present case, the defendant would have been charged not with the full offence of using personal data, but with an attempt to do so. If the defendant had been so charged, the jury would have had to consider whether, on the evidence before them, the defendant's actions coupled with his state of mind showed that he was committing no more than acts preparatory for the commission of an offence, for example if he was just finding out whether there was information available which might be of use to him in assisting Capital Investigations in their debt-collecting business; or whether he had embarked on the commission of the offence of using personal data for an improper purpose because, when he caused his colleague to operate the computer to reveal the information about the owners of the two vehicles in question, he had a firm intention to put that information to an improper use if it proved to be useful for that purpose. In the latter circumstances the case would, as I see it, have been little different from that of a man who puts his hand in another man's pocket with an intention to steal anything he finds inside; even if he finds nothing, he will nevertheless be guilty of an attempt to steal. . . ."

Lord Griffiths (dissenting):

". . . Whilst I have found this to be a difficult question I have come to the conclusion that 'use' should be given a broad construction as otherwise the purpose of the Act will not be achieved, there will be a serious lacuna in the protection it provides, and there will be difficulties in its enforcement. . . .

It is not straining the meaning of language to say that a person is using the information stored in a computer if he informs himself of its contents. Whether or not he then goes on to apply the information for a particular purpose, and to use it in that sense, will depend on the value of the information to him: but whether or not he applies the information does not alter the fact that he has wrongly invaded the privacy of the individual, and now has the information available to apply at any time in the future.

Once information has entered the public domain it is impractical to attempt to place any restraints on its use or further dissemination. The Act therefore concentrates its protective provisions in s.5 upon the conduct of those who hold or have access to personal data, in an attempt to ensure that they do not abuse the data, and confine it to the proper purpose for which it is required.

The purpose of the offences created by s.5 of the Act is clearly to protect the integrity and security of the data. A servant or agent of the holder of data is guilty of an offence if he uses data for any purpose not described in the register, if he discloses it to any person not described in the register, if he obtains it from a source not described in the register, and if he transfers it to a territory outside the United Kingdom not described in the register. So what would be the position of a police officer who deliberately falsified personal data held in the computer? He undoubtedly processed the data within the meaning of s.1(7); but if he was not 'using' the data by processing it he committed no offence. I cannot believe that in the Data Protection Act it was intended that wrongful interference with the data by those with access to it should not be an offence. But such is the result if 'use' is given the limited meaning adopted by the Court of Appeal.

This police officer had no business to be reading the personal data on the police computer for debt-collecting purposes, and I see no hardship in adopting a construction of the section that creates an offence if he does so. If on the other hand an obligation is laid on the prosecution to prove not only that illegitimate access to the information in the computer was obtained, but also how that information was subsequently applied I can see great practical difficulties in the enforcement of the Act and the protection of personal data that the convention and the Act intended to achieve."

[Lord Hoffmann delivered separate reasons which were substantially in agreement with those of Lord Goff. Lord Browne-Wilkinson concurred with Lord Hoffmann. Lord Jauncey of Tullichettle concurred with Lord Griffiths in dissent.]

QUESTIONS

- How would you classify the judgments in *R. v Brown* in terms of Goodrich's two models of judicial interpretation?

- Do you think there is an "ordinary and natural meaning" to the word "use" which is of assistance in interpreting this statute?

If judges approach the task of interpretation through a determination of the "ordinary" meaning of words, then the question remains where that ordinary meaning is to be found. Parliament has enacted the Interpretation Act, which provides very limited assistance in the interpretation of a narrow range of terms. But, in most cases, the judiciary is left to turn to more mundane sources in order to determine meaning. An obvious place to turn is the dictionary and, for better or worse, it is a source which is sometimes relied upon.

R. v Fulling [1987] Q.B. 426, CA.

Lord Lane C.J.:
"On 6 August 1986 in the Crown Court at Leeds before his Honour Judge Hurwitz and a jury the appellant was convicted by a majority verdict of ten to two of obtaining property by deception. She faced a further similar count, the trial of which was adjourned. No sentence has yet been passed. She appeals against conviction by leave of the single judge.

The facts which gave rise to the charge were these. In September 1981 the appellant claimed some £5,665 from her insurers in respect of what she claimed was a burglary at her flat in Leeds. The insurance company in July 1982 paid her £5,212 in settlement of the claim.

Many months later a man called Turnpenny, an acknowledged criminal, gave to the police a mass of information about the activities of other criminals, which resulted in a large number of people being arrested, among them being the appellant. Turnpenny gave evidence that the appellant had told him that her 'burglary' was bogus, that a man called Maddon had committed it and that she knew the whereabouts of the stolen property. She gave him to understand that the idea of the bogus burglary had been initiated by one Drewery, with whom the appellant had been living and with whom she was infatuated. Turnpenny conceded that he had good reasons for wishing to harm Drewery.

As a result of this information the appellant was arrested in the early hours of Friday, 12 July 1985. Drewery was arrested at the same time. She was interviewed twice on that day, but exercised her right to say nothing despite persistent questioning by the police. She was interviewed again on the following day, Saturday. The interview was split into two, with a break in between, according to the police of 50 minutes, according to her of about 5 or 10 minutes.

The police witnesses described how, after initially refusing to answer questions, her attitude started to change. One of the officers, Det Sgt Beech, said:

'Q. You've obviously got a lot on your mind, are you finding it difficult?

A. Yes.

Q. Would I be right in saying that you want to talk about this but every bone in your body is telling you you shouldn't?

A. Something like that.'

Then came the break already described.

When the interview was resumed, in answer to questions from the officer she admitted a number of offences. Amongst them was the setting up of the bogus burglary: 'I approached a man in a pub because I was short of money and asked him if he would break in for me.' She admitted obtaining money from her insurers. She said that she had spent some of it on a holiday for herself and Drewery. She expressed her sorrow at having committed the offences and said she felt relieved that she had confessed. She sought, it should be added, to exculpate Drewery.

Thus there were two legs to the prosecution case. Turnpenny's evidence and the police account of her confession. The only corroboration of the former was the latter. The prosecution concede that if the confession goes, then the appeal should be allowed. They would not seek to rely on Turnpenny's uncorroborated evidence.

The only issue in the appeal is whether or not the confession was properly admitted. A submission was made to the judge that the confession should be ruled inadmissible by virtue of the provisions of s.76 of the Police and Criminal Evidence Act 1984, which provides as follows:

'(1) In any proceedings a confession made by an accused person may be given in evidence against him in so far as it is relevant to any matter in issue in the proceedings and is not excluded by the court in pursuance of this section.

(2) If, in any proceedings where the prosecution proposes to give in evidence a confession made by an accused person, it is represented to the court that the confession was or may have been obtained—(a) by oppression of the person who made it; or (b) in consequence of anything said or done which was likely, in the circumstances existing at the time, to render unreliable any confession which might be made by him in consequence thereof, the court shall not allow the confession to be given in evidence against him except in so far as the prosecution proves to the court beyond reasonable doubt that the confession (notwithstanding that it may be true) was not obtained as aforesaid.'

It was represented to the judge that the confession was or might have been obtained by oppression of the appellant within the meaning of sub-s (2)(a).

The appellant's evidence on the voir dire as to her reason for making the confession was this. After the break in the final interview one of the police officers, Det Con Holliday, told her that Drewery, her lover, had been having for the last three years or so an affair with a woman called Christine Judge. Now Christine Judge was one of the many people who had been arrested as a result of Turnpenny's disclosures. She was in the next cell to the appellant and, said the appellant, Det Con Holliday told her so. These revelations, said the appellant, so distressed her that she 'just couldn't stand being in the cells any longer'. Then later in her evidence she said: 'As soon as the matter about Christine came out, Det Con Holliday left the room and my head was swimming. I felt numb and after a while I said to Det Sgt Beech, "Is it true?" and he said, "Ronnie shouldn't have said that, he gets a bit carried away. Look Ruth, why don't you make a statement?"'.

She said that she knew Drewery had in 1982 had an affair with a woman called Christine. She had before the interview noticed that the cell next door to hers had the name Christine Judge on its door, but said she did not realise that this was the same Christine until the police told her. After she had made her confession she had shouted to Christine to ask her if what the police told her was true. Up to that point she said she was not particularly expressing her distress, but once she had spoken to Christine she just cried and cried. Later in cross-examination she said, 'I agreed to a statement being taken, it was the only way I was going to be released from the cells', but she conceded that she was not suggesting that she had been offered bail in return for a statement. The officers denied that they had made to her any such revelation as she suggested.

The basis of the submission to the judge was that the information given to her by the police about Christine amounted to oppression, and that the confession was, or might have been, obtained thereby, and that the prosecution had failed to discharge the burden of proving beyond a reasonable doubt that the confession was not so obtained.

In his ruling on the matter the judge declined to make any express finding of fact as to whether the appellant or the police were correct in their account of events. He was prepared to assume for the purposes of argument that the appellant's version of events was the true one and to judge the matter on that basis. That is the subject of criticism by counsel for the appellant, but we think he has no proper ground for complaint on that score.

The material part of the ruling runs as follows:

'Bearing in mind that whatever happens to a person who is arrested and questioned is by its very nature oppressive, I am quite satisfied that in s.76(2)(a) of the Police and Criminal Evidence Act 1984, the word oppression means something above and beyond that which is inherently oppressive in police custody and must import some impropriety, some oppression actively applied in an improper manner by the police. I do not find that what was done in this case can be so defined and, in those circumstances, I am satisfied that oppression cannot be made out on the evidence I have heard in the context required by the statutory provision. I go on to add simply this, that I have not addressed my mind as to whether or not I believe the police or the defendant on this issue because my ruling is based exclusively on the basis that, even if I wholly believed the defendant, I do not regard oppression as having been made out. In those circumstances, her confession (if that is the proper term for it), the interview in which she confessed, I rule to be admissible.'

Counsel for the appellant has drawn our attention to a number of authorities on the meaning of 'oppression'. Sachs L.J. in *R. v. Priestly* (1967) 51 Cr App R 1 said:

'. . . to my mind this word [oppression] in the context of the principles under consideration imports something which tends to sap, and has sapped, that free will which must exist before a confession is voluntary . . . the courts are not concerned with ascertaining the precise motive of a particular statement. The question before them is whether the prosecution have shown the statement to be voluntary, whatever the motive may be, and that is always the point to which all arguments must return. To solve it, the court has to look to the questions which I have already mentioned. First, was there in fact something which could properly be styled or might well be oppression? Secondly, did whatever happened in the way of oppression or likely oppression induce the statement in question?'

R. v. Prager [1972] 1 All ER 1114, [1972] 1 WLR 260 was another decision on para (e) of the introduction to the Judges' Rules 1964 (see *Practice Note* [1964] 1 All ER 237, [1964] 1 WLR 152), which required that a statement by the defendant before being admitted in evidence must be proved to be 'voluntary' in the sense that it has not been obtained by fear of prejudice or hope of advantage or by oppression. In the judgment of the court, delivered by Edmund Davies L.J., appears the following passage ([1972] 1 All ER 1114 at 1119, [1972] 1 WLR 260 at 266):

'As we have already indicated, the criticism directed in the present case against the police is that their interrogation constituted "oppression". This word appeared for the first time in the Judges' Rules 1964, and it closely followed the observation of Lord Parker CJ in *Callis v Gunn* [1963] 3 All ER 677 at 680, [1964] 1 QB 495 at 501 condemning confessions "obtained in an oppressive manner" . . . In an address to the Bentham Club in 1968 (see 21 CLP 10), Lord MacDermott described "oppressive questioning" as—"questioning which by its nature, duration or other attendant circumstances (including the fact of custody) excites hopes (such as the hope of release) or fears, or so affects the mind of the

subject that his will crumbles and he speaks when otherwise he would have stayed silent."
We adopt these definitions or descriptions . . .'

DPP v. Ping Lin [1975] 3 All ER 175, [1976] AC 574 was again a case in which the question was whether a statement by the defendant was shown to be voluntary. It was held that a trial judge faced by the problem should approach the task in a commonsense way and should ask himself whether the prosecution had proved that the contested statement was voluntary in the sense that it was not obtained by fear of prejudice or hope of advantage excited or held out by a person in authority. Lord Wilberforce, Lord Morris and Lord Hailsham expressed the opinion that it is not necessary, before a statement is held to be inadmissible because not shown to have been voluntary, that it should be thought or held that there was impropriety in the conduct of the person to whom the statement was made. What has to be considered is whether a statement is shown to have been voluntary rather than one brought about in one of the ways referred to.

Finally counsel for the appellant referred us to a judgment of this court in *R. v. Rennie* [1982] 1 All ER 385, [1982] 1 WLR 64.

Counsel for the appellant submits to us that on the strength of those decisions the basis of the judge's ruling was wrong, in particular when he held that the word 'oppression' means something above and beyond that which is inherently oppressive in police custody and must import some impropriety, some oppression actively applied in an improper manner by the police. It is submitted that that flies in the face of the opinions of their Lordships in *DPP v. Ping Lin*.

The point is one of statutory construction. The wording of the 1984 Act does not follow the wording of earlier rules or decisions, nor is it expressed to be a consolidating Act, nor yet to be declaratory of the common law. The title runs as follows:

'An Act to make further provision in relation to the powers and duties of the police, persons in police detention, criminal evidence, police discipline and complaints against the police; to provide for arrangements for obtaining the views of the community on policing and for a rank of deputy chief constable; to amend the law relating to the Police Federations and Police Forces and Police Cadets in Scotland; and for connected purposes.'

It is a codifying Act, and therefore the principles set out in *Bank of England v. Vagliano Bros* [1891] AC 107 at 144–145, [1891–4] All ER Rep 93 at 113 apply. Lord Herschell, having pointed out that the Bills of Exchange Act 1882 which was under consideration was intended to be a codifying Act, said:

'I think that the proper course is in the first instance to examine the language of the statute and to ask what is its natural meaning, uninfluenced by any considerations derived from the previous state of the law, and not to start with inquiring how the law previously stood, and then, assuming that it was probably intended to leave it unaltered, to see if the words of the enactment will bear an interpretation in conformity with this view. If a statute, intended to embody in a code a particular branch of the law, is to be treated in this fashion, it appears to me that its utility will be almost entirely destroyed, and the very object with which it was enacted will be frustrated. The purpose of such a statute surely was that on any point specifically dealt with by it, the law should be ascertained by interpreting the language used instead of, as before, by roaming over a vast number of authorities in order to discover what the law was, extracting it by a minute examination of the prior decisions, dependent upon a knowledge of the exact effect even of an obsolete proceeding such as a demurrer to evidence.'

Such observations are to be found in *Bristol Tramways Carriage Co. Ltd v Fiat Motors Ltd* [1910] 2 KB 831 at 836 *per* Cozens-Hardy M.R.

Section 76(2) of the 1984 Act distinguishes between two different ways in which a confession may be rendered inadmissible: first, where it has been obtained by oppression (para (a)); second, where it has been made in consequence of anything said or done which was likely in the circumstances to render unreliable any confession which might be made by the defendant in consequence thereof (para (b)). Paragraph (b) is wider than the old formulation, namely that the confession must be shown to be voluntary in the sense that it was not obtained by fear of prejudice or hope of advantage, excited or held out by a person in authority. It is wide enough to cover some of the circumstances which under the earlier rule were embraced by what seems to us to be the artificially wide definition of oppression approved in *R. v. Prager* [1972] 1 All ER 1114, [1972] 1 WLR 260.

This in turn leads us to believe that 'oppression' in s.76(2)(a) should be given its ordinary dictionary meaning. *The Oxford English Dictionary* as its third definition of the word runs as follows: 'Exercise of authority or power in a burdensome, harsh, or wrongful manner; unjust or cruel treatment of subjects, inferiors, etc.; the imposition of unreasonable or unjust burdens.' One of the quotations given under that paragraph runs as follows: 'There is not a word in our language which expresses more detestable wickedness than *oppression*.'

We find it hard to envisage any circumstances in which such oppression would not entail some impropriety on the part of the interrogator. We do not think that the judge was wrong in using that test. What however is abundantly clear is that a confession may be invalidated under s.76(2)(b) where there is no suspicion of impropriety. No reliance was placed on the words of s.76(2)(b) either before the judge at trial or before this court. Even if there had been such reliance, we do not consider that the policeman's remark was likely to make unreliable any confession of the appellant's own criminal activities, and she expressly exonerated (or tried to exonerate) her unfaithful lover.

In those circumstances, in the judgment of this court, the judge was correct to reject the submission made to him under s.76 of the 1984 Act. The appeal is accordingly dismissed."

NOTES AND QUESTIONS

- Although it provides a good illustration of how judges sometimes turn to dictionaries in order to discern the ordinary meaning of words, the *Fulling* case is now rather dated in terms of its relevance to policing. By virtue of s.34 of the Criminal Justice and Public Order Act 1994, if a defendant, during questioning, fails to mention a fact which he wishes to rely on in his defence and it is a fact which he could reasonably have been expected to mention, then a court or jury may draw "such inferences from the failure as appear proper". By virtue of s.35, an accused must be told that if he or she refuses to be sworn at trial, or to answer questions, then an adverse inference may be drawn from silence by a jury. See Fiona Cownie and Anthony Bradney, *English Legal System in Context* (2nd ed., Butterworths, London, 2000), pp.282–283.

- Why did the problem of statutory interpretation arise in the case?

- What choices of interpretation were open to the Court?

- What arguments did the Court use to justify the interpretation it adopted?

- What arguments could have been used to support other possible interpretations?

- Did you agree with the interpretation adopted by the Court? Give reasons for your point of view.

- Redraft the statutory provision so as to avoid the problem which arose in the case.

- What are your views on the policy merits of the statutory provision?

CASE BRIEFING EXERCISE

- Making a case brief is an essential legal skill. It is not the quantity of cases or the length of judgments that you read that matters, but rather the quality of your reading and note taking. It is important to read cases *actively*, noting key material facts, the principles on which the case was decided, and important policy considerations.

- Write a case brief of *R v Fulling* in no more than 250 words. In your summary you should set out (with headings) the material facts, the legal issue in dispute, the reasoning of the judge, the result reached, and your view on the significance of the case. The *Fulling* case has not been edited from its original form, so as to give you experience with reading a case exactly as it was written by the judge.

THE DISTINCTION BETWEEN FACT AND LAW

The distinction between questions of fact and law has been described as "one of the most vexed questions in the whole topic of legal classification".[6] It is an issue of particular importance in administrative law because a decision of an administrative body is more easily challengeable on judicial review if it is characterised as an issue of law rather than fact. The assumption is that the tribunal is in the best position to make determinations on questions of fact, but that the role of courts is to ensure that questions of law have been properly decided by the original decision maker. The classic statement of the distinction between "fact" and "law" was provided by Denning L.J.:

> "It is important to distinguish between primary facts and the conclusions from them. Primary facts are facts which are observed by witnesses and proved by oral testimony or facts proved by the production of a thing itself, such as original documents. Their determination is essentially a question of fact for the tribunal of fact, and the only question of law that can arise on them is whether there was any evidence to support the finding. The conclusions from primary facts are, however, inferences deduced by a process of reasoning from them. If, and in so far as, those conclusions can as well be drawn by a layman (properly instructed on the law) as a lawyer, they are conclusions of fact for the tribunal of fact: and the only questions of law which can arise on them are whether there was a proper direction in point of law; and whether the conclusion is one which could reasonably be drawn from the primary facts. . . . If, and in so far, however, as the correct conclusion to be drawn from primary facts requires, for its correctness, determination by a trained lawyer—as, for instance, because it involves the interpretation of documents or because the law on the point cannot properly be understood or applied except by a trained lawyer—the conclusion is a conclusion of law."[7]

The distinction between questions of fact and law has proven important in the context of the interpretation of statutes. Is the interpretation of a word or phrase in

---

[6] Ian McLeod, *Legal Method* (4th ed., Macmillan, Basingstoke, 2002), p.33.
[7] *British Launderers' Association v Central Middlesex Assessment Committee and Hendon Rating Authority* [1949] 1 All E.R. 21 at 25–26.

a statute a question of fact (and therefore a matter primarily for the determination of the original decision maker) or a question of law (and, as a consequence, readily open to review by a judicial body on appeal or judicial review)? The law in this area is far from clear, but a succinct explanation of the law/fact distinction has been provided by Vandevelde.

Kenneth J. Vandevelde, *Thinking Like a Lawyer* (Westview Press, Boulder, 1996), pp.11–12:

"Because there are only three things to be decided in a dispute, there are only three types of issues that can arise in legal reasoning. These are issues of fact, issues of law, and issues requiring application of law to fact.

Issues of fact all pose essentially the same basic question: What is the situation to which the law must be applied? In other words, what events have occurred to create the dispute?

Issues of law also pose essentially one basic question: What are the rules of law governing this situation?

Issues requiring the application of law to fact similarly pose one general question: What rights or duties exist between the parties under the governing law in this situation? These issues are sometimes called mixed questions of law and fact.

A single dispute may present all three types of issues or any combination of them. For example, assume that a man sues a physician claiming that she was negligent in failing to administer a particular diagnostic test to him and that, as a result, he sustained injuries three years later that would have been preventable had his disease been diagnosed earlier.

The physician may put at issue some of the plaintiff's factual allegations. She may raise as issues of fact two questions: Would the diagnostic test actually have revealed that the patient was suffering from the disease? Would the disease have been less injurious had it been discovered earlier?

The parties may also disagree on the applicable law. For example, the physician may raise this question as an issue of law: Does the statute of limitations for negligence claims against a medical practitioner require the claims to be filed within two years of the time the negligence *occurred* or within two years of the time the negligence was discovered? If the law requires the claim to be filed within two years of the time the negligence occurred, then the patient would have no right to compensation from the physician.

In addition, the parties may disagree about the application of the law to the facts. For example, the parties may present another question to the court as a mixed issue of law and fact: In this situation, did the physician's failure to administer the test constitute negligence? This is a mixed question of law and fact because it requires the court to apply the legal definition of negligence to the facts to determine whether the physician's conduct constitutes negligence. If the physician was not negligent, then the patient has no right to compensation."

The courts in this country have grappled with the law/fact distinction, and the results at times have been far from clear.

Brutus v Cozens [1972] 2 All E.R. 1297, HL.

Lord Reid:

"My Lords, the charge against the appellant is that on 28 June 1971, during the annual tournament at the All England Lawn Tennis Club, Wimbledon, he used insulting behaviour whereby a breach of the peace was likely to be occasioned, contrary to section 5 of the Public Order Act 1936, as amended.

While a match was in progress on no 2 court he went on to the court, blew a whistle and threw leaflets around. On the whistle being blown nine or ten others invaded the court with banners and placards. I shall assume that they did this at the instigation of the appellant although that is not made very clear in the case stated by the justices. Then the appellant sat down and had to be forcibly removed by the police. The incident lasted for two or three minutes. This is said to have been insulting behaviour.

It appears that the object of this demonstration was to protest against the apartheid policy of the government of South Africa. But it is not said that that government was insulted. The insult is said to have been offered to or directed at the spectators. The spectators at no 2 court were upset; they made loud shouts, gesticulated and shook their fists and while the appellant was being removed some showed hostility and attempted to strike him. The justices came to the conclusion that the appellant's behaviour was not insulting within the terms of the offence alleged. They did not consider the other points raised in argument but dismissed the information without calling on the appellant.

On a case stated a Divisional Court set aside the judgment of the justices and remitted the case to them to continue the hearing of the case. They certified as a point of law of general public importance:

'Whether conduct which evidences a disrespect for the rights of others so that it is likely to cause their resentment or give rise to protests from them is insulting behaviour within the meaning of s.5 of the Public Order Act 1936.'

Section 5 is in these terms:

'Any person who in any public place or at any public meeting—(a) uses threatening, abusive or insulting words or behaviour . . . with intent to provoke a breach of the peace or whereby a breach of the peace is likely to be occasioned, shall be guilty of an offence.'

Subsequent amendments do not affect the question which we have to consider.

It is not clear to me what precisely is the point of law which we have to decide. The question in the case stated for the opinion of the court is 'Whether, on the above statements of facts, we came to a correct determination and decision in point of law'. This seems to assume that the meaning of the word 'insulting' in s.5 is a matter of law. And the Divisional Court appear to have proceeded on that footing.

In my judgment that is not right. The meaning of an ordinary word of the English language is not a question of law. The proper construction of a statute is a question of law. If the context shows that a word is used in an unusual sense the court will determine in other words what that unusual sense is. But here there is in my opinion no question of the word 'insulting' being used in any unusual sense. It appears to me . . . to be intended to have its ordinary meaning. It is for the tribunal which decides the case to consider, not as law but as fact, whether in the whole circumstances the words of the statute do or do not as a matter of ordinary usage of the English language cover or apply to the facts which have been proved. If it is alleged that the tribunal has reached a wrong decision then there can be a question of law but only of a limited character. The question would normally be whether their decision was unreasonable in the sense that no tribunal acquainted with the ordinary use of language could reach that decision. . . .

We were referred to a number of dictionary meanings of 'insult' such as treating with insolence or contempt or indignity or derision or dishonour or offensive disrespect. Many things otherwise unobjectionable may be said or done in an insulting way. There can be no definition. But an ordinary sensible man knows an insult when he sees or hears it. . . . If the view of the Divisional Court was that in this section the word 'insulting' has some special or unusually wide meaning, then I do not agree. Parliament has given no indication that the word is to be given any unusual meaning. Insulting means insulting and nothing else.

If I had to decide, which I do not, whether the appellant's conduct insulted the spectators in this case, I would agree with the justices. The spectators may have been very angry and justly so. The appellant's conduct was deplorable. Probably it ought to be punishable. But I cannot see how it insulted the spectators.

I would allow the appeal with costs."

[Lord Morris of Borth-y-Gest, Viscount Dilhorne, Lord Diplock, and Lord Kilbrandon agreed that the appeal should be allowed].

NOTES AND QUESTIONS

- Why does Lord Reid state that he does not have to decide whether the appellant's conduct was "insulting"?

- Do you think that the appellant's strategy of drawing attention to the apartheid regime in South Africa was successful? Why or why not? Remember that these events occurred in 1971.

- It is interesting that no mention is made in the judgments of the South African regime against which the protest was aimed. It is perhaps ironic that the appellant's behaviour is described as deplorable, when its impact was simply to interrupt a tennis game for a few minutes in an attempt to gain international publicity regarding a government widely viewed as deplorable.

- The distinction between fact and law in the context of statutory interpretation is not as settled as the judgments in *Brutus v Cozens* might suggest. See, *e.g.*, *Energy Conversion Devices Incorporated's Applications* [1982] F.S.R. 544, H.L; *R. v Spens* [1991] 4 All E.R. 421, CA; *Edwards v Bairstow* [1955] 3 All E.R. 48, H.L. For a thorough discussion of the distinction, see Ian McLeod, *Legal Method* (4th ed., Macmillan, Basingstoke, 2002), pp.33–40.

CASE STUDY ON STATUTORY INTERPRETATION: THE RACE RELATIONS ACT

The best way of understanding how courts approach statutory interpretation is through examples. In this section, we will examine one controversial instance of statutory interpretation in which the courts were sharply divided on the application of a statute: the Race Relations Act. We begin with what is now a "classic" case, *Mandla v Dowell Lee*, in which the Court of Appeal and House of Lords differed sharply on the interpretation of the word "ethnic" in the context of Sikhs in Britain. We will then compare the way in which the Court of Appeal subsequently applied the reasoning of the House of Lords in *Mandla* to what appears to be a very similar set of facts in *Dawkins v Department of the Environment*. A commentary on the cases which explores the relationship between "law" and "race" then follows.

Mandla v Dowell Lee and another [1982] 3 All E.R. 1108, CA.

Lord Denning M.R.:
"How far can Sikhs in England insist on wearing their turbans? A turban is their distinctive headgear. They do not cut their hair but plait it under their turbans. Some of them feel

so strongly about it that, when they are motorcyclists, they do not wear crash helmets; and when they are barristers they do not wear wigs.

Sewa Singh Mandla is a Sikh and rightly proud of it. He is a solicitor of the Supreme Court, practising in Birmingham. In 1978 he applied to send his son Gurinder to a private school in Birmingham called the Park Grove School. Gurinder was then aged 13. The school was very suitable for him. It had a high reputation. It took boys of all races. There were 305 boys altogether. Over 200 were English, but there were many others. Five were Sikhs, 34 Hindus, 16 Persians, six Negroes, seven Chinese and about 15 from European countries.

Mr Mandla took his son to see the headmaster. Both he and his son were wearing their turbans. The headmaster felt that it might give rise to difficulties if Gurinder wore his turban in school. He asked the father: 'Will you consent to his removing his turban and cutting his hair?' The father said: 'No. That is completely out of the question.' The headmaster said that he would think about it. Then on 24 July 1978 he wrote:

> 'Thank you for bringing your son to see me. As I promised, I have given much thought to the problem and I have reluctantly come to the conclusion that on balance it would be unwise to relax the School Rules with regard to uniform at the moment. I do not see any way in which it would be possible to reconcile the two conflicting requirements. May I wish you well in your efforts to promote harmony and peace, and I hope you find a suitable school for Gurinder without difficulty.'

Mr Mandla did find another school for Gurinder where he is allowed to wear his turban. So all is now well with them. But Mr Mandla reported the headmaster to the Commission for Racial Equality. They took the matter up with the headmaster. On 19 September 1978 the headmaster wrote this letter:

> 'To make my position quite clear, the boy was not rejected because he was a Sikh since we do not make racial distinctions and we have several Sikhs in the School. It was the turban that was rejected, and I believe your Acts cover people, not clothes.'

The commission, however, did not let the matter rest. They pursued the headmaster relentlessly. They interviewed him. They demanded information from him. Eventually they decided to assist Mr Mandla in legal proceedings against him. With their assistance in money and advice Mr Mandla issued proceedings against the headmaster of the school in the Birmingham County Court. He claimed damages limited to £500 and a declaration that the defendants had committed an act of unlawful discrimination. The county court judge heard the case for five days in February and June 1980, with many witnesses and much argument. The judge dismissed the claim. The Commission for Racial Equality, in Mr Mandla's name, appeal to this court.

The headmaster appeared before us in person. He has not the means to instruct counsel and solicitors. He put his case moderately and with restraint. He has himself done much research in the India Office library and elsewhere. It must have taken him many hours and many days. Now we have to consider what it all comes to.

The Law

The case raises this point of great interest: what is a 'racial group' within the Race Relations Act 1976? If the Sikhs are a 'racial group' no one is allowed to discriminate against any of their members in the important fields of education and employment and so forth. No matter whether the discrimination is direct or indirect, it is unlawful. But, if they are not a 'racial group' discrimination is perfectly lawful. So everything depends on whether they are a 'racial group' or not.

The statute in s.3 (1) of the 1976 Act contains a definition of 'racial group'. It means a 'group of persons defined by reference to colour, race, nationality or ethnic or national origins'. That definition is very carefully framed. Most interesting is that it does not include religion or politics or culture. You can discriminate for or against Roman Catholics as much as you like without being in breach of the law. You can discriminate for or against

Communists as much as you please, without being in breach of the law. You can discriminate for or against the 'hippies' as much as you like, without being in breach of the law. But you must not discriminate against a man because of his colour or of his race or of his nationality, or of 'his ethnic or national origins'. It is not suggested that the Sikhs are a group defined by reference to colour or race or nationality. Nor was much stress laid on national origins. But it is said most persuasively by counsel for the plaintiffs that the Sikhs are a group of persons 'defined by reference to ethnic origins'. It is so important that I will consider each word of that phrase.

'Ethnic'

The word 'ethnic' is derived from the Greek word '$\check{\epsilon}\theta\nu\acute{o}\varsigma$' which meant simply 'nation'. It was used by the 72 Palestinian Jews who translated the Old Testament from Hebrew into Greek (in the Septuagint). They used it to denote the non-Israelitish nations, that is, the Gentiles. When the word 'ethnic' was first used in England, it was used to denote peoples who were not Christian or Jewish. This was the meaning attached to it in the great *Oxford English Dictionary* itself in 1890.

But in 1934 in the *Concise Oxford Dictionary* it was given an entirely different meaning. It was given as: 'pertaining to race, ethnological'. And 'ethnological' was given as meaning: 'corresponding to a division of races'. That is the meaning which I, acquiring my vocabulary in 1934, have always myself attached to the word 'ethnic'. It is, to my mind, the correct meaning. It means 'pertaining to race'.

But then in 1972 there was appended a second supplement of the *Oxford English Dictionary*. It gives a very much wider meaning than that which I am used to. It was relied on by counsel for the plaintiffs:

'Also, pertaining to or having common racial, cultural, religious or linguistic characteristics, especially designating a racial or other group within a larger system; hence (U.S. colloquial), foreign, exotic.'

As an example of this new meaning, the second supplement refers to a book by Huxley and Haddon called *We Europeans* (1935). It mentions 'the non-committal terms *ethnic group*' and refers to the 'special type of *ethnic* grouping of which the Jews form the best-known example' (my emphasis). This reference to the Jews gives us a clue to the meaning of ethnic.

Why are 'the Jews' given as the best-known example of 'ethnic grouping'? What is their special characteristic which distinguishes them from non-Jews? To my mind it is a racial characteristic. *The Shorter Oxford Dictionary* describes a Jew as 'a person of Hebrew race'. Some help too can be found in our law books. . . . If a man desires that his daughter should only marry 'a Jew' and cuts her out of his will if she should marry a man who is not 'a Jew', he will find that the court will hold the condition void for uncertainty. The reason is because 'a Jew' may mean a dozen different things. It may mean a man of the Jewish faith. Even if he was a convert from Christianity, he would be of the Jewish faith. Or it may mean a man of Jewish parentage, even though he may be a convert to Christianity. It may suffice if his grandfather was a Jew and his grandmother was not. The Jewish blood may have become very thin by intermarriage with Christians, but still many would call him 'a Jew'. All this leads me to think that, when it is said of the Jews that they are an 'ethnic group', it means that the group as a whole share a common characteristic which is a racial characteristic. It is that they are descended, however remotely, from a Jewish ancestor. When we spoke of the 'Jewish regiments' which were formed and fought so well during the war, we had in mind those who were of Jewish descent or parentage. When Hitler and the Nazis so fiendishly exterminated 'the Jews', it was because of their racial characteristics and not because of their religion.

There is nothing in their culture of language or literature to mark out Jews in England from others. The Jews in England share all of these characteristics equally with the rest of us. Apart from religion, the one characteristic which is different is a racial characteristic.

'Origins'

The statute uses the word 'ethnic' in the context of 'origins'. This carries the same thought. I turn once again to the *Shorter Oxford Dictionary*. When the word 'origin' is used of a person it means 'descent, parentage'. I turn also to the speech of Lord Cross in *Ealing London Borough v. Race Relations Board* [1972] 1 All ER 15 at 117, [1972] AC 342 at 365:

'To me it suggests a connection subsisting at the time of birth . . . The connection will normally arise because the parents or one of the parents of the individual in question are or is identified by descent . . .'

So the word 'origins' connotes a group which has a common racial characteristic.

'Ethnic Origins'

If I am right in thinking that the phrase 'ethnic origins' denotes a group with a common racial characteristic, the question arises: why is it used at all? The answer is given by Lord Cross in the *Ealing London Borough case* ([1972] 1 All ER 15 at 117–118, [1972] AC 342 at 366):

'The reason why the word "ethnic or national origins" were added to the words "racial grounds" which alone appear in the long title was, I imagine, to prevent argument over the exact meaning of the word "race."'

In other words, there might be much argument whether one group or other was of the same 'race' as another, but there was thought to be less whether it was a different 'ethnic group'.

'Racial Group'

This brings me back to the definition in the statute of a 'racial group'. It means 'a group of persons defined by reference to colour, race, nationality or ethnic or national origins'.

The word 'defined' shows that the group must be distinguished from another group by some definable characteristic. English, Scots or Welsh football teams are to be distinguished by their national origins. The Scottish clans are not distinguishable from one another either by their ethnic or national origins, but only by their clannish or tribal differences. French Canadians are distinguished from other Canadians by their ethnic or national origins. Jews are not to be distinguished by their national origins. The wandering Jew has no nation. He is a wanderer over the face of the earth. The only definable characteristic of the Jews is a racial characteristic. I have no doubt that, in using the words 'ethnic origins', Parliament had in mind primarily the Jews. There must be no discrimination against the Jews in England. Anti-Semitism must not be allowed. It has produced great evils elsewhere. It must not be allowed here.

But the words 'ethnic origins' have a wider significance than the Jews. The question before us today is whether they include the Sikhs.

The Sikhs

The word 'Sikh' is derived from the Sanskrit 'Shishya', which means 'disciple'. Sikhs are the disciples or followers of Guru Nanak, who was born on 5 April 1469. There are about 14 m Sikhs, most of whom live in the part of the Punjab which is in India. Before the partition of the province in 1947 half of them lived in that portion which is now Pakistan; but on the partition most of them moved into India. There was tragic loss of life.

There is no difference in language which distinguishes the Sikhs from the other peoples in India. They speak Punjabi or Hindi or Urdu, or whatever the vernacular may be. There is no difference in blood which distinguishes them either. The people of India are largely the product of successive invasions that have swept into the country. They have intermingled to such an extent that it is impossible now to separate one strain from the other. The Sikhs do not recognise any distinction of race between them and the other peoples of India. They freely receive converts from Hinduism, or vice versa. Not only from outside, but even within the same family. The outstanding distinction between the Sikhs and the other peoples of India is in their religion, Sikhism, and its accompanying culture.

This is so marked that Dr Ballard, who is a lecturer in race relations in the University of Leeds, thought it was an ethnic difference. But, if you study his evidence, it is plain that he was using the word 'ethnic' in a special sense of his own. For him it did not signify any racial characteristic at all. These are some illuminating passages from his evidence:

'Sikhs, most obviously, are not a race in biological terms. Their origins are extremely diverse, probably more diverse than us English . . . I think they are a classic example of an ethnic group because of their distinctive cultural traditions . . . We are busy coining lots of new words here. I think ethnicity is the proper word to coin . . .'

The evidence shows that Sikhs as a community originate from the teaching of Guru Nanak. About the fifteenth century he founded the religious sect. There were a series of Gurus who followed Nanak, but the tenth and last is most important. Early in the nineteenth century he instituted major social and cultural reforms and turned the Sikhs into a community. He laid down the rules by which the hair was not to be cut and it was to be covered by a turban. By adopting this uniform Sikhs made their communal affiliation very clear, both to each other and to outsiders. But they remained at bottom a religious sect.

It is sometimes suggested that the Sikhs are physically a different people. But that is not so. In an important book on *The People of Asia* (1977) p.327 Professor Bowles of Syracuse University, New York, says:

'The difference [between Muslims, Sikhs and Hindus] are mainly cultural, not biological. Much has been written about the tallness . . . and excellent physique of the Sikh, qualities often attributed to their well-balanced vegetarian diet. In part this may be true, but the Sikhs are matched in physique by several other Punjab populations—meateating as well as vegetarian. Muslims as well as Hindus. Some of the neighbouring Pathan tribesmen are even taller. The Sikh physique is probably due to the fact that many have entered professions that have given them an economic advantage over their compatriots, Indians or Pakistanis. A correlation between nutrition and physique holds throughout the entire subcontinent, but it may be more noticeable in the Punjab, where there is such a variety of merchants and traders . . .'

On all this evidence, it is plain to me that the Sikhs, as a group, cannot be distinguished from others in the Punjab by reference to any racial characteristic whatever. They are only to be distinguished by their religion and culture. That is not an ethnic difference at all.

Conclusion

I have dealt with the evidence at length because of the differences on the point in the lower courts and tribunals. In our present case the evidence has been more fully canvassed than ever before. It has been most well and carefully considered by His Honour Judge Gosling here. I agree with his conclusion that Sikhs are not a racial group. They cannot be defined by reference to their ethnic or national origins. No doubt they are a distinct community, just as many other religious and cultural communities. But that is not good enough. It does not enable them to complain of discrimination against them.

You must remember that it is perfectly lawful to discriminate against groups of people to whom you object, so long as they are not a racial group. You can discriminate against the Moonies or the skinheads or any other group which you dislike or to which you take objection. No matter whether your objection to them is reasonable or unreasonable, you can discriminate against them, without being in breach of the law.

No doubt the Sikhs are very different from some of those groups. They are a fine community upholding the highest standards, but they are not a 'racial group'. So it is not unlawful to discriminate against them. Even though the discrimination may be unfair or unreasonable, there is nothing unlawful in it.

In our present case the headmaster did not discriminate against the Sikhs at all. He has five Sikh boys in his school already. All he has done is to say that, when the boy attends school, he must wear the school uniform and not wear a turban. The other Sikh boys in the school conform to this requirement. They make no objection. Mr Mandla is, I expect, strictly orthodox. He feels so strongly that he insists on his son wearing his turban at all times. But that feeling does not mean that the headmaster was at fault in any way. He was not unfair or unreasonable. It is for him to run his school in the way he feels best. He was not guilty of any discrimination against the Sikhs, direct or indirect.

I cannot pass from this case without expressing some regret that the Commission for Racial Equality thought it right to take up this case against the headmaster. It must be very difficult for educational establishments in this country to keep a proper balance between the various pupils who seek entry. The statutes relating to race discrimination and sex discrimination are difficult enough to understand and apply anyway. They should not be used so as to interfere with the discretion of schools and colleges in the proper management of their affairs.

In the circumstances I need say nothing as to the contentions about the word 'can' or 'justifiable' in the statutes. They do not arise.

I would dismiss the appeal."

Oliver L.J.

[Oliver L.J. delivered separate concurring reasons, and concluded with some comments on the actions of the Commission for Racial Equality in this case]:

". . . In the result, I agree that the appeal fails. I would add only this. Without in any way minimising the great assistance which counsel for the plaintiffs have given the court in this difficult case, it is right that some tribute should be paid to the courtesy, skill and patience with which Mr Dowell Lee has conducted in person a case which must have caused him immense personal distress and anxiety. I cannot help observing that the events of which complaint have been made took place as long ago as the summer of 1978, four years ago. Throughout Mr Dowell Lee appears to have behaved with the greatest courtesy and restraint. After an entirely courteous correspondence with the first plaintiff, he found himself the subject of a visitation from a representative of the Commission for Racial Equality and the papers before us contain the notes of an interview with him at which he appears to have been deliberately interrogated with a view to extracting admissions of racial bias and at which barely concealed threats of 'investigation' were made unless he modified the stance which he had adopted. Thereafter he, whose proper business was running his school in a way which to him seemed most suited to the needs of his students, found himself involved in an action fostered and supported by the commission. The proceedings were commenced two years later and have throughout been maintained by the commission in the name of better race relations, although it emerged, ironically, at the trial that the first plaintiff would not, if the matter of his son's entry had been pursued, have been willing in any event for him to go to a school where he would have been expected to attend religious classes of the Christian faith as part of the normal curriculum. There is, and this should be made, I think, entirely clear, absolutely no foundation, in my judgment, for the suggestion that Mr Dowell Lee is seeking or has sought to exclude children from the school either on racial or religious grounds. . . . Mr Dowell Lee's objection to the wearing of the turban at school is precisely, as I understand it, because he feels that it would tend to accentuate those very religious and social distinctions which it is his desire to minimise in trying to effect a homogenous school community. Whether that is an objection which all or any of the members of this court would equally feel is immaterial. It is, in my judgment, a perfectly respectable viewpoint and is the sincerely held and responsible opinion of a man who is running a multiracial school in a difficult area. I have to say that, speaking entirely for myself, I regard it as lamentable that Mr Dowell Lee's entire livelihood and the future of his school should have been put at risk at the instance of a publicly financed body designed to foster better racial relations. Anything less likely to achieve that result than this case I find it difficult to imagine. As it is Mr Dowell Lee has been compelled to waste a great deal of his time and the resources of the school in defending himself against charges which could hardly have been levelled at any target less deserving of them. He has been dragged through two courts at enormous expense in order, apparently, to establish a point which no doubt is a difficult and important one, but is now entirely academic for both plaintiffs. It seems to me a great pity that it should have been thought necessary to test it at the expense of an entirely blameless individual who has done no more than to seek in the best way that he knows how to run his own business in his own way. What makes it, perhaps, particularly ironic is the evidence of the plaintiffs' expert Mr Indarijit Singh:

> 'Tolerance is the willingness, and a Sikh should be willing, to fight in every way including, if need be, eventually to give his life, to upholding the next person's right to determine his own particular way of life.'

For my part, I find it regrettable that this unimpeachable sentiment should not have been applied here and that machinery designed specifically for the protection of the weak and disadvantaged should have operated as, it seems to me, it has in this case, albeit no doubt with the loftiest of motives, as an engine of oppression.

I should only add that, in saying this, I am making no criticism whatever of counsel for the plaintiffs or those instructing him, who have conducted the appeal in accordance with their clients' instructions with the most punctilious fairness and propriety.

I too would dismiss the appeal."

Kerr L.J.

[Kerr L.J. delivered concurring reasons, concluding with the following comment]:

"... I would add my disquiet to what Lord Denning M.R. and Oliver L.J. have already said about the events which have led up to these proceedings. The Commission for Racial Equality is clearly highly motivated and does useful work in cases where there is clear evidence, or real ground for suspicion, that racial discrimination exists and is practised. But this is not such a case. This school was demonstrably conducted harmoniously on a multi-racial basis. I have read in this evidence the notes of the interview of the headmaster by an official of the commission. In parts this reads more like an inquisition than an interview, and I can see no basis whatever for what I can only describe as harassment of this headmaster. All that the commission has achieved in this case, as it seems to me, is to create racial discord where there was none before."

QUESTIONS

- Consider Lord Denning's description of the ethnic mix of the school. Is there anything problematic about his description? What does he mean by "English" students?

- Is Lord Denning's explanation of why "ethnic" was included in the statutory language convincing? Can you come up with an alternative explanation?

- In Lord Denning's reasons, a substantial amount of expert evidence (that is, evidence given by experts in the area under consideration) is presented. On what basis is this evidence accepted or rejected? Specifically, on what basis does Lord Denning reject Dr Ballard's definition of Sikhs as an ethnic group?

- All of the judges are loathe to interfere with the "discretion" of the headmaster in running his school as he sees fit. Is that attitude potentially problematic in the face of the application of the Race Relations Act to education? Is not the point of the legislation to constrain the exercise of discretion when its impact is discriminatory?

- Lord Oliver mentions that Mr Mandla would not have sent his son to this school in any event because it conducted Christian religious education. Could you argue that such services are themselves in contravention of the Race Relations Act? Note here that Lord Denning stated that Jews definitely do constitute an "ethnic group" for the purposes of the legislation.

ESSAY QUESTION

Describe and evaluate the attitude of the members of this Court of Appeal to "race relations" and, in particular, the work of the Commission for Racial Equality.

The case was then appealed to the House of Lords.

***Mandla v Dowell Lee* [1983] 1 All E.R. 1062, HL.**

[Lord Fraser described the facts and the issue of statutory interpretation, before considering whether Sikhs constituted an ethnic group]:

Lord Fraser of Tullybelton
". . . My Lords, I recognise that 'ethnic' conveys a flavour of race but it cannot, in my opinion, have been used in the 1976 Act in a strict racial or biological sense. For one thing it would be absurd to suppose that Parliament can have intended that membership of a particular racial group should depend on scientific proof that a person possessed the relevant distinctive biological characteristics (assuming that such characteristics exist). The practical difficulties of such proof would be prohibitive, and it is clear that Parliament must have used the word in some more popular sense. For another thing, the briefest glance at the evidence in this case is enough to show that, within the human race, there are very few, if any, distinctions which are scientifically recognised as racial. . . .
    I turn, therefore, to the third and wider meaning which is given in the *Supplement to the Oxford English Dictionary* vol I (A–G) (1972). It is as follows: 'pertaining to or having common racial, cultural, religious, or linguistic characteristics, esp. designating a racial or other group within a larger system . . .' Counsel for the appellants, while not accepting the third (1972) meaning as directly applicable for the present purpose, relied on it to this extent, that it introduces a reference to cultural and other characteristics, and is not limited to racial characteristics. The 1972 meaning is, in my opinion, too loose and vague to be accepted as it stands. It is capable of being read as implying that any one of the adjectives, 'racial, cultural, religious or linguistic' would be enough to constitute an ethnic group. That cannot be the sense in which 'ethnic' is used in the 1976 Act, as that Act is not concerned at all with discrimination on religious grounds. Similarly, it cannot have been used to mean simply any 'racial or *other* group'. If that were the meaning of 'ethnic', it would add nothing to the word group, and would lead to a result which would be unacceptably wide. But in seeking for the true meaning of 'ethnic' in the statute, we are not tied to the precise definition in any dictionary. The value of the 1972 definition is, in my view, that it shows that ethnic has come to be commonly used in a sense appreciably wider than the strictly

racial or biological. That appears to me to be consistent with the ordinary experience of those who read newspapers at the present day. In my opinion, the word 'ethnic' still retains a racial flavour but it is used nowadays in an extended sense to include other characteristics which may be commonly thought of as being associated with common racial origin.

For a group to constitute an ethnic group in the sense of the 1976 Act, it must, in my opinion, regard itself, and be regarded by others, as a distinct community by virtue of certain characteristics. Some of these characteristics are essential; others are not essential but one or more of them will commonly be found and will help to distinguish the group from the surrounding community. The conditions which appear to me to be essential are these: (1) a long shared history, of which the group is conscious as distinguishing it from other groups, and the memory of which it keeps alive; (2) a cultural tradition of its own, including family and social customs and manners, often but not necessarily associated with religious observance. In addition to those two essential characteristics the following characteristics are, in my opinion, relevant: (3) either a common geographical origin, or descent from a small number of common ancestors; (4) a common language, not necessarily peculiar to the group; (5) a common literature peculiar to the group; (6) a common religion different from that of neighbouring groups or from the general community surrounding it; (7) being a minority or being an oppressed or a dominant group within a larger community, for example a conquered people (say, the inhabitants of England shortly after the Norman conquest) and their conquerors might both be ethnic groups. . . .

The result is, in my opinion, that Sikhs are a group defined by a reference to ethnic origins for the purpose of the 1976 Act, although they are not biologically distinguishable from the other people living in the Punjab. That is true whether one is considering the position before the partition of 1947, when the Sikhs lived mainly in that part of the Punjab which is now Pakistan, or after 1947, since when most of them have moved into India. It is, therefore, necessary to consider whether the respondent has indirectly discriminated against the appellants in the sense of s.1(1)(b) of the 1976 Act. That raises the two subsidiary questions. . . .

'Can comply'

It is obvious that Sikhs, like anyone else, 'can' refrain from wearing a turban, if 'can' is construed literally. But if the broad cultural/historic meaning of ethnic is the appropriate meaning of the word in the 1976 Act, then a literal reading of the word 'can' would deprive Sikhs and members of other groups defined by reference to their ethnic origins of much of the protection which Parliament evidently intended the 1976 Act to afford to them. They 'can' comply with almost any requirement or condition if they are willing to give up their distinctive customs and cultural rules. On the other hand, if ethnic means inherited and unalterable, as the Court of Appeal thought it did, then 'can' ought logically to be read literally. The word 'can' is used with many shades of meaning. In the context of s.1 (1)(b)(i) of the 1976 Act it must, in my opinion, have been intended by Parliament to be read not as meaning 'can physically', so as to indicate a theoretical possibility, but as meaning 'can in practice' or 'can consistently with the customs and cultural conditions of the racial group'. . . . Accordingly I am of opinion that the 'no turban' rule was not one with which the second appellant could, in the relevant sense, comply.

'Justifiable'

The word 'justifiable' occurs in s.1(1)(b)(ii). It raises a problem which is, in my opinion, more difficult than the problem of the word 'can'. But in the end I have reached a firm opinion that the respondent has not been able to show that the 'no turban' rule was justifiable in the relevant sense. Regarded purely from the point of view of the respondent, it was no doubt perfectly justifiable. He explained that he had no intention of discriminating against Sikhs. . . . The reasons for having a school uniform were largely reasons of practical convenience, to minimise external differences between races and social classes, to discourage the 'competitive fashions' which he said tend to exist in a teenage community, and to present a Christian image of the school to outsiders, including prospective parents. The respondent explained the difficulty for a headmaster of explaining to a non-Sikh pupil why the rules about wearing correct school uniform were enforced against him if they were relaxed in favour of a Sikh. In my view these reasons could not, either individually or collectively, provide a sufficient justification for the respondent to apply a condition that is prima facie discriminatory under the 1976 Act.

An attempted justification of the 'no turban' rule, which requires more serious consideration, was that the respondent sought to run a Christian school, accepting pupils of all religions and races, and that he objected to the turban on the ground that it was an outward manifestation of a non-Christian faith. Indeed, he regarded it as amounting to a challenge to that faith. I have much sympathy with the respondent on this part of the case and I would have been glad to find that the rule was justifiable within the meaning of the statute, if I could have done so. But in my opinion that is impossible. The onus under para (b)(ii) is on the respondent to show that the condition which he seeks to apply is not indeed a necessary condition, but that it is in all circumstances justifiable 'irrespective of the colour, race, nationality or ethnic or national origins of the person to whom it is applied', that is to say that it is justifiable without regard to the ethnic origins of that person. But in this case the principal justification on which the respondent relies is that the turban is objectionable just because it is a manifestation of the second appellant's ethnic origins. That is not, in my view, a justification which is admissible under para (b)(ii). . . .

Final considerations

Before parting with the case I must refer to some observations by the Court of Appeal which suggest that the conduct of the Commission for Racial Equality in this case has been in some way unreasonable or oppressive. . . .

My Lords, I must say that I regard these strictures on the commission and its officials as entirely unjustified. The commission has had a difficult task, and no doubt its inquiries will be resented by some and are liable to be regarded as objectionable and inquisitive. But the respondent in this case, who conducted his appeal with restraint and skill, made no complaint of his treatment at the hands of the commission. He was specifically asked by some of my noble and learned friends to point out any part of the notes of his interview with the commission's official to which he objected, and he said there were none and that an objection of that sort formed no part of his case. The lady who conducted the interview on behalf of the commission gave evidence in the county court, and no suggestion was put to her in cross-examination that she had not conducted it properly. Opinions may legitimately differ as to the usefulness of the commission's activities, but its functions have been laid down by Parliament and, in my view, the actions of the commission itself in this case and of its official who interviewed the respondent on 3 November, 1978 were perfectly proper and in accordance with its statutory duty.

I would allow this appeal. The appellants have agreed to pay the costs of the respondent in this House and they do not seek to disturb the order for costs in the lower courts in favour of the present respondent made by the Court of Appeal."

[Lord Templeman delivered separate concurring reasons. Lord Edmund-Davies, Lord Roskill, and Lord Brandon of Oakbrook concurred in the reasons of Lord Fraser and Lord Templeman.]

- Lord Fraser expressed his sympathy with the respondent's desire to run a "Christian" school. Could such a desire be legally problematic in terms of the way in which the House of Lords defines "ethnic origins" in the Race Relations Act? Are there other "outward manifestations" of non-Christian faiths, the prohibition of which could lead to action under the legislation? Would it be more "just" if outward manifestations of Christianity were also prohibited?

- Note how Lord Fraser chastises the Court of Appeal for its criticism of the Commission for Racial Equality. How does he employ the doctrine of the supremacy of Parliament to ground his criticism of the Court of Appeal?

Compare the following judgment which seeks to apply the reasoning in *Mandla v Dowell Lee* to what appear to be very similar facts:

Dawkins v Department of the Environment [1993] I.R.L.R. 284, CA.

Neill L.J.:
"This is an appeal by leave of the single Lord Justice by Mr Trevor Dawkins from the order of the Employment Appeal Tribunal dated 24 April 1991 allowing the appeal of Crown Suppliers (SA) Ltd from the decision of the Industrial Tribunal dated 28 March 1989. I shall call Mr Dawkins 'the appellant' and the Crown Suppliers (PSA) Ltd 'the PSA'. . . . The respondent to the appeal is now the Department of the Environment.

The facts

The PSA, which is part of the Home Civil Service, is responsible for *inter alia* providing transport for the government Interdepartmental Despatch Service (IDS). In June 1988 the PSA inserted an advertisement in the South London Press seeking experienced drivers for the IDS. The advertisement stipulated that the applicants should be aged between 25 and 45 with a clean driving licence. The appellant responded to the advertisement and attended at the PSA's premises for interview at 10 am on 28 June 1988.

Before the Industrial Tribunal there was a conflict of evidence as to the appearance of the appellant at the interview. It is sufficient to say that the appellant, who is a Rastafarian, attended wearing a hat and that underneath the hat he had long hair arranged in the form of dreadlocks. Miss Barbara Herbert, who conducted the interview with the appellant, explained to him that the SA expected their drivers to have short hair. The appellant indicated that he was not willing to cut his hair and the interview was then concluded amicably.

On 26 September 1988 the applicant applied to the Industrial Tribunal for a finding whether he had been discriminated against contrary to the Race Relations Act 1976. The appellant's complaint was heard on 16 and 17 January 1989 at London South. By the decision of the Industrial Tribunal which was sent to the parties on 28 March 1989 the tribunal found by a majority that the appellant's claim succeeded. The question of remedies was left over for a later occasion. By their majority decision the Industrial Tribunal held that the PSA had been guilty of both direct and indirect discrimination. They held that the appellant had been refused employment not because he was black but because of the opinion which Miss Herbert formed as to his unsuitability by reason of the length of his hair. The central question at issue before the Industrial Tribunal was whether or not Rastafarians constituted a racial group within the meaning of the 1976 Act. By a majority the Industrial Tribunal decided that Rastafarians did constitute such a group. In reaching this conclusion the Industrial Tribunal made a number of findings of fact which have not been challenged. The difference of opinion between the members of the Industrial Tribunal was as to the application of the law to these facts.

I should set out the findings of fact made by the Industrial Tribunal in paragraph 10 of their reasons. These findings were as follows:

'(i) The Rastafarian movement as such began about 1930. We do not think it is possible to trace it back any further than this. It seems to us that it was in the decade between 1920 and 1930 that the ideas of Marcus Garvey began to crystallise, and that it cannot be said that the movement had any separate existence before 1930.

(ii) That there is a distinct culture which although in some respects is vague and difficult to grasp seems to us nevertheless to exist. The fact that the Rastafarians do not, as most have, distinct centres of worship does not seem to us to be very material. We find that they do, as Dr Cashmore says, meet in groups in order to discuss matters of common interest as outlined in his evidence and that they do observe distinct customs such as a refusal to cut hair or to shave, and observe dietary laws and prohibitions on homosexuality and contraception. They also have, we find, a common language i.e. English and the Jamaican patois.

(iii) They have a common geographical origin in that the majority of them come from Jamaica at least in origin, although by now a large number of Rastafarians in this country will have been born here.

(iv) That there is some literature and some cultural tradition, that is that there is some poetry which is distinctive to the group and there is also reggae music. We feel that if a group shows a musical tradition then this must also be taken into account as well as a written or oral literary tradition.

(v) That they do have a sense of being a minority and of being oppressed in that their distinctive appearance is likely to single them out for criticism by other members of the community thus causing them to have a feeling that they are a peculiar minority among other people.

(vi) We also find that there has been continuity, albeit tenuous, from 1930. We think the answer here is that until about 1970 Rastafarians, at least in this country, were few and far between. This is probably why not many were noticed between the 1950s, when immigration from the West Indies to this country started, and 1970 when the movement seems to have been noticed. We think, however, that it can be shown that the movement has either here or in Jamaica or in other parts of the world been continuous since 1930.'

I shall have to return later to consider how the Industrial Tribunal applied the relevant law to these facts.

The Law

The complaint by the appellant was brought before the Industrial Tribunal in accordance with s.54(1) of the Race Relations Acts 1976 which provides that a complaint that another person has committed an act of discrimination against the complainant which is unlawful by virtue of art.II of the Act may be presented to an Industrial Tribunal. [Neill L.J. then explained the content and structure of the statutory regime]. . . .

In the present case the appellant claims that he was subjected to both direct and indirect racial discrimination in that he was refused employment by the PSA by reason of his membership of a particular racial group, namely the Rastafarians. It is contended on his behalf that Rastafarians constitute a group of persons who are defined by reference to their ethnic origins.

On behalf of the PSA it is accepted that the appellant was refused employment because he was a Rastafarian, but it is denied that Rastafarians constitute a group of persons defined by reference to their ethnic origins. It will be seen therefore that the crucial question to be decided by the Industrial Tribunal was whether or not Rastafarians were a group defined by reference to their ethnic origins. . . .

The decision of the Industrial Tribunal

In their full and careful reasons the Industrial Tribunal referred to the decisions in *Mandla* and in *King-Ansell*.[8] In addition they referred to the decision of the Court of Appeal in England in *Commission for Racial Equality v. Dutton* [1989] IRLR 8 (CA) where the question for decision was whether gypsies constituted an ethnic group within the meaning of the 1976 Act.

In paragraph 12 of their reasons the Industrial Tribunal considered whether Rastafarians satisfied the first of the 'essential' conditions set out in Lord Fraser's speech [*i.e.* whether the group can show a shared history]. . . .

The Industrial Tribunal were divided on the question whether a shared tradition of just under 60 years was long enough. Two members of the Tribunal were of the opinion that in the circumstances the test of a long shared history was satisfied because the test had to be examined not only in relation to its actual length but also by reference to its continuity and persistence. The third member disagreed on the basis that a far longer period of time than 60 years was required before it could be said that a group possessed a long shared history.

In paragraph 13 of the reasons the Industrial Tribunal considered the other conditions set out in Lord Fraser's speech. The majority considered that the condition of a cultural tradition was satisfied. In addition there was a unanimous finding that Rastafarians had a common geographical origin in that their ancestors came from Jamaica. The reasons continued:

> 'There is some sort of common literature, there is not a common religion, they do have a sense of being a minority or being an oppressed group because of their peculiar customs.'

In the light of their findings the Industrial Tribunal decided by a majority of two to one that Rastafarians constituted a racial group within the definition in s.3(1) of the 1976 Act. The PSA appealed.

The decision of The Employment Appeal Tribunal

The judgment of the Employment Appeal Tribunal was delivered by Tucker J. By a majority the appeal by the PSA was allowed. In their judgment the Employment Appeal Tribunal referred to the *Mandla* case and the *Dutton* case . . . . At [1991] ICR 583, 594 Tucker J. said:

> 'Applying those tests to Rastafarians, we ask whether they possess any of the characteristics of a race? We very much doubt whether the majority of Rastafarians can claim that they are of group descent, though some of them may be. Their geographical origin is Jamaica. We doubt whether they can be said to have a group history. . . . There is in our view insufficient to distinguish them from the rest of the Afro-Caribbean community so as to render them a separate group defined by reference to ethnic origins. They are a religious sect and no more.

In any event returning to Lord Fraser's test, we are unable to agree with the majority of the Industrial Tribunal that Rastafarians have a long shared history. It cannot reasonably

---

[8] *King-Ansell v Police* [1979] 2 N.Z.L.R. 531, a decision of the New Zealand Court of Appeal.

be said that a movement which goes back for only 60 years, i.e. within the living memory of many people, can claim to be long in existence. Its history, in the judgment of the majority, is insufficiently sustained. The fact that the movement has maintained itself and still exists is insufficient. We have no hesitation in disagreeing with the conclusion of the majority of the Tribunal on this point, because first we do not regard it as a finding of fact, and secondly, even if it were we would regard it as a finding which no reasonable Tribunal could make, and therefore perverse.

So far as Lord Fraser's second essential test is concerned, that of a cultural tradition of its own, our view is that Rastafarians are a group with very little structure, no apparent organisation and having customs and practices which have evolved in a somewhat haphazard way. Nevertheless, notwithstanding these reservations and placing them in the context of a formerly enslaved people striving for an identity, there may be a sufficient cultural tradition to satisfy the test, and we are not prepared to disagree with the finding of the Tribunal on this point.

These are the views of the majority of the members of the Tribunal. One member dissents from them. On the basis of a book *One Love Rastafari: History, Doctrine and Livity* by Jah Bones (not referred to in argument before us) he is of the view that Rastafarians have a sufficiently long shared history to fulfil the test. In addition he would hold that they are more than a religious sect. However, by a majority, we allow the appeal for the reasons which we have expressed.' . . .

Do the Rastafarians constitute a racial group?

. . . I am unable to accept that the Industrial Tribunal's decision by a majority that Rastafarians had a sufficiently long shared history to satisfy Lord Fraser's first condition was merely a finding of fact with which an appellate court cannot interfere. The finding that a group originated in 1930 was indeed a finding of fact, but a decision as to the length of a shared history, which is necessary for the purpose of satisfying a statutory test, is a very different matter. In any event it is important to remember that the relevant words in the statute are 'ethnic origins'. . . .

It is clear that Rastafarians have certain identifiable characteristics. They have a strong cultural tradition which includes a distinctive form of music known as reggae music. They adopt a distinctive form of hairstyle by wearing dreadlocks. They have other shared characteristics of which both the Industrial Tribunal and the Employment Appeal Tribunal were satisfied. But the crucial question is whether they have established some separate identity by reference to their ethnic origins. In speaking about Rastafarians in this context I am referring to the core group, because I am satisfied that a core group can exist even though not all the adherents of the group could, if considered separately, satisfy any of the relevant tests.

It is at this stage that one has to take account of both the racial flavour of the word 'ethnic' and Lord Fraser's requirement of a long shared history. Lord Meston submitted that if one compared Rastafarians with the rest of the Afro-Caribbean community in this country, there was nothing to set them aside as a separate ethnic group. They are a separate group but not a separate group defined by reference to their ethnic origins. I see no answer to this submission.

Mr Whitmore quite rightly stressed that this case is concerned with identity. The question is: have the Rastafarians a separate ethnic identity? Do they stand apart by reason of their history from other Jamaicans?

In my judgment it is not enough for Rastafarians now to look back to a past when their ancestors, in common with other peoples in the Caribbean, were taken there from Africa. They were not a separate group then. The shared history of Rastafarians goes back only 60 years or so. One can understand and admire the deep affection which Rastafarians feel for Africa and their longing for it as their real home. But, as Mr Riza recognises, the court is concerned with the language of the statute. In the light of the guidance given by the House of Lords in Mandla, I am unable to say that they are a separate racial group.

I would dismiss the appeal.
Beldam L.J: I agree.
Sir John Megaw: I also agree.
Appeal dismissed with costs. Application for leave to appeal to the House of Lords refused."

QUESTIONS

- After reading *Dawkins*, do you have a clear sense of when a "shared history" becomes long?

- The majority of the Employment Appeal Tribunal described Rastafarian culture as "haphazard" and as lacking in structure and organisation. Are those relevant considerations? Is the development of a culture not always somewhat haphazard given that it depends upon historical circumstance? Why is the degree of structure and organisation relevant to a statute which deals with discrimination?

- Note how the Employment Appeal Tribunal and the Court of Appeal employ the fact-law distinction to overturn the Industrial Tribunal's finding that Rastafarians have a long shared history. Both the Employment Appeal Tribunal and the Court of Appeal held that this was a legal inference rather than a finding of fact. Is the fact-law distinction any clearer in your mind after reading this case (hint: it shouldn't be!)?

- Remember that nowhere in the statute is there a definition of ethnicity which depends upon the existence of a long shared history. Reread Lord Fraser's judgment in *Mandla v Dowell Lee*. Is the existence of a long shared history a necessary requirement for the finding of an ethnic group in Lord Fraser's analysis?

Consider the following analysis of "race" in legal discourse:

Werner Menski, "Race and Law" in *The Critical Lawyers' Handbook 2* (Paddy Ireland and Per Laleng, eds., Pluto Press, London, 1997), pp.67–69:

"Western legal systems have long operated a pattern of selective toleration and recognition of 'ethnic' needs and claims. This approach is problematic, since recognition of diversity has tended to be viewed as a favour which may be withheld by those in authority, not as an integral structural element. Such strategies of selective recognition inevitably produce conflicts. In fact, they end up discriminating: not only in Britain does 'ethnic' recognition by the official law clearly discriminate between different claimant groups. Although we cannot explore this in detail here, while various forms of Asian ethnicity are widely accepted in English law, those of African and Afro-Caribbean groups have tended to be dismissed, probably because they were assumed to be racial rather than cultural.

The underlying argument against the recognition of racial diversities, that colour is only socially but not legally relevant, and that at any rate uniformity is best, so that diversities and pluralisms should be ignored as far as possible, has landed English race relations law in a conceptual mess: while the purpose of the law would appear to be protection against discrimination, the case-law shows that even when racial discrimination admittedly took place, the law as it stands now will not protect victims of discrimination unless they can bring themselves under the increasingly arbitrary judicial definition of 'racial group' in s.3 of the Race Relations Act 1976. The case-law confirms this: Trevor Dawkins, a Rastafarian driver told to cut his hair if he wanted a job, found that the decision in his case contrasted somewhat illogically with the leading case of Mandla, in which a Sikh schoolboy had been told to cut his hair if he wanted admission to a particular school. The Sikh boy achieved the full protection of English law, but not the Rastafarian appellant. Thus, in virtually identical factual situations, English law today protected only members of certain 'racial groups', and on the basis of heavily contested criteria.

While principled arguments against the recognition of diversity appear rather too defensive at the end of the twentieth century, they do not take into account the apparent fact that even codified Western legal systems have been making all kinds of allowances for various forms of diversity. Presumably guided by sociolegal and 'race relations' expertise, the historical development of English law in this regard has relied on extra-legal expertise and political pressure rather than legal analysis. The law has been reactive, rather than proactive. The results seem deeply unsatisfactory in terms of intellectual clarity and cohesiveness. They are also politically insensitive, to say the least: the very legal framework which is supposed to improve 'race relations' actually does the reverse. Curiously, the general public in Britain as well as many lawyers remain unaware that the law has been protecting only certain 'racial groups', so that it remains perfectly possible to discriminate against the majority of non-white citizens and co-residents. Leading judges, in critical moments, have been looking for general dictionaries rather than specialist legal analysis. Such simplistic techniques of law-making, almost inevitably, lead to strange mistakes which then have to be rectified.

Lack of research and of clarity about 'race' and 'ethnicity' have been coupled with an aversion to address religious issues in legal contexts, especially in Parliament, granting privileged status to the Sikhs as a 'racial group' under the Race Relations Act. But the Court of Appeal in 1993, faced with a claim by Rastafarians to the same effect, and in almost identical circumstances, refused them recognition as a 'racial group', sidelining the questions of religion and ethnic identity. Yet what distinguished the Sikhs from other Punjabis other than their religion? Clearly, the liberal dreams of a progressive, protective evolution of the relevant definitions in the 1976 Act have been shattered."

ESSAY QUESTION

"The canon of literal interpretation enjoys an exaggerated authority and is believed to be far more productive of automatic solutions than it really is. As already stated, the judge's view of meaning is always coloured by his view of the particular facts before him, and he often makes a meaning for those facts without realizing it. So he frequently legislates unconsciously and therefore necessarily in accordance with his own private view of policy. This, of course, is undesirable and it is, to a great extent, unnecessary. The democratic method requires that policy should be determined by discussion and vote. And on the whole, the policy of legislation is largely determined by public pressure upon the legislature by means of public opinion and periodic elections. Though the intention of the legislature is a fiction, the purpose or object of the legislation is very real. No enactment is ever passed for the sake of its details; it is passed in an attempt to realize a social purpose. It is what is variously called the aim and object of the enactment, the spirit of the legislation, the mischief and the remedy. Though real, it is not always easily discoverable, even if the rules of interpretation permitted a proper search to be made for it. . . . The statute must be treated as a means to an end; the end should be determined by the social forces which brought it about and not by private choices of the judge. On the highroad of plain meaning, he follows the signposts as they appear. In the deep—and widespread—forests of ambiguity, the details in the foreground merely adds to the confusion. He should follow the compass—the object and purpose of the legislation. Where that fails, as it sometimes will, he can only trust himself."

[J.A. Corry, "Administrative Law and the Interpretation of Statutes" (1935) 1 University of Toronto Law Journal 286 at 292–293.]

Although Corry was writing in 1935, are his sentiments still relevant to the task of judicial interpretation of statutes? Use examples drawn from this chapter to support your argument.

8

STATUTORY INTERPRETATION:
THE SEARCH FOR LEGISLATIVE INTENTION

In this chapter, we continue our focus on statutory interpretation. The emphasis, however, changes. In Chapter 7, we looked primarily to the meaning of statutory language itself. By contrast, in this chapter, we will turn to what judges often see as their primary role in statutory interpretation: determining the intention of the legislature which enacted the statute. We begin with an examination of the meaning of legislative "intent" and the idea of purposive interpretation. Then, we look at ways in which the courts engage in the pursuit of intention, both through "internal aids" to interpretation and "external aids" such as *Hansard* (the record of Parliamentary debates). We then focus on a central tension in statutory interpretation between the desire to interpret statutes in accordance with the intention of the legislature, and the need for interpretation to reflect (and help consolidate) social *change*. Following on from this, we look at what are commonly known as the rules or "canons" of interpretation.

<small>THE ROLE OF INTENTION AND PURPOSE IN STATUTORY INTERPRETATION</small>

Judges frequently justify the statutory interpretations which they adopt through the claim that they are advancing the "intention" of Parliament. This justification is wedded to the idea of Parliamentary supremacy: that judges simply apply the law which Parliament has enacted. However, the idea of legislative intention is a more slippery concept than one would think by reading the cases.

John Bell and Sir George Engle, *Cross on Statutory Interpretation* (3rd ed., Butterworths, London, 1995), pp.24–27:

"The 'intention of Parliament' with regard to a particular statute cannot mean the intention of all those who were members of either House when the royal assent was given, for many of them might have been out of the country at all material times and never have heard of the statute. Equally plainly the phrase cannot mean the intention of the majority who voted for the statute as this will almost certainly have been constituted by different persons at the different stages of the passage of the Bill and, in any event, it would be rash to assume that all those who vote for it have the same intentions with regard to a particular piece of legislation. For example, it has been pointed out that, in a debate on what became the Statute of Westminster 1931, Winston Churchill and the Solicitor-General agreed that there was no obscurity in the provisions concerning the Irish Free State, although they took diametrically opposite views concerning their effect.

Someone bent on identifying the intention of specific human beings as that to which reference is made when people speak of the intention of Parliament might resort to the notion of agency. It could be said that the promoters of a Bill must have some consequences in mind as its general and particular effects, but promoters, whoever they may be, are initiators who place proposals before Parliament rather than act as its agents; and many Bills contain amendments which are not the work of the promoters. . . .

The court may justify the meaning it ultimately attaches to statutory words by suggesting that this is the meaning which, it believes, members of the legislature would have attached to them had the situation before the court been present to their minds. But, . . . the following words of a South African judge surely hold good for English law:

> 'Evidence that every member who voted for a measure put a certain construction upon it cannot affect the meaning which the court must place upon the statute, for it is the product, not of a number of individuals, but of an impersonal Parliament.'

This last quotation helps to make clear . . . that the question of legislative intention is not about the historical or hypothetical views of legislators, but rather concerns the meaning of words used in a particular context. The objective is not to reconstruct a psychological model of Parliament or the promoters of a Bill, or even of the drafter, and then to use it to determine what was meant by them when they used certain words, or what would have been provided had a particular eventuality been envisaged at the time of drafting or enactment. . . . Judges are concerned instead with using the conventions of ordinary language and of statutory interpretation to determine the meaning of words in their context. . . .

In the context of the interpretation of statutes there are three principal situations in which people in general and judges in particular speak of the intention of Parliament. In the first place, whenever the meaning of specific words is under consideration, the idea that a particular meaning is that which would or would not have been attached to a word or phrase by the average member of Parliament, sitting at the time when the statute was passed, may be expressed or refuted by some such statement as 'that is (or is not) what Parliament intended by those words'. Second, when the consequences of a particular construction are under consideration, the idea that a particular consequence might well have been in the mind of the average member of Parliament is often expressed by some such statement as 'that was likely (or unlikely) to have been the intention of Parliament'. Finally, although it is impossible to identify the individual members whose purpose it was, it is common to speak of the purpose, aim or object of a statute as the intention of Parliament. The third situation is the most important if only because reflection upon it shows that those who feel uncomfortable about the use of the expression 'intention of Parliament' ought not to feel any more at ease if they abandon the phrase for some other one such as 'the intention of the statute', 'legislative purpose' or 'the object of the statute'. Only human beings can really have intentions, purposes or objects, but, in the situation under consideration, the intentions, purposes or objects are not those of identifiable human beings. The words are used by close analogy to the intentions of a single legislator. The analogy is more remote when the 'intention of Parliament' is used as a synonym for what the average member of Parliament of a particular epoch would have meant by certain words or expected as the consequences of a statutory provision."

In addition, although we have suggested that judges frequently turn to the "ordinary meaning" of statutory language in interpretation, this approach also is closely connected to the idea of legislative purpose.

John Bell and Sir George Engle, *Cross on Statutory Interpretation* (3rd ed., Butterworths, London, 1995), p.32:

"'[T]he context of ordinary language' already involves a certain number of assumptions. Even in ordinary language, words have more than one meaning, *e.g.* a 'chair' can be something to sit on, the president of a meeting, or a job as a professor. The ordinary user of language selects the appropriate 'ordinary meaning' according to the context in which a communication takes place. Certain assumptions are made about the most likely use of the words in this context. Those assumptions relate, in part, to the purpose of the speaker or writer—if the word 'chair' is used by a university in an advertisement on the jobs page of a newspaper, it is unlikely to intend to refer to furniture. We still refer to this as an interpretation by reference to 'ordinary meaning' because the reader is able to rely on an immediate understanding of the purpose behind the use of the words without engaging in any further research. If this interpretation of the writer's words proves to be wrong, the reader can rightly complain that a warning should have been given that it was necessary to read the words in a different, less immediate context. Thus, an 'ordinary meaning' or 'grammatical meaning' does not imply that the judge attributes a meaning to the words of a statute independently of their context or of the purpose of the statute, but rather that he adopts a meaning which is appropriate in relation to the immediately obvious and unresearched context and purpose in and for which they are used. By enabling citizens (and their advisers) to rely on ordinary meanings unless notice is given to the contrary, the legislature contributes to legal certainty and predictability for citizens and to greater transparency in its own decisions, both of which are important values in a democratic society".

The judicial role in relation to purpose of the statute and intention of the legislature sometimes has been explicitly considered by the judiciary.

Duport Steels Ltd and others v Sirs and others [1980] 1 All E.R. 529, HL.

[The appeal concerned the interpretation of the Trade Union and Labour Relations Act 1974 and, in particular, whether the decision of a union in dispute with (the publicly owned) British Steel Corporation to extend a strike to the private steel sector was an action "in . . . furtherance of a trade dispute" and therefore not subject to a potential prosecution in tort. The House of Lords unanimously reversed the decision of the Court of Appeal (which included Lord Denning M.R.) which had found against the union.][1]

Lord Scarman:
". . . [I]n the field of statute law the judge must be obedient to the will of Parliament as expressed in its enactments. In this field Parliament makes and unmakes the law, the judge's duty is to interpret and to apply the law, not to change it to meet the judge's idea of what justice requires. Interpretation does, of course, imply in the interpreter a power of choice where differing constructions are possible. But our law requires the judge to choose the construction which in his judgment best meets the legislative purpose of the enactment. If the result be unjust but inevitable, the judge may say so and invite Parliament to reconsider its provision. But he must not deny the statute. Unpalatable statute law may not be disregarded or rejected, merely because it is unpalatable. Only if a just result can be achieved without violating the legislative purpose of the statute may the judge select the construction which best suits his idea of what justice requires. Further, in our system the *stare decisis* rule applies as firmly to statute law as it does to the formulation of common law and equi-

---

[1] For a discussion of this and related cases, see J.A.G. Griffith, *The Politics of the Judiciary* (4th ed., Harper Collins, London, 1999), pp.93–99.

table principles. And the keystone of *stare decisis* is loyalty throughout the system to the decisions of the Court of Appeal and this House. The Court of Appeal may not overrule a House of Lords decision; and only in the exceptional circumstances set out in the practice statement of 26 July 1966 will this House refuse to follow its own previous decisions.

Within these limits, which cannot be said in a free society possessing elective legislative institutions to be narrow or constrained, judges, as the remarkable judicial career of Lord Denning M.R. himself shows, have a genuine creative role. Greater judges are in their different ways judicial activists. But the Constitution's separation of powers, or more accurately functions, must be observed if judicial independence is not to be put at risk. For, if people and Parliament come to think that the judicial power is to be confined by nothing other than the judge's sense of what is right (or, as Selden put it, by the length of the Chancellor's foot), confidence in the judicial system will be replaced by fear of it becoming uncertain and arbitrary in its application. Society will then be ready for Parliament to cut the power of the judges. Their power to do justice will become more restricted by law than it need be, or is today."

INTERNAL AIDS TO DISCERNING INTENTION

To this point, our analysis of statutory interpretation has focused primarily upon the particular words which give rise to interpretive questions. But judges often find guidance to interpretation in *other* words within the context of the statute as a whole.[2] For example, it is commonly stated that "an act should be read as a whole". Thus, in order to understand the meaning of a word or phrase, it may well be helpful to look at the broader context of the statute as a whole, which may shed light on the particular interpretive question.

As well, there are a number of "rules" regarding the *admissibility* and *weight* of what are referred to as "internal aids" to the construction of statutes; that is, parts of a statute other than the enacted clauses themselves. These "rules" may seem quite arbitrary, but you should at least be aware that they exist.

Ian McLeod, *Legal Method* (4th ed., Palgrave Macmillan, Basingstoke, 2002), pp.281–285:

The anatomy of a statute

Preambles

"Where there is a preamble to a statute it will recite the reasons why the statute was passed. However, modern drafting practice in relation to Public Bills has almost entirely dispensed with the use of preambles, although they still appear in Private Bills, and therefore in Private Acts. It follows that their status for the purposes of interpretation is relatively insignificant in quantitative terms. Nevertheless, in those cases where preambles are encountered, their status is clear. According to Lord Normand in *Attorney-General v Prince Ernest Augustus of Hanover* [1957] 1 All ER 49, 'It is only when it conveys a clear and definite meaning in comparison with relatively obscure or indefinite enacting words that the preamble may legitimately prevail'. . . .

Long titles

Long titles are much more important than preambles in practice, since all modern statutes have them. Moreover, as the leading cases show, they have much the same effect in practice.

---

[2] See *e.g. Courtauld v Legh* (1869) L.R. 4 Exch. 126; *R. v Allen* (1872) L.R. 1 CCR 367; *R. v Millward* [1985] 1 All E.R. 859.

For example, in *R. v Galvin* [1987] 2 All ER 851, Lord Lane CJ, speaking of the Official Secrets Act 1911, and its predecessor of 1889, said:

> 'One can have regard to the title of a statute to help resolve an ambiguity in the body of it, but it is not, we consider, open to a court to use the title to restrict what is otherwise the plain meaning of the words of the statute simply because they seem to be unduly wide.' . . .

Short titles

The short title is almost always found towards the end of the statute. The leading case is *Re Boaler* [1915] 1KB 21, where it is acknowledged that the short title is part of the Act, and as such the court can and should consider it. However, it is by definition a *short* title and therefore, as Scrutton LJ said, 'accuracy may be sacrificed to brevity'. Moreover, particular care should be taken when dealing with the short titles of old Acts. Before 1896 it was not the practice for Acts to have short titles, but the Short Titles Act of that year conferred short titles on many older Acts. However, all the short titles were not necessarily appropriate, so that, for example, the short title of the Criminal Procedure Act was given to a statute passed in 1865 which dealt with both criminal and civil procedure.

Headings and marginal notes

A glance at any substantial statute will reveal a collection of *headings* (also know as *cross-headings*) between groups of sections, and *marginal notes* (also known as *side-notes* or *shoulder notes*) in the margin. These are both inserted by the drafter and are never subject to debate by Parliament.

There is reasonably clear judicial consensus that marginal notes and headings are relevant to the process of interpretation, 'provided that we realize that they cannot have equal weight with the words of the Act'. (Lord Reid in *Director of Public Prosecutions v Schildkamp* [1969] 3 All ER 1640.)

More particularly, marginal notes may be used to identify the mischief at which the section is aimed, as Upjohn LJ explained in *Stephens v Cuckfield RDC* [1960] 2 QB 373:

> 'While the marginal note to a section cannot control the language used in the section, it is a least permissible to approach a consideration of its general purpose and the mischief at which it is aimed *with the note in mind*.' [Emphasis added.]

Schedules

Although some comments may be found which suggest there is some significance in the distinction between the main (or operative) part of an Act and a Schedule to an Act, in reality the distinction is purely a matter of form and not of substance, as Bennion explains:

> 'It is often convenient to incorporate part of the operative provisions of an Act in the form of a Schedule. The Schedule is often used to hive off provisions which are too long or detailed to be put in the body of the Act. This does not mean they are unimportant.' (*Statutory Interpretation*, 3rd edn, 1997, p.554.)

Judicial authority to the same effect may be found in the judgment of Brett LJ in *Attorney-General v Lamplough* (1878) 3 ExD 214:

> 'A schedule in an Act is a mere question of drafting, a mere question of words. The schedule is as much part of the statute, and is as much an enactment, as any other part.'

Transitional provisions

A statute which amends an existing statute may well contain provisions which regulate the transition from the old scheme to the new. These transitional provisions will be found towards the end of the statute, and their substance is not uncommonly contained in Schedules. For example, the provisions of the Magistrates' Courts Act 1980, which amended the procedure to be followed by a magistrates' court when committing a defendant for trial at the Crown Court, came into force on 6 July 1981. A Schedule to the Act contained transitional provisions relating to proceedings which had begun before 6 July.

Definition sections

Definition sections, which are commonly found towards the end of statutes but towards the beginning of statutory instruments, contain provisions of two types. First there are those which simply state that the defined terms shall 'mean' whatever the provision states them to mean.

Secondly, there are those which state that the defined terms shall 'include' whatever the provision states them to include. In cases falling within the latter category the words will have not only their special statutory meaning but, according to Lord Selbourne LC in *Robinson v Baron-Eccles Local Board* (1883) 8 App Cas 798, they will also possess their 'ordinary, popular and natural sense whenever that would be applicable'. In other words, this category does not enact definitions in the strict sense of the term, since it is the nature of a definition to restrict, rather than simply to illustrate, the meaning of a word.

Commencement sections

Commencement sections are generally found towards the end of statutes. Section 4 of the Interpretation Act 1978, whose ancestry can be traced to the Acts of Parliament (Commencement) Act 1793, states that, where provision is made for an Act or part of an Act to come into force on a particular day, it comes into force at the beginning of that day; and that, where no such provision is made, an Act comes into force at the beginning of the day on which it receives Royal Assent. The limited degree of retrospectivity inherent in this provision appears to cause no injustice in practice, and is in any event a marked improvement over the pre-1793 position, when Acts took effect from the beginning of the Parliamentary session in which they were passed.

Section 4 of the 1978 Act is seldom relevant in practice, because statutes commonly state that they will come into force either on a particular future date, or on the expiry of a stated period after they receive Royal Assent, or on whatever day may be appointed by the appropriate Secretary of State, who will usually be empowered to make a commencement order by way of a statutory instrument. Appointed days and commencement orders are frequently used when the successful implementation of an Act depends on things such as setting up administrative machinery, appointing staff, making delegated legislation, and so on."

EXTERNAL AIDS TO DISCERNING INTENTION

If the task of the judiciary in interpreting legislation is to seek out the intention of the legislature, then intuitively it would seem reasonable that judges turn to those materials produced by Parliament which might well describe what Parliament had in mind when it was enacting new law. Although a variety of documents are produced by Parliament which might provide some insight into its intention regarding a statutory word or phrase, the most obvious source undoubtedly is *Hansard*: the record of the debates in the two Houses of Parliament. It will perhaps come as a surprise to you that historically these debates were not admissible in courts, (*i.e.* counsel was not allowed to introduce them as evidence into court) in order to assist in determining the meaning of a statute. As Lord Simonds explained:

> "The part which is played in the judicial interpretation of a statute by reference to the circumstances of its passing is too well known to need re-statement. It is sufficient to say that the general proposition that it is the duty of the court to find out the intention of

Parliament—and not only of Parliament but of Ministers also—cannot by any means be supported. The duty of the court is to interpret the words that the legislature has used. Those words may be ambiguous, but, even if they are, the power and duty of the court to travel outside them on a voyage of discovery are strictly limited."[3]

The relationship between what may have been intended by the legislature, and what was actually enacted, was described by the Earl of Halsbury L.C. As Lord Chancellor (a member of the government), he had been responsible for legislation. Yet, as a member of the House of Lords, he was charged with the ultimate judicial function. In *Hilder v Dexter* [1902] A.C. 474, the Earl of Halsbury discussed this anomalous situation, and decided to remove himself from the task of statutory interpretation in that case:

"My Lords, I have more than once had occasion to say that in construing a statute I believe the worst person to construe it is the person who is responsible for its drafting. He is very much disposed to confuse what he intended to do with the effect of the language which in fact has been employed. At the time he drafted the statute, at all events, he may have been under the impression that he had given full effect to what was intended, but he may be mistaken in construing it afterwards just because what was in his mind was what was intended, though, perhaps, it was not done. For that reason I abstain from giving any judgment in this case myself; but at the same time I desire to say, having read the judgments proposed to be delivered by my noble and learned friends, that I entirely concur with every word of them. I believe that the construction at which they have arrived was the intention of the statute. I do not say my intention, but the intention of the Legislature. I was largely responsible for the language in which the enactment is conveyed, and for that reason, and for that reason only, I have not written a judgment myself, but I heartily concur in the judgment which my noble and learned friends have arrived at (pp.477–478)."

Note especially how the Earl of Halsbury differentiates between the intention of the individual responsible for the drafting of a piece of legislation, and the intention of the legislature as a whole. This distinction remains an important one, which we will explore in this chapter. The traditional approach to *Hansard* was substantially modified in 1992, when the House of Lords took the opportunity to change the rule.

Pepper (Inspector of Taxes) v Hart and related appeals [1993] 1 All E.R. 42, HL.

[The background to the case has been summarised by Bale]:

"*Pepper v Hart* was initially a run of the mill tax case involving the valuation of a fringe benefit. The taxpayers were nine teachers and the bursar of Malvern College who took advantage of a scheme which permitted staff members to have their children educated at the school for only 2% of the fees payable by the public. As higher-paid employees they were required to include in their income, as a benefit of employment, the cash equivalent of the benefit which s.63(1) of the Finance Act 1976 defined as 'an amount equal to the cost of benefit less so much (if any) of it as is made good by the employee to those providing the benefit.' The taxpayers contended that the cost of the benefit was the additional or marginal cost of educating an additional student in a school that had surplus capacity and, since this was less than the concessionary fees paid by them, the cash equivalent of the benefit was nil. The Revenue contended the cost of the benefit was the same for all pupils, namely, the average cost of educating each pupil. The taxpayers won before the special commissioner but the decision was reversed by Vinelott J., and that decision was affirmed

[3] *Magor and St Mellons Rural District Council v Newport Corporation* [1951] 2 All E.R. 839 at 841, HL.

by the Court of Appeal. The taxpayers then appealed to the House of Lords. After the first hearing before a panel of five Law Lords, three supported the assessment made by the Revenue and two would have held for the taxpayers. However, before the Lords rendered their decision, the debate in the House of Commons in 1976 concerning the Finance Bill came to their attention. The Financial Secretary in reply to a specific question about the tax treatment of concessionary fees for children of school staff stated that 'the benefit will be assessed on the cost to the employer, which would be very small indeed in this case.' *Hansard* clearly indicated that in determining the benefit to the employee the marginal cost and not the average cost was intended under the Finance Act 1976."[4]

Lord Mackay of Clashfern L.C., dissenting [Lord Mackay's discussion of the factual background to the case has been omitted]:

". . . But much wider issues than the construction of the Finance Act 1976 have been raised in these appeals and for the first time this House has been asked to consider a detailed argument on the extent to which reference can properly be made before a court of law in the United Kingdom to proceedings in Parliament recorded in Hansard. . . .

The principal difficulty I have on this aspect of the case is that in Mr Lester's submission reference to parliamentary material as an aid to interpretation of a statutory provision should be allowed only with leave of the court and where the court is satisfied that such a reference is justifiable (a) to confirm the meaning of a provision as conveyed by the text, its object and purpose, (b) to determine a meaning where the provision is ambiguous or obscure or (c) to determine the meaning where the ordinary meaning is manifestly absurd or unreasonable.

I believe that practically every question of statutory construction that comes before the courts will involve an argument that the case falls under one or more of these three heads. It follows that the parties' legal advisers will require to study Hansard in practically every such case to see whether or not there is any help to be gained from it. I believe this is an objection of real substance. It is a practical objection, not one of principle. . . .

Your Lordships are well aware that the costs of litigation are a subject of general public concern and I personally would not wish to be a party to changing a well-established rule which could have a substantial effect in increasing these costs against the advice of the Law Commission and the Renton Committee unless and until a new inquiry demonstrated that that advice was no longer valid.

I do not for my part find the objections in principle to be strong and I would certainly be prepared to agree the rule should no longer be adhered to were it not for the practical consideration to which I have referred and which my noble and learned friend agrees to be of real substance. . . . If reference to parliamentary material is permitted as an aid to the construction of legislation which is ambiguous, or obscure or the literal meaning of which leads to an absurdity, I believe as I have said that in practically every case it will be incumbent on those preparing the argument to examine the whole proceedings on the Bill in question in both Houses of Parliament. Questions of construction may be involved on what is said in Parliament and I cannot see how if the rule is modified in this way the parties' legal advisers could properly come to court without having looked to see whether there was anything in the Hansard report on the Bill which could assist their case. If they found a passage which they thought had a bearing on the issue in this case, that passage would have to be construed in the light of the proceedings as a whole.

I fully appreciate, and feel the force of the narrowness of the distinctions which are taken between what is admissible and what is not admissible, but the exception presently proposed is so extensive that I do not feel able to support it in the present state of our knowledge of its practical results in this jurisdiction. For these reasons, I agree that these appeals should be allowed, although I cannot agree on the main issue for the discussion of which this further hearing was arranged."

---

[4] Gordon Bale, "Parliamentary Debates and Statutory Interpretation: Switching on the Light or Rummaging in the Ashcans of the Legislative Process" (1995) 74 *Canadian Bar Review* 1 at 13.

Lord Browne-Wilkinson [The discussion of the factual and legislative background has been omitted]:

Should the rule prohibiting reference to parliamentary privilege be relaxed?

"Under present law, there is a general rule that references to parliamentary material as an aid to statutory construction is not permissible (the exclusionary rule) (see *Davis v. Johnson* [1978] 1 All ER 1132, [1979] AC 264 and *Hadmor Productions Ltd v. Hamilton* [1981] 2 All ER 724, [1983] 1 AC 191). This rule did not always apply but was judge-made. Thus, in *Ash v. Abdy* (1678) 3 Swan 664, 36 ER 114 Lord Nottingham L.C. took judicial notice of his own experience when introducing the Bill in the House of Lords. The exclusionary rule was probably first stated by Willes J. in *Millar v. Taylor* (1769) 4 Burr 233 at 2332, 98 ER 21 at 217. However, *Re Mew and Throne* (1862) 31 L.J. Bcy 87 shows that even in the middle of the last century the rule was not absolute: in that case Lord Westbury L.C. in construing an Act had regard to its parliamentary history and drew an inference as to Parliament's intention in passing the legislation from the making of amendment striking out certain words.

The exclusionary rule was later extended so as to prohibit the court from looking even at reports made by commissioners on which legislation was based (see *Salkeld v. Johnson* (1848) 2 Exch 256 at 273, 154 ER 487 at 495). This rule has now been relaxed so as to permit reports of commissioners, including Law Commissioners, and white papers to be looked at for the purpose solely of ascertaining the mischief which the statute is intended to cure but not for the purpose of discovering the meaning of the words used by Parliament to effect such cure. . . . Indeed, in *Factortame Ltd v. Secretary of State for Transport* [1989] 2 All ER 692, [1990] 2 AC 85 your Lordships' House went further than this and had regard to a Law Commission report not only for the purpose of ascertaining the mischief but also for the purpose of drawing an inference as to parliamentary intention from the fact that Parliament had not expressly implemented one of the Law Commission's recommendations. . . .

[T]he reasons put forward for the present rule are, first, that it preserves the constitutional proprieties, leaving Parliament to legislate in words and the courts (not parliamentary speakers) to construe the meaning of the words finally enacted, second, the practical difficulty of the expense of researching parliamentary material which would arise if the material could be looked at, third, the need for the citizen to have access to a known defined text which regulates his legal rights and, fourth, the improbability of finding helpful guidance from *Hansard*.

The Law Commissions of England and Scotland in their joint report on *Interpretation of Statutes* and the Renton Committee on *Preparation of Legislation* both recognised that there was much to be said in principle for relaxing the rule but advised against a relaxation at present on the same practical grounds as are reflected in the authorities. However, both bodies recommended changes in the form of legislation which would, if implemented, have assisted the court in its search for the true parliamentary intention in using the statutory words. . . .

My Lords, I have come to the conclusion that, as a matter of law, there are sound reasons for making a limited modification to the existing rule (subject to strict safeguards) unless there are constitutional or practical reasons which outweigh them. In my judgment, subject to the questions of the privileges of the House of Commons, reference to parliamentary material should be permitted as an aid to the construction of legislation which is ambiguous or obscure or the literal meaning of which leads to an absurdity. Even in such cases references in court to parliamentary material should only be permitted where such material clearly discloses the mischief aimed at or the legislative intention lying behind the ambiguous or obscure words. In the case of statements made in Parliament, as at present advised I cannot foresee that any statement other than the statement of the minister or other promoter of the Bill is likely to meet these criteria.

I accept Mr Lester's submissions, but my main reason for reaching this conclusion is based on principle. Statute law consists of the words that Parliament has enacted. It is for the courts to construe those words and it is the court's duty in so doing to give effect to the intention of Parliament in using those words. It is an inescapable fact that, despite all the care taken in passing legislation, some statutory provisions when applied to the circumstances under consideration in any specific case are found to be ambiguous. One of the reasons for such ambiguity is that the members of the legislature in enacting the statutory provision may have been told what result those words are intended to achieve. Faced with a given set of words which are capable of conveying that meaning it is not surprising if the words are accepted as having that meaning. Parliament never intends to enact any ambiguity. Contrast with that the position of the courts. The courts are faced simply with a set of words which are in fact capable of bearing two meanings. The courts are ignorant of the underlying parliamentary purpose. Unless something in other parts of the legislation discloses such purpose, the courts are forced to adopt one of the two possible meanings using highly technical rules of construction. In many, I suspect most, cases references to parliamentary materials will not throw any light on the matter. But in a few cases it may emerge that the very question was considered by Parliament in passing the legislation. Why in such a case should the courts blind themselves to a clear indication of what Parliament intended in using those words? The court cannot attach a meaning to words which they cannot bear, but if the words are capable of bearing more than one meaning why should not Parliament's true intention be enforced rather than thwarted?

A number of other factors support this view. As I have said, the courts can now look at white papers and official reports for the purpose of finding the 'mischief' sought to be corrected, although not at draft clauses or proposals for the remedying of such mischief. A ministerial statement made in Parliament is an equally authoritative source of such information; why should the courts be cut off from this source of information as to the mischief aimed at? In any event, the distinction between looking at reports to identify the mischief aimed at but not to find the intention of Parliament in enacting the legislation is highly artificial. Take the normal Law Commission report which analyses the problem and then annexes a draft Bill to remedy it. It is now permissible to look at the report to find the mischief and at the draft Bill to see that a provision in the draft was not included in the legislation enacted (see *Factortame v. Secretary of State for Transport* [1989] 2 ALL ER 692, [1990] 2 AC 85). There can be no logical distinction between that case and looking at the draft Bill to see that the statute as enacted reproduced, often in the same words, the provision in the Law Commission's draft. Given the purposive approach to construction now adopted by the courts in order to give effect to the true intentions of the legislature, the fine distinctions between looking for the mischief and looking for the intention in using words to provide the remedy are technical and inappropriate. Clear and unambiguous statements made by ministers in Parliament are as much the background to the enactment of legislation as white papers and parliamentary reports. . . .

It is said that parliamentary materials are not readily available to, and understandable by, the citizen and his lawyers, who should be entitled to rely on the words of Parliament alone to discover his position. It is undoubtedly true that Hansard and particularly records of committee debates are not widely held by libraries outside London and that the lack of satisfactory indexing of committee stages makes it difficult to trace the passage of a clause after it is redrafted or renumbered. But such practical difficulties can easily be overstated. It is possible to obtain parliamentary materials and it is possible to trace the history. The problem is one of expense and effort in doing so, not the availability of the material. In considering the right of the individual to know the law by simply looking at legislation, it is a fallacy to start from the position that all legislation is available in a readily understandable form in any event: the very large number of statutory instruments made every year are not available in an indexed form for well over a year after they have been passed. Yet, the practitioner manages to deal with the problem, albeit at considerable expense. Moreover, experience in New Zealand and Australia (where the strict rule has been relaxed for some years) has not shown that the non-availability of materials has raised these practical problems.

Next, it is said that lawyers and judges are not familiar with parliamentary procedures and will therefore have difficulty in giving proper weight to the parliamentary materials. Although, of course, lawyers do not have the same experience of these matters as members of the legislature, they are not wholly ignorant of them. If, as I think, significance should only be attached to the clear statements made by a minister or other promoter of the Bill, the difficulty of knowing what weight to attach to such statements is not overwhelming. In the present case, there were numerous statements of view by members in the course of the debate which plainly do not throw any light on the true construction of s.63. What is persuasive in this case is a consistent series of answers given by the minister, after opportunities for taking advice from his officials, all of which point the same way and which were not withdrawn or varied prior to the enactment of the Bill.

Then it is said that court time will be taken up by considering a mass of parliamentary material and long arguments about its significance, thereby increasing the expense of litigation. In my judgment, though the introduction of further admissible material will inevitably involve some increase in the use of time, this will not be significant as long as courts insist that parliamentary material should only be introduced in the limited cases I have mentioned and where such material contains a clear indication from the minister of the mischief aimed at, or the nature of the cure intended, by the legislation. Attempts to introduce material which does not satisfy those tests should be met by orders for costs made against those who have improperly introduced the material. Experience in the United States of America, where legislative history has for many years been much more generally admissible than I am now suggesting, shows how important it is to maintain strict control over the use of such material. That position is to be contrasted with what has happened in New Zealand and Australia (which have relaxed the rule to approximately the extent that I favour): there is no evidence of any complaints of this nature coming from those countries.

There is one further practical objection which, in my view, has real substance. If the rule is relaxed legal advisors faced with an ambiguous statutory provision may feel that they have to research the materials to see whether they yield the crock of gold, *i.e.* a clear indication of Parliament's intentions. In very many cases the crock of gold will not be discovered and the expenditure on the research wasted. This is a real objection to changing the rule. However, again it is easy to overestimate the cost of such research: if a reading of *Hansard* shows that there is nothing of significance said by the minister in relation to the clause in question, further research will become pointless.

In sum, I do not think that the practical difficulties arising from a limited relaxation of the rule are sufficient to outweigh the basic need for the courts to give effect to the words enacted by Parliament in the sense that they were intended by Parliament to bear. Courts are frequently criticised for their failure to do that. This failure is due not to cussedness but to ignorance of what Parliament intended by the obscure words of the legislation. The courts should not deny themselves the light which parliamentary materials may shed on the meaning of the words Parliament has used and thereby risk subjecting the individual to a law which Parliament never intended to enact.

Is there, then, any constitutional objection to a relaxation of the rule? The main constitutional ground urged by the Attorney General is that the use of such material will infringe s.1, Art.9 of the Bill of Rights as being a questioning in any court of freedom of speech and debates in Parliament. As I understand the submission, the Attorney General was not contending that the use of parliamentary material by the courts for the purposes of construction would constitute an 'impeachment' of freedom of speech since impeachment is limited to cases where a member of Parliament is sought to be made liable, either in criminal or civil proceedings, for what he has said in Parliament, *e.g.* by criminal prosecution, by action for libel or by seeking to prove malice on the basis of such words. The submission was that the use of *Hansard* for the purpose of construing an Act would constitute a 'questioning' of the freedom of speech or debate. The process, it is said, would involve an investigation of what the minister meant by the words he used and would inhibit the minister in what he says by attaching legislative effect to his words. This, it was submitted, constituted 'questioning' the freedom of speech or debate.

Article 9 is a provision of the highest constitutional importance and should not be narrowly construed. It ensures the ability of democratically elected members of Parliament to discuss what they will (freedom of debate) and to say what they will (freedom of speech).

But, even given a generous approach to this construction, I find it impossible to attach the breadth of meaning to the word 'question' which the Attorney General urges. It must be remembered that art.9 prohibits questioning not only 'in any court' but also in any 'place out of Parliament'. If the Attorney General's submission is correct, any comment in the media or elsewhere on what is said in Parliament would constitute 'questioning' since all members of Parliament must speak and act taking into account what political commentators and others will say. Plainly art.9 cannot have effect so as to stifle the freedom of all to comment on what is said in Parliament, even though such comment may influence members in what they say.

In my judgment, the plain meaning of art.9, viewed against the historical background in which it was enacted, was to ensure that members of Parliament were not subjected to any penalty, civil or criminal, for what they said and were able, contrary to the previous assertions of the Stuart monarchy, to discuss what they, as opposed to the monarch, chose to have discussed. Relaxation of the rule will not involve the courts in criticising what is said in Parliament. The purpose of looking at *Hansard* will not be to construe the words used by the minister but to give effect to the words used so long as they are clear. Far from questioning the independence of Parliament and its debates, the courts would be giving effect to what is said and done there. . . .

According to my judgment the use of clear ministerial statements by the court as a guide to the construction of ambiguous legislation would not contravene art.9. No doubt all judges will be astute to ensure that counsel does not in any way impugn or criticise the minister's statement or his reasoning.

The Attorney General raised a further constitutional point, namely that for the court to use parliamentary material in construing legislation would be to confuse the respective roles of Parliament as the maker of law and the courts as the interpreter. I am not impressed by this argument. The law, as I have said, is to be found in the words in which Parliament has enacted. It is for the courts to interpret those words so as to give effect to that purpose. The question is whether, in addition to other aids to the construction of statutory words, the courts should have regard to a further source. Recourse is already had to white papers and official reports not because they determine the meaning of the statutory words but because they assist the court to make its own determination. I can see no constitutional impropriety in this.

Finally, on this aspect of the case, the Attorney General relied on considerations of comity: the relaxation of the rule would have a direct effect on the rights and privileges of Parliament. To the extent that such rights and privileges are to be found in the Bill of Rights, in my judgment they will not be infringed for the reasons which I have given. . . .

I therefore reach the conclusion . . . that the exclusionary rule should be relaxed so as to permit reference to parliamentary materials where: (a) legislation is ambiguous or obscure, or leads to an absurdity; (b) the material relied on consists of one or more statements by a minister or other promoter of the Bill together if necessary with such other parliamentary material as is necessary to understand such statements and their effect; (c) the statements relied on are clear. Further than this, I would not at present go."

[Lord Keith of Kinkel, Lord Bridge of Harwich, Lord Griffiths, Lord Ackner, Lord Oliver of Aylmerton all concurred in their reasons with Lord Browne-Wilkinson on the admissibility of *Hansard* in judicial proceedings. The appeal was allowed with costs.]

The decision in *Pepper v Hart* undoubtedly has been and will continue to be of significance for statutory interpretation in the years to come. The reasons why the House of Lords decided to alter its historical approach to Parliamentary materials are varied.

Gordon Bale, "Parliamentary Debates and Statutory Interpretation: Switching on the Light or Rummaging in the Ashcans of the Legislative Process" (1995) 74 Canadian Bar Review 1 at 17:

"A number of reasons combined to bring about the demise of the exclusionary rule. Perhaps the most important is the move toward a purposive approach to statutory interpretation that has gained momentum in Britain in the last four decades. Also the volume and complexity of modern statutes has required the judiciary to seek greater knowledge of the legislative context in order to construe them properly. There has been growing realization that the canons of interpretation are simply a grab bag of conflicting presumptions that offer little guidance to the proper interpretation of statutes. The powerful European influence exerted through greater contact with decisions of the European Court of Justice and the European Court of Human Rights has reinforced the advantage of a purposive approach to legislation in place of literal interpretation. Commonwealth countries, particularly Australia and New Zealand, have thrown out the traditional exclusionary rule. That this has been achieved without adverse consequences has exerted an influence in Britain. Another factor is that in spite of the rule judges frequently do look to the debates for guidance or to check that their interpretation accords with the purpose of the statute. Many counsel regarded this surreptitious peek at Hansard to be unfair to litigants because the exclusionary rule prevented them from making any submissions about the relevance and weight to accord the parliamentary record. Finally courts do not focus solely on the statute but look to extrinsic aids such as Reports of Royal Commissions, Law Commission Reports and White Papers at least to perceive the problem with which the statute was intended to cope. Admitting these extrinsic aids while excluding the sometimes more relevant parliamentary debates became logically indefensible. In view of the purposive approach to statutory interpretation the highly artificial distinction between looking for the mischief and not the intent appeared increasingly technical and inappropriate. Finally, counsel by wisely arguing for only limited modification of the exclusionary rule finessed the rule of law requirement that the statute book must remain a reliable guide to the citizen. Hansard will only be consulted when legislation is ambiguous, obscure or leads to an absurdity. The courts as interpreters will still be confined by the text but in the case of ambiguity they will not be confined *to* it. The appropriate separation of powers between parliament and the courts will be preserved."

The impact of the House of Lords decision in *Pepper v Hart* will be felt by practitioners, courts, and Parliament alike. The impact on the practitioner was explicitly recognised by the Law Lords, and is significant, with a resulting impact on the users of legal services.

T.St.J.N. Bates, "The Contemporary Use of Legislative History in the United Kingdom" (1995) 54 C.L.J. 127 at 136:

"The majority of the Law Lords may have considered these various difficulties would have a limited practical effect because the relaxation of the exclusionary rule was thought to have been carefully circumscribed and would, in any event, be policed by orders for costs. . . . However that may be, the assessment of the majority of the Law Lords has not been shared by the experienced practitioner nor is it borne out by practice. For example James Goudie Q.C. has observed that standing committee debates, where much relevant material is likely to be found, are not held at all by the (English) Law Society, by the Supreme Court Library, or by the libraries of three of the Inns of Court and only partially by the fourth; and a few other libraries in London have incomplete sets on closed access or in store requiring advance notice. He described the position outside London as 'dire almost to the point of being non-existent'. In times of economic stringency the position of academic law libraries may be even worse. On a visit to Cambridge, the writer was informed that in 1991, as an economy measure, the Squire Law Library ceased even to take the Hansard reports of proceedings on the floor of the Commons and the Lords, let alone of standing committee debates, although they are still held by the University Library. . . .

The concerns of the practitioner are further exacerbated by the possibility that if there is a failure to research the full parliamentary material in advising a client on a question of statutory interpretation the practitioner may be liable for a breach of professional duty. Indeed some members of the English Bar have adopted the practice in their opinion work, both to avoid liability and reduce costs for the client, of including a disclaimer that the opinion has not involved researching the parliamentary material which as a result of *Pepper v. Hart* may be relevant to a question of interpretation. The client, for a further fee, may then presumably request the research to be undertaken."

The impact of *Pepper v Hart* is also felt by Parliament.

David Miers, "Taxing Perks and Interpreting Statutes: Pepper v. Hart" (1993) 56 M.L.R. 695 at 706:

". . . But what are the longer term implications of *Pepper v. Hart* upon the preparation and interpretation of legislation? Consider first the impact of the House's decision on the function of parliamentary debate on Bills. As *Pepper v. Hart* gives the government the opportunity to say in other words what the legal effect of a clause is to be, there will be an incentive to use the opportunity whenever some particularly difficult piece of legislation is to be debated, as a way of increasing the chances that the courts will interpret the section as the government wishes. Are we therefore to see (like planted Parliamentary Questions) carefully framed amendments at the Committee stage (which will of course need to be selected by the Chairman) permitting Ministers to clarify what kinds of conduct fall within a given clause? But precisely because judicial reliance may be placed upon their remarks, Ministers will have to be careful not to deviate from the advice that has been prepared by their civil servants and by Parliamentary Counsel, as the following remarks made by Lord Henley, a Government Minister, at the Committee Stage of the Education Bill 1992 make abundantly clear:

'I very carefully said that I am advised that this is the case. In the light of the recent court case, *Pepper v. Hart* . . . it is very important that I know exactly what I am saying from the Dispatch Box.'

For the inexperienced Minister, the desirability of keeping to the brief will thus be the more powerful. This advice will apply as much when Ministers are moving new government amendments as when they are responding to probing amendments put by opposition parties. If their remarks are self-contradicting, then they will presumably fail to meet the new criteria, which include clarity: this suggests that Ministers will be discouraged from doing much more than repeating the advice they have been given. This, it may be argued, places too great a significance to sticking to the script at the cost of allowing worthwhile change to occur through debate. Merely nodding assent or dissent to assertions put by the other side, on the other hand, would presumably not count as a 'statement' and thus no reliance could be placed upon such indications. These considerations will also apply where amendments to private Members' Bills are debated, since the new rule includes remarks made by their sponsors. Since few private Members' Bills succeed that are not supported by the government (and indeed may be government Bills in all but name), departments will also have to consider what responses are likely to be made by the sponsor, and correct them if necessary. All this suggests more work for Parliamentary Counsel."

Finally, what is the impact on statutory interpretation in the courts? Miers gives one hypothesis.

David Miers, "Taxing Perks and Interpreting Statutes: *Pepper v Hart*" (1993) 56 M.L.R. 695 at 709:

"*Pepper v. Hart* accords primacy to ministerial statements in the event of absurdity, obscurity and ambiguity. To put it mildly, this is a significant break with tradition. Even recent statements on what has long been called the 'golden rule' of interpretation, that is, that the court may select a secondary meaning of a statutory word or phrase where its ordinary meaning in context yields an absurdity in this case, have emphasised that this secondary meaning must be one that can be linguistically sustained by the words in dispute. In short, *Pepper v. Hart* is of the first constitutional importance: it has brought about a reversal in the relative authority of two kinds of parliamentary statement. In formulating its relaxation of the exclusionary rule, the House said, in the person of Lord Browne-Wilkinson, 'Further than this, I would not at present go.' In Australia, where judicial access to 'any relevant report of a committee of the Parliament or of either House of the Parliament that was made to the Parliament or to that House of the parliament before the time when the provision was enacted' is a statutory permission, the courts have sought since its introduction in 1984 to limit the effect of the Minister's words. This is particularly so 'when the intention stated by the Minister but unexpressed in the law is restrictive of the liberty of the individual.' In such cases, however unfortunate it may be that the executive's intentions have been thwarted by statutory oversight or inadvertence, 'the function of the court is to give effect to the will of Parliament as expressed in the law.' What then will be the response of courts here? Will they give priority to the Minister's clear views (and irrespective of the quality of the Minister) over unclear legislation whether the effect is to the advantage or disadvantage of the citizen; or will they adopt the view that where the Minister's intentions benefit the citizen, those wishes will prevail; but that otherwise the executive is bound by the enacted law? *Yes, Minister* may yet prove to be an interpretive policy that does not receive unqualified approval."

The reaction to the decision in *Pepper v Hart* was not, by any means, unqualified support. A critical analysis of the decision is provided by Baker.

J.H. Baker, "Statutory Interpretation and Parliamentary Intention" (1993) 52 C.L.J. 353 at 354:

"It is submitted that evidence of ministerial statements is not relevant evidence because, allowing that statutes should be interpreted according to the intention of Parliament, no individual member of Parliament is in a position to state what that intention is or to speak for the silent majority. Parliament acts as a corporate body and the only expression of its common intention is the text to which the Queen and both Houses have given their unqualified assent. What passes in one House is not formally known to the other, or to the sovereign. Even if it is thought that the intention of Parliament is the same thing as the common intention of the greatest number of its members, what one individual member says in debates cannot be cogent evidence of what every other member intends. His remarks may be based on a sound and impartial legal understanding of the issues, but they may not. They may persuade some, but they may not persuade others. There is no debate in which every member speaks, or even a majority of members, and so the prevailing view cannot be ascertained from the speeches. Nor does the fact that a Bill secured the necessary assents enhance the evidentiary value of previous statements. It is not uncommon to vote for motions even when one disagrees with some of the statements and arguments of the person proposing them, because one is satisfied with the wording and one is voting for the wording and its effect rather than for the sentiments expressed orally by its proposer. In other cases one may be persuaded to vote in favour by the different reasoning of a speaker following the first mover, though any consideration of such speeches is apparently excluded under the new rule. Certainly there is no procedure for members of Parliament to register assent to a Bill coupled with dissent from all or some of the reasons given by its promoters. Silence by members is therefore equivocal. . . ."

It is remarkable that these well-known principles were not properly discussed in *Pepper v Hart*. The nearest we find to an implied response is the argument that the courts now take a purposive rather than a literal approach to construction. . . . The question is not whether the approach to interpretation is or should be purposive, which is not disputed, but how the purpose behind a document may properly and logically be established. In the case of statutes, it is axiomatic that the purpose to be sought is that of Parliament, and not that of the government. A minister speaks for the government, but not for Queen, Lords and Commons all at once. If the words of a minister are to be considered as evidence of parliamentary intention, should the minister be called as a witness so that he may be cross-examined? Apparently not. Again and again in the Lordships' speeches, the intention of the minister is equated with the intention of Parliament and is not regarded as a matter of evidence: the minister's words are to be read as a source of law, attached as it were to the Act. The exclusionary rule is consequently treated merely as a form of blindfold which for purely technical reasons serves to conceal the truth from the court. Yet what is in fact being concealed from the court is not the intention of Parliament, which can only be expressed in written form, but rather the policy of the government, which should be of no concern to the courts. It is, of course, a notorious fact that while a government remains in power it may whip in a majority of members of the House of Commons to vote in favour of its Bills. . . . It does not follow from *de facto* recognition of our party system, and is not a fact, that members belonging to the party in power may be whipped in to support the legal reasoning of a government minister, or the interpretation which he places on a particular Bill. The whip drives members' bodies into the lobby but is not used to correct their states of mind or to teach them law. It is surely an unwarranted assumption that a minister's interpretation of an ambiguous Bill indicates the intention even of the House of Commons, let alone of Parliament.

The government-centred approach of the House of Lords is, with respect, rather chilling. It is true that in the instant case it operated in favour of the taxpayer, but it must obviously work either way. In future, when an Act is unclear, the intention of Parliament is apparently to be equated with the policy of the government or with what a minister chose to say about that policy in the House of Commons. It took many centuries of constitutional struggle to eliminate the notion that the policy of the government should have the force of law; now, it seems, something very like it is slipping through the back door."

More recently, a critical analysis of the *Pepper v Hart* decision has been developed by Lord Steyn, one of the Law Lords, in a lecture given at University College Oxford.

Johan Steyn, "*Pepper v Hart*; A Re-examination" (2001) *Oxford Journal of Legal Studies* 59 at 60–61, 63–69, 72:

"In our democracy the primary law-making function is entrusted to citizens assembled in two separate chambers of Parliament. The legislature enacts statutes in accordance with the law of Parliament for a European liberal democracy. Subject to general presumptions of constitutional importance, such as the rule of law and the principle of constitutionality, the critical thing is what the text of the law so enacted by Parliament provides. When controversy arises the contextual meaning of the enacted text is controlling. The intention of the majority of members of the legislature on the subject under discussion, assuming such a fact to be discoverable, does not have legal significance. Similarly, the views of the government, ministers, and whips—decisive as their decisions may be on the outcome of debates—do not have any relevance to the meaning of the legislation. Under our constitution Parliament enacts legislation, the courts interpret and apply the enacted laws and the executive acts in conformity with the law as interpreted by the courts. The executive is enormously powerful in getting its proposals enacted. But it has no law-making function and it has no authority to declare what the law is or will be if a Bill is enacted. . . .

My concern is with the effect and consequences of the central ruling in *Pepper v Hart*.

Initially, my untutored view was that it must be right to let in *Hansard* material which can cast light on an ambiguous provision. And in 1996 I expressed that opinion in a public lecture. Recently, without expressing a view on the rival arguments of principle, I argued in a published essay that in the light of practical experience in the operation of *Pepper v Hart* it may have become an expensive luxury in our legal system. This was a view based on the meagre results yielded by the resort to *Hansard* set against the cost of producing such material. It has become the duty of lawyers to conduct such searches at pain of being judged to have been professionally negligent. . . .

Almost invariably such searches are fruitless. It remains my view that *Pepper v Hart* has substantially increased the cost of litigation to very little advantage. Many appellate judges share this view. . . .

It is sometimes meaningful and appropriate for a judge to refer to the intention of Parliament in recognition of its supreme law-making power. It is also perfectly sensible to say that legislation as duly promulgated reflects the will of Parliament. But it is quite a different matter to ascribe to a composite and artificial body such as a legislature a state of mind deduced from exchanges in debates. I am not saying that the law cannot ascribe to legal persons, such as companies and state agencies, an intention to commit particular acts. It can and often does. . . . But the argument that a legislature, operating through two chambers, each consisting of hundreds of members, may have an intention revealed by statements in debates raises distinctive problems. And until *Pepper v Hart* the common law, the law of Parliament, and our constitution knew no rule of attribution, or rule of recognition, treating statements of ministers as Acts of Parliament.

It is important to bear in mind precisely what is involved. The intention under consideration is one targeted on the meaning of language contained in a clause in a Bill and employed in a ministerial statement. A Bill is unique as a written document. First Parliamentary Counsel recently explained:

> '[a] Bill is not there to inform, to explain, to entertain or to perform any of the other usual functions of literature. A Bill's sole reason for existence is to change the law. The resulting Act *is* the law. A consequence of this unique function is that a Bill cannot set about communicating with the reader in the same way that other forms of writing do. It cannot use the same range of tools. In particular, it cannot repeat important points simply to emphasize their importance or safely explain itself by restating a proposition in different words. To do so would risk creating doubts and ambiguities that would fuel litigation. As a result, legislation speaks in a monotone and its language is compressed.'

Parliament can legislate only through the combined action of both Houses acting in accordance with the elaborate stages prescribed by the rules of Parliament. Although the legislative powers of Parliament are exercised by human beings, Parliament as an abstraction cannot have a state of mind like an individual. Parliament legislates by the use of general words. It would be strange use of language to say even of an individual legislator that he intended something in regard to the meaning of a Bill which was never present in his mind. To ascribe to all, or a plurality of legislators, an intention in respect of the meaning of a clause in a complex Bill and how it interacts with a ministerial explanation is difficult. The ministerial explanation in *Pepper v Hart* was made in the House of Commons only. What is said in one House in debates is not formally or in reality known to the members of the other House. How can it then be said that the minister's statement represents the intention of Parliament, i.e. both Houses? The Appellate Committee took the view that opposing views expressed by a person other than the promoter can safely be disregarded whenever a statement by a promoter is admitted. The statement of the promoter is treated as canonical. This is also an assumption which seems inherently implausible in respect of the ebb and flow of parliamentary debates. The relevant exchanges sometimes take place late at night in nearly empty chambers. Sometimes it is a party political debate with whips on. The questions are often difficult but political warfare sometimes leaves little time for reflection. These are not ideal conditions for the making of authoritative statements about the meaning of a clause in a Bill. In truth a minister speaks for the government and not for Parliament. The statements of a minister are no more than indications of what the government would like the law to be. In any event, it is not discoverable from the printed record whether individual members of the legislature, let alone a plurality in each chamber, understood and accepted a ministerial explanation of the suggested meaning of the words. For many the spectre of the ever watchful whips will be enough. They may agree on only one thing, namely, to vote yes. And they have no means of voting yes and registering at the same time disagreement with the explanation of the minister. Their silence is therefore equivocal. When one ponders such realities of parliamentary life the idea of determining from *Hansard* the true intention of Parliament on the meaning of a clause in a Bill, and an associated ministerial statement, looks more and more far fetched. In *Black-Clawson* Lord Reid, speaking with enormous parliamentary experience, said: 'We often say that we are looking for the intention of Parliament but that is not quite accurate. We are seeking the meaning of the words which Parliament used.'[5] It would have been a fiction for the House to say in *Pepper v Hart* that as a matter of historical fact the explanation of the Financial Secretary reflected the intention of Parliament. Such a fact cannot in the nature of things be deduced from *Hansard*. Arguably, the House may have had in mind in *Pepper v Hart* that an intention derivable from the Financial Secretary's statement ought to be imputed to Parliament. If that were the case, the reasoning would rest on a complete fiction. My view is that the only relevant intention of Parliament can be the intention of the composite and artificial body to enact the statute as printed. If there is substance in this part of my analysis, it tends to undermine the very core of the reasoning in *Pepper v Hart*.

It is now necessary to examine *Pepper v Hart* against a broader canvas. This requires consideration of the legal and practical consequences of the decision. I would argue that four propositions are sustainable. First, if the foundation requirements for the admission of a statement in *Hansard* are established it must be admitted. The court has no discretion. Secondly, the occasion to admit such a statement arises where, after exhausting normal methods of interpretation, there is an ambiguity, obscurity or absurdity in respect of the particular point of statutory interpretation and a promoting minister's statement is clear on the very question. In these circumstances it seems likely that a properly admitted statement will be a trump card or at the very least of considerable weight. Thirdly, in the real world of litigation it is impossible for a court to decline *in limine* to receive such a statement on the ground that the requirements of ambiguity, obscurity or absurdity are not satisfied. Such a refusal before all arguments have been deployed would be seen as a prejudgment of the case. This factor creates the opportunity for the full deployment of *Hansard* in a wide category of cases. Fourthly, it is in practice inevitable that the courts will from time to time allow such statements to determine whether there is ambiguity. Lord Browne-Wilkinson said: 'Having once looked at what was said in Parliament, it is difficult to put it out of mind'. This is underlined by the fact that, but for *Hansard*, the majority in *Pepper v Hart* would have decided in favour of the Revenue. In the real world it will be difficult to hold to a line that ambiguity, and so forth, must be determined only be reference to normal methods of interpretation. The third and fourth points are not critical to the rest of my argument but they underline the potential scope of *Pepper v Hart*.

There is a case for allowing a statute to be interpreted in favour of the taxpayer in accordance with a considered explanation given by a minister promoting the Bill. It is the argument that the executive ought not to get away with saying in a parliamentary debate that the proposed legislation means one thing in order to ensure the passing of the legislation and then to argue in court that the legislation bears the opposite meaning. That is what happened in *Pepper v Hart*. Lord Bridge of Harwich said that the Financial Secretary 'assured' the House that it was not intended to impose the relevant tax. He must have taken the view, as did other members of the majority, that the Revenue in imposing the tax were going back on an assurance to the House of Commons. That would have been an unfair result in a mature democracy. If such a consequence prevailed it might tend to undermine confidence in the legal system. Presented in this way the reasoning begins to look like an estoppel argument. An analogy springs to mind. English law adopts an objective approach

---

[5] *Black-Cawson International Ltd v Papierwerke Waldhoff Anschaffenberg AG* [1975] A.C. 591 at 613–615.

to the construction of written contracts. The question is not what the parties subjectively intended. The task of the judge is to ascertain what in the context of the contract the language must reasonably be taken to mean. Evidence of what the parties intended is generally excluded. On the other hand, if one party has led the other to act in the belief that in their dealings the contract will have a certain meaning the first party will be estopped from raising a contrary contention. In this way English law tempers the rigidity of the objective theory and the relevant exclusionary rules. Whether one calls it an estoppel or not *Pepper v Hart* as decided on its facts can similarly be viewed as a tempering of the exclusionary rule in the interests of fairness. On this basis the impact of the decision could be confined to the admission against the executive of categorical assurances given by ministers to Parliament. This may be a defensible and principled justification of *Pepper v Hart*. And it does not involve a search for the phantom of a parliamentary intention.

But that is not how the reasoning of the House in *Pepper v Hart* was formulated. The House had before it a ministerial statement which it regarded as favouring the taxpayer. This framework dictated the shape of the arguments and the judgments. The converse case was not considered. What would the position have been if the statutory position had been truly ambiguous and the ministerial statement favoured the Revenue? *Ex hypothesi* the statement would have come from a minister promoting the Bill and would have been clear on the very question in issue. It would therefore have been a trump card. A judge who declined to give effect to it would, on the reasoning in *Pepper v Hart*, be thwarting the intention of Parliament. What then happens to the principle that if a taxation provision is reasonably capable of two alternative meanings, the courts will prefer the meaning more favourable to the subject? *Pepper v Hart* does not address this question. It also does not address the position where, in the face of an ambiguity, presumptions of general application with constitutional import, e.g. restrictively construing general words in a statute which appear wide enough to trench on the rule of law, would otherwise have been regarded as decisive. The criteria laid down for the admissibility of statements made by a minister are wide enough to cover any case where the statement supports the government view. Nevertheless, as I have explained, there may be a new but respectable argument that in the field of taxation and elsewhere, *Pepper v Hart* may only be used against the executive.

The basis on which the exclusionary rule was relaxed ignores constitutional arguments of substance. Lord Bridge described the rule as 'a technical rule of construction'. And implicitly that is how the majority approached the matter. Surely, it was much more. It was a rule of a constitutional importance which guaranteed that only Parliament, and not the executive, ultimately legislates; and that the courts are obliged to interpret and apply what Parliament has enacted, and nothing more or less. To give the executive, which promotes a Bill, the right to put its own gloss on the Bill is a substantial inroad on a constitutional principle, shifting legislative power from Parliament to the executive. Given that the ministerial explanation is *ex hypothesi* clear on the very point of construction, *Pepper v Hart* treats qualifying ministerial policy statements as canonical. It treats them as a source of law. It is in constitutional terms a retrograde step: it enables the executive to make law. It is to be noted that the objection is not to the idea of a judge looking at *Hansard*. For example, it may be unobjectionable for a judge to identify the mischief of a statute from *Hansard*. What is constitutionally unacceptable is to treat the intentions of the government as revealed in debates as reflecting the will of Parliament.

Let me look at some of the wider consequences of *Pepper v Hart*. *Prima facie* the statutes of our Parliament are regarded as 'always speaking' and not tied to the circumstances in which they were passed. A statute 'has a legal existence independently of the historical contingencies of its promulgation, and accordingly should be interpreted in the light of its place within the system of legal norms currently in force'.[6] This is a benign principle which allows for statutes to apply despite the inevitable changes in social conditions of society. It seems to me, it may be said that the position is crystallized as explained by the minister at

---

[6] Sir Rupert Cross, *Statutory Interpretation* (3rd ed., 1995) 52; *Reg. v Ireland* [1998] A.C. 147 at 158C–D; see also S.A. De Smith, Lord Woolf and J. Jowell, *Judicial Review of Administrative Action* (5th ed.) para.6–07.

the time. In the result the reference to *Hansard* settles an interpretation within the contemporary understanding of government and this introduces a new form of literalism. If that is so, a valuable capacity of our legal system to cope with changing conditions is lost. Another feature of our system which must be considered is the principle of legality. It does not permit general wording in statutes to erode basic rights and freedoms. There is too great a risk that the implications of general words may go unnoticed in the democratic process. If Parliament wishes to make inroads on basic rights it must squarely confront what it is doing. But what happens if the minister made a *Pepper v Hart* statement indicating an intention by general words to modify a basic right? Lord Lester of Herne Hill, the barrister who so ably and successfully argued *Pepper v Hart* in the House of Lords, has subsequently written that the courts will not 'permit ministers to interfere with basic rights and freedoms on the basis of what ministers say in Parliament'. But how can that be guaranteed if the legislation is ambiguous and there is a clear ministerial statement indicating that such an inroad on fundamental rights is intended? After all, under *Pepper v Hart* the court has no element of discretion. Another consequence of *Pepper v Hart* is on the drafting of statutes. That draftsmen will continue to draft with care and precision I do not doubt. But when political issues arise and ministers become involved *Pepper v Hart* offers an opportunity to call off a search for precision by making a statement. A likely effect of *Pepper v Hart* is to encourage imprecision in drafting in controversial measures.

A matter not considered in *Pepper v Hart* is the likely impact of the relaxation of the exclusionary rule on executive practice. It was always predictable that the behaviour of ministers would alter in response to the change announced in *Pepper v Hart*. After all, why should ministers not take advantage of the opportunity under *Pepper v Hart* to explain the effect of the legislation in the way in which the government would like to be understood? If this happens it must mark a constitutional shift of power from Parliament to ministers. . . .

I have challenged a judgment of Lord Browne-Wilkinson. His contribution to the development of English law as a judge, Vice-Chancellor, Law Lord and eventually Senior Law Lord has been immense. He is a great judge. But our allegiance must always be to the law. As lawyers our duty is to follow the evidence and arguments where they lead. I hope I have demonstrated that in *Pepper v Hart* issues of high principle were not examined and that a re-examination of that case is necessary. It is for you to judge whether I have succeeded in this task."

NOTES

- For the perspective of a legislative drafter on *Pepper v Hart*, see Francis Bennion, "Hansard—Help or Hindrance? A Draftsman's View of *Pepper v Hart*" (1993) 14 Statute Law Review 149.

- For an analysis of the much more liberal American approach to legislative history in statutory interpretation, see Stephen D. Grivin, "Hansard and the Interpretation of Statutes" (1993) 22 Anglo-American Law Review 475; and, for a discussion of other jurisdictions, see Gordon Bale, "Parliamentary Debates and Statutory Interpretation: Switching on the Light or Rummaging in the Ashcans of the Legislative Process" (1995) 74 Canadian Bar Review 1.

- In *Pepper v Hart*, Lord Browne-Wilkinson discusses the admissibility of other Parliamentary materials as extrinsic aids to statutory interpretation. The "leading" case on the admissibility of material such as Parliamentary committee reports, which may contain draft legislation, is *Black-Clawson International Ltd v Papierwerke Waldhof Aschaffenburg AG* [1975] 1 All E.R. 81, HL.

- *Pepper v Hart* is sometimes explained as an example of the penetration of a European approach to interpretation. We consider approaches to interpretation in the particular context of European law in Chapter 10.

The decision in *Pepper v Hart* has been applied extensively by courts, and McLeod summarises the way in which the law has developed in the years since the House of Lords delivered this landmark judgment:

Ian McLeod, *Legal Method* (4th ed., Palgrave Macmillan, Basingstoke, 2002), pp.292–294:

"Turning to the case-law on the application of *Pepper v Hart*, it is necessary to consider how the courts decide whether an ambiguity exists in a particular case. Although a judge may take a robust view of the matter, as Millett LJ did when he declared that the meaning of s.56(4) of the Taxes Management Act 1970 was 'too plain for argument' (*Petch v Gurney* [1994] 3 All ER 731), it is clear that some judges may not regard their own opinions as being necessarily decisive of the matter. In *Restick v Crickmore* [1994] 2 All ER 112, Stuart-Smith LJ considered there was no ambiguity in the relevant provision, but nevertheless said:

'Perhaps it may be said that the difference of judicial opinion between the judges in the courts below and this court shows that there is an ambiguity (see *Chief Adjudication Office v Foster* [1993] 1 All ER 705 at 717 *per* Lord Bridge of Harwich).'

When applying *Pepper v Hart*, the courts will not go behind the statement which is reported in *Hansard*. In *R. v Secretary of State for Foreign and Commonwealth Affairs ex parte Rees-Mogg* [1994] 1 All ER 457, the court was invited to disregard a ministerial statement which had been made on the advice of the Attorney-General, as that advice was demonstrably wrong. Lloyd LJ said that this argument, 'would, if correct, undermine the utility of *Pepper v Hart* in every case in which it would otherwise apply. Ministers act on advice. It cannot make any difference whether the source of the advice is made explicitly.'

As the decision in *Pepper v Hart* has become more deeply embedded in the law, the courts have started to take a more relaxed view of it in various ways. For example, where it is doubtful whether the criteria in *Pepper v Hart* are satisfied, the court may be willing to permit a citation provided the other side does not object. (See *Richardson v Pitt-Stanley* [1995] 1 All ER 460.)

The courts have even referred to *Hansard* without mentioning *Pepper v Hart* at all, as illustrated by Lord Mustill's lengthy references to a speech of the Minister of State at the Home Office, relating to the Bill which became the Criminal Justice Act 1991. (See *Doody v Secretary of State for the Home Department* [1993] 3 All ER 92.)

A statement in Parliament as to the meaning of an existing Act is not within the *Pepper v Hart* principle (*Hillsdown Holdings plc v Pensions Ombudsman* [1997] 1 All ER 862), but where an existing provision is replaced by one expressed in different words, the absence of any Ministerial indication that a change in the law is intended may result in the court attaching no significance to the change of wording (*Berkovits v Grinberg (Attorney-General Intervening)* [1995] 2 All ER 681).

However, the House of Lords has seen the danger which only Lord Mackay LC perceived in *Pepper v Hart* itself, namely that references to *Hansard* may cost more than they are worth. More particularly, in *Melluish v BMA (No 3) Ltd* [1995] 4 All ER 453, Lord Browne-Wilkinson, giving the only substantial speech, emphasized that only statements specifically related to the provision in question could be brought within *Pepper v Hart*, and that where attempts were made to introduce other material:

'judges should be astute to check such misuse of the new rule by making appropriate orders as to costs wasted. In the present case, if it were otherwise appropriate to order the taxpayers to pay the costs of this issue, I would advise your Lordships to disallow any costs incurred by the Crown in the improper attempt to introduce this irrelevant Parliamentary material.' . . .

Lord Brown-Wilkinson's comment could easily be applied more widely to cases where the material in *Hansard* was relevant to the provision before the court, but nevertheless did not assist in the process of interpretation.

In *Three Rivers District Council v Bank of England* [1996] 2 All ER 363, the High Court said that a purposive approach to statutory interpretation, which it accepted as being generally appropriate, is particularly important when the court is seeking a construction which is consistent with a Community obligation. More particularly, in these circumstances, reference to Ministerial statements in *Hansard* is permissible in order to identify the purpose of a statute, even though the criteria specified in *Pepper v Hart* may not be satisfied."

NOTES AND QUESTIONS

- To what extent has the application of *Pepper v Hart* by the courts been faithful to the original precondition for the admissibility of *Hansard* imposed by the House of Lords?

- There are numerous other external aids to the interpretation of statutes which courts routinely draw upon in deciding cases, including academic textbooks. However, unlike the civilian tradition, common law judges tend not to rely on academic writing to a significant extent, although this may be changing somewhat.

- "Both the principled and the practical objections to the admissibility of *Hansard* in courts are more compelling than any benefits that might be derived therefrom." Do you agree?

LEGISLATIVE INTENTION AND SOCIAL CHANGE

Up to this point, we have assumed that the courts, in interpreting legislation, focus upon discerning the intention of the legislature. However, statutory language often must be interpreted over a long period. During that time, social conditions and mores may well have changed substantially, in such a way that the interpretation which will seem reasonable and, indeed, necessary to a majority of the population, may not have been that which would have been intended by those who voted for a statute in Parliament. To what extent, then, should courts adapt interpretation to meet the changing needs of a society? Should statutory interpretation be a *dynamic* or a *static* process? The issue has been confronted by courts on many occasions, some of them now legendary.

Henrietta Muir Edwards and others v Attorney-General for Canada [1930] A.C. 124, PC.

Lord Sankey L.C.:
"By s.24 of the British North America Act, 1867, it is provided that 'The Governor General shall from time to time, in the Queen's name, by instrument under the Great Seal of Canada, summon qualified persons to the Senate; and, subject to the provisions of this Act, every person so summoned shall become and be a member of the Senate and a senator.'

The question at issue in this appeal is whether the words 'qualified persons' in that section include a woman, and consequently whether women are eligible to be summoned to and become members of the Senate of Canada.

Of the appellants, Henrietta Muir Edwards is the Vice-President for the province of Alberta of the National Council of Women for Canada; Nellie L. McClung and Louise C. McKinney were for several years members of the Legislative Assembly of the said Province; Emily F. Murphy is a police magistrate in and for the said Province; and Irene Parlby is a member of the Legislative Assembly of the said Province and a member of the Executive Council thereof.

On August 29, 1927, the appellants petitioned the Governor General in Council to refer to the Supreme Court certain questions touching the powers of the Governor General to summon female persons to the Senate, and upon October 19, 1927, the Governor General in Council referred to the Supreme Court the aforesaid question. The case was heard before Anglin C.J., Duff, Mignault, Lamont, and Smith J.J., and upon April 24, 1928, the Court answered the question in the negative; the question being understood to be 'Are women eligible for appointment to the Senate of Canada.'

The Chief Justice, whose judgment was concurred in by Lamont and Smith JJ., and substantially by Mignault J., came to this conclusion upon broad lines mainly because of the common law disability of women to hold public office and from a consideration of various cases which had been decided under different statutes as to their right to vote for a member of Parliament.

Duff J., on the other hand, did not agree with this view. He came to the conclusion that women are not eligible for appointment to the Senate upon the narrower ground that upon a close examination of the British North America Act, 1867, the word 'persons' in s.24 is restricted to members of the male sex. The result therefore of the decision was that the Supreme Court was unanimously of the opinion that the word 'persons' did not include female persons, and that women are not eligible to be summoned to the Senate.

Their Lordships are of opinion that the word 'persons' in s.24 does include women, and that women are eligible to be summoned to and become members of the Senate of Canada.

In coming to a determination as to the meaning of a particular word in a particular Act of Parliament it is permissible to consider two points—namely: (i) The external evidence derived from extraneous circumstances such as previous legislation and decided cases. (ii) The internal evidence derived from the Act itself. As the learned counsel on both sides have made great researches and invited their Lordships to consider the legal position of women from the earliest times, in justice to their argument they propose to do so and accordingly turn to the first of the above points—namely: (i) The external evidence derived from extraneous circumstances. . . ."

[Lord Sankey then reviewed the historical position of women in relation to the holding of public office.]

"No doubt in any code where women were expressly excluded from public office the problem would present no difficulty, but where instead of such exclusion those entitled to be summoned to or placed in public office are described under the word 'person' different considerations arise.

The word is ambiguous, and in its original meaning would undoubtedly embrace members of either sex. On the other hand, supposing in an Act of Parliament several centuries ago it had been enacted that any person should be entitled to be elected to a particular office it would have been understood that the word only referred to males, but the cause of this was not because the word 'person' could not include females but because at common law a woman was incapable of serving a public office. The fact that no woman had served or has claimed to serve such an office is not of great weight when it is remembered that custom would have prevented the claim being made or the point being contested.

Customs are apt to develop into traditions which are stronger than law and remain unchallenged long after the reason for them has disappeared.

The appeal to history therefore in this particular matter is not conclusive. . . .

Their Lordships now turn to the second point—namely, (ii) the internal evidence derived from the Act itself. . . .

The British North America Act planted in Canada a living tree capable of growth and expansion within its natural limits. The object of the Act was to grant a Constitution to Canada. 'Like all written constitutions it has been subject to development through usage and convention': *Canadian Constitutional Studies*, Sir Robert Borden (1922), p.55.

Their Lordships do not conceive it to be the duty of this Board—it is certainly not their desire—to cut down the provisions of the Act by a narrow and technical construction, but rather to give it a large and liberal interpretation so that the Dominion to a great extent, but within certain fixed limits, may be mistress in her own house, as the provinces to a great extent, but within certain fixed limits, are mistresses in theirs. 'The Privy Council, indeed, has laid down that Courts of law must treat the provisions of the British North America Act by the same methods of construction and exposition which they apply to other statutes. But there are statutes and statutes; and the strict construction deemed proper in the case, for example, of a penal or taxing statute or one passed to regulate the affairs of an English parish, would be often subversive of Parliament's real intent if applied to an Act passed to ensure the peace, order and good government of a British Colony': see Clement's *Canadian Constitution* (3rd ed., p.347). . . .

A heavy burden lies on an appellant who seeks to set aside a unanimous judgment of the Supreme Court, and this Board will only set aside such a decision after convincing argument and anxious consideration, but having regard: (1) To the object of the Act—namely, to provide a constitution for Canada, a responsible and developing State; (2) that the word 'person' is ambiguous, and may include members of either sex; (3) that there are sections in the Act above referred to which show that in some cases the word 'person' must include females; (4) that in some sections the words 'male persons' are expressly used when it is desired to confine the matter in issue to males; and (5) to the provisions of the Interpretation Act; their Lordships have come to the conclusion that the word 'persons' in s.24 includes members both of the male and female sex, and that, therefore, the question propounded by the Governor General should be answered in the affirmative, and that women are eligible to be summoned to and become members of the Senate of Canada, and they will humbly advise His Majesty accordingly."

NOTES AND QUESTIONS

- The Judicial Committee of the Privy Council, composed primarily of the Law Lords, was the final court of appeal against decisions of colonial courts. It still exists, although most former British colonies have abolished appeals to the Privy Council.

- The "Persons Case", as it is widely known, is also famous for Lord Sankey's description of the British North America Act as a "living tree". What does this imply for the way in which courts approach the task of statutory interpretation? In this regard, what does Lord Sankey's comment that "there are statutes, and then there are statutes" mean?

The "Persons Case" is not solely of historical interest. Mossman argues that it exemplifies the way in which legal method itself is gendered.

Mary Jane Mossman, "Feminism and Legal Method: The Difference it Makes", in *At the* *Boundaries of Law* **(Martha Albertson Fineman and Nancy Sweet Thomadsen, eds.,** **Routledge, New York, 1991), pp.285–298:**

"Just a few years before the nineteenth century drew to a close, Clara Brett Martin was admitted to the practice of law in Ontario, the first woman to become a lawyer in the British Commonwealth. Her petition for admission was initially denied by the Law Society on the basis that there were no precedents for the admission of women as lawyers. However, in 1892 a legislative amendment was passed permitting women to be admitted as solicitors; three years later, another legislative amendment similarly permitted women to be admitted as barristers. Clara Brett Martin herself was finally admitted in February 1897 as a barrister and solicitor.

Because of the admission arrangements in Ontario, it was the Law Society of Upper Canada, rather than a superior court, which reviewed the issue of Clara Brett Martin's entitlement to admission as a lawyer. By contrast, there was a court challenge in the Province of New Brunswick when Mabel Penury French sought admission as a lawyer there in 1905. When her application was presented to the court, the judges decided unanimously that there were no precedents for the admission of women, and denied her application. In the next year, however, after the enactment of a legislative amendment, French was admitted as a lawyer in New Brunswick. The same pattern (judicial denial of the application followed by legislative amendment) occurred again some years later when she applied for admission by transfer in British Columbia, and in a number of other Canadian provinces when women applied for admission as lawyers.

In contrast to the cases where women sought to enter the legal profession and were denied admission by the courts, the celebrated Privy Council decision in the Persons case determined that Canadian women were eligible to participate in public life. . . .

The decisions in these cases offer an interesting historical picture of legal process in the cultural milieu of the early twentieth century. In the cases about the admission of women to the legal profession, judges accepted the idea that there was a difference between men and women, a difference which 'explained' and 'justified' the exclusion of women from the legal profession. Yet, the Privy Council's decision in the Persons case completely discounted any such difference in relation to the participation of women in public life.

The issue is why there were these differing approaches: was it the nature of the claims, the courts in which they were presented, or the dates of the decisions? More significantly, what can we learn from the reasoning in these cases about the nature of legal method, especially in the context of challenges to 'deeply-held beliefs, vested interests, and the status quo'? In other words, what do these cases suggest about the potential impact of feminism on legal method?

French's case in New Brunswick provides a good illustration of judicial decision making on the issue of women in law. Her case was presented to the court for direction as to the admissibility of women by the president of the Barristers' Society of New Brunswick (as *amicus curiae*), and the court decided that women were not eligible for admission. Indeed, Mr Justice Tuck emphatically declared that he had no sympathy for women who wanted to compete with men; as he said: 'Better let them attend to their own legitimate business'.
. . .

The stated reasons in these cases were consistent with well-established principles of legal method. The principles can be analyzed in terms of three aspects: (1) the characterization of the issues; (2) the choice of legal precedents to decide the validity of the women's claims; and (3) the process of statutory interpretation, especially in determining the effect of statutes to alter common law principles. Both the principles themselves and their application to these specific claims are important for an understanding of the potential impact of feminism on legal method.

Characterizing the issue

In both *French* and the Persons case, the judges consistently characterized the issues as narrowly as possible, eschewing their 'political' or 'social' significance, and explaining that the court was interested only in the law. . . .

Equally clearly, the women claimants never intended to bring to the court a 'neutral' legal issue for determination; they petitioned the court to achieve their goals, goals which were unabashedly political. In the face of such claims, however, the court maintained a view of its process as one of neutral interpretation. More significantly, the court's power to define the 'real issues' carried with it an inherent absence of responsibility on the part of the (male) judges for any negative outcome. It was the law, rather than the (male) person interpreting it, which was responsible for the decision. The result of such a characterization process, therefore, is to reinforce the law's detachment and neutrality rather than its involvement and responsibility; and to extend these characteristics beyond law itself to judges and lawyers.

Yet, how can we accommodate this characterization of detachment and neutrality with the opinions expressed, especially in *French*, about the role of women? The ideas about gender-based difference expressed forcefully by Mr Justice Barker in that case appear very close to an expression about the 'desirability' of women as lawyers and not merely a dispassionate and neutral application of legal precedents. Thus, at least in *French*, there is inconsistency between the legal method declared by the judges to be appropriate, and the legal method actually adopted in making their decisions. In this context, the expressed idea of detachment and neutrality both masks and legitimates judicial views about women's 'proper' sphere.

Using precedents in the Common Law tradition

The existence of women's common law disability was regularly cited in both these cases as the reason for denying their claims to be admitted to the legal profession and to take part in public life. The judges used numerous precedents for their conclusion. . . . Obviously, the Privy Council was less concerned with the absence of precedent in their decision making than the judges in *French*. Is this approach simply an early example of a court of highest jurisdiction deciding not to be bound by precedent in appropriate cases, or is there some other explanation?

In terms of the legal method described by the judges, of course, there is no answer to this question. Neither the judgments in the Supreme Court of Canada nor Lord Sankey's opinion in the Privy Council expressly consider the reality of women's experience at that time at all, and they specifically do not consider the reality of experience for the actual women claimants in the Persons case. Thus, even if the judges' perspectives on women's place were different in the two courts, there is virtually nothing in the judgments expressly reflecting them. For this reason, it is impossible to demonstrate that Lord Sankey's differing perspective was the reason for the different outcome in the Privy Council. At the same time, it is hard to find any other convincing explanation.

What does, of course, seem clear is the existence of judicial choice in the application of precedents. In the process of choosing earlier cases and deciding that they are binding precedents, judges make choices about which aspects of earlier cases are 'relevant' and 'similar,' choices which are not neutral but normative. In suggesting that the earlier decisions (relied on by the Supreme Court of Canada as binding precedents) were not determinative, Lord Sankey was declaring that the earlier decisions should not be regarded as exactly the same as the situation before the court in the Persons case. In this way, Lord Sankey's decision demonstrates the availability of choice in the selection of facts, in the categorization of principles and in the determination of relevance. At the same time, his opinion completely obscures the process and standards which guided the choice he actually made. To the myth of 'neutrality,' therefore, Lord Sankey added the 'mystery' of choice.

Interpreting statutes and Parliament's intent

Even in the statutes which used gender-neutral language, however, there were problems of statutory interpretation in relation to these cases. The legislation reviewed in the Persons case, as well as that at issue in the admission of both Martin and French, used the word 'person' in describing the qualifications for being appointed to the Senate and called to the bar respectively. In the Persons case in the Supreme Court of Canada, Chief Justice Anglin expressed his surprise that such a monumental change in the position of women could be conferred by Parliament's use of such insignificant means; as he stated rhetorically: 'Such an extraordinary privilege is not conferred furtively'. Not surprisingly, he concluded that the women's claim must be dismissed because there was no evident express intent on the part of Parliament to effect the change advocated by them; the use of the word 'person' was not, by itself, sufficient. . . .

Once again, however, the opinion of the Privy Council is different. After reviewing at some length the legislative provisions of the B.N.A. Act, Lord Sankey stated conclusively:

> 'The word 'person' . . . may include members of both sexes, and to those who ask why the word should include females, the obvious answer is why should it not. In these circumstances the burden is upon those who deny that the word includes women to make out their case.'[7]

Lord Sankey cited no precedent to support this presumption in favour of the most extensive meaning of the statutory language, even though it expressly contradicted the principles of statutory interpretation adopted by all the judges in the decision of the Supreme Court of Canada.

In the end, just as the Privy Council decision was puzzling in relation to the effect of legal precedents about women's common law disabilities, it is also difficult to reconcile Lord Sankey's conclusions about the interpretation of the statute to the principles and precedents accepted in the Supreme Court of Canada. Clearly, the Privy Council departed from the Supreme Court's approach to legal method in reaching its conclusion to admit the women's claim. What remains unclear are Lord Sankey's reasons for doing so.

Feminism and legal method

In such a context, what conclusion is appropriate about feminism's potential for perspective transforming in the context of legal method?

The analysis of these cases illustrates the structure of inquiry identified as legal method. First of all, legal method defines its own boundaries: questions which are inside the defined boundaries can be addressed, but those outside the boundaries are not 'legal' issues, however important they may be for 'politics' or 'morals,' etc. Thus, the question of women becoming lawyers or Senators was simply a matter of interpreting the law; it did not require any consideration of utility or benefit to the women themselves or to society in general. The purpose and the result of the boundary-defining exercise is to confer 'neutrality' on the law and on its decision makers; in so doing, moreover, the process also relieves both the law and its decision makers of accountability for (unjust) decisions—('our whole duty is [only] to construe . . . the provisions of the [constitution]').

More serious is the potential for judicial attitudes to be expressed, and to be used in decision making (either explicitly or implicitly), when there is no 'objective' evidence to support them; because of the myth of neutrality which surrounds the process, such attitudes may acquire legitimacy in a way which strengthens and reinforces ideas in 'politics' and 'morals' which were supposed to be outside the law's boundary. After the decision in *French*, for example, women were different as a matter of law, and not just in the minds of people like Mr Justice Barker. Thus, the power to name the boundaries of the inquiry (and to change them, if necessary) makes legal method especially impervious to challenges from 'the outside.'

---

[7] This portion of the judgment has not been included in the excerpted case.

Second, legal method defines 'relevance' and accordingly excludes some ideas while admitting others. Some facts, such as inherent gender-based traits, were regarded as relevant in *French*, for example, while in both cases the actual conditions in which women lived their lives were not relevant at all. What was clearly relevant in both cases were earlier decisions about similar circumstances from which the judges could abstract principles of general application. That all of the earlier cases had been decided by men, who were interpreting legislation drafted when women had no voting rights, was completely irrelevant to the decision making in the cases analyzed; even though the cases represented direct and significant challenges to the continuation of gender-exclusive roles and the circumstances of the historical context may seem quite significant to women now. The irony of solemn judicial reliance on precedent in the context of significant efforts by women to change the course of legal history underlines the significant role of legal method in preserving the status quo.

Finally, the case analysis demonstrates the opportunity for choice in legal method: choice as to which precedents are relevant and which approach to statutory interpretation is preferred; and choice as to whether the ideas of the mainstream or those of the margins are appropriate. The existence of choice in legal method offered some possibility of positive outcomes in the women's rights cases, at the same time as legal method's definitions of boundaries and concept of relevance ensured that positive outcomes would seldom occur. Lord Sankey's opinion in the Privy Council is an example of choice in legal method, however, which is as remarkable for its common sense as it is for its distinctiveness in legal method. Yet because Lord Sankey obscured the reasons for his choice, he also preserved the power and mystery of legal method even as he endowed women with the right to be summoned to the Senate. Thus, the opportunity for choice of outcome, positive as it appears, will not automatically lead to legal results which successfully challenge 'vested interests' or the 'status quo,' especially in relation to the law itself.

The conclusion that legal method is structured in such a way which makes it impervious to a feminist perspective is a sobering one. Within the women's movement, it has concrete consequences for the design of strategies for achieving legal equality: it suggests, for example, the general futility of court action for achieving significant change in women's rights, even though such action may be useful to monitor interpretation by courts or to focus attention on legal problems. For a feminist who is also a lawyer, however, the effort of 'double-think' may be both taxing and ultimately frustrating; the needs of clients require her to become highly proficient at legal method at the same time as her feminist commitment drives her to challenge the validity of its underlying rationale.

This dilemma also exists for feminist scholars. Feminist legal scholars are expected to think and write using the approaches of legal method: defining the issues, analyzing relevant precedents, and recommending conclusions according to defined and accepted standards of legal method. A feminist scholar who chooses instead to ask different questions or to conceptualize the problem in different ways risks a reputation for incompetence in her legal method as well as lack of recognition for her scholarly (feminist) accomplishments. Too often, it seems almost impossible to be both a good lawyer and a good feminist scholar.

This dilemma is similarly acute for feminist law teachers and students. With the advent of large numbers of women law students and increased numbers of women on law faculties, many have concluded that there is now a feminist perspective in the law school. Such a conclusion ignores the power of legal method to resist structural change. For example, discussions about whether feminist law teachers should create separate courses with feminist approaches and content, or whether we should use such approaches and content in 'malestream' courses, or whether we should do both at once, etc clearly confirm the 'reality' of the existing categories of legal knowledge, and reinforce the idea of the feminist perspective as 'Other'. While the separate course approach marginalizes the feminist perspective, the process of 'tacking on' feminist approaches to malestream courses only serves to emphasize what is really important in contrast to what has been 'tacked on.' Even efforts to give equal time to the feminist perspective and to reveal the essential maleness of the 'neutral' approach may underline that what is male is what really has significance. On this basis, adding women's experience to the law school curriculum cannot transform our perspective of law unless it also transforms legal method.

Taking this conclusion seriously, as I think we must, leads to some significant conclusions for women who are feminists and who are lawyers, law teachers and law students. It is simply not enough just to introduce women's experience into the curriculum or to examine the feminist approach to legal issues, although both of these activities are important. Yet, especially because there is so much resistance in legal method itself to ideas which challenge the status quo, there is no solution for the feminist who is a law teacher except to confront the reality that gender and power are inextricably linked in the legal method we use in our work, our discourse, and our study. Honestly confronting the barriers of our conceptual framework may at least permit us to begin to ask more searching and important questions."

Notes and questions

- Why is the idea of precedent *inherently* conservative? As a consequence, why is Lord Sankey's judgment so significant—both for what it reveals and for what it conceals?

- Mossman mentions Clara Brett Martin, the first woman lawyer in the British Commonwealth. Martin became a powerful symbol for equality in the legal profession but, after Mossman's article was published, it became apparent from Martin's private writings that she was vehemently anti-Semitic. It is worth remembering that historically the legal profession was closed not only to women, but also discriminated (and still does) on the basis of race, religion, ethnicity, class, sexuality, and other relations of power, which intersect in various ways.

Another example of the contested relationship between legislative intention, precedent, and social change can be found in the definition of a "family" in law and "society". These cases deal with the situation of death of a "statutory tenant" in rent protected housing. Under the law, a member of the tenant's "family" living with him or her cannot be evicted.

Gammans v Ekins [1950] 2 K.B. 328, CA.

[The claimant, David Gammans, the owner of number 177, Avery Lane, Gosport, a house within the Rent Restriction Acts, let it to a Mrs Smith who lived there until her death in 1949. The defendant, J.J. Ekins, had lived with her for a number of years, and had taken her name. In the neighbourhood they were thought to be man and wife.

On the tenant's death the defendant refused to quit the premises claiming to be a member of the tenant's "family" within the meaning of s.12(1)(g) of the Increase of Rent and Mortgage Interest (Restrictions) Act, 1920. The landlord in these proceedings claimed possession on the ground that the defendant was a trespasser.

The county court judge gave judgment for the defendant, finding him to be a member of the tenant's family. The landlord appealed.]

Asquith L.J. [after stating the facts]:

"It has been held that 'family' in s.12(1)(g) of the Act of 1920 should be given its popular meaning. Consanguinity is not a prerequisite of membership of the same family. On the authorities, not only are children members of their parents' family, but a husband is a member of his wife's, an adopted child a member of the adopter parents', and a husband, on unusual facts, has been held to be a member of the same family as his wife's niece. Mr Blundell, I think, was right in saying that the material decisions limit membership of the same 'family' to three relationships: first, that of children; secondly, those constituted by way of legitimate marriage, like that between a husband and wife; and thirdly, relationships whereby one person becomes *in loco parentis* to another. Beyond that point the law has not gone. I do not think that we should be justified in saying that the defendant was a member of the tenant's family. Either the relationship was platonic or it was not. The judge has not found which, and says that it makes no difference; but if their relations were platonic, I can see no principle on which it could be said that these two were members of the same family, which would not require the court to predicate the same of two old cronies of the same sex innocently sharing a flat.

If, on the other hand, the relationship involves sexual relations, it seems to me anomalous that a person can acquire a 'status of irremovability' by living or having lived in sin, even if the liaison has not been a mere casual encounter but protracted in time and conclusive in character.

But I would decide the case on a simpler view. To say of two people masquerading, as these two were, as husband and wife (there being no children to complicate the picture) that they were members of the same family, seems to be an abuse of the English language, and I would accordingly allow the appeal."

Jenkins L.J.:

"I agree. If the matter were free from authority, speaking for myself I would have little hesitation in holding that the defendant was not a member of the tenant's family within any ordinary accepted use of that expression or within the meaning of s.12(1)(g). There has, however, been a series of decisions, each of them addressed to the particular facts of the case before the court, which taken together have so extended the meaning of the word 'family' for the purposes of the sub-section as to make it possible to argue with a considerable degree of plausibility that there is no reason why the benefit of the sub-section should not be extended also to the defendant. But when the cases are examined, it will, I think, be found that none of them goes so far as we are invited to go in the present case. The defendant was not in my view a member of the tenant's family in any reasonable sense whatever. The parties for reasons of convenience, had chosen to live together and the defendant, to avoid as he said gossip, had taken the tenant's name of Smith. The neighbours assumed that they were husband and wife and accepted them as such. I cannot regard this as giving the defendant the same claim to be considered a member of the tenant's family as if they had been lawfully man and wife. . . .

If the county court judge's decision were to stand, an alarming vista would, it seems to me, be opened up: if, for instance, brothers and sisters are members of the tenant's family, I see no reason why two friends should not set up house together, one changing his or her name to that of the other, and then give out that they were sisters or brother and sister as the case might be; in which case, provided that they were accepted as such in the neighbourhood, there would, by parity of reasoning, be no ground why, when one of them, being a statutory tenant of the house in which they both resided died, the other should not claim to be a member of the statutory tenant's family on account of the artificial relationship which they had chosen for their own purposes to adopt. I agree that the appeal should be allowed."

Evershed M.R. [Evershed M.R. delivered concurring reasons and concluded with the comment]:

"It may not be a bad thing that by this decision it is shown that, in the Christian society in which we live, one, at any rate, of the privileges which may be derived from marriage is not equally enjoyed by those who are living together as man and wife but who are not married."

- Why are all of the members of the Court of Appeal so troubled by the legal implications of a finding in favour of Ekins in this case? In their minds, what are the implications? Half a century later, do those implications seem unacceptable?

- What is the *purpose* of the statutory provision in issue in this case? In light of that *purpose*, how would you define "family", *for the purposes of this statutory provision*?

Times change, and sometimes, so does the interpretation of a statutory provision, as the following judgment demonstrates.

Dyson Holdings Ltd v Fox [1975] 3 All E.R. 1031, CA.

Lord Denning M.R.:

"So far as we know, Jack Wright was a bachelor and Olive Agnes Fox was a spinster, who met 4 years ago and lived happily ever after. They lived together as man and wife. She took his name and was known as Mrs Wright. In 1940 they were bombed out and went to live at 3 Old Road, Lewisham. The rent book was in the name of Mr J Wright. They both went out to work and used their earnings to run the house. In every respect they were man and wife save that they had not gone through a ceremony of marriage.

After 21 years in the house, on 28 August 1961 Mr Jack Wright died. She remained on in the house and paid the rent, using the name Mrs Wright. The rent book remained in the name of 'J Wright' and the records of the landlord still showed the tenant as 'J Wright'.

I expect that the ownership changed hands from time to time, but in March 1973 the owners were a property company, Dyson Holdings Ltd. By this time Mrs Wright (as she was known) was herself getting on in years. She was 73. She wrote to the landlord asking for a statement of the weekly rent. She signed herself 'OA Wright'. This put the property company on enquiry. They asked their agents to call at the house. She told them that Mr Jack Wright died on 28 August 1961 and that she was his widow. The property company asked their agents to check up on the electoral roll. They did so. They found that she had given her name there as 'Olive Fox'. The property company inferred that she was not really his widow. If she had been his widow, she could, of course, have had protection under the Rent Acts. But, if she was not his widow, they thought they were entitled in law to get her out. So on 27 March 1973 they wrote to her:

'We are addressing you as Mrs O Wright although we understand from the Electoral Register that the person in occupation is Olive Fox and perhaps you would explain this in your reply. Until this matter is clarified, we are unable to accept any rent . . .'

So after all those years, the truth was out. She was not his widow. She was only a woman who had lived with him as his wife for 21 years. The property company refused to receive any rent from her and brought proceedings against her for possession on the ground that she was not protected by the Rent Act 1968. She had, they said, no tenancy and was a trespasser. They had accepted the rent from her, not knowing that the tenant had died. As soon as they discovered it, and that she was not his widow, they were entitled to possession. The judge accepted their argument. He held that he was bound by the decision of this court in *Gammans v. Ekins*. It was sad, he said, to have to turn this lady of 74 out; but felt he had no alternative. He ordered her out in 28 days. She appeals to this court.

Ever since 1920 the Rent Acts have protected a 'member of the tenant's family' in these words:

'. . . the expression 'tenant' includes a widow of a tenant . . . who was residing with him at the time of his death, or where a tenant . . . leaves no widow or is a woman, such member of the tenant's family so residing aforesaid as may be decided in default of agreement by the county court.'

So in the present case the lady is protected if she was a 'member of the tenant's family'; but not otherwise. Those words have often been considered by the courts. The cases collected are in Megarry on the Rent Acts. The word 'family' in the 1968 Act is not used in any technical sense, but in a popular sense. It is not used in the sense in which it would be used by a studious and unworldly lawyer, but in the sense in which it would be used by a man who is 'base, common and popular', to use Shakespeare's words . . . ."

[Lord Denning then considered *Gammans v Ekins*]:

"But is this court at liberty to reject the distinction? Are we bound by *Gammans v Ekins*? That case can be distinguished on narrow grounds, such as that the woman was the tenant and not the man, or that their relationship might perhaps have been platonic. But I dislike the device of distinguishing a case on narrow grounds. I prefer to say, as I have often said, that this court is not absolutely bound by a previous decision when it is seen that it can no longer be supported. At any rate, it is not so bound when, owing to the lapse of time, and the change in social conditions, the previous decision is not in accord with modern thinking. . . . I am glad to find that we are all of one mind on this, but in case there are some who are doubtful, I can put the case on a conventional ground.

It has been decided by the House of Lords that, when an Act uses an ordinary English word in its popular meaning as distinct from its legal meaning, it is for the tribunal of fact to decide whether or not that popular meaning covers the case in hand. The tribunal of fact must use its own understanding of the word and apply it to the facts which have been proved. A Court of Appeal should not interfere with its decision unless it was unreasonable in the sense that no tribunal acquainted with the ordinary use of language could reasonably reach that decision. That was the very ground of the decision of the House of Lords in *Brutus v. Cozens*.[8] In the light of that decision, it appears to me that *Gammans v. Ekins* was wrongly decided. In that case, the tribunal of fact — the county court judge — gave judgment for the man, finding him to be a 'member of the tenant's family'. The Court of Appeal recognised that the words were to be given their ordinary and popular meaning, but nevertheless they reversed the county court judge. I do not think they should have done. To my mind the decision of the county court judge in that case was a perfectly reasonable decision, as Evershed M.R. recognised. And, on the authority of *Brutus v. Cozens*, the Court of Appeal ought not to have interfered with it. They went wrong just as the Divisional Court did in *Brutus v. Cozens*.[9] Their decision cannot stand with that subsequent decision of the House of Lords. We are not, therefore, bound by it: see *Young v. Bristol Aeroplane*.[10]

I would, however, add a word of caution about *Brutus v. Cozens*. When an ordinary word comes to be applied to similar facts, in one case after another, it is very important that the various tribunals of fact should each apply it in the same way. For instance, if the question comes up: is an unmarried woman (living for many years as a man's wife) a member of his family? Each tribunal of fact should give the same answer. It would be intolerable if half of the judges gave one answer; and the other half another. . . .

So here in the present case, I think this court should give a definite ruling. We should rule that in this case this lady was a member of the tenant's family residing with him at the time of his death. As such, she was entitled to the protection of the Rent Acts. The property company were not entitled to turn her out. I would allow the appeal accordingly."

[8] [1972] 2 All E.R. 1297. [1973] A.C. 854.
[9] [1972] 2 All E.R. 1, [1972] 1 W.L.R. 484.
[10] [1944] 2 All E.R. 293 at 298, [1944] K.B. 718 at 725.

James L.J. [James L.J. reviewed the decision in *Gammans v Ekins* and continued]:
"It is not so easy to decide whether in 1961 the ordinary man would have regarded the appellant as a member of Mr Wright's family. The changes of attitude which have taken place cannot be ascribed to any particular year. Had we to consider the position as at 1955 I would not be satisfied that the attitude reflected in the words of Asquith L.J. in *Gammans v. Ekins* had changed. I am confident that by 1970 the changes had taken place. There is no magic in the date 1961. I think that, having regard to the radical change which has by 1975 taken place, it would be a harsh and somewhat ossified approach to the present case to hold that in 1961 the appellant was not in the popular sense a member of the family.

I turn to the issue whether there is any rule of law which precludes the appellant being a member of the family for the purposes of the Rent Acts. If there is, it is to be found only in the decision of this court in *Gammans v. Ekins*. I confess that I have been troubled in the course of argument as to how far the decision of this court in that case is conclusive of the present appeal. The court in *Gammans v. Ekins* reversed the trial judge. They could not have done so unless the issue was a question of law. It is not a decision which can be explained on the basis of a question of fact. The cases which are said to be inconsistent with the decision are in my judgment not shown to be inconsistent. They are based on the added fact of birth of a child or children to the illicit union. . . . I cannot take the view that *Gammans v. Ekins* was wrongly decided. The decision is binding on this court, but it is binding only on the meaning to be given to 'family' at that time. The point decided was that applying the popular meaning of the word 'family' as it was used and understood in 1949 the evidence of relationship could not support a finding that the defendant was a member of the tenant's family. The decision is not authority for the proposition that at some later time a person in a similar position to Mr Ekins could not in law be a member of the tenant's family within the meaning of the increase of Rent and Mortgage Interest (Restrictions) Act 1920 and the Rent Act 1968. The word 'family' must be given its popular meaning at the time relevant to the decision in the particular case.

To hold that *Gammans v. Ekins* precludes the appellant from bringing herself within the Act would be to apply a precedent slavishly in circumstances to which it is not appropriate having regard to reality.

I would therefore allow this appeal."

Bridge L.J. [Bridge L.J. considered *Gammans v. Ekins* and continued]:
"Can we give effect to this change in social attitude and consequent change in the scope of a common English word without doing violence to the doctrine of judicial precedent and notwithstanding that in this case the appellant's status must be considered at the date of the original tenant's death in 1961? I have felt some hesitation on both these points, but in the end have concluded that it would be unduly legalistic to allow either consideration to defeat the appellant's claim. On the first point, if language can change its meaning to accord with changing social attitudes, then a decision on the meaning of a word in a statute before such a change should not continue to bind thereafter, at all events in a case where the courts have consistently affirmed that the word is to be understood in its ordinary accepted meaning. On the second point, where the modern meaning is plain, we should, I think, be prepared to apply it retrospectively to any date, unless plainly satisfied that at that date the modern meaning would have been unacceptable.

Accordingly I agree that this appeal should be allowed."

Appeal allowed. Leave to appeal to the House of Lords refused.

NOTES AND QUESTIONS

• How do the members of the Court of Appeal in *Dyson Holdings v Fox* avoid the impact of the rules of horizontal precedent? Are the reasons convincing?

- The law-fact distinction is used by Lord Denning to justify his departure from the precedent of *Gammans v Ekins*. How? Is the distinction clearer to you after reading his reasons? (*hint*: probably not!).

Reading the case law on family members should make you think of other situations, some of which were raised by the judges themselves, that might come up in litigation. The following is a more recent example, where the surviving partner was successful when the case reached the House of Lords.

Fitzpatrick v. Sterling Housing Association Ltd [1999] 4 All E.R. 705, HL.

Lord Slynn of Hadley:
"My Lords, throughout this century Parliament has provided statutory protection for residential tenants and for certain persons with what can be called derived rights from those tenants. . . .

The Rent Act 1977 consolidated the existing law, but s.76 of the Housing Act 1980 extended the rights to take over the tenancy to a surviving spouse of either sex and not just to the widow. The 1977 Act was amended by the Housing Act 1988. The result was that at the relevant time for the present case by Sch 1 to the 1977 Act as amended, an 'original tenant' was defined as the person 'who immediately before his death, was a protected tenant of the dwelling-house or the statutory tenant of it by virtue of his previous protected tenancy' (see para 1). Then it is provided in paras 2 and 3 that:

'2.—(1) The surviving spouse (if any) of the original tenant, if residing in the dwelling-house immediately before the death of the original tenant, shall after the death be the statutory tenant if and so long as he or she occupies the dwelling-house as his or her residence.

    (2) For the purposes of this paragraph, a person who was living with the original tenant as his or her wife or husband shall be treated as the spouse of the original tenant.

    (3) If, immediately after the death of the original tenant, there is, by virtue of sub-paragraph (2) above, more than one person who fulfils the conditions in sub-paragraph (1) above, such one of them as may be decided by agreement or, in default of agreement, by the county court shall be treated as the surviving spouse for the purposes of this paragraph.

3.—(1) Where paragraph 2 above does not apply, but a person who was a member of the original tenant's family was residing with him in the dwelling-house at the time of and for the period of 2 years immediately before his death then, after his death, that person or if there is more than one such person such one of them as may be decided by agreement, or in default of agreement by the county court, shall be entitled to an assured tenancy of the dwelling-house by succession.'

It is unnecessary for present purposes to set out the remainder of Sch 1. It is however to be noted that since the 1988 Act it is only the spouse (actual or deemed) who gets a statutory tenancy. Other family members get an assured tenancy which does not pass on to that person's successor whereas in the case of the spouse there may be further succession.

There are differences between this legislation and the Housing Acts dealing with public sector housing, but it does not seem to me necessary to set out those provisions here.

Mr John Thompson was the 'original tenant' of a flat known as 75A Ravenscourt Road, London W6 from 1972 until his death in his sixties on 9 November, 1994. That flat is part of a two-flat building of which the respondent is the registered freehold owner. Mr Martin

Fitzpatrick, the appellant in these proceedings, lived with Mr Thompson in the flat from 1976 until the latter's death and has continued to live there since. It is agreed between the parties that the appellant and the deceased has been partners in a longstanding, close, loving and faithful, monogamous, homosexual relationship.

The appellant sought a declaration that he had succeeded to the tenancy under the Rent Act 1977, as amended. He claimed that he was 'a spouse' of the deceased in that he had been living with Mr Thompson 'as his wife or husband' or alternatively that he was a member of Mr Thompson's family.

Judge Colin Smith QC, in a sensitive and sympathetic judgment, found the relationship to have been of the description agreed by the parties to which I have referred. He related an accident in 1986 when Mr Thompson fell down the stairs and sustained a blood clot to the brain which led to his being in a coma for some months. When he came round he never spoke again. As the judge said:

> 'Eventually, after various unfortunate incidents at the hospital, the applicant took Mr Thompson home in April 1986 to care for him full time himself. The applicant took over the total care 24 hours a day for Mr Thompson, feeding him and nursing him until his death in 1994. The applicant gave up his job and received benefit because he was unable to work, due to his full time care of Mr Thompson. Despite the loving and dedicated care of the applicant, Mr Thompson died in November 1994.'

The learned judge held, however, that the applicant could not succeed to the tenancy under either of the ways he put his claim. Waite and Roch LJJ ([1974] 4 All ER 991, [1998] Ch 304) agreed with him in the result, though expressing considerable sympathy and under-standing of the position in which same-sex partners living together found themselves under the legislation as they, and in the case of Roch LJ with hesitation in respect of the second way of putting the claim, held it to be. They both considered that there were matters which Parliament ought to consider. Ward LJ, in a trenchant and detailed judgment, concluded that the appellant succeeded as a spouse of, but, if not, then as a member of the family of, the original tenant.

On this appeal to your Lordships' House the appellant put forward both grounds but he relies in the first place on para 2 of Sch 1 to the 1977 Act, as amended. 'Spouse', he says, is to be interpreted in the present climate as including two persons of the same sex inti-mately linked in a relationship which is not merely transient and which has all the indicia of a marriage save that the parties cannot have children. In the second place, he says that the intimacy of the relationship of two persons living together as he and Mr Thompson were is such that they should be regarded as constituting a family.

It has been suggested that for your Lordships to decide this appeal in favour of the appellant would be to usurp the function of Parliament. It is trite that that is something the courts must not do. When considering social issues in particular judges must not sub-stitute their own views to fill gaps. They must consider whether the facts 'fall within the parliamentary intention' (see *Royal College of Nursing of the UK v Dept of Health and Social Security* [1981] 1All ER 545 at 565, [1981] AC 800 at 822 per Lord Wilberforce). Thus in the present context if, for example, it was explicit or clear that Parliament intended the word 'family' to have a narrow meaning for all time, it would be a court's duty to give effect to it whatever changes in social attitudes a court might think ought to be reflected in the legislation. Similarly, if it were explicit or clear that the word must be given a very wide meaning so as to cover relationships for which a court, conscious of the traditional views of society might disapprove, the court's duty would be to give effect to it. It is, however, for the court in the first place to interpret each phrase in its statutory context. To do so is not to usurp Parliament's function; not to do so would be to abdicate the judicial function. If Parliament takes the view that the result is not what is wanted it will change the legislation.

The question is, therefore, was the appellant the spouse of, or a member of the family of, Mr Thompson within the meaning of this Act? I stress 'within the meaning of this Act' since it is all that your Lordships are concerned with. In other statutes, in other contexts, the words may have a wider or a narrower meaning than here. I refer to the judgment of

McHugh J in *Re Wakim, ex p McNally, Re Wakim, ex p Darvall, Re Brown, ex p Amann, Spinks v Prentice* (1999) 73 ALJR 839 at 850 in the High Court of Australia which recognises that changes in attitudes and perceptions may require a wider meaning to be given to a word such as 'marriage', at any rate in some contexts.

The first question then is whether the appellant was the 'spouse' of Mr Thompson within the meaning of para 2 of Sch 1 to the 1977 Act as amended. I recognise that if the non-gender specific noun 'spouse' stood alone the matter might be more debatable as Mr Blake QC contends, though the ordinary meaning is plainly 'husband' or 'wife'. In the context of this Act, however, 'spouse' means in my view legally a husband or wife. The 1988 amendment extended the meaning to include as a 'spouse' a person living with the original tenant 'as his or her wife or husband'. This was obviously intended to include persons not legally husband and wife who lived as such without being married. That *prima facie* means a man and a woman, and the man must show that the woman was living with him as 'his' wife; the woman that he was living with her as 'her' husband. I do not think that Parliament as recently as 1988 intended that these words should be read as meaning 'my same-sex partner', rather than specifically 'husband' or 'wife'. If that had been the intention, it would have been spelled out. The words cannot in my view be read as the appellant contends. I thus agree as to the result with the decision in *Harrogate BC v Simpson* (1984) 17 HLR 205. The appellant accordingly fails in the first way he puts his appeal. Whether that result is discriminatory against same-sex couples in the light of the fact that non-married different sex couples living together are to be treated as spouses, so as to allow one to succeed to the tenancy of the other may have to be considered when the Human Rights Act is in force. Whether the result is socially desirable in 1999 is a matter for Parliament.

Is it fatal to a claim to be a member of the family of the original tenant that the appellant cannot show that he was living with Mr Thompson as his husband or wife, the nearest family relationship he asserts? In my view it is not. If a person does not succeed on the first he may still succeed on the second category. Here the partner fails because the first category requires partners of different sexes. That he cannot satisfy. If he satisfies the definition of family he may still qualify.

I turn then to the second question which I, at any rate, have found a difficult one—difficult largely because of preconceptions of a family as being a married couple and, if they have children, their children; difficult also because of the result of some of the earlier cases when applying the law to the facts. It is, however, obvious that the word 'family' is used in a number of different senses, some wider, some narrower. 'Do you have any family?' usually means 'do you have children?' 'We're having a family gathering' may include often distant relatives and even close friends. The 'family of nations', 'the Christian family' are very wide. This is no new phenomenon. Roman law, as I understand it, included in the family all members of the social unit though other rights might be limited to spouses or heirs.

It is not an answer to the problem to assume (as I accept may be correct) that if in 1920 people had been asked whether one person was a member of another same-sex person's family, the answer would have been 'no'. That is not the right question. The first question is what were the characteristics of a family in the 1920 Act, and the second whether two same-sex partners can satisfy those characteristics so as today to fall within the word 'family'. An alternative question is whether the word 'family' in the 1920 Act has to be updated so as to be capable of including persons who today would be regarded as being of each other's family, whatever might have been said in 1920 . . .

If 'family' could only mean a legal relationship (of blood or by legal ceremony of marriage or by legal adoption) then the appellant would obviously fail. Over the years, however, the courts have held that this is not so. . . .

Given, on the basis of these earlier decisions that the word is to be applied flexibly, and does not cover only legally binding relationships, it is necessary to ask what are its characteristics in this legislation and, to answer that question, to ask further what was Parliament's purpose. It seems to me that the intention in 1920 was that not just the legal wife but also the other members of the family unit occupying the property on the death of the tenant with him should qualify for the succession. The former did not need to prove a qualifying period; as a member of the tenant's family a two-year residence had to be shown.

If more than one person qualified, then, if no agreement can be reached between them, the court decided who should succeed.

The hallmarks of the relationship were essentially that there should be a degree of mutual inter-dependence, of the sharing of lives, of caring and love, of commitment and support. In respect of legal relationships these are presumed, though evidently they are not always present, as the family law and criminal courts know only too well. In de facto relationships these are capable, if proved, of creating membership of the tenant's family. If, as I consider, this was the purpose of the legislation, the question is then who in 1994 or today (I draw no distinction between them) are capable in law of being members of the tenant's family. It is not who would have been so considered in 1920. In considering this question it is necessary to have regard to changes of attitude. The point cannot have been better put than it was by Bingham MR in *R v Ministry of Defence, ex p Smith* [1996] 1 All ER 257 at 261–263, [1996] QB 517 at 552–554 when, although dealing with the validity of an administrative decision rather than the meaning of a few words in a statute, he said, after referring to changes of attitude in society towards same-sex relationships:

> 'I regard the progressive development and refinement of public and professional opinion at home and abroad, here very briefly described, as an important feature of this case. A belief which represented unquestioned orthodoxy in Year X may have become questionably by Year Y, and unsustainable by Year Z. Public and professional opinion are a continuum.'

If 'meaning' is substituted for 'opinion' the words are no less appropriate. In *Barclays Bank plc v O'Brien* [1993] 4 All ER 417 at 431, [1994] 1 AC 180 at 198 Lord Browne-Wilkinson (with whom other members of the House agreed) said that in relation to the equity arising from undue influence in a loan transaction:

> 'But in my judgment the same principles are applicable to all other cases where there is an emotional relationship between cohabitees. The "tenderness" shown by the law to married women is not based on the marriage ceremony but reflects the underlying risk of one cohabitee exploiting the emotional involvement and trust of the other. Now that unmarried cohabitation, whether heterosexual or homosexual, is widespread in our society, the law should recognise this.'

In particular, if the 1988 amendment had not been made ('as his or her wife or husband') I would have no hesitation in holding today when, it appears, one-third of younger people live together unmarried, that where there is a stable, loving and caring relationship which is not intended to be merely temporary and where the couple live together broadly as they would if they were married, that each can be a member of the other's family for the purpose of the 1977 Act.

If, as I think, in the light of all the authorities this is the proper interpretation of the 1920 Act I hold that as a matter of law a same-sex partner of a deceased tenant can establish the necessary familial link. They are capable of being, in Russell LJ's words in *Ross v Collins*, a broadly recognisable *de facto familial nexus*' (see [1964] 1 All ER 861, [1964] 1 WLR 425 at 432). It is then a question of fact as to whether he or she does establish the necessary link.

It is accordingly not necessary to consider the alternative question as to whether by 1999 the meaning of the word in the 1920 Act needs to be updated. I prefer to say that it is not the meaning which has changed but those who are capable of falling within the words have changed. . . .

It seems to be suggested that the result which I have so far indicated would be cataclysmic. In relation to this Act it is plainly not so. The onus on one person claiming that he or she was a member of the same-sex original tenant's family will involve that person establishing rather than merely asserting the necessary indicia of the relationship. A transient superficial relationship will not do even if it is intimate. Mere cohabitation by friends as a matter of convenience will not do. There is, in any event, a minimum residence qualification: the succession is limited to that of the original tenant. Far from being cataclysmic it is, as both the county court judge and the Court of Appeal appear to recognise, and as I consider, in accordance with contemporary notions of social justice. In other statutes, in other contexts, the same meaning may or may not be the right one. If a narrower meaning is required, so be it. It seems also to be suggested that such a result in this statute undermines the traditional (whether religious or social) concept of marriage and the family. It does nothing of the sort. It merely recognises that, for the purposes of this Act, two people of the same sex can be regarded as having established membership of a family, one of the most significant human relationships which both gives benefits and imposes obligations.

It is plain on the findings of the county court judge that in this case, on the view of the law which I have accepted, on the facts the appellant succeeds as a member of Mr Thompson's family living with him at his death.

On that ground I would allow the appeal.'

Lord Nicholls of Birkenhead:

'My Lords, this appeal raises an important point on the interpretation of a provision in the Rent Acts. For many years certain residential tenants have enjoyed the benefits of fair rentals and protection from eviction conferred by successive Rent Acts. Ever since the earliest days of this legislation in 1920, these benefits have not been confined to the original tenant. Under the Increase of Rent and Mortgage Interest (Restrictions) Act 1920, s.12(1)(g), 'tenant' included the widow of a tenant in certain circumstances and, in other case, such 'member of the tenant's family' residing with him when he died as might be agreed or decided by the court. In addition to protecting the tenant personally, Parliament has always been concerned to protect the family unit of which the deceased tenant was a part. . . .

The question calling for decision in the present case is a question of statutory interpretation. It is whether the same-sex partner is capable of being a member of the other partner's family for the purposes of the Rent Act legislation. I am in no doubt that this question should be answered affirmatively. A man and woman living together in a stable and permanent sexual relationship are capable of being members of a family for this purpose. Once this is accepted, there can be no rational or other basis on which the like conclusion can be withheld from a similarly stable and permanent sexual relationship between two men or between two women. Where a relationship of this character exists, it cannot make sense to say that, although a heterosexual partnership can give rise to membership of a family for Rent Act purposes, a homosexual partnership cannot. Where sexual partners are involved, whether heterosexual or homosexual, there is scope for the intimate mutual love and affection and long-term commitment that typically characterise the relationship of husband and wife. This love and affection and commitment can exist in same-sex relationships as in heterosexual relationships. In sexual terms a homosexual relationship is different from a heterosexual relationship, but I am unable to see that the difference is material for present purposes. As already emphasised, the concept underlying membership of a family for present purposes is the sharing of lives together in a single family unit living in one house. . . .

This submission raises the question whether the word 'family' as used in the Rent Acts may change its meaning as ways of life and social attitudes change. Can the expression family legitimately be interpreted in 1999 as having a different and wider meaning than when it was first enacted in 1920? The principles applicable were stated cogently by Lord Wilberforce in *Royal College of Nursing of the UK v Dept of Health and Social Security* [1981] 1 All ER 545 at 564–565, [1981] AC 800 at 822. A statute must necessarily be interpreted having regard to the state of affairs existing when it was enacted. It is a fair presumption that Parliament's intention was directed at that state of affairs. When circumstances change, a court has to consider whether they fall within the parliamentary intention. They may do so if there can be detected a clear purpose in the legislation which can only be fulfilled if an extension is made. How liberally these principles may be applied must depend upon the nature of the enactment, and the strictness or otherwise of the words in which it was expressed.

In the present case Parliament used an ordinary word of flexible meaning and left it undefined. The underlying legislative purpose was to provide a secure home for those who share their lives together with the original tenant in the manner which characterises a family unit. This purpose would be at risk of being stultified if the courts could not have regard to changes in the way people live together and changes in the perception of relationships. This approach is supported by the fact that successive Rent Acts have used the same undefined expression despite the far-reaching changes in ways of life and social attitudes meanwhile. It would be unattractive, to the extent of being unacceptable, to interpret the word 'family' in the 1977 Act without regard to these changes.

The change in attitudes towards unmarried couples cohabiting as husband and wife exemplifies this point. In *Gammans v Ekins* [1950] 2 KB 328 the court's decision was affected by its perception of the immorality of such a relationship. An immoral relationship did not come within the ambit of family in the Rent Acts. Asquith LJ said it would be anomalous that a person could acquire protection by living in sin even if the liaison was protracted in time and conclusive in character. Jenkins LJ described the relationship as no more than a liaison between two elderly people who chose to pose as husband and wife when they in fact were not. Evershed MR was more hesitant, but his conclusion was that it might be no bad thing to show that one of the privileges derivable from marriage was not equally enjoyed by those living together as man and wife but in fact unmarried.

In one respect of crucial importance there has been a change in social attitudes over the last half-century. I am not referring to the change in attitude toward sexual relationships between a man and woman outside marriage or toward homosexual relationships. There has been a widespread change in attitude toward such relationships, although differing and deeply felt views are held on these matters. These differing views are to be recognised and respected. The crucial change to which I am referring is related but different. It is that the morality of a lawful relationship is not now regarded as relevant when the court is deciding whether an individual qualifies for protection under the Rent Acts. Parliament itself made this clear in 1988, when amending the Rent Acts in the 1988 Act. Paragraph 2(3) of Sch 1 envisages that more than one person may be living with the tenant as a surviving spouse under the extended definition. In so enacting the law, Parliament was not expressing a view, either way, on the morality of such relationships. But by this provision Parliament made plain that, for purposes of Rent Act protection, what matters is the factual position. The same must be true of homosexual relationships.

It is for this reason that I do not accept the argument that the inclusion of a tenant's homosexual partner within the ranks of persons eligible to qualify as members of his family is a step which should be left to Parliament. It really goes without saying that in cases such as this the courts must always proceed with particular caution and sensitivity. That is not to say the courts can never proceed at all. That is not what the Court of Appeal did in 1975 when deciding the *Dyson Holdings* case. Nor should this course commend itself to your Lordships in the present case.

In this regard, at the risk of repetition, it is necessary to stress the limited nature of the decision in this case. The courts have already decided that the undefined expression 'family' is to be given a wide meaning in the context of the Rent Acts. The courts have already decided that family included relationships other than those based on consanguinity or affinity. To include same-sex partners is to do no more than apply to them the same rationale as that underlying the inclusion of different sex partners. The decision goes no further than this. The decision leaves untouched questions such as whether persons of the same sex should be able to marry, and whether a stable homosexual relationship is within the scope of the right to respect for family life in art.8 of the Convention for the Protection of Human Rights and Fundamental Freedoms (Rome, 5 November 1950; TS 71 (1953); Cmd 8969).

I would allow this appeal. It is not disputed that if a same-sex partner can qualify as a member of the tenant's family, the appellant does in fact qualify. He and the original tenant, until the latter's death, lived together for many years in a stable homosexual relationship. The judge found they enjoyed a very close, loving and monogamous homosexual relationship. In my view the appellant falls within para 3."

Lord Clyde:

". . . The problem in the present case is to determine what, short of blood or marriage, may evidence the common bond in a partnership of two adult persons which may entitle the one to be in the common judgment of society a member of the other's family. It seems to me that essentially the bond must be one of love and affection, not of a casual or transitory nature, but in a relationship which is permanent or at least intended to be so. As a result of that personal attachment to each other, other characteristics will follow, such as a readiness to support each other emotionally and financially, to care for and look after the other in times of need, and to provide a companionship in which mutual interests and activities can be shared and enjoyed together. It would be difficult to establish such a bond unless the couple were living together in the same house. It would also be difficult to establish it without an active sexual relationship between them or at least the potentiality of such a relationship. If they have or are caring for children whom they regard as their own, that would make the family designation immediately obvious, but the existence of children is not a necessary element. Each case will require to depend eventually upon its own facts.

The concept of the family has undergone significant development during recent years, both in the United Kingdom and overseas. Whether that is a matter for concern or congratulation is of no relevance to the present case, but it is properly part of the judicial function to endeavour to reflect an understanding of such changes in the reality of social life. Social groupings have come to take a number of different forms. The form of the single parent family has been long recognised. A more open acceptance of differences in sexuality allows a greater recognition of the possibility of domestic groupings of partners of the same sex. The formal bond of marriage is now far from being a significant criterion for the existence of a family unit. While it remains as a particular formalisation of the relationship between heterosexual couples, family units may now be recognised to exist both where the principle members are in a heterosexual relationship and where they are in a homosexual or lesbian relationship. . . .

It was suggested that if the present appeal was allowed there would be great uncertainty in the ascertainment of successors to statutory tenancies. I am not persuaded that such fears are justified. There may at present be need on occasion to explore the facts of particular cases to discover whether a person was living with the original tenant 'as his or her wife or husband'. In relation to the word 'family', it is difficult to devise a construction which will obviate inquiry unless a very restrictive view of the scope of a family is taken. Once it is accepted, as it has been in the cases, that the application extends beyond the scope of strictly legal relationships, some inquiry may well be involved into the facts which are alleged to be sufficient to constitute the necessary nexus. It does not seem to me that the recognition that a person living together with another in a homosexual relationship may qualify as a member of the other's family is likely to lead to any significant uncertainties in the application of the statutory provision.

Ward LJ expressed an anxiety that he might be exceeding the limits of the judicial function in reaching his decision. Judicial activism certainly has to be tempered by due restraint, and the drawing of the boundary of the judicial task is often delicate and sometimes controversial. I do not consider that the boundary is being passed in the present case. What we are concerned with is the application of a word recognised as being loose and flexible. Parliament has in other contexts provided definitions of the kind of relationships which it intends should be affected by particular provisions. For example, under s.113 of the Housing Act 1985 a person was a 'member of another's family' if he was the spouse of that person, or if he and that person lived together as husband and wife, or if he was that person's parent, grandparent, child, grandchild, brother, sister, uncle, aunt, nephew or niece. In marked distinction to that kind of approach Parliament has in relation to protected tenancies under the Rent Act 1977 left the word 'family' to be applied by the courts without the guidance of statutory definition. The court in the *Dyson Holdings* case accordingly applied the word as was appropriate to the social circumstances prevailing at that period, innovating on its earlier application. If, as I believe, the word is now appropriate to cover a homosexual partnership of the kind which existed in the present case, it seems to me consistent with the intention of Parliament that it should be applied.

I would allow the appeal."

Lord Hutton (dissenting): . . .

"The second issue: para 3(1) of Sch 1

The secondary submission advance on behalf of Mr Fitzpatrick was that if the wording of para 2(2) excluded the relationship of a couple of the same sex, the consideration that the relationship is akin to marriage nevertheless qualifies it as being familial in character so that, within the meaning of para 3(1), Mr Fitzpatrick was a member of Mr Thompson's family. In considering this submission it is relevant at the outset to have regard to the scheme of Sch 1 to the 1977 Act. Whilst in earlier provisions in the Rent Acts legislation a distinction was not drawn between a widower of the tenant and a member of the tenant's family, so that under the Increase of Rent and Mortgage Interest (Restrictions) Act 1920 it was held that a widower was a member of the tenant's family (see *Salter v Lask, Lask v Cohen* [1925] 1KB 584), it is apparent that Sch 1 to the 1977 Act deals separately with the surviving spouse of the tenant and a person living with the tenant as his or her wife or husband on the one hand and with a member of the tenant's family on the other hand. If Mr Fitzpatrick were entitled to claim the protection given by Sch 1 it would appear appropriate that he should obtain protection under para 2 and not under para 3, because the essence of his claim is that the relationship which he shared with Mr Thompson was the same relationship as that shared between a husband and wife or a couple living together as husband and wife, save that the relationship was homosexual and not heterosexual. Therefore, if (as I would hold) Parliament did not intend that a homosexual partner should obtain protection under para 2, it would appear to be a somewhat strained and artificial construction to hold that Mr Fitzpatrick is entitled to obtain protection under para 3.

In *Harrogate BC v Simpson* (1984) 17 HLR 205 at 210 Watkins LJ stated:

> 'Mrs Davies, who appears for the plaintiffs, contends that, if Parliament had wished homosexual relationships to be brought into the realm of the lawfully recognised state of a living together of man and wife for the purpose of the relevant legislation, it would plainly have so stated in that legislation, and it has not done so. I am bound to say that I entirely agree with that.'

If it was the intention of Parliament that a homosexual partner should have the same protection under the Rent Acts as a heterosexual partner I think that in 1988 Parliament would have used express words in para 2(2) of Sch 1 to place a homosexual partner in the same position as an unmarried heterosexual partner rather than leave it to the courts to extend the meaning of the phrase 'a member of the original tenant's family' in para 3(1) to include a homosexual relationship. Instead in para 2(2) Parliament used terminology similar to that recently held by the Court of Appeal in *Simpson*'s case to be confined to a heterosexual relationship. . . .

I fully recognise the strength of the argument, eloquently stated at the conclusion of Waite LJ's judgment that Parliament should change the law to give protection to the homosexual partner of a deceased tenant and also to other persons who lived with and gave devoted care to deceased tenants. But in my opinion such changes can only be made by Parliament and accordingly I would dismiss the appeal."

Lord Hobhouse of Woodborough (dissenting):

". . . The statutory provisions upon which Mr Fitzpatrick relies form part of a scheme for the transfer of protected tenancies following the death of the original tenant which Parliament has substantially revised from time to time. Since legislation of this type was first introduced in 1915, the provisions have gone through a number of versions and most of the decided cases have inevitably dealt with those earlier versions. In my judgment, the current wording must be construed having regard to the revised scheme of which it now forms part. Parliament has from time to time considered and decided to what extent the rights of succession should be increased or varied, most recently in 1988, and has amended the Act. The Act is social legislation. There are competing social policies and choices that are relevant to the decision what statutory rights of succession should be granted. The situation is complex. There are conflicting interests; indeed the subject matter of these provisions is private law property rights. Inevitably, boundaries have to be drawn which may on occasions give rise to hard cases.

I mention this aspect not only because it is important but also because it is possible to have sympathy for those in the position of Mr Fitzpatrick. A social argument can be made on their behalf for sympathetic treatment. They are at least as meritorious as some of those who clearly come within the scheme. But likewise they are not less meritorious than some of those who clearly fall outside the scheme—devoted and caring friends who have lived for a long time with the tenant in the premises but have never engaged in sexual relations with the tenant. Similarly, some may argue that, in view of changing social attitudes to homosexual relationships, the time has come as a matter of policy to equate such relationships with heterosexual ones. But such matters are for Parliament, not the courts. It is an improper usurpation of the legislative function, for a court to adopt social policies which have not yet been incorporated in the relevant legislation.

In the present case, the courts have been urged to extend by a process of liberal interpretation the concept of family to cover homosexual relationships and relationships of close long-lasting friendship. It is submitted that the usage of the word 'family' may vary from time to time and that it has no constant meaning; that accordingly it should now in 1999 be given an up-to-date meaning; that spouse includes a homosexual relationship 'akin' to marriage; that immigration law has recently been revised to take account of such relationships. This type of argument and its proper limits were considered in the speech of Lord Wilberforce in *Royal College of Nursing of the UK v Dept of Health and Social Security* [1981] 1 All ER 545 at 564–565, [1981] AC 800 at 822, to which we were referred by Mr Blake QC who appeared for Mr Fitzpatrick on this appeal. Lord Wilberforce said:

'In interpreting an Act of Parliament it is proper, and indeed necessary, to have regard to the state of affairs existing, and known by Parliament to be existing, at the time. It is a fair presumption that Parliament's policy or intention is directed to that state of affairs . . . when a new state of affairs, or a fresh set of facts bearing on policy, comes into existence, the courts have to consider whether they fall within the parliamentary intention. They may be held to do so if they fall within the same genus of facts as those to which the expressed policy has been formulated. They may also be held to do so if there can be detected a clear purpose in the legislation which can only be fulfilled if the extension is made . . . In any event there is one course which the courts cannot take under the law of this country: they cannot fill gaps; they cannot by asking the question, "What would Parliament have done in this current case, not being one in contemplation, if the facts had been before it?", attempt themselves to supply the answer, if the answer is not to be found in the terms of the Act itself.'

Applying this to the present case, the relevant Act was passed in 1977 and has been amended since. On any view it is difficult to see what fresh set of facts has since come into existence. Homosexual relationships have been known about and existed throughout any relevant period of time and homosexual couples have shared accommodation. Not much has changed; the highest that it can be put is that the public attitude to such relationships has changed. This has nothing to do with any social policy concerning statutory tenancies by succession. If, contrary to what I have just said, it does have relevance, it is a matter for Parliament to consider, not for the courts to ask themselves: 'What would Parliament do now?' But even then one has to take into account that this legislative scheme was amended as recently as 1988. . . .

The word 'family' is as has often been said not a term of art.but describes a unit which has the familial characteristics. One such characteristic is the existence of blood relationships. Thus, in *Hawes v Evenden* [1953] 2 All ER 737, [1953] 1 WLR 1169, a group which consisted of the tenant, his mistress of some 12 years and their two children was easily recognised as being a family (cf *Gammans v Ekins* [1950] 2 All ER 140, [1950] 2 KB 328). In *Brock v Wollans* [1949] 1 All ER 715, [1949] 2 KB 388 a woman, who had at the age of five in 1912 been informally adopted by the tenant and brought up as his daughter and who returned later in her life (after her husband had died) to live with the tenant, was held to be a member of his family. even though not a blood relation. It was his de facto adoption of her whilst a child that made her a part of his family.

The limits upon the ambit of the word family were most forcefully expressed in

Gammans v Ekins [1950] 2 All ER 140, [1950] 2 KB 328. A childless couple were living together as man and wife but they had not married. The woman was not part of the man's family. Asquith LJ, using language which would scarcely be acceptable today, unequivocally rejected the idea that mere friendship or a sexual relationship between two people of the same or a different sex could amount to a family. He and other members of the Court of Appeal affirmed that the concept of family must involve blood or affinity. The only exception was relationships whereby one person becomes in loco parentis to another, *e.g. Brock v Wollans.*

Returning to the speech of Lord Diplock in the *Carega Properties* case, he left open the questions raised by *Dyson Holdings Ltd v Fox* [1979] 2 All ER 1084 at 1085, [1979] 1 WLR 928 at 930. As I have already observed, the legislature has, by the amendments which it has chosen to make to the 1977 Act, already addressed the implications of that decision. Lord Diplock's ratio decidendi follows on a reference to *Gammans v Ekins* and *Ross v Collins.* Lord Diplock chose to adopt as his own what was said by Russell LJ in the second of these cases: 'Granted that "family" is not limited to cases of strict legal familial nexus, I cannot agree that it extends to a case such as this. It still requires, it seems to me, at least a broadly recognisable de facto familial nexus. This may be capable of being found and recognised as such by the ordinary man—where the link would be strictly familial had there been a marriage or where the link is through adoption of a minor, de jure or de facto, or where the link is "step", or where the link is "in-law" or by marriage. But two strangers cannot, it seems to me, ever establish artificially for the purposes of this section a familial nexus by acting as brothers or as sisters, even if they call each other such and consider their relationship to be tantamount to that. Nor, in my view, can an adult man and woman who establish a platonic relationship establish a familial nexus by acting as a devoted brother and sister or father and daughter would act, even if they address each other as such and even if they refer to each other as such, and regard their association as tantamount to such. Nor, in my view, would they indeed be recognised as familial links by the ordinary man.' (See [1979] 2 All ER 1084 at 1087, [1979] 1 WLR 928 at 931.)

This ratio decidendi is binding upon your Lordships. It is consistent with the arguments of Mr Fitzpatrick. Living together as homosexual lovers is not a familial relationship. It is a different relationship: for present purposes, as counsel said, no better and no worse—no less or more meritorious, just different. At one stage of his submissions, Mr Blake expressly disavowed any reliance upon the existence of sexual relations between Mr Fitzpatrick and Mr Thompson. But Mr Blake would have been wrong to abandon, if this was what he was doing, this plank of his case. Absent a sexual relationship, the relationship would have been no more than one of caring friendship which on any view does not suffice. He has to be able to say that the existence of a (formerly active) homosexual relationship makes all the difference. Stripped of that feature he cannot, on the English authorities, succeed.

It is understandable why Mr Blake shrank from putting his client's case in that way. It would expose the degree of the extension of the previous authorities for which he has to contend and points up the lack of support for his argument in the drafting of paras 2 and 3 of Sch 1. If Parliament had wished to take this further radical step, extending the rights of succession to protected tenancies, it would have given some hint of its intention in the amendments which it made after 1977. It has manifested no such intention. The *Dyson Holdings* decision has been recognised by the legislature in its amendment of para 2. The argument of Mr Blake would seem to treat as family two persons of the opposite sex living together in the same flat or house who have or have had a long term stable sexual relationship but do not choose to be known as man and wife. Regardless of the reason for their choice, para 2(2) makes it essential that each should be living as the wife or husband of the other. If your Lordships are being asked to say that nevertheless the survivor should still qualify as family under para 3 on the strength of the decision in the *Dyson Holdings* case, the invitation should in my judgment be rejected. The amendment to para 2 has laid down the relevant criterion which the relationship must satisfy. By a parity of reasoning, the *Dyson Holdings* case does not now provide Mr Fitzpatrick with a route down which he can pass asserting an equivalence between homosexual and heterosexual relationships.

The word 'family', as I have previously observed, is not a term of art. It is a word which is used to refer to a scheme of relationships having certain characteristics. All those characteristics may not be present in every case; this is the nature of descriptive words. But in any case there must be sufficient of the relevant characteristics to justify the application of the descriptive term. In deciding a legal question it is necessary to decide on which side of the line the individual case falls. This exercise is not one of choosing what social policy to support. It involves looking at the language of the statute construed in its legislative context and having regard to the previous decisions of the courts. The decided authorities have told us what the relevant characteristics are. The legislative context has been made clear by the history of the amendments made. The fundamental difficulty for Mr Fitzpatrick is that he is seeking to establish a legal right against the owners of the property, the plaintiffs in the action, based upon the advocacy of a social policy which may one day be adopted by the legislature but which has not yet been incorporated in legislation and which anticipated the essential policy and drafting decisions which would have to be taken by the legislature."

NOTES AND QUESTIONS

- The *Dyson* approach to statutory interpretation is quite unique to this particular statutory regime. Far more common is a judicial focus on the intention of the legislature at the time a statute was enacted. The focus on contemporary understandings of the term "family", and the recognition that the term changes its meaning over time, is exceptional.

- If you were counsel arguing that your client had the requisite 'familial link' in a tenancy case, how would you seek to convince the court? What factors seem to be most important and why?

- Identify passages from the judgments in *Fitzpatrick* in which the majority attempt to answer the 'floodgates' argument.

- Evaluate the judgments of the Law Lords in terms of the degree to which they exemplify 'judicial activism' or 'judicial conservatism'. Provide evidence from the judgments to support your assessment.

- Of what relevance is the fact that—as Lord Hobhouse writes—"the subject matter of these provisions is private law property rights"? What are the "competing social policies" to which he refers? Which policy does he prioritise in this case?

INTERPRETIVE POLICIES AND PRESUMPTIONS

Over the course of the history of statutory interpretation, numerous presumptions —both linguistic and policy-based—have grown up in the law. A familiarity with their existence is necessary so that you can recognise their relevance should a set of facts come along to which one of them applies.

Peter Goodrich, *Reading the Law* (Blackwell, Oxford, 1986), pp.57–59:

"Special rules prescribing how certain commonly used combinations of words are to be interpreted have arisen. For example, the *ejusdem generis* rule deals with the combination of specific and general terms. It requires that where three or more specific examples are followed by a general word, then the parameters of the general category are to be determined by the common characteristics of the specific words (*Palmer v Snow* [1900] 1 QB 725, at 727). The *noscitur a sociis* rule prescribes that words are to take their meaning from their context (*Muir v Keay* [1875] LR 10 QB 594). A further category of aids to interpretation are general principles by which the task of interpretation is to be assisted. Many of the principles are general guides describing the attributes of the activity of legislation. For example in *Morris v Beardmore* [1980] 2 All ER 753, the court had to consider the legislative provisions relating to the taking of specimens of breath by the police. The dispute related to the power of the police to enter private premises to effect a breathalyser test. In interpreting the statutory provision, Lord Scarman made the following reference to a general principle:

> 'When for the detection, prevention or prosecution of crime Parliament confers on a constable a power or right which curtails the rights of others it is to be expected that Parliament intended the curtailment to extend no further than its express authorisation. A constable, who in purported execution of his duty has infringed rights which Parliament has not expressly curtailed, will not, therefore, be able to show that he has acted in execution of his duty, unless (and this will be rare) it can be shown by necessary implication that Parliament must have intended to authorise such infringement (763 b–c).'

The narrow construction of penal provisions is another example of a similar principle, as seen in *R. v. Cuthbertson* [1980] 2 All ER 41 where Lord Diplock applied a restrictive principle to the interpretation of the Misuse of Drugs Act 1971, s.23 in the following fashion: 'the fact that the section is a penal provision is in itself a reason for hesitating before ascribing to phrases used in it a meaning broader than they would normally bear' (404). The above selection of secondary techniques is not exhaustive; it is merely a selection to draw attention to various categories of method and technique.

A final matter which demands consideration again focuses upon the relationship between the judiciary and the legislature. As has already been noted, the act of interpretation through the ascription of meaning to the text may be viewed as a law-making function. Whilst reference has been made to strategies available to the courts which purport to deny the law-making nature of interpretation, such strategies are not completely successful; even in explicit practice, successive readings purporting to follow a literal interpretation, for example, may not be in total agreement as to the meaning of the text. In the event of such an outcome a question arises as to the status of the respective interpretations. Suggestions that one judicial interpretation may or must be privileged can be read to imply that the interpretation is a source of law superior to the actual words of the statutory text, which directly challenges the position of the text as the supreme source of law. In *Ogden Industries v. Lucas* [1970] AC 113, Lord Upjohn considered the matter and concluded:

> 'It is quite clear that judicial statements as to the construction and intention of an Act must never be allowed to supplant or supersede its proper construction *and courts must beware of falling into the error of treating the law to be laid down by the judge in construing the Act rather than found in the Act itself*. No doubt a decision on particular words binds inferior courts on the construction of those words on similar facts but beyond that the observations of the judges on the construction of statutes may be of the greatest help and guidance but are entitled to no more than respect and cannot absolve the court from its duty in exercising an independent judgment [emphasis added by Goodrich].'

His observations provide a striking illustration of the narrow political line formally espoused by the judiciary, one which in the last instance predictably asserts the superiority of the legal text over its interpreters and wittingly or unwittingly denies that the ritual claim to 'literal obedience' to the statutory text may mask any number of strategies of interpretation."

The presumptions of interpretation can be illustrated through examples.

Gregory v Fearn [1953] 1 W.L.R. 974, CA.

"Appeal from Judge Caporn sitting at Nottingham County Court.

The plaintiff, A. R. Gregory, acting in the course of his normal business as an estate agent, on April 2, 1952, which was a Sunday, signed a contract of agency for the sale of a house, whereby the vendor, the defendant, George Fearn, agreed to pay to the plaintiff £100 when the property was sold, the property to be deemed to have been sold 'and the commission payable on the receipt of a deposit or a purchase agreement being entered into by a purchaser.' Subsequently, the estate agent brought proceedings to recover the commission, alleging that he had introduced a purchaser, one Owen, who had entered into a purchase agreement, but had subsequently refused to complete because he found that he would not be able to use the premises for business purposes. Owen alleged that the plaintiff had misrepresented to him that it could be so used.

Judge Caporn held that as the contract appointing the plaintiff agent for the vendor had been made on a Sunday and involved the doing by the plaintiff of his ordinary business as an estate agent, it offended against section 1 of the Sunday Observance Act, 1677, and, consequently, that the plaintiff could not rely on it. He further decided, on other grounds which are not material to this report, that the plaintiff would not have been able to establish his claim to the commission even if the contract had been valid.

The plaintiff appealed.

Evershed M.R., after referring to the facts: Judge Caporn concluded against the plaintiff on the ground among others, that the agreement fell within the prohibition of section 1 of the Sunday Observance Act, 1677, as having involved the doing on the Lord's Day of business or work by a tradesman, that is, an estate agent, in his ordinary calling.

On the view which I take, it is not strictly necessary to decide that point. But it seems to me, as at presently advised, that Mr Heald is right when he says that an estate agent is not a 'tradesman' within the contemplation of that section, even if the execution by him of a contract of this kind was the doing of business or work in his ordinary calling. At first sight, Mr Heald's argument appeared to be difficult, because the formula in section 1 of the Act of 1677 is 'no tradesman, artificer, workman, labourer, or other person whatsoever'; and assuming that an estate agent is not a tradesman, he would be, prima facie, within the formula 'other person whatsoever.' It has, however, long been established that those words 'other person whatsoever' are to be construed *ejusdem generis* with those which precede it: so that, for the defendant to succeed on this point, it must be shown that an estate agent is a tradesman or something sufficiently like a tradesman to be covered by the *ejusdem generis* rule. . . ."

[Evershed M.R. dismissed the appeal. Birkett L.J. and Romer L.J. concurred].

McBoyle v United States 293 U.S. 25 (1930).

Mr Justice Holmes delivered the opinion of the US Supreme Court:

"The petitioner was convicted of transporting from Ottawa, Illinois, to Guymon, Oklahoma, an airplane that he knew to have been stolen, and was sentenced to serve three years' imprisonment and to pay a fine of $2,000. The judgment was affirmed by the Circuit Court of Appeals for the Tenth Circuit 43 F (2d) 273. A writ of certiorari was granted by this Court on the question whether the National Motor Vehicle Theft Act applies to aircraft. . . . That Act provides: 'Sec 2. That when used in this Act:

(a) The term 'motor vehicle' shall include an automobile, automobile truck, automobile wagon, motor cycle, or any other self-propelled vehicle not designed for running on rails; . . . Sec 3. That whoever shall transport or cause to be transported in interstate or foreign commerce a motor vehicle, knowing the same to have been stolen, shall be punished by a fine of not more than $5,000, or by imprisonment of not more than five years, or both.'

Section 2 defines the motor vehicles of which the transportation in interstate commerce is punished in section 3. The question is the meaning of the word 'vehicle' in the phrase 'any other self-propelled vehicle not designed for running on rails.' No doubt etymologically it is possible to use the word to signify a conveyance working on land, water or air, and sometimes legislation extends the use in that direction. . . . But in everyday speech 'vehicle' calls up the picture of a thing moving on land. . . . For after including automobile truck, automobile wagon and motor cycle, the words 'any other self-propelled vehicle not designed for running on rails' still indicate that a vehicle in the popular sense, that is a vehicle running on land, is the theme. It is a vehicle that runs, not something, not commonly called a vehicle, that flies. Airplanes were well known in 1919, when this statute was passed; but it is admitted that they were not mentioned in the reports or in the debates in Congress. It is impossible to read words that so carefully enumerate the different forms of motor vehicles and have no reference of any kind to aircraft, as including airplanes under a term that usage more and more precisely confines to a different class. . . .

Although it is not likely that a criminal will carefully consider the text of the law before he murders or steals, it is reasonable that a fair warning should be given to the world in language that the common world will understand, of what the law intends to do if a certain line is passed. To make the warning fair, so far as possible the line should be clear. When a rule of conduct is laid down in words that evoke in the common mind only the picture of vehicles moving on land, the statute should not be extended to aircraft, simply because it may seem to us that a similar policy applies, or upon the speculation that, if the legislature had thought of it, very likely broader words would have been used. Judgment reversed."

PROBLEM QUESTION

You are a junior solicitor in a law firm. A senior partner has come to you for your legal opinion so that he can advise a client named Anne Artiste. Anne is a painter of watercolours who owns a small piece of land outside Stoketon. She has pulled an old caravan on this land. The caravan is still "on wheels". Anne uses this caravan as her studio and retreat. When inspired, she will often spend several days at a time working long hours in the caravan (and eating and sleeping there). Lately, she has been spending even more time at the caravan because she is not getting along with her partner. Anne also sells her paintings to people who come from far and wide to buy them. She has built a small shed next to the caravan which has a sign on it— "Anne's Gallery"—where her works are displayed and sold. Last month, a stray spaniel showed up. Anne tried to chase the dog away without success. However, one day she felt sorry for the dog and gave it some food and water. She has repeated this practice on occasion. The dog often goes away for fairly long periods, but lately it has rather taken to Anne and sometimes sleeps immediately outside the shed. Anne also has been concerned with her safety while staying in the caravan. She is comforted by the spaniel's loud and vicious barking whenever strangers are in the area. Purely as a further security measure, Anne has displayed a sign on the shed which reads "Warning: Dangerous Guard Dog on Premises".

Last week, an earnest local authority dog warden from Stoketon came to view some of Anne's watercolours. He found the spaniel running loose on Anne's property and barking earnestly and aggressively. Seeing the warning sign, the warden immediately charged Anne with a violation of s.1 of the Guard Dogs Act 1975. Anne has now retained your firm to represent her.

Your senior partner has asked you to write a 1,500 word memorandum of law, in which you explain the bases upon which a legal argument can be made before the Magistrates' Court that Anne has not acted in violation of the relevant statute. You are also asked to assess the likely chances of success of such an argument.

In order to answer this assignment, you will need to undertake legal research. In particular, you should find a copy of the Guard Dogs Act 1975, any cases which are of assistance to the issues of interpretation raised by the problem, and the relevant debates in *Hansard*, portions of which *might* be admissible in court.

9

STATUTORY INTERPRETATION: THE IMPACT OF THE LAW OF THE EUROPEAN UNION AND EUROPEAN HUMAN RIGHTS LAW

In this, our final chapter on the interpretation of statutes, we focus on the implications of the law of the European Union and European human rights law for the principles of statutory interpretation which we have examined in previous chapters. Our focus is twofold. First, we look at the law of the European Union, and we begin with an examination of the approaches to statutory interpretation adopted by the European Court of Justice. Our interest is in how the interpretation of European Union law by the ECJ differs from the "traditional" approaches to interpretation in a common law system. We then turn to the interpretation of European Union law in common law courts and look at how our own courts approach European law, as well as how *domestic* law must be interpreted in light of Britain's legal obligations as a member of the European Union. In the second part of the chapter, our focus shifts to European human rights law, in the form of the European Convention on Human Rights. We will see that the Convention has had an increasing importance within UK law, one which is growing significantly as a result of the enactment of the Human Rights Act 1998.

STATUTORY INTERPRETATION IN THE EUROPEAN COURT OF JUSTICE

We looked at the constitutional implications of membership in the European Union in Chapter 5. In this chapter, we examine the implications of that membership for statutory interpretation. We begin with a consideration of the European Court of Justice which, along with the Court of First Instance, is the judicial arm of the EU.

Paul Craig and Gráinne de Búrca, *EU Law: Text, Cases and Materials* (3rd ed., Clarendon Press, Oxford, 2003), pp.96–99:

Role and methodology of the court

"The specific tasks to be performed by the Court are described in the Treaties. The main provisions governing its jurisdiction are Articles 226–243 (ex Articles 169–186) of the EC Treaty, and Article 46 (ex Articles L) of the TEU [Treaty on European Union]. The TEU enhanced the Court's jurisdiction under Article 228 (ex Article 171) EC, by giving it power to impose a pecuniary penalty on a Member State which failed to comply with a previous judgment against it. In accordance with Article 238 (ex Article 181) ToA [Treaty of Amsterdam] it is to have jurisdiction in any dispute between Member States where the subject matter is covered by the Treaty and the dispute is submitted to it by agreement of the parties. A number of international agreements concluded between the Member States also confer jurisdiction on the ECJ, such as the Convention on Jurisdiction and the Enforcement of Judgments in Civil and Commercial Matters made pursuant to Article 293 (ex Article 220) of the Treaty, and the Convention on Jurisdiction and the Recognition and Enforcement of Judgments in Matrimonial Matters pursuant to what was then Article K.3 of the TEU, which gave the Court jurisdiction to give preliminary rulings. Under the European Economic Area (EEA) Agreement, too, the national courts of EFTA States may, if those States permit, make references on the interpretation of the Agreement to the ECJ.

However, it is Article 220 (ex Article 164) which perhaps figured most prominently in the Court's shaping of its own sphere of influence. The ECJ used this provision over the years to define its role broadly. This Article, which was amended by the TN [Treaty of Nice] to include the CFI [Court of First Instance], provides that 'the Court of Justice and the Court of First Instance, each within its jurisdiction, shall ensure that in the interpretation and application of this Treaty the law is observed'. . . . The Court has utilized this provision to extend its review jurisdiction to cover bodies which were not expressly subject to it, and measures which were not listed in the Treaty. In the name of preserving 'the rule of law' in the Community, the Court has extended its functions beyond those expressly outlined in the Treaty under which it was established. Since the competence of the Community, and hence of its institutions, is an attributed competence, limited by Article 5 (ex Article 3b) EC to what is given by the Treaty an inherent jurisdiction for the Court could be considered problematic, despite its distinctive judicial role.

In addition to extending its own review jurisdiction under Article 220 (ex Article 164), the gap-filling role of the Court has also extended to developing principles of a constitutional nature as part of Community law, to which it then holds both the institutions and the Member States bound when they act within the Community sphere. As interpreter of the Treaties and their limits, the Court also has to adjudicate not just among the EC institutions in disputes over their respective powers, but also, and more contentiously, in questions concerning the proper sphere of the Community as against that of the Member States. These issues arise in many guises, either in direct challenges to Community action by Member States, in actions between the institutions, in preliminary references which may relate to the scope of areas of substantive Community law, or in non-contentious advisory proceedings involving the compatibility of an international agreement with the Treaties.

In the years of so-called institutional malaise or stagnation, the Court arguably played a 'political' role through law, attempting to render the Treaty effective when its provisions had not been implemented as required by the Community, and to render secondary legislation effective when it had not been properly implemented by the Member States. It took an active part in the creation of the internal market through the litigation which came before it, by requiring the 'negative' removal of national barriers to trade, at a time when progress towards completing the Single Market through positive legislative harmonization was hindered by institutional inaction.

The Court has achieved the hobby-horse status which it occupies amongst European lawyers as much on account of its reasoning and methodology as on account of the impact of its decisions. Its approach to interpretation is generally described as purposive or teleological, although not in the sense of seeking the purpose or aim of the authors of the text. The fact that the *travaux préparatoires* to the original Treaties were never published meant these were never used as a source, and this is reflected in the Court's case law. In the case of secondary legislation, although the discussions at Council and Commission meetings are not published, declarations and extracts from the minutes have occasionally been relied on as aids to interpretation before the Court. Occasionally the ECJ has referred to such material for assistance, but in most cases it has denied its relevance if it does not appear in the text of the legislation itself.

Rather than adopting a narrower historical-purposive approach, the Court tends to examine the whole context in which a particular provision is situated, and gives the interpretation most likely to further what the Court considers that provision in its context sought to achieve. Often this is far from a literal interpretation of the Treaty or of legislation in question, even to the extent of flying in the face of the express language. This aspect of the Court's methodology has attracted considerable criticism, although it has also had robust defenders from amongst the academic community, from its former personnel, and from amongst practitioners.

Probably the most famous of the Court's earlier critics was Hjalte Rasmussen, whose 1986 critique of the Court's policy-making was one of the earliest sustained attacks on what the author viewed as its illegitimate practices. His thesis was that the Court has sought 'inspiration in guidelines which are essentially political in nature and hence, not judicially applicable. This is the root of judicial activism which may be a usurpation of power'.[1] He did not criticize all 'activism', but rather that which he believed to have lost popular legitimacy. In discussing Judge Pescatore's celebrated comment about the judges of the early ECJ having '*une certaine ideé de l'Europe*' of their own, Rasmussen's book, using terms which, although written more than fifteen years ago, could equally well be used today, referred to 'society's declining taste for a precipitated process of integration'.

There were mixed reactions to Rasmussen's strongly argued and polemical work from an academic community which had largely been supportive of the Court's strategy. Mauro Cappelletti in particular argued that Rasmussen's critique lacked a historical dimension, that any constitutional court should have the courage to enforce its 'higher law' against temporary pressures, and that the ECJ's vision 'far from being arbitrary, is fully legitimate, for it is rooted in the text, most particularly in the Preamble and the first articles of the EEC Treaty'. Some years ago a high-profile and more political attack on the methodology of the ECJ was made by Sir Patrick Neill, in his 'case study in judicial activism', in which he argued that the Court was a dangerous institution, skewed by its own policy considerations and driven by an elite mission.

In defence of the Court's 'constitutional' role, however, Advocate General Jacobs has argued that it plays an essential role in preserving the balance between the Community and the Member States, and in developing constitutional principles of judicial review."

A good example of the primacy of a broad, contextual approach to interpretation can be found in the ECJ's interpretation of the "free movement" provisions of the EC Treaty. The relevant Treaty provision is Art.39(3) (formerly 48(3)), which provides that the freedom of movement of workers shall entail the right "(a) to accept offers of employment actually made; (b) to move freely within the territory of the Member States for this purpose. . .". The question was whether the right of free movement included the right of a citizen of the EC (as it then was) to look for work in another member state.

The Queen v Immigration Appeal Tribunal, Ex p. Antonissen [1991] E.C.R. 1–745, ECJ.

European Court of Justice:

"1. By an order of 14 June 1989, which was received at the Court on 21 September 1989, the High Court of Justice, Queen's Bench Division, referred to the Court for a preliminary ruling under Article 177 of the EEC Treaty two questions on the interpretation of the provisions of Community law governing the free movement of workers as regards the scope of the right of residence of nationals of Member States seeking employment in another Member State.

[1] H. Rasmussen, *On Law and Policy in the European Court of Justice* (Nijoff, 1986), 62.

2. The questions arose in proceedings between Mr Gustaff Desiderius Antonissen, a Belgian national, and the Secretary of State for Home Affairs, who on 27 November 1987 decided to deport him from the United Kingdom.

3. Mr Antonissen arrived in the United Kingdom in October 1984. He had not yet found work there when, on 3 March 1987, he was sentenced by the Liverpool Crown Court to two terms of imprisonment for unlawful possession of cocaine and possession of that drug with intent to supply. He was released on parole on 21 December 1987.

4. The decision to order Mr Antonissen's deportation was based on section 3(5)(b) of the Immigration Act 1971 ('the 1971 Act'), which authorizes the Secretary of State to deport foreign nationals if he considers that it would be 'conducive to the public good'.

5. Mr Antonissen lodged an appeal against the Secretary of State's decision with the Immigration Appeal Tribunal. Before the Tribunal Mr Antonissen argued that since he was a Community national he must qualify for the protection afforded by Council Directive 64/221/EEC of 25 February 1964 on the coordination of special measures concerning the movement and residence of foreign nationals which are justified on grounds of public policy, public security or public health. The Tribunal took the view that, since he had been seeking employment in the United Kingdom for more than six months, he could no longer be treated as a Community worker and claim that the directive should apply in his case. The Tribunal based this part of its decision on paragraph 143 of the Statement of Changes in Immigration Rules (HC169), adopted pursuant to the 1971 Act, under which a national of a Member State may be deported if, after six months from admission to the United Kingdom, he has not yet found employment or is not carrying on any other occupation.

6. His appeal being dismissed, Mr Antonissen made an application for judicial review to the High Court of Justice, Queen's Bench Division, which stayed the proceedings and referred the following questions to the Court of Justice for a preliminary ruling:

'1 For the purpose of determining whether a national of a Member State is to be treated as a 'worker' within the meaning of Article 48 of the EEC Treaty when seeking employment in the territory of another Member State so as to be immune from deportation save in accordance with Council Directive 64/221 of 25 February 1964, may the legislature of the second Member State provide that such a national may be required to leave the territory of that State (subject to appeal) if after six months from admission to that territory he has failed to enter employment?

2 In answering the foregoing question what weight if any is to be attached by a court or tribunal of a Member State to the declaration contained in the minutes of the meeting of the Council when the Council adopted Directive 68/36?'

7. Reference is made to the Report for the Hearing for a fuller account of the facts of the case before the national court, the applicable legislation and the written observations submitted to the Court, which are mentioned or discussed hereinafter only in so far as is necessary for the reasoning of the Court.

8. By means of the questions submitted to the Court for a preliminary ruling the national court essentially seeks to establish whether it is contrary to the provisions of Community law governing the free movement of workers for the legislation of a Member State to provide that a national of another Member State who entered the first State in order to seek employment may be required to leave the territory of that State (subject to appeal) if he has not found employment there after six months.

9. In that connection it has been argued that, according to the strict wording of Article 48 of the Treaty, Community nationals are given the right to move freely within the territory of the Member States for the purpose only of accepting offers of employment actually made (Article 48(3)(a) and (b)) whilst the right to stay in the territory of a Member State is stated to be for the purpose of employment (Article 48(3)(c)).

10. Such an interpretation would exclude the right of a national of a Member State to move freely and to stay in the territory of the other Member States in order to seek employment there, and cannot be upheld.

11. Indeed, as the Court has consistently held, freedom of movement for workers forms

one of the foundations of the Community and, consequently, the provisions laying down that freedom must be given a broad interpretation.

12. Moreover, a strict interpretation of Article 48(3) would jeopardize the actual chances that a national of a Member State who is seeking employment will find it in another Member State, and would, as a result, make the provision ineffective.

13. It follows that Article 48(3) must be interpreted as enumerating, in a non-exhaustive way, certain rights benefiting nationals of Member States in the context of the free movement of workers and that that freedom also entails the right for nationals of Member States to move freely within the territory of the other Member States and to stay there for the purposes of seeking employment.

14. Moreover, this interpretation of the Treaty corresponds to that of the Community legislature, as appears from the provisions adopted in order to implement the principle of free movement, in particular Articles 1 and 5 of Regulation No 1612/68/EEC of the Council of 15 October 1968 on freedom of movement for workers within the Community, which presuppose that Community nationals are entitled to move in order to look for employment, and hence to stay, in another Member State.

15. It must therefore be ascertained whether the right, under Article 48 and the provisions of Regulation No 1612/68, to stay in a Member State for the purposes of seeking employment can be subjected to a temporal limitation.

16. In that regard, it must be pointed out in the first place that the effectiveness of Article 48 is secured in so far as Community legislation or, in its absence, the legislation of a Member State gives persons concerned a reasonable time in which to apprise themselves, in the territory of the Member State concerned, of offers of employment corresponding to their occupational qualifications and to take, where appropriate, the necessary steps in order to be engaged.

17. The national court referred to the declaration recorded in the Council minutes at the time of the adoption of the aforesaid Regulation No 1612/68 and of Council Directive 68/36/EEC (of the same date) on the abolition of restrictions on movement and residence within the Community for workers of Member States and their families. That declaration read as follows:

'Nationals of a Member State as referred to in Article 1 [of the directive] who move to another Member State in order to seek work there shall be allowed a minimum period of three months for the purpose; in the event of their not having found employment by the end of that period, their residence on the territory of this second State may be brought to an end.

However, if the above mentioned persons should be taken charge of by national assistance (social welfare) in the second State during the aforesaid period they may be invited to leave the territory of this second State.'

18. However, such a declaration cannot be used for the purpose of interpreting a provision of secondary legislation where, as in this case, no reference is made to the content of the declaration in the wording of the provision in question. The declaration therefore has no legal significance. . . .

21. In the absence of a Community provision prescribing the period during which Community nationals seeking employment in a Member State may stay there, a period of six months, such as that laid down in the national legislation at issue in the main proceedings, does not appear in principle to be insufficient to enable the persons concerned to apprise themselves, in the host Member State, of offers of employment corresponding to their occupational qualifications and to take, where appropriate, the necessary steps in order to be engaged and, therefore, does not jeopardize the effectiveness of the principle of free movement. However, if after the expiry of that period the person concerned provides evidence that he is continuing to seek employment and that he has genuine chances of being engaged, he cannot be required to leave the territory of the host Member State.

22. It must therefore be stated in reply to the questions submitted by the national court that it is not contrary to the provisions of Community law governing the free movement of workers for the legislation of a Member State to provide that a national of another

Member State who entered the first State in order to seek employment may be required to leave the territory of that State (subject to appeal) if he has not found employment there after six months, unless the person concerned provides evidence that he is continuing to seek employment and that he has genuine chances of being engaged."

The judgment in *Antonissen* is interesting, not only for the method of interpretation —which is far from literal—but also for the style of the judgment, which is representative of ECJ judgments more generally. The method of interpretation adopted in *Antonissen* has been subject to criticism.

Trevor C. Hartley, "Five Forms of Uncertainty in European Community Law" (1996) 55 C.L.J. 265 at 278:

"As is well known, the European Court adopts a different method of interpretation from that usually followed by English courts. Where a provision is clear and unambiguous, English courts will usually follow the plain meaning of the words used; the European Court, on the other hand, gives much greater emphasis to ensuring that the objective of the measure is attained. In order to do so, it will sometimes depart from the plain meaning.

The objection to this from a constitutional point of view is that it involves the Court taking on a legislative role and revising the work of the legislator. From a more general point of view, it raises the question how the objective of a measure is to be determined. The Treaties express the will of the Member States; most EC legislation is adopted by the Council, which is made up of the representatives of the Member States. In either case, therefore, the objective of a provision must depend on the intention of the Member States. As was said previously, however, the Member States often have no common intention, and are united only in their agreement to adopt a certain form of words. In such a case, an objective cannot be ascribed to the measure beyond that implied by the words themselves.

This question has been discussed recently in another article, in which examples were given of cases in the constitutional sphere in which it was thought that the European Court had departed from the plain meaning of the words used. Here, a different example will be chosen, the *Antonissen* case. The provision in question in that case, Article 48(3) EC, is clear and unambiguous in so far as it concerns person migrating to find work: it does not cover them. The Court, however, refused to accept that this was the correct interpretation. It gave three reasons: first, that such an interpretation would exclude the right of a Community migrant to move freely to another Member State to seek employment; secondly, that the Court had previously held that provisions—such as Article 48—that lay down the right of free movement of workers must be given a broad interpretation, since such freedom constitutes one of the foundations of the Community; and finally, that a 'strict' interpretation of Article 48(3) 'would jeopardise the actual chances that a national of a Member State who is seeking employment will find it in another Member State, and would, as a result, make the provision ineffective.'

The argument may be set out as follows: first, it is assumed—reasonably enough—that the objective of Article 48 is to allow nationals of one Member State to obtain employment in another; secondly, it is assumed—again reasonably—that this will be more difficult if workers cannot travel to another Member State to look for employment on the spot: from these two assumptions the conclusion is drawn that the plain meaning of the words must be ignored so as to ensure that workers have this right.

The objection to this is that it fails to recognise the possibility that, though the authors of the Treaty may have wished to make it easier for Community nationals to work in another Member State, this might not have been the only consideration they had in mind. Law-making almost always involves balancing conflicting interests and objectives. The words of a provision express the way the balance is struck by the legislator. To assume that there is only one objective, or that one objective must be pursued irrespective of all other considerations, is both irresponsible and naïve.

In the case of Article 48 EC, another objective that the Member States presumably had in mind was to avoid an influx of unemployed migrants who might be unable to support themselves. The wording of Article 48(3) reflects the balance struck by the Member States when they signed the Treaty in 1957. No doubt the situation changed as the years passed, and by 1968 the Member States were willing to take a further step. They could have done this by granting a right of entry in the legislation they adopted that year. They did not do this. Instead, they made the 'secret' declaration. The purpose of this was apparently to ensure that the right was granted under national law, rather than under Community law, thus allowing the Member States to decide its precise extent. This may have represented a compromise between those Member States that wanted to give further rights to migrant workers and those that were concerned about the economic and social consequences.

Where the text of a provision is itself unclear, the European Court's method of interpretation may not lead to any greater uncertainty; in some cases, indeed, it may be a good solution. Where the words of the provision are clear, however, it produces uncertainty, since it is never possible to predict with accuracy what the Court will regard as the objectives of the provision, what it will consider necessary to ensure their attainment and how far it will be willing to go in departing from the words of the provision in order to achieve those objectives."

NOTES

- Another unique characteristic of European legislation is the fact that there are 12 official languages of the EU (Danish, Dutch, English, Finnish, French, Gaelic, German, Greek, Italian, Portuguese, Swedish, and Spanish). With the exception of Gaelic, they are also all working languages of the EU! As Millett argues:

  "Because all . . . language versions are authentic, the literal meaning of a Community legislative text in one language cannot be relied on as a conclusive guide to its meaning. It has to be compared with the other language versions, and in the practice of the Court of Justice—usually also checked against another criterion of interpretation, such as the purpose of the provision in question. Thus the multilingual nature of Community legislation necessarily reduces the importance of the literal method of interpretation, which contrasts with the predominant place it enjoys in the interpretation of British domestic legislation."[2]

- Also of importance to note is that "every provision of Community law must be placed in its context and interpreted in the light of the provisions of Community law as a whole, regard being had to the objectives thereof and to its state of evolution at the date on which the provision in question is to be applied."[3]

- Finally, "although the Treaties contain the fundamental provisions on which the Community's legal order is based, when it comes to Regulations, Directives and Decisions, the Community know no doctrine of legislative supremacy. For example, the Court may quash Community legislation which contravenes the general principles of Community law."[4]

---

[2] Timothy Millett, "Rules of Interpretation of EEC Legislation" (1989) 10 *Statute Law Review* 163.
[3] *CILFIT v Ministry of Health* [1982] E.C.R. 3415.
[4] Ian McLeod, *Legal Method* (4th ed., Palgrave Macmillan, Basingstoke, 2002), p.322.

THE IMPACT OF EUROPEAN COMMUNITY LAW ON INTERPRETATION IN DOMESTIC COURTS

As we saw in Chapter 5, the principle of the supremacy of Parliament has had to be modified by the courts in light of Britain's membership in the European Community and European Union. In Chapter 5, we looked at the decision of the European Court of Justice and House of Lords in *Factortame No 2* [1991] 1 All E.R. 70, in which it was held to be the duty of national courts to override rules of national law which were in conflict with directly enforceable rules of European Community law. Our focus in this section is on a distinct, but related, matter: the approaches which domestic courts take to the interpretation of European legislation. As we discussed in the previous section, the European Court of Justice, in keeping with its continental European roots, takes a rather different approach to statutory interpretation than is typical of a common law court. Thus, we can ask, to what extent should (and do) common law courts adapt their approach to statutory interpretation when dealing with EC legislation? Although national courts sometimes will refer questions concerning the interpretation of EC law to the ECJ pursuant to Art.234 (formerly 177) of the EC Treaty, in some cases they will interpret legislation themselves in light of European law. An early, and at that time unorthodox approach, was advocated some years ago by Lord Denning:

> "Seeing these differences, what are the English courts to do when they are faced with a problem of interpretation? They must follow the European pattern. No longer must they examine the words in meticulous detail. No longer must they argue about the precise grammatical sense. They must look to the purpose or intent. To quote the words of the European Court in the *Da Costa*[5] case: they must limit themselves to deducing from 'the wording and the spirit of the treaty the meaning of the Community rules . . .'. They must not confine themselves to the English text. They must consider, if need be, all the authentic texts, of which there are now eight. They must divine the spirit of the treaty and gain inspiration from it. If they find a gap, they must fill it as best they can. They must do what the framers of the instrument would have done if they had thought about it. So we must do the same. Those are the principles, as I understand it, on which the European Court acts."[6]

The cynic might argue that for Lord Denning, Britain's entry into the European Community provided a ready justification for a more liberal, "gap filling" approach to statutory interpretation; one which was more in keeping with his long preferred approach.

Some years later, Lord Diplock pointed to both similarities and differences between the approach of the European Court of Justice and English courts:

> "The European court, in contrast to English courts, applies teleological rather than historical methods to the interpretation of the Treaties and other Community legislation. It seeks to give effect to what it conceives to be the spirit rather than the letter of the Treaties; sometimes, indeed, to an English judge, it may seem to the exclusion of the letter. It views the Communities as living and expanding organisms and the interpretation of the provisions of the Treaties as changing to match their growth. For these reasons the European Court does not apply the doctrine of precedent to its own decisions as rigidly as does an English court. Nevertheless, as any browsing in the Common Market Law Reports will show, the

[5] [1963] C.M.L.R. 224 at 237.
[6] *H.P. Bulmer Ltd and another v J. Bollinger SA and others* [1974] 2 All E.R. 1226 at 1237–1238, CA.

The impact of the law

European Court too seeks to maintain consistency in its decisions in the interest of legal certainty. Consequently in the opinions of the Advocates General and the judgments of the court itself, citations of previous judgments in the court are as frequent as citations of previous authority in judgments of English courts. Thus, when there is a *cursus curiae*, a series of decisions to the same effect, or what is described in the court's own rules (article 95) as 'an established body of case law' an English court if the case before it is one to which an established body of case law plainly applies, may properly take the view that no real question of interpretation is involved that makes reference under article 177 necessary in order to give judgment."[7]

In *Henn and Darby*, Lord Diplock also explicitly warned of the "danger of an English court applying English canons of statutory construction to the interpretation of the Treaty or, for that matter, of Regulations or Directives".[8]

The question of interpretive approaches is made more complex when domestic legislation is enacted in order to fulfil obligations under European Community law. In this situation, courts here may be faced with the task of interpreting law made in this country in order to comply with European law. How should our courts interpret in that situation? The following case represents a judicial response.

Litster and others v Forth Dry Dock and Engineering Co. Ltd and another [1989] 1 All E.R. 1134, HL.

Lord Oliver of Aylmerton:
"My Lords, this appeal raises, not for the first time, the broad question of the approach to be adopted by courts in the United Kingdom to domestic legislation enacted in order to give effect to this country's obligations under the EEC Treaty. The legislation with which the appeal is concerned is a statutory instrument made on 14 December 1981 pursuant to para 2(2) of Sch 2 to the European Communities Act 1972 and entitled the Transfer of Undertakings (Protection of Employment) Regulations 1981, SI 1981/1794. The regulations were made by the Secretary of State, and this is common ground, in order to give effect to EC Council Directive 77/187 adopted by the Council of the European Communities on 14 February 1977 to provide for the approximation of the laws of the member states relating to the safeguarding of employees' rights in the event of transfer of undertakings, businesses or parts of businesses. The question which arises is whether it has achieved this object.

The approach to the construction of primary and subordinate legislation enacted to give effect to the United Kingdom's obligations under the EEC Treaty have been the subject matter of recent authority in this House (see *Pickstone v Freemans plc* [1988] 2 All ER 803, [1989] AC 66) and is not in doubt. If the legislation can reasonably be construed so as to conform with those obligations, obligations which are to be ascertained not only from the wording of the relevant directive but from the interpretation placed on it by the Court of Justice of the European Communities, such a purposive construction will be applied even though, perhaps, it may involve some departure from the strict and literal application of the words which the legislature has elected to use.

It will, I think, be convenient to consider the terms of the directive and the regulations before outlining the circumstances in which the instant appeal arises. The broad scope of the directive appears from the following two recitals:

'Whereas economic trends are bringing in their wake, at both national and Community level, changes in the structure of undertakings, through transfers of undertakings, businesses or parts of businesses to other employers as a result of legal transfers or mergers;

---

[7] *Henn and Darby v Director of Public Prosecutions* [1981] A.C. 850 at 905, HL.
[8] *ibid.*, at 904.

Whereas it is necessary to provide for the protection of employees in the event of a change of employer, in particular, to ensure that their rights are safeguarded . . .'

By art.1 it is provided that the directive shall apply to the transfer of an undertaking, business or part of a business to another employer. Article 2 contains definitions, the relevant ones for present purposes being:

'(a) "transferor" means any natural or legal person who, by reason of a transfer within the meaning of Article 1(1), ceases to be the employer in respect of the undertaking, business or part of the business; (b) 'transferee' means any natural or legal person who, by reason of a transfer within the meaning of Article 1(1), becomes the employer in respect of the undertaking, business or part of the business . . .'

Section II is headed '*Safeguarding of employees' rights*' and contains three articles of which the relevant ones for present purposes are arts 3 and 4. Article 3 provides (so far as material):

'1. The transferor's rights and obligations arising from a contract of employment or from an employment relationship existing on the date of a transfer within the meaning of Article 1(1) shall, by reason of such transfer, be transferred to the transferee. . .' . . .

Article 4 is, so far as material, in the following terms:

'1. The transfer of an undertaking, business or part of a business shall not in itself constitute grounds for dismissal by the transferor or the transferee. This provision shall not stand in the way of dismissals that may take place for economic, technical or organisational reasons entailing changes in the workforce . . .

2. If the contract of employment or the employment relationship is terminated because the transfer within the meaning of Article 1(1) involves a substantial change in working conditions to the detriment of the employee, the employer shall be regarded as having been responsible for termination of the contract of employment or of the employment relationship.' . . .

Turning now to the 1981 regulations, which came into operation in 1982 and which represent the British government's perception at that time of its obligations under the directive, these provide for relevant purposes as follows: . . .

'5(1) A relevant transfer shall not operate so as to terminate the contract of employment of any person employed by the transferor in the undertaking or part transferred but any such contract which would otherwise have been terminated by the transfer shall have effect after the transfer as if originally made between the person so employed and the transferee.

(2) Without prejudice to paragraph (1) above, on the completion of a relevant transfer
—(a) all the transferor's rights, powers, duties and liabilities under or in connection with any such contract, shall be transferred by virtue of this Regulation to the transferee; and (b) anything done before the transfer is completed by or in relation to the transferor in respect of that contract or a person employed in that undertaking or part shall be deemed to have been done by or in relation to the transferee.

(3) Any reference in paragraph (1) or (2) above to a person employed in an undertaking or part of one transferred by a relevant transfer is a reference to a person so employed immediately before the transfer, including, where the transfer is effected by a series of two or more transactions, a person so employed immediately before any of those transactions . . .

8(1) Where either before or after a relevant transfer, any employee of the transferor or transferee is dismissed, that employee shall be treated for the purposes of art.V of the 1978 Act and Articles 2 to 41 of the 1976 Order (unfair dismissal) as unfairly dismissed if the transfer or a reason connected with it is the reason or the principal reason for his dismissal. . . .'

It will be seen that, as is to be expected, the scope and purpose of both the directive and the regulations are the same, that is to ensure that on any transfer of an undertaking or part of an undertaking, the employment of the existing workers in the undertaking is preserved or, if their employment terminates solely by reason of the transfer, that their rights arising out of that determination are effectively safeguarded. It may, I think, be assumed that those who drafted both the directive and the regulations were sufficiently acquainted with the realities of life to appreciate that a frequent, indeed, possibly the most frequent, occasion on which a business or part of a business is transferred is when the original employer is insolvent, so that an employee whose employment is terminated on the transfer will have no effective remedy for unfair dismissal unless it is capable of being exerted against the transferee. It can hardly have been contemplated that, where the only reason for the determination of the employment is the transfer of the undertaking or the relevant part of it, the parties to the transfer would be at liberty to avoid the manifest purpose of the directive by the simple expedient of wrongfully dismissing the workforce a few minutes before the completion of the transfer. The European Court has expressed, in the clearest terms, the opinion that so transparent a device would not avoid the operation of the directive, and if the effect of the regulations is that under the law of the United Kingdom it has that effect, then your Lordships are compelled to conclude that the regulations are gravely defective and the government of the United Kingdom has failed to comply with its mandatory obligations under the directive. If your Lordships are in fact compelled to that conclusion, so be it; but it is not, I venture to think, a conclusion which any of your Lordships would willingly embrace in the absence of the most compulsive content rendering any other conclusion impossible.

My Lords, the circumstances in which the question has arisen for decision in the instant case are these. The first respondents, Forth Dry Dock and Engineering Co Ltd, carried on a business of ship repairers at the Edinburgh dry dock, premises which they held under a lease from the Forth Ports Authority. At the material time, the 12 appellants were tradesmen employed in that business. They were part of a permanent workforce of skilled shipworkers of various trades who had been continuously employed by the first respondents since 1981 or 1982. In the year 1983 the group of companies of which the first respondents formed part was in financial difficulties and the receiver of the various companies in the group (including the first respondents) was appointed by the debenture holder, Lloyd's Bank, on September 28, 1983. The workforce was then told by the receiver's representative, a Mr Page, that the intention was to sell the business as a going concern and that their jobs would be safe. That belief may have been genuinely entertained at the time, but it was falsified in the event.

On 23 November 1983 the second respondents, Forth Estuary Engineering Ltd (Forth Estuary) was incorporated. A few days before the transfer of the first respondents' assets, which took place on 6 February 1984, the capital of Forth Estuary was increased from £1,000 to £20,000: 85% of the issued capital became vested in a Mr Brooshooft, who had been a financial adviser to the first respondents' company, and 10% in a Mr Hughes, who had been a director of and had managed the business of the first respondents. On 6 February 1984 an agreement was entered into between the first respondents, the receivers and Forth Estuary under which (a) all the first respondents' business assets, consisting of plant, machinery, equipment, furniture and office equipment specified in a schedule, were acquired by Forth Estuary at a price of £33,500 payable on execution of the agreement, (b) the first respondents undertook to cease business at close of business on that day (at which time the sale and purchase was to be carried into effect) and (c) the first respondents undertook forthwith to relinquish their rights under the lease of the dry dock which they held from the ports authority. Before this, it is not clear exactly when, Forth Estuary had obtained from the Forth Ports Authority a new lease of the property previously let to the first respondents (with the exception of one shed). It is interesting to note that under cl 14 of this agreement, its construction, validity and performance were to be governed by English law and the courts of England were given exclusive jurisdiction. As a matter of

English law, therefore, the ownership of the assets transferred passed in equity to Forth Estuary on the execution of the agreement and those assets were, assuming, as we must assume, that the consideration was then paid as provided by the agreement, then held by the transferor as a bare trustee for the transferee. Up to this point the appellants had continued to be employed by the first respondents. It had, however, clearly been determined by the receivers, and, one infers, by Forth Estuary, that that situation was not to be permitted to continue and it is difficult, if not impossible, to resist the inference that the reason why it was not to be permitted to continue was that both parties were well aware of the provisions of the regulations to which I have already referred. It can hardly have been merely a fortunate coincidence that officers from the redundancy payments section of the Department of Employment were already at the dock on that afternoon when Mr Hughes and Mr Page arrived at approximately 3 pm having come straight from the office of Messrs Brodies, where the agreement had been signed. They addressed the workforce and told them that the business was to close down at 4.30 pm that day and that they were dismissed 'with immediate effect'. Each of the appellants was given a letter from the receivers under the first respondents' letterhead which was dated 6 February 1984 and was, so far as material, in the following terms:

> 'We would advise you that no further funds can be made available to pay your wages with effect from the close of business today and accordingly we have to inform you that your employment with the company is terminated with immediate effect. No payments will be made in respect of your accrued holiday pay, or the failure to give you your statutory period of notice. Under the Insolvency provisions of the Employment Protection Act, any claim you may have for the above will, subject to certain limitations, be paid to you by the Department of Employment out of the Redundancy Fund . . . Your wages up to the date of dismissal will be paid in the normal way and you will be issued with a P45 from the company's head office.'

One of the less creditable aspects of the matter is that one of the appellants, Mr Walker, who was the union shop steward, asked specifically whether the business was being taken over by Forth Estuary, and was told by Mr Hughes that he knew nothing about a new company taking over, while Mr Page said that he knew nothing about a company called Forth Estuary Engineering. This indicates a calculated disregard for the obligations imposed by reg 10 of the 1981 regulations. Within 48 hours of their dismissal, the appellants learned, at the local job centre, that Forth Estuary was recruiting labour and a group of them went to fill in application forms for employment. None was successful and indeed only three former employees of the first respondents were taken on. Work which was in progress on the vessels on 6 February was subsequently continued and completed by Forth Estuary, which very soon had a workforce of similar size to that of the first respondents, embracing the same trade but recruited at lower rates of pay elsewhere than from the existing employees. . . .

Two questions then arise. First, was the time which elapsed between the dismissals and the transfer of so short a duration that, on the true construction of reg 5, the appellants were 'employed immediately before' the transfer, as required by para (3) of that regulation? Second, if the answer to that question is in the negative, what difference (if any) does it make that the reason, or the principal reason, for the dismissals was, as it clearly was, the imminent occurrence of the transfer so that the dismissals were, by reg 8(1), deemed to be unfair dismissals? . . .

Regulation 8(1) does not follow literally the wording of Art.4(1). It provides only that if the reason for the dismissal of the employee is the transfer of the business, he has to be treated 'for the purposes of art.V of the 1978 Act' as unfairly dismissed so as to confer on him the remedies provided by ss.69–79 of the Act (including, where it is considered appropriate, an order for reinstatement or re-engagement). If this provision fell to be construed by reference to the ordinary rules of construction applicable to a purely domestic statute and without reference to treaty obligations, it would, I think, be quite impermissible to regard it as having the same prohibitory effect as that attributed by the European Court to art.4 of the directive. But it has always to be borne in mind that the purpose of the directive and of the regulations was and is to 'safeguard' the rights of employees on a transfer and that there is a mandatory obligation to provide remedies which are effective and not merely symbolic to which the regulations were intended to give effect. The remedies provided by the 1978 Act in the case of an insolvent transferor are largely illusory unless they can be exerted against the transferee as the directive contemplates and I do not find it conceivable that, in framing regulations intending to give effect to the directive, the Secretary of State could have envisaged that its purpose should be capable of being avoided by the transparent device to which resort was had in the instant case. . . . Having regard to the manifest purpose of the regulations, I do not, for my part, feel inhibited from making such an implication in the instant case. The provision in reg 8(1) that a dismissal by reason of transfer is to be treated as an unfair dismissal, is merely a different way of saying that the transfer is not to 'constitute a ground for dismissal' as contemplated by art.4 of the directive and there is no good reason for denying to it the same effect as that attributed to that article. In effect this involves reading reg 5(3) as if there were inserted after the words 'immediately before the transfer' the words 'or would have been so employed if he had not been unfairly dismissed in the circumstances described in reg 8(1)'. For my part, I would make such an implication which is entirely consistent with the general scheme of the regulations and which is necessary if they are effectively to fulfil the purpose for which they were made of giving effect to the provisions of the directive. . . .

In the instant case it is quite clear that the reason for the dismissal of the appellants was the transfer of the business which had just been agreed and was going to take place almost at once. The effect of reg 5, construed as I have suggested that it should be, is that their employment continued with Forth Estuary. I would therefore allow the appeal. . . ."

[Lord Keith of Kinkel, Lord Brandon of Oakbrook, Lord Templeman, and Lord Jauncey of Tullichettle also allowed the appeal].

NOTES

- The Acquired Rights Directive has become a fairly controversial area of the regulation of employment relations; in particular, the decision of the ECJ that the "contracting out" of services could constitute a "legal transfer" within the meaning of the Directive.[9] This decision had enormous consequences within the U.K., involving "individuals and trade unions who had been adversely affected by the government's policies in relation to the compulsory competitive tendering of services by the National Health Service and by local authorities, or by the transfer of the provision of services from the public sector to the private or 'quasi-private' sector".[10] As More argues, the ECJ has been criticized for giving undue weight to employee rights in a series of cases involving the Acquired Rights Directive, to the detriment of employer "flexibility". As More concludes, however, "the Court's teleological interpretation of the Acquired Rights Directive has allowed it to be adapted to meet the needs of employment protection, albeit in a changed economic environment".[11] *Forth Dry Dock* is an

---

[9] *Rask v ISS Kantineservice A/S* [1992] E.C.R. I-5755: *Schmidt v Spar- und Leikhkasse der früheren Ämter Bordesholm, Kiel und Cronshagen* [1994] E.C.R. I-1311.

[10] Gillian More. "The Acquired Rights Directive: Frustrating or Facilitating Labour Market Flexibility", in *New Legal Dynamics of European Union* (J. Shaw and G. More, eds., Clarendon Press, Oxford, 1995), pp.129, 134.

[11] *ibid.*, p.145.

example of such an interpretive approach in the *domestic* courts, when interpreting a domestic statutory instrument designed to implement *European* law.

THE INTERPRETATION OF EUROPEAN HUMAN RIGHTS LAW

In Chapter 5, we examined the impact of the European Convention on Human Rights on the principle of the supremacy of Parliament through the role of the European Court of Human Rights in Strasbourg. Courts in this country also operate under the presumption that Parliament in the legislation it enacts intended to comply with *international* law. As a consequence, courts have been prepared to examine international treaties, to which the United Kingdom is a signatory, as an aid in the interpretation of *ambiguous* legislation.[12]

This has been of importance with respect to the European Convention on Human Rights. Prior to incorporation into English law, the Convention has only been of assistance to domestic courts as an aid in interpreting ambiguous legislation.[13] The extent to which the Convention could be and should be turned to by domestic courts has been the subject of considerable academic comment.[14] With the coming into force of the Human Rights Act 1998, the role of the European Convention on Human Rights in the interpretation of domestic law is changing significantly.

Human Rights Act 1998:

"An Act to give further effect to rights and freedoms guaranteed under the European Convention on Human Rights; to make provision with respect to holders of certain judicial offices who become judges of the European Court of Human Rights; and for connected purposes.

Introduction

1(1)   In this Act, 'the Convention rights' means the rights and fundamental freedoms set out in–

    (a)   Articles 2 to 12 and 14 of the Convention,
    (b)   Articles 1 to 3 of the First Protocol, and
    (c)   Articles 1 and 2 of the Sixth Protocol,

as read with Articles 16 to 18 of the Convention.

(2)   Those Articles are to have effect for the purposes of this Act subject to any designated derogation or reservation (as to which see sections 14 and 15).

---

[12] See *James Buchanan & Co. Ltd. v Babco Forwarding & Shipping (UK) Ltd* [1978] A.C. 141, HL; *Fothergill v Monarch Airlines Ltd* [1981] A.C. 251, HL.

[13] See *e.g. Brind v Secretary of State for the Home Department* [1991] 1 All E.R. 720, HL; *Derbyshire County Council v Times Newspapers and Others* [1992] 3 All E.R. 65, CA; *R. v Secretary of State for the Home Department and Another* Ex p. *Norney and others* (1995) 7 Admin. L.R. 861, HC.

[14] See *e.g.* Michael K. Addo, "The Role of English Courts in the Determination of the Place of the European Convention on Human Rights in English Law" (1995) 46 N.I.L.Q 1; Brian Bix and Adam Tomkins, "Unconventional Uses of the Convention?" (1992) 55 M.L.R. 721; Nicholas Grief, "The Domestic Impact of the European Convention on Human Rights as Mediated Through Community Law" [1991] P.L. 555; Eric Barendt, "Libel and Freedom of Speech in English Law" [1993] P.L. 449.

(3)   The Articles are set out in Schedule 1.

(4)   The Lord Chancellor may by order make such amendments to this section or Schedule 1 as he considers appropriate to reflect the effect, in relation to the United Kingdom, of a protocol.

(5)   In subsection (4) 'protocol' means a protocol to the Convention–

    (a)   which the United Kingdom has ratified; or
    (b)   which the United Kingdom has signed with a view to ratification.

(6)   No amendment may be made by an order under subsection (4) so as to come into force before the protocol concerned is in force in relation to the United Kingdom.

2(1)   A court or tribunal determining a question which has arisen under this Act in connection with a Convention right must take into account any–

    (a)   judgment, decision, declaration or advisory opinion of the European Court of Human Rights,
    (b)   opinion of the Commission given in a report adopted under Article 31 of the Convention,
    (c)   decision of the Commission in connection with Article 26 or 27(2) of the Convention, or
    (d)   decision of the Committee of Ministers taken under Article 46 of the Convention,

whenever made or given, so far as, in the opinion of the court or tribunal, it is relevant to the proceedings in which that question has arisen. . . .

Interpretation of legislation

3(1)   So far as it is possible to do so, primary legislation and subordinate legislation must be read and given effect in a way which is compatible with the Convention rights.

(2)   This section–

    (a)   applies to primary legislation and subordinate legislation whenever enacted;
    (b)   does not affect the validity, continuing operation or enforcement of any incompatible primary legislation; and
    (c)   does not affect the validity, continuing operation or enforcement of any incompatible subordinate legislation if (disregarding any possibility of revocation) primary legislation prevents removal of the incompatibility.

4(1)   Subsection (2) applies in any proceedings in which a court determines whether a provision of primary legislation is compatible with a Convention right.

(2)   If the court is satisfied that the provision is incompatible with a Convention right, it may make a declaration of that incompatibility.

(3)   Subsection (4) applies in any proceedings in which a court determines whether a provision of subordinate legislation, made in the exercise of a power conferred by primary legislation, is compatible with a Convention right.

(4)   If the court is satisfied—

    (a)   that the provision is incompatible with a Convention right, and
    (b)   that (disregarding any possibility of revocation) the primary legislation concerned prevents removal of the incompatibility, it may make a declaration of that incompatibility. . . .

8(1)   In relation to any act (or proposed act) of a public authority which the court finds is (or would be) unlawful, it may grant such relief or remedy, or make such order, within its jurisdiction as it considers just and appropriate.

(2) But damages may be awarded only by a court which has power to award damages, or to order the payment of compensation, in civil proceedings.

(3) No award of damages is to be made unless, taking account of all the circumstances of the case, including—

    (a) any other relief or remedy granted, or order made, in relation to the act in question (by that or any other court), and

    (b) the consequences of any decision (of that or any other court) in respect of that act, the court is satisfied that the award is necessary to afford just satisfaction to the person in whose favour it is made.

(4) In determining–

    (a) whether to award damages, or

    (b) the amount of an award,

the court must take into account the principles applied by the European Court of Human Rights in relation to the award of compensation under Article 41 of the Convention.

Remedial action

10(1) This section applies if—

    (a) a provision of legislation has been declared under section 4 to be incompatible with a Convention right and, if an appeal lies—
        (i) all persons who may appeal have stated that they do not intend to do so;
        (ii) the time for bringing an appeal has expired and no appeal has been brought within that time; or
        (iii) an appeal brought within that time has been determined or abandoned; or

    (b) it appears to a Minister of the Crown or Her Majesty in Council that, having regard to a finding of the European Court of Human Rights made after the coming into force of this section in proceedings against the United Kingdom, a provision of legislation is incompatible with an obligation of the United Kingdom arising from the Convention.

(2) If a Minister of the Crown considers that there are compelling reasons for a proceeding under this section, he may by order make such amendments to the legislation as he considers necessary to remove the incompatibility.

(3) If, in the case of subordinate legislation, a Minister of the Crown considers—

    (a) that it is necessary to amend the primary legislation under which the subordinate legislation in question was made, in order to enable the incompatibility to be removed, and

    (b) that there are compelling reasons for proceeding under this section, he may by order make such amendments to the primary legislation as he considers necessary.

(4) This section also applies where the provision in question is in subordinate legislation and has been quashed, or declared invalid, by reason of incompatibility with a Convention right and the Minister proposes to proceed under paragraph 2(b) of Schedule 2.

(5) If the legislation is an Order in Council, the power conferred by subsection (2) or (3) is exercisable by Her Majesty in Council. . . .

14(1) In this Act, 'designated derogation' means any derogation by the United Kingdom from an Article of the Convention, or of any protocol to the Convention, which is designated for the purposes of this Act in an order made by the Lord Chancellor.

(2)   [*repealed*].

(3)   If a designated derogation is amended or replaced it ceases to be a designated derogation.

(4)   But subsection (3) does not prevent the Lord Chancellor from exercising his power under subsection (1) to make a fresh designation order in respect of the Article concerned.

(5)   The Lord Chancellor must by order make such amendments to Schedule 2 as he considers appropriate to reflect–

    (a)   any designation order; or
    (b)   the effect of subsection (3).

(6)   A designation order may be made in anticipation of the making by the United Kingdom of a proposed derogation.

15(1)   In this Act, 'designated reservation' means–

    (a)   the United Kingdom's reservation to Article 2 of the First Protocol to the Convention; and
    (b)   any other reservation by the United Kingdom to an Article of the Convention, or of any protocol to the Convention, which is designated for the purposes of this Act in any order made by the Lord Chancellor.

(2)   The text of the reservation referred to in subsection (1)(a) is set out in Part II of Schedule 3.

(3)   If a designated reservation is withdrawn wholly or in part it ceases to be a designated reservation.

(4)   But subsection (3) does not prevent the Lord Chancellor from exercising his power under subsection (1)(b) to make a fresh designation order in respect of the Article concerned.

(5)   The Lord Chancellor must by order make such amendments to the Act as he considers appropriate to reflect—

    (a)   any designation order; or
    (b)   the effect of subsection (3).

16(1)   If it has not already been withdrawn by the United Kingdom, a designated derogation ceases to have effect for the purposes of this Act at the end of the period of five years beginning with the date on which the order designating it was made.

(2)   At any time before the period—

    (a)   fixed by subsection (1), or
    (b)   extended by an order under this subsection,

comes to an end, the Lord Chancellor may be order extend it by a further period of five years.

(3)   An order under section 14(1) ceases to have effect at the end of the period for consideration, unless a resolution has been passed by each House approving the order.

(4)   Subsection (3) does not affect—

    (a)   anything done in reliance on the order; or
    (b)   the power to make a fresh order under section 14(1).

(5)   In subsection (3) 'period for consideration' means the period of forty days beginning with the day on which the order was made.

(6) In calculating the period for consideration, no account is to be taken of any time during which–

    (a) Parliament is dissolved or prorogued; or
    (b) both Houses are adjourned for more than four days.

(7) If a designated derogation is withdrawn by the United Kingdom, the Lord Chancellor must by order make such amendments to this Act as he considers are required to reflect that withdrawal.

17(1) The appropriate Minister must review the designated reservation referred to in section 15(1)(a)—

    (a) before the end of the period of five years beginning with the date on which section 1(2) came into force; and
    (b) if that designation is still in force, before the end of the period of five years beginning with the date on which the last report relating to it was laid under subsection (3).

(2) The appropriate Minister must review each of the other designated reservations (if any)—

    (a) before the end of the period of five years beginning with the date on which the order designating the reservation first came into force; and
    (b) if the designation is still in force, before the end of the period of five years beginning with the date on which the last report relating to it was laid under subsection (3).

(3) The Minister conducting a review under this section must prepare a report on the result of the review and lay a copy of it before each House of Parliament."

The 'Convention rights' to which the Human Rights Act 1998 refers are as follows:

European Convention for the Protection of Human Rights and Fundamental Freedoms:

Article 2

"1. Everyone's right to life shall be protected by law. No one shall be deprived of his life intentionally save in the execution of a sentence of a court following a conviction of a crime for which this penalty is provided by law.

2. Deprivation of life shall not be regarded as inflicted in contravention of this Article when it results from the use of force which is no more than absolutely necessary:

    (a) in defence of any person from unlawful violence;
    (b) in order to effect a lawful arrest or to prevent the escape of a person lawfully detained;
    (c) in action lawfully taken for the purpose of quelling a riot or insurrection.

Article 3

No one shall be subjected to torture or to inhuman or degrading treatment or punishment.

Article 4

1. No one shall be held in slavery or servitude.

2. No one shall be required to perform forced or compulsory labour.

3. For the purpose of this Article the term 'forced or compulsory labour' shall not include:

    (a) any work required to be done in the ordinary course of detention imposed according to the provisions of Article 5 of this Convention or during conditional release from such detention;
    (b) any service of a military character or, in case of conscientious objectors in countries where they are recognized, service exacted instead of compulsory military service;
    (c) any service exacted in case of an emergency or calamity threatening the life or well-being of the community;
    (d) any work or service which forms part of normal civic obligations.

Article 5

1. Everyone has the right to liberty and security of person. No one shall be deprived of his liberty save in the following cases and in accordance with a procedure prescribed by law;

    (a) the lawful detention of a person after conviction by a competent court;
    (b) the lawful arrest or detention of a person for non-compliance with the lawful order of a court or in order to secure the fulfilment of any obligation prescribed by law;
    (c) the lawful arrest or detention of a person effected for the purpose of bringing him before the competent legal authority on reasonable suspicion of having committed an offence or when it is reasonably considered necessary to prevent his committing an offence or fleeing after having done so;
    (d) the detention of a minor by lawful order for the purpose of educational supervision or his lawful detention for the purpose of bringing him before the competent legal authority;
    (e) the lawful detention of persons for the prevention of the spreading of infectious diseases, of persons of unsound mind, alcoholics or drug addicts, or vagrants;
    (f) the lawful arrest or detention of a person to prevent his effecting an unauthorized entry into the country or of a person against whom action is being taken with a view to deportation or extradition.

2. Everyone who is arrested shall be informed promptly, in a language which he understands, of the reasons for his arrest and of any charge against him.

3. Everyone arrested or detained in accordance with the provision of paragraph 1(c) of this Article shall be brought promptly before a judge or other officer authorized by law to exercise judicial power and shall be entitled to trial within a reasonable time or to release pending trial. Release may be conditioned by guarantees to appear for trial.

4. Everyone who is deprived of his liberty by arrest or detention shall be entitled to take proceedings by which the lawfulness of his detention shall be decided speedily by a court and his release ordered if the detention is not lawful.

5. Everyone who has been the victim of arrest or detention in contravention of the provisions of this Article shall have an enforceable right to compensation.

Article 6

1. In the determination of his civil rights and obligations or of any criminal charge against him, everyone is entitled to a fair and public hearing within a reasonable time by an independent and impartial tribunal established by law. Judgment shall

be pronounced publicly but the press and public shall be excluded from all or part of the trial in the interests of morals, public order or national security in a democratic society, where the interest of juveniles or the protection of the private life of the parties so require, or to the extent strictly necessary in the opinion of the court in special circumstances where publicity would prejudice the interests of justice.

2.   Everyone charged with a criminal offence shall be presumed innocent until proved guilty according to law.

3.   Everyone charged with a criminal offence has the following minimum rights:

    (a)   to be informed promptly, in a language which he understands and in detail, of the nature and cause of the accusation against him;

    (b)   to have adequate time and facilities for the preparation of his defence;

    (c)   to defend himself in person or through legal assistance of his own choosing or, if he has not sufficient means to pay for legal assistance, to be given it free when the interests of justice so require;

    (d)   to examine or have examined witnesses against him and to obtain the attendance and examination of witnesses on his behalf under the same conditions as witnesses against him;

    (e)   to have the free assistance of an interpreter if he cannot understand or speak the language used in court.

Article 7

1.   No one shall be held guilty of any criminal offence on account of any act or omission which did not constitute a criminal offence under national or international law at the time when it was committed. Nor shall a heavier penalty be imposed than the one that was applicable at the time the criminal offence was committed.

2.   This Article shall not prejudice the trial and punishment of any person for any act or omission which, at the time when it was committed, was criminal according to the general principles of law recognized by civilized nations.

Article 8

1.   Everyone has the right to respect for his private and family life, his home and his correspondence.

2.   There shall be no interference by a public authority with the exercise of this right except such as in accordance with the law and is necessary in a democratic society in the interests of national security, public safety or the economic well-being of the country, for the prevention of disorder or crime, for the protection of health or morals, or for the protection of the rights and freedoms of others.

Article 9

1.   Everyone has the right to freedom of thought, conscience and religion; this right includes freedom to change his religion or belief, and freedom, either alone or in community with others and in public or private, to manifest his religion or belief, in worship, teaching, practice and observance.

2.   Freedom to manifest one's religion or beliefs shall be subject only to such limitations as are prescribed by law and are necessary in a democratic society in the interests of public safety, for the protection of public order, health or morals, or for the protection of the rights and freedoms of others.

Article 10

1. Everyone has the right to freedom of expression. This right shall include freedom
    to hold opinions and to receive and impart information and ideas without interfer-
    ence by public authority and regardless of frontiers. This Article shall not prevent
    States from requiring the licensing of broadcasting, television or cinema enter-
    prises.

2. The exercise of these freedoms, since it carries with it duties and responsibilities,
    may be subject to such formalities, conditions, restrictions or penalties as are pre-
    scribed by law and are necessary in a democratic society in the interests of national
    security, territorial integrity or public safety, for the prevention of disorder or crime,
    for the protection of health and morals, for the protection of the reputation or
    rights of others, for preventing the disclosure of information received in confidence,
    or for maintaining the authority and impartiality of the judiciary.

Article 11

1. Everyone has the right to freedom of peaceful assembly and to freedom of associ-
    ation with others, including the right to form and to join trade unions for the pro-
    tection of his interests.

2. No restrictions shall be placed on the exercise of these rights other than such as are
    prescribed by law and are necessary in a democratic society in the interests of
    national security or public safety, for the prevention of disorder or crime, for the
    protection of health or morals or for the protection of the rights and freedoms of
    others. This Article shall not prevent the imposition of lawful restrictions on the
    exercise of these rights by members of the armed forces, of the police or of the
    administration of the State.

Article 12

Men and women of marriageable age have the right to marry and found a family, according to the national laws governing the exercise of this right.

Article 13

Everyone whose rights and freedoms as set forth in this Convention are violated shall have
an effective remedy before a national authority notwithstanding that the violation has been
committed by persons acting in an official capacity.

Article 14

The enjoyment of the rights and freedoms set forth in this Convention shall be secured
without discrimination on any ground such as sex, race, colour, language, religion, political or other opinion, national or social origin, association with a national minority, property, birth or other status. . . .

Article 16

Nothing in Articles 10, 11 and 14 shall be regarded as preventing the High Contracting
Parties from imposing restrictions on the political activity of aliens.

Article 17

Nothing in this Convention may be interpreted as implying for any State, group or person any right to engage in any activity or perform any act aimed at the destruction of any of the rights and freedoms set forth herein or at their limitation to a greater extent than is provided for in the Convention.

Article 18

The restrictions permitted under this Convention to the said rights and freedoms shall not be applied for any purpose other than those for which they have been prescribed."

At the time of its enactment, there was much speculation as to the possible impact of the Human Rights Act 1998 on statutory interpretation.

Geoffrey Marshall, "Interpreting Interpretation in the Human Rights Bill" [1998] P.L. 167 at 167:

The meaning of "possible" in Clause 3

"In the first place it is not clear how the phrase 'so far as it is possible to do so' is to be understood. In some sense or other anything is possible if those who apply rules of interpretation are willing to stretch, change or apply them differently. Is Clause 3 intended to change the existing rules of interpretation whenever a question of Convention rights is an issue? The Government White Paper 'Rights Brought Home' implies that some change is intended. It says that the Bill 'goes far beyond the present rule which authorises the courts to take the Convention into account in resolving any ambiguity in a legislative provision'. What the authors of the White Paper mean by going beyond the present rule is uncertain. At the Committee stage of the Bill in the House of Lords, Lord Cooke of Thorndon suggested that what is prescribed by Clause 3 differs from the present rules in that 'it enjoins a search for possible meanings as distinct from the true meaning which has been the traditional approach'. But the disjunction between the meaning now to be sought and the true meaning is an odd one, particularly as Lord Cooke went on to say that the new kind of interpretation now enjoined 'is not a strained interpretation but one that is *fairly* possible'. Does that mean that the courts should be encouraged to disregard the true (or most obvious or likely) meaning in some degree, but not to strain or distort it too grossly? Another possibility as to the meaning of 'possible' is of course that it means that if, when the normal rules of construction are applied, it is possible fairly to say that a legislative provision has a particular meaning and if that meaning is compatible with the Convention it should be so interpreted and if not, not. But if that is what it means, Clause 3 is redundant. On the other hand, if Clause 3 is not redundant, then we do not know what it means.

Legislative ambiguity and convention rights

In introducing the Bill the Lord Chancellor explained the purpose of Clause 3 by saying that 'If it is possible to interpret a statute in two ways—one compatible with the Convention and one not—the courts will always choose the interpretation which is compatible'. But leaving aside the difficulty of knowing what it means to say that there is a possibility of such an interpretation what are we to understand by an interpretation that is 'compatible with Convention rights'? Is this the same as an ambiguity that is resolved by reference to Convention rights or (in the language of the White Paper) interpreting legislation 'so as to uphold Convention rights'? In what kinds of cases will Convention rights be relevant to the resolving of ambiguity in a statutory provision?

Issues of construction that arise in the application of the language of statutes generally raise a question as to whether particular persons or circumstances fall within the general terms of the statutes. *Harris v DPP*[15] is a not untypical example. That involved the interpretation of section 139 of the Criminal Justice Act 1988. The guilt of the accused, who was charged with possession of a prohibited article, namely a sharply pointed blade, depended on the meaning of 'folding pocket knife' since such knives were excluded from the operation of the statute. It was held that a small bladed knife whose blade could only be folded by operating a locking button was a fixed blade knife, not a folding pocket knife. Here the statute could be said to be capable of being interpreted in two ways. But is this the kind of case in which the existence of the Human Rights Bill and its putatively new rule of interpretation is relevant? Can it be said that since the Convention protects the right to liberty of the person and the right to fair trials, it becomes relevant in every criminal proceeding on the grounds that criminal conviction involves a loss of liberty and that guilt has to be established in accordance with the provisions of the Convention? If so, which of the two interpretations of 'folding pocket knife' is more compatible with the Convention? Is either? There is already said to be a presumption enjoining in some degree strict construction of penal statutes so as to give the benefit of the doubt to an accused where there is genuine uncertainty as to the proper application of statutory language. The principle seems to have been somewhat submerged in recent times when public policy and purposive interpretation have appeared to suggest that the courts will only apply the presumption 'if there are no considerations indicating the desirability of a wider interpretation', and public policy together with the intention of Parliament may often suggest a wider interpretation.

But is it to be supposed that Clause 3 of the Human Rights Bill creates a new or extended version of that presumption, so that the courts are to lean towards the construction that will lead to acquittal whenever any possible construction of statutory language might lead to that result? It would be odd to suppose that the Convention could prescribe such a conclusion whenever anyone alleged its relevance, or that Clause 3 is intended to change the approach to such questions of construction throughout the criminal law. . . .

'Reading or giving effect'

Although Clause 3 is headed 'Interpretation of legislation' what it says is that primary and subordinate legislation should be 'read and given effect' in a way which is compatible with the Convention. 'Read and given effect' may be intended to be read as meaning 'interpreted', but it would seem that it must involve not merely the resolution of ambiguity in statutory provisions but also the question whether a provision of primary or secondary legislation can be treated as being compatible or incompatible with rights guaranteed in the Convention. This seems not so much a question of interpretation or construction of language but of assessment or characterisation or proper description of the relevant legislative provision when placed alongside the relevant right or rights in the Convention. It is only as a result of such assessment or reading of the statutory provision that the court can be in a position to make—when necessary—the determination of incompatibility which should lead to parliamentary remedial action under Clause 10 of the Bill. If a litigant establishes that the statutory provision in question is incompatible with, or infringes the Convention, his right under the Convention is upheld (though the legislation remains valid under the provisions of Clause 3(b)) and his only remedy is a declaration of incompatibility until remedial action is taken. If the court finds that the legislation is compatible with the Convention the litigant fails to establish that he is entitled to protection under the Convention over and above that provided by the United Kingdom legislation.

At this point a startling paradox suggests itself about the wording of Clause 3. What it commands is the opposite of what might be assumed from a reading of the White Paper and the parliamentary statements made in introducing Clause 3. The White Paper says that the courts will be required to uphold the Convention rights unless it is impossible to do so. So a hopeful litigant under the Human Rights Bill might assume that the courts would lean

---

[15] [1993] 1 W.L.R. 82.

towards holding that the Convention right in issue should prevail over the legislative provision under attack, which it can only do if the legislation is inconsistent or incompatible
with the Convention right. But what Clause 3 urges the court to do, wherever possible, is
to find that the legislation is *compatible* with the Convention rights. If it is so compatible,
the Convention has no bite on the legislation and the litigant seeking protection under the
Convention not provided for by the legislation loses his case. The more faithfully the courts
follow the injunction to read legislation as being compatible with the Convention the less
effect the Convention will have. If it were to have the advertised effect of allowing the
Convention more easily to trump legislation that threatens rights, Clause 3 should presumably have provided that, whenever the possibility arises, primary and secondary legislation
should be treated as *incompatible* with the Convention rights unless such a finding is ruled
out because the legislation is clearly compatible. But then the only remedy would be a declaration of incompatibility until (and if) remedial action is taken under Clause 10.

Many speakers in the debate on the Human Rights Bill praised its drafting as ingenious
and subtle. Perhaps, as with the failure of Clauses 3 and 4 to implement the White Paper's
commitment to incorporate the Convention rights in United Kingdom law, the so-called
interpretation provision in Clause 3 is a further example of ingenuity gone wrong. What
interpretation the courts will place on Clause 3 is impossible to know."

Not surprisingly, a more optimistic forecast of the impact of the Human Rights Act
was made by the Lord Chancellor at the time it was enacted.

**Lord Irvine of Lairg, "The Development of Human Rights in Britain under an Incorporated
Convention on Human Rights" [1998] P.L. 221 at 225:**

"On October 23, I introduced the Human Rights Bill into Parliament. It will incorporate
into the domestic law of the United Kingdom the rights and liberties guaranteed by the
European Convention on Human Rights. It will mean that our citizens can secure their
rights from our own United Kingdom courts. They will not have to take the long slow road
to the Court in Strasbourg. It is one of the major constitutional changes which this
Government is making. . . .

The implications of the change

What then are the practical implications of this change to a rights based system within the
field of civil liberties?

Domestication of freedom

First, the Act will give to the courts the tools to uphold freedoms at the very time their
infringement is threatened. Until now, the only remedy where a freedom guaranteed by the
Convention is infringed and domestic law is deficient has been expensive and slow proceedings in Strasbourg. They could not even be commenced until after all the domestic avenues
of complaint and appeal had been exhausted. The courts will now have the power to give
effect to the Convention rights in the course of proceedings when they arise in this country
and to grant relief against an unlawful act of a public authority (a necessarily widely drawn
concept). The courts will not be able to strike down primary legislation. But they will be
able to make a declaration of incompatibility where a piece of primary legislation conflicts
with a Convention right. This will trigger the ability to use in Parliament a special fast-
track procedure to bring the law into line with the Convention.

This innovative technique will provide the right balance between the judiciary and
Parliament. Parliament is the democratically elected representative of the people and must
remain sovereign. The judiciary will be able to exercise to the full the power to scrutinise
legislation rigorously against the fundamental freedoms guaranteed by the Convention but
without becoming politicised. The ultimate decision to amend legislation to bring it into

line with the Convention, however, will rest with Parliament. The ultimate responsibility for compliance with the Convention must be Parliament's alone.

Prioritising rights

That point illustrates the second important effect of our new approach. If there are to be differences or departures from the principles of the Convention they should be conscious and reasoned departures, and not the product of rashness, muddle or ignorance. This will be guaranteed both by the powers given to the courts but also by other provisions which will be enacted. In particular, Ministers and administrators will be obliged to do all their work keeping clearly and directly in mind its impact on human rights, as expressed in the Convention and in the jurisprudence which attaches to it. For, where any Bill is introduced in either House, the Minister of the Crown, in whose charge it is, will be required to make a written statement that, either in his view, the provisions of the Bill are compatible with the Convention rights; or that he cannot make that statement but the Government none-theless wishes the House to proceed with the Bill. . . .

Substantive rights

Thirdly, the Convention will enable the courts to reach results in cases which give full effect to the substantive rights guaranteed by the Convention. It would not be appropriate for me to deal with individual aspects of the law which may come up for decision in the courts in future, but some general observations are possible. . . .

It is moreover likely—although individual cases will be for the courts to determine and I should not attempt to prejudge them—that the position will in at least some cases be different from what it would have been under the pre-incorporation practice. The reason for this lies in the techniques to be followed once the Act is in force. Unlike the old Diceyan approach where the Court would go straight to what restriction had been imposed, the focus will first be on the positive right and then on the justifiability of the exception. Moreover, the Act will require the courts to read and give effect to the legislation in a way compatible with the Convention rights 'so far as it is possible to do so . . .'. This, as the White Paper makes clear, goes far beyond the present rule. It will not be necessary to find an ambiguity. On the contrary the courts will be required to interpret legislation so as to uphold the Convention rights unless the legislation itself is so clearly incompatible with the Convention that it is impossible to do so. Moreover, it should be clear from the Parliamentary history, and in particular the Ministerial statement of compatibility which will be required by the Act, that Parliament did not intend to cut across a Convention right. Ministerial statements of compatibility will inevitably be a strong spur to the courts to find means of construing statutes compatibly with the Convention.

Whilst this particular approach is innovative, there are some precedents which will assist the courts. In cases involving European Community law, decisions of our courts already show that interpretative techniques may be used to make the domestic legislation comply with the Community law, even where this requires straining the meaning of words or reading in words which are not there. An illustrative case is *Litster*[16] concerning the con-struction of the Transfer of Undertakings Regulations. The issue was whether protection in the Regulations, limited to those employed in the business 'immediately before' the time of the transfer, extended to employees unfairly dismissed very shortly before the transfer. The applicants had clearly not been employed in the business immediately before the trans-fer as those words would normally be interpreted. Nor were the words ambiguous. Yet the House of Lords interpreted the Regulations (so as to accord with the European Court's existing interpretation of the underlying Community obligation which the Regulations were intended to implement) by implying additional words 'or would have been so employed if they had not been unfairly dismissed [by reason of the transfer]'. . . .

Guidance may also be found in the jurisprudence of the New Zealand courts. Under the

---

[16] *Litster v Forth Dry Dock and Forth Estuary Engineering* (1990) 1 A.C. 546, HL, which we examined earlier in this Chapter.

New Zealand Bill of Rights Act 1990 a meaning consistent with the rights and freedoms contained in the Bill of Rights is to be given in preference to any other meaning 'wherever an enactment can be given [such] a meaning'. The existing New Zealand decisions seem to show that the only cases where the legislation will *not* be interpreted consistently with the protected rights are those where a statutory provision contains a clear limitation of fundamental rights. The difference from the approach until now applied by the English courts will be this: the Court will interpret as consistent with the Convention not only those provisions which are ambiguous in the sense that the *language* used is capable of two different meanings, but also those provisions where there is *no* ambiguity in that sense, unless a *clear* limitation is expressed. In the latter category of case it will be 'possible' (to use the statutory language) to read the legislation in a conforming sense because there will be no clear indication that a limitation on the protected rights was intended so as to make it 'impossible' to read it as conforming.

Principled decision-making

The fourth point may be shortly stated but is of immense importance. The courts' decisions will be based on a more overtly principled, and perhaps moral, basis. The Court will look at the positive right. It will only accept an interference with that right where a justification, allowed under the Convention, is made out. The scrutiny will not be limited to seeing if the *words* of an exception can be satisfied. The Court will need to be satisfied that the interference with the protected right *is* justified in the public interest in a free democratic society. Moreover, the courts will in this area have to apply the Convention principle of proportionality. This means the Court will be looking *substantively* at that question. It will not be limited to a secondary review of the decision making process but at the primary question of the merits of the decision itself.

In reaching its judgment, therefore, the Court will need to expand and explain its own view of whether the conduct is legitimate. It will produce in short a decision on the *morality* of the conduct and not simply its compliance with the bare letter of the law."

Two years after the Human Rights Act 1998 came into force (the coming into force of the legislation did not occur until 2000), the impact of the legislation upon statutory interpretation could begin to be felt. The trends in the case law involving statutory interpretation were described by Klug and O'Brien.

Francesca Klug and Claire O'Brien, "The First Two Years of the Human Rights Act" (2002) P.L. 649–654:

"Last year, 12 months after the Human Rights Act 1998 ('HRA') came into force, we asked whether incorporation 'through the front door' had led—as was intended—to the adoption of new principles of interpretation and judicial reasoning to render the standards of the European Convention effective for individuals in the United Kingdom. Although the HRA was still in its very early days, our 'snapshot' analysis of all reported cases in the higher courts up to that point led us to reach a tentative 'yes' in answer to those questions —although doubts remained in a number of key areas.

Now, two years into the life of what is effectively our first modern bill of rights, we review what further effects this 'higher law' is having on legislative interpretation, the development of the common law and judicial review of public bodies.

What is beyond doubt is that Convention rights are being raised in domestic courts and tribunals of all kinds and at all levels. While there is a consensus that the HRA did not lead to an avalanche of challenges, the flow of HRA cases shows no sign yet of abating. Out of 316 cases where the ECHR was cited in the domestic courts over two decades prior to incorporation, we estimated that in only 11 cases did the ECHR influence statutory interpretation and in 59 cases was it used to 'develop' the common law. Now, using a similar methodology, we have estimated that in the first 18 months of its life the HRA affected the outcome, reasoning or procedure in 318 cases out of 431 cases in the higher courts where it was cited. An HRA claim was upheld in 94 of these cases, and remedies granted in 91 of these. A total of eight declarations of incompatibility have been made, although at the present time only two remain in place and not subject to appeal.

Statutory interpretation

Before and after; reconciliation or declaration

The duty imposed on the courts by section 3 of the HRA—to construe legislation compatibly with Convention rights 'so far as it is possible to do so'—represents a significant departure from the past. Prior to the HRA, the domestic courts refrained from interpreting legislation in the light of human rights norms unless there was ambiguity or uncertainty in the wording of the statute. Already within the first 12 months of the HRA, there was clear evidence of a shift in approach to statutory interpretation by the courts, even if this was not always consistently applied.

In *R. v Offen*,[17] *R. v A (No. 2)*[18] and *R. v Lambert*[19] the courts applied s.3 of the HRA significantly to alter the effects of statutory provisions—even in the face of recent, pre-HRA authority to the contrary[20]—in order to achieve compatibility with ECHR rights.[21]. . .

The landmark case of *R. v A (No. 2)*, concerning recently enacted 'rape shield' legislation, signalled that there would be real differences of opinion as to where to draw this line. Lord Steyn, for the majority, held that it would sometimes be permissible to adopt an interpretation which was 'linguistically . . . strained'.[22] In defence of stretching the meaning of statutory provisions in this way, Lord Steyn referred to the fact that Parliament had rejected the option of legislating for a 'reasonable interpretation' only (under section 3) and that the government had made clear statements that a 'declaration of incompatibility' (under section 4) must be avoided unless compatible interpretation was 'plainly impossible'. In his view, this would be the case '[i]f a *clear* limit on Convention rights is stated *in terms*'.[23]

Lord Hope, dissenting, found that interpretation was plainly not 'possible' if a contended meaning contradicted the clear intention of Parliament in the legislation.[24] In *R. v Lambert*,[25] Lord Hope returned to section 3 and observed that: [t]he obligation [in section 3(1)], powerful though it is, is not to be performed without regard to its limitations'. Section 3(1) preserved the sovereignty of Parliament, therefore judges were not empowered to 'overrule decisions which the language of the statute shows have been taken on the very point at issue by the legislator.'[26] More recent cases addressing the intersection between sec-

---

[17] [2001] 1 W.L.R. 253.
[18] [2002] 1 A.C. 45.
[19] [2001] 3 W.L.R. 206.
[20] In *Offen*, this was *R. v Kelly* [2000] Q.B. 198 where Lord Bingham held that to be exceptional a circumstance need not be unique, or unprecedented, but could be one that is regularly, or routinely, or normally encountered. But Lord Woolf reasoned on Arts 3 and 5 that both prohibited arbitrary detention and, consequently, since it was *possible*, s.2 of the 1997 Act was to be interpreted to avoid that result.
[21] See also *Ashworth Security Hospital v MGN Ltd* [2001] 1 W.L.R. 515.
[22] See n. 18 above, para. 44.
[23] *ibid*. emphasis in the original.
[24] *ibid*. para. 108.
[25] See n. 19 above.
[26] *ibid*. para. 79.

tions 3 and 4 of the HRA shed further light on this difference in approach.[27] In the Children Act case, the Court of Appeal[28] had found a risk to Article 8 under Parts III and IV of the Children Act 1989 for children subject to full care orders.[29] It therefore applied section 3 HRA to 'read in' a new procedure for ongoing judicial supervision of such cases.[30]

The House of Lords[31] however took the view that this was 'judicial innovation' beyond the licence of section 3. According to Lord Nicholls, the interpretation the Court of Appeal arrived at had given rise to a scheme that substantially departed from a 'cardinal principle' of Parliament's intention in enacting the Children Act 1989 which entrusted to local authorities (and not the courts) parental responsibility once a care order is in place.[32] This he said, was a sure sign of illegitimate 'statutory amendment' as opposed to 'legislative interpretation'.[33] To add to this, 'far-reaching practical ramifications' for local authorities resulted from the Court of Appeal's judgements, which materially impacted on resource allocation. In words reminiscent of Lord Hope's in *R. v. A*, Lord Nicholls observed that in such a 'highly sensitive and carefully research field' the design of a new scheme was 'impossible for a court to evaluate'.[34]

Lord Hope provided a further refinement to his approach to the intersection between sections 3 and 4 in *R. v Shayler*.[35] If 'compatibility cannot be achieved without . . . mak[ing] the statute unintelligible or unworkable' then the court would have no option but to make a section 4 declaration. This would leave to Parliament decisions as to whether, and how, to amend the offending legislation.[36]

In *R. (on the application of International Transport Roth GmbH) v Secretary of State for the Home Department*, the High Court found that, notwithstanding its 'strong obligation', where the measure of reinterpretation required to ensure compatibility would 'turn the statutory language . . . inside out',[37] section 3's ambit was outstripped. In consequence, the court issued a section 4 declaration,[38] later upheld by the Court of Appeal.[39] In relation to the High Court's use of section 3 in 'compatibilising' a *second* provision that had

---

[27] The interaction of ss.3 and 4 distinguishes the HRA model of rights protection from other bills of rights. S. 4 declarations of incompatibility are the flip side of s.3 and may well define in negative terms the extent of the force of s.3.

[28] *W and B (Children); W (children)* [2001] 2 F.L.R. 582 (Thorpe, Sedley and Hale L.JJ.).

[29] By virtue of the Act's omission to provide for independent oversight of a responsible local authority's implementation of a court-ordered care plan, where default might lead to violation of Art. 8.

[30] Involving conferral of "starred status" on the "essential milestone" of the care plan, and monitoring of their achievement, by the trial court.

[31] *Re W and B (Children) (Care Plan), Re W (Children) (Care Plan)* [2002] 2 W.L.R. 720 (Lords Nicholls, Browne-Wilkinson, Hutton, Mackay and Mustill).

[32] *ibid.* p.732, para.42. Lord Nicholls noted that the enactment of the Children Act 1989 had represented a change of law on this point, and also described the boundary of responsibility as delineated by that legislation "with complete clarity" (p.728, paras 25, 27).

[33] para.43.

[34] paras 43, 44. One further important issue emerged from the Children Act case. Finding a breach of Art. 8 rights under the legislation, the Court of Appeal refused applications for s.4 declarations because it found "the problem is more with what the Act does not say than with what it does" (n. 37 above, para.50). While this led the court to conclude itself obliged to fill the gap in protection left by the Act's omission, the House of Lords, taking a different view of what s.3 can and cannot do, found that if a lacuna exists, then it may be the case that neither s.3 nor s.4 provides a solution (n. 37, at p.740, paras 85 and 86).

[35] [2002] 2 W.L.R. 754.

[36] p.781, para 52.

[37] para.181.

[38] (2002) 99 L.S.G. 27. Note that Sullivan J held that, if the regime determined civil obligations within Art. 6(1) ECHR, rather than a criminal charge under Art. 6(2), then Immigration and Asylum Act 1999 could, on a "strained" interpretation, have been read as enabling a defence to be raised at the debt recovery stage (as suggested in *R. (on the application of Balbo B & C Auto Transporti Internazionali) v Secretary of State for the Home Department)* [2001] 1 W.L.R. 1556), avoiding incompatibility.

[39] [2002] S.T.C. 347, which found s.3 reinterpretation blocked by the need to reinterpret the "statutory scheme inside out", and to "create a wholly different scheme" to achieve compatibility (para.66).

been challenged, Simon Brown L.J. (Laws L.J. concurring) found that section 3 had been correctly applied by the High Court in reading the word 'must [take steps if he objects]' as 'may [take steps . . .]',[40] on the footing that this interpretation in fact achieved the meaning the Home Office had always intended to apply.

Matthews v Ministry of Defence[41] concerned Crown immunity against negligence claims by armed forces personnel. Because section 10 of the 1947 Act[42] could only be interpreted compatibly if read as subject to a lengthy implied qualifying clause,[43] this went beyond even the 'linguistically strained' interpretation possible under *R. v A*.[44]

Finally, in the *SIAC*[45] case, the Anti-Terrorism, Crime and Security Act 2001 was held incompatible under section 4 of the HRA because of its discriminatory treatment of foreign nationals. This was the first successful challenge in a domestic forum to emergency legislation under a derogation from an international human rights treaty, and an undeniably significant step forward in the protection of human rights yielded by the HRA.

This range of HRA cases under sections 3 and 4 suggests three provisional conclusions on the court's new powers of statutory interpretation in the post-HRA era. First, they demonstrate that, despite many failed challenges, the HRA's scheme can alter law and practice to give substantive protection for individual rights. This can follow the form of 'dialogue' —initiated by a declaration of incompatibility and subsequent government action—as well as through interpretation of legislation.[46] Secondly, the courts are most likely to apply section 3 forthrightly to reinterpret legislation where their own powers are at issue,[47] and are least likely to do so where questions of resource allocations or decisions outside their traditional expertise are at stake.[48] Thirdly, it is undeniable that section 3 of the HRA has significantly altered the relationship between the courts and Parliament with regard to statutory interpretation in the context of human rights. What can be agreed so far is that section 3 can require a court to 'read down' over-broad legislation,[49] 'read in necessary safeguards' or give a statutory provision a meaning 'it would not ordinarily bear'.[50] But the emerging view is that the 'plain meaning' of statutory language cannot be 'ignored or simply changed in the cause of securing compatibility'—courts are not to be driven by an

---

[40] In IAA 1999, s.35(1).

[41] [2002] A.C.D. 42 (Keith J.).

[42] Which so far as relevant provides that: "(2) No proceedings in tort shall lie against the Crown for death or personal injury due to anything suffered by a member of the armed forces, if–a) that thing is suffered by him in consequence of the nature or condition of any such land, ship, aircraft or vehicle . . . equipment or supplies and . . . b) [the Secretary of State] certifies [that his suffering of that thing has been or will be treated as attributable to service for the purposes of entitlement to an award . . .relating to the disablement or death of members of the force of which he is a member]".

[43] *i.e.* that the "Secretary of State would only issue an appropriate certificate in exceptional circumstances *e.g.* when death or personal injury resulted from risk greater than could be expected of someone in comparable circumstances in civilian life" (para.50).

[44] *R. v A (No. 2)* (in n. 18 above). The High Court's ruling in *Matthews* on s.3 HRA was approved by the Court of Appeal, [2002] EWCA Civ 773 (Lord Phillips MR, Mummery, Hale LJJ), which found that the required reinterpretation would "go beyond the bounds" of s.3 and "amount to legislation" (para.76), although the declaration was rescinded on the basis of no substantive violation of Art. 6.

[45] *A and Other v Secretary of State for the Home Department* (Special Immigration Appeals Commission, July 30, 2002; Collins J., Kennedy L.J., Mark Ockleton).

[46] See *e.g.*, *R. (on the application of H) v London North & East Region Mental Health Tribunal* [2002] Q.B. 1 and the remedial order (Mental Health Act 1983 (Remedial) Order 2001 (S.I. 2001 No. 3712) made pursuant to the court's declaration of incompatibility. Additionally, the Secretary of State for Health approved an *ex gratia* scheme for compensation of those who had been affected. Following the declaration issued in *International Transport Roth*, provisions were included in the Immigration Asylum and Nationality bill to address the incompatibility identified.

[47] See *R. v Offen, R. v. A (No. 2)*, and *R. v Lambert*, above.

[48] *Re W and B (Children) (Care Plan), Re W (Children (Care Plan)*, n. 37 above; see also *R. (on the application of Reynolds) v Secretary of State for Work and Pensions* [2002] EWHC 426 (Admin); though *cf R.(on the Application of H) v Mental Health Tribunal (North & East London)*.

[49] See Lord Steyn in *R v A (No 2)*, n. 18 above, para.44.

[50] See Lord Hope in *R. v Lambert*, n. 19 above, para.80.

'imperative to find compatibility at all costs'[51]. As Sedley L.J. has put it: section 3 is not a 'supplanting mechanism but a 'strong canon of construction'[52]—a distinction the 'rule of law' justification for which has been neatly recapitulated by Auld L.J.[53]: '[t]hose who are governed by, and seek to order their conduct according to statutory words, are entitled to a broad measure of certainty as to what they mean, not some contrary or wholly different meaning which a court, if and when the matter reaches it, might or might not consider permissible'."

Although the cases described above suggest the *significance* of the Human Rights Act 1998 for statutory interpretation by judges, it should also be appreciated that the courts may sometimes be reluctant to accept arguments that Convention rights have been breached. A good example of *deference* to Parliament by the Court of Appeal with respect to rights arguments can be seen in the following case, in which the Court was required to interpret the Housing Act 1988. This case raises the important issue of what constitutes a "public" authority under the Act, as well as the substantive rights which were alleged to have been breached.

Poplar Housing Regeneration Community Association Ltd v Donoghue [2001] 4 All ER 604, CA.

Lord Woolf C.J.:

The background

"This is an appeal from an order of District Judge Naqvi dated 5 December 2000. The judge gave permission to appeal and directed that the appeal should be heard by the Court of Appeal pursuant to CPR 52.14 on the ground that the appeal raises important points of principle and practice.

The proceedings started in the Bow County Court as a straightforward claim for possession of 31 Nairn Street London E14 0LQ, of which the defendant was the tenant and which is owned by the claimant housing association, Poplar Housing and Regeneration Community Association Ltd (Poplar). On the day of the hearing, 5 December, 2000, the proceedings were in the ordinary housing list. It had not been appreciated that the defendant wished to raise the issue that to make an order for possession would contravene her rights to respect for her private and family life and respect for her home contrary to art.8 of Sch 1 to the Human Rights Act 1998. Fortunately, notwithstanding the novel nature of the contention, District Judge Naqvi was in a position to consider the arguments which were advanced before him and give judgment straight away. We have a copy of the judgment and we commend the judge on the manner in which he dealt with the case.

---

[51] *R. v Daniel* [2002] EWCA Crim 959 (Auld L.J., Newman and Roderick Evans JJ., para 2.7). On this basis Auld L.J. rejected the House of Lords' conclusion in *Lambert* that "proves" might be read as meaning "gives sufficient evidence" in order to transform a persuasive into an evidential burden under Misuse of Drugs Act 1971, s.28.

[52] *R. (on the application of Wooder) v Feggetter and Mental Health Act Commission* [2002] 3 W.L.R. 591 (Brooke, Potter and Sedley L.JJ.). The *ration* applied s.3 to the Mental Health Act 1983: para.48.

[53] See n. 51 above. Note also Auld L.J.'s comment (para.28) that where there is plain incompatibility between statutory words' ordinary meaning and Art. 6(2), "*whatever the context*" courts should strive not to exceed what is "possible" within s.3 JRA—without doubt in allusion, and apparent contradistinction, to Lord Steyn's principle in *Ex p. Daly* that in determining the intensity of judicial review "context is everything" (para.28).

The approach of the judge

As he points out in his judgment, although this was not how the case was initially presented, the tenancy was an assured shorthold tenancy subject to s.21 of the Housing Act 1988. Section 21 deals with the recovery of possession on the expiry or termination of assured shorthold tenancies. Under the section, the court's discretion not to make an order for possession is strictly limited.

Section 21(1) applies to orders for possession of dwelling houses after the coming to an end of an assured shorthold tenancy for a fixed term. The defendant did not have a fixed term tenancy. She had a periodic tenancy. Periodic tenancies are dealt with by s.21(4). Section 21(4) provides:

> 'Without prejudice to any such right as is referred to in subsection (1) above, a court *shall* make an order for possession of a dwelling-house let on an assured shorthold tenancy which is a periodic tenancy if the court is satisfied—(a) that the landlord, or, in the case of joint landlords, at least one of them has given to the tenant a notice in writing stating that, after a date specified in the notice, being the last day of a period of the tenancy and not earlier than two months after the date the notice was given, possession of the dwelling-house is required by virtue of this section; and (b) that the date specified in the notice under paragraph (a) above is not earlier than the earliest day on which, apart from section 5(1) above, the tenancy could be brought to an end by a notice to quit given by the landlord on the same date as the notice under paragraph (a) above.' (My emphasis.)

It will be observed that s.21(4) appears to be mandatory in its terms. The court has to make an order for possession if there is a tenancy to which the subsection applies and the appropriate notice has been given. There is no requirement for the court to be satisfied that it is *reasonable* to make an order.

The first point taken on behalf of the defendant before the judge was that the notice which had been given did not comply with s.5 of the Protection from Eviction Act 1977. The judge held that s.5 only applied to purely common law notices to quit and not to statutory notices under s.21(4) of the 1988 Act. No appeal has been pursued in respect of that holding.

The judge then turned his attention to the Human Rights Act argument. It was contended that to make an order for possession would contravene arts 6 and 8 of the European Convention for the Protection of Human Rights and Fundamental Freedoms (Rome, 4 November 1950; TS 71 (1953); Cmd 8969) (as set out in Sch 1 to the 1998 Act) and would involve interpreting s.21(4) in a manner which is not compatible with the 1998 Act. The judge rejected these contentions as well. He said:

> 'If I were to read s.21(4) of the 1988 Act in the way in which I am being enjoined to do, this would, in effect, enable people who were intentionally homeless, and that is a finding that has been already made by the local authority, which has been reviewed and has not been challenged, the final decision having been made a year ago in November 1999, to jump the housing queue, that would impede the human rights of others and that is the proviso to Art.8(2) that I have got in mind, "the protection of the rights and freedoms of others".'

He did, however, postpone the date on which the order came into force for 42 days. This was the maximum extension which he was entitled to give. This was because of the defendant's exceptional personal circumstances. In addition, as already stated, the judge gave permission to the defendant to appeal directly to the Court of Appeal.

It is the defendant's contention that the judge should have adjourned the hearing so as to enable her to place before the court the substantial evidence, which is now before this court, in support of her appeal. The evidence is directed to the issues of whether the housing association is a public body or performing a public function and whether any breach of art.9 could be justified on the grounds set out in art.8(2).

In our judgment, where it is possible for a judge to give a decision summarily, as the judge did here, in a case where there will almost certainly be an appeal, there can be substantial advantages in adopting this approach. It can avoid expense and delay being incurred both at first instance and in the Court of Appeal.

The facts

The defendant moved into 31 Nairn Street in March 1998. She then had three children aged three, four and five. At the time of the possession proceedings she was expecting her fourth. The tenancy was granted by the London Borough of Tower Hamlets (Tower Hamlets) pursuant to its duties as the local housing authority under s.188 of the Housing Act 1996. The tenancy was a weekly non-secure tenancy under para 4 of Sch 1 to the Housing Act 1985. This was recorded in the written agreement dated 25 February 1998. The property was later transferred to Poplar. Poplar was created as a housing association by Tower Hamlets in order to transfer to it a substantial proportion of the council's housing stock.

The defendant had been provided with housing by Tower Hamlets pending a decision as to whether she was intentionally homeless. On 16 September 1999, Tower Hamlets decided she was intentionally homeless and notified the defendant to this effect (s 184 of the 1996 Act). The reason given was that the defendant had left an assured shorthold tenancy to live with her sister. A review of this decision was conducted by Tower Hamlets at the request of the defendant on 29 November 1999. The decision was confirmed. Previously the defendant would have been able, if she wished, to challenge the decision on an application for judicial review. However, by November 1999, the procedure for challenging the decision was by way of appeal to the county court. The defendant did not appeal.

In January or February 2000, Tower Hamlets issued proceedings for possession against the defendant. The authority then discovered that it was not the landlord and proceedings were withdrawn. On 26 June 2000, Tower Hamlets wrote to the defendant informing her that she was a tenant of Poplar and was subject to an assured shorthold tenancy. On 27 June, a notice was served by Poplar under s.21(4) of the 1988 Act. On 19 October 2000, the present proceedings were commenced. . . .

The issues to which this appeal gives rise

If it were not for contentions based on the 1998 Act, there would be no possible basis for interfering with the judge's decision. There is no ambiguity in the terms of s.21(4) of the 1988 Act. Poplar could not obtain possession without an order of a court but the court was required to make the order if the defendant had a tenancy which was subject to s.21(4) and the proper notice was served (which in this case are now not in dispute).

On this appeal, as in the court below, the contentions of the defendant depend upon art.8, coupled with art.6, of the convention set out in Sch 1 to the 1998 Act. Article 8 is in the following terms:

'Right to respect for private and family life

1. Everyone has the right to respect for his private and family life, his home and his correspondence.

2. There shall be no interference by a public authority with the exercise of this right except such as is in accordance with the law and is necessary in a democratic society in the interests of national security, public safety or the economic well-being of the country, for the prevention of disorder or crime, for the protection of health or morals, or for the protection of the rights and freedoms of others.'

In considering art.1, it is helpful in this context to have in mind art.1 of the First Protocol of the convention set out in Pt II of Sch 1 to the 1998 Act. Article 1 provides: 'Every natural or legal person is entitled to the peaceful enjoyment of his possessions. No one shall be deprived of his possessions except in the public interest and subject to the conditions provided for by law . . .

Article 6 entitles the defendant to a fair trial of her right to remain in her home. There is no question of that right being infringed. If we hold that she is entitled to rely on art.8, it may be necessary for the case to be remitted to the county court to determine whether it is reasonable to make an order of possession. As to art.8, it appears to us that the following issues require consideration. (1) Did the judge adopt an appropriate procedure to determine the art.8 issue? (The procedural issue.) (2) Is Poplar a public body or was it performing functions of a public nature? (The public body issue.) (3) Did making an order for possession contravene art.8? (The art.8 issue.) (4) If it did, is a declaration of incompatibility the appropriate remedy? (The remedy issue.)

The procedural issue

As already indicated, the defendant complains that the judge dealt with the art.8 issues in far too summary a manner. Poplar, on the other hand, contends, though not with much enthusiasm, that this was the only appropriate way for the judge to deal with the issue. It would have been wrong of the judge to grant an adjournment so that the defendant could place before the court the evidence that she contended was required since this would have contravened the clear terms of s.21(4) of the 1988 Act. Even if art.8 was contravened, the correct remedy would be to grant a declaration of incompatibility, which would be available on an appeal. It was not for the judge to interpret s.21(4) in a way which gave him discretion to decide whether or not to make an order for possession.

In general terms, we have already indicated our approval of the approach of the judge. This does not mean that we consider that the judge was not required to deal with the art.8 issue once it was raised before him. In our judgment, the judge was required to deal with the defendant's contention, notwithstanding the language of s.21(4). Section 7 of the 1998 Act provides, so far as relevant:

'(1) A person who claims that a public authority has acted (or proposes to act) in a way which is made unlawful by section 6(1) may . . . (b) rely on the Convention right or rights concerned in any legal proceedings, but only if he is (or would be) a victim of the unlawful act.'

If the defendant is right in her contentions as to the manner in which art.8 applies to her tenancy, then she is a 'victim'. Furthermore, if she is right, Poplar is a public authority. She is therefore entitled to rely on art.8 'in any legal proceedings'. The judge clearly accepted that this was the situation and that is why he set out his views as to why art.8 did not apply to her tenancy. If the defendant is right, the question of incompatibility will have to be considered, but unless 21(4) is found to be incompatible, the case will have to be remitted so that a judge can, in the light of her circumstances, decide how he should exercise the discretion he would then have. The issue is there confined to whether the judge was entitled to decide the matter on the limited material that was then available without granting and adjournment.

For reasons we have partly explained, we consider that the judge was entitled to dispose of the case as he did. He sensibly cut through the issues by accepting for the purpose of his decision that Poplar was at least performing a public function in terminating the defendant's tenancy and seeking possession and that art.8(1) therefore applied. He focused on art.8(2) and decided s.21(4) did not offend art.8 on the ground that the purpose s.21(4) serves is within art.8(2). A district judge is familiar with housing issues and is perfectly entitled to apply his practical experience and common sense to an issue of this sort. It is not necessary at his level to hold a state trial into successive governments' housing policies in order to balance the public and private issues to which art.8 gives rise. A great deal of expense and delay was avoided in a case which he was aware would be likely to come before this court in any event. (There is no power to make a declaration of incompatibility in the county court.)

Mr Luba QC, on behalf of the defendant, advanced an argument based on the fact that the court is itself a public authority (s 6(3)(a) of the 1998 Act). However, if there is no contravention of art.8 on which the defendant is entitled to rely, this argument does not avail the defendant.

If courts of first instance are encouraged to deal with Human Rights Act issues summarily, we appreciate, and the present appeal makes clear, that the Court of Appeal will have to be flexible in relation to its own procedures. The outcome of this appeal to a substantial extent depends upon the legislative framework. However, that legislation has to be interpreted against the factual background of how the legislation works on the ground. When it became apparent that this court was going to decide for itself the principal issues involved rather than remit the appeal, if successful, to the court below, the parties wished to place additional evidence before the court. This was done, with our agreement, after the completion of the oral argument. It inevitably meant that the preparation of this judgment was somewhat delayed.

We are very grateful to the parties for the manner in which they have marshalled the evidence and for the further written argument which they have provided. We have considered whether we needed to hear further oral argument but have come to the conclusion that this is not necessary. The evidence, together with the written arguments, makes the positions of the parties clear. We need no further assistance in order to give our decision as to the outcome of this appeal.

The legislative framework

In order to determine the remaining issues, it is critical to have in mind the manner in which the legislative framework, which sets out the duties which are owed to tenants in the position of the defendant, and under which a registered social landlord (RSL) such as Poplar operates, has evolved.

The law affecting tenants of domestic accommodation has suffered from a failure to conduct a satisfactory review and consolidation of the legislation. This is despite a continuous process of amendment as the various governments of the day struggled to address the expense and chronic lack of accommodation for the less well-off members of society. The Law Commission has now been given the responsibility of remedying this situation. Until this happens, in order to understand the present legislative position, it is helpful to give the historic position in mind.

At one time, the private sector was heavily controlled in order to mitigate the hardship caused to tenants by a shortage of housing. Rents were carefully controlled and tenants were given a substantial measure of statutory protection against eviction. So far as the private sector has been concerned, generally the policy has been to reduce this control. The change of policy reflected the belief of governments that excessive control resulted in a deterioration in the quality and quantity of housing available in the private sector. This, it is said, has a variety of undesirable economic consequences for the public in general and the poorer members of society in particular.

The statutory responsibility of providing for those who do not have homes was and is that of local government, acting through housing authorities. In particular, boroughs such as Tower Hamlets are subject to a range of statutory duties to provide social housing. For this purpose, as Mr Gahagan points out in his written evidence on behalf of the Department, until the 1990s, local government authorities were not only responsible for the availability of local housing, but in addition acted as social landlords with their own housing stock. However, over the last decade, a number of local housing authorities have transferred their stock of housing to RSLs. This policy is considered to have been successful and is being expanded.

Part IV of the 1996 Act governs the allocation of housing accommodation by local housing authorities. A housing authority can select someone to be a secure tenant, or an introductory tenant, or nominate someone to be an assured tenant of RSL stock. Before the housing authorities can allocate accommodation, the person to whom the accommodation is to be allocated must fulfil the qualifying requirements. For this purpose, housing authorities establish and maintain a register of qualifying persons (s 162 of the 1996 Act). Applicants have a right of review of decisions by authorities not to place them on a register or to remove them from a register. Housing authorities must also publish a scheme for determining priorities and procedures. The policy behind the 1996 Act, according to Mr Gahagan, was to create a 'single route' through the housing register into social housing and remove a perceived fast track into such housing for households accepted as statutorily homeless. . . .

Mr Gahagan in his statement makes it clear that in may areas, particularly in London and the South East, demand for social housing far outweighs supply and therefore allocation must be made according to the degree of housing need and how long the applicants have been waiting. He also states:

'47. The purpose of the homelessness legislation is to provide a safety net for people who have become homeless through no fault of their own and would be vulnerable if they were not provided with temporary accommodation until a more settled housing solution becomes available. If people accepted as unintentionally homeless and in priority need were provided with accommodation with security of tenure, this would displace applicants with greater claim to scarce social housing. This would not be in the interests of public policy since it would amount to a fast track into a secure social tenancy for people accepted as statutorily homeless and would create a perverse incentive for people to apply for homelessness assistance. 48. The provision of temporary accommodation can be expensive for authorities, particularly in areas of high demand where they do not have sufficient accommodation of their own and must make arrangements with other landlords. A guiding principle underlying the legislation is that authorities are not obliged to secure accommodation, other than very briefly if the applicant has priority need, for people who have made themselves homeless intentionally. Such applicants are expected to make their own arrangements to find accommodation for themselves. 49. The interim duty to accommodate those applicants who appear to be homeless and have a priority need, pending completion of inquiries and a decision as to whether a substantive duty is owed, is a very important aspect of the safety net. It is essential to the public policy interest, however, that authorities can bring such interim accommodation to an end where they are satisfied that the applicant does not qualify for further assistance.'

The role of housing associations in providing accommodation has equally been affected by government policy.

Housing associations were very much the 'legal embodiment of the voluntary housing movement' as Mr Brockway, another witness on behalf of the Department, stated. Originally, many were small local charities, though others were large entities endowed by wealthy employers or philanthropists. The legal definition of a housing association is contained in s.1(1) of the Housing Associations Act 1985. This section makes it clear that a housing association may be a charity, an industrial and provident society, or a company which does not trade for profit and which has among its objects the provision of housing accommodation. Some are fully mutual co-operative organisations. Throughout the twentieth century many housing associations were funded by grants or loans usually through local authorities. In 1964, the Housing Corporation (the Corporation) was created and thereafter most of the public funding was channelled through the Corporation. The Corporation was granted supervisory powers by the Housing Act 1974. There are now 4,000 housing associations, of which approximately 2,200 are registered with the Corporation as RSLs. Since 1988, RSLs have been required to borrow funds in the private markets to supplement public funding. To date, some £20bn has been raised outside the public sector borrowing requirement. The other major development has been the growth in the transfer of housing stock from local authorities to RSLs. Both under the previous and the present government, some 500,000 dwellings have been transferred in this way. Today, there are 1.5 million dwellings in the ownership of RSLs.

Under Pt I of the 1996 Act, the Corporation is given two basic roles. These are to provide funding to RSLs and to regulate them. The funding is payable by way of grant under s.18 of the 1996 Act. Regulation covers the area of governance, finance and housing management. If performance fails, the Corporation can exercise a number of powers; it can withdraw funding, make appointments to the governing body of the RSL and remove employees or governing body members (Sch 1 of the Act).

Section 170 of the 1996 Act importantly provides:

> 'Where a local housing authority so request, a registered social landlord shall co-operate to such an extent as is reasonable in the circumstances in offering accommodation to people with priority on the authority's housing register.'

Section 213 of the 1996 Act also requires 'other bodies' to co-operate with housing authorities to assist in the discharge of their functions, subject to the request for co-operation being reasonable in the circumstances. 'Other bodies' includes RSLs: s.213(2)(a). Mr Brockway states that in most local authority areas, the housing authority will have nomination agreements with RSLs. These agreements enable the authority to nominate tenants, to whom the RSLs should grant tenancies, from the housing registers.

Many local authorities have transferred some or all of their housing stock to one or more RSL. This has happened so far as Poplar is concerned. Poplar was created for the purpose of taking over part of the housing stock of the borough of Tower Hamlets. It was a condition of Tower Hamlets receiving funding that this should happen. The funding came from the government under a scheme (the Estates Renewal Challenge Fund) designed to bring about the repair and improvement of old housing stock, the improvement of security for occupants of estates, to tackle anti-social behaviour and crime and to develop community initiatives. The transfer of the council stock to Poplar was only possible where there was a majority vote by tenants in favour of the transfer of the particular housing stock involved. No payment was involved for the transfer. The properties transferred were regarded as having a negative value because of their state of repair. Mr Brockway makes it clear that the government's policy was that the RSLs should be private sector bodies. The way they were funded was dependent on this. Mr Brockway states that as a matter of policy the Corporation has always asked RSLs to grant the most secure form of tenure available to its tenants. This will usually be achieved by granting periodic tenancies of which possession can only be achieved on discretionary grounds. Such tenancies are accepted by Mr Luba as providing the necessary protection which he submits is necessary to comply with art.9 of the convention. The Corporation requires that if a tenant has an assured tenancy, then an order for possession can only be sought if it is reasonable to seek the order.

However, guidance has been given by the Corporation to RSLs to grant assured shorthold tenancies where special circumstances exist. Those circumstances include where the provision of accommodation is to be temporary, as was the position in the case of the defendant.

Mr Christopher Holmes, the director of Shelter, has provided evidence for the defendant. Based on his experience, he states that in practical terms, particularly where large-scale voluntary transfers have occurred, housing associations provide the means whereby accommodation is made available to homeless persons. This can include interim accommodation under s.188 of the 1996 Act while the priority of an applicant is being determined and where, as in the case of the defendant, the applicant has been found to be homeless intentionally. Mr Holmes goes on to point out:

> 'To enable the statutory duties imposed on local authorities to be discharged appropriately, close co-operation with housing associations continues beyond the point where accommodation is made available. When duties come to an end and accommodation is to be recovered, notification will pass from the authority to the association and possession will be recovered in due course. In effect, the association acts as a conduit for the authority's decision on whether a duty arises or has come to an end.'

He adds:

> 'Although there is no doubt that housing associations have their own constitutions and mechanisms for governance, in the practical day-to-day management of both long-term and short-term provision for the homeless, they are inextricably linked to the statutory framework imposing duties on local authorities and associations alike.'

He further adds:

'The complex nature of housing associations, run as they are, by unpaid persons and with their own constitutions, is apparent. And yet the associations are free to decide key issues regarding investment of funds and the nature of refurbishment and development works. Although tied in with local authorities in terms of allocations and homelessness, this does not, of itself, alter the fundamentally private nature of associations. There are many bodies which are required to act in accordance with public powers, duties and functions but which remain essentially private bodies. Railtrack is an example.'

Later, having referred to Mr Brockway's approach that any RSL taking over the stock of a housing authority will be a private sector body, Mr Holmes adds: 'This is, of course, the case but the day-to-day management of that stock may in my view be properly categorised as a public function in the circumstances I have described in this statement.'

He also refers to the fact that RSLs are subject to the scheme introduced by s.51 of the 1996 Act for the investigation of complaints by the independent housing ombudsman.

Mr Holmes does not accept that the use of assured shorthold tenancies by RSLs is necessary. His complaints include the fact that:

'More and more tenants are losing their homes on mandatory grounds. The government's own homelessness statistics show that, between 1992 and 1999, there was an increase of nearly 63% in the number of households accepted as homeless and in priority need following the recovery of possession of premises let on an assured shorthold tenancy. The loss of a shorthold is now the third most common reason for homelessness given by persons accepted as homeless by local authorities. In some areas of high housing demand it is the most common reason.'

He supports his view by referring to cases which illustrate the disadvantage of assured shorthold tenancies.

Public bodies and public functions

The importance of whether Poplar was at the material times a public body or performing public functions is this: the 1998 Act will only apply to Poplar if it is deemed to be a public body or performing public functions. Section 6(1) of the 1998 Act makes it unlawful for a public authority to act in a way which is incompatible with a convention right. Section 6(3) states that a 'public authority' includes 'any person certain of whose functions are functions of a public nature'. Section 6(5) provides: 'In relation to a particular act, a person is not a public authority by virtue only of subsection (3)(b) if the nature of the act is private.'

The defendant relies on the witness statements of Mr David Cowan, a lecturer of law at the University of Bristol (specialising in housing law and policy) and of Professor Alder of the University of Newcastle in support of her contention that Poplar is a public authority within s.6. Both Mr Cowan and Professor Alder acknowledge that the questions raised are ones of importance and of some debate in academic circles. However, Mr Cowan says it is 'tolerably clear that RSLs do fall within the definition of public authority under s.6(1)' as they are performing public functions.

Mr Cowan says:

'The obligation to provide interim accommodation under Pt VII (homelessness) of the Housing Act 1996 pending inquiries is owed by the local authority to the homeless applicant. That is clearly a public function. The accommodation can be provided by an RSL (see s.206(1)(b)). An RSL which provides that accommodation is thus fulfilling a public function. Where, as here, the accommodation provided to the homeless household in satisfaction of the duty was originally owed by the local authority, but subsequently transferred to the RLS *whilst the duty was ongoing*, then the public nature of a function is made all the clearer. The decision to seek possession of the property once the relevant inquiries and a decision on the homelessness application have been made are all part and parcel of that function. It is therefore clear that this case does not fall within the exemption of activities covered by s.6(5).'

We agree with Mr Luba's submissions that the definition of who is a public authority, and what is a public function, for the purposes of s.6 of the 1998 Act, should be given a generous interpretation. However, we would suggest that the position is not as simple as Mr Cowan suggests. The fact that a body performs an activity which otherwise a public body would be under a duty to perform cannot mean that such performance is necessarily a public function. A public body in order to perform its public duties can use the services of a private body. Section 6 should not be applied so that if a private body provides such services, the nature of the functions are inevitably public. If this were to be the position, then when a small hotel provides bed and breakfast accommodation as a temporary measure, at the request of the housing authority that is under a duty to provide that accommodation, the small hotel would be performing public functions and required to comply with the 1998 Act. This in not what the 1998 Act intended. The consequence would be the same where a hospital uses a private company to carry out specialist services, such as analysing blood samples. The position under the 1998 Act is necessarily more complex. Section 6(3) means that hybrid bodies, who have functions of a public and private nature are public authorities, but *not* in relation to acts of a private nature. The renting out of accommodation can certainly be of a private nature. The fact that through the act of renting by a private body a public authority may be fulfilling its public duty, does not automatically change into a public act what would otherwise be a private act. . . .

The purpose of s.6(3)(b) is to deal with hybrid bodies which have both public and private functions. It is not to make a body, which does not have responsibilities to the public, a public body merely because it performs acts on behalf of a public body which would constitute public functions were such acts to be performed by the public body itself. An act can remain of a private nature even though it is performed because another body is under a public duty to ensure that that act is performed. . . .

The approach of Professor Alder differs from that of Mr Cowan. He states that there is no single factor that determines whether a function is a public function. He adds:

'The meaning of "public function" is not necessarily the same in the different contexts where the matter arises . . . Analogies, particularly in respect to the test for determining which bodies are susceptible to judicial review in the Administrative Court may be helpful, given that one purpose of judicial review is to ensure that public bodies are subject to high standards of conduct the same being true of the [convention]. There is also an analogy with the test that is being developed in European Community law for determining whether a body is a public body, namely "a body, whatever its legal form, which has been made responsible, pursuant to a measure adopted by the state, for providing a public service under the control of the state and which has for that purpose special powers beyond those which result from the normal rules applicable in relations between individuals . . ." (*Foster v British Gas plc* Case C-188/89 [1990] 3 All ER 897 at 922, [1991] 1 QB 405 at 427, [1990] ECR I-3313 at 3348–3349 (par 20)).'

In coming to his conclusion that in this case the activities of Poplar are within s.6, the professor relies upon the charitable status of Poplar; the fact that Poplar is subject to the control of the Corporation; the sanctions which the Corporation can apply; the provision of public funding to Poplar; the standards which Poplar is required to adopt in the exercise of its powers; the control which the Corporation can exert over the exercise of Poplar's powers; and local authority involvement.

Both the Department and Poplar dispute that Poplar is a public authority. Mr Philip Sales helpfully adopts the distinction correctly identified by Clayton and Tomlinson *The Law of Human Rights* (2000) vol 1, p 189 (para 5.08) between *standard public* authorities, *functional* public authorities and courts and tribunals. Mr Sales submits, and we, like Professor Alder and Mr Holmes, would agree that housing associations as a class are not standard public authorities. If they are to be a public authority this must be because a particular function performed by an individual RSL is a public as opposed to a private act. The RSL would then be a functional, or hybrid, public authority.

In support of his contention, Mr Sales draws attention to the following features of housing associations. (a) They vary vastly in size. (b) Their structure is that of an ordinary private law entity. (c) As to regulation by the Corporation he points to the fact that many financial institutions are regulated by the Bank of England but this does not make them public bodies. Furthermore, the Corporation gives each RSL freedom to decide how it achieves what is expected of it. (d) Members of the RSL are not appointed by, or answerable to, the government but are private individuals who volunteer their services. Even in the rare cases where the Corporation makes appointments, the appointee owes his duty to the RSL. (e) In *R v Servite Houses, ex p Goldsmith* [2001] BLGR 55 Moses J decided a housing association was not subject to judicial review. (f) Although an RSL is funded in part out of public funds, the major source of its income is its rental income. In any event, this is not by any means conclusive (see *Peabody Housing Association Ltd v Green* (1979) 38 P&CR 644 at 660, 662).

In coming to our conclusion as to whether Poplar is a public authority within the 1998 Act meaning of that term, we regard it of particular importance in this case that (i) while s.6 of the 1998 Act requires a generous interpretation of who is a public authority, it is clearly inspired by the approach developed by the courts in identifying the bodies and activities subject to judicial review. The emphasis on public functions reflects the approach adopted in judicial review by the courts and text books since the decision of the Court of Appeal (the judgment of Lloyd LJ) in *R v Panel on Take-overs and Mergers, ex p Datafin plc (Norton Opax plc intervening)* [1987] 1 All ER 564, [1987] QB 815. (ii) Tower Hamlets, in transferring its housing stock to Poplar, does not transfer its primary public duties to Poplar. Poplar is no more than the means by which it seeks to perform those duties. (iii) The act of providing accommodation to rent is not, without more, a public function for the purposes of s.6 of the 1998 Act. Furthermore, that is true irrespective of the section of society for whom the accommodation is provided. (iv) The fact that a body is a charity or is conducted not for profit means that it is likely to be motivated in performing its activities by what it perceives to be the public interest. However, this does not point to the body being a public authority. In addition, even if such a body performs functions that would be considered to be of a public nature if performed by a public body, nevertheless, such acts may remain of a private nature for the purpose of s.6(3)(b) and (5). (v) What can make an act, which would otherwise be private, public, is a feature or a combination of features which impose a public character or stamp on the act. Statutory authority for what is done can at least help to mark that act as being public; so can the extent of control over the function exercised by another body which is a public authority. The more closely the acts that could be of a private nature are enmeshed in the activities of a public body, the more likely they are to be public. However, the fact that the acts are supervised by a public regulatory body does not necessarily indicate that they are of a public nature. This is analogous to the position in judicial review, where a regulatory body may be deemed public but the activities of the body which is regulated may be categorised private. (vi) The closeness of the relationship which exists between Tower Hamlets and Poplar. Poplar was created by Tower Hamlets to take a transfer of local authority housing stock; five of its board members are also members of Tower Hamlets; Poplar is subject to the guidance of Tower Hamlets as to the manner in which it acts towards the defendants. (vii) The defendant, at the time of the transfer, was a sitting tenant of Poplar and it was intended that she would be treated no better and no worse than if she remained a tenant of Tower Hamlets. While she remained a tenant, Poplar therefore stood in relation to her in very much the position previously occupied by Tower Hamlets.

While these are the most important factors in coming to our conclusion, it is desirable to step back and look at the situation as a whole. As is the position on applications for judicial review, there is no clear demarcation line which can be drawn between public and private bodies and functions. In a borderline case, such as this, the decision is very much one of fact and degree. Taking into account all the circumstances, we have come to the conclusion that while activities of housing associations need not involve the performance of public functions, in this case, in providing accommodation for the defendant and then seeking possession, the role of Poplar is so closely assimilated to that of Tower Hamlets that it was performing public and not private functions. Poplar therefore is a functional public authority, at least to that extent. We emphasise that this does not mean that all Poplar's functions are public. We do not even decide that the position would be the same if the defendant was a secure tenant. The activities of housing associations can be ambiguous. For example, their activities in raising private or public finance could be very different from those under consideration here. The raising of finance by Poplar could well be a private function.

The art 8 issue

To evict the defendant from her home would impact on her family life. The effect of art.8(2) of the convention is therefore critical. The starting point is the fact that after the order for possession was obtained, Tower Hamlets continued to owe a limited duty to provide the defendant with assistance as a person who was found to be intentionally homeless. This was so even though Poplar's responsibility came to an end. If the defendant had not fallen into one of the special categories, she would have been provided with greater security of occupation.

Mr Holmes recognises that the defendant could not expect security of tenure, but he submits that there should be a residual discretion to protect the defendant's basic human rights. He also submits that this would not in practice give rise to undesirable consequences, to which the witnesses for the Department refer, but this is very much a matter of judgment.

There is certainly room for conflicting views as to the social desirability of an RSL being able to grant assured shorthold tenancies which are subject to s.21(4) of the 1988 Act. Mr Holmes considers the present policy mistaken. However, in considering whether Poplar can rely on art.8(2), the court has to pay considerable attention to the fact that Parliament intended when enacting s.21(4) to give preference to the needs of those dependent on social housing *as a whole* over those in the position of the defendant. The economic and other implications of any policy in this area are extremely complex and far-reaching. This is an area where, in our judgment, the courts must treat the decisions of Parliament as to what is in the public interest with particular deference. The limited role given to the court under s.21(4) is a legislative policy decision. The correctness of this decision is more appropriate for Parliament than the courts and the 1998 Act does not require the courts to disregard the decisions of Parliament in relation to situations of this sort when deciding whether there has been a breach of the convention.

The defendant's lack of security is due to her low priority under the legislation because she was found to be intentionally homeless. She was and must be taken to be aware that she was never more than a tenant as a temporary measure. In the case of someone in her position, even if she is a mother of young children, it is perfectly understandable that Parliament should have provided a procedure which ensured possession could be obtained expeditiously and that Poplar should have availed itself of the procedure.

Tenants in the position of the defendant have remedies other than under s.21(4) which are relevant when considering art.8. There are provisions for appeal against the decision that a person is intentionally homeless. There is a regulatory role of the corporation and there is the ombudsman. There is also the fact that RSLs are subject to considerable guidance as to how they use their powers.

We are satisfied, that notwithstanding its mandatory terms, s.21(4) of the 1988 Act does not conflict with the defendant's right to family life. Section 21(4) is certainly necessary in a democratic society in so far as there must be a procedure for recovering possession of property at the end of a tenancy. The question is whether the restricted power of the court is legitimate and proportionate. This is the area of policy where the court should defer to the decision of Parliament. We have come to the conclusion that there was not contravention of art.8 or of art.6.

The incompatibility issue

As we have decided that there is no contravention of arts 6 and 8, strictly, there is no need for us to speculate as to whether, if there had been a contravention, this would have created a situation of incompatibility. We note that if we decided that there was a contravention of art.8, the Department would prefer us not to interpret s.21(4) 'constructively' but instead to grant a declaration of incompatibility. However, so far, the sections of the 1998 Act dealing with interpretation and incompatibility have been subject to limited guidance and for that reason we hope it will be helpful if we set out our views even though they are strictly obiter.

The relevant sections of the 1998 Act are ss.3 and 4. They are in the following terms:

'3. *Interpretation of legislation.*—(1) So far as it is possible to do so, primary legislation and subordinate legislation must be read and given effect in a way which is compatible with the Convention rights.

(2) This section—(a) applies to primary legislation and subordinate legislation whenever enacted; (b) does not affect the validity, continuing operation or enforcement of any incompatible primary legislation; and (c) does not affect the validity, continuing operation or enforcement of any incompatible subordinate legislation if (disregarding any possibility of revocation) primary legislation is compatible with a Convention right.

4. *Declaration of incompatibility.*—(1) Subsection (2) applies in any proceedings in which a court determines whether a provision of primary legislation is compatible with a Convention right.

(2) If the court is satisfied that the provision is incompatible with a Convention right, it may make a declaration of incompatibility.

(3) Subsection (4) applies in any proceedings in which a court determines whether a provision of subordinate legislation, made in the exercise of a power conferred by primary legislation, is compatible with a Convention right.

(4) If the court is satisfied—(a) that the provision is incompatible with a Convention right, and (b) that (disregarding any possibility of revocation) the primary legislation concerned prevents removal of the incompatibility, it may make a declaration of that incompatibility.

(5) In this section "court" means—(a) the House of Lords; (b) the Judicial Committee of the Privy Council; (c) the Courts-Martial Appeal Court; (d) in Scotland the High Court of Justiciary sitting otherwise than as a trial court or the Court of Session; (e) in England and Wales or Northern Ireland, the High Court or the Court of Appeal.

(6) A declaration under this section ("a declaration of incompatibility")—(a) does not affect the validity, continuing operation or enforcement of the provision in respect of which it is given; and (b) is not binding on the parties to the proceedings in which it is made.'

It is difficult to overestimate the importance of s.3. It applies to legislation passed both before and after the 1998 Act came into force. Subject to the section not requiring the court to go beyond that which is possible, it is mandatory in its terms. In the case of legislation predating the 1998 Act where the legislation would otherwise conflict with the convention, s.3 requires the court to now interpret legislation in a manner which it would not have done before the 1998 Act came into force. When the court interprets legislation usually its primary task is to identify the intention of Parliament. Now, when s.3 applies, the courts have to adjust their traditional role in relation to interpretation so as to give effect to the direction contained in s.3. It is as though legislation which predates the 1998 Act and conflicts with the convention has to be treated as being subsequently amended to incorporate the language of s.3. However, the following points. which are probably self-evident, should be noted: (a) unless the legislation would otherwise be in breach of the convention s.3 can be ignored (so courts should always first ascertain whether, absent s.3, there would be any breach of the convention); (b) if the court has to rely on s.3 it should limit the extent of the modified meaning to that which is necessary to achieve compatibility; (c) s.3 does not entitle the court to *legislate* (its task is still one of *interpretation*, but interpretation in accordance with the direction contained in s.3); (d) the views of the parties and of the Crown as to whether a 'constructive' interpretation should be adopted cannot modify the task of the court (if s.3 applies the court is required to adopt the s.3 approach to interpretation); and (e) where despite the strong language of s.3, it is not possible to achieve a result which is compatible with the convention, the court is not *required* to grant a declaration and presumably in exercising its discretion as to whether to grant a declaration or not it will be influenced by the usual considerations which apply to the grant of declarations.

The most difficult task which courts face is distinguishing between legislation and interpretation. Here practical experience of seeking to apply s.3 will provide the best guide. However, if it is necessary in order to obtain compliance to radically alter the effect of the legislation this will be an indication that more interpretation is involved.

In this case Mr Luba contends that all that is required is to insert the words 'if it is reasonable to do so' into the opening words of s.21(4). The amendment may appear modest but its effect would be very wide indeed. It would significantly reduce the ability of landlords to recover possession and would defeat Parliament's original objective of providing certainty. It would involve legislating.

Finally, we are prepared to grant the parties declarations if this will assist them to seek permission to appeal. Despite this, the parties should not assume permission to appeal will be granted. The decision whether to grant permission or to leave the decision to grant permission to the Lords, should not be affected by the fact that the appeal involves the 1998 Act. The House of Lords should normally be allowed to select for itself the appeals which it wishes to hear. The appeal is dismissed.

Appeal dismissed. Permission to appeal refused."

NOTES AND QUESTIONS

- Summarise the facts of the case, explaining particularly why Poplar Housing served a notice to quit on Donoghue.

- Lord Woolf states that there are four issues in this case: (i) the procedural issue; (ii) the public body issue; (iii) the Art.8 issue; (iv) the remedy issue. For each issue, state in the form of a question precisely what the Court of Appeal was called upon to answer. In other words, frame each issue as a question which states the underlying substantive legal issue.

- Give the Court of Appeal's answer to each of the questions you have just posed. Try to limit your answer to one sentence for each issue.

- With respect to the public body issue, why will this be of such importance, not only in this case, but in Human Rights Act case law more generally? What section of the Human Rights Act is relevant to this issue? What factors motivated the Court to reach the conclusion it did on this issue?

- How widely do *you* think Art.8 should be interpreted? Why?

- Explain the basis on which the defendant argued that her article 8 European Convention rights were infringed by the actions of Poplar Housing.

- With respect to the incompatibility issue, Lord Woolf distinguishes between the functions of *legislating* and *interpreting*. What point is Lord Woolf trying to make? Why does Lord Woolf suggest that a finding in favour of Donoghue would have crossed the line between interpretation and legislation? Do you think that distinction can be maintained in the "Human Rights Act era"?

Finally, we include a more sceptical voice on the desirability of the Human Rights Act 1998 and the implications it has, not only for statutory interpretation, but more widely for society.

Adam Tomkins, "Introduction: on being sceptical about human rights", in *Sceptical Essays on Human Rights* (K.D. Ewing and Adam Tomkins, eds., Oxford University Press, Oxford, 2001), pp.110:

"Human rights have played a central role in the rhetoric (if not the reality) of international relations—from the United Nations down—ever since the mid-twentieth century. But over the past two decades human rights have additionally come to enjoy an ever more dominant position in national constitutional or public law. This has been as true for Canada and New Zealand as it has been for Poland and Hungary. One of the last countries in the common law world, and one of the last countries in Europe, to allow its domestic legal system to embrace human rights is the United Kingdom. At the turn of the millennium, however, human rights are beginning to be paraded as a central pillar of even the UK's rapidly changing legal order. After years of argument, Parliament in 1998 at last enacted legislation to 'bring rights home' as the government rather jingoistically put it. The Human Rights Act 1998, which came fully into force in October 2000, gives effect to a unique form of 'domestic incorporation' of (most of) the substantive provisions of the European Convention on Human Rights, a treaty which the UK had been bound by (but only as a matter of international law—and not therefore within the UK's own domestic legal system) since the Convention first came into force, in 1953. The Human Rights Act is, loosely, the UK's Bill of Rights, the UK's approximate equivalent of the Canadian Charter on Fundamental Freedoms (1982), of the New Zealand Bill of Rights Act (1990), and of the constitutional texts of countless emergent democracies from the Baltic States of northeast Europe to the turbulent but thrilling polity of the new South Africa. Human rights law is a global phenomenon to which, it seems, the UK is no longer immune. . . .

The Human Rights Act 1998 was one of the most widely celebrated statutes to have been passed by Parliament in many years. Nowhere were the celebrations more pronounced or more intense than among communities of lawyers. The celebration has taken many forms: from the self-congratulatory back-slapping of Tony Blair's Lord Chancellor to the publication of an enormous pile of both academic and practitioner-oriented literature which seeks to explain, to expound and to expand lawyers' understandings of the manifold changes which this legislation is assumed to necessitate. . . . In the clamour for liberal self-congratulation, and in the rush to explain how the UK has at last brought rights home, there has been little space for dissent, for critique, or even for doubt. . . ."

[Tomkins goes on to consider the broad sets of reasons to be sceptical of human rights.]

"A good number of different reasons can be identified, for example, in support of the proposition that we should be sceptical of rights (our first category of scepticism). First, rights-talk is inherently antagonistic, and encourages litigation. Secondly, human rights law imagines a paradigm in which there are two parties (the individual rights-holder and the public authority), a model which squeezes out any room for the *res publica*, for the public interest, along with any third party interests which, in the absence of their being 'victims', find it incredibly difficult to get into or otherwise be heard in court. Thirdly, human rights law reduces the relationship between the citizen and the state to one of regulation and quasi-contract—a bill of rights is a list of the clauses in the contract of good governance. The state will be allowed to tax you, to coerce you, to imprison you, to impose restrictions and constraints on you, and you will tolerate (and indeed support and protect —even be prepared to die for) the political, regulatory, military, and economic coercive power of the state on condition that the state respects your rights. Not only does this result in the state being portrayed in unambiguously negative terms, seemingly denying the good that the state is in a unique position to provide in terms of housing the homeless, healing the sick, educating both young and old, and providing welfare for the disadvantaged, and so on, but it also imagines that the individual wants nothing more than to be left alone, that freedom from government, rather than participation in government, is the goal. It also apparently—and dangerously—imagines that any political grievance can be successfully remedied by filing a lawsuit.

Fourthly, human rights law is insufficiently sensitive to the hegemonic power of its own discourse. Rights are an incredibly powerful rhetorical tool, and they get everywhere, strangling other devices, stymieing alternative developments. . . . Similarly, but more broadly, locating the task of enforcing rights in the courts can lead to the suffocating of alternative avenues for dispute resolution. What fate awaits ministerial responsibility, or the Parliamentary Commissioner for Administration (the ombudsman) after the Human Rights Act?

That there is life beyond the courtroom, but that institutions such as Parliament, ombudsmen, and others are likely to find it more difficult to make their scrutineering voices fully heard in the new post Human Rights Act legal order, connects with the second category of scepticism . . .: scepticism about judges. Why should it be the unrepresentative, overwhelmingly white male upper-middle-class judiciary of the UK's creaking courts who enjoy the emancipation that will come to them with the Human Rights Act? There are two questions here: why give power to *these* people, and why *not* give it to others? Even if the reasons for being sceptical about rights can be overcome, and we decide that we do properly want rights-talk to play a greater role in our polity, why give the job of talking that talk to the judges? After all, what have they done to show either that they deserve, or that they are the appropriate body to enjoy, this newfound role of constitutional referee. By inflating the power and responsibility of the judiciary, the influence and contribution which could be offered from other less well-dressed, but perhaps better-suited, institutions has been sidelined and overlooked. . . .

As to the third and final category of scepticism, namely scepticism about the specific content of, and omissions from, the ECHR and the HRA, this really speaks for itself, and little needs to be added here. Clearly the rights protected under the terms of the ECHR are partial in two senses. They are incomplete, in that there are many, many other social or political goods which we might want to be protected, or at least respected, in our polity but which do not find their way into the Act. But they are also partial in the more profound, and more disturbing, sense in that they represent a particular political—and party-political—vision of what it is that society should privilege and prioritize. In the ECHR, and thereby in the HRA, for example, we find the paradigmatic right of liberal political theory (freedom of expression) but not the core of republican philosophy or deliberative democracy (freedom of information, open government, and guarantees of full participation). Property is protected for those who possess it, but the homeless have no right to be housed. Religious freedom is protected, but not the right to an adequate standard of health care. And so on, and on. Social and economic rights are nowhere to be seen in the new liberal order: only a select few rights have been 'brought home' in the Not-Very-Many-Human-Rights Act of 1998."

- What are the various grounds on which Tomkins is sceptical of the Human Rights Act 1998? To what extent are you persuaded by his arguments?

- To what extent and how can the decision of the Court of Appeal in *Poplar Housing* be explained and analysed in terms of Tomkins' analysis?

PART FOUR: INTERPRETING CASES

10

JUDGE MADE LAW: AN INTRODUCTION TO COMMON LAW REASONING

In this chapter, our attention turns to "judge made law"; that is, the common law, described as the foundation of our legal system. We will examine the fundamentals of the common law method of reasoning. The chapter begins with some definitions of key concepts and then turns to look at the historical development of the common law tradition. We look at the *process* of common law reasoning, including the impact of membership in the European Union. In the closing section, we focus upon common law reasoning from a more theoretical perspective, and address the fundamental question of the extent to which judges in a common law system *make* the law.

KEY CONCEPTS AND TERMINOLOGY

It can be confusing for new law students to listen to discussion about the common law because it actually has a number of meanings and is used in different contexts. The abstract from Downes maps out the main uses of the phrase. It also draws our attention to the rather piecemeal fashion in which the concepts emerged.

T.A. Downes, *Textbook on Contract* (5th ed., Blackstone Press, London, 1997), pp.2–4:

Three meanings of "Common Law"

Historical: common law and equity

"After the Norman conquest of England local laws gave way to a general law of the country, which became known as the common law. The king's courts became the most important forum for the resolution of disputes between citizens. An action could only be brought in these courts by obtaining (purchasing) a writ. Over time the forms of such writs became fixed, and only Parliament could approve a new type of writ designed to meet a claim which could not be accommodated within the existing writs and forms of action. This rigidity in the legal system was often the cause of hardship to individual litigants, and the practice grew of petitioning the king for justice in the individual case. The petitions were dealt with by the chancellor, who in this period was a man of the church and who was regarded as the 'conscience' of the king. In due course a formal procedure for such petitions evolved, culminating in a Court of Chancery, presided over by the Lord Chancellor, applying a system of rules known as 'equity' rather than the common law of the ordinary courts.

Although the Court of Chancery was effective in remedying injustices, the existence of parallel jurisdictions brought problems and injustices of its own. Chancery developed procedures separate from, but at least as complex as, those of the common law courts. A litigant had to be sure of the classification of the rule he sought to have applied, in order to commence his action in the right court. The equity of the Chancery Court became a set of rules almost as precise as those of the common law. In the case of conflict between the two systems, the rules of equity prevailed. Parliament sought to put an end to these divisions with the Judicature Acts 1873–1875, which established a unified system of courts which were charged with applying both the common law and equity.

To the non-lawyer 'equity' is probably synonymous with the idea of natural justice. Although that was the origin of the Chancery jurisdiction, it has long since disappeared from the rules of equity. The rules of equity are just as capable today as those of the common law of producing resolutions of disputes which may be viewed as just or unjust. Indeed, since the two types of rules are now applied by the same courts, there is little significance left in the distinction. Nevertheless, in two respects it has left a legacy which still has an impact on today's courts. In the first place, while common law rules are available to plaintiffs as of right, equitable remedies are discretionary in the sense that they are subject to some general conditions of availability. For example, there is no absolute right to specific performance of a contract. Secondly, the existence of parallel systems of rules, the one based on formal procedures, the other based originally on the idea of substantial justice, has allowed some judges to invoke the tension between the two systems as a source of judicial creativity in developing the law to meet new situations. For example, Lord Denning has used this device in relation to the enforceability of promises and in relation to contracts affected by mistake.

Common law and statute

In another sense, the common law is the law applied by the courts developed through the system of precedent without reference to legislation passed by Parliament. Although statute has become the most prolific source of law in this country, this has only relatively recently been the case. Centuries ago, much of the law was applied by the courts independently of any statutory source. The constitutional fiction was that the judges merely declared what the law was, as though it was already there and merely had to be discovered. Today it is accepted that the courts created the law, although there is no reason to suppose they often acted arbitrarily in so doing. No doubt they acted in response to the values and needs of society, as they perceived them, in making law. This process created the body of the common law, which in this sense includes the law made by all the courts, including those of Chancery.

Common law as a 'family' of legal systems

A wider meaning still of 'common law' is a description of a group of related legal systems. The English legal system was exported around the world wherever British influence dominated. The legal systems of the USA, and of the 'old' Commonwealth countries, are all based on the English common law. In much the same way, the legal systems of continental European countries were exported around the world. They are usually described as the civil law systems, of which the most influential has been that of France, because by producing the Code Civil Napoleon gave to France the first modern European legal system, which was copied elsewhere.

Criminal law, civil law and public law

Criminal law

Most people have some understanding of what criminal law is. It deals with actions, or failures to act, which are contrary to the interests of society as a whole, and for which some penalty has been prescribed. Criminal law is a species of public law, in the sense that prosecutions of those accused of committing crimes are (except rarely) brought by public officials in the name of the state. It must be remembered that a crime which is contrary to society's general interest may also cause particular loss or injury to an individual. It would then also be a civil wrong (called a 'tort'), for which the individual would be able to claim compensation. Such compensation would normally be claimed by civil action in the civil courts, but in a criminal trial the courts have power to award compensation to persons injured, payable by a person convicted at trial (s.35, Powers of Criminal Courts Act 1973, as amended by the Criminal Justice Acts of 1982, 1988 and 1991).

Civil law

As well as denoting the continental European family of legal systems, civil law is the title of one category of English law. In one sense civil law is all law other than criminal law. . . . By civil law, today we often mean English *private* law.

Public law

The expression public law has existed for some time, but had little significance other than to indicate that the subject-matter in some way involved a public authority. Continental European legal systems, on the other hand, had developed the idea of public law into a separate and specialised body of rules applicable only to cases involving the administration. English law has not yet taken such a radical step, but in *O'Reilly v Mackman* [1982] 3 All ER 1124 the House of Lords drew a distinction between private law and public law rights. The latter can be asserted only by means of a special procedure which provides certain safeguards for the administration which do not exist in ordinary actions for private law rights. The full impact of this development in English law is still to be seen, and recently there have been some indications that not all judges favour making the distinction stronger.

Substantive law and procedure

The distinction between substantive law and procedure is, in simple terms, the distinction between the rules applicable to the merits of a dispute and the rules governing the manner of resolution of a dispute. For those who practise law the rules of procedure are very important, but at the academic stage of legal studies the focus is on the substantive rules. It is nevertheless important to have some understanding of procedure, because procedure can affect the application of the substantive rules. In fact, the rules of procedure were in the past of great significance in shaping the substantive rules, since English law has, from the time of the need to frame one's action within the form of an existing writ, proceeded from the existence of a remedy to the establishment of a right. It might almost be said that procedure came before substantive rights."

NOTES AND QUESTIONS

- Imagine that you have been asked to give a five-minute presentation to your seminar group on the notion of common law. Sketch out in rough how you would approach the task.

- Reflect for a minute on the law you have studied so far in your course. How much of it has been common law?

We will consider many of the points which Downes raises throughout this chapter and the rest of this text. For our purposes, he provides a good introduction to many of the terms which we will be using in considering common law reasoning. Central to that method of reasoning are the ideas of "case law" and "precedent".

Rupert Cross and J.W. Harris, *Precedent in English Law* (4th ed., Clarendon Press, Oxford, 1991), pp.3–5:

"The strongly coercive nature of the English doctrine of precedent is due to rules of practice, called 'rules of precedent', which are designed to give effect to the far more fundamental rule that English law is to a large extent based on case-law. 'Case-law' consists of the rules and principles stated and acted upon by judges in giving decisions. In a system based on case-law, a judge in a subsequent case *must* have regard to these matters; they are not, as in some other legal systems, merely material which he *may* take into consideration in coming to his decision. The fact that English law is largely a system of case-law means that the judge's decision in a particular case constitutes a 'precedent'. If we place ourselves in the position of a judge in a later case, there may be said to be many different kinds of precedent. The judge may simply be obliged to consider the former decision as part of the material on which his present decision could be based, or he may be obliged to decide the case before him in the same way as that in which the previous case was decided unless he can give a good reason for not doing so. Finally, the judge in the instant case may be obliged to decide it in the same way as that in which the previous case was decided, even if he can give a good reason for not doing so. In the last-mentioned situation the precedent is said to be 'binding' or of 'coercive effect' as contrasted with its merely 'persuasive' effect in the other situations in which the degree of persuasiveness may vary considerably.

Some branches of our law are almost entirely the product of the decisions of the judges whose reasoned judgments have been reported in various types of law report for close on 700 years. Other branches of our law are based on statutes, but, in many instances, case-law has played an important part in the interpretation of those statutes. As the sovereignty of Parliament is more complete in England than practically anywhere else in the world, it might be thought that the rigidity of the doctrine of precedent in this country is of no particular importance because any unsatisfactory results of case-law can be swept away by legislation, but the promotion of a statute on matters of this nature is often slow and difficult. There are many instances in which the recommendations of Royal Commissions and Law Revision Committees, designed to ameliorate the situation produced by case-law have been ignored, apparently for no other reason than pressure on parliamentary time.

Perhaps the number of such instances will be reduced in the future because there are now in existence several very important law-reforming agencies, notably the Law Reform Committee dealing with the reform of the civil law on matters referred to it by the Lord Chancellor, the Criminal Law Revision Committee dealing with the reform of the criminal law on matters referred to it by the Home Secretary, and, most important of all, the Law Commission. The Commission was set up by statute in 1965, and it is charged with the task of reviewing the law with a view to systematic development and reform, including, in particular, codification. When the work of the Law Commission results, as it probably will do, in codes of the more important branches of English law, the role of case-law will, *pro tanto*, be diminished."

NOTES

- You might find it useful to look at the Law Commission website (at *www.lawcom.gov.uk*) which contains details of its publications and the areas of law that it currently has under review. In addition to explaining its own programmes of reform the "Law Under Review" section contains summarised official law reform projects by other government bodies.

Cross and Harris raise the issue of the relationship between statute and common law, and suggest that there has been a historical process in which the role of statutes has increased, at the expense of judge made common law. We have already examined extensively the role of statutes in our legal system, but understanding the relationship between statutes and common law is a vital element in appreciating common law reasoning and the interface between these two sources of law. In the following classic extract Llewellyn teases out some other more fundamental distinctions.

K.N. Llewellyn, *The Bramble Bush* (Oceana Publications, New York, 1996), pp.87–88:

"Now the essential differences between statutes and the law of case decisions are these. A judge makes his rule in and around a specific case, and looking backward. The case shapes the rule; the judge's feet are firmly on the particular instance; his rule is commonly good sense, and very narrow. And any innovation is confined regularly within rather narrow limits—partly by the practice of trying hard to square the new decision with old law; it is hard to keep daring innovations even verbally consistent with old rules. And partly innovation is confined through conscious policy: case law rules (though new) are applied as *if* they had always been the law; this derives from our convention that 'judges only declare and do not make the law'. Knowing that the effect of their ruling will be retroactive, and unable to foresee how many men's calculations a new ruling may upset, the judges move very cautiously into new ground. Then, when a case has been decided, it enters into the sea of common law—available to any court within the Anglo-American world, and peculiarly, within this country. Finally, and important here, case law is flexible around the edges; the rules are commonly somewhat uncertain in their wording, and not too easy to make definite. Else why your study?

But statutes are made relatively in the large, to cover wider sweeps, and looking forward. They apply only to events and transactions occurring *after* they have come into force; that element of caution disappears. They are, moreover, recognized machinery for readjustment of the law. They represent not single disputes, but whole classes of disputes. They are political, not judicial in their nature, represent readjustments along the lines of balance of power, decide not single cases by a tiny shift of a rule, but the rearrangement of a great mass of clashing interests. Statute-making, too, is confined within what in relation to society at large is a straightened margin of free movement; but in comparison to courts the legislature is a horse without a halter."

William Geldart, *Introduction to English Law* (11th ed., Oxford University Press, Oxford, 1995), pp.2–6:

"1. In spite of the enormous and ever-growing bulk of the Statute Law—our statutes begin with the reissue of Magna Carta in 1225 in the reign of Henry III, and a large volume is now added every year—much of the fundamental part of our law is still Common Law. No statute, for instance, yet prescribes in general terms that a man must pay his debts or perform his contracts or pay damages for trespass or libel or slander. The statutes assume the existence of the Common Law. Except in so far as they restate in the form of a code some particular branch of the law, they are the addenda and errata of the book of the Common Law; and they would have no meaning except by reference to the Common Law. If all the statutes of the realm were repealed, we should still have a system of law, though, it may be, an unworkable one; if we could imagine the Common Law swept away and the Statute Law preserved, we should have only disjointed rules torn from their context, and no provision at all for many of the most important relations of life. The Law Commissions Act 1965, however, established a body of Commissioners whose task it is to prepare legislation which shall reform and simplify the law, and the Commissioners stated, in announcing their first programme of work, that they intended to prepare a codification of the laws of contract and of landlord and tenant. These major codes have not yet been completed (the Annual Report of the Law Commission for 1972–3 stated that work on the preparation of a code of the law of contract had been suspended, and so it is now doubtful whether it will ever be completed), but certain codes dealing with more restricted areas of law have been enacted in recent years, *e.g.* the Theft Act 1968, the Animals Act 1971, the Forgery and Counterfeiting Act 1981, and the Criminal Attempts Act 1981 . . . The work of the Law Commission has in recent years also led to much obsolete legislation being repealed. For example, much of the old Sunday Observance legislation was swept away by the Statute Law (Repeals) Act 1969.

2. Where Statute Law and Common Law come into competition, it is the former that prevails. Our law sets no limits to the power of Parliament. As the constitutionalist A.V. Dicey wrote a century ago, 'The sovereignty of Parliament is (from a legal point of view) the dominant characteristic of our political institutions.' No court or judge can refuse to enforce an Act of Parliament, though in the exercise of its duty to interpret an Act a court may sometimes alter considerably the effect that the legislators had intended the Act to have. No development of the Common Law can repeal an Act of Parliament, but large parts of the Common Law have from time to time been abolished by Act of Parliament, and their place has been taken by statutory rules. . . .

3. How do we know the law? Here there is a great difference between Statute and Common Law. A statute is drawn up in a definite form of words, and these words have been approved by Parliament and have received the Royal assent. In general there is no difficulty in ascertaining the words of a statute. At the present day two identical printed copies are made, each bearing a certificate of the Clerk of Parliaments that the Royal assent has been given, and in the last resort reference can be made to these copies for the purpose of ascertaining the true words of the statutes. For practical purposes any copy made by the Queen's printer is sufficient. In the case of some old statutes there is a possible doubt not only as to the exact words of a statute, but even whether such a statute was ever made; but in practice such doubts hardly ever arise. . . .

On the other hand we have no authoritative text of the Common Law. There is no one form of words in which it has as a whole been expressed at any time. Therefore in a sense one may speak of the Common Law as unwritten law in contrast with Statute Law, which is written law. Nevertheless the sources from which we derive our knowledge of the Common Law are in writing or print. First among these come the reported decisions of the judges of the English courts. Ever since the reign of Edward I there have been lawyers who have made it their business to report the discussions in court and the judgments given in cases which seemed of legal interest. The earliest of these reports are the Year-Books. They are reports of cases made by anonymous reporters from the time of Edward I to that of Henry VIII. These are followed by reports produced by lawyers reporting under their own names. They were at first published (like textbooks) only as and when the author, or the representatives of a deceased author, saw fit to do so. It was not until the end of the eighteenth century that reports began to be regularly published contemporaneously with the decisions of the cases reported. At the beginning these reports seem to have served mainly the purpose of instruction and information. The fact that a judge had stated that such and such was the law was evidence, but not more than evidence, that such was the law. He might have been mistaken; another judge might perhaps decide differently. But in course of time we find a change in the attitude of judges and lawyers towards reported decisions. The citation of decided cases becomes more frequent; greater and greater weight is attached to them as authorities. From the sixteenth century onwards we may say that decided cases are regarded as a definite authority, which, at least in the absence of special reasons to the contrary, must be followed for the future. For the last 35 years, at any rate, the decisions of judges of the higher courts have had a binding force for all similar cases which may arise in the future."

This historical development of the common law, and the rules of precedent in particular, have also been traced by Goodrich who raises important questions about the rhetoric and reality of common law reasoning.

Peter Goodrich, *Reading the Law* (Blackwell, Oxford, 1986), pp.66–72:

"Based in custom and in the 'natural reason' or will of the people, the common-law tradition is supposedly the unique product of the English people and their legal class and is supposedly vernacular in its form and democratic in its functioning. While there is some measure of historical truth in such a perception of the common law as a distinctive tradition, it both exaggerates the national quality of the common law and actively misleads the student of the contemporary legal order, which is effectively the product of much wider political and economic developments dating from the late seventeenth century to the present day. However politically pleasing or doctrinally desirable it might be to view the national legal system as a unique national product, we will argue here and subsequently that such a view is very far from being an accurate account of either the historical or contemporary workings of the common law. To the limited extent that the early common law was systematized into any coherent form of jurisprudence, the important intellectual influences upon it during its formative periods were those of Christianity and of Roman law, while as a body of disparate customary norms, the common law was distinctive primarily for its inaccessibility, obscurity and formality. Neither of such features supports the popular image of a native system of law emanating from the people or from below. They suggest rather the necessary complexity and, more specifically, the political and economic dependency of law upon other strata of the social whole. We shall look briefly at each of the two features mentioned, first at the formal or intellectual basis of the common law and secondly at the content and accessibility of the purportedly national customary law.

The conceptual source of the common law can be traced with considerable precision to the Anglo-Saxon monarchies of the period before the Norman conquest of 1066. In keeping with the general historical tradition which displays so close a relationship between law, power and writing, it is interesting to note that the earliest known law within the common-law tradition was both sacred and written. The tradition in question is one of a theocratic kind, rule being the rule of God as represented through the king, and the law of God was collected and promulgated in a codified, written form from a very early date, with major collections being associated with Aethelbert (602–3), Wihtred and most famously with King Cnut (1016–38). The single distinctive feature of these codes was that they were written in the vernacular, rather than in Latin, while their content was principally and fairly directly drawn from the Creed and other biblical passages. The model of law upon which these early codes were based was that of Rome: the codes were theocratic in their form and expressed fairly directly the political authority of government both in the elaboration of a relatively sophisticated body of penal norms but also in the growing use of charters as a means of conferring, 'by the grace of god', rights, duties and concessions upon individuals, groups, institutions and so on. The most famous example of such a charter is the very much later Great Charter (Magna Carta) of 1215, a concessionary charter extracted from King John, which commences, significantly and typically enough: 'First, we have granted to God, and by this our present charter have confirmed for us and our heirs for ever, that the English church shall be free and shall have all her rights and liberties, whole and inviolable. We have also given and granted to freemen of our realm, for us and our heirs for ever, these liberties underwritten, to have and to hold to them and their heirs, of us and our heirs for ever.' The early charters provided a formal expression of the king's will and were of greater practical importance, in all probability, than the general law promulgated by the king.

The influence of Christian law and the sacred status of the royal source of law tends to undermine more democratic conceptions of the origins of the common law. The other influence, of course, was Roman law and Roman ideas of government which played an increasing role throughout Europe. The early English legal tradition did not escape the latinization of European culture and by the time of the conquest Latin was the major legal language. More importantly, the centralization of the legal system which occurred soon after the Norman conquest was very much an exercise in developing and systematizing native law according to the precepts and principles of Roman law. The first centralized courts were royal courts and the first judges were royally appointed from amongst the clergy and legally trained in canon law and Roman law. It was precisely the king's courts, located at Westminster, and the king's judges, who first fashioned the 'general custom' of the land into a system of legal rules and provided, in a highly complex set of royal 'writs' governing the situations in which remedies were available from the courts, the rudiments of the centralized administration of justice or common law.

Remaining with 'general custom' and the early centralization of authority, the crucial period would appear to run from the late twelfth century through to the end of the thirteenth century. It was during this period that Henry II consolidated the central control of the king's courts and royal judges, both based in Westminster though increasingly peripatetic, and the early emergence of the legal profession based around the Inns of Court followed soon after. The theocratic tradition of law-making was supplemented by the influence of Roman law and the first literary expositions of the common law, most notably those of Glanvill (*De Legibus*) which appeared around 1187 and that of Bracton (*De Legibus et consuetudinibus Angliae*) which is dated 1256 and was praised by the historian Maitland as the 'crown and flower of English medieval jurisprudence'. Bracton was himself both a prominent cleric, eventually becoming chancellor of Exeter Cathedral, and also a royally appointed judge; his work on the law and customs of England draws extensively upon his experience as a judge and his knowledge of and access to earlier transcripts of pleadings before the royal courts. The form of systematization which Bracton brought to the common law was, however, that of the Roman law in which, as a cleric, he had originally been trained. . . .

The rapid development and stabilization of a system of common law during the thirteenth century was accompanied by the emergence of an early professional legal class, based at Westminster and skilled in oral pleading. Paradoxically the notions of oral pleading (narrators) and of an unwritten law were short-lived and the history of the common law is by and large a history of the recording and documentation of custom in a professional and extremely obscure language, that of law French, and hidden in technical and often verbose reports, initially of pleadings (plea rolls) and later of arguments and judgments (*Year Books*). In many senses it would be inaccurate to regard the common law as ever having been wholly unwritten in its character; it is simply unwritten in the technical sense of not being 'written law' (*ius scriptum*) or legislation. From a very early date, and certainly from the ninth century, the basic rules of general custom—of royally approved practices—were collected and recorded, most famously by King Alfred who compiled a dome-book or *liber judicialis* for use throughout the kingdom of Wessex. The book was lost but is known to have been a resource for information and knowledge of common law until the mid-fifteenth century and is said by Blackstone to have 'contained, we may probably suppose, the principal maxims of the common law, the penalties for the misdemeanours and the forms of judicial proceedings'. The substantive significance of the dome-book as a record of law and procedures is limited, however, by the subsequent Danish and Norman invasions and the separation of local and general customs.

At the level of particular custom, the Norman monarchy brought with it feudal law based upon the grant of land and the rights and duties which went with the land. It was feudal law which, in general, the common lawyers sought originally to systematize and record as common law. Originally the recording of the unwritten law was in the exclusive hands of the royal judges and emanated fairly directly from the monarch in the form of writs (the writ—originally referring to sacred writ or writings—means both command and writing) devised and issued by the king's secretariat, the Chancery. The system of writs was extremely formalistic from its earliest days and by 1258, by edict (*the Provisions of Oxford*), had congealed into a largely static and closed system of extremely complex pleadings. More general evidence of the common law was no less specialized. The plea rolls were written records of pleadings made at Westminster which frequently did not include the judgment in the case while the *Year Books*, which started reporting cases from 1292, report the oral arguments before the courts in law French and are, in terms of the legal knowledge they presuppose, extremely demanding upon the reader. The law administered as the common law from Westminster was already inaccessible, esoteric and extremely technical, an 'occult science' which needed to be extracted with great difficulty and skill from the lengthy and arcane books of the law. These reports of arguments and judgments were neither official nor necessarily accurate. As Plucknett describes them:

> 'The whole business of pleading orally . . . was an immensely skilful and recondite game, conducted with great virtuosity by the leaders of the bar, and keenly relished by all others who were sufficiently learned to understand what it was all about. After such a display, it was an anti-climax to think of a decision. Time after time the Year Books will give pages of subtle fencing until we get the words: "and so to judgment". What the judgment was, nobody knew and nobody cared; what interested the reader was not the substantive law involved in a case, but the technique of conducting the pleadings. . . .'

The *Year Books* were eventually superseded by the ad hoc development of law-reporting from the early sixteenth century, when named private reporters would recall and publish more or less detailed and more or less accurate accounts of cases; Plowden, Dyer and Coke were among the most significant of the early reporters. The quality and content of the reports produced by the named reporters between 1550 and 1790 varied greatly and while frequent reference was made to earlier decisions, the reporting was frequently 'casual and careless' and on occasions 'grossly inadequate'. Again we would observe that such a haphazard written record of the common law hardly indicates any great certainty, predictability or widespread knowledge of law and procedure. Nor could one view the system of common-law judgment as a coherent and complete system of legal rules or as, in its modern sense, a legal order. It is only in the late eighteenth and early nineteenth centuries, with the renewed influence of Roman-law doctrines and classifications, with the shift from law French to the vernacular and with the emergence of professional and later official law reports that it becomes possible even to contemplate referring to the common law as a coherent system of rules or as an order of precedent. . . .

The modern and purportedly highly distinctive conception of a common-law system of binding precedent, of *stare rationibus decidendi*, meaning to follow the reasoning of previous decisions (*stare decisis*), dates back to the early years of the nineteenth century, if not before. In broad terms, the conception of binding precedent refers to the following of the rules (*rationes decidendi*) laid down in previous decisions and its logical form and entailment are classically set out by Justice *Parke in Mirehouse v. Rennell* [1833] 1 Cl and F 527, 546, in the following terms:

'Our common law system consists in the applying to new combinations of circumstances those rules which we derive from legal principles and judicial precedents; and for the sake of attaining uniformity, consistency and certainty, we must apply those rules, where they are not plainly unreasonable and inconvenient, to all cases which arise; and we are not at liberty to reject them, and to abandon all analogy to them, in those to which they have not yet been judicially applied. . . . It appears to me to be of great importance to keep this principle of decision steadily in view, not merely for the determination of a particular case, but for the interests of law as a science.'

In short, legal decisions are to be arrived at, where the dispute is governed by the unwritten or common law, by reference, either directly or by analogy, to the rules set down in previously decided cases. Such pre-existent rules or principles (reasonings) are to be followed, according to Justice Parke, even where the deciding judge does not view them to be necessarily the best means to deciding the disputed issue: predictability and consistency of legal decision-making are accorded greater value than particular justice.

This early view of precedent was developed during the nineteenth century into what is traditionally regarded as one of the strictest and most extreme systems of precedent known in the history of western legal systems. While the rest of Europe entered the age of codifications and the emergent nation-states placed their faith in publicly available written codes of national law, the English developed and refined an antiquated system of highly technical and highly particular legal decisions into the modern common law. The motives behind the development belong firmly in the European political and economic context of the nineteenth century. For the common-law system, the nineteenth century was also an age of statute law, of partial codifications and of consolidating Acts, the great upsurge coming in the 1830s and continuing unabated to the present day. Parallel to this development of what were seen as systematizing, simplifying and democratizing statute laws was the development of the common law as national law, it being the peculiar view of English lawyers that common law represented a unique and jealously guarded national legal achievement. It was, however, only with the aid of principles drawn from the academics and the civil law, that the common law could be developed into a coherent and largely self-sufficient system of legal decision-making. In 1861, in *Beamish v Beamish* [1861] 9 H.L. Cases 274, the House of Lords decided that precedent decisions of the House were to be binding in future cases, even upon the House itself. Only Parliament could alter the decisions of the House of Lords, a view reiterated in *London Street Tramways Co. Ltd v London County Council* [1898] A.C. 375, 38, by Lord Halsbury in a succinct statement that 'a decision of the House on a question of law is conclusive', a view which remained the law until 1966 when the House of Lords issued a Practice Statement declaring that, in a limited number of circumstances, the House would no longer be bound to follow its earlier decisions. The lower courts, the Court of Appeal in particular (see *Davis v Johnson* [1979] A.C. 264), however, remain bound by their own earlier decisions and the system of precedent in general is still doctrinally stated to be one of binding or strict precedent. The strongest legal argument is one which cites the *ratio decidendi* of a relevant precedent case; the issue of the forms which a precedent may take and the manner of its discovery and application are still the central methodological issues within the common law, although, paradoxically, 'theorists have not been able to agree upon an answer to the question, what is a *ratio*? Nor is there agreement as to the test to be used to identify a *ratio*, once the basic meaning of the term has been defined'."

NOTES AND QUESTIONS

- How would you define the idea of precedent? In what sense is it coercive?

- What is the *ratio decidendi* of a case? Why is it so important to the idea of precedent?

- Explain the relationship between common law and statutory law. To what extent are they symbiotic?

- What is meant by the claim that the common law is "unwritten"? In what way is the claim misleading?

- In your view does the connection between law, power and writing that Goodrich refers to still exist in society?

- In Chapter 12 we will return to a discussion of the mystique of legal language in our consideration of the role of the legal profession. For present purposes it would be interesting for you to reflect on the number of new words and phrases you have learnt as a law student which would not be understood by those who had not studied law.

- Before you read the following extract from Cownie and Bradney, write down what you consider to be the advantages of the doctrine of precedent. Then read the extract and consider the extent to which you concur with them.

Fiona Cownie and Anthony Bradney, *English Legal System in Context* (2nd ed., Butterworths, London, 2000), pp.88–90:

"Law is not just a mechanism for settling disputes. It is also a way of avoiding disputes; of telling people how they might order their lives so that disputes can be avoided. If people are to do this they must know what the law is; they must know how judges will settle a dispute should a matter come to court. Law must be predictable. Lawyers must be able to tell their clients how to run their affairs. Judges must be able to announce what the law will be to the world at large. One must be able to know what the law is before going to court, for this would be expensive both financially and socially. Moreover, the law must be removed from the judges. Judges must be there not to decide cases on their own initiative. They must be there to apply a known set of rules to the facts before them. The job of the judge must be stripped of any subjective or personal element. Law must be a system of rules not of men. It has been argued that a system of precedent can be of assistance in allowing all these things to be done.

The previous Lord Chancellor, Lord MacKay, has described the advantages of precedent in this way:

'. . . a scheme of precedent is clearly capable of providing important benefits. It assists litigants to assess the nature and scope of legal obligations and, to the extent that it enables them to predict the likely outcome of disputes, it restricts the scope of litigation. By allowing the vast bulk of disputes to be settled in the shadow of the law, a system of precedent prevents the legal apparatus from becoming clogged by a myriad of single instances. It reflects a basic principle of the administration of justice that like cases should be treated alike and therefore generates a range of expectations from different participants in the legal process. Rules of law based on a system of precedent are therefore likely to exhibit characteristics of certainty, consistency and uniformity.'

Precedent, on this argument, provides certainty, consistency and thus a measure of clarity. People know not only what the law is but also what it will be. In principle, the ordinary person, the ordinary lawyer, the humblest judge is in just as good a position as the judge in the highest court to look back and see what the law was and, thus, see what the law will be. However, in providing this consistency, precedent also carries a disadvantage.

Precedent carries with it the unlikely message that those that came before us knew as much as we do now; that those in the past are good judges of what we should do in the present. One past Lord Chancellor, in a book of political philosophy, has caricatured the lawyer's idea of precedent thus:

'Failing all else, their last resort will be: "This was good enough for our ancestors and who are we to question their wisdom? Then they'll settle back in their chairs, with an air of having said the last word on the subject—as if it would be a major disaster for anyone to be caught being wiser than his ancestors!'

Precedent is conservative. It favours the status quo. Precedent slows down the pace of change within the legal system. In a world where things are constantly in flux, where things are always changing and where the pace of change seems to ever increase, the very advantages of precedent can thus be a disadvantage. By making the law predictable, precedent also makes it predictable that law will be suitable for old social conditions but not for those that presently obtain. Law is certain but also certainly out-dated. Law is consistent but also consistently wrong.

For traditional theorists the solution to these problems are clear. The legislature exists to change legal rules. Parliament has the political legitimacy to amend the rules of the game. The judiciary, being unelected professionals who merely have a particular technical competence, are simply there to apply those rules which the legislature have made, or by implication, approved.

There are several problems with this account of the judge's role. One difficulty is its political naiveté. The parliamentary timetable is a crowded matter. There is not the time to debate all the legislation that the government would like to put forward in order to fulfil its own programme. There is still less time for measures which may be of great moment or importance within a narrow area of law but which are of no pressing weight for the population taken as a whole. There is almost no time at all for ideas for legislation which are not favoured by the government. A second problem for this traditional account of precedent is that most people, including most judges, now accept that judges do indeed make law."

THE PROCESS OF COMMON LAW REASONING: "THINKING LIKE A LAWYER"

As Goodrich's historical analysis of the common law demonstrated, the history of the common law has been a rather haphazard process, in which general rules emerged from remedies granted in particular disputes. This process of moving from specific disputes to the development of general rules, (*i.e.* precedents), which are then applicable to a wide range of cases, is central to common law reasoning. It is a method of reasoning known as inductive (moving from the specific to the general), and is fundamental to our legal method.

In the following extract from his seminal series of lectures to new law students, Llewellyn advises students of the key tasks they need to perform when they come to read a case and determine how useful it will be to them.

K.N. Llewellyn, *The Bramble Bush* (Oceana Publications, New York, 1996), pp.84–86:

"1) (a) There is first the question of what the court *actually decided* in a given case; judgment reversed, and a new trial ordered. And the question of what express *ratio decidendi* it announced. These are facts of observation. They are the starting point of all discussion. Until you have them there is no use doing any arguing about anything.

1) (b) There is the question of *what the rule of the case is*, as derived from its comparison with a number of other cases. This is not so simple, but the technical procedures for determining it are clear. Skilled observers should rather regularly be able to agree on two

points: (i) the reasonably safe maximum rule the case can be used for; (ii) the reasonably certain minimum rule the case must be admitted to contain.

2) As against both of these, there is the question of the manner, attitude and accuracy of the court's *interpretation* or transformation of the raw evidence. Here judgment factors enter, and you and I may not agree about it. But at least we can keep the level of discussion separate from the levels just above. There we *presuppose* facts as they *result* from this interpretation we are here discussing; and we look to the rule laid down upon the facts already transformed.

3) There is the question of what the *probable* precedent value of the case is, in a given court or in general. Here, too, judgment factors enter very largely, and objective agreement is not to be expected; for we must draw into our thinking the results of our work on the second level, and must draw further things as well. Yet here, too, as to the *level* of discourse all can agree: it is a question of predicting what some court will in fact do. You can phrase this, if you will, in terms of Ought: what some court will understand this case to tell it to do. I think this latter phrasing slightly misleading, and certainly cumbersome; but defensible it surely is.

4) There is the question of *estimating what consequences the case* (and its effects on other cases) will have to laymen: the relation between the *ways* of the court and the *ways* of those affected by the court. This I take again to be purely on the level of description or prediction, but to be a very complicated matter, and one which involves even more information from outside the cases than does problem 3. The consequences may turn, for instance, on the persons concerned making quite inaccurate prediction of how later cases will eventuate—on their quite misinterpreting the case, on their readjusting their own ways not to their actual environment, but to an *imaginary* environment of court ways.

5) (a) There is the question of *evaluating* the court's action in the case—of concluding how desirable it is. And this is of course the most complicated of all, because it includes all the foregoing, and various premises also as to what values are to be taken as the baseline and the goal. What is utterly vital to see at least is that you cannot begin on this *until you have settled* the matters in the first and second problems, and grappled with those in the third and fourth. And, finally, that this matter of evaluation, while it presupposes the others, in no way touches the *level* on which they are discussed.

5) (b) There is the evaluation of the court's decision or ratio from the angle of *doctrine*. Here some premise or concept is *assumed*, as authoritatively given, and the court's action is tested for whether it is or is not dogmatically *correct*, when compared with the premise. Less dogmatically minded thinkers use the same technique, on the same *logical* level, to see not whether the case is 'correct', but whether it *squares* with a given hypothesis (either of doctrine or of prediction)—*i.e.*, to test its consistency with some formulation of a 'rule' derived inductively from other cases. It should be clear that this touches neither 3, nor 4, nor (really) 5a."

Vandevelde explores these points in much more detail and suggests specific techniques which might be of value to students learning their trade.

Kenneth J. Vandevelde, *Thinking Like a Lawyer* (Westview Press, Boulder, 1996), pp.49–55:

"The lawyer synthesizes the new rule by a method similar to the logical process of induction. Induction is a method of reasoning that, in essence, proceeds from the particular to the general.

For example, after tasting several raisins and finding that each of them is sweet, one may reason by induction that all raisins taste sweet. Induction produces a conclusion that is probable, though not certain. No matter how many raisins one eats, the possibility always exists that the next one may taste different from the others.

Nevertheless, courts formulate rules of law by a process that is inductive in form. If a number of cases have been decided in which a particular right or duty was found to exist, then the court may conclude that the same right or duty exists in all similar cases. By studying several particular instances, the court formulates a general rule.

For example, assume that various courts decide a number of cases imposing a duty on landowners to warn guests about various conditions on the land, such as a concealed pit, quicksand, or an unstable slope. As the number of cases grows, it becomes possible to think of these cases as collectively establishing a rule that requires the landowner to warn guests about hazards. In this situation, a rule is formulated by a process of induction. The rule, however, is broader than any of the specific cases on which it was based. The whole thus becomes greater than the sum of the parts.

By creating a rule broader than any one prior case, the court creates a rule broad enough to apply to the novel case. The novel case, accordingly, can be decided by application of the newly synthesized rule.

As noted above, induction does not compel a particular conclusion but can only suggest that the conclusion is probable. In the same way, the court is not compelled to accept the new, broader rule. Just as tasting a few raisins does not force one to conclude that all raisins taste the same, the prior decisions in cases involving certain specific hazards do not require the court to decide that other hazards are subject to the same rule. The court may correctly note that the holdings in the prior cases did not reach beyond quicksand, a concealed pit, and an unstable slope and may decide not to extend the holdings beyond those situations. . . .

The problem of indeterminacy

The premise for using inductive reasoning is that several similar items have been identified about which a generalization can safely be made. Yet, the lawyer will find that the process of formulating a generalization is not a mechanical one. Rather, it is a process that requires the exercise of judgment and that can lead to more than one result.

The lawyer must make at least two decisions in synthesizing the rule. First, the lawyer must decide which facts to include in the factual predicate, thus determining how to characterize the prior cases. Each of the prior cases may be subject to multiple characterizations, depending upon which facts of those cases the lawyer chooses to emphasize. In deciding how to characterize the cases included in the rule, the lawyer in effect is choosing the elements of the rule.

For example, the lawyer may characterize the cases involving the quicksand, the concealed pit, and the unstable slope as cases involving abnormal conditions, provided that each condition was abnormal for that area. Or, the lawyer may characterize them as cases involving hazards, because each condition was dangerous. Alternatively, the lawyer may characterize them as cases involving concealed hazards, on the theory that none of the hazards was obvious to the casual observer. Or, the cases may be characterized as involving natural hazards, if they were not the result of human activity. Finally, the lawyer may choose to emphasize the especially dangerous nature of the hazards and characterize the cases as involving life-threatening hazards.

All of these characterizations may be equally accurate. No one characterization is the 'correct' one that must be chosen to the exclusion of the others. The process of characterizing the facts is indeterminate. The lawyer can reach a particular characterization only by the exercise of judgment.

A second decision the lawyer must make is to set the level of generality at which the new rule should be formulated. This means deciding whether the prior cases are to be described in broad, general terms or in narrow, specific terms.

In the case of the concealed pit, the unstable slope, and the quicksand, for example, the lawyer must decide at what level of generality to characterize the conditions on the land that give rise to a duty to warn. At one extreme, they could be characterized as hazards. In that case, the lawyer could conclude that the various cases identified by research establish a general rule that the landowner has a duty to warn guests about all hazards on the land.

At the other extreme, the lawyer could characterize the conditions as falling within the three narrow categories of quicksand, concealed pits, and unstable slopes. Each of these categories might be characterized even more narrowly so that, under the lawyer's characterization of the rule, a landowner has a duty to warn only of concealed pits of a certain depth, unstable slopes of a specified angle, and quicksand pools of a particular size.

Between these extremes is a range of possible rules of differing levels of generality. The term 'life-threatening hazards,' for example, is more specific than the term 'hazards.'

Each of these levels of generality may yield a rule that is equally accurate. No particular level of generality is correct to the exclusion of the others. The choice of the level of generality at which to state the rule is indeterminate. The lawyer's selection of a particular level of generality must therefore be based on the exercise of judgment. Different lawyers generalizing about the same group of cases will produce rules at different levels of generality.

The judgments concerning which facts to include in the factual predicate and the level of generality at which to state a rule are interrelated. The more general the rule, the fewer the facts that need to be specified. For example, if the rule is formulated as applying to all hazards, then whether the hazards are natural or life-threatening is irrelevant and would not be specified in the rule. Put another way, stating the rule at a high level of generality allows the lawyer to be agnostic about which of various specifics to include in the factual predicate. The corollary, of course, is that if the lawyer decides to include numerous detailed facts in the factual predicate, then, necessarily, the rule cannot be stated at a high level of generality.

Addressing indeterminacy through policy judgments

The lawyer may attempt to solve the indeterminacy involved in synthesizing a rule by referring to the policies underlying the cases. In this situation, the lawyer uses the underlying policies as a guide in selecting the facts to include in the factual predicate of the rule and in choosing the level of generality at which to state the rule. As will be seen, however, use of the underlying policies does not entirely solve the problem of indeterminacy.

The first decision the lawyer must make is to select the facts to include in the factual predicate of the rule. As an initial matter, some of the prior cases may have specified that certain facts were dispositive. For example, the case involving the pit may have specified that a duty to warn was imposed because the pit was a concealed hazard; that is, the case made clear that the holding imposing a duty was based on the presence of two facts—the fact that the condition was hazardous and the fact that it was concealed.

To the extent that the prior cases leave unclear which facts were dispositive, the lawyer selects for inclusion in the newly synthesized rule those facts in the prior cases that were relevant to accomplishing the underlying policies. For instance, if the policy was solely the protection of personal safety, then the fact that the conditions were natural probably should not matter, since a condition may be hazardous whether it is natural or not. Nor perhaps should it matter that the conditions were concealed, since even an obvious hazard can threaten safety. If the policy, however, was to encourage people to be responsible for their own safety, then the fact that the condition was concealed becomes more relevant. In such situations, the court may wish to deny recovery to guests who put themselves at risk by encountering an obvious hazard.

A second decision the lawyer must make is to select the level of generality at which to state the elements in the newly synthesized rule. As a practical matter, the lawyer must state the elements in terms general enough to include the facts of any prior case from which the rule is being synthesized. Thus, if the lawyer wishes to include the quicksand, the slope, and the pit cases, then a term at least as general as 'hazard' may have to be used. Any narrower term could arguably exclude some of the cases.

The lawyer must also state the elements in terms at least general enough to include the novel case to which the rule will be applied. For example, assume that the lawyer concluded that, in the prior cases, the quicksand, the pit, and the slope were all in some way concealed, and thus the term 'concealed hazard' would include all prior cases. The lawyer's client, however, was injured by a hazard that was not really concealed, although the client unfortunately did not notice it. If the lawyer characterizes the facts of the prior cases as involving concealed hazards, the very case for which a rule is being formulated will be excluded. Accordingly, the lawyer characterizes the facts of the prior cases in still more general terms —perhaps as 'hazards'—in order to include the case under consideration.

The lawyer, however, also has the choice of synthesizing a rule in terms broader than is absolutely necessary in order to include the prior cases and the current case. Assume for a moment that the term 'concealed hazard,' in fact, would embrace all of the cases, then so would the more general term 'hazards' and the even more general term 'potentially dangerous conditions.' The lawyer must decide whether to use one of these more general characterizations or to be only as general as is absolutely necessary to include the current case.

In choosing the level of generality, the lawyer must avoid overreaching. In other words, the lawyer cannot formulate the rule in terms so broad that it includes new cases that make the policy judgments underlying the prior cases inapplicable. If the rule is too broad, application of the rule can yield undesirable results.

For example, assume that in the quicksand, pit, and slope cases the courts were attempting to strike a balance between, on the one hand, compensating injury and, on the other hand, encouraging safety by refusing to compensate the careless. In each case, the court held that because the hazard was concealed, the victim could not have avoided injury by exercising care. Thus, the policy of encouraging safety did not preclude imposing liability on the landowner.

The lawyer who characterizes these cases as imposing liability for all 'hazards' may well be overreaching, because the policy judgments in the prior cases would not apply to any case in which the hazard was obvious. In the case of an obvious hazard, the victim might well have avoided injury by exercising care, and thus the policy judgment made in the prior cases does not apply. In cases in which the hazard is obvious, the policy of encouraging safety could require leaving the careless plaintiff uncompensated by not imposing liability on the landowner.

Thus, the lawyer must state the newly synthesized rule at a level of generality sufficient to include the prior cases and the client's case. At the same time, the rule must not be stated at a level of generality high enough to encompass new cases in which the policies underlying the prior cases would require a different result.

Between these extremes, however, the lawyer may well have some degree of choice. Thus, reference to the underlying policies may not eliminate all of the indeterminacy in synthesizing a new rule.

Using rule synthesis as an advocate

The discussion in the previous section implicitly assumed to some extent that the lawyer, in synthesizing a new rule, was acting as a dispassionate observer, looking for the 'true' nature of the rule that would explain the prior cases as well as govern the new case.

Yet, the lawyer engaged in the synthesis of a new rule is very often acting as an advocate, with the purpose of either constructing a new rule that will compel the result the client seeks or opposing the creation of the new rule. Let us consider the tactical moves that a lawyer in either situation may make in support of a client's position.

Supporting the new rule

First, the lawyer attempting to create the rule probably wants to generalize from as many cases as possible. Recall that the lawyer would probably argue that the rule being advocated is not a new rule at all but rather a well-established rule perhaps not previously articulated in explicit terms. The more cases that have recognized the rule, the more the rule looks like a well-established rule of law that the court must apply and the less the courts feel that it has ventured onto new terrain.

Second, the lawyer obviously wants to include in the factual predicate of the rule only those facts that clearly have counterparts in the current case. At times, that may be difficult because the court in a prior case may have stated explicitly that a particular fact—say, the fact that the hazard was concealed—was dispositive. If the fact was dispositive in the prior case from which the new rule is to be synthesized, then the fact generally has to be included in the new rule as well.

There is at least one argument the lawyer can make for excluding the dispositive fact from the new rule, and this is to contend that the dispositive fact was a sufficient, but not a necessary, condition for the result reached in the prior case. Thus, the fact need not be an element of the rule. This argument is bolstered considerably if the dispositive fact was absent from some prior cases. Even if it was present in all of them, the lawyer can argue that it was only a sufficient fact. This is done by demonstrating that the policies underlying the rule do not dictate that it be present. The lawyer might argue, for example, that the only policy mentioned by the court in the prior case was protecting persons against avoidable injury and that policy would have required imposition of a duty to warn whether the hazard was concealed or not. The lawyer is arguing, in effect, that the fact of concealment was not truly necessary to the result and any statements about the necessity of the fact should be considered dictum. Further, because the policy underlying the rule does not require that the hazard be concealed, the prior court's dictum to the effect that a concealed condition was a necessary fact should not be followed.

Third, the lawyer probably wants to formulate the rule in the most general terms possible, without overreaching. A more general rule embraces more prior cases because the broad language used obscures the minor differences among the cases, thus allowing more cases to fall within the rule. As explained above, the more cases that seem to have embraced the rule, the more willing the court will be to apply it in the novel case. At the same time, the broader the rule, the more likely it is to encompass the lawyer's case.

Opposing the new rule

A lawyer opposing recognition of the new rule may also employ a set of standard tactical moves. First, the lawyer attempts to restrict the number of cases on which the generalized rule may be based. This is done by confining the prior cases to their facts. That is, the lawyer points out that the quicksand case addressed only quicksand; the concealed pit case, only concealed pits; the unstable slope case, only unstable slopes. Therefore, anything beyond quicksand, concealed pits, and unstable slopes is mere dictum that need not be followed. Ultimately, the argument is that no general rule exists; there are only several specific rules, none of which applies here. This argument, in essence, is an appeal to the reluctance of courts to make new law.

Second, the lawyer tries to identify dispositive facts in the prior cases that are not present in the novel situation, searching through the prior cases for as many details as can be found and arguing that all of these details were necessary to (not merely sufficient for) the decisions and thus belong in the factual predicate of any newly synthesized rule. Thus, for example, the lawyer may argue that the quicksand, pit, and slope are all concealed, life-threatening natural hazards and thus the rule should be limited to concealed, life-threatening natural hazards. Obviously, the strategy is to formulate a rule that excludes the current case.

Third, the lawyer tries to formulate the rule as narrowly as possible, again with the hope that it will exclude the current case. One way to do this is to characterize the facts narrowly —a concealed pit would be called a concealed pit, not a hazard or an abnormal condition. For this argument to be effective, the lawyer must be prepared to explain why the policy judgments that underlie the rule do not apply in the same way when the rule is formulated in more general terms; that is, the lawyer must explain why a rule formulated in more general terms would overreach."

NOTES AND QUESTIONS

• Define inductive reasoning and explain its relevance to common law analysis.

- What does Vandevelde mean by his use of the term dispositive? How would you go about determining which facts are dispositive in a case?

- What does it mean to develop a synthesised rule? Think of a leading case you have read recently and consider how the judges moved from the specific facts of a case to consideration of a general rule.

Vandevelde's description of common law advocacy provides a good introduction to how lawyers deal with precedent in a common law system. From his explanation, it is clear that the process involves fitting the precedents together in such a way to form a general rule, that can then be applied (or not) to a new factual situation. It should also be clear to you now that there is no one way in which the cases can fit together; after all, a new factual situation is a legal dispute with parties (and legal representatives) on both sides trying to make the precedents fit together to reach the outcome they desire. Thus, when dealing with common law problem cases in your legal education, it is imperative that you realize that there is no one "right answer". Instead, there are good answers, which engage with the cases creatively, while not trying to construct rules from them which the facts of those cases cannot realistically support. Vandevelde mentions in the passage above that a lawyer may characterise a statement in a precedent as merely "dictum"; and, therefore, as not "binding" on a future court. We have already examined the idea of decisions being binding or merely persuasive, under the principle of *stare decisis* earlier in this chapter. However, even if a precedent is binding according to the hierarchy of courts, there is a crucial distinction in common law reasoning between the *ratio decidendi* of a precedent, and those parts of a judgment which are merely *obiter dicta*. Understanding common law reasoning requires an appreciation of the often difficult distinction between those two elements of a common law precedent.

R. Cross and J.W. Harris, *Precedent in English Law* (4th ed., Clarendon Press, Oxford, 1991), pp.39–43:

"[E]very court is bound to follow any case decided by a court above it in the hierarchy, and appellate courts (other than the House of Lords) are bound by their previous decisions. This statement is too concise because it does not indicate that the only part of a previous case which is binding is the *ratio decidendi* (reason for deciding). . . .

The *ratio decidendi* is best approached by a consideration of the structure of a typical judgment. . . . It consists of a review of facts and arguments and a discussion of relevant questions of law. Several opinions are frequently delivered in appellate courts because appeals are always heard by more than one judge.

It is not everything said by a judge when giving judgment that constitutes a precedent. In the first place, this status is reserved for his pronouncements on the law, and no disputed point of law is involved in the vast majority of cases that are tried in any year. The dispute is solely concerned with the facts. For example, the issue may be whether a particular motorist was driving carelessly by failing to keep a proper look-out or travelling at an excessive speed. No one doubts that a motorist owes a legal duty to drive carefully and, very frequently, the only question is whether he was in breach of that duty when he caused damage to a pedestrian or another motorist. Cases in which the only issues are questions of fact are usually not reported in any series of law reports, but it is not always easy to distinguish law from fact and the reasons which led a judge of first instance or an appellate court to come to a factual conclusion are sometimes reported at length. For example, an employer is under a legal duty to provide his employees with a reasonably safe system of working. The question whether that duty has been broken is essentially one of fact, but the law reports contain a number of cases in which judges have expressed their views concerning the precautions which an employer should have taken in particular instances. When an injury would not have occurred if a workman had been wearing protective clothing it has been said that his employer ought to have insisted that such clothing should have been worn instead of merely rendering it available for those who desired to wear it, but the House of Lords has insisted that observations of this nature are not general propositions of law necessarily applicable to future cases and the decisions based upon them do not constitute a precedent. There is no point in endeavouring to ascertain the *ratio decidendi* of such cases.

The second reason why it is not everything said by a judge in the course of his judgment that constitutes a precedent is that, among the propositions of law enunciated by him, only those which he appears to consider necessary for his decision are said to form part of the *ratio decidendi* and thus to amount to more than an *obiter dictum*. If the judge in a later case is bound by the precedent according to the English doctrine of *stare decisis*, he must apply the earlier *ratio decidendi* however much he disapproved of it, unless, to use the words of Lord Reid, he considers that the two cases are 'reasonably distinguishable'. Dicta in earlier cases are, of course, frequently followed or applied, but dicta are never of more than persuasive authority. There is no question of any judge being bound to follow them. Even when the *ratio decidendi* of a previous case is merely a persuasive authority, it must be followed in later cases unless the judge has good reason to disapprove of it. It constitutes a precedent, and the difference between a persuasive precedent and an *obiter dictum* is only slightly less significant than that between binding and persuasive precedents. If, for example, a High Court judge of first instance comes to the conclusion that a proposition of law contained in a previous opinion of another High Court judge of first instance is ratio, he will be a great deal more reluctant to differ from it than would be the case if he was satisfied that it was merely a *dictum*, although a judge of first instance is not bound to follow the decision of another judge of first instance.

The distinction between *ratio decidendi* and *obiter dictum* is an old one. As long ago as 1673 Vaughan C.J. said:

> 'An opinion given in court, if not necessary to the judgment given of record, but that it might have been as well given if no such, or a contrary had been broach'd, is no judicial opinion; but a mere gratis dictum. . . .'

There are undoubtedly good grounds for the importance attached to the distinction between *ratio decidendi* and *obiter dictum*. In this context an *obiter dictum* means a statement by the way, and the probabilities are that such a statement has received less serious consideration than that devoted to a proposition of law put forward as a reason for the decision. It is not even every proposition of this nature that forms part of the *ratio decidendi*. To quote Devlin J., as he then was:

> 'It is well established that if a judge gives two reasons for his decision, both are binding. It is not permissible to pick out one as being supposedly the better reason and ignore the other one; nor does it matter for this purpose which comes first and which comes second. But the practice of making judicial observations *obiter* is also well established. A judge may often give additional reasons for his decisions without wishing to make them part of the *ratio decidendi*; he may not be sufficiently convinced of their cogency as to want them to have the full authority of a precedent, and yet may wish to state them so that those who later may have the duty of investigating the same point will start with some guidance. This is a matter which the judge himself is alone capable of deciding, and any judge who comes after him must ascertain which course has been adopted from the language used and not by consulting his own preferences.'

One thing which a judge cannot do is to prevent his decision on a point of law from constituting a precedent.

The above remarks of Lord Devlin represent orthodox judicial theory, and, at first sight, the power they concede to those who decide a case may seem somewhat surprising. If a judge has this amount of freedom to determine which of his observations is *ratio decidendi* and which *obiter dictum*, is there not a grave danger that he will exercise an undue influence on the future development of the law? He only has to state twenty propositions and say that he bases his decision on each of them to have created twenty new legal rules. It is true that the majority of the judges of former times would have denied that they possessed any power to make new law, but we are primarily concerned with the contemporary situation in which the declaratory theory of judicial decision no longer holds sway. It is also true that the last thing any modern English judge would wish to do is to fetter his successors by laying down a multitude of superfluous rules. But just now we are concerned with legal theory. The answer to the question raised is that there are several considerations which may be said to redress the balance in favour of the judges who come afterwards. No doubt the *ratio decidendi* of a previous case has to be gathered from the language of the judge who decided that case, but it is trite learning that the interpreter has nearly as much to say as the speaker so far as the meaning of words is concerned. Of even greater significance is the existence of certain rules of judicial practice concerning the construction to be placed by a future judge upon past decisions. By stressing the necessity of having regard to the facts of the previous case and the language of prior or subsequent judgments, these rules greatly curtail the influence that can be exercised on legal development by means of the reasons which a particular judge sees fit to give for his decisions."

One of the primary ways in which judges in future cases can exercise a high degree of control over the meaning of a precedent is through the use of analogical reasoning. That is, judges can extend the scope of a precedent to cover new situations by drawing *analogies* between the facts of the case at hand, and the precedent. Alternatively, the judge may *distinguish* the immediate case from the precedent on the basis that there is a *material* difference between them; which means the precedent will not be applied to the facts at issue. The "art" of applying and distinguishing case law is one of the most important skills for the student of the common law to develop and, indeed, for any legal advocate.

In the extract below, Vandevelde reviews the various options open to advocates in their treatment of previous cases. He describes processes which may appear complex at this stage of your studies but will become much easier to understand and appreciate the more cases you read.

Kenneth J. Vandevelde, *Thinking Like a Lawyer* (Westview Press, Boulder, 1996), pp.91–98:

Arguments for following the precedent

"As an initial matter, the lawyer arguing that a prior case should be followed in a later case emphasizes the numerous factual similarities between the two cases. Strictly speaking, the only relevant facts are those whose existence would further or impede one of the underlying policies. The advocate arguing that a prior case should be followed, however, rarely limits the argument to those facts. Rather, the advocate includes in the recitation of similarities virtually any fact that is not a trivial coincidence.

Second, the advocate argues that the inevitable dissimilarities are irrelevant, the basic contention being that none of the facts that make the cases different is relevant to furthering or impeding any of the underlying policies. Obviously, for example, the fact that the parties' names differ is irrelevant to any legitimate policy. To the extent possible, the advocate makes a parallel argument with respect to any dissimilarity between the cases.

This argument may be difficult to make where the court in the prior case has stated explicitly that a particular fact, not present in the current case, is dispositive. The best argument for following the case in that situation is to point out that in light of the policies underlying the prior case, the prior case would have been decided the same way even without the so-called dispositive fact. The lawyer is arguing, in effect, that the fact was not truly necessary to the result. Since it was not actually necessary to the result, any discussion of that fact should be considered dictum and need not be followed. It may be difficult to prevail in this argument because it requires the court to disregard how another court characterized its own decision.

A third technique for arguing that a precedent should be followed is to state the factual predicate of the precedent at a higher level of generality. For example, if the prior case held that the presence of a concealed pit on the land gives rise to a duty on the part of the landowner to warn a guest, but the current case involves a guest who fell down a slope, the lawyer for the injured guest may characterize the prior case as involving a 'hazard' rather than a concealed pit. As the language becomes more general, it will tend to encompass the facts of the current situation. . . .

A fourth technique is to characterize the prior case, not in terms of its facts but in terms of the underlying policy judgments, which the lawyer argues should be followed. For example, the lawyer seeking to impose on a landowner a duty to warn customers about concealed hazards on the land may rely on cases holding that a manufacturer has a duty to warn consumers of product defects. The lawyer would then argue that the prior cases adopted a policy of protecting the unwary against physical injury and that such policy should prevail in the current case as well. This technique may require manipulating the level of generality at which the policy underlying the precedent is stated. The product defect cases, for example, may have described the underlying policy as protecting the stream of commerce against unsafe instrumentalities. By restating the policy more generally as protecting the unwary, the lawyer makes the policy seem applicable to the subsequent case. That is, the impression is created that the result the lawyer seeks in the later case would further the policies articulated in the earlier case.

Arguments for distinguishing the precedent

The arguments for distinguishing a prior case mirror those for following it. First, the lawyer emphasizes every possible difference between the two cases, being especially alert to facts that the court in the prior case regarded as dispositive. Even if the facts were only sufficient for the holding and not necessary, the lawyer notes that the dispositive facts are not present in this case. If the later case differs concerning some such dispositive fact, then it is likely the court will distinguish the two cases. Assuming that the cases do not differ concerning any fact explicitly considered dispositive in the earlier case, the lawyer attempting to distinguish the precedent may nevertheless point to differences in other facts in an effort to make the cases appear as different as possible.

Second, the lawyer attempts to dismiss similarities between the cases as irrelevant. If possible, the lawyer argues that particular facts in the precedent that are similar to those in the later case were not explicitly found to be dispositive and are therefore irrelevant coincidences. If the facts were held to be dispositive, the lawyer can attempt to argue that the facts were not relevant to accomplishing the underlying policy, although this can obviously be a difficult argument to make.

Third, the lawyer attempting to distinguish the cases characterizes the precedent in the narrowest possible terms. The lawyer states the facts and the legal consequence with great specificity, noting that any broader reading would constitute dictum, which the court need not follow. By stating the facts at very specific levels, the lawyer produces new dissimilarities. Thus, a pit is not merely a pit, but a concealed, life-threatening, 20-foot-deep pit.

Fourth, the lawyer may contend that the policy judgments underlying the prior case do not apply to the current case. This argument may follow any of several different approaches.

One approach is to argue that the policies that prevailed in the prior case require a different result in this case than was reached in the prior case. For example, assume that the prior case held that the government has the power to prohibit the use of offensive language on a television broadcast because the danger that a youngster might be injured by hearing the language outweighed the broadcaster's right to use it. In a later case, a television station broadcasts a documentary that realistically portrays the lives of young drug users in an effort to persuade juveniles that drug use could ruin their lives. To make the documentary more realistic and thus more credible, the station broadcasts film of drug users engaged in conversation with the police, their families, and each other—conversation involving the use of the same offensive language. The lawyer might argue that, in this case, the policy of protecting children actually would be *furthered* by permitting the offensive language to be broadcast. Thus, to further the policy that prevailed in the prior case the court should distinguish the prior case and void, rather than uphold, the ban on offensive language. . . .

Finally, the lawyer can argue that if the precedent is applied to this case, *stare decisis* would require that it also be applied to other cases in which it would produce a clearly undesirable result. This, again, is the parade of horribles or the slippery slope argument. The lawyer demonstrates that this case is indistinguishable from other hypothetical cases in which application of the precedent would lead to undesirable results. As with legal reasoning in the deductive form, this argument is distinguished by not requiring a demonstration that following the precedent would lead to a bad result in this case, only that it would entail application of the precedent to other cases in which it would produce an undesirable result. . . .

The problem of competing analogies

The prior discussion has assumed that the lawyer was attempting to determine whether one precedent should be followed or distinguished in deciding a current dispute. The precedent must be followed if it is like the current case.

Often, however, the lawyer encounters a situation where there are two or more precedents, each of which is like the current case in some respects. The problem is that the two precedents reached opposite results and thus both cannot be followed. In other words, the lawyer must choose between competing analogies. . . .

The lawyer nevertheless chooses between the competing analogies using the same techniques that are used to decide whether to follow or distinguish a single precedent. The correct analogy is the one that seems most like the current case, taking into account all similarities and dissimilarities."

This passage makes clear that lawyers can have considerable impact on the development of common law. The application of precedent is far from being a mechanical act. On the contrary, the tactical devices employed by lawyers in their attempts to ensure that the outcome of the case is most favourable to their client can lead to shifts in the values which underpin the treatment of particular cases. The potential for this to occur will be made clear in the case study on negligence that we visit in the next chapter. The tension between creativity and conservatism is summarised by Lord Denning in his typically flamboyant style.

Lord Denning, *The Discipline of Law* (Butterworths, London, 1979), p.285:

"To a student of jurisprudence this doctrine of precedent exercises a particular fascination. He is hypnotised by it. To a practising lawyer it is *Mr. Facing-both-ways*. He is attracted or repelled by it according as to whether it is for him or against him. He can argue either way, as you please. To a Judge it comes, if he chooses, as a way of escape. He does not have to think for himself or to decide for himself. It has already been decided by the previous authority. But not so for most Judges. Whilst ready to applaud the doctrine of precedent when it leads to a just and fair result, they become restless under it when they are compelled by it to do what is unjust or unfair. This restlessness leads them to various expedients to get round a previous authority. But never to depart from it altogether—except for an absolution recently granted by the House of Lords to themselves, though not vouchsafed by them to others."

EXERCISE

Consider the following problem. Construct arguments for the claimant and defendant, and then consider how, as a judge, you would decide the case and prepare reasons. You should draw upon the material on precedent which we have examined thus far as a guide for discerning the *ratio decidendi* of your precedent, and how to apply or distinguish it.

Edmund M.A. Kwaw, *The Guide to Legal Analysis, Legal Methodology and Legal Writing* (Emond Montgomery, Toronto, 1992), p.198:

"You are a judge in a case in which Jason, a truck driver, and Louis, a pedestrian, are suing a day nursery. You learn from the evidence that as Jason was driving, he saw a little girl dart through the gate of the day nursery onto the road. He swerved to avoid hitting her. In doing so, he knocked down Louis, who happened to be walking on the sidewalk at that moment, and his truck also struck a lamp post. Jason suffered shock and Louis sustained bruises and a fractured leg. You learn from the evidence that the gate of the day nursery should not have been opened without a teacher or other adult being present. No one can explain how the gate got open. The only precedent is the (hypothetical) case that follows.

Samson v Dunlop

Dunlop was a local farmer who had a flock of sheep. He was assisted in his work by three sheep dogs, Wolfie, Blackie, and Spotty. The three dogs were regarded as the best sheep dogs in the county. One day something peculiar happened. Instead of rounding up the sheep as they were supposed to, the three dogs began attacking the sheep. There was a stampede and the fence that kept the sheep in was broken. As the sheep rushed out, Samson the letter carrier, who happened to be riding along on his bicycle, swerved to avoid colliding with the sheep. Samson lost control of the bicycle and smashed into a tree. In an action brought by Samson against Dunlop, the court held that farmers who were in control of livestock owed a legal duty to ensure that the livestock did not injure other people."

THE IMPLICATIONS OF MEMBERSHIP IN THE EUROPEAN UNION ON COMMON LAW REASONING

As we have seen in previous chapters, membership in the European Union (EU) legal order is now a central element of our legal system. Consequently, an understanding of how precedent works within a common law system must be supplemented by a recognition that "classic" common law reasoning must now take into consideration the impact of the EU. After all, the EU emerged from the *civilian* rather than the *common law* tradition, in which precedent does not hold the same power. Here, our interest is in how the role of precedent must be modified to take

European law into account. We have already considered the basic structure of that legal order in Chapter 5. We begin here with the status of cases decided by the European Court of Justice (ECJ), when they are considered by domestic courts.

Colin Manchester, David Salter and Peter Moodie, *Exploring the Law: The Dynamics of Precedent and Statutory Interpretation* (Sweet and Maxwell, London, 2000):

"Although sections 2 and 3 [of the European Communities Act 1972] leave a number of matters unclear, the ECJ has nevertheless provided some indication of its views, where a case has been referred to it under Article 177, of how its ruling in that case should be regarded on return of the case to the (English or other national) court which referred it. The ECJ stated in *Milchkontor v Haupzollamt Saarbrucken* Case 29/68 [1969] ECR 165 (*Milchkontor*) that a ruling given by it is binding on the court receiving it. To this extent, the notion of one court binding another court is introduced into the EC legal order. This is not, however, a departure from the principle of *res judicata, i.e.* that the decision in a case is generally final and binding only as between the parties to that case, since the ruling given by the ECJ on an Article 177 reference is confined to the particular case in question. This ruling consists of an interpretation or exposition of EC law, formulated in the abstract as a proposition of law rather than one which is dependent upon the material facts of the case, although the proposition will be formulated by reference to those facts. Although binding only on the parties to the case, the ruling is, however, one which the ECJ (presumably) expects English courts in future to follow, although it would (presumably) be a matter for the English courts to determine in what way that should be achieved. Not only might the ECJ expect English courts to follow rulings under Article 177 following references from English courts, but it may also expect any of its other decisions (including rulings under Article 177 following references from courts in other Member States) to be followed, although again it would (presumably) be a matter for the English courts to determine how those decisions should be followed. However, it is clear that, as a matter of EC law, it would be open to an English court in any future case to refer the case before it to the ECJ under Article 177 for a ruling on EC law, notwithstanding the existence of a previous ruling or any other ECJ decision on the particular point.

On receipt of a ruling under Article 177 from the ECJ, it will be for the English court to apply the ruling to the facts of the case before it. When a ruling is so applied, it may, from a traditional English perspective, become part of the *ratio* of that case and thus become part of a proposition of law based on the material facts of that case. As such, the ruling, as part of the *ratio* of the case, would therefore (presumably) be capable of forming a binding precedent, in the English sense, for application in future cases, although, of course, it would be open to a subsequent court to limit the scope of such *ratio* (and thus ruling) by distinguishing it on the ground that the case before it had materially different facts.

Whilst a ruling by the ECJ returned to an English court may become part of the *ratio* of a case in the manner indicated above, it is less clear how any ruling returned to a national court of another Member State or any other decision of the ECJ may do so. In any event, to the extent that any ECJ ruling or decision *has* become part of the *ratio* of a case, this may be seen as being inconsistent with the view that it must always remain open to a court in any future case to make a reference to the ECJ under Article 177.

It is clear from the above that ECJ cases may have a number of implications for the English doctrine of precedent. The extent of such implications, as will be seen below, may vary depending upon whether a court, when considering a point of EC law, decides to refer the case to the ECJ under Article 177 or decides itself to interpret that point.

(i) Implications of a decision to refer to the ECJ under Article 177

When cases have been referred to the ECJ and rulings on points of EC law have been received by the courts which referred the cases, those courts invariably seem to have accepted the rulings as binding on them (in accordance with the ECJ's stated view in *Milchkontor*). On receipt of such rulings, it is necessary for English courts to decide how the interpretations or expositions of EC law contained therein should be applied to the facts of the case. This may involve a consideration of the impact of the ruling on the provision in question in the English legislation and, as seen, different approaches have been adopted on this matter. In some cases, courts have regarded rulings as setting out a proposition of EC law which should be applied in preference to a provision in English legislation deemed to be inconsistent with that proposition (Priority Approach), an approach adopted, for instance, by the Court of Appeal in *Macarthys*, in which Lord Denning M.R. stated (at [1981] 1 All ER 111, 120):

> 'We have now been provided with the decision of that court [the ECJ]. It is important now to declare, and it must be made plain, that the provisions of article 119 of the EEC Treaty [as interpreted by the ECJ on an Article 177 reference from the present case] take priority over anything in our English statute on equal pay which is inconsistent with art.119.'

In other cases, courts have regarded the rulings as an aid to interpretation of a provision in English legislation. Thus courts have, on some occasions, used the ruling as an aid to resolving an ambiguity (Ambiguity Interpretation Approach) and, on other occasions, to interpret a provision in English legislation (not regarded as containing any ambiguity) in whatever manner is necessary to secure compliance with EC law (General Interpretation Approach). An instance of a court using a ruling as an aid to interpretation can be seen in *Garland*, where the House of Lords used a ruling to resolve an ambiguity in section 6(4) of the Sex Discrimination Act 1975 and where Lord Diplock stated (at [1982] 2 All ER 402, 416) that it was necessary to obtain a ruling from the ECJ 'so as to provide the House with material necessary to aid it in construing s.6(4) of the Sex Discrimination Act 1975.'

On occasions, courts receiving rulings have also expressed views (*obiter*) as to the status that such rulings will have in future cases. Thus, when the Court of Appeal in *Macarthys* received a ruling from the ECJ that article 119 of the EC Treaty required equal pay for men and women even where they were not employed at the same time, Lord Denning M.R. stated (at [1981] 1 All ER 111, 120): 'That interpretation must now be given by all the courts in England. It will apply in this case and in any such case hereafter.' Similarly, Lord Diplock in the House of Lords in *Garland*, reflecting on the decision in that case to make a reference to the ECJ under Article 177, stated (at [1982] 2 All ER 402, 415) that 'it was desirable to obtain a ruling of the European Court that would be binding on all courts in England, including this House.'

This means that the interpretation or exposition of EC law will be of general application, *i.e.* not limited in scope to future cases in which the *ratio* of the particular case in question might be considered applicable in view of the materially similar facts, and will apply irrespective of the position in the court hierarchy of either the court receiving the ruling or of any later court applying it. By regarding rulings returned to English courts as being generally binding in this way (subject to exercise of the right to refer under Article 177), the above statements appear to regard these rulings in much the same way as any other decisions of the ECJ (including rulings under Article 177 following references from courts in other Member States), a matter which is considered immediately below.

(ii) Implications of a decision by an English court to interpret EC law

... English courts may have regard to ECJ cases. These cases may include previous rulings under Article 177 following references from English courts or from courts in other Member States, as well as any other decisions of the ECJ. English courts appear to regard ECJ cases in each instance as being binding generally. As a consequence, interpretations of EC law contained in such ECJ cases may be binding on an English court in a particular case, irrespective of the presence or absence of similar material facts between the ECJ case(s) and the case in question and irrespective of the position of the English court in the court hierarchy.

Instances of where English courts have had regard to ECJ case law when interpreting EC law have included the decision of the Court of Appeal in *Pickstone* and the decision of the House of Lords in *Henn*. The Court of Appeal in *Pickstone* was concerned with interpreting two points of EC law, determining the scope of the principle of equal pay based on Article 119 and determining whether that principle had direct effect as regards work of equal value. On the first point, two of the three members of the Court of Appeal, Nicholls and Purchas L.JJ. found guidance on the interpretation of Article 119 in different decisions of the ECJ, notwithstanding material differences in the facts of those cases from the case in question. Nicholls L.J. referred to the case of *Macarthys*, an earlier ECJ case in which a ruling had been given under Article 177 following a reference from the English Court of Appeal, whilst Purchas L.J., found guidance on the interpretation of Article 119 in *Defrenne*, an earlier case in which a ruling had been given under Article 177 following a reference from a Belgian court. On the second point, Nicholls and Purchas L.JJ. referred to two ECJ decisions, *Jenkins v Kingsgate (Clothing Productions) Ltd*, Case 96/80 [1981] 1 ECR 911 and *Worringham*, in which rulings had been given under Article 177 following references from English courts. These cases provided interpretations on the direct effectiveness of the principle of equal pay based on Article 119 and were considered to have application in preference to an earlier Court of Appeal decision on direct effectiveness, *O'Brien v Sim-Chem Ltd.* [1980] 2 All E.R. 307. In *Henn*, the House of Lords had regard to a 'well-established body of case law of the European court' (*per* Lord Diplock at [1981] AC 850, 905), that provided guidance on the interpretation of Article 3 of the EC Treaty, under which quantitative restrictions on importation of goods as between Member States were prohibited, when determining the scope of that article."

THEORETICAL PERSPECTIVES ON COMMON LAW REASONING

In this final section, our emphasis shifts to a more reflective mode, and we look at the broader, more theoretical implications of the common law system of precedent. Central to that inquiry, first of all, is the question of the extent to which we can say that judges are "makers" of law; rather than simply engaged in the task of "declaring" a common law that is already "there". Although it may seem obvious to us, at the start of the twenty-first century, that judges are lawmakers, this viewpoint at one time would have been considered very radical. The common law was assumed to be already "there", and had always been there, just waiting to be declared by judges in the interpretation of cases. Cotterrell describes this as a "paradox" of the common law.

Roger Cotterrell, *The Politics of Jurisprudence* (Butterworths, London, 1989), pp.26–30:

"A paradox seems to lie at the heart of classical common law thought. Common law as the embodiment of ancient wisdom is revealed by judges, not created by them. It is, therefore, always already existent. Yet obviously it develops with the accumulation, reinterpretation and restatement of precedents and the adjustment of legal doctrine to new circumstances reflected in the never-ending succession of cases brought before courts. How is the evolution of law explained in this conception? And why is it not possible to assert openly that judges *make* law, even if only within strict limits which would fix them as clearly subordinate to recognised legislators, such as (in the context of English history) a parliament or the monarch?

The formal answer to this last question is that law embodies an ancient wisdom which may, according to some conceptions of common law, be considered timeless or, according to others, be seen as continually evolving through collective experience. On either view judges can only reflect this wisdom and not change it. In some classical common law thought the claim of timelessness is taken to fantastic lengths. Influential seventeenth century lawyers, such as Sir Edward Coke, 'argued on the flimsiest of evidence that the common laws, including their most detailed procedural provisions, dated from the earliest times'. Even Magna Carta was treated as declaring ancient law, confirming and making enforceable rights which had long existed. Coke claimed that in all its major parts the law and constitution had remained unchanged since the Saxon era and even before. These strange views were always controversial but the reason for asserting them at times when the authority of common law was seriously challenged (as in the early seventeenth century) is not hard to see. This authority was traditional in nature. Rooting it in a distant or even mythical past emphasised that it was certainly not derived from the present power of any monarch or other political authority.

The authority or legitimacy of common law as a legal order entitled to the highest respect was seen as residing not in the political system but in the community. If a judge *made* law this could only be as an exercise of political power. The deliberate making of law would be a political act. But according to common law theory, the authority of the judge is not as a political decision-maker (certainly not as delegate of the king or parliament) but as representative of the community. Hence he has authority only to *state* the community's law, not to impose law upon the community as if he were a political ruler or the servant of one. And the community is to be thought of here as something uniting past and present, extending back through innumerable past generations as well as encompassing the present one. Clearly, if the term 'community' were to be defined rigorously in this context it would be necessary to ask who exactly is within this community and what is its nature. It would also be necessary to consider the compatibility of this communitarian conception of law with the fact that the judges referred to here are judges of the *royal* courts, the instruments of a centralised justice promoted by kings. But such issues are typically absent from classical common law thought. Thus, common law is, for Coke, simply 'the most ancient and best inheritance that the subjects of this realm have'.

The usual way of conceptualising this apparently unchanging inheritance in classical common law thought is as *custom*. As Brian Simpson remarks, it is odd nowadays to think of law in this way because lawyers are used to treating this law as posited by the judges. But this is another example of the tendency to impose alien modern theoretical conceptions on common law. Just as common law is not strictly to be thought of, in the classical conception, as rules, neither is it to be thought of as decisions. To term it 'a residue of immutable custom' is more accurate, but does not confront the fact that common law thought embraces complex notions explaining and justifying past practices (not just stating them as custom) and providing guidance for future conduct. Equally common law thought allows the development of new doctrines and ideas, so has a dynamism which custom may lack. Because of these characteristics Simpson prefers to term common law customary law, rather than custom. But this hardly seems to solve the theoretical problem of its development. Customary law still has the character of custom, looking back to the past rather than guiding the future. It is concerned with stating established practice rather than with means of developing legal doctrine to meet changing times.

The problem here is not that custom is changeless. There is no reason why it cannot be considered to change over time. Law as an expression of custom can, therefore, also change. The problem is that common law thought itself cannot really address this change or explain it as a *legal* process. The mechanisms of change are in society (or the community). Law changes solely through the mysterious processes by which custom changes. To explain or even recognise explicitly processes of legal change, classical common law thought would require some kind of sociological or anthropological insight. But the common lawyers were hardly sociologists. Common law thought predated any modern social science and, in any event, its practical case-by-case view of legal development would have found little room for any explicit general theory of social or cultural change. So classical common law thought emphasised continuity (which it could interpret legally in terms of precedents and fundamental principles), rather than change (for which it could find no specifically legal criteria of evaluation).

Historically, the conundrum of law as changeless yet always changing was avoided by devices made possible by cultural conditions. Common law was considered to be unwritten. Blackstone, following Hale, distinguished 'the common law, or *lex non scripta* of this kingdom' from the written law of Acts of Parliament. Even though this unwritten law was eventually reported in written form, the fact that the law itself was still considered unwritten presumably allowed individual innovation to be forgotten, subsumed in the image of a changeless collective legal knowledge. As the anthropologist Jack Goody has noted about societies lacking writing, it is not that the creative element is absent in them or that 'a mysterious collective authorship, closely in touch with the collective consciousness, does what individuals do in literate cultures. It is rather that the individual signature is always getting rubbed out in the process of generative transmission'. Certainly common law's unwritten character was seen as one of its strengths, making possible 'a flexible system which had developed along with the English people itself'.

In the early ages of common law the lack of writing allowed a convenient amnesia. Blackstone wrote in the eighteenth century that 'in our law the goodness of a custom depends upon its having been used time out of mind; or, in the solemnity of our legal phrase, time whereof the memory of man runneth not to the contrary. This it is that gives its weight and authority'. The traditional authority of common law required that its customs be shrouded in antiquity. But in the Middle Ages two or three lifetimes would be enough to make a principle of common law immemorial; 'in ten or twenty years a custom was of long standing; in forty years it was "age-old"'. Later the flexibility of memory was less satisfactory. When, in the seventeenth century, lawyers such as Coke found it necessary to assert with the greatest possible force the traditional authority of common law against the king, the 'idea of the immemorial . . . took on an absolute colouring . . . It ceased to be a convenient fiction and was heatedly asserted as literal historical truth'. It can easily be seen, therefore, that common law thought eventually backed itself into a corner. First, the idea that the law was unwritten eventually became a mere fiction as the common law was recorded — preserved, explained and digested in written form in public records, law reports and 'the authoritative writings of the venerable sages of the law'. Secondly, the purely traditional authority of the law eventually demanded an utterly unrealistic claim of unbroken continuity from ancient times. And, finally, the declaratory theory of common law judging had to be maintained in the face of abundant evidence of conscious judicial innovation in legal doctrine.

Three responses to this situation were possible. One was to declare that common law possessed no authority by which it could develop further. Legal innovation could only come through Acts of Parliament, or other legislative acts. Thus, as one judge put the matter, 'It is in my opinion impossible for us now to create any new doctrine of common law'. A second response was to embrace openly the idea that judges sometimes make law, discard all fictions and go on to ask serious questions as to *how* and under what conditions they should make it. But this pragmatic approach also involved discarding all the standard assumptions underpinning the authority and legitimacy of common law. Traditional authority would need to be replaced with something else—perhaps the charismatic authority of individual wise judges, a conception of delegated political power or, as in the United States, the authority of a specific constitutional document providing the ultimate foundation of legal and judicial systems. In any event such a new foundation of judicial authority, if it could be found, would be something different from that presupposed in classical common law thought.

A third solution was to discard the notion of common law as custom and the formal idea of an unchanging ancient law, and to emphasise instead the complex conception of the judge as spokesman of the community—neither individual creator of law nor mere restator of ancient truths, but representative of an evolving collective consciousness."

- Why do you think that commentators such as Edward Coke found it necessary to argue that common law is the embodiment of ancient wisdom?

- Although modern observers of the use of precedent are much more likely to acknowledge that judges play an active role in creating law there may be dangers in taking this argument to its logical conclusion. Think of as many reasons as you can as to why this might be the case.

The issue of whether judges merely "declare" the law which is already "there", and the degree to which precedent operates as an effective constraint upon judicial decision making, have long been the subject of vigorous debate. Beginning in the 1930s, "American legal realism" drew into question these established "truths". One of the members of this school, Jerome Frank, was particularly sceptical of the constraints which the common law mode of thought claimed to impose upon judges. It has been argued that most lawyers today are realists in one form or another, but Frank was particularly radical in his claim that there was a great divergence between what judges say in their decisions, (*i.e.* what they claim is the basis for their decisions, such as precedent), and what *really* is operating on judges in the process of decision making (which Frank viewed as an emotional response to the particular facts of the case). Thus, for legal realists, the gap between the rhetoric of common law judging, and its reality, was potentially vast.

Jerome Frank, *Law and the Modern Mind* (Peter Smith, Gloucester, MA, 1970), pp.159–162:

"Lawyers and judges purport to make large use of precedents; that is, they purport to rely on the conduct of judges in past cases as a means of procuring analogies for action in new cases. But since what was actually decided in the earlier cases is seldom revealed, it is impossible, in a real sense, to rely on these precedents. What the courts in fact do is to manipulate the language of former decisions. They could approximate a system of real precedents only if the judges, in rendering those former decisions, had reported with fidelity the precise steps by which they arrived at their decisions. The paradox of the situation is that, granting there is value in a system of precedents, our present use of illusory precedents makes the employment of real precedents impossible.

The decision of a judge after trying a case is the product of a unique experience. 'Of the many things which have been said of the mystery of the judicial process,' writes Yntema, 'the most salient is that *decision is reached after an emotive experience in which principles and logic play a secondary part.* The function of juristic logic and the principles which it employs seem to be like that of language, to describe the event which has already transpired. These considerations must reveal to us the impotence of general principle to control decision. Vague because of their generality, they mean nothing save what they suggested in the organized experience of one who thinks them, and, because of their vagueness, they only remotely compel the organization of that experience. The important problem . . . is not the formulation of the rule but the ascertainment of the cases to which, and the extent to which, it applies. And this, even if we are seeking uniformity in the administration of justice, will lead us again to the circumstances of the concrete case . . . The reason why the general principle cannot control is because it does not inform . . . It should be obvious that when we have observed a recurrent phenomenon in the decisions of the courts, we may appropriately express the classification in a rule. But the rule will be only a mnemonic device, a useful but hollow diagram of what has been. It will be intelligible only if we *relive again the experience of the classifier'*.

The rules a judge announces when publishing his decision are, therefore, intelligible only if one can relive the judge's unique experience while he was trying the case—which, of course, cannot be done. One cannot even approximate that experience as long as opinions take the form of abstract rules applied to facts formally described. Even if it were desirable that, despite its uniqueness, the judge's decision should be followed, as an analogy, by other judges while trying other cases, this is impossible when the manner in which the judge reached his judgment in the earlier case is most inaccurately reported, as it now is. You are not really applying his decision as a precedent in another case unless you can say, in effect, that, having relived his experience in the earlier case, you believe that he would have thought his decision applicable to the facts of the latter case. And as opinions are now written, it is impossible to guess what the judge did experience in trying a case. The facts of all but the simplest controversies are complicated and unlike those of any other controversy; in the absence of a highly detailed account by the judge of how he reacted to the evidence, no other person is capable of reproducing his actual reactions. The rules announced in his opinions are therefore often insufficient to tell the reader why the judge reached his decision.

Dickinson admits that the 'personal bent of the judge' to some extent affects his decisions. But this 'personal bent,' he insists, is a factor only in the selection of new rules for unprovided cases. However, *in a profound sense the unique circumstances of almost any case make it an 'unprovided case' where no well-established rule 'authoritatively' compels a given result*. The uniqueness of the facts and of the judge's reaction thereto is often concealed because the judge so states the facts that they appear to call for the application of a settled rule. But that concealment does not mean that the judge's personal bent has been inoperative or that his emotive experience is simple and reducible."

NOTES AND QUESTIONS

- Frank's views were radical in his time and, to some extent, would still be considered unorthodox in many legal circles. Although they may accord with many "common sense" assumptions about human nature, why would they be threatening to common law judges, and those who place great "faith" in the common law?

- Having read some of his ideas, why do you think Frank was described as a "realist"?

- If you subscribe to Frank's views, what does that suggest about the sort of skills that are important for legal advocacy? In other words, in order to achieve a "good" result for your client, is an intricate knowledge of the relevant precedents of prime importance, or are other skills at least as crucial? What might those skills be?

Frank's scepticism, which was directed to the traditional understanding of precedent, seems less radical today. In part, this is because many writers and commentators on the law recognise quite openly that the process of deciding whether cases are analogous or distinguishable is itself laden with political and social values, and is not a "neutral", formalistic process.

Fiona Cownie and Anthony Bradney, *English Legal System in Context* (2nd ed., Butterworths, London, 2000), pp.104–106:

"We can see an alternative to the traditional approach to precedent if we return to one of the essential features of any theory of precedent; the desire to treat similar cases in the same fashion and thus bring both certainty and consistency to the law. Here the basic question is how do we decide that two cases are or are not alike? Traditional theories approach this question on the basis that it is simply a matter of close reasoning to see what are and what are not the significant and trivial aspects of the two cases in issue. However, we have seen that, in law, as in other disciplines, what makes something trivial or significant does not depend solely on linguistic features. Nothing is essentially significant or essentially trivial. Meaning is socially defined by the small community of English lawyers.

Thinking like a lawyer means not arguing more rigorously than others but, literally, thinking in the way that a lawyer would. . . . Prediction is achieved not just because the same rules are followed but because of an ability to empathise with those whose thought processes are being considered. One seeks to use words and judgments in the way other English lawyers would use them.

Several writers have argued that in considering how this social effect of language occurs we need to consider the influence of what they have called the legal canon in legal reasoning. . . . A canon is an accepted body of literature which it is said one should know if one is to be knowledgeable about a particular area. But a canon is more than simply a certain set of books (or in the case of a legal system, judgments). The works that constitute the canon are chosen for their alleged value. This value is moral or political. Works in the canon say something about the spirit of the system. However, since the canon reflects values in the system the selection of what is and what is not in the canon is in itself a value-laden act. The canon reflects and reinforces the politics of those who constitute the community for whom it operates. In the context of law this means that the influence of the canon on legal argument is itself not a value-free act. Arguments which are not reflective of the values of the canon will find it harder to find a purchase within the system.

The notion of the canon provides a framework within which the more traditional accounts of ratio and obiter can work. It allows us to understand how legal arguments can be acceptable even if they are not logical. The idea of a canon helps to explain how, on the one hand, there can be irresolvable problems in traditional accounts of precedent and yet, on the other hand, there can still be a reasonable degree of consistency and certainty in English legal reasoning. Social pressures supplement the principles of English legal reasoning to produce comparatively predictable outcomes to legal arguments. This explanation, though, has consequences for our understanding of the nature of legal reasoning. If reasoning is in part social, in part about values, who does the reasoning matters. The social background of judges and lawyers will affect how they respond to, and help construct, the atmosphere which in turn creates the canon."

Cownie and Bradney make an important point that one of the tasks of a legal method course must be to teach students how "to use words and judgments in the way other English lawyers would use them". Thus, even if judges decide cases on a basis other than formal legal reasoning, it remains important for the lawyer to be able to speak within that "traditional" legal discourse—since that is what is expected of him or her. In that sense, law (unfortunately, many would argue) remains a conservative enterprise, in the sense that one must use a language expected of you. It remains difficult to alter and broaden the scope of legal reasoning, so as to encompass broader perspectives. However, that is not to say that legal method and discourse forecloses innovation. Instead, it suggests that for the critical or radical lawyer, the task becomes particularly challenging. He or she must be able to converse in traditional legal discourse *at least as well* as his or her adversaries, but at the same time, must try to expand its scope and achieve outcomes more in keeping with his or her view of what "social justice" demands. At the same time, the barrister may need to convince a judge that what he or she is asking the judge to do is not too dramatic, by couching it within a language with which he (and it probably will be a "he") is most comfortable. It is no small task!

The job is not helped for the lawyer (and, indeed, for the law student) by the traditional differentiation between "law" (supposedly neutral, apolitical, and value-free) and "policy" (which is assumed to be something other than law). As Sugarman argues, the categories of common law thought, which have been entrenched through traditional legal education, have served to create this law/policy dichotomy, which conveniently serves to disguise the politics of law.

David Sugarman, "'A Hatred of Disorder': Legal Science, Liberalism and Imperialism" in *Dangerous Supplements* (Peter Fitzpatrick, ed., Pluto Press, London, 1991), pp.34–35:

"The 'black letter' tradition continues to overshadow the way we teach, write and think about law. Its categories and assumptions are still the standard diet of most first-year law students and they continue to organise law textbooks and casebooks. Stated baldly it assumes that although law may appear to be irrational, chaotic and particularistic, if one digs deep enough and knows what one is looking for, then it will soon become evident that the law is an internally coherent and unified body of rules. This coherence and unity stems from the fact that law is grounded in, and logically derived from, a handful of general principles, and that whole subject areas such as contract and torts are distinguished by some common principles or elements which fix the boundaries of the subject. The exposition and systematisation of these general principles and the techniques required to find and to apply both them and the rules that they underpin, are largely what legal education and scholarship are all about.

The claim that law is unified and coherent is also sustained by a battery of dualisms: common law/statute law, law/politics, law/state, law/morality, legal/empirical, technique/substance, form/substance, means/ends, private law/public law, law/history, law/theory, which make it more tenable to regard law as 'pure' and 'scientific'.

Despite the variety of producers and consumers of legal discourse, it is what the judges say and the supposed needs of the legal profession as narrowly defined, that have had the greatest magnetic pull over the nature and form of legal education and scholarship. Other aspects that are equally important to understanding law, such as legislation, the operation of law in practice, as well as the history, theory, morality and politics of law, are ignored or marginalised.

The 'black letter' tradition is also the bearer of an important political message. The message is that the law (primarily through case law) and the legal profession (centrally, the judiciary) play a major role in protecting individual freedom; and that the rules of contract, torts and constitutional law, for example, confer the maximum freedom on individuals to act as they wish without interference from other individuals or the state. Policing the boundaries within, and between, legal subject areas constitutes a major foundation of the rule of law. In this way, the form as well as the content of the law become synonymous with our very definitions of individual freedom and liberty, and thereby acquire an additional patina of reverence and universality. The world, as pictured within the conceptual categories of legal thought, is basically sound. It is more or less the best that is realisable. In so far as a better world is possible, it would not fundamentally differ from the present.

Like any closed model of rationality, the 'black letter' tradition is shot through with contradictions, omissions and absurdities, which generations of judges and jurists have sought to repress. For instance, the notion of law as resting upon an objective body of principle founders when we consider that the quest for underlying principles must involve a selection from the sum of principles available and, therefore, has a strong evaluative element. Principles are thus inseparable from interpretation and theory which, in turn, are determined by values. Thus, the schizophrenia of the first-year law student: when is it that s/he is supposed to talk about 'law', and when is it that s/he can talk about 'policy'? We are heirs of this schizophrenia."

Because, as Sugarman argues, the common law is founded upon a set of legal categories and principles, it becomes necessary for people to "translate" social disputes and problems into those legal categories; *i.e.* to "fit" the issue into an existing category, no matter how inappropriate it might be. This is a process of *abstraction*, and it is central to common law reasoning. However, one of the key problems with such a form of reasoning is that "common sense" is frequently lost sight of as analogies are drawn between factual situations and legal disputes which seem to bear little resemblance to each other, as Mansell, Meteyard, and Thomson illustrate through three cases.

Wade Mansell, Belinda Meteyard, and Alan Thompson, *A Critical Introduction to Law* (Cavendish, London, 1999), pp.57–59:

"The first, *Ashford v. Thornton* is very much a case which marks the transition, albeit a late one, from the explicit avoidance of issues to the new format which decides hard cases by reference not to social facts but to structured legal categories and technicalities. *Ashford v Thornton* is a case decided in 1818 in which it was held that under some circumstances trial by battle was still available to an accused. The Chief Justice Lord Ellenborough held, in words which take us back very explicitly to rule magic, as follows:

'The general law of the land is in favour of the wager of battles, and it is our duty to pronounce the law as it is, and not as we may wish it to be. Whatever prejudices therefore may justly exist against this mode of trial, still as it is the law of the land, the Court must pronounce judgment for it.'

Incidentally, but as a matter of interest, the authorities considered, in reaching that decision, went all the way back to the law of Normandy before the Norman Conquest of 1066.

Ashford v Thornton also provides us with an (admittedly) extreme example of the translation process used by law to put questions into a resolvable form. The application against Abraham Thornton at the behest of William Ashford, the deceased woman's brother was put in the following terms:

'. . . For that he the said Abraham Thornton not having the fear of God before his eyes, but being moved and seduced by the instigation of the devil, on the 27th day of May, in the 57th year of the reign of our Sovereign Lord George the Third by the Grace of God, &c with force of arms at the parish of Sutton-Coldfield in the county of Warwick, in and upon the said Mary Ashford spinster, in the peace of God and our said lord the King, then and there being feloniously, wilfully, and of his malice aforethought, did make an assault, and that the said did take the said Mary Ashford into both his hands, and did then and there feloniously, wilfully, violently, and of his malice aforethought, case, throw, and push the said Mary Ashford into a certain pit of water, wherein there was a great quantity of water, situation in the parish of Sutton-Coldfield aforesaid in the county aforesaid, by means of which said casting, throwing, and pushing of the said Mary Ashford into the pit of water aforesaid by the said A Thornton in form aforesaid, she, the said M Ashford in the pit of water aforesaid with the water aforesaid, was then and there choaked, suffocated, and drowned, of which said choking, suffocating, and drowning she, the said M Ashford, then and there instantly died. And so the said A

Thornton, her the said Mary Ashford in manner and form aforesaid feloniously and wilfully, and of his malice aforethought, did kill and murder against the peace of our said lord the King his Crown and dignity.' (*Ashford v Thornton* (1818) 106 ER 149).

While we would not now expect to see charges framed in such a way this *reductio ad absurdum* does make manifest the legal method of translating social events into legal format.

The second English case which we can use to illustrate both the sidestepping of the issues and the way law justifies decisions by referring to pre-existing rules is the case of *Thompson v London and Midland Railway* [1930] 1 KB 41 which, although over 60 years old, seems almost contemporaneous to lawyers.

The facts of that case as heard by the court were that the tragic Mrs Thompson had wished to travel for a day's outing from Manchester to Darwin on the London and Midland Railway. Mrs Thompson could neither read nor write and she requested her niece to purchase her rail ticket for her. When the niece bought the ticket she might have seen on the front of the ticket the words: 'excursion. For conditions see back.' Had Mrs Thompson's niece then turned the ticket over she would have seen a notice to the effect that the ticket was issued subject to the conditions in the rail company's timetables. The timetables were on sale at the ticket office and one of the conditions attaching to the issue of excursion tickets, according to the timetable was that all liability for injury to excursion passengers, however caused, was excluded.

Without being aware of these conditions Mrs Thompson set off for Darwin. Unfortunately, when the train arrived at Darwin and its arrival was announced to passengers, Mrs Thompson stepped out only to discover that there was no platform outside her door as the train in which she was a passenger was longer in length than the Darwin station platform. Mrs Thompson was injured in the fall and sought compensation from the railway company. The *legal* issue of the case did not concern itself with Mrs Thompson's injuries except extraordinarily indirectly. Mrs Thompson must have been amazed to discover what the question of her compensation turned upon. The legal question to be answered by the court was: 'was the clause excluding liability for injury, to be found in the timetable which was available at the ticket office, a part of the contract of carriage entered into by Mrs Thompson via her niece as agent and the railway company?'.

The court held that Mrs Thompson was unable to recover. They did so by referring to previous cases and the rules that they had laid down. The questions they asked were not concerned with what seemed the most socially relevant facts—the injury to Mrs Thompson and her need for compensation—but rather to the rules and circumstances under which it would be held that a party to a contract had had 'constructive' notice of the existence of a clause which purported to limit liability. Having said that it must be conceded, that, to many law students, the legal question will seem the obvious one. So commonsensical has contract become that many on hearing the facts of Mrs Thompson's case will want to know immediately the terms which governed the transaction. . . .

For a more modern and equally striking example of the 'translation' process at work readers may wish to turn to the decision of the European Court of Justice in *SPUC v Grogan* [1991] 3 CMLR 689. The case arose out of a decision of the Irish Supreme Court to grant an injunction to restrain a student organisation from publishing and distributing guides to abortion clinics in the UK. It appeared to raise fundamental questions relating to the protection of human rights and to necessitate a balancing of the 'right to life' contained in the Irish Constitution on the one hand, and freedom of expression protected by Community law, on the other. Translated into a form susceptible to adjudication by a reluctant European Court, however, the case was deemed to hinge rather upon the meaning of 'services' within the European Community Treaty and the capacity of the Irish restriction upon the provision of information to interfere with the cross-border supply of services in the Community's internal market. Ultimately the decision of the Court was predicated upon the fact that the students responsible for the distribution of the information were not financially rewarded for their activities and hence not economically tied to the clinics in the UK whose services they were advertising. For the European Court, 'buying' an abortion was seen in the same light as the purchase of an insurance policy."

QUESTION

- Compare the "common sense" and "legal" construction of the issues in the three cases. To what extent do you think that "translation" of the issues into legal discourse distorted what was really going on in the cases?

11

JUDGE MADE LAW:
A CASE STUDY ON THE LAW OF NEGLIGENCE

In this chapter, we apply the material on case law which we examined in Chapter 10 to the development of a particular area of law: the general duty of care in tort. The focus is on the historical development of this area of judge made common law, in order to help make more concrete some of the theory which we have looked at thus far. This material is designed to help you to get a better "feel" for the central common law concepts of precedent, *ratio decidendi, obiter dictum,* and the application and distinguishing of cases. It is also designed to give you practice reading common law judgments, and we conclude this chapter with an exercise to test your ability to work with precedents and to engage in common law analysis.

We have chosen the law of negligence as our case study for several reasons. First and foremost, we believe that it provides a particularly good illustration of the way in which new areas of the common law develop, and how the development of one area is linked to the limitations of another field of the common law (contract). Second, the historical development of the law of negligence vividly demonstrates the importance of the personal contribution of individual judges to the development of the common law. Third, the case law underscores the difficulty of discerning the *ratio decidendi* of a case given the dynamic character of common law reasoning. Finally, negligence demonstrates a relationship between "law" and "morality", which we have touched upon already in earlier chapters.

<h4 style="text-align:center">HISTORICAL BACKGROUND TO THE LAW OF TORTS</h4>

We begin with some historical background to help you understand from where our modern conception of the duty of care principle—which will be the central focus of this chapter—emerged.

Peter Cane, *The Anatomy of Tort Law* (Hart Publishing, Oxford, 1997), pp.2–8:

"I shall argue that the traditional approach to tort law conceals its nature as a system of ethical principles of personal responsibility. My claim is that organizing the law around the ideas of correlativity, protected interests, sanctioned conduct and sanctions provides a much deeper understanding of its inner logic than the traditional approach, and also a more satisfactory way of sorting out the relationship between tort law and other legal categories. In my view the framework I offer provides, both for theoretical and practical purposes, a much better way of thinking about and organizing tort law than the traditional division of the law into 'torts'.

If you look at a typical text on the law of tort in any common law jurisdiction (that is, where the applicable law is, or is derived from or based on English law), you will find the law discussed and expounded in terms of a number of 'torts'. These include the tort of negligence, the tort of nuisance, the tort of conversion, the tort of defamation, and so on. Indeed, one author has constructed an 'alphabetical list of known torts' containing more than 70 entries. This approach to expounding tort law I shall call the 'common law approach'. This approach is in notable contrast to that adopted in civil law jurisdictions (that is, where the law is derived from or based on Roman law). France provides, perhaps, the most extreme example of the civil law approach: there, much of the law of delict (or 'tort') is derived from a few very general provisions in the *Code Civil*, such as Article 1382: 'Every act whatever . . . which causes damage to another obliges him by whose fault the damage occurred to repair it'. This provision has two notable features: first, it is very general, and secondly, it bases liability directly on a principle of personal responsibility for damage caused by faulty conduct. The common law approach, by contrast, has at least two important characteristics relevant to the present discussion. First, and putting the point very crudely, whereas a French lawyer might see the process of deciding particular legal disputes as involving the application of broad general principles to particular facts, the common lawyer is more likely to think of that process in terms of determining whether a particular fact situation fits into a framework of rules and quite narrow principles which define the elements of 'tort'. Secondly, the common lawyer tends to view the elements of particular torts as technical requirements of the law rather than as applications of ethical principles of personal responsibility concerned with what people ought or ought not to do, such as that people ought not to cause damage deliberately. The common lawyer's understanding of the law of tort consists largely of knowledge about the technical definitions of legal terms and concepts and about fact situations which have, in the past, been held to give rise to tort liability. The typical common lawyer would not (in a professional capacity, at least) think of the law of tort as a set of ethical principles of personal responsibility, principles about how people ought and ought not to behave in their dealings with others.

The common law way of thinking about tort law can be traced historically to the 'forms of action' which were central to the 'formulary system' of pleading cases before courts. Under a formulary system of litigation, an action can be started (and will succeed) only if the facts of the plaintiff's case fit one of the formulae which the courts recognize, or if the plaintiff can persuade the court to recognize a new formula. In the heyday of the English formulary system, the courts would process a claim only if it could be and was appropriately 'packaged'. If a container (called a 'writ') of the right shape was not available, the claim would fail even if, had the court processed the claim, it would have found the claim to be meritorious. In short, under a formulary system, the way a claim is packaged is as important as the claim's strength. Changing the metaphor, forms of action were a bit like recipes — recipes for success in litigation. The prime concern of the lawyer in a formulary system is to follow the recipe faithfully.

The English formulary system was gradually replaced in the 19th century by the modern system under which what matters (in theory, anyway) is not how a complaint is packaged but whether the complaint is a good one. In other words, what is important is not the 'form' of the claim but rather whether it states a 'good cause of action'. The forms of action have been replaced by causes of actions. A cause of action provides a court with a legally recognized ground for granting a remedy to a claimant. This change from forms to causes of action was of enormous importance in the history of the law and of legal thought because it shifted attention away from the mechanics and procedure of making legal claims (were they properly packaged?) to the substance and merits of claims. Under a formulary system it is impossible to understand the law without also understanding procedures for litigating, because claims have to be packaged in a way which is recognized by the processing authorities, the courts. By contrast, the typical modern text on the law of contract or tort, for instance, contains almost nothing about procedural law but is primarily concerned with the '*substance*' of the law or, in other words, the grounds on which courts will award legal remedies.

Because, in practice, the procedures of making legal claims have subtle and complex effects on the substance of the law relevant to resolving such claims, this distinction between procedure and substance is, to a certain extent, misleading—but only to a certain extent. We can gain a great deal of useful knowledge about the law without knowing much, if anything, about the procedures for litigation. One important reason for this is that civil law (as opposed to criminal law), of which the law of tort is a 'department', has both backward-looking functions and forward-looking functions. The backward-looking functions are concerned with the resolution of disputes and the provision of remedies. The procedures which were central to the formulary system were procedures for resolving disputes in the courts and for obtaining judicial remedies. Even under our modern, non-formulary system, a knowledge and understanding of relevant procedures for resolving legal disputes is important to success in making a legal claim. This is true whether the claim is heard by a court or, as is most commonly the case, it is resolved by an out-of-court settlement. For instance, if a legal claim is not made within a specified period (the 'limitation period'), it will fail, however strong the substance of the claim might be; and one of the commonest causes of complaint against solicitors is delay beyond the limitation period in making legal claims.

One of the forward-looking functions of civil law is to guide conduct. If people know the sorts of conduct the law allows and those it prohibits, or the interests which the law protects and those it does not, people can attempt to plan their lives in such a way as to minimize the chance of being involved in a legal dispute or of breaching the law. Knowledge of procedures for resolving disputes is quite unimportant if one's interest is in using the law in this prophylactic or precautionary way. Moreover, for most people most of the time, the law is much more important as a guide to conduct than as a set of rules for resolving disputes. Relatively speaking, only a tiny proportion of human conduct which is regulated or affected by law gives rise to legal disputes which become the subject of litigation or other formal modes of dispute resolution. For this reason alone, knowledge and understanding of the substance of the law is much more important than knowledge of the procedures of litigation.

The emergence of legal textbooks as we know them today was partly as a result of the demise of the formulary system. This encouraged lawyers to think about the substantive principles underlying the forms of action and to organize causes of action according to these principles. One of the most important products of this new intellectual approach was the development of what is now often referred to as 'the classical law of contract', that is, a set of rules and principles governing the formation and termination of contracts. Exposition of these rules and principles (concerned with offer and acceptance, consideration and so on) occupies a substantial part of most modern contract texts; and although the law recognizes specific contracts, such as contracts for the sale of goods and contracts of guarantee, which are governed by special sets of rules, these special rules are usually seen as applications or adaptations of the general principles of the law of contract to meet particular circumstances. No one doubts that we have a law of contract (singular) rather than (or, perhaps, in addition to) a law of contracts (plural).

However, although the forms of action were replaced by causes of action, the thinking underlying the formulary system continued to exert a powerful influence on the way textbook writers (and courts) thought about the law in general and tort law in particular. So, for instance, some of the old forms of action, such as trespass or nuisance, took on new life as causes of action: and today, texts on the law of tort still contain sections dealing with trespass and nuisance in their various manifestations. Furthermore, in certain respects, such causes of action are just as formulaic as the forms of action were. If some 'element' of a modern cause of action 'in tort' is not present in the plaintiff's claim, the plaintiff may lose even if some notion of fairness or justice would suggest that the plaintiff should win. For instance, since the days of the formulary system, it has been the law that in order to succeed in an action in nuisance, the plaintiff must have an 'interest in land'. This means, for example, that if a family has noisy neighbours, the only member of the family who can bring a nuisance action against the neighbours is the member who owns or rents their house, even if the whole family suffers equally from the noise. In some contexts, this rule is now thought by many to produce unsatisfactory results; but judges have had great difficulty in deciding whether to allow a person who does not have an interest in land to bring a nuisance action or whether, instead, the law should recognize a new tort which would not be encumbered with the 'interest in land' requirement and which might be used to deal, for instance, with cases of 'harassment' of people in their homes, whatever the nature of their interest in the property. . . .

Despite the abolition of the formulary system, the prevalent approach to tort law is still essentially formulaic. Under this approach, the modern torts are treated as formulae, or sets of technical legal rules which define the conditions for success in litigation: winning a tort action depends largely on finding a formula which fits one's case. Causes of action in tort operate in a similar way to the forms of action—they regulate and shape the resolution of legal disputes by litigation and other modes of dispute settlement. However, causes of action in tort are also important in relation to the forward-looking functions of the law, because through them we organize the substantive law of tort liability into manageable portions. A lawyer advises a client whether planned action might attract tort liability by surveying the causes of action in tort and determining whether the proposed activity falls within any of them. The mind of the tort lawyer, whether as litigator or adviser, tends to be dominated by the recipes for forensic success which the individual torts represent."

- What are the differences between the common law and civil law approaches to thinking about tort?

- What is the difference between the formulary and the modern system of tort?

- What are the "backward-looking" and "forward-looking" functions of tort?

- Note that one of the early textbook writers was A.V. Dicey whom we encountered earlier in this book. Law professors such as Dicey to a considerable extent are responsible for the way in which the categories of common law are disseminated across the generations of lawyers.

The development of a general law of negligence in English common law did not come about easily or quickly. There were particular obstacles faced by those who advocated such a view.

David Howarth, *Textbook on Tort* (Butterworths, London, 1995), pp.26–27:

"Negligence originally meant in English law what it means in everyday speech, not a wrong in itself but a way of committing wrongs. Negligence is to be contrasted with maliciousness or wickedness as a state of mind that people who do harm to others may have. By the end of the nineteenth century, a study of negligence in the English law of torts would have been about the various torts that could be committed without malice (or, in more modern terms, intentionality) but by wrongful inattention, for example the actions 'on the case' arising from collisions on the street and at sea and from various accidents that result in personal injuries.

Furthermore, 'negligence' would have been a sufficient condition of liability when certain legal relationships went wrong—that between an innkeeper and a customer, for example, or between a bailor and a bailee (that is, a person who deposits a thing with somebody else and that somebody else).

But there were various obstacles to the creation of a general principle along the lines of articles 1382 and 1383 [of the French Civil Code]. One was that in the accident cases, the action 'on the case' alleging negligence had a rival in the action 'for trespass'—that is for the direct application of unlawful force. Confusion reigned as the courts appeared to say that for road accidents the proper action in a collision case was 'trespass', but that, exceptionally, the plaintiff had to prove fault, whether intention or negligence, but in other accident cases where there was a 'direct' application of force, there could be a 'trespass' action in which it was up to the defendant to disprove fault.

A second obstacle to the creation of a general principle was the notorious 'privity fallacy'. Many nineteenth century judges were impressed by the idea of the 'bargain', the idea . . . that for economists the only sure ground for saying that people want something is that they are prepared to exchange something for it. This idea was expanded into the notion of 'privity of contract', according to which people who had not taken part in making a bargain had no legal right to sue if the bargain was not fulfilled. But it also expanded in another direction, namely that bargain and exchange should be the only basis of civil liability either in all novel cases or in all cases in which the plaintiff could have formed a bargain with the defendant but did not do so.

The effect of the privity doctrine was that, for example, the ultimate consumer of a product had no legal recourse against the manufacturer of a product if it caused injury. The victim would be told either that he or she should sue the retailer in contract, or, if the victim had received the product as a gift, that since there was no contractual link or bargain between the plaintiff and anyone, there was no legal liability at all. It also meant that the wife of a tenant could not sue if she was injured by the fault of the landlord. The husband had a contract with the landlord in the form of the lease, but the wife had not contracted and therefore had no rights at all."

The undermining of the privity of contract fallacy is closely related to the development of a general principle of liability for negligence at common law. The development of that principle can best be understood through an examination of a series of cases. Our story begins in the late nineteenth century.

Heaven v Pender (1883) 11 QBD 503, CA.

Brett M.R.:

"In this case the plaintiff was a workman in the employ of Gray, a ship painter. Gray entered into a contract with a shipowner whose ship was in the defendant's dock to paint the outside of his ship. The defendant, the dock owner, supplied, under a contract with the shipowner, an ordinary stage to be slung in the ordinary way outside the ship for the purpose of painting her. It must have been known to the defendant's servants, if they had considered the matter at all, that the stage would be put to immediate use, that it would not be used by the shipowner, but that it would be used by such a person as the plaintiff, a working ship painter. The ropes by which the stage was slung, and which were supplied as a part of the instrument by the defendant, had been scorched and were unfit for use and were supplied without reasonably careful attention to their condition. When the plaintiff began to use the stage the ropes broke, the stage fell, and the plaintiff was injured. The Divisional Court held that the plaintiff could not recover against the defendant. The plaintiff appealed. The action is in form and substance an action for negligence. That the stage was, through want of attention of the defendant's servants, supplied in a state unsafe for use is not denied. But want of attention amounting to a want of ordinary care is not a good cause of action, although injury ensue from such want, unless the person charged with such want of ordinary care had a duty to the person complaining to use ordinary care in respect of the matter called in question. Actionable negligence consists in the neglect of the use of ordinary care or skill towards a person to whom the defendant owes the duty of observing ordinary care and skill, by which neglect the plaintiff, without contributory negligence on his part, has suffered injury to his person or property. The question in this case is whether the defendant owed such a duty to the plaintiff.

If a person contracts with another to use ordinary care or skill towards him or his property the obligation need not be considered in the light of a duty; it is an obligation of contract. It is undoubted, however, that there may be the obligation of such a duty from one person to another although there is no contract between them with regard to such duty. Two drivers meeting have no contract with each other, but under certain circumstances they have a reciprocal duty towards each other. So two ships navigating the sea. So a railway company which has contracted with one person to carry another has no contract with the person carried but has a duty towards that person. So the owner or occupier of house or land who permits a person or persons to come to his house or land has no contract with such person or persons, but has a duty towards him or them. It should be observed that the existence of a contract between two persons does not prevent the existence of the suggested duty between them also being raised by law independently of the contract, by the facts with regard to which the contract is made and to which it applies an exactly similar but a contract duty. We have not in this case to consider the circumstances in which an implied contract may arise to use ordinary care and skill to avoid danger to the safety of person or property. We have not in this case to consider the question of a fraudulent misrepresentation express or implied, which is a well recognised head of law. The questions which we have to solve in this case are—what is the proper definition of the relation between two persons other than the relation established by contract, or fraud, which imposes on the one of them a duty towards the other to observe, with regard to the person or property of such other, such ordinary care or skill as may be necessary to prevent injury to his person or property; and whether the present case falls within such definitions. When two drivers or two ships are approaching each other, such a relation arises between them when they are approaching each other in such a manner that, unless they use ordinary care and skill to avoid it, there will be a danger of an injurious collision between them. This relation is established in such circumstances between them, not only if it be proved that they actually know and think of this danger, but whether such proof be made or not. It is established, as it seems to me, because any one of ordinary sense who did think would at once recognise that if he did not use ordinary care and skill under such circumstances there would be such danger. And every one ought by the universally recognised rules of right and wrong, to think so much with regard to the safety of others who may be jeopardised by his conduct; and if, being in such circumstances, he does not think, and in consequence neglects, or if he neglects to use ordinary care or skill, and injury ensue, the law, which takes cognisance of and enforces the rules of right and wrong, will force him to give an indemnity for the injury. In the case of a railway company carrying a passenger with whom it has not entered into the contract of carriage the law implies the duty, because it must be obvious that unless ordinary care and skill be used the personal safety of the passenger must be endangered. With regard to the condition in which an owner or occupier leaves his house or property other phraseology has been used, which it is necessary to consider. If a man opens his shop or warehouse to customers it is said that he invites them to enter, and that this invitation raises the relation between them which imposes on the inviter the duty of using reasonable care so to keep his house or warehouse that it may not endanger the person or property of the person invited. This is in a sense an accurate phrase, and as applied to the circumstances a sufficiently accurate phrase. Yet it is not accurate if the word 'invitation' be used in its ordinary sense. By opening a shop you do not really invite, you do not ask A. B. to come in to buy; you intimate to him that if it pleases him to come in he will find things which you are willing to sell. So, in the case of shop, warehouse, road, or premises, the phrase has been used that if you permit a person to enter them you impose on yourself a duty not to lay a trap for him. This, again, is in a sense a true statement of the duty arising from the relation constituted by the permission to enter. It is not a statement of what causes the relation which raises the duty. What causes the relation is the permission to enter and the entry. But it is not a strictly accurate statement of the duty. To lay a trap means in ordinary language to do something with an invitation. Yet it is clear that the duty extends to a danger the result of negligence without intention. And with regard to both these phrases, though each covers the circumstances to which it is particularly applied, yet it does not cover the other set of circumstances from which an exactly similar legal liability is inferred. It follows, as it seems to me, that there must be some larger proposition which involves and covers both sets of circumstances. The logic of inductive reasoning requires that where two major propositions lead to exactly similar minor premisses there must be a more remote and larger premiss which embraces both of the major propositions. That, in the present consideration, is, as it seems to me, the same proposition which will cover the similar legal liability inferred in the cases of collision and carriage. The proposition which these recognised cases suggest, and which is, therefore, to be deduced from them, is that whenever one person is by circumstances placed in such a position with regard to another that every one of ordinary sense who did think would at once recognise that if he did not use ordinary care and skill in his own conduct with regard to those circumstances he would cause danger of injury to the person or property of the other, a duty arises to use ordinary care and skill to avoid such danger. Without displacing the other propositions to which allusion has been made as applicable to the particular circumstances in respect of which they have been enunciated, this proposition includes, I think, all the recognised cases of liability. It is the only proposition which covers them all. It may, therefore, safely be affirmed to be a true proposition, unless some obvious case can be stated in which the liability must be admitted to exist, and which yet is not within this proposition. There is no such case. Let us apply this proposition to the case of one person supplying goods or machinery, or instruments or utensils, or the like, for the purpose of their being used by another person, but with whom there is no contract as to the supply. The proposition will stand thus: whenever one person supplies goods, or machinery, or the like, for the purpose of their being used by another person under such circumstances that every one of ordinary sense would, if he thought, recognise at once that unless he used ordinary care and skill with regard to the condition of the thing supplied or the mode of supplying it, there will be danger of injury to the person or property of him for whose use the thing is supplied, and who is to use it, a duty arises to use ordinary care and skill as to the condition or manner of supplying such thing. And for a neglect of such ordinary care or skill whereby injury happens a legal liability arises to be enforced by an action for negligence. This includes the case of goods, &c., supplied to be used immediately by a particular person or persons or one of a class of persons, where it would be obvious to the person supplying, if he thought, that the goods would in all probability be used at once by such persons before a reasonable opportunity for discovering any defect which might exist, and where the thing supplied would be of such a nature that a neglect of ordinary care or skill as to its condition or the manner of supplying it would probably cause danger to the person or property of the person for whose use it was supplied, and who was about to use it. It would exclude a case in which the goods are supplied under circumstances in which it would be a chance by whom they would be used or whether they would be used or not, or whether they would be used before there would probably be means of observing any defect, or where the goods would be of such a nature that a want of care or skill as to their condition or the manner of supplying them would not probably produce danger of injury to person or property. The cases of vendor and purchaser and lender and hirer under contract need not be considered, as the liability arises under the contract, and nor merely as a duty imposed by law, though it may not be useless to observe that it seems difficult to import the implied obligation into the contract except in cases in which if there were no contract between the parties the law would according to the rule above stated imply the duty. . . .

I cannot conceive that if the facts were proved which would make out the proposition I have enunciated, the law can be that there would be no liability. Unless that be true, the proposition must be true. If it be the rule the present case is clearly within it. This case is also, I agree, within that which seems to me to be a minor proposition—namely, the proposition which has been often acted upon, that there was in a sense, an invitation of the plaintiff by the defendant, to use the stage. The appeal must, in my opinion, be allowed, and judgment must be entered for the plaintiff."

Cotton L.J.:

"Bowen, L.J., concurs in the judgment I am about to read. In this case the defendant was the owner of a dock for the repair of ships, and provided for use in the dock the stages necessary to enable the outside of the ship to be painted while in the dock, and the stages which were to be used only in the dock were appliances provided by the dock owner as appurtenant to the dock and its use. After the stage was handed over to the shipowner it no longer remained under the control of the dock owner. But when ships were received into the dock for repair and provided with stages for the work on the ships which was to be executed there, all those who came to the vessels for the purpose of painting and otherwise repairing them were there for business in which the dock owner was interested, and they, in my opinion, must be considered as invited by the dock owner to use the dock and all appliances provided by the dock owner as incident to the use of the dock. To these persons, in my opinion, the dock owner was under an obligation to take reasonable care that at the time the appliances provided for immediate use in the dock were provided by him they were in a fit state to be used—that is, in such a state as not to expose those who might use them for the repair of the ship to any danger or risk not necessarily incident to the service in which they are employed. . . . I think that the same duty must exist as to things supplied by the dock owner for immediate use in the dock, of which the control is not retained by the dockowner, to the extent of using reasonable care as to the state of the articles when delivered by him to the ship under repair for immediate use in relation to the repairs. For any neglect of those having control of the ship and the appliances he would not be liable, and to establish his liability it must be proved that the defect which caused the accident existed at the time when the article was supplied by the dockowner. . . .

This decides this appeal in favour of the plaintiff, and I am unwilling to concur with the Master of the Rolls in laying down unnecessarily the larger principle which he entertains, inasmuch as there are many cases in which the principle was impliedly negatived. . . .

In declining to concur in laying down the principle enunciated by the Master of the Rolls, I in no way intimate any doubt as to the principle that anyone who leaves a dangerous instrument, as a gun, in such a way as to cause danger, or who without due warning supplies to others for use an instrument or thing which to his knowledge, from its construction or otherwise, is in such a condition as to cause danger, not necessarily incident to the use of such an instrument or thing, is liable for injury caused to others by reason of his negligent act.

For the reasons stated I agree that the plaintiff is entitled to judgment, though I do not entirely concur with the reasoning of the Master of the Rolls."

NOTES AND QUESTIONS

• How did you determine which of the facts are material in *Heaven v Pender*?

• How does the judgment of Brett M.R. differ from that of Cotton L.J.? What rule for determining liability is formulated by Brett M.R.? By contrast, on what basis does Cotton L.J. find the defendants liable? Which is the broader rule (that is, of wider application)?

• What is the *ratio decidendi* of *Heaven v Pender*?

- The contrasting approaches in *Heaven v Pender* underscore a tension at the heart of the historical development of the law of negligence. As Howarth has explained:

> "The English legal system has never quite decided whether it is a general principle system or a specific interest or circumstance system. In the nineteenth century, the English judges leant heavily towards the specific interest or circumstance view, although discontent with that approach produced a few notable counterblasts, most famously that of Brett M.R. in *Heaven v Pender*. The view appeared to be that to allow legal liability to extend beyond the bounds of contract, that is beyond the bounds of what people had subjected themselves to voluntarily, would be to impose an intolerable burden of state interference upon them. In consequence, the presumption had to be against liability, a presumption displaced only by established rules of custom and practice."[1]

- The reluctance to develop a general duty-imposing principle outside of the realm of contract, apparent in the judgment of Cotton LJ, is also exemplified by the decision of the House of Lords a few years later in *Derry v Peek* (1889) 14 App.Cas. 337, HL. In *Derry v Peek*, the material facts were as follows. The promoters of a company were sued for a false statement written in a document designed to invite the public to purchase shares in a company. The statement, although false, was made honestly but the promoters may have been careless in determining whether it was true or not. If Brett MR's test had been widely accepted and applied to these facts, might the promoters have been liable for damages? In fact, in *Derry v Peek* the promoters were found not to be liable in damages. Lord Herschell explained:

> "I have arrived with some reluctance at the conclusion to which I have felt myself compelled, for I think those who put before the public a prospectus to induce them to embark their money in a commercial enterprise ought to be vigilant to see that it contains such representations only as are in strict accordance with fact, and I should be very unwilling to give any countenance to the contrary idea. I think there is much to be said for the view that this moral duty ought to some extent to be converted into a legal obligation, and that the want of reasonable care to see that statements, made under such circumstances, are true, should be made an actionable wrong. But this is not a matter fit for discussion on the present occasion. If it is to be done the legislature must intervene and expressly give a right of action in respect of such a departure from duty."[2]

This passage demonstrates a judicial mindset, which you will encounter frequently in your legal studies, whereby a judge refuses to take a course of action, but encourages the legislature to embark on it instead. Why do you think Lord Herschell felt unable to create (or "find") a duty of care whereby the promoters of the company

---

[1] David Howarth, *Textbook on Tort* (Butterworths, London, 1995), pp.162–163.
[2] *Derry v Peek* (1889) 14 App. Cas. 337 at 376, HL.

could be held responsible for their statements of encouragement to investors? In fact, the legislature did intervene with the Directors' Liability Act 1890.

In the years following *Heaven v Pender*, Brett M.R. became Lord Esher. He figures prominently in another famous negligence case, *Le Lievre and Dennes v Gould*.[3] The case concerned the liability of a surveyor to a mortgagee for statements made as to the progress of a building. There was no contractual relationship between the parties (a vitally important point in all of these cases). The Court of Appeal found no liability, and Lord Esher goes on at some length to interpret the earlier decision of the Court of Appeal in *Heaven v Pender*. The passage usefully demonstrates the way in which the *ratio* of a common law case can only be determined definitively in light of the way in which courts subsequently interpret it.

Le Lievre and Dennes v Gould [1893] 1 Q.B. 491, CA.

Lord Esher M.R.:

". . . No doubt the defendant did give untrue certificates; it was negligent on his part to do so, and it may even be called gross negligence. But can the plaintiffs rely upon negligence in the absence of fraud? The question of liability for negligence cannot arise at all until it is established that the man who has been negligent owed some duty to the person who seeks to make him liable for his negligence. What duty is there when there is no relation between the parties by contract? A man is entitled to be as negligent as he pleases towards the whole world if he owes no duty to them. The case of *Heaven v Pender* has no bearing upon the present question. That case established that, under certain circumstances, one man may owe a duty to another, even though there is no contract between them. If one man is near to another, or is near to the property of another, a duty lies upon him not to do that which may cause a personal injury to that other, or may injure his property. For instance, if a man is driving along a road, it is his duty not to do that which may injure another person whom he meets on the road, or to his horse or his carriage. In the same way it is the duty of a man not to do that which will injure the house of another to which he is near. If a man is driving on Salisbury Plain, and no other person is near him, he is at liberty to drive as fast and as recklessly as he pleases. But if he sees another carriage coming near to him, immediately a duty arises not to drive in such a way as is likely to cause an injury to that other carriage. So, too, if a man is driving along a street in a town, a similar duty not to drive carelessly arises out of contiguity or neighbourhood. That is the effect of the decision in *Heaven v Pender*, but it has no application to the present case. . . . A charge of fraud is such a terrible thing to bring against a man that it cannot be maintained in any Court unless it is shewn that he had a wicked mind. That is the effect of *Derry v Peek*. What is meant by a wicked mind? If a man tells a wilful falsehood, with the intention that it shall be acted upon by the person to whom he tells it, his mind is plainly wicked, and he must be said to be acting fraudulently. Again, a man must also be said to have a fraudulent mind if he recklessly makes a statement intending it to be acted upon, and not caring whether it be true or false. I do not hesitate to say that a man who thus acts must have a wicked mind. But negligence, however great, does not of itself constitute fraud. The official referee who tried this case and heard the evidence came to the conclusion that the defendant, though he had acted negligently, had not wilfully made any false statement, or been guilty of any fraud. All that he had done was to give untrue certificates negligently. Such negligence, in the absence of contract with the plaintiffs, can give no right of action at law or in equity. All the grounds urged on behalf of the plaintiffs fail, and the appeal must be dismissed."

---

[3] [1893] 1 Q.B. 491, CA.

- How does Lord Esher reformulate *Heaven v Pender* in light of the judgment of the House of Lords in *Derry v Peek*? How does Lord Esher distinguish the case of *Heaven v Pender*? How would you frame the *ratio* of Lord Esher's judgment in *Le Lievre v Gould*?

- The distinction between negligence and fraud is an important one. Fraud is a state of mind which is not easy to prove in court. Negligence, also a state of mind, implies carelessness (as opposed to "wickedness") and therefore is easier to establish.

- You may well have noticed an important feature of both *Derry v Peek* and *Le Lievre v Gould*. Unlike *Heaven v Pender*, the facts of these cases do not involve claimants who have been physically injured, nor has the property of the claimants been physically damaged. As a consequence, we say that these claimants have suffered "economic loss" rather than "physical damage". This is a vitally important distinction in the law of torts, one which you no doubt will spend a great deal of time grappling with in your tort law courses! For our purpose, the important point is that the judiciary has been very reluctant to allow recovery for "pure" economic loss in its various forms, for a number of reasons. The cases of *Derry v Peek* and *Le Lievre v Gould* provide early examples of that unwillingness. The cases demonstrate the power of judges to restrict or to encourage the development of doctrine.

THE DEVELOPMENT OF A GENERAL DUTY OF CARE

The development of a general duty of care—which as noted above the judiciary was reluctant to recognise—finally appeared to be accepted in what is widely viewed as the most famous and important negligence case in the common law world. It is a Scottish case and, as a consequence, some of the procedural terminology appears 'foreign' to English lawyers. However, its importance in the development of a general duty of care in negligence transcends its Scottish roots.

M'Alister (or Donoghue) (Pauper) v Stevenson **[1932] A.C. 562, HL.**

[By an action brought in the Court of Session the appellant, who was a shop assistant, sought to recover damages from the respondent, who was a manufacturer of aerated waters, for injuries she suffered as a result of consuming part of the contents of a bottle of ginger-beer which had been manufactured by the respondent, and which contained the decomposed remains of a snail. The appellant by her condescendence averred that the bottle of ginger-beer was purchased for the appellant by a friend in a café at Paisley, which was occupied by one Minchella; that the bottle was made of dark opaque glass and that the appellant had no reason to suspect that it contained anything but pure ginger-beer; that the said Minchella poured some of the ginger-beer out into a tumbler, and that the appellant drank some of the contents of the tumbler; that her friend was then proceeding to pour the remainder of the contents of the bottle into the tumbler when a snail, which was in a state of decomposition, floated out of the bottle; that as a result of the nauseating sight of the snail in such circumstances, and in consequence of the impurities in the ginger-beer which she had already consumed, the appellant suffered from shock and severe gastro-enteritis. The appellant further averred that the ginger-beer was manufactured by the respondent to be sold as a drink to the public (including the appellant); that it was bottled by the respondent and labelled by him with a label bearing his name; and that the bottles were thereafter sealed with a metal cap by the respondent. She further averred that it was the duty of the respondent to provide a system of working his business which would not allow snails to get into his ginger-beer bottles, and that it was also his duty to provide an efficient system of inspection of the bottles before the ginger-beer was filled into them, and that he had failed in both these duties and had so caused the accident.

The respondent objected that these averments were irrelevant and insufficient to support the conclusions of the summons.

The Lord Ordinary held that the averments disclosed a good cause of action and allowed a proof.

The Second Division by a majority (the Lord Justice-Clerk, Lord Ormidale, and Lord Anderson; Lord Hunter (dissenting) recalled the interlocutor of the Lord Ordinary and dismissed the action].

Lord Buckmaster (dissenting):

". . . In my view, therefore, the authorities are against the appellant's contention and apart from authority it is difficult to see how any common law proposition can be formulated to support her claim.

The principle contended for must be this—that the manufacturer, or, indeed, the repairer, of any article, apart entirely from contract, owes a duty to any person by whom the article is lawfully used to see that it has been carefully constructed. All rights in contract must be excluded from consideration of this principle, for such rights undoubtedly exist in successive steps from the original manufacturer down to the ultimate purchaser, embraced in the general rule that an article is warranted as reasonably fit for the purpose for which it is sold. Nor can the doctrine be confined to cases where inspection is difficult or impossible to introduce. This conception is simply to misapply to tort doctrines applicable to sale and purchase.

The principle of tort lies completely outside the region where such considerations apply, and the duty, if it exists, must extend to every person who, in lawful circumstances, uses the article made. There can be no special duty attaching to the manufacture of food, apart from those implied by contract or imposed by statute. If such a duty exists it seems to me it must cover the construction of every article, and I cannot see any reason why it should not apply to the construction of a house. If one step, why not 50? Yet if a house be, as it sometimes is, negligently built, and in consequence of that negligence the ceiling falls and injures the occupier or anyone else, no action against the builder exists according to English law, although I believe such a right did exist according to the laws of Babylon. Were such a principle known and recognised, it seems to me impossible, having regard to the numerous cases that must have arisen to persons injured by its disregard, that with the exception of *George v Skivington*[4] no case directly involving the principle has ever succeeded in the courts, and

[4] (1869) L.R. 5 Exch. 1.

were it well known and accepted much of the discussion of the earlier cases would have been waste of time. . . ."

Lord Atkin:

"My Lords, the sole question for determination in this case is legal: Do the averments made by the pursuer in her pleading, if true, disclose a cause of action? I need not restate the particular facts. The question is whether the manufacturer of an article of drink sold by him to a distributor, in circumstances which prevent the distributor or the ultimate purchaser or consumer from discovering by inspection any defect, is under any legal duty to the ultimate purchaser or consumer to take reasonable care that the article is free from defect likely to cause injury to health. I do not think a more important problem has occupied your Lordships in your judicial capacity: important both because of its bearing on public health and because of the practical test which it applies to the system under which it arises. The case has to be determined in accordance with Scots law; but it has been a matter of agreement between the experienced counsel who argued this case, and it appears to be the basis of the judgments of the learned judges of the Court of Session, that for the purposes of determining this problem the laws of Scotland and of England are the same. I speak with little authority on this point, but my own research, such as it is, satisfies me that the principles of the law of Scotland on such a question as the present are identical with those of English law; and I discuss the issue on that footing. The law of both countries appears to be that in order to support an action for damages for negligence the complainant has to show that he has been injured by the breach of a duty owed to him in the circumstances by the defendant to take reasonable care to avoid such injury. In the present case we are not concerned with the breach of the duty; if a duty exists, that would be a question of fact which is sufficiently averred and for present purposes must be assumed. We are solely concerned with the question whether, as a matter of law in the circumstances alleged, the defender owed any duty to the pursuer to take care.

It is remarkable how difficult it is to find in the English authorities statements of general application defining the relations between parties that give rise to the duty. The Courts are concerned with the particular relations which come before them in actual litigation, and it is sufficient to say whether the duty exists in those circumstances. The result is that the Courts have been engaged upon an elaborate classification of duties as they exist in respect of property, whether real or personal, with further divisions as to ownership, occupation or control, and distinctions based on the particular relations of the one side or the other, whether manufacturer, salesman or landlord, customer, tenant, stranger, and so on. In this way it can be ascertained at any time whether the law recognizes a duty, but only where the case can be referred to some particular species which has been examined and classified. And yet the duty which is common to all the cases where liability is established must logically be based upon some element common to the cases where it is found to exist. To seek a complete logical definition of the general principle is probably to go beyond the function of the judge, for the more general the definition the more likely it is to omit essentials or to introduce non-essentials. The attempt was made by Brett M.R. in *Heaven v Pender*, in a definition to which I will later refer. As framed, it was demonstrably too wide, although it appears to me, if properly limited, to be capable of affording a valuable practical guide.

At present I content myself with pointing out that in English law there must be, and is, some general conception of relations giving rise to a duty of care, of which the particular cases found in the books are but instances. The liability for negligence, whether you style it such or treat it as in other systems as a species of 'culpa,' is no doubt based upon a general public sentiment of moral wrongdoing for which the offender must pay. But acts or omissions which any moral code would censure cannot in a practical world be treated so as to give a right to every person injured by them to demand relief. In this way rules of law arise which limit the range of complainants and the extent of their remedy. The rule that you are to love your neighbour becomes in law, you must not injure your neighbour; and the lawyer's question, Who is my neighbour? Receives a restricted reply. You must take reasonable care to avoid acts or omissions which you can reasonably foresee would be likely to injure your neighbour. Who, then, in law is my neighbour? The answer seems to be—

persons who are so closely and directly affected by my act that I ought reasonably to have them in contemplation as being so affected when I am directing my mind to the acts or omissions which are called in question. This appears to me to be the doctrine of *Heaven v Pender*, as laid down by Lord Esher (then Brett M.R.) when it is limited by the notion of proximity introduced by Lord Esher himself and A.L. Smith L.J. in *Le Lievre v Gould*. Lord Esher says: 'That case established that, under certain circumstances, one man may owe a duty to another, even though there is no contract between them. If one man is near to another, or is near to the property of another, a duty lies upon him not to do that which may cause a personal injury to that other, or may injure his property.' So A.L. Smith L.J.: 'The decision of *Heaven v Pender* was founded upon the principle, that a duty to take due care did arise when the person or property of one was in such proximity to the person or property of another that, if due care was not taken, damage might be done by the one to the other.' I think that this sufficiently states the truth if proximity be not confined to mere physical proximity, but be used, as I think it was intended, to extend to such close and direct relations that the act complained of directly affects a person whom the person alleged to be bound to take care would know would be directly affected by his careless act. That this is the sense in which nearness or 'proximity' was intended by Lord Esher is obvious from his own illustration in *Heaven v Pender* of the application of his doctrine to the sale of goods. 'This' (i.e. the rule he has just formulated) 'includes the case of goods, etc., supplied to be used immediately by a particular person or persons, or one of a class of persons, where it would be obvious to the person supplying, if he thought, that the goods would in all probability be used at once by such persons before a reasonable opportunity for discovering any defect which might exist, and where the thing supplied would be of such a nature that a neglect of ordinary care or skill as to its condition or the manner of supplying it would probably cause danger to the person or property of the person for whose use it was supplied, and who was about to use it. It would exclude a case in which the goods are supplied under circumstances in which it would be a chance by whom they would be used or whether they would be used or not, or whether they would be used before there would probably be means of observing any defect, or where the goods would be of such a nature that a want of care or skill as to their condition or the manner of supplying them would not probably produce danger of injury to person or property.' I draw particular attention to the fact that Lord Esher emphasizes the necessity of goods having to be 'used immediately' and 'used at once before a reasonable opportunity of inspection.' This is obviously to exclude the possibility of goods having their condition altered by lapse of time, and to call attention to the proximate relationship, which may be too remote where inspection even of the person using, certainly of an intermediate person, may reasonably be interposed. With this necessary qualification of proximate relationship as explained in *Le Lievre v Gould*, I think the judgment of Lord Esher expresses the law of England; without the qualification, I think the majority of the Court in *Heaven v Pender* were justified in thinking the principle was expressed in too general terms. There will no doubt arise cases where it will be difficult to determine whether the contemplated relationship is so close that the duty arises. But in the class of case now before the Court I cannot conceive any difficulty to arise. A manufacturer puts up an article of food in a container which he knows will be opened by the actual consumer. There can be no inspection by any purchaser and no reasonable preliminary inspection by the consumer. Negligently, in the course of preparation, he allows the contents to be mixed with poison. It is said that the law of England and Scotland is that the poisoned consumer has no remedy against the negligent manufacturer. If this were the result of the authorities, I should consider the result a grave defect in the law, and so contrary to principle that I should hesitate long before following any decision to that effect which had not the authority of this House. I would point out that, in the assumed state of the authorities, not only would the consumer have no remedy against the manufacturer, he would have none against any one else, for in the circumstances alleged there would be no evidence of negligence against any one other than the manufacturer; and, except in the case of a consumer who was also a purchaser, no contract and no warranty of fitness, and in the case of the purchase of a specific article under its patent or trade name, which might well be the case in the purchase of some articles of food or drink, no warranty protecting even the purchaser-consumer. There are other instances than of articles of food and drink where goods are sold intended to be used immediately by the consumer, such as many forms of goods sold for cleaning purposes, where the same liability must exist. The doctrine supported by the decision below would not only deny a remedy to the consumer who was injured by consuming bottled beer or chocolates poisoned by the negligence of the manufacturer, but also to the user of what should be a harmless proprietary medicine, an ointment, a soap, a cleaning fluid or cleaning powder. I confine myself to articles of common household use, where every one, including the manufacturer, knows that the articles will be used by other persons than the actual ultimate purchaser—namely, by members of his family and his servants, and in some cases his guests. I do not think so ill of our jurisprudence as to suppose that its principles are so remote from the ordinary needs of civilized society and the ordinary claims it makes upon its members as to deny a legal remedy where there is so obviously a social wrong. . . .

If your Lordships accept the view that the appellant's pleading discloses a relevant cause of action, you will be affirming the proposition that by Scots and English law alike a manufacturer of products which he sells in such a form as to show that he intends them to reach the ultimate consumer in the form in which they left him, with no reasonable possibility of intermediate examination, and with the knowledge that the absence of reasonable care in the preparation or putting up of the products will result in injury to the consumer's life or property, owes a duty to the consumer to take that reasonable care.

It is a proposition that I venture to say no one in Scotland or England who was not a lawyer would for one moment doubt. It will be an advantage to make it clear that the law in this matter, as in most others, is in accordance with sound common sense. I think that this appeal should be allowed."

Lord Thankerton:

". . . We are not dealing here with a case of what is called an article *per se* dangerous or one which was known by the defender to be dangerous, in which cases a special duty of protection or adequate warning is placed upon the person who uses or distributes it. The present case is that of a manufacturer and a consumer, with whom he has no contractual relation, of an article which the manufacturer did not know to be dangerous, and, unless the consumer can establish a special relationship with the manufacturer, it is clear, in my opinion, that neither the law of Scotland nor the law of England will hold that the manufacturer has any duty towards the consumer to exercise diligence. In such a case the remedy of the consumer, if any, will lie against the intervening party from whom he has procured the article. . . .

The special circumstances, from which the appellant claims that such a relationship of duty should be inferred, may, I think, be stated thus, namely, that the respondent, in placing his manufactured article of drink upon the market, has intentionally so excluded interference with, or examination of, the article by any intermediate handler of the goods between himself and the consumer that he has, of his own accord, brought himself into direct relationship with the consumer, with the result that the consumer is entitled to rely upon the exercise of diligence by the manufacturer to secure that the article shall not be harmful to the consumer. If that contention be sound, the consumer, on her showing that the article has reached her intact, and that she has been injured by the harmful nature of the article owing to the failure of the manufacturer to take reasonable care in its preparation before its enclosure in the sealed vessel, will be entitled to reparation from the manufacturer.

In my opinion, the existence of a legal duty in such circumstances is in conformity with the principles of both the law of Scotland and the law of England. The English cases demonstrate how impossible it is finally to catalogue, amid the ever-varying types of human relationships, those relationships in which a duty to exercise care arises apart from contract, and each of these cases relates to its own set of circumstances, out of which it was claimed that the duty had arisen. In none of these cases were the circumstances identical with the present case as regards that which I regard as the essential element in this case, namely, the manufacturer's own action in bringing himself into direct relationship with the party injured."

[Lord Thankerton would allow the appeal.]

Lord Macmillan:
". . . The law takes no cognizance of carelessness in the abstract. It concerns itself with carelessness only where there is a duty to take care and where failure in that duty has caused damage. In such circumstances carelessness assumes the legal quality of negligence and entails the consequences in law of negligence. What then are the circumstances which give rise to this duty to take care? In the daily contacts of social and business life human beings are thrown into or place themselves in an infinite variety of relationships with their fellows, and the law can refer only to the standards of the reasonable man in order to determine whether any particular relationship gives rise to a duty to take care as between those who stand in that relationship to each other. The grounds of action may be as various and manifold as human errancy, and the conception of legal responsibility may develop in adaptation to altering social conditions and standards. The criterion of judgment must adjust and adapt itself to the changing circumstances of life. The categories of negligence are never closed. The cardinal principle of liability is that the party complained of should owe to the party complaining a duty to take care and that the party complaining should be able to prove that he has suffered damage in consequence of a breach of that duty. Where there is room for diversity of view is in determining what circumstances will establish such a relationship between the parties as to give rise on the one side to a duty to take care and on the other side to a right to have care taken.

To descend from these generalities to the circumstances of the present case I do not think that any reasonable man or any twelve reasonable men would hesitate to hold that if the appellant establishes her allegations the respondent has exhibited carelessness in the conduct of his business. For a manufacturer of aerated water to store his empty bottles in a place where snails can get access to them and to fill his bottles without taking any adequate precautions by inspection or otherwise to ensure that they contain no deleterious foreign matter may reasonably be characterised as carelessness without applying too exacting a standard. But, as I have pointed out, it is not enough to prove the respondent to be careless in his process of manufacture. The question is: Does he owe a duty to take care, and to whom does he owe that duty? I have no hesitation in affirming that a person who for gain engages in the business of manufacturing articles of food and drink intended for consumption by members of the public in the form in which he issues them is under a duty to take care in the manufacture of these articles. That duty, in my opinion, he owes to those whom he intends to consume his products. He manufactures his commodities for human consumption; he intends and contemplates that they shall be consumed. By reason of that very fact he places himself in a relationship with all the potential consumers of his commodities, and that relationship, which he assumes and desires for his own ends, imposes upon him a duty to take care to avoid injuring them. He owes them a duty not to convert by his own carelessness an article which he issues to them as wholesome and innocent into an article which is dangerous to life and health.

It is sometimes said that liability can arise only where a reasonable man would have foreseen and could have avoided the consequences of his act or omission. In the present case the respondent, when he manufactured his ginger-beer, had directly in contemplation that it would be consumed by members of the public. Can it be said that he could not be expected as a reasonable man to foresee that if he conducted his process of manufacture carelessly he might injure those whom he expected and desired to consume his ginger-beer? The possibility of injury so arising seems to me in no sense so remote as to excuse him from foreseeing it. Suppose that a baker through carelessness allows a large quantity of arsenic to be mixed with a batch of his bread, with the result that those who subsequently eat it are poisoned, could he be heard to say that he owed no duty to the consumers of his bread to take care that it was free from poison, and that, as he did not know that any poison had got into it, his only liability was for breach of warranty under his contract of sale to those who actually bought the poisoned bread from him? Observe that I have said 'through carelessness' and thus excluded the cases of a pure accident such as may happen where every care is taken. I cannot believe, and I do not believe, that neither in the law of England nor in the law of Scotland is there redress for such a case. The state of facts I have figured might well give rise to a criminal charge, and the civil consequences of such carelessness can scarcely be less wide than its criminal consequences. Yet the principle of the decision appealed from is that the manufacturer of food products intended by him for human consumption does not owe to the consumers whom he has in view any duty of care, not even the duty to take care that he does not poison them.

. . . It must always be a question of circumstances whether the carelessness amounts to negligence and whether the injury is not too remote from the carelessness. I can readily conceive that where a manufacturer has parted with his product and it has passed into other hands it may well be exposed to vicissitudes which may render it defective or noxious and for which the manufacturer could not in any view be held to be to blame. It may be a good general rule to regard responsibility as ceasing when control ceases. So also where between the manufacturer and the user there is interposed a party who has the means and opportunity of examining the manufacturer's product before he reissues it to the actual user. But where, as in the present case, the article of consumption is so prepared as to be intended to reach the consumer in the condition in which it leaves the manufacturer and the manufacturer takes steps to ensure this by sealing or otherwise closing the container, so that the contents cannot be tampered with, I regard his control as remaining effective until the article reaches the consumer and the container is opened by him. The intervention of any exterior agency is intended to be excluded, and was in fact in the present case excluded. It is doubtful whether in such a case there is any redress against the retailer."

[Lord Macmillan would allow the appeal.]
[Lord Tomlin (dissenting) delivered reasons for dismissing the appeal.]

NOTES AND QUESTIONS

- What are the material facts of *Donoghue v Stevenson*? What is the legal issue?

- Note that the factual question—whether *in fact* there was a snail in the ginger beer—was never considered, as the case did not go to trial. The judgment deals with the prior question whether, even if the facts are true, there is any cause of action. Thus, the Law Lords, for the purposes of argument on this point, assumed the facts as alleged by the claimant to be true. Had the case then gone to trial, those factual allegations would have had to be proven.

- The majority consisted of three Law Lords. How would you state the *ratio decidendi* of the case? Are there a variety of ways in which it can be stated? List a series of different possible *ratios*, in order of their breadth of scope. Do Lords Atkin, Macmillan and Thankerton seem to be in agreement as to what their ruling in this case stands for?

- Does Lord Atkin's formulation of the duty of care in negligence differ from Lord Esher's formulation in *Le Lievre v Gould*? If so, how?

- The judgments in *Donoghue v Stevenson* again exemplify the point made earlier in this chapter: that the history of negligence in this country is a story of tension between the imposition of a general duty of care, and a number of discrete duties applicable to different situations. Try to find specific references to this tension in the various judgments in *Donoghue v Stevenson*.

- For further reading on the internal history of negligence law, see P.H. Winfield, "The History of Negligence in the Law of Torts" (1926) 42 L.Q.R. 184; and, for a critical analysis of the impact of *Donoghue v Stevenson*, see J.C. Smith and P. Burns, "Donoghue v Stevenson—The Not so Golden Anniversary" (1983) 46 M.L.R. 147.

Although you were asked to state the *ratio decidendi* of *Donoghue v Stevenson*, you should not be concerned if you found no easy answer to the question! In fact, it was pointed out by Heuston, on the 25th anniversary of the decision, that the determination of the *ratio* of *Donoghue v Stevenson* is a far from straightforward task.

R.F.V. Heuston, "*Donoghue v Stevenson* in Retrospect" (1957) 20 M.L.R. 1 at 5:

The *ratio decidendi* of the case

"The ascertainment of the *ratio decidendi* of any decision given by an appellate court in the course of which several judgments have been delivered is notoriously a difficult task. One problem may be disposed of at once. It was agreed between counsel and stated by the judges in all the courts that the relevant principles of Scots and English law were identical. Now it has always been assumed that in such a case a decision of the House of Lords on an appeal from the Court of Session is binding on all courts in the English hierarchy. Those who adhere to a mechanical test for distinguishing *ratio decidendi* from *obiter dictum* would no doubt be obliged to deny this, for in a Scots appeal the only issue in the case is Scots law, and any statement as to the meaning or effect of English law must necessarily be *obiter*. It seems safer to say that the principles stated in *Donoghue v Stevenson* have been universally recognised to be authoritative in England as well as in Scotland, and to turn to the more difficult task of discovering what those principles are. Lord Wright has appropriately referred to the decision to illustrate the proposition that 'Notwithstanding all the apparatus of authority, the judge has nearly always some degree of choice. . . . The higher the court, the less is the decisive weight of authority and the freer the choice.' On the assumption that it is possible to draw from a given decision as many general propositions as there are possible combinations of distinguishable facts, Professor Stone has observed that the decision could be restricted to mean that there is a duty not to sell opaque bottles of beverage containing dead snails to Scots widows, or expanded to mean that there is a duty not to distribute defective objects of any kind whatsoever which cause damage of any kind to any person into whose hands the object may come.

Now as between the parties themselves there can be no doubt that the case decided that if the pursuer could prove that which she averred she would have a good cause of action. So the case decided at least something to do with the duty owed by a supplier of chattels. There are some authorities who would deny that the case decided any more. This appears to have been the view taken by the experienced reporter who framed the 'somewhat conservatively worded headnote,' and in several later cases we find clear statements that the *ratio decidendi* is so confined. Nevertheless there has been a persistent belief that the case is authority for something more. Lord Normand has put this most clearly. 'The argument for the defender was that there were certain relationships, such as physical proximity or contract, which alone give rise to duties in the law of quasi-delict or tort, and that the relationship between the pursuer and defender was not one of them.' The decision was that the categories of negligence are not closed and that duties of care are owed, not only to physical neighbours, but to anyone who is 'my neighbour' in the wider sense, as stated by Lord

Atkin, 'of a person . . . "so closely and directly affected by my act that I ought reasonably to have (him) in contemplation as being so affected when I am directing my mind to the acts or omissions which are called in question."' This is the neighbour principle so familiar to us all. Our inquiry at the moment is limited to discovering how far this principle can fairly be said to form a, or part of the, *ratio decidendi* of the judgment of (i) Lord Atkin himself, (ii) the majority of the House of Lords.

(i) A fair reading of the whole judgment in its context, not concentrating on this or that passage to the exclusion of others, makes it plain that Lord Atkin intended to show (a) that the liability of a supplier of chattels is not limited to cases in which the parties are in physical proximity to each other: a duty of care may exist even in the absence of spatial or temporal 'proximity' if there is a probability of harm inherent in the relationship of the parties, and the facts of the case before him provided a model for such a relationship; (b) that 'there must be, and is, some general conception of relations giving rise to a duty of care, of which the particular cases found in the books are but instances.' He then states the 'neighbour principle' in the term which we have already cited, and concludes that this 'appears to me to be the doctrine of *Heaven v Pender* as laid down by Lord Esher when it is limited by the notion of proximity introduced by Lord Esher himself and A.L. Smith L.J. in *Le Lievre v Gould*.' It is impracticable to draw a clear line anywhere between the two parts of the judgment. The reasoning is everywhere dovetailed and interlocked. The neighbour principle is part of the *ratio decidendi* of Lord Atkin's judgment, for it is a step in the argument, a vital link in the chain of reasoning which led to the formulation of the principle about manufacturers' liability. The significance to be attached to the neighbour principle will be discussed in detail later: it is enough to say here that it has been accepted by many as showing that *Donoghue v Stevenson* provides a general criterion of liability—at least in the tort of negligence, and possibly throughout the whole field of tort. So that when Dean Wright tells us that 'Whether that decision will be expanded into a broad revolutionary principle or confined to a narrow category is one of the most important decisions that modern courts must make' it seems clear that he is not referring only to the part of the decision which deals with manufacturers' liability. Even those who, like Mr Landon, say that 'all that *Donoghue v Stevenson* has done is to add a new category of negligence to our law' have been obliged to meet the argument that at least one law lord attempted to state the principle upon which such an addition had been made.

(ii) Whatever the status of the 'neighbour principle' in Lord Atkin's own judgment, it hardly seems possible to say that it forms part of the *ratio decidendi* of the decision, for the two other members of the majority seem to have been careful to avoid expressing their concurrence with it. Lord Thankerton said that he agreed with Lord Atkin's speech, but it is the proper inference from the context of this remark that his agreement was confined to that part of the speech which analyses the English cases on manufacturers' liability. In any case, he expressly said that it was impossible to catalogue finally the circumstances in which a duty of care might arise. Lord Macmillan recognised that new duties might be created— 'the categories of negligence are never closed'—but maintained a cautious silence about the principle or principles upon which this might be done.

Two further points may be made. First, it is preferable to refer to this particular part of the judgment as enshrining a 'principle' and not a 'rule.' The former word connotes a degree of flexibility and adaptability which the latter does not. 'A principle is the broad reason which lies at the base of a rule of law: it has not exhausted itself in giving birth to that particular rule but is still fertile.' If, as is generally believed, Lord Atkin's judgment forms a guide for the future as well as an appraisal of the past, it is best to describe it in a way which will enable us to use its potentialities to the utmost. Secondly, there seems to be little profit in an attempt to discover the sources of the ideas expounded in the neighbour principle. Lord Atkin himself expressly refers to Lord Esher and indirectly to the lawyer's question to Jesus which inspired the story of the Good Samaritan. . . .

The conclusion is that there are four propositions for which the case commonly is (or can be) cited as authority: (1) that negligence is a distinct tort; (2) that the absence of privity of contract between plaintiff and defendant does not preclude liability in tort; (3) that manufacturers of products owe a duty of care to the ultimate consumer or user; and (4) that the criterion of the existence of a duty in the law of negligence (or perhaps in any part of the law of tort) is whether the defendant ought reasonably to have foreseen that his acts or omissions would be likely to result in damage to the plaintiff. Of these, only the second and third, and possibly the first, can truly be said to form part of the *ratio decidendi* of the decision. The fourth proposition, although perhaps the most commonly cited and in many ways the most significant, cannot properly be regarded a part of the *ratio decidendi* of the decision. No amount of posthumous citation can of itself transfer with retrospective effect a proposition from the status of *obiter dictum* to that of *ratio decidendi*; no doubt it will serve to magnify greatly the interest and importance of the case, but that is another matter."

Given the variety of propositions for which the case of *Donoghue v Stevenson* might stand, it should seem increasingly clear to you that the *ratio* of a case is a fairly flexible concept. In fact, it could be argued that we can only approach a definitive *ratio* in light of how a case is interpreted by courts. The idea that there is necessarily a single, clear, and uncontentious *ratio* to any given case thus becomes unsustainable, as MacCormick illustrates using the example of *Donoghue v Stevenson*.

Neil MacCormick, *Legal Reasoning and Legal Theory* (Clarendon Press, Oxford, 1978), pp.84–86:

"[T]here is a possibility that some precedents contain relatively clear rulings on fairly sharply defined points of law, and that others contain implicit rulings of similar, but perhaps less, relative clarity. Yet others because of judicial disagreement or simply confusion contain none. It is only a dogmatic fiction that the third class has anything which could reasonably be called a *ratio* at all, and the truth is that in relation to that type of case even the most rigid doctrine of binding precedent cannot in practice obligate the judge in a later case to do more than find some 'explanatory' proposition which is consistent with the actual decision of the precedent case and also relevant to the instant case; all the better if his 'explanatory' proposition squares in some degree with some at least of what was said in the confused or conflicting opinion or opinions given in the precedent.

It should be remarked also that even where an express ruling is given encapsulating the kind of 'proposition' wherewith Lord Atkin concluded his speech in *Donoghue*, the doctrine of precedent even in its English form leaves the subsequent court with a significant 'explanative' discretion: it is at best the proposition, not the particular words in which it was couched, that is binding. Therefore the later Court is free to re-express the proposition, together with further conditions or qualifications which may be deemed appropriate to novel types of circumstance as revealed by the later case. That the norms of the system leave its operators with that discretion gives interpreters of the system a problem which has sometimes been mistakenly supposed to be more than a problem of words: in *Donoghue v Stevenson* a certain 'proposition' was laid down about the manufacturer's duty to consumers of his products; in *Haseldine v Daw* ([1941] 2 KB 343; [1941] 3 All E.R. 156) for example, the negligent repair of a defective lift was brought within the doctrine and the repairers held liable to those injured in its collapse (observe that the dissents of Lords Tomlin and Buckmaster had dealt with the case of repairers, though none of the affirming majority did); is the 'ratio' of *Donoghue v Stevenson* the explicit ruling as given by the judges in *Donoghue* itself, or that ruling as re-expressed and extended in *Haseldine*?

The only observation I wish to make is that answering that question does not add to our knowledge of the real world at all. All that it does is to stipulate a particular usage for the technical term *ratio*, which is in fact somewhat ambiguous in its ordinary use, precisely because it is variably used in practice. Sometimes it is used as referring to the proposition as actually laid down in the original decision of a case, sometimes to that proposition as explained reinterpreted qualified or whatever in later cases.

There is not the least probability of any stipulation by me determining usage, so I offer none; I only observe that among judges and practitioners the predominant operational usage of the term *ratio* seems to be as referring to express statements of propositions of law made by judges in their justifying opinion in recorded cases, and (if my opinion matters) that seems to be the least confusing usage available for the term."

MacCormick makes the important point that often the *ratio* of a case can only be determined in light of what judges subsequently make of it. That is particularly apt in the case of *Donoghue v Stevenson*. The central question of whether the majority of the Lords sought to establish a general duty of care in negligence only can be answered by examining how other courts then applied their reasoning. Four years after *Donoghue v Stevenson*, an indication of its scope—as applying more broadly than, for example, to common household goods or food and beverage—was apparent in a judgment of the Judicial Committee of the Privy Council. In reading this excerpt, think about how the material facts may be similar to those in *Donoghue v Stevenson*, despite their superficial difference.

Grant v Australian Knitting Mills Ltd [1936] A.C. 85, PC.

Lord Wright:
"The appellant is a fully qualified medical man practising at Adelaide in South Australia. He brought his action against the respondents, claiming damages on the ground that he had contracted dermatitis by reason of the improper condition of underwear purchased by him from the respondents, John Martin & Co., Ld, and manufactured by the respondents, the Australian Knitting Mills, Ld. The case was tried by Sir George Murray, Chief Justice of South Australia, who, after a trial lasting for twenty days, gave judgment for the appellant against both respondents for 245l and costs. On appeal the High Court of Australia set aside that judgment by a majority. Evatt J. dissented, and agreed in the result with the Chief Justice though he differed in regard to the Sale of Goods Act, 1895. Of the majority, the reasoning of Dixon J., with whom McTiernan J. concurred, was in effect that the evidence was not sufficient to make it safe to find for the appellant. Starke J., who accepted substantially all the detailed findings of the Chief Justice, differed from him on his general conclusions of liability based on these findings.

The appellant's claim was that the disease was caused by the presence, in the cuffs or ankle ends of the underpants which he purchased and wore, of an irritating chemical, namely, free sulphite, the presence of which was due to negligence in manufacture, and also involved on the part of the respondents, John Martin & Co., Ltd, a breach of the relevant implied conditions under the Sale of Goods Act.

The underwear, consisting of two pairs of underpants and two singlets, was bought by the appellant at the shop of the respondents, John Martin & Co., Ld, who dealt in such goods, and who will be hereafter referred to as 'the retailers,' on June 3, 1931. The retailers had in ordinary course at some previous date purchased them with other stock from the respondents, the Australian Kntting Mills, Ld, who will be referred to as the manufacturers; the garments were of that class of the manufacturers' make known as Golden Fleece. The appellant put on one suit on the morning of Sunday, June 28, 1931; by the evening of that day he felt itching on the ankles but no objective symptoms appeared until the next day, when a redness appeared on each ankle in front of an area of about two and a half inches by one and a half inches. The appellant treated himself with calamine lotion, but the irritation was such that he scratched the places till he bled. On Sunday, July 5, he changed his underwear and put on the other set which he had purchased from the retailers; the first set was washed and when the appellant changed his garments again on the following Sunday he put on the washed set and sent the others to the wash; he changed again on July 12. Though his skin trouble was getting worse, he did not attribute it to the underwear, but on July 13 he consulted a dermatologist, Dr Upton, who advised him to discard the underwear, which he did, returning the garments to the retailers with the intimation that they had given him dermatitis; by that time one set had been washed twice and the other set once. The appellant's condition got worse and worse; he was confined to bed from July 21 for seventeen weeks; the rash became generalized and very acute. In November he became convalescent and went to New Zealand to recuperate. He returned in the following February, and felt sufficiently recovered to resume his practice, but soon had a relapse, and by March his condition was so serious that he went in April into hospital, where he remained until July. Meantime, in April, 1932, he commenced this action, which was tried in and after November of that year. Dr Upton was his medical attendant throughout and explained in detail at the trial the course of the illness and the treatment he adopted. Dr de Crespigny also attended the appellant from and after July 22, 1931, and gave evidence at the trial. The illness was most severe, involving acute suffering, and at times Dr Upton feared that his patient might die.

It is impossible here to examine in detail the minute and conflicting evidence of fact and of expert opinion given at the trial: all that evidence was meticulously discussed at the hearing of the appeal before the Board. It is only possible to state briefly the conclusions at which the Lordships, after careful consideration, have arrived.

[Lord Wright reviewed the evidence and concluded that the Chief Justice's findings of fact at trial should be upheld]. . . .

That conclusion means that the disease contracted, and the damage suffered by the appellant, were caused by the defective condition of the garments which the retailers sold to him, and which the manufacturers made and put forth for retail and indiscriminate sale. The Chief Justice gave judgments against both respondents, against the retailers on the contract of sale, and against the manufacturers in tort, on the basis of the decision in the House of Lords in *Donoghue v Stevenson*. The liability of each respondent depends on a different cause of action, though it is for the same damage. It is not claimed that the appellant should recover his damage twice over; no objection is raised on the part of the respondents to the form of the judgment, which was against both respondents for a single amount.

So far as concerns the retailers, Mr Greene conceded that if it were held that the garments contained improper chemicals and caused the disease, the retailers were liable for breach of implied warranty, or rather condition, under s.14 of the South Australia Sale of Goods Act, 1895, which is identical with s.14 of the English Sale of Goods Act, 1893. . . .

The retailers, accordingly, in their Lordships' judgment are liable in contract: so far as they are concerned, no question of negligence is relevant to the liability in contract. But when the position of the manufacturers is considered, different questions arise: there is no privity of contract between the appellant and the manufacturers: between them the liability, if any, must be in tort, and the gist of the cause of action is negligence. The facts set out in the foregoing show, in their Lordships' judgment, negligence in manufacture. According to the evidence, the method of manufacture was correct: the danger of excess sulphites being left was recognized and was guarded against: the process was intended to be fool proof. If excess sulphites were left in the garment, that could only be because some one was at fault. The appellant is not required to lay his finger on the exact person in all the chain who was responsible, or to specify what he did wrong. Negligence is found as a matter of inference from the existence of the defects taken in connection with all the known circumstances: even if the manufacturers could by apt evidence have rebutted that inference they have not done so

[Lord Wright went on to consider the relevance of *Donoghue v Stevenson*]. . . .

It is clear that the decision treats negligence, where there is a duty to take care, as a specific tort in itself, and not simply as an element in some more complex relationship or in some specialized breach of duty, and still less as having any dependence on contract. All that is necessary as a step to establish the tort of actionable negligence is to define the precise relationship from which the duty to take care is to be deduced. It is, however, essential in English law that the duty should be established: the mere fact that a man is injured by another's act gives in itself no cause of action: if the act is deliberate, the party injured will have no claim in law even though the injury is intentional, so long as the other party is merely exercising a legal right: if the act involves lack of due care, again no case of actionable negligence will arise unless the duty to be careful exists. In *Donoghue's* case the duty was deduced simply from the facts relied on — namely, that the injured party was one of a class for whose use, in the contemplation and intention of the makers, the article was issued to the world, and the article was used by that party in the state in which it was prepared and issued without it being changed in any way and without there being any warning of, or means of detecting, the hidden danger: there was, it is true, no personal intercourse between the maker and the user; but though the duty is personal, because it is *inter partes*, it needs no interchange of words, spoken or written, or signs of offer or assent; it is thus different in character from any contractual relationship; no question of consideration between the parties is relevant: for these reasons the use of the word 'privity' in this connection is apt to mislead, because of the suggestion of some overt relationship like that in contract, and the word 'proximity' is open to the same objection; if the term 'proximity' is to be applied at all, it can only be in the sense that the want of care and the injury are in essence directly and intimately connected; though there may be intervening transactions of sale and purchase, and intervening handling between these two events, the events are themselves unaffected by what happened between them: 'proximity' can only properly be used to exclude any element of remoteness, or of some interfering complication between the want of care and the injury, and like 'privity' may mislead by introducing alien ideas. Equally also may the word 'control' embarrass, though it is conveniently used in the opinions in *Donoghue's* case to emphasize the essential factor that the consumer must use the article exactly as it left the maker, that is in all material features, and use it as it was intended to be used. In that sense the maker may be said to control the thing until it is used. But that again is an artificial use, because, in the natural sense of the word, the makers parted with all control when they sold the article and divested themselves of possession and property. An argument used in the present case based on the word 'control' will be noticed later.

It is obvious that the principles thus laid down involve a duty based on the simple facts detailed above, a duty quite unaffected by any contracts dealing with the thing, for instance, of sale by maker to retailer, and again by retailer to consumer or to the consumer's friend.

It may be said that the duty is difficult to define, because when the act of negligence in manufacture occurs there was no specific person towards whom the duty could be said to exist: the thing might never be used: it might be destroyed by accident, or it might be scrapped, or in many ways fails to come into use in the normal way: in other words the duty cannot at the time of manufacture be other than potential or contingent, and only can become vested by the fact of actual use by a particular person. But the same theoretical difficulty has been disregarded in cases like *Heaven v Pender*, or in the case of things dangerous *per se* or known to be dangerous . . . . In *Donoghue's* case the thing was dangerous in fact, though the danger was hidden, and the thing was dangerous only because of want of care in making it; as Lord Atkin points out in *Donoghue's* case, the distinction between things inherently dangerous and things only dangerous because of negligent manufacture cannot be regarded as significant for the purpose of the questions here involved.

One further point may be noted. The principle of *Donoghue's* case can only be applied where the defect is hidden and unknown to the consumer, otherwise the directness of cause and effect is absent: the man who consumes or uses a thing which he knows to be noxious cannot complain in respect of whatever mischief follows, because it follows from his own conscious volition in choosing to incur the risk or certainty of mischance.

If the foregoing are the essential features of *Donoghue's* case, they are also to be found, in their Lordships' judgment, in the present case. The presence of the deleterious chemical in the pants, due to negligence in manufacture, was a hidden and latent defect, just as much as were the remains of the snail in the opaque bottle: it could not be detected by any examination that could reasonably be made. Nothing happened between the making of the garments and their being worn to change their condition. The garments were made by the manufacturers for the purpose of being worn exactly as they were worn in fact by the appellant: it was not contemplated that they should be first washed. It is immaterial that the appellant had a claim in contract against the retailers, because that is a quite independent cause of action, based on different considerations, even though the damage may be the same. Equally irrelevant is any question of liability between the retailers and the manufacturers on the contract of sale between them. The tort liability is independent of any question of contract.

It was argued, but not perhaps very strongly, that *Donoghue*'s case was a case of food or drink to be consumed internally, whereas the pants here were to be worn externally. No distinction, however, can be logically drawn for this purpose between a noxious thing taken internally and a noxious thing applied externally: the garments were made to be worn next the skin: indeed Lord Atkin specifically puts as examples of what is covered by the principle he is enunciating things operating externally, such as 'an ointment, a soap, a cleaning fluid or cleaning powder.'

Mr Greene, however, sought to distinguish *Donoghue*'s case from the present on the ground that in the former the makers of the ginger-beer had retained 'control' over it in the sense that they had placed it in stoppered and sealed bottles, so that it would not be tampered with until it was opened to be drunk, whereas the garments in question were merely put into paper packets, each containing six sets, which in ordinary course would be taken down by the shopkeeper and opened, and the contents handled and disposed of separately, so that they would be exposed to the air. He contended that though there was no reason to think that the garments when sold to the appellant were in any other condition, least of all as regards sulphur contents, than when sold to the retailers by the manufacturers, still the mere possibility and not the fact of their condition having been changed was sufficient to distinguish *Donoghue*'s case: there was no 'control' because nothing was done by the manufacturers to exclude the possibility of any tampering while the goods were on their way to the user. Their Lordships do not accept that contention. The decision in *Donoghue*'s case did not depend on the bottle being stoppered and sealed: the essential point in this regard was that the article should reach the consumer or user subject to the same defect as it had when it left the manufacturer. That this was true of the garment is in their Lordships' opinion beyond question. At most there might in other cases be a greater difficulty of proof of the fact.

Mr Greene further contended on behalf of the manufacturers that if the decision in *Donoghue*'s case were extended even a hair's-breadth, no line could be drawn, and a manufacturer's liability would be extended indefinitely. He put as an illustration the case of a foundry which had cast a rudder to be fitted on a liner: he assumed that it was fitted and the steamer sailed the seas for some years: but the rudder had a latent defect due to faulty and negligent casting, and one day it broke, with the result that the vessel was wrecked, with great loss of life and damage to property. He argued that if *Donoghue*'s case were extended beyond its precise facts, the maker of the rudder would be held liable for damages of an indefinite amount, after an indefinite time, and to claimants indeterminate until the event. But it is clear that such a state of things would involve many considerations far removed from the simple facts of this case. So many contingencies must have intervened between the lack of care on the part of the makers and the casualty that it may be that the law would apply, as it does in proper cases, not always according to strict logic, the rule that cause and effect must not be too remote: in any case the element of directness would obviously be lacking. . . .

In their Lordships' opinion it is enough for them to decide this case on its actual facts. No doubt many difficult problems will arise before the precise limits of the principle are defined: many qualifying conditions and many complications of fact may in the future come before the Courts for decision. It is enough now to say that their Lordships hold the present case to come within the principle of *Donoghue*'s case, and they think that the judgment of the Chief Justice was right in the result and should be restored as against both respondents, and that the appeal should be allowed, with costs here and in the Courts below, and that the appellant's petition for leave to adduce further evidence should be dismissed, without costs."

- The case of *Grant v Australian Knitting Mills* usefully illustrates how the breadth of *Donoghue v Stevenson* was a live issue at that time. In what ways (sometimes imaginatively) did counsel for Australian Knitting Mills try to convince the Law Lords that the *ratio decidendi* should be read narrowly, so that the facts of *Grant* could be distinguished from *Donoghue v Stevenson*? What responses to those arguments were made by Lord Wright? Note in particular the "floodgates argument" made by counsel (that is, if this case is decided in favour of the appellant, the floodgate of claims will be opened). How did Lord Wright respond?

- To what extent does it appear, on reading *Grant v Australian Knitting Mills*, that a general principle of liability was emerging within English law?

- The tension between a general principle of liability and specific duties giving rise to liability continued. For example, in *Deyong v Shenburn* [1946] 1 K.B. 227, CA, a case which concerned stolen garments and a pantomime dame, Du Parcq, L.J. held:

  > "There are well-known words of Lord Atkin in *Donoghue v Stevenson* as to the duty towards one's neighbour. It has been pointed out (and this only shows the difficulty of stating a general proposition which is not too wide) that unless one somewhat narrows the term of the proposition as it has been stated, one would be including in it something which the law does not support. It is not true to say that wherever a man finds himself in such a position that unless he does a certain act another person may suffer, or that if he does something another person will suffer, then it is his duty in the one case to be careful to do the act and in the other case to be careful not to do the act. Any such proposition is much too wide. There has to be a breach of a duty which the law recognizes, and to ascertain what the law recognizes regard must be had to the decisions of the courts. There has never been a decision that a master must, merely because of the relationship which exists between master and servant, take reasonable care for the safety of his servant's belongings in the sense that he must take steps to ensure, so far as he can, that no wicked person shall have an opportunity of stealing the servant's goods. That is the duty contended for here, and there is not a shred of authority to suggest that any such duty exists or ever has existed (p.233)."

You will recall that in the cases of *Derry v Peek* and *Le Lievre v Gould*, the Courts were not prepared to find a duty of care in the case of economic loss, as opposed to physical damage to person and property. In the wake of *Donoghue v Stevenson*, the question remained of interest: does *Donoghue v Stevenson* apply only to physical injury to person or property, or does its logic extend to economic loss? After all, economic loss is a form of injury to property: it is an injury to the claimant's wallet! This issue became tied up with the distinction between negligent words and negligent acts, and whether one could be held liable for negligent words. That distinction, as you will discover in your tort law course, is a rather confused one, and has not been a particularly helpful way in which to analyse these issues. In any event, the extent to which *Donoghue v Stevenson* could be read as establishing a general principle applicable to economic loss—which would allow courts to revisit the issue raised in cases such as *Derry v Peek* and *Le Lievre v Gould*—came before the Court of Appeal.

Candler v Crane, Christmas & Co. [1951] 2 K.B. 164, CA.

[The claimant was considering the possibility of his investing 2,000*l* in a limited liability company, but, before deciding to do so, desired to see the accounts of the company. The managing director of the company accordingly instructed the defendants, the accountants of the company, who were getting out the accounts, to press on and complete them, informing a clerk of the accountants, who had been requested by them to prepare the accounts, that they were required to be shown to the claimant who to his knowledge was a potential investor in the company. The clerk accordingly prepared the accounts and at the request of the managing director showed them to and discussed them with the claimant who took a copy of them and submitted them to his own accountant for advice. As a result the claimant invested his money in the company. The accounts were carelessly prepared, contained numerous false statements and gave a wholly misleading picture of the state of the company, which was wound up within a year, the claimant losing the whole of his investment. In an action brought by the claimant against the defendants, Lloyd-Jacob, J., found that the clerk was not guilty of fraud, but had been "extremely careless in the preparation of the accounts", and that the resulting damage to the claimant was plain. He held that the clerk had acted within the course of his employment, but dismissed the action on the ground that the defendants owed no duty of care to the claimant. The claimant appealed.]

Denning L.J. [who was asked to read his judgment first]:
"... This case raises a point of law of much importance; because Mr Lawson on behalf of the plaintiff submitted that, although there was no contract between the plaintiff and the accountants, nevertheless the relationship between them was so close and direct that the accountants did owe a duty of care to him within the principles stated in *Donoghue v Stevenson*; whereas Mr Foster on behalf of the accountants submitted that the duty owed by the accountants was purely a contractual duty owed by them to the company, and therefore they were not liable for negligence to a person to whom they were under no contractual duty. ... The only defences raised by the accountants at the hearing of the appeal were: (1) that Fraser was not acting in the course of his employment; and (2) that, even if he were, they owed no duty of care to the plaintiff [Lord Denning then considered the first issue, and found that Fraser was acting in the course of his employment]. ...

Now I come to the great question in the case: did the accountants owe a duty of care to the plaintiff? If the matter were free from authority, I should have said that they clearly did owe a duty of care to him. They were professional accountants who prepared and put before him these accounts, knowing that he was going to be guided by them in making an investment in the company. On the faith of those accounts he did make the investment, whereas if the accounts had been carefully prepared, he would not have made the investment at all. The result is that he has lost his money. In the circumstances, had he not every right to rely on the accounts being prepared with proper care; and is he not entitled to redress from the accountants on whom he relied? I say that he is, and I would apply to this case the words of Knight Bruce, L.J. in an analogous case ninety years ago: 'A country whose administration of justice did not afford redress in a case of the present description would not be in a state of civilization'.

Turning now to authority, I can point to many general statements of principle which cover the case made by some of the great names in the law . . . [b]ut it is said that effect cannot be given to these statements of principle, because there is an actual decision of this court in 1893 which is to the contrary, namely *Le Lievre v Gould*.

Before I consider the decision in *Le Lievre v Gould* itself, I wish to say that, in my opinion, at the time it was decided current legal thought was infected by two cardinal errors. The first error was one which appears time and time again in nineteenth century thought, namely, that no one who is not a party to a contract can sue on it or on anything arising out of it. This error has had unfortunate consequences both in the law of contract and in the law of tort. So far as contract is concerned, I have said something about it in *Smith v River Douglas Catchment Board*.[5] So far as tort is concerned, it led the lawyers of that day to suppose that, if one of the parties to a contract was negligent in carrying it out, no third person who was injured by that negligence could sue for damages on account of it . . ., except in the case of things dangerous in themselves, like guns. This error lies at the root of the reasoning of Bowen, L.J., in *Le Lievre v Gould*, when he said that the law of England 'does not consider that what a man writes on paper is like a gun or other dangerous instrument', meaning thereby that, unless it was a thing which was dangerous in itself, no action lay. This error was exploded by the great case of *Donoghue v Stevenson*, which decided that the presence of a contract did not defeat an action for negligence by a third person, provided that the circumstances disclosed a duty by the contracting party to him.

The second error was an error as to the effect of *Derry v Peek*, an error which persisted for thirty-five years at least after the decision, namely, that no action ever lies for a negligent statement even though it is intended to be acted on by the plaintiff and is in fact acted on by him to his loss. . . .

Let me now be constructive and suggest the circumstances in which I say that a duty to use care in statement does exist apart from a contract in that behalf. First, what persons are under such duty? My answer is those persons such as accountants, surveyors, valuers and analysts, whose profession and occupation it is to examine books, accounts, and other things, and to make reports on which other people—other than their clients—rely in the ordinary course of business. Their duty is not merely a duty to use care in their reports. They have also a duty to use care in their work which results in their reports. Herein lies the difference between these professional men and other persons who have been held to be under no duty to use care in their statements, such as promoters who issue a prospectus: *Derry v Peek* (now altered by statute), and trustees who answer inquiries about trust funds: *Low v Bouverie*.[6] Those parties do not bring, and are not expected to bring, any professional knowledge or skill into the preparation of their statements: they can only be made responsible by the law affecting persons generally, such as contract, estoppel, innocent misrepresentation or fraud. But it is very different with persons who engage in a calling which requires special knowledge and skill. From very early times it has been held that they owe a duty of care to those who are closely and directly affected by their work. . . .

Secondly, to whom do these professional people owe this duty? I will take accountants, but the same reasoning applies to the others. They owe the duty, of course, to their employer or client; and also I think to any third person to whom they themselves show the accounts, or to whom they know their employer is going to show the accounts, so as to induce him to invest money or take some other action on them. But I do not think the duty can be extended still further so as to include strangers of whom they have heard nothing and to whom their employer without their knowledge may choose to show their accounts. Once the accountants have handed their accounts to their employer they are not, as a rule, responsible for what he does with them without their knowledge or consent. . . .

Thirdly, to what transactions does the duty of care extend? It extends, I think, only to those

---

[5] [1949] 2 K.B. 500 at 514–17.
[6] [1891] 3 Ch. 82.

transactions for which the accountants knew their accounts were required. For instance, in the present case it extends to the original investment of 2,000*l* which the plaintiff made in reliance on the accounts, because the accountants knew that the accounts were required for his guidance in making that investment; but it does not extend to the subsequent 200*l* which he made after he had been two months with the company. This distinction, that the duty only extends to the very transaction in mind at the time, is implicit in the decided cases. . . .

My conclusion is that a duty to use care in statement is recognized in English law, and that its recognition does not create any dangerous precedent when it is remembered that it is limited in respect of the persons by whom and to whom it is owed and the transactions to which it applies.

One final word: I think that the law would fail to serve the best interests of the community if it should hold that accountants and auditors owe a duty to no one but their client. Its influence would be most marked in cases where their client is a company or firm controlled by one man. It would encourage accountants to accept the information which the one man gives them, without verifying it; and to prepare and present the accounts rather as a lawyer prepares and presents a case, putting the best appearance on the accounts they can, without expressing their personal opinion of them. This is, to my way of thinking, an entirely wrong approach. There is a great difference between the lawyer and the accountant. The lawyer is never called on to express his personal belief in the truth of his client's case; whereas the accountant, who certifies the accounts of his client, is always called on to express his personal opinion as to whether the accounts exhibit a true and correct view of his client's affairs; and he is required to do this, not so much for the satisfaction of his own client, but more for the guidance of shareholders, investors, revenue authorities, and others who may have to rely on the accounts in serious matters of business. If we should decide this case in favour of the accountants there will be no reason why accountants should ever verify the word of the one man in a one-man company, because there will be no one to complain about it. The one man who gives them wrong information will not complain if they do not verify it. He wants their backing for the misleading information he gives them, and he can only get it if they accept his word without verification. It is just what he wants so as to gain his own ends. And the persons who are misled cannot complain because the accountants owe no duty to them. If such be the law, I think it is to be regretted, for it means that the accountants' certificate, which should be a safeguard, becomes a snare for those who rely on it. I do not myself think that it is the law. In my opinion accountants owe a duty of care not only to their own clients, but also to all those whom they know will rely on their accounts in the transactions for which those accounts are prepared.

I would therefore be in favour of allowing the appeal and entering judgment for the plaintiff for damages in the sum of 2,000*l*."

Asquith, L.J.:

"On two points I entirely agree with the judgment delivered by Denning, L.J. I agree that the cause of action based on an alleged breach of duty occurring after the plaintiff became a shareholder cannot be made out if only because the damage relied on preceded the breach. I also agree, for the reasons he has given, that Fraser was clearly acting within the scope of his employment by the defendant firm in showing the draft accounts and giving certain other information to the plaintiff.

But I have the misfortune to differ from my brother on the more important point raised in this case.

[Asquith, L.J. then considered the case law, culminating with *Donoghue v Stevenson*].
. . .

Apart, however, from any limitation which should be read into Lord Atkin's language by reference to the facts of the case before him—the '*subjecta materies*'—it seems to me incredible that if he thought his formula was inconsistent with *Gould*'s case he would not have said so. This case, now nearly sixty years old, had at that time stood for nearly forty years. He must have considered it closely. Yet his only reference to it is as annexing a valid and essential qualification to Lord Esher's formula in *Heaven v Pender*. Not a word of disapproval of the decision on its merits. The inference seems to me to be that Lord Atkin continued to accept the distinction between liability in tort for careless (but non-fraudulent) misstatements and liability in tort for some other forms of carelessness, and that his formula defining 'who is my neighbour' must be read subject to his acceptance of this overriding distinction. . . .

In what has gone before it has been assumed that the two Law Lords who agreed with Lord Atkin's opinion or result accepted the broad formula about 'my duty to my neighbour' which he laid down, as well as in the narrow proposition limited to the liability of the negligent manufacturer of a chattel which reaches the consumer, without an opportunity of intermediate examination, and injures him. This assumption seems to me more than questionable. Lord Thankerton, though he says that he entirely agreed with Lord Atkin's discussion of the authorities, is clearly considering the authorities in their application to the narrow ambit of a manufacturer's liability, chattels and physical injury. His judgment does not travel outside these limits. Nor do I read Lord Macmillan's judgment as indorsing the wider proposition. There is a passage in which he lays down certain general propositions. It would have been easy for him to have adopted Lord Atkin's formula in terms if he had thought so broad a proposition justified. But when he says in an oft-quoted phrase, 'the categories of negligence are never closed' he is not, in my view, accepting an acid test of liability valid in all circumstances—he does not mention the word 'neighbour'; he is merely saying that in accordance with changing social needs and standards new classes of persons legally bound or entitled to the exercise of care may from time to time emerge—in this case by the addition of a careless manufacturer or circulator of a chattel—as parties bound, *vis-à-vis* consumers, or users, as parties entitled. In other words, what Lord Macmillan envisaged was the addition of another slab to the existing edifice, not a systematic reconstruction of the edifice on a single logical plan.

For these reasons I am of the opinion that *Donoghue*'s case neither reverses nor qualifies the principle laid down in *Gould*'s case. . . .

In the present state of our law different rules still seem to apply to the negligent misstatement on the one hand and to the negligent circulation or repair of chattels on the other; and *Donoghue*'s case does not seem to me to have abolished these differences. I am not concerned with defending the existing state of the law or contending that it is strictly logical —it clearly is not. I am merely recording what I think it is.

If this relegates me to the company of 'timorous souls', I must face that consequence with such fortitude as I can command. I am of opinion that the appeal should be dismissed."

Cohen L.J. [Cohen L.J. delivered a judgment in substantial agreement with Asquith L.J. He reasoned the decision in *Le Lievre v Gould* was binding upon him]:

"The principle of that decision seems to me directly in point in the present case. It is binding on us unless it can be said to be inconsistent with some other decision of this court or of the House of Lords. I am unable to find any such decision. Mr Lawson asked us to say that it is inconsistent with the principle laid down by Lord Atkin in *Donoghue v Stevenson*. It is to be observed that in *Donoghue v Stevenson* Lord Atkin himself cited with approval some passages from the judgments of Lord Esher, M.R. and A.L. Smith, L.J. in *Le Lievre v Gould*, and I am unable to believe that if he had thought the *ratio decidendi* in that case was wrong he would have cited those passage without making it clear that he was not approving the decision. I think, therefore, that although the relevant passages in Lord Atkin's speech are couched in such general terms that they might possibly cover the case of negligent misstatement, that question was not present to Lord Atkin's mind or intended to be covered by his statement. . . .

I would only add that despite the observations of my brother Denning, I do not think the conclusion I have reached will encourage accountants to fall short of the high standard of conduct which the Institutes to which they belong have laid down for their members.

In the result this appeal will be dismissed."

- The judgment in *Candler v Crane, Christmas & Co.* is of particular interest for the way in which it demonstrates how judges engage in the process of applying and distinguishing precedents which are binding, and which may not be easy to reconcile. In this case, at issue was the impact of *Le Lievre v Gould*, in light of the subsequent decision of the House of Lords in *Donoghue v Stevenson*. How does the interpretation placed on these two decisions by Denning L.J. differ from that of Asquith and Cohen L.JJ.? Which did you find more convincing and why?

- Denning L.J. justifies his approach through an appeal to "policy". What policy arguments are deployed by him? How does Cohen L.J. seek to respond to them?

- The judgment of Asquith L.J. might be described as an example of judicial conservatism in the development of the common law (something Denning L.J. would never be accused of!). Which portion of his judgment explicitly adopts a conservative approach to the role of a Court of Appeal judge in the development of the common law? Did you find this approach satisfying? Why or why not?

- To what extent do the judgments suggest that the judges see themselves as having different roles to play in the development of doctrine?

Given the hierarchy of courts in the United Kingdom, and the nature of a system of binding precedent, it was ultimately up to the House of Lords to consider the impact of *Derry v Peek* and *Le Lievre v Gould* in light of *Donoghue v Stevenson*. The question of the extent of a duty of care owed in the making of negligent misstatements was finally resolved by the House of Lords in 1963.

Hedley Byrne & Co. Ltd v Heller & Partners Ltd [1964] A.C. 465, HL.

Lord Reid:
"My Lords, this case raises the important question whether and in what circumstances a person can recover damages for loss suffered by reason of his having relied on an innocent but negligent misrepresentation. I cannot do better than adopt the following statement of the case from the judgment of McNair J.: 'This case raised certain interesting questions of law as to the liability of bankers giving references as to the credit-worthiness of their customers. The plaintiffs are a firm of advertising agents. The defendants are merchant bankers. In outline, the plaintiffs' case against the defendants is that, having placed on behalf of a client, Easipower Ltd, on credit terms substantial orders for advertising time on television programmes and for advertising space in certain newspapers on terms under which they, the plaintiffs, became personally liable to the television and newspaper companies, they caused inquiries to be made through their own bank of the defendants as to the credit-worthiness of Easipower Ltd who were customers of the defendants and were given by the defendants satisfactory references. These references turned out not to be justified, and the plaintiffs claim that in reliance on the references, which they had no reason to question,

they refrained from cancelling the orders so as to relieve themselves of their current liabilities. . . . [His Lordship stated the facts and continued:] The appellants now seek to recover
this loss from the respondents as damages on the ground that these replies were given negligently and in breach of the respondents' duty to exercise care in giving them. In the judgment McNair J. said: 'On the assumption stated above as to the existence of the duty, I have
no hesitation in holding (1) that Mr Heller was guilty of negligence in giving such a reference without making plain—as he did not—that it was intended to be a very guarded reference, and (2) that properly understood according to its ordinary and natural meaning the
reference was not justified by facts known to Mr Heller.

Before your Lordships the respondents were anxious to contest this finding, but your
Lordships found it unnecessary to hear argument on this matter, being of opinion that the
appeal must fail even if Mr Heller was negligent. Accordingly I cannot and do not express
any opinion on the question whether Mr Heller was in fact negligent. But I should make it
plain that the appellants' complaint is not that Mr Heller gave his reply without adequate
knowledge of the position, nor that he intended to create a false impression, but that what
he said was in fact calculated to create a false impression and that he ought to have realised that. And the same applies to the respondents' letter of November 11.

McNair J. gave judgment for the respondents on the ground that they owed no duty of
care to the appellants. He said: 'I am accordingly driven to the conclusion by authority
binding upon me that no such action lies in the absence of contract or fiduciary relationship. On the facts before me there is clearly no contract, nor can I find a fiduciary relationship. It was urged on behalf of the plaintiff that the fact that Easipower Ltd were heavily
indebted to the defendants and that the defendants might benefit from the advertising campaign financed by the plaintiffs, were facts from which a special duty to exercise care might
be inferred. In my judgment, however, these facts, though clearly relevant on the question
of honesty if this had been in issue, are not sufficient to establish any special relationship
involving a duty of care even if it was open to me to extend the sphere of special relationship beyond that of contract and fiduciary relationship.'

The judgment was affirmed by the Court of Appeal both because they were bound by
authority and because they were not satisfied that it would be reasonable to impose upon
a banker the obligations suggested. . . .

The appellants' first argument was based on *Donoghue v Stevenson*. That is a very important decision, but I do not think that it has any direct bearing on this case. That decision
may encourage us to develop existing lines of authority, but it cannot entitle us to disregard them. Apart altogether from authority, I would think that the law must treat negligent words differently from negligent acts. The law ought so far as possible to reflect the
standards of the reasonable man, and that is what *Donoghue v Stevenson* sets out to do.
The most obvious difference between negligent words and negligent acts is this. Quite
careful people often express definite opinions on social or informal occasions even when
they see that others are likely to be influenced by them; and they often do that without
taking that care which they would take if asked for their opinion professionally or in a business connection. The appellant agrees that there can be no duty of care on such occasions,
and we were referred to American and South African authorities where that is recognised,
although their law appears to have gone much further than ours has yet done. But it is at
least unusual casually to put into circulation negligently made articles which are dangerous. A man might give a friend a negligently-prepared bottle of home-made wine and his
friend's guests might drink it with dire results. But it is by no means clear that those guests
would have no action against the negligent manufacturer.

Another obvious difference is that a negligently made article will only cause one accident,
and so it is not very difficult to find the necessary degree of proximity or neighbourhood
between the negligent manufacturer and the person injured. But words can be broadcast
with or without the consent or the foresight of the speaker or writer. It would be one thing
to say that the speaker owes a duty to a limited class, but it would be going very far to say
that he owes a duty to every ultimate 'consumer' who acts on those words to his detriment.
It would be no use to say that a speaker or writer owes a duty but can disclaim responsibility if he wants to. He, like the manufacturer, could make it part of a contract that he is not

to be liable for his negligence: but that contract would not protect him in a question with a third party, at least if the third party was unaware of it.

So it seems to me that there is good sense behind our present law that in general an innocent but negligent misrepresentation gives no cause of action. There must be something more than the mere misstatement. I therefore turn to the authorities to see what more is required. The most natural requirement would be that expressly or by implication from the circumstances the speaker or writer has undertaken some responsibility, and that appears to me not to conflict with any authority which is binding on this House. . . .

A reasonable man, knowing that he was being trusted or that his skill and judgment were being relied on, would, I think, have three courses open to him. He could keep silent or decline to give the information or advice sought: or he could give an answer with a clear qualification that he accepted no responsibility for it or that it was given without that reflection or inquiry which a careful answer would require: or he could simply answer without any such qualification. If he chooses to adopt the last course he must, I think, be held to have accepted some responsibility for his answer being given carefully, or to have accepted a relationship with the inquirer which requires him to exercise such care as the circumstances require.

If that is right, then it must follow that *Candler v Crane, Christmas & Co.* was wrongly decided. . . . This seems to me to be a typical case of agreeing to assume a responsibility: they knew why the plaintiff wanted to see the accounts and why their employers, the company, wanted them to be shown to him, and agreed to show them to him without even a suggestion that he should not rely on them.

The majority of the Court of Appeal held that they were bound by *Le Lievre v Gould* and that *Donoghue v Stevenson* had no application. In so holding I think that they were right. The Court of Appeal have bound themselves to follow all *rationes decidendi* of previous Court of Appeal decisions, and, in face of that rule, it would have been very difficult to say that the *ratio* of *Le Lievre v Gould* did not cover *Candler*'s case. Denning L.J., who dissented, distinguished *Le Lievre v Gould* on its facts, but, as I understand the rule which the Court of Appeal have adopted, that is not sufficient if the *ratio* applies; and this is not an appropriate occasion to consider whether the Court of Appeal's rule is a good one. So the question which we now have to consider is whether the *ratio* of *Le Lievre v Gould* can be supported. . . . [Lord Reid went on to conclude that the *ratio* in *Le Lievre v Gould* was "wrong".]

Now I must try to apply these principles to the present case. What the appellants complain of is not negligence in the ordinary sense of carelessness, but rather misjudgment, in that Mr Heller, while honestly seeking to give a fair assessment, in fact made a statement which gave false and misleading impression of his customer's credit. It appears that bankers now commonly give references with regard to their customers as part of their business. I do not know how far their customers generally permit them to disclose their affairs, but, even with permission, it cannot always be easy for a banker to reconcile his duty to his customer with his desire to give a fairly balanced reply to an inquiry. And inquirers can hardly expect a full and objective statement of opinion or accurate factual information such as skilled men would be expected to give in reply to other kinds of inquiry. So it seems to me to be unusually difficult to determine just what duty beyond a duty to be honest a banker would be held to have undertaken if he gave a reply without an adequate disclaimer of responsibility or other warning. . . . [H]ere the appellants' bank, who were their agents in making the inquiry, began by saying that 'they wanted to know in confidence and without responsibility on our part,' that is, on the part of the respondents. So I cannot see how the appellants can now be entitled to disregard that and maintain that the respondents did incur a responsibility to them. . . .

I am therefore of opinion that it is clear that the respondents never undertook any duty to exercise care in giving their replies. The appellants cannot succeed unless there was such a duty and therefore in my judgment this appeal must be dismissed."

[Lord Morris of Borth-y-Gest, Lord Hodson, Lord Devlin and Lord Pearce agreed that the appeal should be dismissed.]

NOTES AND QUESTIONS

- It is important to realise that while *Hedley Byrne* is significant for its recognition of the possibility that a negligent misstatement can give rise to a duty of care, on the facts of this case liability had been excluded by contract. If you were giving legal advice to a bank, the day after *Hedley Byrne* was decided, what would you advise they do to protect themselves?

- Note the comments about *stare decisis* delivered by Lord Reid. How convinced is Lord Reid by Denning L.J.'s attempt in *Crane Christmas* to distinguish *Le Lievre v Gould*? Given that Lord Reid disagreed with the approach taken by the majority in *Crane Christmas* and with the decision in *Le Lievre v Gould*, why do you think he was not more positive about Denning L.J.'s dissent in *Crane Christmas*?

The reasoning of the House of Lords in *Hedley Byrne* was part of a move towards the general principle of liability approach which, it might be argued, began with Lord Atkin's judgment in *Donoghue v Stevenson*. The tension between the specific duty versus general duty approaches has continued in tort law to the present day.

David Howarth, *Textbook on Tort* (Butterworths, London, 1995), pp.164–165:

"[I]n the 1960s and 1970s, the general principle view came to the fore. In *Hedley Byrne v Heller* [1964] AC 465, *Home Office v Dorset Yacht* [1970] AC 1004 and ultimately in *Anns v Merton London Borough Council* [1978] AC 728 the House of Lords came to the conclusion that there ought to be a presumption in favour of liability for harm caused by carelessness. The *Anns* 'two- stage' test, as formulated by Lord Wilberforce, was simply that there ought to be liability for harm caused by fault (stage 1) unless there were good reasons why not (stage 2). *Anns* inspired judges such as Lord Scarman to say in *McLoughlin v O'Brian* [1983] 1 AC 410 that principle required the application of *Donoghue* 'untrammelled by spatial, physical or temporal limits'.

But a reaction set in after *Anns* and *McLoughlin*, led by Lord Keith of Kinkel. . . . Lord Keith's favourite text in cases such as *Yuen Kun Yeu v A-G* (Hong Kong) [1988] AC 175 and *Murphy v Brentwood District Council* [1991] 1 AC 398 and Lord Bridge's favourite text in *Caparo v Dickman* [1990] 2 AC 605 and *Curran v Northern Ireland Co-ownership Housing Association* [1987] AC 718 was a passage from the judgment of the Australian judge Brennan J. in *Sutherland Shire Council v Heyman* (1985) 6 ALR 1. Brennan J. had said that:

> 'It is preferable, in my view, that the law should develop novel categories incrementally and by analogy with established categories, rather than by a massive extension of a prima facie duty of care restrained only by indefinable 'considerations which ought to negative, or to reduce or limit the scope of the duty or the class of person to whom it is owed.'

Ultimately, Lord Bridge went the whole way back to the pre-*Donoghue* circumstances and interests approach and declared in *Caparo* that:

> 'I think the law has now moved in the direction of attaching greater significance to the more traditional categorisation of distinct and recognisable situations as guides to the existence, scope and the limits of the varied duties of care which the law imposes.'

It seems, however, that just as *Anns* and *McLoughlin v O'Brian* marked the high point of the last upswing of the general principles approach, *Caparo* may mark the high point of the swing in the opposite direction. Cases such as *Spring v Guardian Assurance* [1994] 3 All E.R. 129 and *Henderson v Merrett Syndicates Ltd* [1994] 3 All E.R. 506 seem to point to the construction of general principles of liability that cut across the traditional categories of tort and contract and if they do not point to the return to the *Anns* approach or, even more, to a French approach, at least there is again a consciousness that it is possible to construct principles and rules that go beyond mere analogies with the existing case law."

The significance of the decision of the House of Lords in *Donoghue v Stevenson*, and particularly the judgment of Lord Atkin, cannot be underestimated. Both the rhetorical style and the reasoning provide a model of the analytical power of common law reasoning. Lord Atkin's biographer also notes, however, that the importance of the decision in the development of the law of negligence was recognised far more quickly in the Commonwealth than it was at home.

Geoffrey Lewis, *Lord Atkin* (Butterworths, London, 1983) pp.62–63, 65–67:

"The decision worked a legal revolution. According to the style of the modern appellate judgment, the majority did not content themselves with a conclusion wide enough only to decide the dispute. They surveyed the entire field and found the state of the law wanting. In order that the debris of the old cases should not stand in the way of development which was consonant with both common sense and social needs, a framework had to be worked out within which the law of negligence could grow, unconstrained by illogical or nice distinctions. To achieve this the reactionaries had first to be beaten out of their entrenchments. When seven years later Lord Atkin was presented for an Honorary doctorate at Liverpool University, his eulogium described him as 'what is very rare in England, a legal scientist, a judge who is not content merely to settle present disputes, but seeks to expand and develop those underlying principles which are to be applied to other disputes'; and went on to contrast him with those judges 'who lack his imaginative courage'.

'They are content to be guided and seek for authority as an easy substitute for independent action. They take refuge in precedent as in a protective shell: like the mollusc, they attain safety at the price of flexibility and mobility, and practitioners and students alike search their judgments in vain for those general ideas which are the life of the law.'

Courage of that order was necessary, and judgment too, for however obvious the good sense of the decision now seems, it was less evident then than the dangers of the limitless field which had been opened up.

Yet the revolution was not destructive. That was why Atkin particularly, but his fellow judges of the majority also, took such pains in analysing and explaining the old cases. They were not tempted to smash the clay and start again. The growth was organic and was later described by Lord Devlin in these words:

'What *Donoghue v Stevenson* did may be described as the widening of an old category or as the creation of a new and similar one. The general conception can be used to produce other categories in the same way. An existing category grows as instances of its application multiply until the time comes when the cell divides.'

It is a feature of English law that most of its best modern jurisprudence is to be found in the great opinions and judgments in the Law Reports and not in academic writings. The most thoughtful attempts to analyse the methods and effects of the decision of the majority in *Donoghue v Stevenson* are to be found in two later decisions of the House of Lords in the same field which were themselves milestones. *Hedley Byrne* in 1963[7] and the *Dorset Yacht* Case in 1970.[8] Here it was said for the first time with authoritative clarity that Lord Atkin's 'general conception' of neighbourhood is not a universal rule of law to be applied literally as if it were a statute, but is a guide to the circumstances in which a duty of care may be held to exist. The most lasting value of the case will be to show 'how the law can be developed to solve particular problems'. . . .

Considering that Lord Atkin thought and said that no more important problem had occupied the Law Lords, their decision on *Donoghue v Stevenson* received only a modest welcome in the professional journals of the day. Sir Frederick Pollock contributed a short article to the *Law Quarterly Review* entitled 'The Snail in the Bottle, and Thereafter'[9] in which he praised 'the Scots Lords of Appeal for overriding the scruples of English colleagues who could not emancipate themselves from the pressure of a supposed current of authority in English Courts'. Professor Winfield wrote: 'it cannot be doubted that the decision meets the needs of the community',[10] and the opinion of the *Solicitors' Journal* was that it would 'govern millions of small transactions every day in the whole of the United Kingdom'.[11] But no writer appreciated the significance of the general conception of foreseeability which Atkin had propounded. Where it was discussed it was generally misunderstood. Within a few weeks of the House of Lords' decision, the Court of Appeal presided over by Lord Justice Scrutton had to decide a case in which it was argued that *Donoghue v Stevenson* had changed the law.[12] The jib of a crane had fallen and killed a skilled erector who had noticed that some cogwheels did not fit well, but had not appreciated the extent of the danger and had started to work the crane. His widow's claim against the manufacturer had been withdrawn from the jury by Mr Justice McCardie, and the Court of Appeal refused to disturb the decision. Scrutton adopted a minatory tone: 'English judges' he said, 'have been slow in stating principles going beyond the facts they are considering. They find themselves in a difficulty if they state too wide propositions and find that they do not suit the actual facts.' In his view Lord Atkin had stated his general proposition too widely, and the real ground of the decision was no more than the definition of 'a manufacturer's liability to the ultimate consumer when there is no reasonable possibility of intermediate examination of the product'.

Fears about the implications of Atkin's general conception continued to trouble some. As late as 1941, the writer of a note in the *Law Quarterly Review* seized on a phrase of Atkin's in a recent case that 'Every person, whether discharging a public duty or not, is under a common law obligation to some persons *in some circumstances* to conduct himself with reasonable care so as not to injure those who are likely to be affected by his want of care', and supposed that in so saying Atkin had repented and accepted that 'the criterion of "neighbourly duty", was not a universal one'. The qualification would, the writer thought, 'bring tranquillity to many minds that, for the past nine years, have been sorely harassed in the attempt to reconcile the decision in that case with the normal trend of the development of our law'.[13]

The reception which was accorded to the decision in the Commonwealth showed more understanding than at home. A full and thoughtful article in the *Canadian Bar Review*, although written from Oxford, said that 'Lord Atkin's judgment is at once stamped as perhaps the most impressive and certainly the most authoritative effort ever made to generalise the English law of negligence', and described the neighbour principle as 'a guide to judges where before there was none'.[14]

And Mr Justice Evatt, with whom Atkin seems to have corresponded regularly, wrote from the High Court of Australia in March 1933:

---

[7] [1964] A.C. 465.
[8] [1970] A.C. 1004.
[9] 49 L.Q.R. 22.
[10] 51 L.Q.R. 249 at 254.
[11] 76 Sol. Jo. 387. The writer noted in passing that the decision had not attracted much public notice.
[12] *Farr and Butters Bros* [1932] 2 K.B. 606.
[13] P.A. Landon 57 L.Q.R. 179 at 183.
[14] F.C. Underhay, 10 Can. Bar Rev. 615.

'. . . The Snail Case has been the subject of the keenest interest and debate at the Bar and in the Sydney and Melbourne Law Schools: on all sides there is profound satisfaction that, in substance, your judgment and the opinion of Justice Cardozo of the U.S.A. coincide, and that the common law is again shown to be capable of meeting modern conditions of industrialisation, and of striking through forms of legal separateness to reality. There is an article in the *Canadian Bar Review* which expresses the Australian view as well as that of Canada. . . .

The revolution brought about by *Donoghue v Stevenson* was so quiet that it passed completely unnoticed by the general public who were so closely affected by it: and its true nature was perhaps not fully understood even by the profession until Lord Devlin's speech in 1963 in the *Hedley Byrne* Case. The general conception of neighbourly duty was not a proposition which had been stated too widely. It was a statement which called the law of negligence into existence as a separate civil wrong, and enabled that branch of the law to develop on common sense lines so as to become the most important and far-reaching of all civil wrongs. In the fifty years which have passed since the decision it has renewed itself again and again, and has demonstrated its usefulness in all manner of circumstances. There is no sign that its power of adaptability is waning, nor is there any reason why it should. This power is due more than anything else to the moral spirit which animated Lord Atkin's speech, an object lesson, as Lord Wright said, of liberal thought in the handling of principles which has influenced the common law in all its branches.

Atkin and his colleagues found a tangled mass of old decisions but no decision of the House directly in point. The step which they took to bring order to the chaos was one which was impelled by the ordinary needs of British society and the assumptions which it made about right and wrong. They were doing something which every legal system requires of its law makers, parliamentary or judicial, that of constantly relating the law to the tacitly accepted moral principles of their own society.

In retrospect the decision now seems so clearly right and just that it makes one marvel at the state of the law before 1932; but the increasing certainty which time brings that an important decision is right is the highest tribute that can be accorded to the judgment of those who made it."

THE CASE LAW IN HISTORICAL CONTEXT

We started this chapter with a consideration of the historical development of the common law cases which formed the foundations of the modern law of negligence. We now return to history, but the history not of the cases themselves (an internal perspective), but of the wider ideological context in which the cases emerged (an external perspective). Through an understanding of this history, we can gain insights into the underlying reasons *why* the common law developed in the particular way it did. Conaghan and Mansell identify a number of historical perspectives which shed light on the historical patterns of negligence jurisprudence.

Joanne Conaghan and Wade Mansell, *The Wrongs of Tort* (2nd ed., Pluto Press, London, 1999) pp.81–103:

"A marked characteristic of most conventional accounts of the tort of negligence (and, indeed, of legal doctrine generally) is the complete absence of any historical perspective. Leading textbooks make little or no reference to the historical origins of legal doctrine. Even texts which purport to be in some sense 'critical' or 'contextual' lack any significant historical dimension. Such a seemingly glaring omission raises a number of important questions. First, and most obviously, *why* is history regarded as so completely irrelevant to an account of legal doctrine? Second, why is this neglect of history not more often noticed, criticised and commented upon? Finally, and perhaps most importantly, what is the effect of presenting legal doctrine in a timeless ahistorical way?

The most manifest effect of a traditional legal neglect of history is to render insignificant dates and times. Reading a contract text, it makes little difference to the student whether *Hyde v. Wrench* (1840) was decided in 1840 or 1940. What matters is that it supports the rule that a counter-offer does not make a contract. Likewise, in tort, the student of negligence attaches no particular significance to the timing of the finding in favour of the consumer in *Donoghue v. Stevenson* (1932).She is not provoked to ask why the House of Lords decided then, and not before, to eschew the doctrine of privity and its dubious relevance to the availability of a tort claim. She is not encouraged to explore the wider 'social context' of *Donoghue* in terms of, for example, the huge expansion in the market for consumer goods in the twentieth century and the observable shift away from protection of industry (the manufacturer's immunity) towards protecting the consumer. For the student of the expository legal tradition, dates are little more than a useful mechanism for organising and absorbing the relevant material.

In this way, law and legal doctrine are presented as timeless and ageless. The doctrine of consideration in contract appears not as a historical product of the social and economic conditions of the nineteenth century but rather as a universal principle of reciprocity reflecting man's underlying human nature. Likewise, the fault principle in tort emerges as the common sense embodiment of a concept of social justice which is good for all time. In other words, the absence of a historical perspective on legal doctrine tends to reinforce the view of law as consisting of a series of universally accepted and uncontentious principles of common sense rather than as comprising and promulgating historically and politically specific policies and values. To the extent that changes in legal doctrine *are* located historically—*Donoghue v Stevenson*, for example, is often presented as laying to rest the 'older' principle of privity 'originating' in *Winterbottom v Wright* (1842)—they are usually presented as the *application* of a general and universal principle (in this case the fault principle) to a novel situation. In other words, the 'history' of legal doctrine which is employed by conventional texts is not so much a history of the adoption and evolution of a principle or maxim but rather of its *discovery* and subsequent application. Essentially. then, a neglect of history depoliticises law by robbing it of context. At the same time it deifies law by making it immortal.

A further effect of ignoring history is that it gives the student a sense of law as static rather than dynamic. Law is experienced as a set of relatively fixed rules which are simply 'there' to be applied. Thus, for example, no duty is owed in the absence of a relationship of proximity; a plaintiff can recover damages for nervous shock but not for ordinary grief; economic loss is generally not recoverable in negligence. Such highly rule-oriented assertions of legal doctrine in no way communicate the essential fluidity of the common law, its existence and manifestation as a living, moving thing. The textbook tendency to present a picture of the law 'as is' simply fails to provide students with the knowledge and understanding of legal discourse necessary to the process of 'lawyering'. By perceiving law as a framework of rules rather than as a series of arguments the weight of which varies according to time and circumstance, students develop a rigid and unimaginative approach towards case law. They experience case analysis as a mechanism rather than as a creative exercise which, in the end, breeds technicians rather than advocates. It is only by viewing law historically that it can be understood as progressive rather than static; and it is that experience of law's dynamism and vitality which facilitates both an understanding of the system and an ability to manipulate it successfully.

Thus, the absence of any historical perspective in conventional presentations of tort law has a significant effect on the way in which it is experienced and understood. It constitutes a particular 'knowledge' of law, but not one which easily admits to its partiality or to its imperialistic tendencies. At the same time, by so constituting itself, the expository tradition has no need to explain or defend its cavalier disregard for the past because by its very nature, as a set of timeless and universal principles of which the cases are a mere elaboration, it has defined itself as ahistorical except in the narrowest senses accorded by the doctrine of precedent. . . .

Internal historiography: Professor Percy H. Winfield

In the 1920s and 1930s, Percy H. Winfield, original author of the eminent and enduring *Winfield and Jolowicz on Tort*, wrote a series of articles on the historical emergence of negligence. Most of what he wrote then still informs conventional legal approaches today. His definition of negligence as 'the breach of a legal duty to take care by an inadvertent act or omission which injures another' still reigns supreme, and his presentation of the tort in terms of three component parts—duty, breach and consequence—is still the mainstay of most texts and syllabuses on the subject in the 1990s. . . .

Winfield's approach to uncovering the history of negligence was to focus solely on case law. From medieval to modern times he bounded back and forth from case to case, citing instances in support of an argument here and against a claim there. What emerged was a long and meandering narration mapping out what he perceived to be the 'relevant' cases and a story of negligence's birth and development which was in no way informed by or informative of the society in which those disputes arose.

The story which Winfield related ran something like this. The modern tort of negligence emerged from the old writ of trespass on the case. Until well into the nineteenth century private law actions were dominated by two cumbersome and mutually exclusive procedures known as trespass and trespass on the case (case). One essential difference in the use of the two procedures, certainly in the later period of their operation, was that trespass was deemed the appropriate form of action for injuries inflicted *directly* while case was the route to be pursued where harm was *indirectly* inflicted by another. According to the old writ system, to use the wrong form of action, trespass instead of case or vice versa, was fatal to a plaintiff's claim regardless of the merits of the case. However, to proceed by way of case, particularly after the decision in *Williams v Holland* (1833), was to incur less risk of issuing the wrong form of action. Hence the emergence of negligence through an action on the case rather than through the writ of trespass and its eventual assumption of a status of independence quite distinct from the tort of trespass. . . .

Negligence and economic subsidisation: Professor Morton J. Horwitz and the transformation of American law

Although it is scarcely evident in the venerated texts of Britain's most famous tort scholar, Percy Winfield, his story of the rise of negligence coincides in time very closely with the course of the Industrial Revolution. Nor is this coincidence generally regarded as accidental or peripheral. Millner acknowledges the debt owed by negligence to 'the favourable climate of the industrial revolution', while the American legal historian, Laurence Friedmann makes the even stronger claim that 'the exposition of tort law and negligence in particular must be entirely attributed to the age of engines and machines'. It is thus relatively undisputed that industrial development in the late eighteenth and nineteenth centuries is of crucial significance in understanding the rise of modern negligence. More significantly, it appears that the idea of a causal connection between law and economic activity enjoys widespread if tentative acceptance. What is more controversial is the precise nature of this causal connection. . . .

It is against this background of industrial accidents that Horwitz addresses the question of how and why negligence emerged and flourished in nineteenth-century American law. . . .

Horwitz's starting point is to see law in instrumentalist terms. For him, the period between 1780 and 1860 witnessed a 'transformation' in American law characterised by an increasing willingness on the part of judges to use law for particular ends; to shape the common law in pursuit of particular goals and to view decision-making as involving not just a consideration of the dispute at hand but of its wider social, economic and political implications also. Law, according to Horwitz, became an *instrument* in the hands of judges, a tool for the promotion of certain interests and objectives. In the context of negligence, this general contention takes the form of a particular allegation, namely that the fault principle prospered in nineteenth-century tort law because it was perceived by, *inter alia*, judges as a means of protecting nascent industry from the huge costs, in terms of accidents, generated by their activities. According to Horwitz, during the course of the nineteenth century, negligence ousted the 'ancient' principle of strict liability, expressed in the maxim *sic utere tuo ut alienum non laedas* ('use your land so as not to injure another'), from its preeminent position under the old writ system, gradually assuming a position of dominance in the field of unintentional injuries. In this way, industrialists were relieved of the crushing burden which strict liability would have imposed upon their enterprises and it was carried instead by the accident victims themselves. . . .

The imposition of a fault standard of liability on industrialists, in conjunction with a range of other common law doctrines such as contributory negligence (barring a plaintiff's claim where she had in any careless way contributed to the injury), *volenti non fit injuria* (barring a claim where the plaintiff was deemed to have accepted the risk) and the doctrine of common employment (whereby the plaintiff could not sue her master for injuries inflicted by a fellow-servant in the course of employment, see below), ensured that the cost of accidents was carried, in the main, by the victims rather than by the perpetrators of such accidents. Thus the legal liability rules effectively *subsidised* industry during this period by shifting costs of entrepreneurial activity away from industry and on to workers, consumers and bystanders. In making this argument, Horwitz's identification of the dominance of strict liability in the pre-industrial era assumes considerable significance. It is the *transformation* from a strict liability to a fault-based standard which is the focus of his attention and the basis of his claim that the judges applied the law in an instrumental fashion to promote the interests of industrialists. . . .

What evidence is there to support these contentions? It is certainly the case, both in England and America, that many judges and statesmen of the day were aware of the way in which the fault principle and other associated doctrines served the interests of industry. In *Ryan v. New York Central Railway Co* (1866), a New York judge refused to apply even the fault principle to a situation involving a negligent railroad company whose carelessness started a fire which destroyed a number of properties, on the grounds that the burden inflicted by liability would be so great as to ensure 'the destruction of civilised society'. He further observed that 'in a commercial country each man, to some extent, runs the hazard of his neighbour's conduct and each, by insurance against such hazards, is enabled to obtain a reasonable security against such loss'.

Thus, in *Ryan* the commercial climate was clearly relevant to judicial consideration of the imposition of liability. In England also there is evidence of an awareness of the impact of tort doctrine on entrepreneurial activity. In 1871 a Select Committee to the House of Commons, considering the doctrine of common employment (whereby a servant, injured by a 'fellow servant' in the 'common employment' of the master was unable to avail himself of the doctrine of vicarious liability entitling him to sue the master, but was confined to an action against his 'fellow servant'), concluded, in favour of the doctrine:

> 'There can be no doubt that the effect of abolishing the defence of "common employment" . . . would effect a serious disturbance in the industrial arrangements of the country. Sooner or later the position of master and workman would find its level by a readjustment of the rate of wages, but in the meantime great alarm would be occasioned, and the investment of capital in industrial undertakings would be discouraged.'

Thus the direct impact of particular tort doctrines on industrial activity was recognised and indeed considered to be a legitimate rationale for their continuance. . . .

But to show that the nineteenth-century tort doctrines had the *effect* of subsidising industry is not to establish that they were *designed* for that express purpose. To show that the law functioned in a particular way is not to demonstrate that it was devised to function so. Thus, Horwitz and others may be claiming too much when they assert that judges used the law instrumentally to serve the needs of the capitalist classes. That is not to say that they did not. It is simply to assert that it cannot be assumed from the evidence of a class-biased effect that they *consciously* did. . . .

Negligence as an independent legal category: G. E. White and the intellectual origins of tort law

For Horwitz, the emergence of negligence and the reshaping of tort law in the nineteenth century was closely bound up with the process of industrialisation. His primary focus is on the relationship between legal doctrine and economic relations, in particular the relations of commodity production and exchange. G. Edward White challenges this almost exclusive focus on the economic determinants of change and points to the importance of intellectual trends in shaping and restructuring nineteenth-century tort law. While industrialisation played a role in developing a notion of fault in the sense of carelessness to resolve the increasing number of disputes between strangers, he argues that the emergence of a *fault principle*, a principle which captured and expressed the basic essence of liability in a vast number of private law cases not governed by contract, was the result of intellectual analysis and synthesis of the existing case law by leading legal academics in 1870s America. Moreover, the same intellectual trend towards 'conceptualisation' led to the emergence of tort as an independent legal category as opposed to the collection of miscellaneous, non-criminal wrongs catalogued by Blackstone a century earlier. Thus, White asserts that 'the emergence of torts as a distinct branch of law owed as much to changes in jurisprudential thought as to the spread of industrialisation'.

To what 'changes in jurisprudential thought' is White referring? It is certainly the case that the second half of the nineteenth century witnessed a growing intellectual interest in a category of civil wrongs commonly if haphazardly subsumed under the mantle of tort. Indeed, until that period one could not accurately speak of tort as a category at all if the idea of a category implies some immediately identifiable and unifying characteristics(s). The existence, however, of a residual categoryless number of non-contractual, non-criminal wrongs encompassing the writs of trespass and case gradually generated some intellectual attention. Thus, the first American Treatise on Torts appeared in 1859. Yet, in 1870, the famous American jurist Oliver Wendell Holmes Jr was still insisting that 'torts is not a proper subject for a lawbook', although only two years later he was attempting to write his own 'Theory of Tort'. Moreover, in 1874, Ames produced the first American tort casebook, and by the end of the century tort was a firmly established legal category with a fast-increasing literature to bolster its credentials. . . .

Can similar claims be made about English legal development? It must at first be pointed out that in the area of tort theorisation, America led the way. Indeed, the first English treatise on tort, by Addison, appeared in 1860, a year after its American counterpart, while the first attempt to articulate a general theory of tort in England did not occur until Sir Frederick Pollock produced the first edition of his textbook in 1887. During the early years of the twentieth century, tort was as popular a subject for legal scholarship in Britain as in America. Indeed, although by the close of the nineteenth century Pollock's *Law of Tort* was in its fourth edition (1895), the idea of a general theory of tortious liability was still contentious when Winfield was writing in the 1920s, as was the claim that negligence operated as an independent tort. On the other hand, as early as 1883, Brett MR was attempting to devise a formula to capture the concept of the duty of care in negligence, thus suggesting that judicial attention was focused on the need for a rationalisation of the case law through the articulation of general principles (*Heaven v Pender* (1883)).

It is also clear that during the period 1850–1907, a period which Sugarman describes as the 'classical period of legal education and scholarship', British jurists were similarly engaged in articulating a scientific approach to the study of law. Sugarman locates the emergence of such an approach in Oxford and identifies Pollock as one of its leading proponents. Indeed, in a lecture given in 1886, Pollock describes the task of the law teacher as guiding the student 'to the distinction of that which is accidental and local from that which is permanent and universal', self-consciously comparing the role of the jurist to that of the mathematician.

It is Sugarman's contention that the development of a legal scientific approach to the study of law was an attempt by legal academics to justify their existence by 'peddling' a 'special expertise', and he credits the Oxford jurists of the late nineteenth century (including the leading tort scholars Pollock and Salmond) with the construction of the 'black-letter tradition' with its emphasis on 'exposition, conceptualisation, systematisation and analysis of existing legal doctrine', which he maintains has continued to inform British approaches to legal education ever since. Like White, Sugarman does not view the exposition of law as science as a neutral exercise, but rather as rooted in the political ideology of the times. He points in this respect to the relationship between law, nationalism and imperialism, and identifies the juristic project as in part a response to problems of social order generated in particular by the extension of the franchised and the middle-class fear of 'majoritarianism'. The scientific approach to law as to other disciplines provided the middle class with a cultural and intellectual basis by which to legitimate their continued control of the social order.

The presence of similar intellectual trends in the study of law in England and America does go some way towards explaining the approach taken towards tort law in particular by academics in both countries during the relevant period. But the evolution of an identifiable body of legal obligations based on relations other than contract, with the principle of no liability without fault at its heart, can also be located within the much broader framework of the essentially liberal values and assumptions informing the Victorian period. Arblaster has identified the rise of individualism as one of the earliest characteristics of modern liberalism. The eighteenth and nineteenth centuries witnessed the emergence of philosophical perspectives based generally on individualism, that is, on the ideas that the individual can be conceived of and understood in isolation from others and from society as a whole (abstract individualism), and that his needs and goals possess value and legitimacy independent of society (individual rights). This tended to produce a version of liberal political philosophy which defined the limits of the state in very narrow terms and extolled the virtues of individual freedom from state interference. In addition, the work of 'classical' economists of the late eighteenth century and early nineteenth century (in particular Adam Smith and David Ricardo), which was widely interpreted as propounding the virtues of a free self-regulating market society, led to the popular espousal of 'political economy' with its concomitant championing of freedom of contract and the pursuit of individual self-interest. . . .

Negligence is also highly individualistic. Reflecting a view of individual responsibility, it carefully delineates the limited situations in which an individual should be liable for the misfortunes of another. Only when an individual is in some sense morally culpable should she be required to assume responsibility for the effects of her activities on others. This moralistic component in tort law is nowhere more evident than in Salmond's remark that 'reason demands that a loss shall lie where it falls, unless some good purpose is to be served by changing its incidence; in general the only purpose so served is that of punishment for wrongful intent or negligence'.

Salmond's statement reflects not only the view that an appropriate reason for imposing a legal obligation includes 'punishment' but also the perception that absent some such 'good purpose' the law should not interfere at all. He thus articulates a point of view which places tort in general and negligence in particular within an abstentionist framework, that is a framework which posits the notion of a limited relationship between the state and the individual."

THE POLITICS OF COMMON LAW REASONING

You will learn more about the tensions in the development of the general duty of care in your tort law courses. For our purposes, one of the important points is that all of these developments have occurred through judicial reasoning, rather than legislative intervention. The development of a general duty of care—as well as attempts by courts to avoid its implications and to return to a series of specific duties to which analogies must be drawn in order to found a duty—is a prime example of how common law reasoning is an ongoing process engaged in by judges. After reading the series of cases on the development of negligence, it would be difficult to say that judges were merely 'declaring' a common law which was already 'there'. The conclusion, rather, seems clearly to be that judges have been engaged in the 'making' of law. The politics of the common law is an obvious issue to consider once we have reached the conclusion that judges are engaged in a process of law 'making'. You might want to consider at this point the different visions that judges have regarding their role and power, as demonstrated by the cases.

Edmund M.A. Kwaw, *The Guide to Legal Analysis, Legal Methodology and Legal Writing* (Emond Montgomery, Toronto, 1992), pp.89–90:

Criticism of traditional Common Law analysis

"Traditional common law legal analysis has been criticized, especially by scholars of the critical legal studies school. These scholars argue that common law legal analysis paints an incomplete and unrealistic picture of the process of adjudication. According to their criticism, the principles of common law legal analysis—the doctrines of precedent, *stare decisis*, and *ratio decidendi*—are based on the misconception that there is a separate and distinct form of legal reasoning and analysis, which ultimately leads to the correct decision. The reality, the critics argue, is that, first, the above principles are so vague that they do not always lead to a logical conclusion or rationale in difficult cases, and some precedents are followed while others are not. Second, the nature of common law legal analysis is such that there are many different interpretations, distinctions, and justifications, which bestow on judges a significant amount of discretion. The principles of common law legal analysis therefore serve only to mask the values, ideology, preferences, and priorities of judges, which ultimately have an effect on the outcome of a case. . . .

The critics argue that the crucial questions always left unanswered are how do judges decide which precedent to follow and what approach do judges adopt in determining the significance of an ambiguous precedent? The answers, it is contended, lies in the values and priorities of different judges; these are the result of a mix of political, social, institutional, and experiential factors. This is clearly shown in the development of the law with regard to negligent misstatements discussed above.

In 1889, the English House of Lords decided in *Derry v Peek* that unless fraud was established, a plaintiff could not bring an action for a statement that was made negligently but in good faith. In 1914, however, this precedent was not followed in *Nocton v Ashburton*. The court said that the decision in *Derry v Peek* had not precluded actions for statements where there existed a fiduciary relationship between the parties. Why the court had not taken into account the relationship between those who issued and prepared the company prospectus and the plaintiff in *Derry*, was not explained. This was followed in 1951 in *Candler v Crane, Christmas & Co*, which also involved the preparation of company accounts. The House of Lords held that no fiduciary relationship existed. Subsequently, however, in *Hedley Byrne & Co Ltd v Heller & Partners Ltd* decided in 1964, the law lords held that *Nocton* did not refer only to fiduciary relationships, but to all special relationships where one party trusted another to do something on his or her behalf. The court offered no explanation for not finding such a special relationship in *Candler*. All that the House of Lords said was that *Candler* had been wrongly decided.

In all these cases the House of Lords never provided any explanation of how it determined if it was bound by a precedent. There was no indication that the majority in the House were not, in reality, deciding the various cases on the basis of what they wished the law to be. Thus, although it was not stated in the discussion of all the precedents, the above cases could not have been decided without some ultimate reference to the values and choices of the judges concerned.

What the above suggests is that the doctrines of precedent and *stare decisis* cannot lead to a specific result or rationale in certain cases. Neither do these doctrines ensure continuity, predictability, rationality, or objectivity. Instead of determining the principles and outcomes of cases, they seem to support such outcomes."

QUESTIONS

- Do you agree with Kwaw's assessment of common law reasoning? Defend your position.

- Is it inevitable that judges must bring their own politics to the process of judicial decision making? Can it be avoided?

Kwaw's focus is on how *stare decisis* in the common law system masks the underlying political and social choices which are made by judges. A further aspect of the development of the duty of care in negligence has also been subject to critique. If you review the judgments which have been excerpted in this chapter, you will notice that frequently judges have referred to the standard of the "reasonable man" as the basis for determining whether a duty of care was breached. Within judicial reasoning, this "reasonable man" standard is assumed, somehow, to operate objectively, neutrally, apolitically, and uncontroversially. Presumably, the question of what standard of behaviour a "reasonable man" would engage in is obvious—at least to judges. Of course, if you think about it, there is no one, universal "reasonable man" standard. The determination of reasonableness inevitably involves social, cultural and political choices, and the standard of reasonableness will vary depending upon one's ideological position. Yet, common law reasoning tends to mask such choices within the language of reasonableness. Feminist tort theory in particular has usefully interrogated the gendering of the "reasonable man".

Joanne Conaghan, "Feminist Perspectives on the Law of Tort" in *The Critical Lawyers' Handbook 2* (Paddy Ireland and Per Laleng, eds., Pluto Press, London, 1997), pp.127–128:

"The feminist critique of negligence's 'reasonable man' raises issues of form as well as substance. In other words, it is not just the content of the standard being applied which is under scrutiny, it is also the application of a single and allegedly objective, universal standard to human behaviour at all. What feminist legal theory reveals (in the company of critical legal theory in general) is that law is neither politically nor morally neutral but is value-laden: it is an expression of particular values and assumptions about the distribution of resources in society (and individual access to them) which has blatantly political consequences. Thus judges when assessing reasonable behaviour, whether they are articulating their own subjective opinions or whether they are engaged in a genuine attempt to give expression to what they believe are prevailing social standards of proper behaviour, are making, in effect, policy-based decisions, that is, decisions which appeal to particular values and moral preferences governing individual relationships with each other and with the state. These are values about which reasonable people may well disagree.

Thus the conventional understanding of the reasonable man as an objective measure of human behaviour is a legal fiction: he is in fact merely a particular expression of appropriate human behaviour inevitably reflecting the values and assumptions, experience and understanding of those responsible for his birth and subsequent upbringing. For this reason it is not enough to simply replace the 'reasonable man' standard with an appeal to the 'reasonable person' as is the practice in some of the more 'politically correct' textbooks. The reasonable person is no more objective than the reasonable man. Indeed the claim to objectivity is itself contentiously male: objectivity, it is alleged, is the method by which men's point of view is privileged and women's silenced."

CASE LAW EXERCISE

Your client, Albert, is a regular patron of a pub. One evening he consumed five pints of lager there, all of which were served to him by Barbara, the proprietor. Albert normally only drinks lemonade, but was upset because of an argument he had had earlier with his wife, Carol. He became extremely intoxicated and then began to abuse other patrons in the pub. He was promptly asked to leave the establishment by Barbara. It was obvious to everyone at that point that Albert was very unsteady on his feet. Because of her long acquaintance with Albert, Barbara was aware that the location of Albert's house required him to cross a very busy road after leaving the pub. In fact, the road has a reputation in the neighbourhood for being dangerous for pedestrians, even when they are sober. Upon leaving the pub, Albert stumbled down the street, into the busy road, was hit by a passing motorist and badly injured. He now wishes to sue Barbara in negligence. The only relevant authorities in this case are *Barrett v Ministry of Defence* [1995] 3 All E.R. 87, CA; and *Crocker v Sundance Northwest Resorts* [1988] 1 S.C.R. 1186, a decision of the Supreme Court of Canada. The relevant portions of Barrett are set out below, and Crocker is sufficiently discussed, for our purposes, within the judgment in *Barrett*. Read the judgment as excerpted, and answer questions which follow it.

Barrett v Ministry of Defence [1995] 3 All E.R. 87, CA.

Beldam L.J.:

"In these proceedings Mrs Dawn Barrett, widow of Terence Barrett, claims damages for herself and her son Liam under the Fatal Accidents Act 1976 and for the benefit of the estate of her deceased husband under the Law Reform (Miscellaneous Provisions) Act 1934. She blames the appellant, the Ministry of Defence, for the death of her husband who was serving in the Royal Navy. On May 12, 1993 Judge Phelan, sitting as a deputy judge of the High Court, gave judgment for the plaintiff for £160, 651.16. . . . The appellant in this appeal challenges one of the two grounds on which the judge found it to have been in breach of duty to the deceased. . . .

At the time of his death Terence Barrett, the deceased, was thirty years of age and a naval airman serving at a shore based establishment of the Royal Navy at Barduffos in northern Norway. The naval base is somewhat isolated and the shore facilities are uninviting. It was used for a series of training exercises known as 'Exercise Clockwork'. On January 6, 1988 detachments of marine commandos, together with No 845 Helicopter Squadron from Royal Naval Air Station, Yeovilton arrived to take part in one of these training exercises. The deceased was attached to the squadron.

Because the recreational facilities ashore were limited, the appellant had installed several

video rooms, computer equipment, a gymnasium, a sauna and other recreational and educational facilities. Within the base there were three bars: the ward room, the senior rates' bar
and the junior rates' bar, at which duty free drink could be obtained. Drinking in these bars
when off duty was one of the main recreations of personnel attached to the base. In January
1988 the senior naval officer at Barduffos was Lt Cdr Lomax. The evidence was to show that
his attitude to the enforcement of the Queen's Regulations for the Royal Navy 1967 (BR 31)
and of standing orders, in particular to excessive drinking and drunkenness, was unusually
lax. As a consequence of the death of the deceased he was charged with and pleaded guilty
to a breach of Art.181 of the Queen's Regulations, which provides: 'It is the particular duty
of all officers, Fleet Chief Petty Officers, Chief Petty Officers and leading ratings actively to
discourage drunkenness, over-indulgence in alcohol and drug abuse by naval personnel both
on board and ashore. . . .' His plea of guilty acknowledged that he had negligently performed the duty of actively discouraging drunkenness and over-indulgence in alcohol. . . .

   The facts leading up to the death of the deceased were not in dispute. He died in his bunk
between 2 am and 2.30 am on the morning of Saturday, January 23, 1988. Friday, January
22 was the deceased's thirtieth birthday. He had recently learned that after some ten years'
service he was to be promoted leading hand and so had additional reason to celebrate.
Friday evening was customarily an evening for heavy drinking. On this Friday a Hawaiian
party event had been organised in the senior rates' bar. A number of the senior rates attend-
ing the party decided they would compete to see who could drink the most. Very substantial quantities of duty free spirits were consumed.

   The deceased went to the junior rates' bar at about 9.15 pm to begin his celebrations.
Having placed money behind the bar to treat his mess mates, the judge found he himself
consumed there three cans of cider and two double Bacardis. At about 10.30 pm he was
invited to the senior rates' bar where he was bought six Bacardis, each of which was a
double measure. By about 11 pm he had consumed a minimum of four ciders and nine
double Bacardis. It was not, however, suggested that the barmen in charge of either bar
had served him personally with this number of drinks. Most of the drinks were bought for
him. At about 11.30 pm he returned to the junior rates' bar to get fuel for his cigarette
lighter and then went back to the senior rates' bar where, shortly afterwards, he became
unconscious. He was carried back to the junior rates' bar where he was placed on a chair
in the lobby. He was seen there by Lt Cdr Parker who had just returned from sledging. The
deceased was then in a collapsed state and insensible. Petty Officer Wells, the duty senior
rate whose office was nearby, organised a stretcher and the deceased was taken to his cabin
where he was placed in his bunk in the recovery position. He was in a coma but tossing and
turning. He was visited on about three occasions by the duty ratings. When his cabin mate
went to turn in at about 2.30 am, he found that the deceased had vomited, had inhaled his
vomit and was apparently asphyxiated. Attempts were made to revive him but without
success. A board of inquiry was held and a ship's inquiry and many statements were taken
from witnesses. Based on these statements and the evidence which he had heard, the judge
found that at this isolated base cases of drunkenness, especially at the weekends, were commonplace and that disciplinary action that might lead to punishment was not taken.

   The judge also found there was a much more relaxed attitude to drinking tolerated at
this base than there would be in the United Kingdom. Drunkenness was common at the
weekends when the men were off duty and especially on Friday nights. The judge summarised the situation disclosed by the evidence as 'a perfectly deplorable situation'.

   The appellant does not challenge this assessment of the discipline at Barduffos. Of the
deceased the judge found that he was quite a heavy drinker and this was widely known.
There was little inducement for anyone to go ashore for recreation for alcohol prices were
remarkably high in Norway and astonishingly low in the base. A good range of recreational
facilities existed but boredom was inevitable and foreseeable. He was under the appellant's
codes of discipline and it controlled all facilities. Disciplinary codes existed which, if implemented, would have greatly reduced drunkenness. He said that the deceased was a heavy
drinker introduced to a potentially dangerous situation. In these circumstances the judge
held that it was foreseeable in this particular environment that the deceased would succumb
to heavy intoxication. Although it was only in exceptional circumstances that a defendant

could be fixed with a duty to take positive steps to protect a person of full age and capacity from his own weakness, he considered in the exceptional circumstances that arose in this case it was just and reasonable to impose a duty to take care on the appellant. He also held that the appellant was in breach of that duty because it failed to enforce the standards it itself set in matters of discipline. . . .

The appellant does not challenge the judge's findings that it was in breach of duty to take care of the deceased once he had collapsed and it had assumed responsibility for him.

The appellant's principal ground of appeal is that the judge was wrong to hold that it was under any duty to take care to see that the deceased, a mature man thirty years of age, did not consume so much alcohol that he became unconscious. If the deceased himself was to be treated as a responsible adult, he alone was to blame for his collapse. . . .

The purpose of Queen's Regulations and standing orders is to preserve good order and discipline in the service and to ensure that personnel remain fit for duty and while on duty obey commands and off duty do not misbehave bringing the service into disrepute. All regulations which encourage self-discipline, if obeyed, will incidentally encourage service personnel to take greater pride in their own behaviour but in no sense are the regulations and orders intended to lay down standards or to give advice in the exercise of reasonable care for the safety of the men when off duty drinking in the bars.

The judge placed reliance on the fact that it was foreseeable that if the regulations and standing orders were not properly enforced in this particular environment the deceased would succumb to heavy intoxication. He also said it was just and reasonable to impose a duty in these circumstances. . . .

In the present case the judge posed the question whether there was a duty at law to take reasonable steps to prevent the deceased becoming unconscious through alcohol abuse. He said his conclusion that there was such a duty was founded on the fact that: 'It was foreseeable in the environment in which the defendant grossly failed to enforce their regulations and standing orders that the deceased would succumb to heavy intoxication.' And in these circumstances that it was just and reasonable to impose a duty.

The respondent argued for the extension of a duty to take care for the safety of the deceased from analogous categories of relationship in which an obligation to use reasonable care already existed. For example employer and employee, pupil and schoolmaster and occupier and visitor. It was said that the appellant's control over the environment in which the deceased was serving and the provision of duty free liquor, coupled with the failure to enforce disciplinary rules and orders were sufficient factors to render it fair, just and reasonable to extend the duty to take reasonable care found in the analogous circumstances. The characteristic which distinguishes those relationships is reliance expressed or implied in the relationship which the party to whom the duty is owed is entitled to place on the other party to make provision for his safety. I can see no reason why it should not be fair, just and reasonable for the law to leave a responsible adult to assume responsibility for his own actions in consuming alcoholic drink. No one is better placed to judge the amount that he can safely consume or to exercise control in his own interest as well as in the interest of others. To dilute self-responsibility and to blame one adult for another's lack of self-control is neither just nor reasonable and in the development of the law of negligence an increment too far. . . .

The respondent placed reliance on *Crocker v Sundance Northwest Resorts Ltd* [1988] 1 SCR 1186, a decision of the Supreme Court of Canada. . . . In [*Crocker*] . . . the defendant was held liable to an intoxicated plaintiff for permitting him to take part in a dangerous ski hill race which caused him to be injured. The defendant had taken the positive step of providing him with the equipment needed for the race knowing that he was in no fit state to take part. The plaintiff had consumed alcohol in the defendant's bars. Liability was based not on permitting him to drink in the bars but in permitting him to take part in the race. . . . [T]he court founded the imposition of a duty on factors additional to the mere provision of alcohol and the failure strictly to enforce provisions against drunkenness.

In the present case I would reverse the judge's finding that the appellant was under a duty to take reasonable care to prevent the deceased from abusing alcohol to the extent he did. Until he collapsed I would hold that the deceased was in law alone responsible for his condition. Thereafter, when the appellant assumed responsibility for him, it accepts that the measures taken fell short of the standard reasonably to be expected. It did not summon medical assistance and its supervision of him was inadequate. . . .

The deceased involved the appellant in a situation in which it had to assume responsibility for his care and I would not regard it as just and equitable in such circumstances to be unduly critical of the appellant's fault. I consider a greater share of blame should rest upon the deceased than on the appellant and I would reduce the amount of the damages recoverable by the respondent by two-thirds holding the appellant one third to blame. . . ."

Saville L.J.: "I agree."

Neill L.J.: "I also agree."

QUESTIONS

- What were the material facts of *Barrett*?

- What was the *ratio decidendi* of *Barrett*?

- In *Barrett*, the trial judge found the appellant in breach of a duty to the deceased on two grounds. Which ground was conceded by the appellant to be a breach of its duty?

- How would you describe the political ideology which underpins the judgment in *Barrett*? Individualist? Welfarist? Why?

- Construct a brief argument on the law in favour of your client Albert, which you could use in civil proceedings launched against Barbara.

ESSAY QUESTION

"The descriptive question that lawyers debate is whether in fact courts resolve issues primarily by the application of rules or by the application of policies. The orthodox view is that judges apply rules through the logical processes of deduction and analogy, turning to policies only in the occasional hard case. The competing theory is that judges in reality intuit the best result, that is, the result that is most satisfactory to them as a matter of policy, and only then do they turn to the rules to explain and justify the result they have reached on other grounds. In this view, the judge may even have the sensation of following the rules, but the interpretation of those rules as the judge applies them is guided by prior intuition about the most desirable resolution. In this way, the rules can seem to produce the correct result."

(Kenneth J. Vandevelde, *Thinking Like a Lawyer* (Westview Press, Boulder, 1996), p.66).

Comment on the above quotation, using the cases discussed in this chapter as the basis for your answer. Describe the 'values and assumptions' which have informed the development of a general duty of care in negligence.

PART FIVE: PEOPLE, SYSTEMS AND METHODS

12

THE LEGAL PROFESSIONS

So far in this collection our focus has been on the courts and methods of legal reasoning. In this chapter we turn our attention to the professionals who provide legal services to the public and prepare cases for litigation. The aim of the chapter is to encourage you to reflect on how legal education and the apprenticeships that lawyers undertaken prepare them for life as a practitioner. We consider what sociologists call the "socialisation process" whereby novices are introduced to and internalise the norms of the professional group to which they aspire to join. Later in the chapter we consider how the values of the university law school and the profession tend towards conservatism and the creation of certain types of lawyers. In the same context we also review the extent to which the notion of the impartiality of the profession, and in particular the judiciary, can be upheld when both tend to be drawn from a small section of society. We start with an overview of the characteristics of modern legal practice.

Martin Partington *An Introduction to the English Legal System* **(Oxford University Press, Oxford, 2000), pp.196–205:**

"There are currently over 71,000 practising solicitors in England and Wales, plus another 12,000 or so barristers. The majority of these are in private practice, though a substantial minority are employed lawyers working 'in-house' for a wide variety of companies, government departments, and agencies. Both these totals have increased very rapidly over the last quarter of a century. They reflect increased demands for legal services resulting from economic growth, structural changes affecting the commercial world such as globalization and involvement in Europe, and numerous other social changes with greater emphasis on citizens' rights. . . .

The organization of the practising legal profession in England and Wales is very different to the position in many other countries. There is still an important distinction in professional identity between *solicitors*, who are professional regulated by the Law Society, and *barristers*, who are regulated by the General Council of the Bar (Bar Council).

Solicitors in private practice usually come together to form partnerships, though a substantial minority practice on their own as 'sole practitioners'. Barristers in private practice come together in 'chambers' but they are self-employed within those chambers. Barristers are not currently permitted to form partnerships.

Independence

One of the key attributes claimed for the legal profession is that it should be independent. This is, constitutionally, an extremely important claim, as it involves lawyers asserting their right to give advice independent of the view of the government of the day. It also involves a professional obligation to take on cases which may be regarded as disagreeable or distasteful. The proposition that a person is innocent until proved guilty depends on lawyers being willing to develop and advance arguments on behalf of their clients no matter how unpleasant those clients may be. The 'cab-rank' principle which applies to the Bar, whereby barristers are professionally obliged to take on whatever case comes to them next, is perhaps the clearest example of the operation of this principle.

This assertion of independence also implies that the professions should be left free to regulate themselves in accordance with their own rules of professional conduct, and without interference from government. As will be seen, there has been significant erosion of the freedom from government intervention in the legal profession over recent years. The abolition of restrictive practices, the changes to legal aid, and modes of dealing with complaints about the quality of work will all be noted as examples of government intervention. Each example of government involvement may be justified, particularly in contexts where the legal profession has not been willing to reform itself in ways in which the public interest might seem to demand. However, the question of where the boundaries should be drawn in the involvement of government in the legal profession is one that needs constant attention, if the role of the legal profession in assisting the individual, often against agencies of the state or other powerful agencies, is not to be compromised.

Trends in legal practice

In the same way that the institutional framework of the legal profession has undergone profound change in recent years, so too has the legal profession. A number of trends affecting the profession are noted here.

The blurring of the distinction between solicitors and barristers

First, though the line between 'solicitor' and 'barrister' can still be drawn as a matter of professional identity, the practical implications of the distinction are much less today than they were twenty years ago. Many of the services which used to be the exclusive preserve of one branch of the profession are now open to all.

The blurring of the distinction is largely the result of a sustained attack on the restrictive practices of lawyers which has lasted for over thirty years. But there has also been a concern that there should be no unnecessary restrictions on the tasks which people might perform with the legal system. The most important change, in this context, has been the adoption by statute of the principle that the highest judicial offices should be open to solicitors, just as much as to barristers (who formerly had the monopoly in these appointments).

Some of the changes have resulted from the professional bodies deciding to change their rules. Others, particularly in the last decade, have been the result of intervention by government. . . .

Growth and globalization

A second trend to be noted is the growth in the size of law firms, and the increasingly global perspective they adopt to practice. These have resulted from the context within which lawyers practice, which cannot be divorced from other changes in the economy at large. The last twenty years have seen a major shift from an economy based on manufacturing to one based on services. Increased globalization of the world economy has led to a growth in the need for lawyers able to advise corporations about all the national contexts within which they are required to operate. There has been a globalization in the provision of legal services which has accompanied the globlization of the economy. British lawyers have responded in a variety of ways:

- Many of the large law firms in the City of London have gone through substantial programmes of merger and expansion.

- Significant groupings of leading firms in provincial commercial centres—for example Leeds, Birmingham, Bristol—have also developed, either through mergers and takeovers, or the creation of networks of legal practices.

- Many of these firms have established presences in other key centres of economic activity, in Europe, the Middle East, the Far East, and the Americas.

- There are beginning to emerge mergers of English law firms with firms in other countries (for example Germany and the US) to create new forms of international partnership.

- There has been a significant increase in the presence of overseas law firms, and in particular US law firms, in London which have added to the competitive pressures on British-based firms.

- There have been moves towards the creation of professional groupings that cut across traditional disciplinary boundaries—in particular, lawyers and accountants. The issue of the establishment of multi-disciplinary partnerships—which has been around for many years—has fast risen up the policy agendas of the professional bodies.

There is every likelihood of further developments of these kinds in the years ahead.

Specialization and niche practices

A third trend to be noted has been the increasing development of specialist/niche practices. In part this is a response to the trend towards 'mega-lawyering' noted in the previous section. Increasingly, small firms of solicitors and sets of barristers chambers have come to specialize in particular areas—family law, criminal law, employment law, and housing law to give some examples. These developments have been supported in part by the legal professional bodies themselves. For example, the Law Society has established a number of specialist panels which practitioners may join, including the Children's Panel, the Mental Health Panel and the Medical Negligence Panel. . . .

Legal services to the poor

A fourth noteworthy trend in the shape of the legal profession has been a complete transformation in the operation of the legal aid scheme. . . . Here the principal point to note is that, whereas ten years ago in effect any firm of solicitors who wished to do legal aid work could do so, now only those firms with a 'franchise' approved by and a contract to provide services from the Legal Services Commission (replacing the Legal Aid Board) will be able to undertake publicly funded legal aid work. Many practitioners of general legal services provided to mainly private clients are affected by these changes.

The likelihood of this happening has been obvious for some time, as successive governments have sought to control legal aid expenditure and obtain better value for money for the legal services they finance. Those who understood how policy in relation to the funding of legal services was likely to develop have been able to take advantage of the new mechanisms for the delivery of funded legal services and offer a service that makes a profit— albeit perhaps not a huge one. Those that resisted these developments or refused to seem them coming have suffered severely and may well go to the wall.

High street practice

A consequence of these last two developments is that the general 'high streets practices', found in the high streets of towns, suburban areas, and other locations, which have in the past tended to provide a general service to private client customers, have come under increasing pressure and face considerable uncertainty. The ability to make a living from a mixed practice of some criminal work, some property work such as conveyancing or probate, a little bit of family and divorce work, and some personal injuries work, which even ten years ago was quite common, is now increasingly difficult. Many of the remaining sole practitioners and small firms fall into this category. The future of the generalist high street practice is under considerable threat, unless those who remain in this sector of the legal services market are prepared to rethink their commercial strategies."

NOTES AND QUESTIONS

- Solicitors and barristers are not the only people who give legal advice. Can you think of others who perform this? Do advisers of this kind have to have law degrees to do their job effectively?

- Is it time for the two branches of the legal profession to fuse so that the roles of adviser and advocate are combined as happens in most other jurisdictions? Can you think of arguments to support the proposition that they should not merge?

- Do you think that lawyers should have a professional obligation to take on cases where they disapprove of the conduct of their client? How does the cab-rank rule allow the profession to claim independence? Give reasons for your answer.

- Should we follow the practice of many other jurisdictions in allowing academics who have not qualified as a practising lawyer to be appointed to the judiciary? What reasons can you think for excluding this disreputable group?

Solicitors and barristers are commonly described as members of the legal profession but what does it mean to be a member of a profession? What is it that makes lawyers different from other workers such as tradespeople or other specialists? Conversely do they share some of the characteristics of other groups which are labelled as professionals such as doctors or teachers? The subject is one on which there has been much debate. In the following extract Phil Harris reviews some of the key arguments which have been put forward in attempts to distinguish the work undertaken by lawyers from other types of employment.

Phil Harris, *An Introduction to Law* (6th ed., Butterworths, London, 2002), pp.439–440.

"Lawyers have traditionally held themselves out as 'professionals', which, sociologically, carries the implication that, as professionals, lawyers occupy key positions within society, respected by lay people as having possession of specialised knowledge and the claimed ability to solve clients' problems. The sociological analyses of professions suggest that professional people are identifiable by reason of their possession of five traits, or characteristics: (i) command of a systematic body of theoretical and specialised knowledge; (ii) professional authority; (iii) the approval and support of the community; (iv) a rigorous code of ethics regulating their activities; and (v) a professional 'culture'. A somewhat similar set of characteristics was listed in the Benson Commission report in 1979, and it has been commented that this approach:

> 'ensured that, among other things, self-regulation would continue and that the "altruistic" nature of the lawyer/client relationship would preclude the introduction of the market. The client would continue to be grateful to the lawyer for a service based on trust, confidentiality, and independence rather than upon competition and economic choice. The term "money" was not to be discussed with or by the client, as the crucial terms were "service" and "justice"—and on justice no price can be placed.'

. . . It is the body of professional knowledge, and the claim to be able to use it to deal with clients' disputes and problems, that maintains and enhances the lawyer's professional authority. Lawyers present themselves to clients, and indeed to the community, as having an *authoritative voice* on all legal matters, and this arguably structures to a great extent the relationship between lawyer and client. Some have argued that the professional-client relationship is one based on *power*: the professional has what the client wants or needs: he or she defines the manner in which the service is to be given and, equally importantly, defines the very *nature* of the client's problem. Typically, the client cannot argue that the professional's opinion or advice is wrong, inaccurate or inappropriate, for it is usually acknowledged by the client that the professional knows best what is in the client's interests.

Abel, drawing up sociological analyses of professions, has produced a substantial analysis of the legal profession in the United Kingdom, and the ways in which it has attempted to respond to both criticism and structural changes in the market for legal services. He notes that:

> "Producers of a service who succeed in constructing a marketable commodity only become an occupation. In order to become a profession they must seek social closure. This project has two dimensions: market control and collective social mobility . . . All occupations are compelled by the market to compete . . .

The professional project is directed not only toward controlling the market but also toward enhancing professional status . . . the lengthy training professionals must complete perhaps may be better understood not as the acquisition of technical skills but as a sacrifice necessary to justify future privilege: only this can make sense of the relative poverty endured by students . . . the tedium of study, the indignities of apprenticeship, the anxiety inflicted by examinations and the lengthy postponement of adulthood."

. . . All lawyers undergo extensive periods of education, both through formal academic learning and through practical training in legal work. In the case of solicitors, this practical training takes the form of a two-year period, after obtaining a law degree and completing the one-year, full-time Legal Practice Course, in a training contract with a firm of practitioners. For intending barristers, the period of training is rather more complicated and less financially secure, but possibly more intensive because of the immersion of the novice in the traditions and practices of the Bar. Apart from undertaking various examinations in law, the prospective barrister must also join one of the four Inns of Court, where the life of the barrister is learned. The various rules and institutions of the Bar serve to socialise the novice into the established ways of that branch of the profession, where customs, tradition and etiquette play so great a part. Barristers' professional, and often much of their social, life involves an exclusive and somewhat socially isolated experience, where the company in which they move comprises, very often, other barristers and judges who are members of the same Inn."

Others have also commented on the close link between professionalisation and the education process. In his discussion of the role of legal skills within the law school curriculum Andrew Boon develops these arguments:

Andrew Boon, "History is Past Politics: A Critique of the Legal Skills Movement in England and Wales", *Journal of Law and Society*, **Vol. 25(1), pp.151–56.**

"The starting point is to recognize the importance of the functional and symbolic role that education played in the English legal profession's claim for respectability and status. At the earliest opportunity both branches of the profession established apprenticeship as the main route into the profession. It is significant to the argument developed in this essay that articles of clerkship were a moral rather than a cognitive training. The decline of professionalism in law was brought about by prospective entrants forsaking the five-year articled clerkship in favour of the law degree. The personal relationships of solicitors had been the cement of the profession, and the means by which it continuously reproduced itself as a club of white, middle-class males. More importantly, articles of clerkship guaranteed the commitment and values of entrants to the profession. They offered 'a period of hardship, drudgery and semi-servitude' which '. . . instilled respect for one's elders, for their experience, for their manners, conventions and ethics and for their sense of corporate honour' and offered 'cast-iron guarantees about the attitudes demeanour and commitment of those who were to enter the profession.' Wider access to educational opportunities, and a rapidly changing practice environment, precipitated a search for new means of ensuring professional inclusiveness and the reproduction of professional values. . . .

The declining fortunes of the profession was a catalyst of the move to a vocational education built about skills. Until the 1970s the legal profession assumed that there was nothing to fear from the state. It acted as if there was a tacit agreement which secured its privileges in return for a commitment to act in the public interest. From the end of the decade, however, the notion that lawyers' perception of the public interest was at best misconceived, or at worst partial and self-interested, gained ground. Sociologists came to see professions as a means of concentrating and exercising power, and their ethical commitments as elements of an ideological weaponry which operated to justify privilege. The benefits offered by professions to clients as consumers, and the wider society, were called into question. The profession's record in relation to conveyancing and criminal legal aid were particularly important for they implied that lawyers systematically exploited two of its main constituencies; the middle classes on the one hand and the state on the other.

The undermining of the profession's public image prepared the ground for the political onslaught on the profession's jurisdiction by the Thatcher governments of the 1980s. In the environment of uncertainty created, competition and levels of competence were causes of deep concern. Until that time professional knowledge had always been inextricably linked with professional power. Professions were seen to exercise market control through the construction of a 'professional commodity' spanning the technical and ideological spheres. The commodity was built on the notion of technical skill and inherent uncertainty such that professional education was preparation for the exercise of discretion. With the failure of the five-year articles, the last association with an educational tradition which had helped to secure professional power, was university style education. Universities were also, however, experiencing change. Their use of transmission modes of teaching assumed that learners were an intellectually and socially homogeneous group, an assumption which was manifestly less true as access widened from the late 1960s. The professional bodies colluded with a hidden agenda of traditional legal education, the belief that, by keeping the arts of practice 'secret' until admission, it was possible to maintain the fine balance between technicality and indeterminacy and, thereby, to maintain professional mystique. The rationalization of technical skills not only signalled the failure of this approach, it threatened two fundamental assumptions. First, the idea that professional expertise was found and transmitted only within the body of the profession and, second, the idea that a rigid distinction between academic and professional programmes was inevitable."

NOTES AND QUESTIONS

- In 1985 the Thatcher government abolished the statutory protection enjoyed by solicitors in their monopoly of conveyancing in the Administration of Justice Act. This allowed licensed conveyancers, who were not required to have a law degree to oversee the transfer of real estate. This provoked outrage amongst solicitors. Why do you think they were so concerned? Did this reform undermine any of the claims to professionalism and social closure identified by Harris?

- Do you think that there are particular types of knowledge or skills which lawyers possess which mark them out from other workers? What are they? Compare yourself with a friend at university who is studying a subject other than law. Do any aspects of your education mark your courses out as different? Are there any similarities?

- In other jurisdictions it is common for solicitors to undertake work which in this country would commonly be referred to an accountant. Are there any jobs which solicitors and barristers undertake which you think others could perform equally as well?

- Do you think that a rigid distinction between academic and professional stages of training is inevitable or desirable? In other jurisdictions, such as Scotland and Australia, the distinction is not nearly as clear as is the case in England. Can you think of any reasons why the academic and practical should be kept separate and those who design these different courses should remain autonomous from each other?

- How many of the people on your course want to become solicitors or barristers? Do you think that a law degree has a purpose other than preparing you for one of the legal professions?

In order to gain a clearer understanding of how lawyers acquire the specialist knowledge they do and why certain types of knowledge are privileged over others it is necessary to look at the role of the law school in the socialisation process.

Fiona Cownie and Anthony Bradney, *English Legal System in Context* (2nd ed., Butterworths, London, 2000), pp.128–132:

"University law schools are not simply one of the bureaucratic divisions of a university. Law schools, like departments of other disciplines in universities, are examples of specific cultures which are separated both from the outside world and from other cultures within the university.

'The tribes of academe . . . define their own identities and defend their own patches of intellectual ground by employing a variety of devices geared to the exclusion of illegal immigrants. Some . . . are manifest in physical form ("the building occupied by the

English department", in Clark's words); others emerge in the particularities of membership and constitution (Waugh's "complex of tribes, each with its own chief and elders
and witch-doctors and braves"). Alongside these structural features of disciplinary communities, exercising an even more powerful integrating force, are their more explicitly
cultural elements: their traditions, customs and practices, transmitted knowledge,
beliefs, morals and rules of conduct, as well as their symbolic forms of communication
and meanings they share.'

It is this culture which helps define the values of university law schools. Identifying the
culture of the university law school is difficult. 'Our law schools, despite sharing a common
culture, are probably too diverse to lend themselves to reliable generalisation.' Individual
variations in practice can appear to be more important that common themes. University
law schools are found in old and new universities. They may be faculties on their own or
departments within a faculty of social sciences. The largest faculties number in excess of
1,000 students, while the smallest may be no more than several hundred, Staff sizes vary in
similar proportions. However, despite all these important variations there are, nevertheless,
some dominant ideas which prevail in most law schools and which constitute the culture
of the university law school. . . .

In an early, very influential article Kennedy argued that '[l]aw schools are intensely political places despite the fact that the modern law school seems intellectually unpretentious,
barren of theoretical ambition or practical vision of what social life might be'.

Kennedy's argument pointed to a number of features which he thought were important
in the ideological impact of the university law school. First, the law school was hierarchical, with the nature of the relationship between lecturer and student being determined by
the lecturer. Second, the study of law involved the study of a new language. Third, law was
put forward as a matter of rules. Fourth, in applying these rules one's emotions or sympathies were deemed to be irrelevant. Finally, the law school provided no overt theory in its
teaching which could act as a source for critique:

> 'Teachers convince students that legal reasoning exists, and is different from policy anal-
> ysis, by bullying them into accepting as valid in particular cases arguments about legal
> correctness that are circular, question-begging, incoherent, or so vague as to be mean-
> ingless. Sometimes these are just arguments from authority, with the validity of the
> authoritative premise put outside discussion by professorial fiat. Sometimes they are
> policy arguments (eg security of transaction, business certainty) that are treated in a par-
> ticular situation as though they were rules that everyone accepts but that will be ignored
> in the next case when they would suggest that the decision was wrong. Sometimes they
> are exercises in formal logic that wouldn't stand up for a minute in a discussion between
> equals (eg the small print in a form contract represents the "will of the parties".)'

Using these methods, black-letter law presents itself, through the cases, statutes and textbooks, as a form of objective knowledge; there is a legally correct outcome to a particular
dispute which, with proper training, the student will discern. A failure to see the objectively
right answer by the student is characterised by the lecturer (and frequently the student) as
a failure to learn the language of law or a failure in knowing the correct rules or an inability to disentangle one's emotional or political sympathies from one's intellectual understanding of the law. However, in Kennedy's view, in fact all there is in law is a distinctive
argumentative technique. This technique does not determine any particular outcome; does
not produce a closure which will require a predestined answer. Legal technique is simply a
form of argument that literally will sound right to another lawyer.

One of the results of the black-letter approach to law teaching is that there appears to
be a strict separation of the question of what law is and what law should be. In learning
the former questions about the latter do not need to be raised. Outcomes of cases do not
need justifying from either an ethical or a political standpoint. They simply are the law.
Thus, in the British context, Fitzpatrick has argued that '[t]he deep complicities between
professional and academic conceptions of law produced an English jurisprudence that . . .
protected law from significant engagement with political and social issues'. Indeed, it has
been argued that raising questions about the social impact of particular legal rules is not

appropriate within a law school. 'The desired result, at the end of legal training, is a competent lawyer who can analyse and apply legal doctrine in an intelligent and disinterested fashion.' Law is seen as a value-free tool.

Kennedy's argument directly opposes this traditional approach. In his view the outcomes to cases are determined not by the content of the rules themselves or by the nature of legal argument but by the policy biases, conscious and unconscious, of those who deal with them.'[E]verything taught [in the university law school], except the formal rules themselves and the argumentative techniques for manipulating them, is policy and nothing more'. The constant repetition of particular policy outcomes in individual cases reinforces a message that such outcomes are natural, inevitable and right. Students are learning an '[I]ndividualism [that] provides a justification for the fundamental legal institutions of criminal law, property, tort and contract'. The fact that these policy outcomes are not explicitly examined or set into any kind of social context further reinforces this message about their naturalness. On this view, by 'learning the law' students are also learning a set of political and ethical values that are oriented towards the status quo."

NOTES AND QUESTIONS

- How have your views about the purpose and relevance of law to wider society changed since you first joined your course? Are you conscious of having altered your views on such subjects as the link between law and justice?

- To what extent do you think it is important to study the impact of law and to place it in a social, political and economic context? What are the arguments against this approach?

The issue of lawyers preserving the status quo is taken up by Cotterell in his consideration of the effects of lawyers on the law. However, it can be seen from the following extract that he is more positive about the prospects of legal creativity than Kennedy.

Roger Cotterrell, *The Sociology of Law: An Introduction* (2nd ed., Butterworths, London, 1992, Chapter 6), pp.201–202, 192–193:

"One writer has suggested that the general conservatism that almost all commentators see as a dominant characteristic of lawyers derives from three sources related specifically to legal practice. First, lawyers are preoccupied with application of a *continuing* set of rules and principles—a stable, monolithic doctrinal structure of order. Secondly, there is the lawyer's 'more immediate and selfish interest in preserving his intellectual capital—the knowledge of the system in which he was trained' and, thirdly, 'there is the tendency of lawyers, and especially of the leading and most able lawyers, to be closely identified in interest with the establishment of the time—the men in power or the men who have prospered'. De Tocqueville wrote of lawyers as 'attached to public order beyond every other consideration', as having 'nothing to gain by innovation'. Morris Finer, himself an eminent British lawyer, remarked that the '*status quo* is part of [the lawyer's] mental capital. Every legal reform robs him of an asset he has worked hard to acquire'.

To write of conservatism in this context may be, however, to use too crude and unenlightening a concept. Throughout modern history there have been 'rebel' or 'radical' lawyers. Lawyers, after all, are not merely concerned with order, but with a particular kind of order: that which can be embodied in the legal doctrine that provides the basis of their professional claim to special expertise. The lawyer's professional commitment to the integrity of doctrine may easily be extended to a professional rejection and condemnation of those forms of order (for example, government by arbitrary terror or unfettered administrative discretion) that are not seen as encompasses by rational, systematic legal doctrine.

Furthermore, certain characteristics of legal doctrine which are adopted as the basis of lawyer's values may assume such importance in elaborated and extended forms that they become the basis of radical legal practice. Thus the concept of the rule of law (with its derivative principles of equal protection under the law and due process of law or natural justice in trial or quasi-judicial proceedings), together with the individualistic orientation of Western law, sometimes become the foundation of forceful advocacy of human rights or civil rights and demands for new forms of representation to bring the claims of the poor and of disadvantaged minorities before the law.

Finally, if lawyers in general have a strong interest in the protection of their 'mental capital', they are also sufficiently close to legal doctrine to recognise its contingent character, its *lacunae* and ambiguities, and to put into perspective (and so identify means of reforming) what appear to others as its awesome complexities. . . .

Maureen Cain, adopting Marx's term, argues that the lawyer is a 'conceptive ideologist': a translator rather than a controller; not dominating the client but translating the client's objectives into the terms of legal discourse and devising the means of achieving them within the framework of law. If this role can be attributed to the solicitors Cain studied and whom she sees as serving middle-class clients if fits more obviously elite lawyers serving powerful business organisations. Their role is to innovate and find ways within the legal system to protect their clients' interests. Today this is clearly a role that takes account of the uncertainties or leeways of legal doctrine—the complex interactions of rule and discretion. . . . Thus the elite legal adviser's role is far from being merely to 'state the law'. The expertise required is one that can use creatively both the certainties and uncertainties of law in strategies that are to the client's advantage. In general, insofar as the business world requires lawyers it needs strategists and troubleshooters, not jurists; experts who can obtain maximum freedom and maximum benefits for the enterprise from government and who can use the threat but rarely the reality of litigation creatively as a precision tool for furtherance of corporate interest. This situation reflects both the increasing significance of legal expertise in a climate of extensive government regulation of business and differences between businessmen's and lawyers' typical views of business transactions."

The issue of membership of, and access to, the legal professions has become a central theme of studies of the legal professions. This is because one of the ways in which the conservatism of lawyers discussed by Cownie, Bradney and Boon is explained is by reference to the narrow sections of society from which the profession is drawn. It has been argued that there is a significantly better gender balance amongst those entering the legal profession than there was 25 years ago. Statistics illustrate that more women than men have entered law school and become solicitors than did so 25 years ago. But this progress seems slow when one considers that women were first admitted to the profession over 80 years ago. Women continue to be poorly represented amongst the judiciary. Statistics published on the Lord Chancellor's Department website show that as of July 2003 no Lords of Appeal in the Ordinary were women, and they made up just six per cent of Lord Justices of Appeal, six per cent of High Court Judges, nine per cent of circuit judges; 12 per cent of Recorders and 19 per cent of district judges. But even this record is impressive when one compares the fate of women to those from ethnic minorities. Phil Harris has considered the record of the professions in relation to gender and ethnicity and also drawn attention to the ongoing significance of class.

Phil Harris, *An Introduction to Law* **(6th ed., Butterworths, London, 2002), pp 449–453:**

"In so far as educational background is an indicator of social class, a survey carried out by the Law Society's Research and Policy Planning Unit in 1989 of a sample of about 1,000 solicitors showed that over one-third had attended a fee-paying independent (or public) school; 11% had attended direct-grant grammar schools; 34% had been to state grammar schools, and only 14% had attended secondary modern or comprehensive schools. the survey report states however that the proportion of solicitors who have attended independent or public school has been declining over the years. There is now clearly a need for new surveys to provide updated information to see how far this trend has progressed.

The peculiarities of recruitment into the legal profession, coupled with its unique position within the social structure, still tend to favour the middle- and upper-middle class aspirant lawyer. The sheer cost of legal education, particularly postgraduate training, is, for many potential recruits, probably prohibitive, and these expenses must be found during the period of training, when novices are not allowed to take on cases for themselves and earn their own fees. Since 1990 the Bar has operated a scheme whereby barristers' chambers pay their pupils during their pupillage year; initially the amount payable was £6,000 per year (though some barristers' chambers paid pupils rather more than that) and has now been increased to £10,000. Even after qualification, however, a high income is not immediately guaranteed, partly because barristers must build up their reputation before cases begin to arrive regularly, and partly because fees earned for the first few cases may well take months to be paid. In many cases, too, pupil barristers will start their careers with substantial debt incurred as a result of the cost of the initial stages of legal education and training.

For an intending solicitor, the two years spent as a trainee are usually fairly lean financially, as they, too, will in all probability have built up substantial debts and are by no means well-paid—in 2000 the minimum starting salary for trainee solicitors was £13,600 in London and £12,000 elsewhere. Such considerations suggest that an intending lawyer, whichever branch of the profession he or she chooses, would do well to come from a background which is financially secure, and preferably have some form of independent income with which to supplement the leaner times of training and early experience. Not surprisingly, surveys have shown that many lawyers *do* come from middle- and upper-middle-class backgrounds: for example, studies of judges, who are traditionally recruited from the ranks of barrister, clearly show a predominance of public school and Oxford or Cambridge university educational backgrounds.

Not only is the legal profession predominantly middle- and upper-middle class; it is also a profession long dominated by *white male* practitioners. The significantly lower proportion of black and other ethnic minority lawyers to white, and the lower numbers of women in the profession (especially the Bar) has attracted considerable criticism over the years. With regard to solicitors, it was not until 1985 that a Race Relations Committee was established by the Law Society to monitor entry by members of black and other ethnic minority communities. In 1986 only 1% of solicitors with practising certificates came from such backgrounds, though this figure had risen to 6% by 1999–2000, and in the same year the Law Society reported that 19% of admissions to the Roll were from ethnic minority backgrounds. There is, however, evidence of discrimination against black students upon graduation, and of difficulties due to ethnic background in the working environment even when jobs can be obtained. And Law Society statistics relating to the year 1999–2000 indicate that over half of solicitors from ethnic minority groups holding practising certificates were employed not in private practice but by other employing organisations.

The picture with respect to barristers is little better. Although the Bar has long attracted —and indeed encouraged—students from overseas, the expectation was that, once qualified, they would return to practise in their home countries. . . .

These is little doubt that the Bar's record on this issue is unimpressive. There remains evidence that black barristers experience discrimination and racism both in obtaining places in chambers and in obtaining work. In order to do something to remedy the situation, the

Bar announced in 1991 a 5% target for the employment of black barristers and solicitors entering practice: in 2000, the Bar's published statistics indicated that just under 9% of barristers came from non-white backgrounds, as did (in July 2001) 18% of registered pupils.

The number of women practising lawyers is rather higher for both branches of the profession but, even here, there is no reason to believe that equality has been achieved. Despite a lamentable history within the solicitors' branch that included a ban on women until 1919 (a change forced on the profession by legislation passed in that year), the proportion of women becoming solicitors has risen dramatically in recent years and in 1999–2000 was 53% of the total admitted to the Roll, with women also accounting for 36% of all solicitors with practising certificates in that year. But this does not mean that there is equality in terms of career progression, although the situation is slowly improving: Law Society figures for 1999–2000 show that of solicitors with 10–19 years' experience in private practice, 84% of men were partners (or sole practitioners) compared with 58% of women. Probably more depressing is a research finding that almost a third of women solicitors have experienced sexual discrimination at work, and one in five have experienced harassment. A survey of 631 members of the Association of Women Solicitors reported in 2001 that 32% said they had experienced sex discrimination at work, compared with 2% and 4% respectively who claimed to have suffered discrimination on grounds of race or disability.

The history of the Bar is similar to that of the Law Society. Abel, reviewing the various surveys carried out over the past 30 years or so, identifies a number of barriers operating to discriminate against women at the Bar: discrimination in obtaining pupillages and tenancies; scholarships awarded by the Inns of Court which are available only to men; the exclusion of women from meetings; the refusal of banks to grant overdraft facilities to women barristers starting out in their careers; the obstacles posed by the profession's unconscious acceptance of the traditional division of labour in childrearing which forced many women to leave the profession for family reasons; and so on. The Benson Commission found that overall, women barristers earn substantially less that their male counterparts. Although the number of women becoming barristers has risen dramatically (women now account for about 30% of all barristers, as compared with about 13% in 1985) there are very few female heads of chambers, and in 1998 women comprised only 7% of QCs."

In their longitudinal study of over 3,000 law students from a range of universities Boon, Duff and Shiner have charted the nature of the 'disadvantages' suffered by many prospective entrants to the legal profession. Their six-year survey charted the progress of a one-year cohort from the second year of their law degree to the point when most of the cohort had been qualified for two years. Their analysis suggests that only a minority of students from minority or disadvantaged backgrounds make it to a point where they are assessed on their abilities rather than their social background.

Andrew Boon, Liz Duff and Michael Shiner, "Career Paths and Choices in a Highly differentiated profession: the position of newly qualified solicitors" (2001) 64(4) M.L.R. 567–569, 591:

"In the early stages of training and qualification sex is not a significant factor, but segmentation on grounds of ethnicity and class begins immediately. Advantage and disadvantage are therefore systemic factors in selection for the profession. Work placements play a key role in selection for traineeship, particularly in City firms and large provincial firms, thus prejudicing those who are unable to work for free during vacations. Lack of finance also prevents many potential applicants from accepting places on the Legal Practice Course (the LPC), the solicitors' vocational course, or the Bar Vocational Course (the BVC), the Bar's equivalent. Sponsorship during the Legal Practice Course was offered by wealthy firms, mainly those in the City, to applicants who took the CPE, studied at Oxbridge and/or

The College of Law. Multivariate analysis suggests that membership of an ethnic minority group or a family where neither parent had a degree or a professional qualification, significantly reduces the chances of receiving an offer of a training contract and of receiving an early offer. What is the impact of these factors on professional demographics once aspiring solicitors have qualified?

The sixth survey found those surviving the attrition of initial selection in a strong position. Those completing the training contract were virtually guaranteed suitable employment and 62 per cent of solicitors qualified for more than two years remained with the firm or organisation in which they had trained. Perhaps surprisingly, given earlier findings, ethnicity was not a significant factor here. Indeed, there was no real evidence of disadvantage, or inequality in the allocations of jobs, or in the initial and medium-term rates of retention of solicitors among those completing their training. Some differences did emerge, however. Graduates from the College of Law were more likely to be retained by the firm with which they trained than students studying the Legal Practice Course at new universities. . . .

The Entry to the Legal Profession project charts the fortunes of a cohort of students as they spread across a range of legal organisations and embark on increasingly specialised legal careers. Just as the profession is increasingly segmented, the selection process is also. Although it distributes entrants according to crude measures of academic achievement, such as the educational establishment attended, it actually allocates individuals to firms according to characteristics such as class and ethnicity. The relative position of women, granted access to training on almost equal terms, is already beginning to deteriorate. The focus of discussion regarding access to the profession has therefore shifted from exclusion to differentiation and subordination."

NOTES AND QUESTIONS

- Discrimination in the profession is clearly a matter for concern amongst professional bodies. Imagine you have just been appointed as a policy officer at the Law Society or Bar Council. How would you set about tackling the problems outlined above?

The extract from Cotterell reproduced above suggested that lawyers are not all conservative. Rather, he argues along with Cain that both radical and other lawyers can create opportunities for change and reform in their everyday tasks of interpretation and argument. However, in his groundbreaking work on the politics of the judiciary, Griffith has argued that this may well be a disadvantage later in life when promotion to the senior ranks of the judiciary becomes an aspiration.

J.A.G. Griffith, *The Politics of the Judiciary* (4th ed., Harper Collins, London, 1991), pp.34–36:

"Judicial independence means that judges are not dependent on governments in ways which might influence them in coming to decisions in individual cases, though their promotion, like their appointment, is effectively in the hands of the Lord Chancellor with, nowadays, a measure of Prime Ministerial intervention. As we have seen, in financial terms, such promotion is not of much significance. But life in the Court of Appeal and, even more, in the House of Lords is not so strenuous as in the High Court (or below), personal prestige and status are higher among the fewer, with a life peerage at the top. These are not inconsiderable rewards for promotion, and the question is whether there are pressures on, particularly, High Court judges to act and to speak in court in certain ways rather than others. Are there decisions which could be classified as popular or unpopular in the eyes of the most important senior judges or the Lord Chancellor? Is a judge ever conscious that his reputation as a judge is likely to be adversely affected in their eyes if he decides one way, and favourably affected if he decides another way?

The answer is that such pressures do exist. For example, a judge who acquires a reputation among his seniors for being 'soft' in certain types of cases where the Lord Chancellor, the Lord Chief Justice, the Master of the Rolls and other senior judges favour a hard line is as likely to damage his promotion prospects as he would if his appointment were found to be unfortunate on other more obvious grounds. But this does not amount to dependence on the political wishes of governments or ministers as such. In no real sense does such direct dependence or influence exist. How far judges consciously or unconsciously subserve the wide interests of governments is another and more important question."

This is a question which has been brought to the forefront in recent years, both by Griffith, and by judicial decisions which have resulted in the now famous "miscarriage of justice" cases.

Phil Harris, *An Introduction to Law* (6th ed, Butterworths, London, 2002), pp.430–434:

"In recent years the English judiciary too, has been 'battered and bruised' by a series of cases in which there was a clear and most serious miscarriage of justice. First came the release from prison of the Guildford Four and the Maguire Seven, and followed by the Birmingham Six—all of whom had been convicted of terrorist activity including the bombing of public houses in Guildford and Birmingham. Later came the release of the men convicted of the murder of the newspaper-boy Karl Bridgewater. It eventually transpired that all of the defendants in these cases had served long periods of imprisonment for crimes they did not commit, though all of the cases had previously been re-examined and duly rejected by the Court of Appeal. Not surprisingly, among the questions asked in the media at the time was simply, why had the court not recognised earlier the weaknesses in the Crown's case against these defendants (and in particular the police and scientific forensic evidence in some cases)? The Birmingham Six case is interesting for, among other things, Lord Denning's previous refusal to grant legal aid to the defendants in 1975 to allow them to bring an action against the West Midlands police:

'If the six men win it will mean that the police were guilty of perjury, that they were guilty of violence and threats, that the confessions were involuntary and were improperly admitted in evidence and that the convictions were erroneous. That would mean the Home Secretary would either have to recommend they be pardoned or he would have to remit the case to the Court of Appeal. This is such an appalling vista that every sensible person in the land would say: "It cannot be right that these actions should go any further".'

In other words, it seemed to his Lordship more important that public confidence in the criminal justice system should not be undermined, than that six innocent men should be freed.

This series of events did little to bolster public confidence in the higher judiciary and there are more cases of people in prison in respect of whose convictions there may be serious doubt. In the wake of the release of the Birmingham Six came the establishment of a Royal Commission on Criminal Justice, chaired by Lord Runciman, whose terms of reference included issues arising after trial and in particular arrangements for considering allegations of miscarriages of justice. The recommendations of the Commission on this point were implemented in the Criminal Appeal Act 1995, which set up the Criminal Cases Review Commission, which has the power to refer cases of convicted persons to the Court of Appeal if it considers that "there is a real possibility that the conviction, verdict, finding or sentence would not be upheld [in the Court of Appeal] because of an argument, or evidence, not raised in the proceedings which led to it or on any appeal or application for leave to appeal against it'. It is to be hoped that this new body will play an important part in effectively preventing miscarriages of justice in the future.

In a more general context, and drawing on many cases from various areas of social activity as illustrations, Griffith has catalogued and discussed the extent to which the role of the judiciary (in particular the judges of the higher courts) can be seen to overlap into the sphere of political decision-making. In particular, Griffith discusses the broad areas of industrial relations, personal rights and freedoms, property rights and squatters, judicial control on ministerial discretion, the uses of conspiracy, and cases involving students and trade union members. He argues that 'judges are part of the machinery of authority within the State and as such cannot avoid the making of political decisions'; and that the senior judges in particular have, by reason of their legal education and their working life as practising barristers, 'acquired a strikingly homogeneous collection of attitudes, beliefs, and principles, which to them represents the public interest'. For Griffith, the idea of an impartial and neutral judiciary, especially in cases involving a political element, is mythical:

'. . .judges in the United Kingdom cannot be politically neutral because they are placed in positions where they are required to make political choices which are sometimes presented to them, and often presented by them, as determinations of where the public interest lies; . . . that interpretation of what is in the public interest and therefore politically desirable is determined by the kind of people they are and the position they hold in our society; . . . this position is part of established authority and so is necessarily conservative and illiberal.'

When first published, Griffith's book met with considerable criticism, particularly, as one might expect, from members and ex-members of the judiciary. Lord Devlin, once a judge in the House of Lords, responded to some of Griffith's assertions and arguments. To a large extent, Devlin's reply may be summarised as a resounding 'so what?' To begin with, he explains, there is no denying the homogeneity of political and other outlooks on the part of the judges, but then the same is true of most other institutions in our society, or at least, those of them which 'like the law are not of a nature to attract the crusading or rebellious spirit'.

Further, argues Devlin, the question posed by Griffith, which is 'do the judges allow their devotion to law and order to distort their application of the law when they apply it to those who do not think as they do?' is beset by the twin difficulties of lack of unanimity among the senior judges whom Griffith, according to Devlin, seeks to present as 'a small group of senior judges who are policy makers': 'The law lords are sometimes divided: more frequently they quarrel with the Court of Appeal.' And the constraints imposed by the length of Griffith's book do not, argues Devlin, allow any rigorous analysis of the cases under discussion. Devlin accepts that Griffith's perspective may be seen as the view from the left, and explains that criticisms of the judiciary might also be made by those taking a different ideological stance: 'Professor Griffith cites cases on the use of police powers which he finds to be "alarming"; someone right of centre could probably produce a list of cases which would alarm him by their tenderness towards crime.' In short, Devlin is inclined to the view that too much is made by Griffith of the 'politics of the judiciary', for 'their politics are hardly more significant than those of the army, the navy and the airforce; they are as predictable as those of any institution where maturity is in command'. . . . [Harris goes on to note one key factor which limits the 'politics' of judicial decision making:]

'[A]n important constraining factor is the necessity, noted by Weber, Frank and others, for judicial decisions to be presented not as the outcome of subjective, arbitrary or capricious reasoning by the judge, but as the result of the application of *objective* criteria. This is the difference between the statement 'in my opinion, you are guilty' and the statement 'according to the law, you are guilty'. The former statement we would regard as somewhat suspect, as being unfair or biased. The issue of public credibility and confidence in the judiciary is once again relevant here: we would not place much faith in a legal system which allowed judges to decide cases according to their whim or their personal views

about the parties to a dispute. We expect judges to decide cases in accordance with existing law, without personal views or prejudices colouring their judgment.'"

The politics of the judiciary frequently becomes more explicit and recognisable
when judges are asked to consider the "public interest". In these situations, ideological assumptions about society often come to the surface. Moreover, judicial decision making in this context often appears to assume that there is a shared system of
values throughout society, and that judges are equipped to identify them, and to
maintain them through the power of law. It is here that the relationship between
"law" and "morality" discussed in the first chapter of this book becomes explicit.

Phil Harris, *An Introduction to Law* (5th ed., Butterworths, London, 1997), pp.445–448:

"[T]he judicial protection of moral standards extends beyond the range of criminal law.
Such concerns are the basis of much judicial comment and decisions in family law, and in
the law of contract we find cases such as that of *Pearce v Brooks* in 1866, where the judges
refused to accept the legality of an agreement between the plaintiffs and the defendant
whereby the former had hired out a carriage to the latter, to be used for the purposes of
prostitution. In *Glynn v Keele University* in 1971, a student who was excluded from residence on the campus for nude sunbathing failed in his attempt to challenge this disciplinary action. Although the court accepted that, in denying him a chance to put his side of
the case, the university official had acted in breach of natural justice, the court none the
less felt that the offence was such as to 'merit a severe penalty according to any standards
current even today'. And in 1971, in *Ward v Bradford Corpn*, the Court of Appeal denied
a remedy to a student teacher who had broken the rules of her hall of residence by permitting her boy-friend to remain in her room overnight for a period of about two months. She
had been expelled by the college and, despite irregularities in the manner in which the disciplinary procedure had been carried out, Lord Denning stated firmly his belief that her
behaviour was not suitable for a trainee teacher: 'she would never make a teacher. No
parent would knowingly entrust their child to her care.'

In such matters of morality, the tension between judicial conservatism and an increased
social tolerance of moral behaviour which is not to everyone's taste, is manifest. It is worth
asking the question whether, in today's climate in which sexual and other moral matters are
relatively freely discussed and practices once regarded as beyond the pale are fairly openly
indulged in, the attitude of the judges may in some cases be too far removed from the 'real
social world', so to speak, to protect the interests of all involved. Having said this, however,
one outstanding case in which the judges showed themselves well aware of modern public
attitudes towards sexual morality was *R. v R.* in 1991—the case which overturned the
common law rule that a husband could not be criminally liable for committing rape upon
his wife. In the Court of Appeal, Lord Lane stated that the old common law rule had
become 'anachronistic and offensive and we consider that it is our duty having reached that
conclusion to act upon it'—a view with which the House of Lords unanimously agreed.
There can be no doubt that this decision was both welcome and long overdue.

Other notable areas where the courts have referred, in the various cases before them, to
the 'public interest', or equivalent terms, include the law of property, where the judges have
consistently upheld the protection of traditional rights to private property as against, for
example, private tenants (through restrictive interpretation of rent legislation) and squatters; the law relating to conspiracy where, until the Criminal Law Act 1977 clarified and
somewhat restricted the range of the offence, the judges had been quite prepared to uphold
convictions for the offence even though the activity allegedly planned by the conspirators
had not been carried out; and the law relating to public order and industrial disputes.

The problems underlying these assumptions and views on the part of the judiciary
revolve around the difficulty of identifying exactly what constitutes the 'public interest' in
a given area—even if such a monolithic entity exists at all. By what criteria do the judges,
who wield considerable power in such cases, discover which particular body of attitudes or

standards in our society constitute *the* public interest? Perhaps Lord Devlin, once again, expressed the view of most judges:

'English law has evolved and regularly uses a standard which does not depend on the counting of heads. It is that of the reasonable man. . . . It is the viewpoint of the man in the street. . . . He might also be called the right-minded man. For my purpose I should like to call him the man in the jury-box, for the moral judgment of society must be something about which any twelve men or women drawn at random might after discussion be expected to be unanimous.'

But how likely is such a consensus? Society is by no means homogeneous: it is composed of many groups and individuals differing in terms of sex, age, ethnic and cultural background, social class and political power. Would it be possible to obtain a unanimous judgment from any group of randomly selected people on the issues of industrial relations, prostitution or any of the other areas where the assumptions held by the judges, particularly in the appellate courts, have come to the fore? Surely any interest group might convincingly register a belief that their policies, beliefs or attitudes were an accurate reflection of a 'public morality' or a 'public interest'? Unless we are, literally, to embark upon a national referendum on all such matters, there would seem to be no clear way of ascertaining what the majority of people believe to be right or acceptable behaviour, with any degree of accuracy.

Furthermore, Lord Devlin and other judges using similar terminology commit a serious analytical error in using phrases such as 'society believes this' or 'society has decided that'. Such loose phrases obscure the fact of pluralistic interests and differential access to policy-making channels within the social structure. What is, therefore, presented as being in the 'public interest' may in fact serve limited, sectional interests. As Coulson and Riddell put it:

'. . . to say that a decision is in the national interest usually means to identify the interests of one group of the population as the National Interest, while conveniently forgetting the interests of those members of the nation who are not benefited by the decision. By the appeal to nationalism, sectional decisions may appear more palatable to people they don't benefit.'"

The ideological underpinnings of judicial decision making are particularly apparent in the way in which the judiciary frequently constructs "common sense" in their reasons. Graycar argues that an underlying gendered perspective is at work in these judicial pronouncements.

Regina Graycar, "The Gender of Judgments: An Introduction" in *Public and Private: Feminist Legal Debates* (Margaret Thornton, ed., Oxford University Press, Melbourne, 1995), pp.266–272:

"I have suggested that the role of judging is gendered and implicitly male, and I think this follows inexorably from a history of social, political and legal practices, and beliefs now deeply entrenched in the substantive body of law with which judges work. Given the fact that women were not even permitted to practise law until well into this century, there is no question that the substantive legal doctrines we use on a day-to-day basis were developed by men, with their problems and concerns in mind, and reflecting their perspectives on the world. Despite the relatively recent entry of women into the profession, and their increasing numbers (though less so on the bench in Australia), legal doctrines and legal reasoning appear to have remained almost completely impervious to perspectives other than those of the (dominant) White, middle-class male. . . .

If law was developed by men in accordance with their needs and experiences and has neither dealt well with women, nor reflected their lives or experiences, then perhaps everything would change if there were some more women in there. But I am not very confident that, simply by adding some women to the bench and stirring, we will automatically change the male-centredness of law and legal reasoning. For a number of reasons—such as the ways in which legal education has been conducted to date and the ways in which certain forms of utterance are privileged by law in the construction of what is authoritative, and by corollary, what (or who) lacks credibility—I am somewhat sceptical of the view that simply as a result of women being there, everything will be different. We may just be adding more women to the bench—nothing more, nothing less. After all, the 'institution' of law remains and its '[i]nstitutional design is a way of allocating authority across different sets of actors', while ensuring that the 'legal texts always operate from a particular strategy of framing facts'. But if we could further our understanding of what judges know, how they know it, how this shapes the construction of reality in judgments—that is, how judges 'orient' their narratives—and how this is all affected by gender, then maybe things *could* change. While there are any number of barriers to women's stories being heard in courts and, even if heard, being given credibility and authority, judges' speech is quintessentially authoritative. Judges are speakers whose verdicts count, both generally, in that they have considerable social status and, most particularly for these purposes, in their power to construct realities in the domain of law.

Consider the following seven examples:

1. A negligence action was brought by a woman who had four children, did not want any more, but became pregnant after having a negligently performed tubal ligation. She sued and sought damages, *inter alia*, for the cost of upkeep of the child. The judge described the plaintiff as 'a motherly sort of woman, nice looking but rather overweight . . . She is not only an experienced mother but, so far as I am able to judge, a good mother, who has all the proper maternal instincts'.

2. A custody dispute in the Family Court of Australia involved two professional parents, both doctors. The judge said, 'the major question mark hanging over the wife . . . is whether she would be prepared to sacrifice her career for the sake of the children'. She was recently remarried and had given evidence that she and her husband planned to have a child, but the judge was not satisfied that she would give up her job and said, 'she wants her cake and eat it too: unremarkable in these days of equality opportunity'. In a decision (subsequently overturned on appeal), the judge awarded the wife (in her late thirties) custody on a conditional basis: 'if she resigned her job and came back to court pregnant two months later, she would be awarded custody; otherwise, custody would be given to the father who was working full time'.

3. Discussing domestic work in the context of a damages claim, the judge said, 'regard must be had to public mores in Australia and, where a husband [and] wife are both working . . . the sharing of domestic burdens with the wife is expected of the husband, even where his wife is perfectly healthy'. The same judge, in another case of an injured woman, commented, 'The appellant and her husband both worked, despite the fact that she had two quite young children . . . The husband will have to do more in the domestic field than he would otherwise have had to. Most Australian males are expected to give domestic assistance to their wives.' And, before leaving this case, another judge remarked, 'Like many migrant women, she had been constantly in work . . . [I]n these days of changed practices of women working, but particularly so in the case of migrant settlers . . .'

4. Explaining why juries in rape cases had to be warned about the dangers of convicting on the uncorroborated evidence of the woman, a judge commented that 'Human experience has shown that in these courts girls and women do sometimes tell an entirely false story which is very easy to fabricate, but extremely difficult to refute. Such stories are fabricated for all sorts of reasons, which I need not now enumerate, and sometimes for no reason at all.' Even after the abolition by statute of the corroboration requirement, we are told: 'Experience has taught the judges that there have been cases where women have manufactured or invented false allegations of rape and sexual attack. It is a very easy allegation to make. It is often very hard to contradict.'

5. The case in which this last remark was made received some public attention in Australia. It involved a prosecution for six counts of rape by a man of his wife: 'There is, of course, nothing wrong with a husband, faced with his wife's initial refusal to engage in

intercourse, in attempting, in an acceptable way, to persuade her to change her mind, and that may involve a measure of rougher than usual handling. It may be, in the end, that handling and persuasion will persuade the wife to agree.'

6. Or, 'it does happen, in the common experience of those who have been in the law as long as I have anyway, that no often subsequently means yes.'

7. And in yet another case, Justice O'Bryan in the Victoria Supreme Court, in the case of sentencing a man to eleven years' jail, commented that a seventeen-year-old girl who was bashed, raped, and had her throat slit was 'not traumatised' by the rape because she was 'probably comatose at the time', having been knocked unconscious by the offender.

It might be tempting to think that these are instances drawn from darkest history; but not one of these examples is more than fifteen years old and, significantly, not all of them are by men. While there are many other quotable quotes that would illustrate the point, merely reproducing them may take us only to an analytical dead end. But perhaps we can learn something from 'the stories judges tell' if we think about the epistemological content of each of them. What are the judges doing? What are they telling us about the things they know about the world? The examples quoted above are deeply politically coloured statements, (as well as being overwhelmingly 'personal'). The knowledge content of these examples goes something like this: in the first, appearance equals character, and a good mother can never be harmed by motherhood; the second is simple—never trust working mothers; the third, the one about domestic work, says that men help with women's work (it also looks like wishful thinking, or perhaps law's famous is/ought distinction). The remaining examples tell us both that we do not even need a stated rationale for our belief in women's mendacity and that rape is simply not a serious form of harm. Further, phrases such as 'as far as I am able to judge' (example 1), 'most Australian males are expected to give domestic assistance' and 'in these days of changed practices' (both from example 3), 'human experience has shown' and 'experience has taught the judges' (both from example 4), 'There is, of course, nothing wrong with a husband' (example 5), and, perhaps the clearest example, 'in the common experience of those who have been in the law as long as I have' (example 6) all illustrate the belief of judges in a pre-existing body of 'knowledge' on which they can, at least in part, base their judgments. Yet, while it may be relatively easy to identify and illustrate a clear problem with at least some judges' common sense understandings of the world and the dissonance between these and how women might experience these events, finding solutions may not be as simple."

We have returned throughout this text to the different ways in which judicial "common sense" reflects, not sense which is "common" to everyone, but a particular perspective on the world, grounded frequently in assumptions about gender, race, sexuality, class, and other relations of power. The question whether a more diverse judiciary, composed of more women and members of ethnic minorities could make a "difference" to the outcome of judicial decision making is questioned by Graycar. Whether her concerns prove to be valid remains to be seen. It seems appropriate since we teach law and you are studying it to return again to the part that legal education plays in the creation and maintenance of discriminatory practice.

Jill Abramczyk, "The Tyranny of the Majority: Liberalism in Legal Education" (1992) 5 *Canadian Journal of Women and the Law* 442 at 451:

"... One of the results of the primacy of liberal objectivity is that one dominant but narrow perspective becomes the most (or only) acceptable approach in the law school classroom, and in legal discourse in general. To the extent that this perspective encodes a particular view of the world, and a particular vision of the way in which the world should be ordered, liberalism can be both 'dominant' and a vehicle for entrenching systemic domination. Ignorance of the experience of others, and disrespect for those who are 'different' from the dominant culture, is thereby legitimized. Those who are different become 'outsiders', the oddities at whom we laugh or shake our heads. Any structural forces are systematically ignored.

Legal reasoning is taught 'as though enduring principles of social organization [are] imbedded in the logic of the doctrines themselves,' rather than as though the doctrines have political and ethical meanings. That law students study rules, which do not take into account backgrounds, socialization, or political beliefs, illustrates that legal reasoning treats people and conflicts as atomistically as liberalism does. When the gender, class, race, age, and gender orientation of the people involved are excluded systematically from discussion, the underlying principles of doctrines and their political and ethical meanings are disregarded. . . . [I]t encourages students to accept at face value what they are told is 'reality' without being encouraged or taught to question it, or to analyze it from any number of critical/analytical perspectives. . . .

Liberal theory directs that the application of 'legal reasoning' leads to 'sound law', which conforms to 'legal conventions concerning interpretation, precedent, rights and so forth, rather than by conformity to political goodness'. Legal reasoning 'says it can take us from legal premises (precedents, notions of rights) to determine answers without resort to political or ethical choice.' The law student is taught that legal reasoning leads us to the 'correct' legal result, and indeed, that there is *one* correct legal result.

This result, and the reasoning produced, is presented as being logical, objective, and neutral. Events are presented 'as they are', in full confidence that the presentation is free from any particular perspective or ideology. But it bears repeating that (legal) reasoning necessarily reflects the perspectives of its participants, and that those perspectives are not neutral. As has been noted, 'most professors, just as most legislators, and judges, and lawyers are white and male and middle-class and heterosexual.'"

Legal education in the United Kingdom has been frequently criticised for its failure to recognise a diversity of racial and ethnic perspectives. This is but one example of Abramczyk's point that a dominant (in this case, "white") perspective is presented as the "universal", thereby erasing the diversity of perspectives which participants in legal education and the practice of law bring to the discipline. University legal education has been slow to recognise the importance of broadening its perspective in this regard.

Aimee Paterson, "The Racial, Ethnic and Cultural Values Underpinning Current Legal Education", in *The Critical Lawyers' Handbook 2* **(Paddy Ireland and Per Laleng, eds., Pluto Press, London, 1997), pp.77–81:**

"An exploration of the courses taught within UK law schools reveals the persisting conservative traditions of the British legal profession. Very few law schools have expanded their curriculum beyond the narrow confines of traditional law courses. It is, surely, important to recognise that 'straight' law courses alone are no longer (if ever they were) sufficient to meet the needs of a multicultural society. Law schools need to adopt a more progressive stance. There is an urgent need for greater academic appreciation of the value of multiculturalism in legal education. Legal education needs to embrace a wider range of disciplines in order to properly inform and serve its new consumers. Equally important, law schools, responsible for producing future lawyers, need to ensure they have the ability to relate to clients of diverse ethnic, cultural and religious backgrounds.

Multiculturalism in legal education would provide a platform for informing and educating students about key race relations issues where ignorance and misconception currently prevail. Training in race relations would help lawyers respond to the needs of contemporary British society. Indeed, this is vitally important if persistent allegations of injustice are

seriously to be addressed and eradicated. The value of this policy has been recently emphasised by the Judicial Studies Board, when it noted that it is 'essential to equip all judges and
magistrates with a basic amount of knowledge and understanding if they are to be seen to
be administering justice fairly to people with whom they have little in common in terms of
upbringing, culture and experience'. . . .

Given the cultural and ethnic diversity of both British society and law students, is there
not a case for 'a wholesale permeation of virtually the entire curriculum with multiracial,
multicultural themes'?. . .

Legal education appears to be structured to create and produce a stereotyped ideal
lawyer. Both the content and delivery of courses, consciously or otherwise, seem designed
to persuade its consumers to adopt a certain image. As noted by the Barrow Report,
'anyone who does not conform and has no wish to, or is unable to, may feel uncomfortable.
This is equally so of pupillage, tenancy and further eminence at the Bar . . .' although '. . .
it is less noticeable then because those who have reached the later stages will already have
successfully conformed'."

A major element in the construction of the "ideal lawyer" through legal education
is indoctrination in the form of legal method which has been analysed in the
excerpts in this section. Williams has illustrated this method of reasoning through
the telling of a story, which highlights the pitfalls of "thinking like a lawyer".

**Patricia J. Williams, *The Alchemy of Race and Rights* (Cambridge, MA: Harvard University
Press, 1991), pp.12–13:**

"Walking down Fifth Avenue in New York not long ago, I came up behind a couple and
their young son. The child, about four or five years old, had evidently been complaining
about big dogs. The mother was saying, 'But why are you afraid of big dogs?' 'Because
they're big,' he responded with eminent good sense. 'But what's the difference between a big
dog and a little dog?' the father persisted. 'They're *big*,' said the child. 'But there's really no
difference,' said the mother, pointing to a large slathering wolfhound with narrow eyes and
the calculated amble of a gangster, and then to a beribboned Pekinese the size of a roller
skate, who was flouncing along just ahead of us all, in that little fox-trotty step that keep
Pekinese from ever being taken seriously. 'See?' said the father. 'If you look really closely
you'll see there's no difference at all. They're all just dogs.'

And I thought: 'Talk about your iron-clad canon. Talk about a static, unyielding, totally
uncompromising point of reference. These people must be lawyers. Where else do people
learn so well the idiocies of High Objectivity? How else do people learn to capitulate so
uncritically to a norm that refuses to allow for difference? How else do grown-ups sink so
deeply into the authoritarianism of their own world view that they can universalize their
relative bigness so completely that they obliterate the subject positioning of their child's
relative smallness? (To say nothing of the position of the slathering wolfhound, from whose
own narrow perspective I dare say the little boy must have looked exactly like a lamb
chop.)'"

NOTES AND QUESTIONS

- You may want to keep Williams' story in mind as you proceed through your
  study of Legal Method. It provides a useful reminder of the dangers of uncritically accepting legal reasoning as a means of discovering the "truth" of things,
  erasing individual perspectives and differences in social positioning in the
  process.

- How might the critics of legal education (*e.g.* Kennedy, Stanley, Williams) respond to the claims of the "law and economics" school of legal reasoning?

- What is your perspective on legal education as a participant? How do you react to the criticisms of legal reasoning and of "thinking like a lawyer"?

- Define "legal method" (you may want to revise your answer at the end of the text and in three years' time).

- In July 2003, the Government published a consultation paper which called for reforms to the way in which judges are appointed. During the course of the year you would be advised to follow this debate. In the meantime, you might like to draft a checklist of changes which you think are necessary in order to secure representation of a broader range of opinions on the bench. Now compare this with what the Government is proposing.

13

DISPUTE RESOLUTION: THE COURTS AND ADJUDICATION

INTRODUCTION

Having considered how lawyers and judges are trained to facilitate the resolution of disputes about legal issues we turn our attention, in this chapter and the next, to the processes used to resolve disputes in the English legal system. We do not attempt to present a comprehensive explanation of the extensive and detailed rules of civil procedure which exist. Instead, we focus on the values and assumptions which underpin the various forms of dispute resolution which are provided or sanctioned by the State. Issues of criminal procedure are beyond the scope of this chapter and are normally covered in criminal law courses although the reader will find that much of what is said about adjudication and negotiation applies equally well to both criminal and civil processes.

Twenty years ago the inclusion of chapters on the principles of adjudication and alternatives to it would have been unthinkable in a book of this kind. For many years law students and legal academics focused their attention almost exclusively on litigation in the higher courts. Indeed, many of the earlier chapters in this book reflect this tendency to prioritise analysis of judicial reasoning. But times have changed. Not only has the government become increasingly interested in reforming the litigation system and diverting cases away from the courts, but consumer groups have begun to call for methods of dispute resolution which are less costly, speedier, less adversarial, more sensitive to non-legal issues in dispute and better able to repair relationships. In recent years the tendency has been for academics to pay more attention to a range of dispute resolution techniques and this has become much more noticeable in the wake of Lord Woolf's review of the civil justice system. His reports published in 1995 and 1996 heralded a radically different approach to the resolution of disputes within the English legal system. The education of law students would now be seriously lacking if they graduated without an understanding of the variety of dispute resolution methods which are commonly used by litigants and their lawyers.

It is important to stress from the outset that *methods* of dispute resolution should not be seen as synonymous with particular forums or places. The extract from Brown and Marriot below makes clear that adjudication, mediation and negotiation each occur in a variety of different settings.

H. Brown and A. Marriot, *ADR Principles and Practice* (Sweet and Maxwell, London, 1993), pp.18–21:

Overview of dispute resolution procedures

"Some ADR writers divide all dispute resolution processes (traditional and alternative into three primary categories: negotiation, mediation and adjudication. Others extend them to up to six primary categories: negotiation, mediation, the judicial process, arbitration, and the administrative and legislative processes. This effectively amounts to a sub-division of adjudication into its constituent parts.

Negotiation

Negotiation must be the 'first among equals' of the dispute resolution processes, standing firmly as such in its own right, as well as falling into the traditional framework as an ancillary part of most cases commenced by adjudication, and being an inherent component of mediation, the mini-trial and other ADR methods.

Negotiation is the way in which individuals communicate with one another in order to arrange their affairs in commerce and everyday life, establishing areas of agreement and reconciling areas of disagreement. Negotiation has been defined as 'the process we use to satisfy our needs when someone else controls what we want.' Most disagreements are dealt with in one way or another by negotiation between the principals themselves; relatively few involve legal intercession.

Negotiation tends often to be a practical skill learned pragmatically by personal experience. There are, however, various theories of negotiation, as well as many different individual styles and approaches.

Adjudication

As a generic term, adjudication is a dispute resolution process in which a neutral has and exercises the authority to hear the respective positions submitted by the disputants and to make a decision on their dispute which will be binding on them. This may occur by:

- *Litigation*, where the process is administered through the Courts and the neutral adjudicator is a judge, a district judge, master, Official Referee or other official appointed by the Court to undertake this function.
- *Arbitration*, where the neutral is privately chosen and paid by the disputants and/or the procedure regulating the dispute follows arbitration rules which may be statutory or imposed by and arbitral organisation.
- *Administrative or statutory tribunals*, where the adjudication follows certain specific statutory requirements, such as establishing rent levels, compensation awards, social security benefits or a range of other matters through tribunals and appeal tribunals.
- *Expert determination*, in which the parties appoint an expert to consider their issues and to make a binding decision or appraisal without necessarily having to conduct an enquiry following adjudicatory rules.
- *Private judging*, in which (in those jurisdictions which have adopted this procedure, not yet within the United Kingdom) the Court refers the case to a referee chosen by the parties to decide some or all of the issues, or to establish any specific facts.

The term 'adjudication' also has a more specialised meaning in some industries including in particular the construction industry, of a procedure by which a neutral, the adjudicator, is empowered and required by contract to make summary binding decisions about disputes arising under that contract without following litigation or arbitration procedures.

Mediation or conciliation

Mediation is a process by which disputing parties engage the assistance of a neutral third party to act as a mediator—a facilitating intermediary—who has no authority to make any binding decisions, but who uses various procedures, techniques and skills to help the parties to resolve their dispute by negotiated agreement without adjudication. The mediator is a facilitator who may in some models of mediation also provide a non-binding evaluation of the merits of the dispute if required, but who cannot make any binding adjudicatory decisions.

Conciliation is a term sometimes used interchangeably with mediation, and sometimes used to distinguish between one of these processes (often mediation) involving a more pro-active mediator role, and the other (conciliation) involving a more facilitative mediator role; but there is no consistency in such usage.

Hybrid processes

Each of the primary processes (litigation, arbitration or mediation) can be used in its own right without adaptation. In addition, by drawing elements from the primary processes and 'tailoring' them, an ADR practitioner can devise a permutation of procedures and approaches which fit all the nuances of the parties' needs and circumstances without being constrained by prescribed rules. For example, it may be appropriate for the practitioner to have informal discussions with the parties, arrange for certain facts or technical questions to be investigated, and then allow each of them to present their respective cases informally to one another before resuming further attempts at settlement. This and any other permutation of requirements can be met by devising a sequence of procedures specifically designed for that dispute and those parties.

Certain common combinations of usage of the primary processes have developed in this way, and have become known as hybrid processes. These include, for example:

- *The mini-trial*, which can be seen as a form of evaluative mediation, or an abbreviated non-binding arbitration, followed by negotiation and/or mediation.
- *Med-arb*, which involves commencing with mediation, and if this does not result in the dispute being resolved, continuing with a binding arbitration.
- *The neutral fact-finding expert*, which involves an investigation by a neutral expert into certain specific issues of fact, technicality and/or law, and thereafter, if required a mediatory role, and eventually participation in an adjudicatory process if required.
- *Early neutral evaluation*, which requires a neutral evaluator to meet parties at an early stage of a case in order to make a confidential assessment of the dispute, partly to help them to narrow and define the issues, and partly to promote efforts to arrive at a settlement.
- *Court-annexed arbitration*, which requires statutory introduction into the court system, and which, depending upon the model adopted, may be binding or initially non-binding, and may or may not provide for a re-hearing by a judge under certain circumstances. . . .

Mediation and hybrid processes generally provide a framework of informal procedures in which a neutral assists the disputing parties with information gathering, clarifying and narrowing issues, facilitating dialogue, negotiation, smoothing out personal conflicts, identifying options, testing the reality of views, risk assessment, impasse resolution and in some cases non-binding evaluation as an aid to reaching agreement."

It is clear from this extract that the notion of adjudication is not synonymous with state funded systems for the resolution of disputes. Rather, adjudication is a particular process which is used in the publicly funded courts as well as in the private resolution of disputes outside of them. By the same token, mediation takes place in the precincts of the courts as well as in the wider community. This point is taken up by Cownie and Bradney who encourage us to place our study of disputes in this broader context.

Fiona Cownie and Anthony Bradney, *English Legal System in Context* (2nd ed., Butterworths, London, 2000), pp.6–8:

"Because the concern in 'English legal system' textbooks is with state courts, and with rules administered by those courts, not all institutions concerned with matters of dispute resolution and dispute avoidance are examined. Thus, for example, 'English legal system' textbooks sometimes consider the role of the police and the rules of law that give them the special powers that they possess. However, such textbooks do not describe the role of private police forces. People who provide security for shopping centres or guard industrial property fall outside the ambit of the area considered by an English legal system textbook. Yet, on one level, both the public police force and private security firms have the same role. They have a police function. Both are concerned with the protection of people or property from the destructive or acquisitive tendencies of others. Given that 'English legal system' texts are state-focused, ignoring private policing is logical but what important aim is served by focusing on the state?

There are many examples of private mechanisms and institutions which mirror the state's attempts to prevent or resolve disputes. All of these mechanisms and institutions are largely ignored in texts on 'the English legal system'.

One reason why some institutions concerned with dispute resolution and avoidance are discussed in English legal system text books and some are not might lie in the different sources of authority that the various institutions have. In the state court system courts operate according to rules of law laid down by Parliament and the judges. These rules of law purport to be universal in their applicability to all of those living in this country. Obedience to these rules is mandatory. In the nineteenth century John Austin described a theory of jurisprudence which regarded this general applicability of the legal system and a habit of obedience to these laws by its subjects as being part of the defining characteristics of law. Law, and thus the legal system, was, for Austin, a quite separate phenomenon from other forms of rules or social forces and was inextricably tied up with notions of the state. Despite the fact that this philosophical position is, in Austin's simple form, no longer accepted by philosophers of law it continues to underlie the boundaries set to much writing about the content of legal rules.

This may seem acceptable. 'The English legal system' is simply 'The Bill' and whatever its civil law equivalent may be. Other forms of dispute resolution are seen as private, voluntary and simply not law. They are therefore either not the province of an 'English legal system' book or, at best, are marginal to such a book.

Separating dispute-resolution mechanisms which owe their authority to the state from voluntary mechanisms and writing only about the former significantly reduces the amount of dispute resolution which is being discussed. Statistically, many disputes are in fact resolved by non-state agencies. The form that such dispute resolution takes varies. Someone mediating between quarrelling friends is a form of dispute resolution; so are arbitration procedures established by retail associations to deal with customer disputes; so are dispute resolution procedures within a Quaker Meeting; so are disciplinary procedures in universities; so are many other things. The essential difference between all of these non-state structures and the state courts is that if parties to a dispute follow the findings of such non-state agency they usually do so of their own volition. Parties choose whether or not they will use these agencies. Both parties must accept their jurisdiction. In the case of state courts the state itself can compel the presence of one of the parties to an action. Parties are obliged to take part in proceedings whether they want to or not.

Non-state dispute resolution agencies must operate within the shadow of the law. They may use state law by, for example, making their decisions the subject of a binding contract. Thus, for example, in the United Kingdom the Jewish Beth Din, a court established under Jewish religious law (though open to both Jews and non-Jews), requires those who wish to use it to accept the provisions of the Arbitration Act 1996."

- Do you agree that it is important for law students to have an understanding of dispute resolution which takes place outside of the courts? Give reasons for your answer.

- Can you think of any reasons why disputants might prefer to have their dispute resolved in a private forum? Can you think of any disadvantages of legal disputes being resolved outside of the courts?

- If the state chooses to legitimate the private ordering of disputants by enforcing mediated or arbitrated agreements through the law of contract, is it true to say that this private ordering is completely separate from formal law and the courts?

- Is the state fulfilling its obligation to provide for redress of citizen grievances by legitimating alternatives to the courts in this way? How far do you think the state's obligation to provide systems for the redress of grievances should extend?

In the remainder of this chapter we will focus on adjudication in courts and tribunals. We will look at the principles which underpin adjudicatory systems, their core characteristics and the different forms they take. The chapter concludes with a consideration of the various ways in which dispute processing in the courts and litigation system is increasingly being viewed as problematic by policy makers and users of these systems. Reactions to criticisms of the courts and adjudication are further explored in the next chapter which looks at the emergence of 'alternative dispute resolution'.

ADJUDICATION

The provision of state-sanctioned systems for the redress of citizen grievances is one of the core rights enshrined in the *Magna Carta* and this obligation has traditionally been satisfied by the adjudication of disputes in public courts funded by the state. In his interim report on the civil justice system Lord Woolf reinforced the continuing need for the state to fulfil this obligation through the litigation system.

Lord Woolf, *Access to Justice: Interim report* (*www.lcd.gov*, June 1995):

The importance of civil justice

"A system of civil justice is essential to the maintenance of a civilised society. The law itself provides the basic structure within which commerce and industry operate. It safeguards the rights of individuals, regulates their dealings with others and enforces the duties of government. The administration of civil justice plays a role of crucial importance in maintaining this structure as Sir Jack Jacob, the doyen of civil proceduralists, observed in 'The Reform of Procedural Law':

> 'It manifests the political will of the State that civil remedies be provided for civil rights and claims and that civil wrongs, whether they consist of infringements of private rights in the enjoyment of life, liberty, property or otherwise, be made good, so far as practicable, by compensation and satisfaction, or restrained, if necessary, by appropriate relief. It responds to the social need to give full and effective value to the substantive rights of members of society which would otherwise be diminished or denuded of worth or even reality.'

Effective access to the enforcement of rights and the delivery of remedies depends on an accessible and effective system of litigation. Lord Diplock drew attention to the constitutional role of our system of justice and the constitutional right which individuals have to obtain access to it in *Bremer v South India Shipping Corporation Ltd* (1981) A.C. 909, 917, when he said:

> 'Every civilised system of government requires that the state should make available to all its citizens a means for the just and peaceful settlement of disputes between them as to their respective legal rights. The means provided are courts of justice to which *every citizen has a constitutional right of access* in the role of plaintiff to obtain the remedy to which he claims to be entitled in consequence of an alleged breach of his legal or equitable rights by some other citizen, the defendant.'

To which statement I would add that he is also entitled to access today in order to seek a remedy for the adverse effects of a breach of public duty."

Adjudication can be defined as a process in which a neutral third party imposes an authoritative and principled decision on the disputants which is supported by reasoned opinion. In coming to a decision, the judge decides between the competing arguments put forward by the two parties to the litigation, so that one party loses and the other wins. Beyond these key characteristics it is clear that many different forms of adjudication exist within the English legal system. The following extract from Elliot and Quinn outlines a number of different courts and tribunals which use a process of adjudication to determine the outcome to a dispute.

C. Elliot and F. Quinn, *English Legal System* (3rd ed., Longman, London, 2000), pp.338–340:

"History

Legal process for civil cases developed in a rather piecemeal fashion, responding to different needs at different times, with the result that at the end of the eighteenth century, civil matters were being dealt with by several different series of courts. Three common law courts, supplemented by the Court of Chancery, did most of the work, but there was also a Court of Admiralty and the ecclesiastical (church) courts. They had separate but often overlapping jurisdictions, and between them administered three different 'systems' of law: civilian law (based on Roman law), common law and equity. The courts were also largely centralized in London, making access difficult for those in the provinces.

With no coordination of the increasingly complex court system, inefficiency, incompetence and delays were common, and the courts acquired a reputation for binding themselves up in cumbersome procedural rules. Until well into the nineteenth century, litigation in the higher courts was an extravagance which could be afforded only by the very rich, and in many respects the system benefited the judges and the legal profession far more than litigants. Reform began in 1846, with the creation of a nationwide system of county courts, designed to provide cheaper, quicker justice at a local level for businessmen. This was followed, in the early 1870s, by the creation of one Supreme Court consisting of the High Court, the Court of Appeal and the Crown Court, although the High Court was still divided into five divisions. In 1881, these were reduced to three: Queen's Bench; Chancery; and what is now known as the Family Division.

The civil courts

There are currently around 300 county courts concerned exclusively with civil work. About 170 of them are designated as divorce county courts and, thereby, have jurisdiction to hear undefended divorces and cases concerning adoption and guardianship.

In the High Court, the three divisions mentioned above remain today—they act as separate courts, with judges usually working within one division only. Lord Woolf recommended that these divisions should remain. The Family Division hears cases concerning marriage, children and the family, such as divorce, adoption and wills. The Chancery Division deals with matters of finance and property, such as tax and bankruptcy. The Queen's Bench Division is the biggest of the three, with the most varied jurisdiction. The major part of its work is handling those contract and tort cases which are unsuitable for the county courts. Sitting as the Divisional Court of the Queen's Bench, its judges also hear certain criminal appeals (originating primarily from the magistrates' courts) and applications for judicial review. High Court judges usually sit alone, but the Divisional Court is so important that two or three judges sit together.

Trials in the High Court are heard either in London or in one of the 26 provincial trial centres. In theory, they are all presided over by High Court judges, but in fact there are not enough High Court judges to cope with the case load. Some cases therefore have to be dealt with by circuit judges, others by barristers sitting as part-time, temporary, deputy judges.

Following the Woolf reforms, trial centres have been identified, headed by a Designated Civil Justice. . . .

Although most civil cases are dealt with by either the county courts or the High Court, magistrates' courts have a limited civil jurisdiction, and some types of case are tried by tribunals."

The English court system is often contrasted with the tribunal system in this country and the court systems of our continental neighbours because it is based on an adversarial rather than an inquisitorial process of adjudication. The following extract from Farrar and Dugdale explains this important distinction further.

John D. Farrar and Anthony M. Dugdale, *Introduction to Legal Method* (3rd ed., Sweet and Maxwell, London, 1990), pp.62–73:

"It might seem obvious that to solve a dispute you must first discover the true facts, but we should remember that this has not always been the case in our legal system and neither is it entirely the case today. For much of the Middle Ages our courts did not find the facts at all, rather they presided over an ordeal. If the disputant survived the ordeal, e.g. his hand had not festered after being burnt by a hot iron, then God had intervened in his favour and that proved his allegations. This method of resolving disputes is often referred to as that of 'Proof' as opposed to 'Trial.' It worked because it was acceptable to the parties. Today it would seem irrational and hence unacceptable but we still accept other methods which do not involve finding the facts, e.g. mediation of industrial disputes. To understand why this is so we should perhaps remember one further point; there is often no absolute, irrefutable way of determining what facts are true. Truth is as elusive in this as in other contexts. Consequently the question is not how we should find the truth but rather what are the acceptable means of dealing with a dispute as to the facts. In this chapter we shall examine the two main approaches taken by adjudicators, the adversarial and inquisitorial methods, and then after comparing the merits of these methods, examine briefly the other approaches adopted in our society.

The adversarial method

The adversarial method is one which gives the parties and their lawyers a great deal of control over the way in which facts are collected and presented. Each party to the dispute will collect its own evidence in the form of witnesses, expert opinions, etc, and will present that evidence to the court in the way most favourable to its own version of the facts and adverse to that of the other party. The role of the judge is limited to that of an umpire, ensuring that the evidence is presented in accordance with certain ground rules such as the rule that a lawyer must not ask his own party's witnesses questions which 'lead' them to a particular answer, *e.g.*, 'You did see X, didn't you?' The judge must not intervene to question a witness himself save to clarify an ambiguity in the witness's answers. When all the evidence has been presented he must decide which version of the facts he prefers. He may very well feel that some important evidence is missing, that the lawyers have failed to ask the right questions or call all the relevant witnesses but there is nothing he can do about that. He must make up his mind on the basis of the evidence presented by the two adversaries.

It is perhaps easier to understand the adversarial method by looking at a particular case, and we will take as our example *Whitehouse v. Jordan*[1] .... Mrs Whitehouse ... had alleged that Mr Jordan, the obstetrician, had negligently pulled too hard with the forceps when attempting to deliver her baby. Her evidence consisted of her own story that she had been lifted *up off* the delivery bed by the pulling and the evidence of two expert witnesses, retired obstetricians, who having read the hospital notes and heard her story concluded that she had been pulled *down off* the bed and that Mr Jordan must therefore have been acting negligently. For Mr Jordan there was his own evidence. He could not remember the facts in any detail but on the basis of his notes concerning the delivery and his usual practice he was certain that he could not have pulled so hard. In his support was the evidence of his junior colleague present at the delivery, that of his superior to whom he reported the events and that of four consultant obstetricians who concluded from the hospital notes that he had not acted negligently. The evidence of the two midwives present at the delivery was not presented by either side seemingly because they could not be traced, a pity as they might have appeared to have been more neutral observers of the facts than either of the parties.

At the trial Mrs Whitehouse's barrister questioned her and her witnesses so as to bring out their story and opinions. This process is known as the *examination in chief*. After he had questioned each witness, Mr. Jordan's barrister cross questioned them, trying to shake their evidence, probing the conflicts as between being pulled *up* or *down* off the bed. This process is called the *cross-examination*. The same method was then applied to Mr Jordan's witnesses. . . .

On the basis of all this conflicting, and in some respects incomplete evidence the judge had to make up his mind and he concluded that on the balance of probabilities Mr Jordan had pulled too hard and was liable. . . . [T]he Court of Appeal and the House of Lords held that the evidence did not justify this conclusion. The conflict of judicial opinion illustrates more clearly than the conflict of the witnesses, the difficulties of finding the facts.

Civil litigation like that in *Whitehouse* is the classic illustration of the adversarial method. The process involves neutrality between the parties. Neither side is forced to disclose more of its evidence before the trial than the other. At the trial although the plaintiff bears the burden of proof, *i.e.* in the absence of any evidence he loses, the standard or extent to which he must prove his case is simply 'on the balance of probabilities' a standard which favours neither party. . . .

---

[1] [1981] 1 W.L.R. 246, (1980) 125 S.J. 167, [1981] 1 All E.R. 267, HL.

The inquisitorial method

The characteristic of this method lies in the fact that the adjudicating body has considerable control over the way in which the evidence is collected and presented. Just as there are varieties of adversarial method, there are also varieties of inquisitorial method. We can illustrate two such by reference to the system for determining disputes about Industrial Injury Benefit. A person is entitled to benefit if he satisfies a number of conditions including (1) that he is an employee rather than being self-employed and (2) that his injury was caused by an accident at work. Disputes as to the first issue are determined by a government minister, the Secretary of State. In practice this usually means that a civil service lawyer will conduct an inquiry and report to the minister who will then make his decision. If the decision goes against the claimant he can appeal to the ordinary courts and have the decision overturned if it was supported by no evidence. Subject to this check, the process is a good illustration of purely inquisitorial method, with the decision maker or his investigator in absolute control of the collection of evidence. Disputes as to the second issue are resolved by a tribunal. At first sight the proceedings before the tribunal may appear adversarial in nature; the claimant will present his case and then the social security officer will present the administration's view of the facts. But appearance deceives; the officer is regarded more as an investigator providing information for the tribunal than as an adversary of the claimant; similarly the claimant's role is to provide information and answer questions. The tribunal controls the proceedings: indeed, it may appoint its own expert assessor. The method is modified inquisitorial: the tribunal does not investigate itself but adopts an inquisitorial attitude whilst relying on the information and investigation of others.

As with the adversarial method, it is easier to appreciate the nature of the inquisitorial method by taking an example, and ours is Ex p. *Moore*,[2] a case concerning . . . causation of injury. Ms Moore had suffered from a form of slipped disc which she claimed was due to her bending at work in her job as a crane driver. The tribunal held against her and she took her case to an appeal tribunal. Before this tribunal a consultant surgeon gave evidence on her behalf. Government medical officers gave evidence suggesting that the disc problem was caused by a pre-existing condition and not the bending. The tribunal also heard reports of the opinions of two other doctors given in previous cases as to the likely causes of disc problems. These doctors did not appear before the tribunal and could not therefore be questioned in an adversarial way by Ms Moore. Nevertheless, the tribunal relied on their opinions and those of the government doctors in concluding that the weight of evidence was against Ms Moore. Ms Moore then asked the ordinary courts to overturn the decision on grounds that by taking account of the reports of the doctors who had not been questioned, the tribunal acted against the principles of natural justice which required a fair hearing. The Court of Appeal dismissed her claim. . . .

Non-adjudicatory methods

. . . It is obvious that some types of disputes are rarely subject to adjudication by either adversarial or inquisitorial methods. Most industrial disputes are resolved by bargaining between the parties or possibly by mediation, *i.e.* a process under which a third party suggests a possible settlement but the two parties are left to decide whether to accept it. . . .

Mediation is being used in the United States, Australia and New Zealand to deal with a range of criminal as well as civil cases involving parties who have some form of continuing relationship with each other, whether as neighbours, fellow workers or members of the same household or organisation. In many such cases, as in labour disputes, the 'win-lose' outcomes of adjudication may work against future harmony between the parties. Moreover, the incident which triggers the legal system intervention, for example an assault, often seems to be only a symptom of underlying tensions. Unlike a court which gives judgment with respect to the particular claim or charge before it, mediators assist

[2] [1965] 1 Q.B. 456, CA.

the disputants to explore their differences and to develop a mutually acceptable formula for future co-existence.

It should also be realised that most civil disputes are settled before trial. In the commercial context the parties will often bargain rather than even start the pre-trial process. In the personal injury context, they will often start the pre-trial process of collecting evidence, but they frequently do this and devise their pre-trial tactics with the aim of forcing a good settlement rather than having the case adjudicated. In recent years American Courts have encouraged parties to use various forms of Alternative Dispute Resolution (ADR) systems in an effort to produce cheaper, faster settlements. The Lord Chancellor's Department has suggested that ADR systems might also have a role to play in the English system. In the context of criminal cases, bargaining is again important. There is considerable evidence to suggest that the practice of plea bargaining, under which the accused pleads guilty in return for a lighter sentence, is rife. Many would see this as undermining criminal justice and the presumption of innocence, trial by jury, etc. But it appears to be acceptable to the participants. It avoids the time, expense and uncertainty of a trial. It enables the parties to control their own fates rather than relinquishing the power to an adjudicator. What it ignores is the wider interest of society in seeing the innocent acquitted and the guilty properly sentenced.

One final comment: there are perhaps some disputes which can be avoided entirely. Lord Justice Lawton suggested in the *Whitehouse* case that the victims of medical mishaps such as the Whitehouse baby 'should be cared for by the community rather than by the hazards of litigation'. This could be achieved by a system of state compensation paid not on proof of negligence but simply on proof of injury. Such a scheme has been introduced in New Zealand. Similarly, it has been suggested that some criminal offences should be de-criminalised, *i.e.* either disregarded or treated as contraventions subject to an on-the-spot fine. Clearly this approach would reduce the number of disputes requiring resolution. These questions obviously raise issues of social policy, but this is true of all methods."

NOTES AND QUESTIONS

- Can you think of cases which are better suited to the adversarial or inquisitorial system? Give reasons for your answers.

- Why do you suppose that common law systems have tended to adopt adversarial forms of adjudication while legal systems based on civil codes have veered towards the inquisitorial?

- The *Whitehouse* case, not surprisingly, has been the subject of some controversy. For further reading see Sally Sheldon, " 'A responsible body of medical men skilled in that particular art . . .' Rethinking the Bolam test", in *Feminist Perspectives on Health Care Law*, Sally Sheldon and Michael Thomson (eds) (Cavendish, London, 1998), p.15.

THE FORMALITY OF PROCEEDINGS

Another way to distinguish between the different forms of adjudication employed within the English legal system is to classify them according to the degree of formality. Court based adjudication can generally be distinguished from other types of dispute resolution by the fact that it is the most formal and ritualised of the primary methods of dispute resolution. As a rule procedures become increasingly formalised as cases proceed up the court hierarchy to the highest appeal courts. It is here, at the apex of the justice system, that most emphasis is placed on pre-determined and highly structured rules of evidence which determine what can be said by whom and in what order.

The distinctions to be made between the courts and tribunals have tended to rest on the degree of formality employed. The question of how "court like" tribunals should be continues to be an important theme in reviews of the justice system. As you read the material which follows, you might reflect again on some of the reasons Dicey was concerned about tribunals (see Chapter 3) and in particular the sugges-tion that the virtues of tribunals are lost when they start to replicate the ordinary courts. Although tribunals were only deserving of a brief mention in the extract from Elliot and Quinn reproduced above, it could be argued that tribunal-based adjudication is the most important form in the English legal system. Numerous areas of life—from social security benefits to unfair dismissal to landlord and tenant disputes—are now handled by tribunals. You may be surprised to learn that tribunals handle several times the number of disputes which are decided by courts of law.

In 1957 the government set up a committee to consider reform of the tribunal system: the Franks Committee. It produced the Report of the Committee on Administrative Tribunals, which was followed in 1958 by the Tribunals and Inquiries Act. The Franks Committee stated that tribunals should be characterised by open-ness, fairness, and impartiality, and that those who chaired tribunals should be legally qualified. It also recommended a Council on Tribunals, to keep under review the workings of tribunals. Also recommended, and implemented, was the principle that representation should be possible before tribunals and, if necessary, represen-tation by a qualified lawyer. Moreover, tribunals in general should give reasons for decisions if requested to do so.

We start our consideration of the function of tribunals by looking in more depth at the differences between adjudication in courts of law and administrative tribu-nals. We begin with two seminal works on the similarities and differences between courts and tribunals which suggest that the distinction between the process of adju-dication in courts and tribunals is that the latter are much more flexible. Tribunals also tend to have three decision makers in contrast to most courts in the English legal system which have just one. They are also less likely to be bound by precedent and to have specialist adjudicators who have a familiarity with the context in which the dispute they are adjudicating arose. The following extract suggests that there may have been more political motive than reason in taking certain disputes out of the court system.

Harry Street, *Justice in the Welfare State* (2nd ed., Stevens & Sons, London, 1975), pp.2–9:

The Welfare State

"We have the main clue once we see that this trend [towards administrative tribunals] started when Lloyd George pioneered his National Health Insurance Act of 1911. It is the extension of the Welfare State which leads to matters being taken away from the courts. When the State provides benefits for citizens it has to devise machinery for ascertaining who has a good claim. When the State imposes controls there has to be a procedure which ensures that the citizen's freedom is not interfered with in an arbitrary manner. The 1911 Act set up special tribunals to handle contested claims for unemployment benefit. These tribunals worked exceptionally well, so much so that the sceptical became convinced that the judges were not the only ones who could do justice in disputes between the government and the public. These unemployment tribunals became the pattern for many others.

We usually call all these bodies administrative tribunals. The name is a good one. It distinguishes them from the ordinary courts. It also reminds us that it is a question of policy to be resolved by the Administration what arrangements are appropriate for deciding a particular set of claims. For instance, the Government decides to introduce a State scheme of unemployment benefits. It works out how the money is to be raised and prescribes the qualification for benefit, and the manner of making payments. It has to meet the situation where a citizen claims benefit and a government official does not accept this claim. It is purely an administrative matter how the Act is going to handle those contested issues. That matter will be resolved, not by laying it down that because there is a dispute it is a judicial question for a judge, but by asking what in the circumstances is the most efficient manner of performing this administrative task.

Links with government

We can readily see how decisions like that are closely linked with the Administration. Plainly the Administration is going to be responsible for the routine day to day payment of benefits. It will be less than say one case in ten thousand where there is an unresolved doubt about a claim to benefit. The Administration will be inclined to regard that one in ten thousand cases as just another administrative problem—calling for a special solution, yes— but it would be natural for it to think of recourse to some institution connected with the responsible department, rather than for it to say: 'This is a judicial issue, which must obviously be decided by one of Her Majesty's judges.' What I have just said about benefits is also true of granting a licence to do something or other, or of other ways in which the State now regulates our activities.

What is needed above all else is a cheap and speedy settlement of disputes. For these cases we do not want a Rolls-Royce system of justice. Some would say that there is too much of the Rolls and not enough of the Mini even in much of our trials in the law courts. If the average claim to benefit is less than £10 we do not want a judge on a pensionable salary of over £12,000 a year[3] with all the trappings (so often foisted on unwilling judges) of special judges' lodgings, private butler, police escort, ushers and marshal, to decide the claim. Nor do we want to wait for years to elapse between the making of the claim and the arrival at a final decision.

We can compile a very long list of matters of this kind which have arisen under the Welfare State for decision by administrative tribunals. Claims for unemployment benefit, family allowances, maternity benefits, death grants, industrial injury benefits, sickness benefits, supplementary benefits (the old National Assistance) and all other social security benefits are settled in this way. The Government decides to regulate rents of houses—and so we have rent assessment committees and rent tribunals. We have a nationalised health service; therefore we need tribunals to investigate complaints against doctors, dentists, opticians and chemists within the service. We interfere with the freedom of businesses to carry goods and passengers on the road where they will; tribunals supervise this regulation of road transport. The right of the Englishman to do as he likes with his land is taken away from him because we recognise the superior claims of public bodies to acquire it on payment of compensation—disputes about compensation go to the Lands Tribunal. We protect the employee by giving him certain rights to compensation if he is made redundant;

---

[3] Note the effect of inflation since 1975!

we interfere with the employer's freedom to dismiss him—industrial tribunals are there to apply these new laws. Injured servicemen may be entitled to a pension—pensions appeal tribunals will decide. When there is compulsory national service, claims for postponement of service and for eventual reinstatement in civilian employment are heard by special tribunals. Regional Health Authorities find it necessary to detain under the Mental Health Act 1959 those who suffer from mental illness or disorder; we have mental health review tribunals to review, on the application of the Secretary of State for Social Services, the patient or his nearest relatives, the case of anyone liable to be detained.

The quest for speed, cheapness and efficiency

There are many other explanations for this movement away from the ordinary courts. Ministers and their top civil servant advisers have in this century frequently come to doubt whether the courts are the appropriate body to decide many of these new cases. They see rightly that many of these disputes are not merely about private rights: the public good on the one hand and the interest of the particular citizen on the other must be weighed in the balance. They look at many decisions in the courts, even at the level of the House of Lords, and find them wanting in that they appear to disregard the social element of a problem. For example, the courts have chosen to hold that there is no law against letting a tumble-down house; even though the landlord knew of the defects, he is held by them not to be liable to anybody injured on the premises because of their defective condition. Again, the courts held that traders who were determined to obtain a monopoly were free to combine together in order to drive a rival trader out of business. Administrators asked themselves whether judges who arrived at such decisions could be relied on to show a proper regard for the public interest, which would often be paramount or decisive in cases referred to them.

There was also a lack of confidence in the way in which courts interpreted Acts of Parliament. This was important because the new kinds of decisions were almost always ones where the meaning of a section of an Act had to be found. . . . Politicians feared that the courts might frustrate the social purposes of their Acts if they approached cases in this constricted literal fashion. A more serious charge has been levelled at the judges; that they brought to statutory interpretation nineteenth-century notions of the inviolability of property; that they would lean over backwards to find that a statute had not taken away an individual's property rights, even if expropriation for public purposes on payment of compensation was the cardinal aim of the Act. Of course it does not matter whether these suspicions and attitudes of our politicians and civil servants were well-founded; I am looking for the reasons why they diverted topics away from the judges. I am not saying that all their reasons were valid.

Whatever his other faults, the politician or civil servant is sometimes prepared to admit that he might have been wrong, and to change his mind. Flexibility is seen as a key attribute in a decision-maker. Yet the courts have long had a different approach: that once a decision has been reached in a case, it should be a binding precedent for other judges to follow in similar future cases. If the new class of cases had been tried by the courts, principles would have become rigid; courts would have to do for evermore what their predecessors had done, even though they were convinced that the earlier decisions were wrong. It was thought that this judicial inflexibility was inappropriate for many of the new kinds of decision.

The ordinary judge has to be a jack of all trades. This week he may try a murderer, and next week he may hear successively running-down claims, industrial accidents, claims by a deceived house buyer for recovery of his purchase price, and actions for breach of contract to deliver goods. Many of the new State schemes are extraordinarily complex; mastery of the laws can be obtained only by intense specialisation. Governments therefore thought it wise to set up tribunals specially to handle cases under any one particular item of social legislation; they felt that judges who were general practitioners could not be expected to have the necessary expertise and ready familiarity with these detailed new provisions. Sometimes it was considered that the necessary consistency of decision could be attained only if all cases were decided by the same person. Rent tribunals are an obvious example. Nobody would pretend that the reasonable rent of a furnished house or flat can be determined with mathematical precision. Public confidence would be lost if, say, comparable flats in the same block were given markedly different rent ceilings—we know how magistrates are criticised for having different ideas about fines for road traffic offences such as speeding. Continuity and consistency of decision should ensue if the same personnel make decisions in a given area.

There is another less obvious but equally important reason for the development of administrative tribunals. The High Court judge and the lawyer who practises before him have an instinctive yearning for certainty; they like their law to be cut and dried, to have it settled once and for all so that lawyers and their clients know exactly where they stand. There is a lot to be said for this view. We are all entitled to know, for instance (or to have our solicitor tell us), whether what we propose to do is a crime. If we buy a house, we do not want to be told that in the present state of the law it is uncertain whether we shall acquire a good title to it. But the administrators maintain that they cannot run the modern State like that. They talk of the formulation of standards. They see a stage between a fixed rule and anarchy. They find it impossible to legislate in advance for every specific instance. For them decision-making is not then some mechanical process; one cannot use a slot machine or even a computer in order to obtain the answer. In their statutes they use words like 'fair', 'adequate' and 'reasonable,' intending that these standards shall be applied to particular cases in the light of experience. They doubt whether judges will find it congenial to work in this way. They also observe that when judges have in the past had to handle such concepts they have been prone to crystallise what should have been merely instances of the standard into rigid legal rules from which they would depart only with reluctance. For instance, courts which had to decide whether a motorist was driving with reasonable care would be tempted to say, once it had been held that a motorist was liable for not being able to pull up within the range of his lights, that a new rule of law had emerged for all circumstances—that it was always careless not to be able to pull up within the limits of one's vision.

Whitehall did not want this to happen to their administrative standards. They see them as flexible. Take some examples from modern administrative schemes. Are premises educationally suitable? Is a building of special architectural interest? Has a man capacity for work? Is employment available in a district? We see that not only must these standards be developed in the light of experience; technical experts must assist in applying them. The working out of these from case to case is not for lawyers-judges alone; the educationist, the architect, the town planner, the valuer, the industrialist and the trade union official have to participate in this task. Neither politicians nor the judges themselves regarded the courts as ideally equipped for duties of this kind.

The judging process in many of these areas demands an adaptability which judges are not accustomed to display. A local valuation court is not content to sit back and listen to what the house owner and rating officer tell them about the rateable value of the house; its members go and see for themselves. A social security tribunal dealing with a claim for industrial injuries can interrupt the hearing for half an hour to go and visit the scene of the accident. Judges do not do this kind of thing (at least publicly); those who decide these new kinds of dispute must.

A related point is the traditional passiveness of courts—they act only when someone takes the initiative in bringing matters before them. If supervision is to be effective, then sometimes representatives of the administrative agency must unearth wrongdoers and bring them before the agency for a hearing. This approach is commonplace in America in such matters, for example, as monopolies, restrictive practices and false advertising, and there are signs that we may follow in some spheres of administrative control.

Unless a litigant engages a lawyer he is never at ease in court. The judge is aloof, the procedure is formal, there is an atmosphere of uncomfortable dignity. A man likes to be able to have his say in his own way, unrestrained by the niceties of the rule against hearsay evidence and the rest. He often does not want to be reprimanded every time—and it will be often—that he fails to distinguish between cross-examining a witness and making a point in his own favour. Administrative tribunals are sufficiently informal to permit these liberties; courts never are."

In contrast, Abel-Smith and Stevens do not see such a clear distinction between courts and tribunals as Street.

Brian Abel-Smith and Robert Stevens, *In Search of Justice: Society and the Legal System* (Penguin, London, 1968), pp.224–228:

The difference between courts and tribunals

"A foreign non-lawyer who was unaware of the prestige of the British judiciary and of traditional concepts such as the separation of powers, which have come to be associated with courts rather than tribunals, might well ask what the difference really is between a court and a tribunal. What does it matter if some particular adversary procedures have come to be called courts while others are described as tribunals? Both are normally established under statutes. Both interpret laws made by or under statute as well as their own case law, although the latter may be more flexible under administrative tribunals. Both are normally chaired by persons appointed by the Lord Chancellor, although in the case of most courts there are no other members of the bench.

We would argue that such differences as there are between them are not in any sense fundamental but at most differences in degree. Tribunals tend to include a much wider range of skills on the bench; and the most significant hallmark of policy-oriented tribunals is specialization. The most cursory examination of the courts shows that the decision-makers consist of lawyers or laymen or both. Trusted laymen (JPs) staff the majority of magistrates' courts. They also sit with legally qualified chairmen at county quarter sessions. . . .

Tribunals, on the other hand, normally use as decision-takers and not just as witnesses, persons with specialized experience (employers or trade unionists) and persons with professional skills other than legal skills. Thus doctors sit on tribunals which assess the degree of disability in National Insurance claims. Those with expertise in housing problems and land prices sit on Rent Assessment Committees and on the Lands Tribunal. Employers and trade unionists sit on social security tribunals because their knowledge of labour practices is considered valuable. Tribunals are developed ad hoc, and their composition is decided to suit the precise function each is intended to serve. Specialization is therefore one of the most obvious aspects of tribunals, and it is the main distinguishing feature between the ordinary courts and the policy-oriented type of tribunal such as the Patents Appeal Tribunal, the Industrial Court, the Lands Tribunal or the Air Transport Licensing Board. Specialization is also a mark of the 'court-substitute' type of tribunal, such as the Rent Tribunals, the Rent Assessment Committees, Industrial Tribunals and the various social security tribunals. But again it is a question of degree rather than basic difference—the Companies Court and the Commercial Court are specialized lists within the court structure.

With respect to the court-substitute type of tribunals we would argue that the chief features which distinguish them from the regular courts are their cheapness, their speed and efficiency, their privacy and their informality. Civil courts, with the exception of Magistrates' courts in certain types of case, charge fees. Tribunals do not. Thus, Rent Tribunals, National Insurance Tribunals and the like emphasize lack of expense. Those appearing before such tribunals can be represented by persons other than lawyers, and this also helps to keep costs down—particularly where parties are represented by trade unionists. Persons must have the permission of the court to be represented by a non-lawyer in a county court or a magistrate's court, and there is no precedent for such representation before the High Court. At the same time, and even bearing in mind the dangers of excessive legalism, we think it dangerous that any form of legal aid is unknown before most tribunals. . . .

Tribunals are as informal as is consistent with an orderly conduct of their affairs. The attempt is usually made to create an atmosphere in which people who appear in person will not feel ill at ease or nervous. While the magistrates' courts, particularly in juvenile cases, go some way in the same direction, the physical layout of courts, the robes and modes of address are forbidding even for persons with considerable poise and self-confidence in any other setting. Moreover, as we have seen, the attitude of some judges and occasionally their remarks can be such as to humiliate litigants. But this difference must not be overestimated. In particular, the increase in legal chairmen and legal representation since 1958 has often eradicated this difference.

Another articulated difference between courts and tribunals as a whole lies in the more restricted rights of appeal found in many of the latter (although the Franks Report, which led to the Tribunal and Enquiries Act, 1958, was in many senses a victory for the lawyers and so led to a wider right of appeal from tribunals). . . .

Some lawyers would argue that there was a further fundamental difference between the two streams. Courts are said to be administering rules of law while tribunals are thought to be administering both law and policy. We would maintain that no such clear line can or should be drawn. Indeed it was the evolution of this myth which helped establish the tribunal system by convincing the judges of the ordinary courts that they were concerned with legal but not with policy questions. But continued insistence on this unsatisfactory distinction makes it increasingly difficult to entrust new matters to the courts or to merge courts and tribunals. Properly understood, tribunals are a more modern form of court. In some cases they may have more discretion than the courts, and this is particularly true of the policy-oriented tribunals. But certainly they have no more discretion than the Chancery Division has in handling trusts, wards or companies. Conversely the court-substitute tribunals are often as precedent-conscious as, and may even exercise a much narrower discretion than, the ordinary courts.

But we would reaffirm our position that there is no fundamental difference between courts and tribunals. We would argue, therefore, that every effort should be made to merge the two. A well-structured court system, with reform and flexible procedures based on the county court or Civil Tribunal, with specialized 'lists', might then offer a general adjudicatory system, with a spectrum of judges specialized in the many fields in which a potential litigant might be interested."

NOTES AND QUESTIONS

- Why are Abel-Smith and Stevens sceptical of the distinction between law and policy?

- Having read the excerpts from Street and Abel-Smith and Stevens, do you think that tribunals and courts are roughly the same, or quite different from each other? Give reasons for your answer?

A recent discussion of the tribunal system by Genn underscores a high degree of continuity in the years since Street and Abel-Smith and Stevens wrote their analyses.

Hazel Genn, "Tribunals and Informal Justice" (1993) 56 M.L.R. 393 at 393:

Tribunals and informal justice

"Informal tribunals that review administrative decisions and adjudicate on disputes between individuals have been part of the British system of civil justice for some time. Their popularity with policy-makers, at least, has led to a remarkable proliferation in the last 50 years, and currently in the UK hear over a quarter of a million cases annually, representing some six times the number of contested civil cases disposed of at trial before the High Court and County Courts together. New tribunals are being created all the time. Such tribunals have historically been viewed as cheap, non-technical substitutes for the ordinary courts for a wide range of grievances and disputes, in which parties can initiate actions without cost or fuss.

Tribunals in the UK have been largely overlooked by scholars concerned with developments in informal justice, who have tended to focus on small claims procedures, conciliation, mediation and arbitration. This omission may be because the history of tribunals predates the contemporary trend towards informalism, and because tribunals do not represent 'alternatives' to courts, unlike, for example, some small claims procedures and arbitration hearings. Tribunals are the only mechanism provided by Parliament for the resolution of certain grievances against the State, and for some specific disputes between individuals. They are the result of deliberate choice, and in the early days of the Welfare State, at least, it has been argued that this choice was underpinned by philosophical as well as practical considerations. Tribunals ought, however, to be of interest to those who study alternative dispute resolution mechanisms. They display many of the characteristics welcomed by proponents of informalism, and some of the historical and modern justifications for the creation of tribunals rest on presumed advantages over ordinary courts which echo the claims made for ADR and criticisms of conventional court adjudication.

Defining tribunals

In the UK there are about 50 different types of tribunals and some 2000 tribunals altogether. Tribunals are supervised on a general basis by the Council on Tribunals, but there is no common procedure followed by these bodies, no general appeal process or appellate body. Some tribunals have lay members, others have specialist qualifications. Some tribunals act in a strictly judicial fashion, while others look more broadly at policy considerations. It is, in fact, impossible to provide a simple definition of a tribunal. The label is given to many different kinds of bodies with widely differing functions, and covering a vast range of subject areas including private as well as public law issues.

The four tribunals included in the study from which this paper has developed are, in effect, court-substitutes.[4] They do not have responsibility for making regulations or devising policy, but are required to act as informal courts, reviewing administrative decisions or adjudicating between disputing parties. There are great differences between tribunals in the degree of informality to be found in proceedings, and in their function. SSATs [social security appeal tribunals] and hearings before immigration adjudicators, for example, provide a first tier of appeal from administrative decisions. Industrial tribunals, on the other hand, adjudicate at first instance on disputes between employers and employees. They are not concerned with administrative decision-making, but with disputes between private parties. There are also many differences in the composition of tribunals. SSATs and industrial tribunals are composed of a legal chairman and two lay members. Immigration cases, on the other hand, are heard before a single legally trained Adjudicator. Although in each of the four tribunals the right to apply for a hearing before a tribunal without incurring cost is virtually automatic, the procedures in each tribunal thereafter are very different. Procedures in SSATs are very informal and defined inaccurately as being 'inquisitorial' with proceedings being conducted around a large table. Immigration hearings and industrial tribunals are considerably more formal and more obviously adversarial, with raised platforms and evidence often given on oath.

Such similarities as there are between tribunals tend to reside in the *absence* of certain features of courts. For example, the absence of strict rules of evidence; the absence of court

---

[4] Genn's study focused on tribunals dealing with welfare benefits, immigration disputes, employment disputes and detention under mental health legislation.

robes; the frequent absence of representatives appearing for applicants, etc. Indeed, it might be argued that the only common, unifying aspects of adjudicative institutions that bear the label 'tribunal' concern their superficially distinctive procedures and personnel. Since it is in the presumed *procedural* advantages over conventional courts that the most compelling arguments for establishing tribunals have been made, it seems appropriate that an analysis of the activities of tribunals should concentrate on the benefit conferred by this procedural innovation on those whose cases are decided by tribunals.

Procedural advantages: tribunals and the 'preferred option'

The arguments for establishing tribunals to deal with certain categories of dispute rather than giving jurisdiction to the ordinary courts have variously been based on constitutional arguments; allegations of class bias in the courts; practical arguments concerning lack of resources in the courts to handle new and potentially huge caseloads; and finally, the positive benefits of tribunals over ordinary courts in terms of their speed, cheapness, informality and expertise. . . .

In the early days of the modern tribunal system, the intention was that tribunals should provide easy access to specialist adjudicators at no cost to applicants. There was no charge for the initiation of applications to tribunals and no cost for applicants if they lost. The hearings were to be 'informal' and there was an assumption that the informality of proceedings would make it possible for applicants to represent themselves at hearings. Tribunal chairmen would take a relatively active role in hearings and adopt flexible procedures. The process was intended to be swift, not bogged down in 'technicality' and not bound by strict rules of evidence. Since there was perceived to be no need for highly trained judges, the system could be operated relatively inexpensively. Although tribunal chairmen would not be of the same calibre as judges, their concentration on specific subject areas would lead to expertise and, presumably, good quality decision-making. Tribunals were therefore presented as being 'good' for applicants who would often be from among the most disadvantaged groups in society and who, it was assumed, would be overawed and dismayed at the prospect of bringing their case to a court.

These attributes of tribunals had evidently already been sufficiently established by 1957 for the Franks Committee to set them out as descriptive characteristics rather than as a set of objectives to be attained by tribunals:

> 'tribunals have certain characteristics which often give them advantages over the courts. These are cheapness, accessibility, freedom from technicality, expedition and expert knowledge of their particular subject.'

This well-worn formulation has been repeated countless times throughout the literature on tribunals since the publication of the Franks Report. The confident assertions about the advantages of tribunals have not always been borne out by empirical studies of the operation of tribunals in practice. Nonetheless, some of the most up-to-date analyses of tribunals by public lawyers continue to repeat the description. For example:

> 'The[se] differences between tribunals and courts are usually seen as being advantages of tribunals, and as reasons for establishing a tribunal rather than a court; both because cheapness, speed, and so on, are good in themselves; and because, in some areas at least, many applicants before tribunals are poor and ill-educated, and so would find a traditional court very intimidating. Tribunals can be seen, therefore, as having both technical and social advantages over courts.'

Other writers, however, argue that decisions to establish rights of appeal to tribunals rather than courts have been based primarily on political and cost considerations, not in the belief that tribunals will provide greater access to justice:

> 'The tribunals were not established to make up for defects in the judicial system. The choice was never between appeal to tribunals and appeal to the courts, but between appeal to tribunals and no appeal. Their introduction did not represent an incorpora-

tion of the idea of legality into new areas of society for its own sake. The provision of a formal right of appeal . . . was introduced as a counter-measure to political protest and as a means of making oppressive changes in the relief of poverty more palatable by giving a symbolic appearance of legality whilst ensuring that this had no real effect.'

The doubts expressed about the political objectives driving the growth of tribunals in the UK during the twentieth century are also to be found in modern criticisms of small claims procedures in this country and other forms of ADR abroad. Theoretical and empirical studies of tribunals, small claims courts, mediation and arbitration contain consistent themes questioning the stimulus for their creation and the extent to which they achieve the benefits claimed for them.

The most commonly stated reasons for establishing informal dispute mechanisms outside of the administrative law field have been either that the courts are overburdened, or that the ordinary courts are in some way inappropriate for dealing with certain classes of dispute because their procedures and the cost of bringing cases before them represent an obstacle to free access to justice. There is, however, a critical strand in the literature on informal justice sceptical of these explanations. Abel has argued that in the civil justice field at least, the modern trend towards informalism, based in efficiency arguments, represents a 'downgrading' of the problems of the poor and a relegation of their disputes to second-class forms of justice. In Abel's analysis, 'informal' tends to be synonymous with 'inferior.' Similar arguments have been made more recently in this country in relation to changes in court jurisdiction designed to reallocate cases down the court hierarchy. Sedley argues that the recent reorganisation has been driven by a desire to free the courts for the resolution of international commercial disputes and in so doing individual rights have been trivialised and diverted to courts of 'poorer' quality.

The suggestion that the problems of the poor have been relegated to inferior adjudicative institutions in order to free the courts for the problems of businessmen may be true. It must be acknowledged, however, that the business community has itself criticised the cost, paraphernalia and lack of speed involved in court litigation. Business is experimenting with alternative methods of settling commercial disputes. In recent years, the rapid growth of arbitration and other innovative forms of ADR in the commercial field in this country and abroad represents a reaction against the disadvantages of attempting to resolve business disputes through the courts. The value of ADR for businesses in long-term relationships has been recognised, in this country, by the establishment of a Centre for Dispute Resolution which provides a mechanism that will spare businesses 'the expensive, time consuming and costly process of litigation.'

The *desire* to establish simplified methods of resolving disputes, and to improve access to justice for *all* sections of society, is a rational response to the perceived shortcomings of the civil courts. However, although there may be a common desire to search for court-alternatives for the problems of the poor and for the problems of commercial men alike, it is highly improbable that the solution for one group will necessarily be appropriate for another. In order to devise court-alternatives which serve the legal needs of the poor and disadvantaged, it is necessary to have a clear understanding of the nature of those needs, and second to appreciate how formal and informal legal institutions operate in practice, rather than in theory. It is possible that some of the shortcomings identified by critics of informal courts and tribunals may lie less in the *principle* than in the *practice* of informal justice."

NOTES AND QUESTIONS

• Assess the argument that the growth of tribunals represents a "downgrading" of the claims of the poor. Could the courts provide a better alternative for such claims?

- List the advantages and disadvantages of tribunals as dispute resolution bodies. For what types of disputes do you think tribunals are best suited (if any)?

To what extent do tribunals *in practice* achieve the objectives ascribed to them in the abstracts considered to date? Baldwin has undertaken an empirical study of the Social Security Appeal Tribunals has found the process to be full of tensions regarding tribunal procedure and the role of the chairperson. We now turn to this as a case study.

John Baldwin, "The adjudication of claims" (June 5, 1992) *New Law Journal* 794 at 795:

"In the wake of the series of damaging criticisms made of supplementary benefit appeal tribunals in the 1970s—criticisms that directly led to the reforms of the 1980s—a determined attempt is nowadays made by the chairmen and members of social security appeal tribunals to facilitate the presentation of cases by ordinary citizens. Lay chairmen have been replaced by qualified lawyers, and a responsibility is placed upon chairmen to enter the arena of dispute to assist unrepresented claimants. 'It makes a mockery of the tribunal system,' as the former President of SSATs explained, 'to leave [the claimant] totally to his own devices to argue his appeal as best he may.'

The tribunals are expected to adopt an inquisitorial approach and take the initiative in questioning both parties in an attempt to elicit all the evidence. In addition, departmental presenting officers are instructed to play the role of *amicus curiae* and not to assume prosecutorial stances. In 45 per cent of the hearings we observed, no appellant turned up, and, even where an appellant was present, only about a third were represented. In such circumstances, the contest between the presenting officer and the appellant would be a most unequal one if the tribunal operated on strictly adversarial lines.

But have these developments improved the position of appellants appearing before tribunals? The idea that life will be made easier for them if the chairmen and members offer assistance and that any imbalance between the parties will be redressed by discouraging presenting officers from acting as advocates for the Department is certainly seductive. It seems almost self-evident that a tribunal that strives to be informal in its approach should lend a helping hand to any appellant who is floundering. Yet our observations of hearings indicated that the chairmen of social security appeal tribunals who seek to play a full inquisitorial role and to assist an appellant who is struggling to present a coherent case are likely to run into difficulty. Nor is it as easy as it might first appear for presenting officers to play a full *amicus* role.

Turning first to the chairman's inquisitorial function, we found two factors in particular limited the extent to which the role could be played. First, because of the removal of discretion from large areas of the social security system, the tribunals often have little or no room for manoeuvre in reviewing an adjudication officer's decision.

Secondly, in almost a half of the cases coming before the tribunal, no appellant is present to be offered assistance. We were frequently told by tribunal chairmen and members that cases in which appellants failed to attend received a more cursory examination than those in which the appellant appeared in person. This was also borne out in our own observations of the hearings themselves.

It soon becomes clear to anyone who attends tribunal hearings that some chairmen play the inquisitorial role much more naturally and effectively than do others. Some chairmen are able to adopt it in a sensitive and expert manner, skilfully eliciting information from claimants and encouraging them to participate fully in the discussion. Others experience evident unease in descending into the fray in this way and revert to adversarial type at the first opportunity. Still others do not strive to play an inquisitorial role at all. On a more general level, the way chairmen run hearings varies enormously. Some are patient and sympathetic, facilitating the difficult task that appellants and other parties face in getting across the essentials of their case. Other chairmen perform these tasks much less satisfactorily.

We looked closely at the way that hearings were conducted, and we assessed the chairman's handling of a case as good or excellent in 57 per cent of the hearings we attended, and as adequate in a further quarter of the hearings. In about one in every six hearings, however, the chairman's conduct of the case was in our view open to serious criticism.

It is not difficult to understand why some chairmen find that adopting a traditional, adversarial approach comes more naturally to them. The body of law with which these tribunals deal is both technical and complex, and it was perhaps remarkable how far chairmen were prepared to allow arguments to be developed which could only cloud the legal issues. Claimants often rely on a commonsense or intuitive notion of what is right or just, in ignorance of the legal merits of their appeal. This means that many cases are in a strict legal sense flimsy, indeed often doomed from the outset.

Many appellants leave the tribunal dissatisfied with decisions which they see as having been based upon the application of objectionable legal rules, and several chairmen conceded to us in interview that they often shared appellants' views about the law. All the chairmen to whom we spoke, however, said that they had no alternative but to apply the regulations regardless of their personal feelings about a case. One appellant in the Midlands made her objection forcefully as follows:

'They just go by the law, and that's it. There's no flexibility in the law, it's rigid. There's no compassion built in. They were all sorry; they were genuinely sorry. The form they give you tells you that you can appeal. This seems to me a bit stupid when there's no chance of you winning the appeal. It's like putting you in a race that you can never win. They slightly raise your hopes, then dash them again. It makes it seem like a sham.'

The tension between the tribunal's sympathy for many claimants and its obligation to apply the law dispassionately runs through the whole of social security adjudication, and chairmen have to find a way in the hearing of allowing appellants to have their say while at the same time steering proceedings along the course that the present law requires. So there is a limit to how far a chairman can be expected to maintain an inquisitorial approach, once the tribunal has satisfied itself that the appeal is based on arguments which have no merit in law."

NOTES AND QUESTIONS

- Note the tension which Baldwin identifies between flexibility and the application of strict legal rules. From reading his analysis, do you think the present approach has the balance right?

- Devise a set of guidelines for chairpersons of tribunals concerning their role. To what extent do you think an inquisitorial role should be adopted?

LEGAL REPRESENTATION BEFORE TRIBUNALS

From Baldwin's analysis it is apparent that the appearance of an unrepresented individual before a tribunal makes a significant difference to the outcome. A related issue is whether that individual should be allowed legal representation before the tribunal. Intuitively, our assumption is probably that representation might make a difference to the result. After all, isn't that what lawyers are supposed to do? On the other hand, we know that tribunals are intended to be informal, relatively inexpensive and speedy. If lawyers get involved, will those values be undermined? Will the tribunal process inevitably become more "court like" if the tribunal is open to lawyers arguing cases? The issue of legal representation thus goes to the heart of the values which inform the tribunal system, and the question of whether tribunals are "different" (and in what ways) from courts. In this country, legal representation is generally allowed to individuals who appear before tribunals, but that right in practice is undermined for many by the fact that legal aid is not available! In her socio-legal analysis of tribunals, Genn has analysed the impact of legal representation on tribunal *outcomes*.

Hazel Genn, "Tribunals and Informal Justice" (1993) 56 M.L.R. 393 at 398:

"Despite the frequent absence of representatives from informal court and tribunal hearings, evidence from empirical research carried out in some tribunals and small claims courts consistently indicates that when present, representation can give an advantage to the represented party. Empirical studies in the UK on the contribution of representation to tribunals generally suggests that represented tribunal applicants are more likely to achieve a favourable outcome to their hearing than unrepresented applicants. However, some of the findings have been criticised for failing to take account of the possibility that representatives select the strongest cases. . . .

One of the chief results of the official view of tribunals in this country is their virtual exclusion from the Legal Aid scheme, although legal or lay representation is permitted in all tribunals.[5] The absence of legal aid is generally explained or defended on the ground that tribunal procedures have been so designed that applicants should be able to bring their cases in person and without legal representation. Tribunal procedures are generally flexible; strict rules of evidence do not apply; applicants are permitted to tell their story in their own words; and tribunal chairs are free to take a more interventionist role than judges in court. Indeed, it is argued not only that legal representation is unnecessary in tribunals, but that the presence of lawyers might undermine the speed and informality that are the hallmarks of tribunal procedures. Despite the absence of legal aid for representation, however, some of those who bring their case before tribunals pay for legal representation or obtain free representation from law centres, tribunal representation units, the Free Representation Unit and a host of specialist advice agencies across the country who provide a limited representation service. Repeated calls for the extension of legal aid to tribunals have fallen on deaf ears, although the research upon which this paper is based was commissioned specifically by the Lord Chancellor's Department to address some of the arguments made about the need for representation to be available to tribunal applicants. . . .

An analysis of the effect of representation on the outcome of hearings established that, in all four tribunals, the presence of a skilled representative significantly and independently increased the probability that a case would succeed. In social security appeals tribunals, the presence of a skilled representative increased the likelihood of success from 30 to 48 per cent. In hearings before immigration adjudicators, the overall likelihood of success was increased by the presence of a representative from 20 to 38 per cent. In mental health review tribunals, the likelihood of a favourable change in conditions rose from 20 to 35 per cent as a result of representation. The effect of representation on the outcome of industrial tribunal hearings is more complicated to state since both parties to hearings are able to appear with a representative. If the respondent was not represented and the applicant was represented by a lawyer, the applicant's success figure was increased from 30 to 48 per cent.

---

[5] Exceptions are the ABWOR scheme for Mental Health Review Tribunals, the Employment Appeals Tribunal (but not Industrial Tribunals) and the Lands Tribunal.

Where the respondent was legally represented and the applicant was unrepresented, the applicant's probability of success fell to 10 per cent.

The research indicated clearly that the presence of a representative influences the substantive outcome of hearings, irrespective of the process value that representation may provide. It also showed that the type of representation used by appellants was very important, and that specialist representatives exerted the greatest influence on the outcome of hearings. . . ."

Genn concludes that the trade-off for the value of informality in the tribunal system is inaccuracy in decision making.

"The potential loss of protection that may accompany informal procedures has been robustly articulated by other writers. Cane, for example, suggests that the 'price' of informality in tribunals 'is a certain amount of legal inaccuracy' and that efforts have to be made to avoid insisting on 'strict legal niceties' if such informality is to be preserved. The problem, however, is in establishing the nature and level of inaccuracy that might represent an acceptable cost of informality. Many of the matters heard by tribunals, for example, constitute win or lose situations because there is no other feasible outcome. The right to remain in the country, or to be released from a mental hospital, or the right to a social security benefit are all or nothing situations in which an 'accurate' decision means the loss of an important right. It is clear, however, that the degree of inaccuracy suffered in informal proceedings could be reduced if knowledge about the operation of informal procedures were used to inform decisions about when such procedures should be adopted and how they should be designed."

NOTES AND QUESTIONS

- While tribunals are often characterised in terms of providing speedy, relatively inexpensive resolution of disputes, it could be argued that the areas with which they deal are no less important than those dealt with by the courts. For example, Mental Health Review Tribunals consider the compulsory detention of the mentally ill; the Immigration Appeal Tribunals consider whether people can remain in this country. These are clearly issues of the greatest importance for the individual, and they are entrusted to tribunals. If you were in charge of designing a new legal system, how would you go about determining which cases should be heard in courts and which in tribunals? Give a detailed explanation of the reasons for your choices.

- What importance would you attach to the financial value of the claim, the seriousness of the alleged abuse, the needs of the litigants or a point of law in developing your new scheme?

BARGAINING IN THE SHADOW OF THE LAW

Focusing as we have done up to now on the resolution of disputes in courts and tribunals is rather artificial. Most cases which enter the litigation system are either abandoned or settled prior to adjudication. Negotiated settlements are agreements in which the claimant undertakes not to pursue their case any further in exchange for payment or another remedy. In the majority of cases, this agreement will be expressed in a written contract which is enforceable in the courts. Negotiated settlement can occur at any time, but traditionally has tended to take place shortly after key events, such as the exchange of expert evidence, or shortly before the parties are due to attend a hearing. The obvious advantage to a negotiated settlement is that it constitutes a quicker end to the dispute, reduces costs and allows greater flexibility because the parties retain control over the terms of the settlement. Most importantly, it can eliminate the risk of having to pay the costs of your opponent should you proceed to a court or tribunal and lose your case.

Whilst negotiation is a different form of dispute resolution, it is a mistake to view adjudication and negotiated settlements as completely separate phenomena. Negotiated settlements often occur in conjunction with an assessment on the part of both sides of the strength of their case were they to have it adjudicated. This means that, among other things, the parties will have to assess whether they have legal precedents in their favour. It is in this way that the courts in particular are said to bestow a bargaining endowment on the parties which will shape the settlement reached. In fact, the relationship between litigation and negotiated settlement is such that Galanter has relabelled the process of agreeing settlement "litigotiation".

Hazel Genn, "Access to Just Settlements: The Case of Medical Negligence" in *Reform of Civil Procedure: Essays on "Access to Justice"*, (A.A.S. Zuckerman and Ross Cranston, eds., Clarendon Press, Oxford, 1995), pp.396–397:

"The vast majority of civil claims are settled without trial and in personal injury and medical negligence cases settlement is clearly the norm. The Oxford study found that 97% of successful personal injury cases settled out of court. In the recent Law Commission study of damages payments in personal injury (including medical negligence) cases it was found that 94% of plaintiffs receiving between £5,000 and £20,000 in damages had settled their claims out of court, and among those who received over £20,000, some 91% had settled their claims out of court.

Settlement is so pervasive that it has been argued that in civil litigation those cases that result in contested hearings are to be considered as deviant. Therefore, when we talk about refining litigation procedures we are considering the procedures by which the parties move toward settlement rather than trial. The conduct of negotiations and the path to settlement are largely dictated by court procedures. There is no separate settlement procedure. Settlement is achieved by preparing for trial—going through the ritualistic procedures determined appropriate for adversarial contest in open court. Parties who want peace and want it on good terms have no alternative, within the context of adversarial court procedures, but to prepare for war. 'There are not two distinct processes, negotiation and litigation; there is a single process of disputing in the vicinity of official tribunals that we might call litigotiation, that is, the strategic pursuit of a settlement through mobilizing the court process.' Once the parties are committed to litigation, there are no procedures that might facilitate creative outcomes or that might minimise conflict. Negotiation within the litigation context is 'fundamentally different from the negotiations that might occur over the purchase of a house or in the context of developing a political agreement'. Indeed, if one were to devise a system in which disputes could be rapidly negotiated to a compromise leaving both parties reasonably content with the outcome, one would be highly unlikely to start with anything resembling the rules of court."

REFORM OF THE LITIGATION SYSTEM

The civil justice system has long been perceived to be in need of reform, and that process has intensified in recent years, culminating with the release of the Woolf Report on Access to Justice and the Middleton Report which followed it. The background to these reforms is described by Darbyshire.

Penny Darbyshire, *Eddey on the English Legal System* (7th ed., Sweet and Maxwell, London, 2001), pp.107–108:

"The problems of English civil procedure have been the subject of constant scrutiny throughout this century and much of the last. Prior to the Lord Chancellor's establishment of the Civil Justice Review in 1985, there had been no fewer than 63 reports, since the turn of the century on the same subject. With tedious and frustrating repetition, they all identify the same core problems so that the opening words of Chapter two of Lord Woolf's interim report, in 1995, give those of us who have been watching the legal system for some years more than a frisson of *dé-jà vu*:

'The process is too expensive, too slow and too complex.'

His Lordship quotes a number of famous judicial critics of the civil process who have all drawn attention to the fact that these problems militate against the provision of an accessible system of civil courts which is necessary if people are to be enabled to enforce their rights in civil law. Indeed, the very title of his Lordship's report, *Access to Justice*, seems like an ironic cliché, after years of concern over the lack of it.

The Civil Justice Review body reported in 1988. The review was remarkable for the breadth and depth of its scrutiny of the system, its radical approach and its success rate, in that many of its recommendations were soon translated into law, in the Courts and Legal Services Act 1990 and subsequent delegated legislation. Yet, despite the fact that its reforms were potentially the most radical since the Judicature Acts of 1893–95, they apparently did not solve those fundamental problems. No sooner had the dust settled on the new legislation than the two sides of the legal profession had established the Heilbron Committee, to produce a 1993 report on the continuing problems of civil justice and their proposals for dealing with them. The Lord Chancellor responded by commissioning Lord Woolf, when a Law Lord, to carry out yet another scrutiny of the system and suggest yet another list of proposed reforms."

Elliot and Quinn take up the story of reform from this point and describe the ills that were identified by the Woolf Report and the solutions that Lord Woolf and his team suggested to the problems.

C. Elliot and F. Quinn, *English Legal System* (3rd ed., Longman, London, 2000) pp.342–349, 355–356:

"In *Access to Justice: Final Report*, published in 1996, [Lord Woolf] stated that a civil justice system should:

- be just in the results it delivers;
- be fair in the way it treats litigants;
- offer appropriate procedures at a reasonable cost;
- deal with cases with reasonable speed;
- be understandable to those who use it;
- be responsive to the needs of those who use it;

- provide as much certainty as the nature of particular cases allows;
- be effective, adequately resources and organized.

Lord Woolf concluded that the system at the time failed to achieve all these goals. It is possible that this failure is inevitable, as some of the aims conflict with others. A system based on cost-efficiency alone would make it difficult to justify claims for comparatively small sums, yet these cases are very important to the parties involved, and wide access to justice is vital. Promoting efficiency in terms of speed can also conflict with the need for fairness. Making the courts more accessible could lead to a flood of cases which would make it impossible to provide a speedy resolution and keep costs down. One practical example of the conflict between different aims is that the availability of legal aid to one party, one of the aims of widening access to justice, can put pressure on the other side if they are funding themselves, and so clash with the need for fairness.

In addition, changes made to the civil justice system may have effects outside it—making it easier to bring personal injury actions, for example, could push up the costs of insurance, and it has been suggested that in the USA this has led to unwillingness on the part of doctors to perform any risky medical treatment.

It is impossible to resolve all of these conflicts and a successful legal system must simply aim for the best possible balance. Lord Scarman has commented:

'To be acceptable to ordinary people, I believe [the] legal process in litigation must be designed to encourage, first, settlement by agreement; secondly, open and speedy trial if agreement is not forthcoming. In other words, justice, not truth is its purpose. It is against the criteria of justice and fairness that the system must be assessed.'

In the final analysis, it is for the Government to decide the balance they wish to strike, and how much they are prepared to spend on it. While conflicting interests may mean it is impossible to achieve a civil justice system that satisfies everyone, there were serious concerns that the civil justice system before April 1999 was giving satisfaction to only a small minority of users for a range of reasons which will be considered in turn.

Too expensive

Research carried out for Lord Woolf's review found that one side's costs exceed the amount in dispute in over 40 per cent of cases where the claim was for under £12,500. Where the claim was for between £12,500 and £25,000 average costs were between 40 per cent and 95 per cent of the claim. The bill for one claim of just £2,000 came to £69,295; that for another of £1,000 was £26,398. The survey concluded that the simplest cases often incurred the highest costs in proportion to the value of the claim.

Because of the complexity of the process, lawyers were usually needed and High Court litigation especially is not a game for the inexperienced, so barristers often draft the pleadings and advise on the evidence. This is expensive. The sheer length of civil proceedings also affected the size of the bill in the end.

Lord Woolf has said that, fifteen years ago, his report would not have been necessary, because most lawyers made their money from other work, such as conveyancing, seeing litigation as a loss maker that they would only undertake reluctantly. But, with the huge increase in the number of lawyers combined with the recession in the property market at the end of the 1980s, lawyers suddenly found that litigation could generate a steady income. He found that costs were now so high that even big companies were wary, with some preferring to fight cases in New York.

Delays

The Civil Justice Review observed that the system was overstretched, and the time between the incident giving rise to the claim and the trial could be up to three years for the county courts and five for the High Court. Research carried out for Lord Woolf found the worst delays in personal injury and medical negligence cases, with these actions taking a median time of 54 and 61 months respectively. The average waiting time for a county court claim was 79 weeks. Time limits were laid down for every stage of an action but both lawyers and the courts disregarded them. Often time limits were waived by the lawyers to create an opportunity to negotiate, which was reasonable, but the problem was that there was no effective control of when and why it was done. The High Court's long vacation (the two months during the summer when the judges do not sit) also contributed to delay.

According to the Civil Justice Review, long delays placed intolerable psychological and financial burdens on accident victims and undermined the justice of the trial, by making it more difficult to gather evidence which was then unreliable because witnesses had to remember the events of several years before. The overall result was to lower public estimation of the legal system as a whole.

The reforms made by the 1990 Courts and Legal Services Act had done little to ease delays. The main complaints were that county courts had not been given enough administrators to cope with their new workload, so High Court delays had simply been transferred to the county courts; the county courts were understaffed and underfunded to cope with the increase in business.

Injustice

Usually an out-of-court settlement is negotiated before the litigants ever reach the trial stage. For every 9,000 personal injury cases commenced only 300 are submitted for judgment. Outside personal injuries, for every 100,000 writs issued before 1999, fewer than 300 actually came for trial. An out-of-court settlement can have the advantage of a quick end to the dispute, and a reduction in costs—although these start to build up from the time each side consults a lawyer—the trial itself is by far the most expensive part. For the claimant, a settlement means they are sure of getting something, and do not have to risk losing the case altogether and probably having to pay the other side's costs as well as their own; but they must weigh this up against the chances of being awarded a better settlement if the case goes to trial and they win. The defendant risks the possibility that they might have won and therefore had to pay nothing, or that they may be paying more than the judge would have awarded if the plaintiff had won the case, against the chance that the plaintiff wins and is awarded more than the settlement would have cost.

The high number of out-of-court settlements creates injustice, because the parties usually held very unequal bargaining positions. In the first place, one party might be in a better financial position than the other, and therefore under less pressure to keep costs down by settling quickly.

Secondly, as Galanter's 1974 study revealed, litigants could often be divided into 'one-shotters' and 'repeat players'. One-shotters are individuals involved in litigation for probably the only time in their life, for whom the procedure is unfamiliar and traumatic; the case is very important to them and tends to occupy most of their thoughts while it continues. Repeat players, on the other hand, include companies and businesses (particularly insurance companies), for whom litigation is routine. They are used to working with the law and lawyers and, while they obviously want to win the case for financial reasons, they do not have the same emotional investments in it as the individual one-shotter. Where a repeat player and a one-shotter are on opposing sides—as is often the case in personal injury litigation, where an individual is fighting an insurance company—the repeat player is likely to have the upper hand in out-of-court bargaining.

A third factor was highlighted by Hazel Genn's 1987 study of negotiated settlements of accident claims. She found that having a non-specialist lawyer could seriously prejudice a client's interest when an out-of-court settlement is made. A non-specialist may be unfamiliar with court procedure and reluctant to fight the case in court. They may, therefore, not encourage their client to hold out against an unsatisfactory settlement. Specialist lawyers on the other side may take advantage of this inexperience, putting on pressure for the acceptance of a low settlement. Repeat players are more likely to have access to their own specialist lawyers whereas, for the one-shotter, finding a suitable lawyer can be something of a lottery, since they have little information on which to base their choice.

Clearly these factors did affect the fairness of out-of-court settlements. In court, the judge would treat the parties as equals, but for out-of-court negotiations one party often had a very obvious advantage.

The rules on payments into court increased the unfairness of the pre-trial procedures. As Zander (1988) observed, the rule was 'highly favourable' to the defendant, putting extra pressure on the plaintiff to accept an offer.

Pressures of time caused injustice. Special continuous trial centres were set up, in which most of the business was heard very quickly, thus allowing the court to hear a number of cases each day. This could lead to an emphasis on processing people through the system at speed, rather than examining the evidence and making a judicial decision. One research report put the average court time spent on local authority repossession cases at 90 seconds, and one judge described the judicial role in such cases as 'purely administrative, somebody independent of the local authority to rubber-stamp the document'.

The adversarial process

Many problems resulted from the adversarial process which encouraged tactical manoeuvring rather than cooperation. It would be far simpler and cheaper for each side to state precisely what it alleged in the pleadings, disclose all the documents they held, and give the other side copies of their witness statements. Attitudes did appear to be slowly changing, with a growing appreciation that the public interest demanded justice be provided as quickly and economically as possible. Some of the procedural rules, for example on expert witnesses, were changed and there was less scope for tactical manoeuvring.

Emphasis on oral evidence

Too much emphasis was placed on oral evidence at trial. This may have been appropriate when juries were commonly used in civil proceedings, but in the twentieth century much of the information the judge needed could be provided on paper and read before the trial. Oral evidence slowed down proceedings, adding to cost and delays.

There were also doubts about the usefulness of oral evidence. In particular, there was a danger that the ordinary witness, often giving evidence years after the events occurred, would be so intimidated by the nature of the questioning and the formality of the proceedings that their evidence would appear far less credible than should be the case; while the evidence of an expert witness familiar with court room antics might well have an aura of authority which it did not deserve.

There had been a limited move away from oral evidence—for example, a 1995 Practice Direction provided that witness statements would be accepted as the evidence-in-chief of that witness.

Enforcement

It was sometimes difficult to enforce judgments against debtors; responsibility for this was largely left to the parties.

Changes in jurisdiction

Though designed to ease the problems of the civil system, the reforms implemented by the 1990 Courts and Legal Services Act to the jurisdiction rules of the High Court and county court had created some new ones of their own. The changes had caused delay in the county courts. There was also a suggestion that the High Court had been preserved as a small, elite court hearing only a few public and commercial cases, while smaller cases, such as accidents at work or on the roads, wrongful arrests, contracts of employment or tenancies and housing conditions—in other words, the problems of the average citizen—were getting second-class justice in the county court.

Lawyers specializing in personal injury litigation (most of whom would previously have been dealing with the High Court) said problems in county courts were considerable; papers lost, letter and phone calls unanswered, inadequate pre-trial procedures, too few administrators and a shortage of experienced, informed judges.

Specialist injury firms also regretted the loss of direct control over the running of cases they enjoyed in the High Court. While solicitors could, with the court's permission, prepare and serve their own documents in county court actions, it was not always possible to do so, and there were long delays in some cities as summonses were sent to typing centres. Even if solicitors took on the work themselves, they had to keep in touch with the court; telephones were often busy and correspondence went unanswered. Many solicitors reported that contact by letter or phone was so difficult that they sent employees to the county court in person several times a week to check on progress with cases.

Not all county courts had the same procedural practices and differing procedures created confusion for firms dealing with a number of different county courts. Some solicitors avoided problematic county courts and, as the news spread about courts to avoid, delays could build up in the more popular courts. There was also concern that the quality of judges would be lower, and that the damages awarded would be smaller than in the High Court.

The civil justice system after April 1999

On 26 April 1999 new Civil Procedure Rules and accompanying Practice Directions came into force. The new rules apply to any proceedings commenced after that date. They constitute the most fundamental reform of the civil justice system this century, introducing the main recommendations of Lord Woolf in his final report, *Access to Justice*. He described his proposals as providing 'a new landscape for civil justice for the twenty-first century'.

The Woolf Report was the product of two years' intensive consultation, and was written with the help of expert working parties of experienced practitioners and academics. The recommendations of the Report received universal support from the senior judiciary, the Bar, the Law Commission, consumer organizations and the media. In 1996, Sir Richard Scott was appointed as Head of Civil Justice with responsibility for implementing the reforms. The Civil Procedure Act 1997 was passed to implement the first stages of the Woolf Report. Following their election into office, the Labour Government set up their own review of the civil justice system and of Lord Woolf's proposed reforms. They quite reasonably wanted a second opinion before adopting the policies of their predecessors on these issues. The review was chaired by Sir Peter Middleton and took four months to complete. The final report was essentially in favour of implementation of Lord Woolf's proposals. His report placed emphasis on the financial implications of the proposals and in particular the opportunities for cost-cutting. In November 1998, an intensive period of training for judges and court staff began to prepare them for the changes, whilst the Treasury made available an additional £2 million to implement the reforms.

The reforms aim to eliminate unnecessary cost, delay and complexity in the civil justice system. The general approach of Lord Woolf is reflected in his statement: 'If "time and money are no object" was the right approach in the past, the it certainly is not today. Both lawyers and judges, in making decisions as to the conduct of litigation, must take into account more than they do at present, questions of cost and time and the means of the parties.' Lord Woolf has suggested that the reforms should lead to a reduction in legal bills by as much as 75 per cent, though it might also mean some lawyers would lose their livelihoods.

The ultimate goal is to change fundamentally the litigation culture. Thus, the first rule of the new Civil Procedure Rules lays down an overriding objective which is to underpin the whole system. This overriding objective is that the rules should enable the court to deal with cases 'justly'. This objective prevails over all other rules in case of a conflict. The parties and their legal representatives are expected to assist judges in achieving this objective. The Woolf report had heavily criticized practitioners, who were accused of manipulating the old system for their own convenience and causing delay and expense to both their clients and the users of the system as a whole. Lord Woolf felt that a change in attitude among the lawyers was vital for the new rules to succeed. According to rule 1.1(2):

'Dealing with a case justly includes, so far as is practicable—

a.   ensuring that the parties are on an equal footing;
b.   saving expense;
c.   dealing with the case in ways which are proportionate—

      i.   to the amount of money involved;
     ii.   to the importance of the case;
    iii.   to the complexity of the issues; and
    iv.   to the financial position of each party;

d.   ensuring that it is dealt with expeditiously and fairly; and
e.   allotting to it an appropriate share of the Court's resources, while taking into account the need to allot resources to other cases.'

The emphasis of the new rules is on avoiding litigation through pre-trial settlements. Litigation is to be viewed as a last resort, with the court having a continuing obligation to encourage and facilitate settlement. Lord Woolf had observed that it was strange that, although the majority of disputes ended in settlement, the old rules had been mainly directed towards preparation for trial. Thus the new rules put a greater emphasis on preparing cases for settlement rather than trial.

The new approach to civil procedure will now be examined in more detail. . . .

Case management

This is the most significant innovation of the 1999 reforms. Case management means that the court will be the active manager of the litigation. The main aim of this approach is to bring cases to trial quickly and efficiently. Traditionally it has been left to the parties and their lawyers to manage the cases. In 1995, the courts had made a move towards case management following a Practice Direction encouraging such methods, but it was only with the new Civil Procedure Rules that case management came fully into force. The new Rules firmly place the management of a case in the hands of the judges, with r.1.4 emphasizing that the court's duty is to take a proactive role in the management of each case. The judges are given considerable discretion in the exercise of their case management role. Lord Woolf does not feel that this will undermine the adversarial tradition, but he sees the legal professions fulfilling their adversarial functions in a more controlled environment.

Once proceedings have commenced, the court's powers of case management will be triggered by the filing of a defence. When the defence has been filed and case management has started, the parties are on a moving train, trial dates will be fixed and will be difficult to postpone, and litigants will not normally be able to slow down or stop unless they settle. The court first needs to allocate the case to one of the three tracks: the small claims track, the fast track or the multi-track (r.24.6(1)), which will determine the future conduct of the proceedings. To determine which is the appropriate track the court will serve an allocation questionnaire on each party. The answers to this questionnaire will form the basis for deciding the appropriate track. When considering the allocation questionnaire, the judge will determine whether a case should be subject to summary judgment, or whether a stay of proceedings should be given for alternative dispute resolution; and if neither of these matters apply, whether there should be an allocation hearing called or whether the matter can be the subject of a paper determination of the allocation to track.

The three tracks

The court allocates the case to the most appropriate track depending primarily on the financial value of the claim, but other factors that can be taken into account include the case's importance and complexity (r.26.6).
Normally:

- small claims track cases deal with actions with a value of less than £5,000;
- fast-track cases deal with actions of a value of between £5,000 and £15,000;
- multi-track cases deal with actions with a value higher than £15,000. . . .

A proactive approach

Gone are the days when the court waited for the lawyers to bring the case back before it or allowed the lawyers to dictate without question the number of witnesses or the amount of costs incurred. In managing litigation the court must have regard to the overriding objective, set out in Part 1, which is to deal with cases justly. To fulfil this key objective of the reformed civil justice system, the court is required to:

- identify issues at an early stage;
- decide promptly which issues require full investigation and dispose summarily of the others;
- encourage the parties to seek alternative dispute resolution where appropriate;
- encourage the parties to cooperate with each other in the conduct of the procedures;
- help the parties to settle the whole or part of the case;
- decide the order in which issues are to be resolved;
- fix timetables or otherwise control the progress of the case;
- consider whether the likely benefits of taking a particular step will justify the cost of taking it;
- deal with a case without the parties' attendance at court if this is possible;
- make appropriate use of technology;
- give directions to ensure that the trial of a case proceeds quickly and efficiently.

Disclosure

Before the 1999 reforms, disclosure was know as 'discovery'. The procedure used to involve each party providing the other with a list of all the documents they had in relation to the action. The parties could then ask to see some or all of this material. The process could be time consuming and costly. Pre-action disclosure was also available in claims for personal injury and death. Lord Woolf recommended that disclosure should generally be limited to documents which were readily available and which to a 'material extent' adversely affected or supported a party's case, though this could be extended in multi-track cases. This change would have altered significantly the disclosure process and risked going against the philosophy of openness between the parties generally advocated by Lord Woolf. He also favoured extending pre-action disclosure to be available for all proceedings and against people who would not have been parties to the future proceedings. However, the new Civil Procedure Rules are actually very similar to the old rules. These require the disclosure of documents on which they rely or which adversely affected or supported a party's case. It is not necessary for this impact to be to a 'material extent'. As under the old rules, additional disclosure will be ordered where it is 'necessary in order to dispose fairly of the claim or to save costs'. The availability of pre-action disclosure was not extended despite the fact that the Civil Procedure Act 1997 provided for its extension. The pre-action protocols are designed to ensure voluntary disclosure is made between likely parties. It seems that the Government wishes to see how the pre-action protocols operate in practice before implementing such changes.

Sanctions

Tough new rules give the courts stringent powers to enforce the new rules on civil procedure to ensure that litigation is pursued diligently. The two main sanctions are an adverse award of costs, and an order for a case or part of a case to be struck out. These sanctions were available under the old rules, but the novelty of the new regime lies in the commitment to enforce strict compliance. There is an increasing willingness of the courts to manage cases with a stick rather than a carrot. The courts can treat the standards set in the pre-action protocols as the normal approach to pre-action conduct and have the power to penalize parties for non-compliance.

Looking first at costs, if a case goes to trial, the winner is usually awarded costs; in other words the loser must pay the legal costs of both parties, as well as any damages ordered. Where a party has not complied with court directions, particularly as to time, they can be penalized by being ordered to pay heavier costs, or by losing the right to have some or all of their costs paid.

A party who fails to comply with the case timetable or court orders may be struck out. The court has the power to strike out a party's statement of case, or part of it where there has been a failure to comply with a rule, practice direction or court order (r.3.4). This power can be exercised on an application from a party, or on the court's own initiative. Mere delay will be enough in itself to deprive a party of the power to bring or defend an action.

It is up to the defaulting party to apply for relief from sanctions using the procedure contained in r.3.9. This is dramatically different to the previous state of affairs where a party in default of a court order was not the subject of any sanction unless the innocent party brought the matter to the Court's attention.

Where, during the trial, any representative of a party incurs costs as a result of their own improper, unreasonable or negligent conduct they will not receive payment for those wasted costs. A wasted costs order is essentially a power to 'fine' practitioners who incur the disapproval of the court."

NOTES AND QUESTIONS

- Imagine that you have been asked to make a short presentation on Radio 4's *Law in Action* programme about the Woolf reforms. Can you summarise the main recommendations of Lord Woolf which are designed to address the problems of the civil justice system. How would you describe the overall approach and the philosophy behind his recommendations?

- Have Lord Woolf's reforms made the courts more accessible? Give detailed reasons for your response.

One important element of Lord Woolf's Interim Report was his recommendation for greater "case management" by the judiciary, which would signal a move away from the traditional adversarial approach to litigation:

Fiona Cownie and Anthony Bradney, *English Legal System in Context* (2nd ed., Butterworths, London, 2000), p.188:

"Under the Woolf system the role of the judge prior to trial would be to be responsible for managing the case and seeing that the timetables . . . were adhered to. At present the litigants are responsible for choosing the venue for the trial and are responsible for pressing the proceedings. Under the Woolf system judges would be responsible for choosing the appropriate track for the individual case and for seeing that the case kept to its allocated timetable. Moreover, prior to trial, there would be an attempt to eliminate as many potential issues as possible and to see whether it was possible to settle the dispute wholly outside the bounds of the civil justice system. Judges would be responsible for trying to encourage a spirit of co-operation between the parties in order to facilitate the quickest and cheapest settlement of the case. In the case of fast track and multi-track cases, case management conferences, involving judges, litigants and their legal advisers would be held as well as pre-trial reviews enabling judges to keep a constant eye on the development of a case."

However, this recommendation for an enhanced role for the judiciary in case management has been subject to criticism as have other aspects of his report.

Michael Zander, "Are there any clothes for the Emperor to wear?" (February 3, 1995) *New Law Journal*, **154 at 538, 542, 545:**

". . . My purpose is to call into question the main thrust of the Woolf Inquiry enterprise. I believe that implementation of many of Lord Woolf's likely main recommendations could make the system worse rather than better and could add to rather than reduce cost and delay.

The terms of reference of the inquiry are very wide: 'to improve access to justice and reduce the cost of litigation, to reduce the complexity of the rules and modernise terminology; and to remove unnecessary distinctions of practice and procedure.' . . .

The starting point for any inquiry into what needs to be done about civil litigation must be to appreciate the nature of the terrain. This was sharply identified by the Cantley Report in 1979:

> 'Most accidents which lead to claims do not lead to writs and most writs do not lead to trial and judgment. These cases are settled and settlement is an essential ingredient in our system of disposing of actions. In round figures, for every 9,000 personal injury writs issued in London there are no more than about 300 judgments (3.3 per cent). Outside the personal injuries field, for every 100,000 writs issued in London there are fewer than 300 judgments after trial (0.3 per cent). The figures for District Registries are not dissimilar. Any solution which concentrates on speeding cases to trial, but which makes settlement less likely or more expensive, might be bought at an unduly high price.'

In other words, the overwhelming majority of cases settle or fall away of their own accord at some point short of trial—without any intervention from the system. If that is so, why do we need new systems, new machinery? The answer given is to reduce cost and to reduce delay—and there are plenty of true horror stories of excessive cost and delay to back this understandable view.

Since the period identified as the Thatcher era it has become official dogma to be concerned about cost and delay and improvements in efficiency. Efficiency scrutinies and their progeny have proliferated all over the place. The Woolf Inquiry is only the latest manifestation of this pervasive modern tendency.

Obviously, there is nothing intrinsically wrong with reducing cost and delay or increasing efficiency. On the contrary. If it can be done without undue adverse consequences, I am wholly in favour. My concern is only to ask whether that is what is in fact likely to be achieved—and to direct attention to what may sometimes be lost in the process.

Plainly it is foolish to create new reform systems unless there is some reasonable expectation that the new systems will improve matters. The trouble is that, at least at present, there is no solid basis for making reform proposals in this field.

The first problem is that most relevant facts are not known. We have virtually no information about either delays or costs and the little information we have is more or less useless. So, for instance, we do not know what proportion of cases suffer delay in the sense of a passage of time beyond what is reasonable. Is it a large proportion or a tiny one? We have virtually no information about the causes of delay, nor how delay is perceived by litigants. We do not know what proportion of cases settle at different stages of the process. There is not even any agreed definition of delay for civil causes (In the US they look at our levels of delay with envy.)

The same ignorance exists with regard to the costs of litigation. Unfortunately, the Woolf Inquiry will produce little new information on these matters.

Lord Woolf has taken the point that the means adopted to move cases forward must be proportionate to the nature of the case. He will certainly propose various levels of pre-trial case management based on allocation of cases to different categories.

But, so far as I am aware, there is no way of identifying which cases might benefit from heavy, medium or light judicial case management—and which cases require none at all since they will settle anyway at a quite early stage. In the absence of such a method the system of allocation of cases is necessarily hit-and-miss.

Even if we had a way of assessing which cases 'need' case management, we would not be much further ahead since there is no sound knowledge anywhere as to what new systems to put in place to cure the perceived problems of cost and delay. In the US they have been working energetically on the problem for the past twenty or more years. The results, to say the least, have been disappointing. . . .

The climate for such reform here is much less favourable. It is clear from what he has said publicly that the main change Lord Woolf envisages is that the pre-trial progress of litigation would be driven by the judges and the system rather than the parties.

Cases would be assigned pre-trial to judges who, depending on the case category, would to varying degrees become responsible for overseeing and directing the progress of the case toward trial—fixing timetables (including the date of trial), dealing with pre-trial motions, holding a robust summons for directions and pre-trial hearings etc.

But English judges have no familiarity with case management as a concept. Their whole professional experience has been with a system that leaves the pace of litigation to the parties. It is difficult to imagine them taking easily to the demands of the new approach required by the Woolf reforms—for example in penalising failure to comply with time-limits. (Not to mention the very considerable administrative hassle and cost for the system of chasing compliance with time-limits and timetables—which may even require more judges.)

Moreover, in England, making judges take responsibility for case-load processing runs up against the major practical difficulty that judges travel on circuit and that so many cases are heard by part-timers. Lord Woolf's solution apparently is to have *teams* of judges responsible for case progressing—a concept likely to boggle the mind of anyone in the LCD [Lord Chancellor's Department] trying to organise the movements of judges. Teams of judges to deal with case management looks to me like a recipe for lowering rather than raising the efficiency of the system.

In my view the only way of being reasonably confident that proposed reforms will reduce delay and costs and increase efficiency is if they do not include significant *additional* procedures. The provisions in last week's important Practice Direction issued by the Lord Chief Justice mainly pass this test. The Practice Direction exhorts judges to place restrictions, *inter alia*, on discovery, on the length of oral submissions, on the time allowed for examination and cross-examination of witnesses, and on reading aloud to the court. . . .

Even, however, if we knew how to increase efficiency, it is by no means certain that this is what litigants most want. A study by the Rand Corporation investigated litigant satisfaction with different procedural systems for handling ordinary, mainly motor car related, tort actions in Virginia, Pennsylvania and Maryland. The study consisted of interviews with 286 litigants—145 plaintiffs and 141 defendants—almost all of whom had been represented by lawyers. The study suggests that litigants are less concerned about cost and delay and even the result of the case than is often supposed.

Winning or losing did correlate with satisfaction with the process. But the amount of money recovered or lost had only a slight impact on litigant satisfaction. The authors concluded, 'it is clearly a mistake to think that litigant evaluations of the tort system and its procedures are driven by how much they win or lose'.

Neither plaintiffs nor defendants registered any significant correlation between delay and their satisfaction with procedural fairness or the overall system. The authors concluded that procedural innovations which cut down delay 'cannot be counted on to enhance tort litigants' satisfaction or perceived fairness'.

Judgments of fairness and satisfaction with the system were equally unrelated to the costs. It made no difference whether the litigant was plaintiff or defendant and whether he paid the whole or part of the cost himself. 'Economic concerns of all sorts seemed to play at most a minor role in determining litigants' attitudes'.

Litigants' satisfaction was, however, very significantly related to their *expectations*. If they did better than they had anticipated in terms of money won or lost, delay and cost, it affected their satisfaction with the system. Most thought their cases had gone on too long —whether in the view of the researchers they had or not. Similarly, there was no correlation between actual costs and the litigants' evaluation of whether the lawyers' fees were justified.

But what seemed to affect litigant satisfaction most was whether the procedure was dignified, careful and unbiased. Impressions of the litigation process were the most powerful determinants of judgments about procedural fairness and about dignity. 'Litigants want procedures with which they can feel comfortable, but this does not mean that they want less formal procedures—informality does not make litigants either more or less comfortable'.

The Rand study certainly does not mean that we should ignore considerations of efficiency. It does suggest however that they are perhaps less important than is often supposed and that there are other considerations that are even more important.

So in regard to the likely Woolf proposals it may signify that, save for obvious and serious delay, it might be better to leave the pace of litigation to the parties than to require them to proceed at a pace determined by the court which may not be right for the parties.

One reason is that because only a small proportion of cases actually need stage management, a court-imposed system would be extremely wasteful of resources of both the system and the litigants. Another reason is that the court-imposed system would probably not deliver greater efficiency anyway. But the third is that the system may be doing more 'justice', actual and perceived, if it normally leaves it to the parties and interferes only when they are clearly behaving unreasonably.

Whichever of Lord Woolf's proposals are in the end implemented, it is vital that there is effective monitoring of the results by proper research. Ideally, changes should be implemented experimentally in a few courts. It is only if the impact of innovation is evaluated by before-and-after studies that we can learn from our mistakes."

NOTES AND QUESTIONS

• Do you find Zander's critique of the philosophy behind the Woolf Report compelling?

• To what extent should economic efficiency be the central goal of the civil justice system?

• The Government are proposing that there should be further reform to the court system by way of abolishing the House of Lords. Can you provide a critique of this suggestion? Are their proposals for reform fuelled by economic expediency or are there other reasons for this constitutional reform?

- To what extent should judges, rather than the parties themselves, control the litigation process?

Baldwin makes a key point regarding the tension in Lord Woolf's recommendations in this area; a tension which is apparent in much of the report.

John Baldwin, "Raising the Small Claims Limit", in A.A.S. Zuckerman and Ross Cranston,
***Reform of Civil Procedure: Essays on Access to Justice* (Clarendon Press, Oxford, 1995),**
p.185:

"It is not clear whether the expansion of the small claims jurisdiction is intended merely to mop up the present overflow of cases from other parts of the civil justice system or whether it represents a genuine effort to enhance access to justice by inducing many people who are at present put off from using the courts to activate the small claims procedure in the future. If the objective is the latter (and there are many indications in the report that Lord Woolf is genuinely concerned about limited access), it is difficult to see how it is to be achieved without substantial corresponding increases in resources—something that Lord Woolf explicitly states in his report will not be needed to implement his proposals in their entirety (p.190)."

The proposed "fast track" procedure has also been criticised on the grounds that it will compromise the pursuit of "truth" itself.

Conrad Dehn, QC, "The Woolf Report: Against the Public Interest?" in *Reform of Civil*
***Procedure: Essays on "Access to Justice"* (A.A.S. Zuckerman and Ross Cranston, eds.,**
Clarendon Press, Oxford, 1995), p.149:

"The principal objective of the English civil justice system up to now has always been justice, to get at the truth as to what happened, who said and did what and why. Until now all proposals to reform the system have been designed to further this objective, by for example reducing the importance of technicalities and avoiding surprise. This Report is I think the first to recommend proposals calculated to make the achievement of this objective less likely.

The Report recognises the conflict between achieving this objective and the expenditure of time and money but in recommending that the achievement of this objective should no longer be put first, it does not in my view give sufficient weight to the fact that there are many parties and witnesses who give false evidence to serve their own interests, or because they are prejudiced, or because they are forgetful of matters inconsistent with their own interests, that it is intolerable and likely to be so regarded by the other party and possibly also by the public if such people can not be properly challenged and can therefore get away with their false evidence, and that it is only by the expenditure of time and money on the two instruments of discovery of documents and cross-examination, fashioned for that purpose, that they can be properly challenged.

It follows therefore that if these minor claims are to be determined in the manner suggested by the Report the chance of the truth being arrived at, of the result being one that accords with justice, must be materially reduced."

In a somewhat different vein, Zuckerman suggests that the problem with the civil justice system lies in the cost system for lawyers in this country, and contrasts it with the German system.

A.A.S. Zuckerman, "Lord Woolf's Access to Justice: *Plus ça change . . ."* **(1996) 59 M.L.R. 773 at 795:**

"It is widely accepted that there is something wrong with a system of civil justice in which the cost of taking a dispute to court is unpredictable, disproportionate and unlimited. Lord Woolf has sought to bring about a cultural change. He has proposed measures for reducing the cost and duration of litigation and for achieving a measure of reasonable proportionality between the value of the subject-matter in dispute and the cost of the legal resolution. His primary aim is to reduce the amount of work involved in litigation, and thereby costs. He proposes to achieve this by judicial case management, which will pass the control over the intensity and pace of the litigious process from lawyers to judges. He also envisages greater standardisation of procedure, whereby straightforward cases will be litigated by a fast simplified process.

Admirable as these proposals are, they do not directly address the cause of high costs. The high level of costs is the natural outcome of the economic incentives possessed by lawyers, whose remuneration rises as litigation becomes more complicated and lengthy. The history of law reform shows that a simplification of procedure is not enough to produce savings as long as there are incentives to devise new complications. Even judicial controls are vulnerable to being subverted by those with an economic interest to do so.

The German system proves the effectiveness of the strategy of reversing the economic incentives. In Germany, lawyers are paid a fixed litigation fee, which represents a small and reasonable proportion of the value of the dispute. As a result, they have no reason to complicate litigation unnecessarily. Access to justice in Germany is affordable by large sections of the public because costs are low. The predictability of costs has led to a thriving litigation cost insurance which places litigation within the reach of even citizens of modest means. Consequently, there is a greater volume of litigation in Germany which, in turn, enables lawyers to generate high incomes without subvention by the public purse.

Lord Woolf felt, presumably, that it was politically impractical to recommend even a mild form of fixed costs litigation due to implacable resistance by the legal profession to any limitation on the fees that lawyers may charge. His suggestions of fixed fees in the fast-track procedure represent a valiant effort to introduce some kind of a fixed cost system. Unfortunately, the fees under this system are neither fixed nor cheap.

Indeed, by comparison to costs in Germany, they are huge. In Germany, the costs in respect of a claim for £8,850 would be as follows. The lawyer will receive £1,260, which is about half of what Lord Woolf envisages as solicitor's fees alone (assuming the top band), and a mere quarter of the combined figure of £5,000 in respect of solicitor's fee and advocacy fee. German law allows only a fixed disbursement fee of £18, whereas there is no limit on the English comparable expenses. However, in Germany there will be a court fee payable of £510, which is considerably higher than the English court fee. Let us assume that some additional disbursements would be incurred in Germany in respect of expert witnesses and that they are of the same level as in England. The total cost in Germany will therefore be £2,288. This is still only about half the £5,500 English figure, which makes no allowance for court fees and which excludes any interlocutory applications.

The history of procedural reform, both recent and remote, shows the ineptness of the indirect approach. Attempts to cut down costs by simplifying procedure, by judicial pressure or by encouraging clients to resist rising costs have all been tried and found wanting. There is no alternative to a direct attack on the economic incentives to complicate and protract the litigation process. But a serious challenge to the vested interests of the legal profession cannot come just from a lone reformer, however bold and exalted. It must involve determined intervention at government level. Until this happens, experience will continue to dispel our hopes of improvement and litigation costs will remain as exorbitant as they have been for a very long time."

Other criticisms of the Woolf report have focused on its avowed aim to promote just settlements. We have already seen that the most common method for the resolution of disputes within the adjudicatory process is settlement. It remains the case, however, that those who lodge a claim in the court system are still expected to prepare their case for litigation, in which they will state their opinions in an adversarial way, rather than from a standpoint of compromise. Despite its focus on early settlement, the Woolf Report may not result in changes to this litigation mindset.

Hazel Genn, "Access to Just Settlements: The Case of Medical Negligence" in *Reform of Civil Procedure: Essays on "Access to Justice"*, (A.A.S. Zuckerman and Ross Cranston, eds., Clarendon Press, Oxford, 1995), pp.393–395:

". . . The assumption of the proposed reforms is that through the twin principles of judicial case control and simplification of the procedures that facilitate adversarialism, problems of cost and delay will resolve themselves—settlements will occur earlier. One of the themes of the report is that 'the philosophy of litigation should be primarily to encourage early settlement of disputes.' The problem, however, resides in the means of promoting settlements. Attacking parties and their lawyers for the legitimate use of adversarial litigation tactics highlights the difficulty of achieving just settlements by means of court procedures. The rules of litigation are geared toward preparation for win or lose adjudication. They have not been designed to facilitate an efficient and relatively bloodless compromise between diametrically opposed positions. Will the new litigation 'tracks' and judicial managers adopt radically different rules designed primarily to promote settlement through bureaucratic case processing? Or might the new system simply represent a cut-down and speeded-up adversarial process which may exacerbate resource inequalities between the parties to the settlement process?

There is great variety in civil litigation: different types of disputes, different types of parties, and different configurations of parties. As a result it is not easy to generalise about the dynamics of litigation or to propose a litigation system appropriate to all. An instructive snippet of information which reinforces this point comes from a small survey of satisfaction with the civil justice system among corporate clients. Somewhat buried among the reported data showing widespread criticism of the length and complexity of the litigation process, frustration at delays and its implications for management time, there is one statistic which reveals that 77% of insurance defendants, expressed satisfaction with the current litigation system. This, up to a point, speaks for itself. It suggests that the current system is operating to the satisfaction of at least some defendants with deep-pockets. What represents a problem or barrier to one party presents an opportunity to another. . . ."

QUESTIONS AND NOTES

- What do you think Lord Woolf hoped to achieve by encouraging disputants to be more co-operative?

- Do you think this is achievable? If not, what changes would you implement to ensure change?

QUESTIONING THE CENTRALITY OF THE COURTS

So far in this chapter, we have worked on the assumption that the notions of law and the courts are symbiotic. This approach has a certain logic. For most people—

lawyers, non-lawyers, and law students alike—an answer to the question "what is law?" would centre on the work of the courts. This "court-oriented view of law", as Atiyah describes, is widespread within the English legal tradition but it might also create a rather incomplete definition of the term "law". In the remainder of the chapter we turn to consider whether the courts are really central to our analysis of law. This leads us on, quite neatly to our consideration of "alternatives" to the courts considered in the next chapter.

P.S. Atiyah, *Law and Modern Society* (2nd ed., Oxford University Press, Oxford, 1995), pp.1–7:

"This association between the law and the legal process, between the rules of law and the courts, is one which lawyers are particularly prone to make. To a lawyer, the courts are the very heart and centre of the law. A modern lawyer would find it impossible to conceive of a legal system which contained rules of law, but no courts. In fact he would probably find it less difficult to imagine a society which contained courts but no rules of law.

Why should this be so? It might seem that logically speaking laws come first, and that courts are merely secondary. After all, in modern society it is the primary function of the courts to apply and enforce the law which actually exists. And anyhow courts and judges are themselves creatures which owe their status, their authority, and in a sense their very existence to the law. It is the law itself which tells us that this elderly gentleman sitting on the dais in that Victorian building in the Strand known as the Royal Courts of Justice, is a judge of the High Court, and that while he sits there he actually is the court.

Moreover, anyone who looks at the whole machinery of government in the broadest sense might find it odd that lawyers should place the courts at the centre of their legal universe. Isn't that a bit like pre-Copernican astronomy? Isn't Parliament the real sun round which the law revolves? Acts of Parliament after all are very real laws, as lawyers would unhesitatingly agree. And Acts of Parliament have a very tangible 'existence'. They are often quite solid documents running to a hundred pages or more. You can buy them, and bind them into volumes, as lawyers do. In them you will find all sorts of rules which often say very little or nothing about the courts or judges who are to enforce them.

Then again, it must be admitted that there are some laws—sometimes extensive and complex bodies of law—which are rarely handled by ordinary courts and judges at all. This is particularly true of modern welfare state legislation, such as the law relating to social security. This enormous mass of law defines the conditions under which people are entitled to a wide variety of welfare benefits, and how these benefits are to be calculated in particular cases. There is a great deal of this law and it is complex and difficult to find. But the point is that it is not generally administered or applied by ordinary courts, judges, or magistrates. For the most part it is administered by civil servants working in the Department of Social Security—the DSS. People who want to claim benefits go to their local DSS office and fill in a form. The form is processed by officials. It is true that a special system of tribunals exists to which the citizen can appeal if he is not satisfied by the initial decisions of the officials. And these tribunals hear cases and decide them according to the law, in much the same way (though with far less formality) as ordinary courts. But lawyers rarely penetrate into these tribunals, and they certainly would not think of them, as they think of the ordinary courts, as being at the very centre of the legal system.

So it may seem curious that lawyers tend to identify 'the law' so heavily with courts and judges. But there are reasons for it, some historical, some practical, and others perhaps less easy to classify.

Among the historical reasons for the modern lawyer's pre-Copernican perception of the legal universe we can identify two factors in particular. The first is that it is not true, in a historical sense, to say that laws came before courts. The central court of the modern English legal system—the High Court of Justice—is the direct descendant of a number of old courts, some of them dating back to the twelfth century, which were never created by a deliberate act of law-making. These courts grew up gradually as offshoots of the authority of the King and, as the very word 'court' indicates, these courts of justice were originally a part of the royal court. They were not created by law in order to administer pre-existing laws. They were created, or grew up, in order to solve pressing practical questions—to dispose of arguments, to solve disputes, and to suppress violence and theft. As they developed into what we would today recognize as courts of law, they actually created the law as they went along. Eventually their decisions began to fall into regular and predictable patterns, people began to take notes of what the judges were deciding, and in due course there emerged the modern 'law reports'. A substantial body of English law was created in this way, and much of it remains in force to this day, modified and modernized in all sorts of respects both by more recent judicial decisions and by Acts of Parliament. This part of the law, usually known as the 'common law', was thus created by the courts in the very process of deciding cases before them.

So when the modern lawyer thinks of the common law it is not surprising if he still tends to think of the courts as in some sense primary, and the law as secondary, rather than the other way around. What is more, the old common law remains in a sense the more fundamental part even of modern English law. In sheer bulk modern legislation is no doubt outstripping the common law, but naturally enough the common law tended to deal with more essential and basic legal issues than much modern legislation. The common law was the first part of the law to be created, and the first part of the law in any society must necessarily deal with essentials. Naturally the common law evolved the basic principles of the criminal law—it was the common law which first prohibited murder, violence, theft, and rape. Similarly, much of our basic property law was first laid down by common law courts, and so was the law of civil liability. The law of contract and the law of torts (or civil wrongs) were very largely created by the courts out of the simplest of ideas—that it is wrong to harm or injure others. Although much of this law has been amended and qualified in all manner of ways in modern times, there is a sense in which the modern lawyer tends still to see the common law as the central repository of legal ideas and principles. Given the very basic values and interests recognized by the common law, this is hardly surprising, and this also helps to explain why courts are still so very central to the way lawyers think about law.

The second historical factor which helps to explain the lawyer's perspective on these matters is that until quite recent times the courts were, relatively speaking, a far more important part of the whole machinery of government than they are today. In modern times the day-to-day administration of government lies in the hands of vast armies of officials in central and local government, including in particular the police; and at the central level, the authority of Parliament is generally undisputed and can readily be used to overturn rules of law laid down by the courts which do not find favour with the government. So in one sense the courts are today a small, though important, part of a very extensive machine. But in historical terms this is all a fairly recent development. Until the eighteenth century the machinery of government was very weak, at both central and local levels. Parliament's law-making activities were confined within fairly narrow limits in practice, and so the role of the courts was then relatively far more important than it is today. Indeed, it is widely thought by historians that the early common law courts were deliberately used as one of the main instruments by which royal authority was extended over the whole country in the twelfth century and onwards. It is from these, and perhaps even earlier, days that the custom began of sending judges out on assize, travelling from town to town, hearing cases, helping to create a body of uniform law across the country, and at the same time, showing the people that the authority of the King extended to every corner of his realm. . . .

There are, in addition, other very practical reasons why lawyers tend to have such a court-oriented view of law. One of them is the simple fact that the courts are where the lawyer goes, on behalf of his clients, when disputes arise which cannot be settled amicably. Just as the civil servant doubtless tends to have a government-oriented vision of law and regulation, because most problems that he deals with tend to get settled within or by governments and government departments, so, for similar reasons, the lawyer sees the courts as the focus of the system of dispute settlement in which he is involved.

A related factor is that when disputes arise it is frequently the case that both the facts and the law applicable to those facts may be unclear. When this happens, a lawyer tends to take a severely practical approach to the question of legal rights and duties: he asks himself what a court is likely to decide if the case comes before it. Indeed, this can quite often be a necessary exercise even where the facts appear clear enough to the client and the lawyer, but there is great difficulty about proving them. To the lawyer, a fact is really a provable fact or it is nothing. Similarly, where the law is uncertain, or where its application is uncertain in particular cases, the lawyer's main concern is with the available lines of argument — he knows that some forms of legal argument are acceptable and others less so — and with the probable outcomes. He is in fact interested in *predicting* what a court is likely to do. This does not, of course, mean that all law is nothing more than a series of predictions about how judges and other officials of the legal system are likely to behave in certain circumstances. It is absurd to suggest that the law prohibiting murder is really just a prediction that anybody who commits murder and is brought before the courts will be sent to gaol for life, or until the Home Secretary chooses to release him. But it is nevertheless a fact of life that practising lawyers, when faced with legal problems, habitually ask themselves: If I had to argue this in court, how would I present the case? How would the judge be likely to react? It is also a fact that making predictions of this kind is not always something that can easily be done by merely looking the law up in books. The lawyer needs a 'feel' for how a judge is likely to react to his case, and this is something which can normally be acquired only by actually practising in the courts and appearing regularly before the judges.

It is this which gives some truth to the aphorism, 'the law is what the court says it is'. Snappy sayings like this can be misleading if pressed too far (for instance, judges themselves do not think the law is merely what they say it is), but there is undoubtedly some truth in them. In this last analysis it doesn't matter what is in the books, the law reports, even Acts of Parliament. If a judge sentences someone to gaol, then to gaol he will assuredly go. The judge may have got it wrong, he may even be perverse, but the immediate result is the same. Of course there may be the possibility of an appeal. But the decision of the appeal court may be equally wrong or perverse. Then what *that* court decides is what matters. Perhaps it is wrong to suggest that this is what counts 'in the last analysis', because obviously if judges habitually flouted Acts of Parliament or established precedents, they would be removed from office. But that is to enter the realms of fantasy. It is because judges don't behave in these extreme ways that one can safely assert that in the last analysis what they decide is the law.

Finally, there are other factors of a less readily identifiable nature which tend to make the lawyer think of courts as the centre of the law. In particular, the leaders of the legal profession tend to be seen, both by the public and also by the profession, as the judges, particularly the high court and appeal court judges. Most able barristers see judicial appointment as the apex of a successful career at the Bar. Judges actually decide cases over which lawyers have pondered and argued. So naturally lawyers are encouraged in their tendency to think of the law as something almost wholly associated with, or even dependent upon, the courts."

NOTES AND QUESTIONS

- What proportion of their time do you think practising lawyers spend in court or preparing for court? Try to find out how realistic your assessment is by asking friends or family who may be lawyers or a tutor who has qualified as a solicitor or barrister.

- What else do lawyers do?

- Atiyah makes reference to the fact that when advising clients, lawyers will use their knowledge and skills to predict the outcome of a case were it to go to court. What other factors might a lawyer and their client take into account when deciding whether to pursue a dispute to court?

In focusing upon the courts as the centre of the legal universe, the implicit assumption is that law is best understood as a tool for the resolution of disputes through the machinery of the state. After all, the common law courts, as Atiyah describes, were created by the King as a means to solve disputes, prevent violence, and to consolidate his authority throughout the realm. Courts today continue to be an important part of the machinery of modern government, although they are *relatively* less important given the rise of other elements of the state, such as the administrative agencies and dispute resolution tribunals described by Atiyah. However, Cownie and Bradney argue that this focus on the institutions of the state as the centre of dispute resolution creates a distorted picture of the meaning of law and legal systems. Their analysis, which draws on the work of the Portuguese legal anthropologist de Sousa Santos, is an attempt to understand law in a broader, social context.

Fiona Cownie and Anthony Bradney, *English Legal System in Context* (2nd ed., Butterworths, London, 2000), pp.8–9:

"There are two possible problems with the state-rule-centred approach. The first is that this approach asserts rather than proves that there is an important difference between what is happening in state agencies concerned with dispute resolution and non-state agencies. The provenance of the authority of the agency, the fact that it comes from the state, is deemed to be significant. This significance has not been obvious to everyone.

De Sousa Santos, a Portuguese legal anthropologist, studied the activities of an institution, the Residents' Association, in a favela or shanty town, Pasargada, in Rio de Janeiro. The land upon which Pasargada was built belonged to the state. The residents were, so far as the Brazilian legal system was concerned, no more than squatters. They had no legal title to the land upon which they had built their houses. However, the Residents' Association was willing to register such sales. Written agreements were drawn up by the association. Standard phrases were used in these agreements. Copies were exchanged, one being kept by the Residents' Association, others by the parties to the sale. Residents of the favela were thus able to pass property amongst each other in a similar way to that in which they would have been able to had they been title-holders under Brazilian state law. When there were disputes about matters relating to housing the Residents' Association were willing to determine which party was in the right. The Residents' Association had no power to do this under Brazilian state law. Its power came from the fact that those who lived in Pasargada regarded it as having a judicial function.

De Sousa Santos concluded that the activities of the Residents' Association could be described as 'Pasargada law' which was 'an example of an informal and unofficial legal system'. According to de Sousa Santos, Pasargada was an example of legal pluralism; a situation where two legal systems, Brazilian state law and Pasargada law, coexisted alongside each other. In deciding which was law there was, for de Sousa Santos, no special significance in the fact that the rules of one legal system, Brazilian state law, emanated from the state. Using the approach which typifies 'English legal system' texts a description of the work of the Residents' Association would form no part of a book on the Brazilian legal system. Yet, for de Sousa Santos, that institution was central to the way in which the inhabitants of the favela brought law into their lives."

- What is meant by the term "legal pluralism"? Give an example of an unofficial legal system which exists in this country.

- Legal pluralism, as exemplified by the research of de Sousa Santos, underscores that in defining what is law, we may need to be careful to avoid privileging the institutions of the state. Dispute resolution and the rules which govern social relations can exist, as they did in the favela, outside of the institutions and rules propagated by government. The law of the state thus might be viewed as one amongst a plurality of legal orders which govern social groups. Mediation and other "alternative" forms of dispute resolution place emphasis on an appreciation of the various normative frameworks which govern disputants behaviour.

14

MEDIATION AND ADR

In this chapter we continue our review of the primary forms of dispute resolution by moving on to consider those processes described under the umbrella of "Alternative" or "Appropriate Dispute Resolution" (ADR). As we saw from Brown and Marriot's typology of dispute resolution processes in the last chapter, ADR can take a number of forms and can be used in a variety of settings. What the different forms share is an underlying attempt to create a more co-operative and less adversarial environment in which disputes can be resolved. ADR is very much on the law reform agenda. It can be seen from the following extract that in his extensive review of the civil litigation system, Lord Woolf strongly recommended ADR as a means of solving some of the problems he identified in the civil justice system.

Lord Woolf, *Access to Justice: Interim Report* (*www.lcd.gov.uk*, June 1995):

"In recent years there has been, both in this country and overseas, a growth in alternative dispute resolution (ADR) and an increasing recognition of its contribution to the fair, appropriate and effective resolution of civil disputes. The fact that litigation is not the only means of achieving this aim, and may not in all cases be the best, is my main reason for including ADR in an Inquiry whose central focus is on improving access to justice through the courts. My second reason is to increase awareness still further, among the legal profession and the general public, of what ADR has to offer. Finally, it is also desirable to consider whether the various forms of ADR have any lessons to offer the courts in terms of practices and procedures.

From the point of view of the Court Service, ADR has the obvious advantage of saving scarce judicial and other resources. More significantly, in my view, it offers a variety of benefits to litigants or potential litigants. ADR is usually cheaper than litigation, and often produces quicker results. In some cases the parties will want to avoid the publicity associated with court proceedings. It may also be more beneficial for them, especially if they are involved in a continuing personal or business relationship, to choose a form of dispute resolution that will enable them to work out a mutually acceptable solution rather than submit to a legally correct adjudication which at least one party would inevitably find disappointing.

Despite these advantages I do not propose that ADR should be compulsory either as an alternative or as a preliminary to litigation. The prevalence of compulsory ADR in some United States jurisdictions is largely due to the lack of court resources for civil trials. Fortunately the problems in the civil justice system in this country, serious as they are, are not so great as to require a wholesale compulsory reference of civil proceedings to outside resolution.

In any event, I do not think it would be right in principle to erode the citizen's existing entitlement to seek a remedy from the civil courts, in relation either to private rights or to the breach by a public body of its duties to the public as a whole. I do, however, believe that the courts can and should play an important part, which I shall consider in more detail later in this chapter, in providing information about the availability of ADR and encouraging its use in appropriate cases.

The scope of ADR

The various forms of ADR include some which resemble litigation in that they follow a relatively formal procedure and produce decisions which are binding on the parties, while others offer a considerably more flexible approach. ADR is used effectively in a wide variety of disputes, ranging from neighbours' quarrels to international commercial actions. Schemes may be court-annexed or independent of the court system, and may be used either before legal proceedings have begun or in the course of litigation. . . .

Developments overseas

The interest in ADR is worldwide. In common law systems, in particular, ADR schemes are being established and innovative experimentation is taking place. The extent of pro bono involvement of the legal profession in the United States is particularly impressive. In the course of preparing this report, I have been able to see some of these schemes at first hand and to discuss the operation of other schemes with those involved. All share an enthusiasm for the schemes with which they are involved and can usually quote impressive statistics to substantiate their effectiveness.

It should not necessarily be assumed, however, particularly in relation to the statistics, that the same results could be achieved within this jurisdiction. This is especially true of the schemes in the United States which are directed to achieving settlement of appeals. My attention was directed principally to those in New York, Washington DC and California. In each case, the models are very efficient and, according to the record, strikingly effective. In considering the results which are achieved, however, it has to be remembered that many of the appeals will be from decisions by juries and that there is a greater tendency to appeal in the United States than in this country. On the other hand, the cautious comments contained in the publication by the Director of the Institute for Civil Justice at the Rand Corporation as to the effectiveness of ADR must also be seen in context. She suggests that the findings of research into the reduction of cost to the public as a result of ADR are proving somewhat disappointing. That conclusion, however, is based on a situation where the existence of compulsory ADR at the court's expense attracts cases into the court system which would not otherwise be there. The result is that 'the aggregate cost to the court of providing arbitration hearings to thousands of cases may offset any public costs savings from reductions in the trial caseload'.

As long as the necessary care is exercised before translating the results experienced in other jurisdictions to what could be achieved here, there can be no doubt that there is an immense amount which would be of value to our court system which can be obtained by studying the initiatives in other jurisdictions. While what may be possible in the immediate future in this country may be limited, it is of great importance that we keep abreast with what is happening abroad, particularly in the United States, Australia and Canada. Fortunately, this is a subject to which the Judicial Studies Board is already directing attention. This should continue, if possible, on a more extensive scale."

Since the publication of Lord Woolf's report the new civil procedure rules have encouraged the use of ADR and empowered judges to direct cases to this alternative forum. Introduced in 1999, the overriding objective of the new rules was to enable the courts to deal with cases through active case management by the judiciary and this included encouraging the parties to use an alternative dispute resolution procedure with or without the agreement of the parties. Since the implementation of the rules there has been a reported 37 per cent drop in the number of claims being issued in the Queen's Bench Division of the High Court and the Centre for Dispute Resolution has claimed that referrals from the courts have risen proportionally year on year from eight per cent in 1999–2000 to 19 per cent in 2000–2001 and to 27 per cent in 2001–2002. They predict that as the judiciary becomes more familiar and confident with the process that these figures will continue to rise (Mackie, 2002). The judiciary has also supported the referral of cases to ADR by imposing cost sanctions on litigants who unreasonably refuse to engage in mediation; upholding the validity of mediated settlements; and enforcing contractual commitments to mediate.

Lord Woolf remarks elsewhere in his report that concerns have focused on the processes leading to the decisions made by the courts, rather than the decisions themselves. But many proponents of ADR have based their support of alternatives to adjudication on the fact that decision-making is qualitatively different from decision-making by adjudicators, is underpinned by an alternative ideology and can produce radically different results. This more radical critique of the need for a wider need for forms of "popular justice" is summarised in the following extract.

H. Brown and A. Marriot, *ADR Principles and Practice* (2nd ed., Sweet and Maxwell, 1999), pp.9–12:

"The references which are sometimes made to the 'ADR movement' and to the 'philosophy of ADR' both in the United Kingdom and the United States could create the impression that there is one single homogeneous group or school of thought guiding the development of ADR processes. While there are indeed supporters and protagonists of ADR, who could be viewed as comprising a movement, it is also a fact that these are drawn from disparate sources, with varying philosophies, cultures and practices. It is questionable whether there can be said to be one single philosophy of ADR, or a consensus that any one of these different approaches properly and authentically represents the 'true spirit' of ADR.

To establish whether and to what extent there is a philosophy of ADR, it may be helpful to examine ADR's main trends and its underlying objectives.

One of the motivations for ADR is commonly said to be the empowerment of the individual. Under traditional processes, dispute resolution is generally in the hands of lawyers, who use procedures and a language and reasoning of their own to resolve the issues for the parties, either by adjudication or by a settlement negotiated by the lawyers before trial. Empowerment of the individual is sometimes linked, especially by some involved in community mediation, with a move away from 'professionalisation'. The 'core of mediation' in the family context has been graphically described as 'reconnecting people to their own inner wisdom or common sense'.

Undoubtedly ADR processes, especially the mediation of inter-personal and family disagreements, commonly tend to help with the empowerment of individuals, giving them greater responsibility for the resolution of their own issues. Insofar as the processes are consensual (which accords with the prevalent view of ADR) the fact that parties need to reach their own resolution and do not depend on a third party to decide for them is itself empowering.

However, not all ADR involves empowerment to any significant extent: in some forms ADR may be a desirable, effective, cost-efficient and speedy form of dispute resolution; but it may not necessarily empower the disputants, other than leaving them with control over the outcome of their dispute, so far as they can jointly agree on this. There is indeed an argument that in some cases, where there are severe power imbalances between the parties, ADR is not empowering and may in fact be inappropriate. That argument . . . is a factor against which the empowerment notion should be viewed. As to the suggestion that ADR is empowering in that it represents a move away from professionalisation, this is countered by the fact that in many forms of ADR there are substantial contributions of skill, expertise and professionalism by the neutral as well as those who may be representing the parties. In any event, even those uneasy about professionalisation acknowledge that it is 'an ambiguous concept' which can refer to elements of professional activity perceived as dubious such as elitism, detachment and client disempowerment; or to those more positive and inherent features of professions, such as independence, training, responsibility, expertise and a commitment to appropriate values.

Another motivation for ADR is sometimes said to be the principle of 'co-operative problem solving'. This them underlies much of the theory of ADR and explains why much of the ADR literature . . . includes sections dealing with theories and strategies of negotiation, including in particular problem-solving theories of negotiation.

However, while experience shows that in many cases there is a shift during the ADR process to a more positive and collaborative approach to the resolution of the issues under negotiation, a significant proportion of parties in ADR cases may well be using the process as a means to an end in getting their case settled, without necessarily feeling any sense of being engaged in mutual problem solving. ADR does not depend for its effectiveness on the parties adopting a problem-solving approach. Such an approach can help to enhance the quality of settlements, but ADR processes are just as effective where the parties adopt positional bargaining, competitive negotiation, problem-solving modes or any permutation of these or any other approaches and strategies.

It is also often said that ADR is able to produce better outcomes than the traditional adversarial system. There are two reasons why this may be so. First, different kinds of disputes may need different kinds of approaches. If parties are not bound by the constraints of conventional litigation but can instead select a process, or permutation of processes, designed for their specific needs to enhance consensual resolution, then there must be an improved prospect of their finding better terms for the settlement of those issues. Secondly, mediation and other ADR forms involving more direct and intensive participation by the parties in settlement negotiations and the intervention of a skilled neutral facilitator will invariably tend to be more creative. There will be greater opportunities to establish the principles and detailed nuances of the settlement terms in a way which the court or an arbitrator could not possibly do, and which negotiations between the lawyers conducting the litigation would have considerable difficult in achieving."

Bush and Folger's description of the four "stories" of the mediation movement extends our understanding of how proponents of mediation differ even further.

R. Bush and J. Folger, *The Promise of Mediation* (Jossey-Bass, San Francisco, 1994) pp.15–24:

"While the growth of mediation in the past two decades is remarkable, what is even more striking is the extraordinary divergence of opinion about how to understand that growth and how to characterize the mediation movement itself. This divergence is so marked that there is no one accepted account of how the mediation movement evolved or what it represents. Instead, the literature of the field reveals several very different accounts or 'stories' of the movement, told by different authors and stressing different dimensions of the mediation process and its societal impacts. Thus, the movement is portrayed by some as a tool to reduce court congestion and provide 'higher quality' justice in individual cases, by others as a vehicle for organizing people and communities to obtain fairer treatment, and by still others as a covert means of social control and oppression. And some, including ourselves, picture the movement as a way to foster a qualitative transformation of human interaction. Indeed, these are the four main accounts of the mediation movement that run through the literature on mediation. We call them, respectively, the *Satisfaction Story* of the movement, the *Social Justice Story*, the *Oppression Story*, and the *Transformation Story*.

The fact that there are four distinct and divergent stories of the movement suggests two important points. On one level, it suggests that the mediation movement is not monolithic but pluralistic—that there are in fact different approaches to mediation practice, with varied impacts. The stories represent these different approaches. On a deeper level, the existence of divergent stories suggests that, while everyone sees the mediation movement as a means for achieving important societal goals, people differ over what goal is most important. The stories thus represent and support different goals, each of which is seen by some people as the most important one for the movement to fulfill.

Recounting the different stories of the movement is therefore a good way both to illustrate the diversity of mediation practice and also to identify the value choices implicit in varying approaches to practice. The following summary of the four stories presents each one as it might be told by its authors and adherents.

The Satisfaction Story

According to this story: 'The mediation process is a powerful tool for satisfying the genuine human needs of parties to individual disputes. Because of its flexibility, informality, and consensuality, mediation can open up the full dimensions of the problem facing the parties. Not limited by legal categories or rules, it can help reframe a contentious dispute as a mutual problem. Also, because of mediators' skills in dealing with power imbalances, mediation can reduce strategic maneuvering and overreaching. As a result of these different features, mediation can facilitate collaborative, integrative problem solving rather than adversarial, distributive bargaining. It can thereby produce creative "win-win" outcomes that reach beyond formal rights to solve problems and satisfy parties' genuine needs in a particular situation. The mediation movement has employed these capabilities of the process to produce superior quality solutions to disputes of all kinds, in terms of satisfaction of parties' self-defined needs, for *all* sides.

Furthermore, in comparison to more formal or adversary processes, mediation's informality and mutuality can reduce both the economic and emotional costs of dispute settlement. The use of mediation has thus produced great *private* savings for disputants, in economic and psychic terms. Also, by providing mediation in many cases that would otherwise have gone to court, the mediation movement has also saved *public* expense. It has freed up the courts for other disputants who need them, easing the problem of delayed access to justice. In sum, the movement has led to more efficient use of limited private *and* public dispute resolution resources, which in turn means a greater overall satisfaction for individual "consumers" of the justice system.

> 'This holds true for all the various contexts in which mediation has been used. Child custody mediation, for example, has produced better-quality results for both children and parents than litigated rulings. Small-claims mediation has resulted in higher party satisfaction with both process and outcome, and higher rates of compliance than litigation. Environmental and public policy mediation have produced creative and highly praised resolutions, while avoiding the years of delay and enormous expense that court action would have entailed. Moreover, mediation in these areas has reduced court caseloads and backlogs, facilitating speedier disposition of those cases that cannot be resolved without trial in court. In these and other kinds of disputes, mediation has produced more satisfaction for disputing parties than could have been provided otherwise.'

The Satisfaction Story is widely told by a number of authors. Many are themselves mediators, either publicly employed or private practitioners or 'entrepreneurs'. Some are academics. Some who are both practitioners and teachers have been very influential in supporting this story of the movement. Also quite influential are the many judges and other justice system officials who tell this story, including former Chief Justice Warren Burger and many other judicial leaders.

The next two interpretations of the mediation movement, the Social Justice Story and the Transformation Story, differ somewhat from the Satisfaction Story. The Satisfaction

Story claims to depict what has generally occurred in the use of mediation thus far, while the other two describe something that has admittedly occurred only in part thus far. In effect, these are 'minor' stories of the movement, but each is still seen by its adherents as representing the movement's most important potential.

The Social Justice Story

According to this story: 'Mediation offers an effective means of organizing individuals around common interests and thereby building stronger community ties and structures. This is important because affiliated individuals are especially subject to exploitation in this society and because more effective community organization can limit such exploitation and create more social justice. Mediation can support community organization in several ways. Because of its capacity for reframing issues and focusing on common interests, mediation can help individuals who think they are adversaries perceive a larger context in which they face a common enemy. As a result, mediation can strengthen the weak by helping establish alliances among them.

'In addition, by its capacity to help parties solve problems for themselves, mediation reduces dependence on distant agencies and encourages self-help, including the formation of effective "grass roots" community structures. Finally mediation treats legal rules as only one of a variety of bases by which to frame issues and evaluate possible solutions to disputes. Therefore, mediation can give groups more leverage to argue for their interests than they might have in formal legal processes. The mediation movement has used these capacities of the process, to some extent at least, to facilitate the organization of relatively powerless individuals into communities of interest. As a result, those common interests have been pursued more successfully, helping ensure greater social justice, and the individuals involved have gained a new sense of participation in civic life.

This picture applies to many, if not all, of the contexts in which mediation is used. Interpersonal neighborhood mediation has encouraged co-tenants or block residents, for example, to realize their common adversaries, such as landlords and city agencies, and to take joint action to pursue their common interests. Environmental mediation has facilitated the assertion of novel (and not strictly legal) claims by groups that have succeeded in redressing imbalances of power favoring land developers. Even mediation of consumer disputes has helped strengthen consumers' confidence in their ability to get complaints addressed, which has led to other forms of self-help and increased consumer power. In short, mediation has helped organize individuals and strengthen communities of interest in may different contexts—and could be used more widely for this purpose.'

The Social Justice Story of the mediation movement has been told for a long time, though by a relatively small number of authors, usually people with ties to the tradition of grass-roots community organizing. Examples include Parul Wahrhaftig, an early figure in community mediation, and Ray Shonholtz, found of the Community Boards Program, long known for its organizing orientation. More recently, Carl Moore and Margaret Herman have echoed this account. While the number of its adherents are few, this story has been told consistently from the earliest stages of the movement.

The third story, the Transformation story, focuses on some of the same features of the mediation process as the first two. However, it characterizes them, and especially their consequences, in distinct and quite different terms than the other stories.

The Transformation Story

According to this story: 'The unique promise of mediation lies in its capacity to transform the character of both individual disputants and society as a whole. Because of its informality and consensuality, mediation can allow parties to define problems and goals in their own terms, thus validating the importance of these problems and goals in the parties' lives. Further, mediation can support the parties' exercise of self-determination in deciding how, or even whether, to settle a dispute, and it can help the parties mobilize their own resources to address problems and achieve their goals. The mediation movement has (at least to some extent) employed these capabilities of the process to help disputing parties strengthen their own capacity to handle adverse circumstances of all kinds, not only in the immediate case but in future situations. Participants in mediation have gained a greater sense of self-respect, self-reliance, and self-confidence. This has been called the *empowerment* dimension of the mediation process.

'In addition, the private, nonjudgmental character of mediation can provide disputants a nonthreatening opportunity to explain and humanize themselves to one another. In this setting, and with mediators who are skilled at enhancing interpersonal communications, parties often discover that they can feel and express some degree of understanding and concern for one another despite their disagreement. The movement has (again, to some extent) used this dimension of the process to help individuals strengthen their inherent capacity for relating with concern to the problems of others. Mediation has thus engendered, even between parties who start out as fierce adversaries, acknowledgment and concern for each other as fellow human beings. This has been called the *recognition* dimension of the mediation process.

While empowerment and recognition have been given only partial attention in the mediation movement thus far, a consistent and wider emphasis on these dimensions would contribute powerfully—incrementally and over time—to the transformation of individuals from fearful, defensive, and self-centered beings into confident, empathetic, and considerate beings, and to the transformation of society from a shaky truce between enemies into a strong network of allies.

This picture captures the potential of all branches of the mediation movement, not just certain areas in which human relationships are considered important (implying that elsewhere they are not). Consumer mediation can strengthen and evoke mutual recognition between merchants and consumers, transforming both the individuals involved and the character of commercial transactions and institutions. Divorce mediation can strengthen and evoke recognition between men and women (even if as childless ex-spouses they will have no further contact), changing both the people involved and the character of male-female interaction generally. Personal injury mediation can strengthen and evoke recognition between individuals who work for loss-coverage institutions and individual accident victims, transforming both the persons involved and the character of compensation processes and institutions in our society. In every area, mediation could, with sufficient energy and commitment, help transform both individuals and society.'

The Transformation Story of the mediation movement is not widely told in the published literature of the field. The few who expound it include practitioners such as Albie Davis (1989) and academics such as Leonard Riskin and Carrie Menkel Meadow, as well as the authors of this volume. Nevertheless, beyond the world of the printed word, this story is given voice in informal discussions among both academics and mediation practitioners. It is, as it were, the underground story of the movement, often the motivating force behind practitioners' involvement. Perhaps it goes unstated because it is not easy to articulate, or perhaps people are hesitant to articulate (or enact) it for fear of seeming too idealistic and impractical. Yet whenever the story *is* told, it generates a remarkably enthusiastic response, which suggests that it has much more currency than its published expressions would indicate.

Here, then, are three very different accounts of the mediation movement. Each of them expresses two different kinds of messages about the movement. On one level, each story is a description, purporting to recount what the mediation movement has actually done and what its actual character is today (in whole or in part). On another level, each story is a prescription, suggesting what the movement *should* do to fulfill what the story's authors see as the most important societal goal or value that mediation can help achieve.

The final story of the movement differs from all the others. The first three all see positive effects of potentials in the movement, although each sees them differently. The fourth, by contrast, sees only negative effects or potentials. It presents not a prescription for the movement but a warning against it. We call it the Oppression Story.

The Oppression Story

According to this story: 'Even if the movement began with the best of intentions, mediation has turned out to be a dangerous instrument for increasing the power of the strong to take advantage of the weak. Because of the informality and consensuality of the process, and hence the absence of both procedural and substantive rules, mediation can magnify power imbalances and open the door to coercion and manipulation by the stronger party. Meanwhile, the posture of "neutrality" excuses the mediator from preventing this. Therefore, in comparison to formal legal processes, mediation has often produced outcomes that are unjust, that is, disproportionately and unjustifiably favorable to the stronger parties. Moreover, because of its privacy and informality, mediation gives mediators broad strategic power to control the discussion, giving free rein to mediators' biases. These biases can affect the framing and selection of issues, consideration and ranking of settlement options, and many other elements that influence outcomes. Again, as a result, mediation has often produced unjust outcomes.

'Finally, since mediation handles disputes without reference to other, similar cases and without reference to the public interest, it results in the "dis-aggregation" and privatization of class and public interest problems. That is, the mediation movement has helped the strong to "divide and conquer". Weaker parties are unable to make common cause and the public interest is ignored and undermined. In sum, the overall effect of the movement has been to neutralize social justice gains achieved by the civil rights, women's, and consumer's movements, among others, and to help reestablish the privileged position of the stronger classes and perpetuate their oppression of the weaker.

This oppressive picture is found in all the movement's manifestations. Divorce mediation removes safeguards and exposes women to coercive and manipulative "bargaining" that results in unjust property and custody agreements. Landlord-tenant mediation allows landlords to escape their obligations to provide minimally decent housing, which results in substandard living conditions and unjust removals for tenants. Employment discrimination mediation manipulates victims into accepting buy-offs and permits structural racism and sexism to continue unabated in businesses and institutions. Even in commercial disputes between businesses, mediation allows the parties to strike deals behind closed doors that disadvantage consumers and others in ways that will never even come to light. In every area, the mediation movement has been used to consolidate the power of the strong and increase the exploitation and oppression of the weak.'

The Oppression Story is clearly a different *kind* of story than the other three. Rather than offering a description of and prescription *for* the mediation movement, it sounds a warning *against* it. This story is almost as widely told as the Satisfaction Story, but by very different authors. They include numerous critics of the mediation movement, such as early and influential figures Richard Abel (1982) and Christine Harrington (1985). Minority critics of the movement, like Richard Delgado (1985), and feminist critics, like Martha Fineman (1988), also tell the Oppression Story. In general, many—although not all—writers and thinkers concerned with equality tend to interpret the mediation movement through the Oppression Story and to see it as a serious threat to disadvantaged groups.

Now that all the stories have been presented, a clarification of one crucial term is in order. Some authors have used the term 'transformation' to mean the *restructuring of social institutions* in a way that redistributes power and eliminates class privilege. It should be clear that as we use the term here—in the Transformation Story and throughout the book —transformation does *not* mean institutional restructuring but rather a change or refinement in the *consciousness and character of individual human beings*. Transformation, in the sense used here, necessarily connotes *individual moral development*, although this kind of change will very likely lead to changes in social institutions as well. On the other hand, when the term is used to mean institutional restructuring, it does not carry any necessary implication of individual moral growth, but rather connotes a reallocation of material benefits and burdens among individuals and groups. We see this aim as encompassed within the concept of social justice or fairness, and in the framework presented here this kind of societal restructuring is the concern of the Social Justice and Oppression Stories, not the Transformation Story."

THE CHARACTERISTICS OF MEDIATION

Despite these differences in approach, most analysts continue to claim that a number of common threads generally run through most types of mediation. In the extract that follows, Genn describes the format of a typical mediation drawn from her own evaluation of the Central London County Court mediation pilot scheme.

Hazel Genn, *Mediation in Action* (Calouste Gulbenkian Foundation, London, 1999) pp.23–25:

What happens in mediation

"Mediation sessions can take place in rooms in a court building, in the offices of a solicitor or barrister or other professional, or even in a hotel. The length of the mediation session tends to depend on the type of dispute and whether or not it is part of a court scheme. Disputes over relatively small sums of money or where the issues are not very complicated can usually be mediated in half a day, whereas in some large commercial disputes the mediation might last for more than a day. The Central London County Court limits its mediation sessions to three hours.

It is important for the mediation sessions to be in comfortable surroundings and to be conducted in an atmosphere that is informal but orderly. The mediator and disputing parties (and their legal or other representatives if present) are usually seated around a table. Mediators have different ways of seating people, but arrangements are generally informal to minimise any sense of confrontation. Sometimes mediators dispense with a table and have everyone sitting in a circle.

Preliminary joint meeting

The parties are usually welcomed at a preliminary joint meeting and congratulated on having taken the step of coming to mediate their dispute. The mediator may then give a little information about him- or herself before going on to explain how the session is going to proceed, what the role of the mediator will be and what the objectives are. He or she will stress that the process is entirely voluntary and that either party is free to leave at any time if they are unhappy with the process.

Sometimes the early stages of these introductory joint meetings can be somewhat tense, especially if it is the first time that the disputing parties have been face to face, or even spoken, since the beginning of the dispute and they feel awkward or embarrassed. The mediator has to reduce tension and create a calm and constructive atmosphere. Solicitors or other representatives, if present, can help by maintaining a courteous and professional approach. Most solicitors are extremely good at this.

The opening joint session is a very important opportunity for both parties to make clear to each other the most serious aspects of their grievance and to communicate exactly what it is that they are concerned about. The mediator will usually give each about fifteen minutes to summarise, in their own words and without interruption, the nature of their complaint against the other side. People tend to find that this opportunity is a very satisfying part of the process and helpful in reaching a compromise agreement to end the dispute.

However, there are some cases where relations between the parties are so bad that they do not want to be in the same room together. If this occurs, mediators will carry out the mediation without any joint sessions, and merely shuttle between the parties.

Private meetings

After the opening joint session each side goes into a separate room for private meetings with the mediator (together with their legal advisers or anyone else who is accompanying them). The mediator then begins a process of 'shuttle diplomacy', exploring with each party alternately the details of their case and discussing the strengths and weaknesses of their claim. Information given to the mediator during these private sessions is strictly confidential and he or she will only pass on information to the other side if given express permission to do so. During this process the mediator tries to establish where there is common ground between the parties and to discover the scope for compromise, and will also try to identify the most important sticking points and to understand why the disputing parties take a different view of those points.

Usually after a period spent in private session the possibilities for agreement begin to emerge. The mediator will spend some time working out the exact terms of any agreement with each side to ensure that both sides are happy with them. This stage can often involve some intense bargaining, with the mediator acting as the go-between.

Concluding joint session

Once a broad agreement has been reached the mediator brings everyone back together for a final joint meeting to work out the details and to draft a document setting out the agreed terms for the disputing parties to sign. The mediator ends the mediation session by congratulating both sides on having reached a settlement and will often invite them to shake hands before they leave.

This final session can be crucially helpful in setting the tone for future relations between the parties and in laying grievances to rest. Even if the parties have not managed to reach an agreement, the mediator uses the final joint session to draw attention to the progress that has been made in clarifying the issues in dispute, and in moving closer to a settlement."

Genn also provides us with a case study of a dispute in which mediation proved to be successful:

Architect v client

"An architect had not received payment of his final bill for work carried out on a private flat. After asking for payment for a year and a half he finally issued court proceedings and the case was mediated. The architect, who had not consulted solicitors, accepted the court's offer of mediation because he did not feel that the money at stake (about £4,000) warranted legal fees, but on the other hand he said, 'it is not a sum of money I am prepared to let go. This has taken ages writing letters and it would take even longer if I went to court.'

The flat-owner's complaint was that the final bill had been much higher than expected, the quality of some of the work was poor and, because of lengthy building works, relations with neighbours had deteriorated. He said: 'This is a classic situation of communication breakdown. For a layman this was a very big project. Supporting walls had to be removed. There was a great deal of stress about the building project, but we went into it with our eyes open and took great care to take precautions. Our consultants and advisers were the best. We asked questions as we went along but no proper answers were given. They never apologised to us. Never once. The effect of that one single project has led to a whole lever-arch file of correspondence with our managing agents and we have been threatened with eviction by our landlord because the owners say that the building might fall down!'

During the course of the mediation an apology from the architect was read out to the flat-owner, which said: 'The plaintiff regrets any inconvenience and stress that has resulted to you and your family.' After this formal apology the parties managed to reach a settlement whereby the flat-owner paid £2,500 of the outstanding bill and both sides agreed that would be an end to litigation. In less than three hours the parties had managed to reach an agreement ending a dispute that had been going on for almost two years. At the end the architect said: 'I think mediation is a very good idea. It just short-circuits the whole business. Although I'm not happy with the outcome, the case was not financially worth pursuing further through the court. I haven't been to business school but even I know that!'"

In the following extract Brown and Marriot draw out the defining characteristics of most forms of mediation.

H. Brown and A. Marriot, *ADR Principles and Practice* (2nd ed., Sweet and Maxwell, 1999), pp.109–111:

Common Features of Mediation

"There are a number of common threads which generally run through the different forms of mediation:

1. **The use of a mediator.** It may be trite, but mediation cannot take place without a mediator. Mediation brings into the dispute resolution process a neutral third party whose very presence creates a new dynamic which does not exist when only the parties themselves or their representatives undertake direct negotiation. It is this element of third party intercession which can be very helpful to the resolution process, but which also some traditional litigators find difficult to accept.

2. **The neutrality of the mediator.** Mediator neutrality and impartiality are fundamental to the mediation process. The mediator should not be associated or connected with any of the disputing parties in a way that would inhibit neutrality or effective intervention.

3. **Nature of the mediator's authority.** If a mediator has authority to make any determination which binds the parties that would be inconsistent with the notion of mediation. The mediator has no power or authority other than that given by the parties expressly or implicitly.

4. **Consensual resolution.** The only binding outcome of mediation is one on which all parties agree. Any process under which there is an imposed binding outcome, whether stipulated by a third party or arrived at in any way other than by agreement of the parties, is not mediation. In that event the process would be arbitration or some other form of adjudication.

5. **Settlement objective.** All mediations have as their primary objective the settlement of differences between the disputants by negotiated agreement. Because of the need to reach agreement and because the process allows more ingenuity and nuances than is usually possible in the adversarial process, mediation aims for resolution which maximises all parties' interests.

6. **Facilitation of negotiation.** The mediator's primary role is to assist the parties with their negotiations. All mediation involves some element of such facilitation, which is enhanced by the mediator's communication and other skills. If the mediator has negotiating skills, that can assist the process; however, the mediator does not negotiate with the parties, but rather assists them to negotiate with one another.

7. **Providing a secure negotiating environment.** One of the main objectives and common practices in mediation is to create conditions which are conducive to discussion, negotiation and the exploration of settlement options and possibilities. This applies to the physical arrangements, to the ambience which is created by the mediators, and to the ground rules regulating the process.

8. **Empowerment of the parties.** Empowerment in relation to the parties collectively means the increase in their ability to make their own decisions and the corresponding

reduction of their dependence on third parties including professional advisers. This arises in mediation first, because the parties retain control over whether they wish to settle and on what terms. Secondly, by their involvement in the process of fact gathering and negotiation as it proceeds, they have a direct connection with the outcome and its detailed shape. In some cases, particularly in family and inter-personal issues, the dynamic of the process, the way in which communications can be improved, and the attention given to power imbalances can all have an empowering effect on an individual party, which means that such a person is better able to make his or her own decisions.

Although the empowerment aspect may sometimes be minimal especially where the parties are represented by lawyers in the mediation, they will always have control over the outcome and will rarely lose power in the way that can happen in conventional litigation representation; and consequently the empowerment aspect can be said to exist to some greater or lesser extent in all mediation.

9. **Confidentiality.** Although parties are free to agree that mediation is to be public or that the outcome is to be publicised in some way, one of the principles in all forms of mediation is that it is by nature a private and confidential process. The mediator will invariably offer confidentiality to the parties, who may be asked also to agree to mutual confidentiality.

10 **No substitute for independent advice.** Whatever model of mediation is followed, and whether or not an evaluation is made, a mediator will not ordinarily give advice to the parties, either individually or jointly, though information may well be furnished. In mediation, parties are responsible for their own decisions, and where appropriate may need to take independent advice, whether on legal, technical or other issues, but not from the mediator.

11. **Containment of escalation.** Whereas the adversarial system has a tendency towards a competitive approach and confrontational communications, the mediation process tends to encourage a problem-solving approach, to facilitate communications and to allow for feelings to be ventilated within a controlled and constructive forum. Consequently, mediation generally has the effect of containing escalation of issues and antagonism. This in turn means that the parties in disagreement who have a relationships with one another, whether business, family or personal, are generally more likely to sustain that relationship, or to vary or end it in a more co-operative way, by using mediation than through the adversarial process."

There are indications that more and more litigants are interested in using mediation. Moreover, interest in mediation from other professionals is also growing. The Chartered Institute of Arbitrators claims to have opened its doors as a "professional home" to mediators in October 1999 and is currently developing a route to Fellowship for 'Chartered Mediators'. Interestingly, a number of large City law firms, including some of the most traditional, have changed the name of their litigation departments to broader terms which encompass arbitration and mediation. Provision for the mediation of consumer disputes which cannot be resolved at service level is becoming common. The Chartered Institute of Arbitrators is involved in a number of schemes such as Brent and Waltham Council's leaseholder dispute resolution schemes and the Finance and Leasing Association Mediation scheme. Large scale consumer mediation schemes have been set up by companies such as Norwich Union.

The increasing importance of alternative dispute resolution in the commercial sphere has also been signalled by a number of recent developments. The City

Disputes Panel which handles many of the disputes which arise in the financial services industry now suggests that a standard mediation clause be inserted in all contracts. Launched in 1994, it claims to have dealt with cases involving a total value in dispute exceeding £4,000m. More recently, Intermediation has been responsible for the setting up of a mediation desk on the floor of Lloyds of London and mediation schemes have been introduced by the British Marine Federation and the British Institute of Architectural Technologists. The Baltic and International Maritime Council has also introduced its own standard dispute resolution clause in a move to increase the shipping industry's awareness and use of mediation techniques and other commercial players in the maritime world are considering the use of mediation clauses as a regular feature of contracts. CEDR, one of the country's largest mediation providers claims that in the 12 months from April 1999 to March 2000, it experienced a 141 per cent increase in the number of commercial disputes referred to it. In the following year, it arranged 467 commercial mediations, of which commercial contract disputes accounted for 31 per cent of cases, some of which involved damages of between £1.1m and £8m.

Government bodies have also taken a steer in these developments at national and international levels. In March 2001 the Lord Chancellor's Department (now the Deparment for Constitutional Affairs) announced that all government departments should seek to avoid litigation by using mediation and a year later the Office of Government Commerce published a dispute resolution guide for all those involved in the drafting of UK procurement contracts. At a European level, the European Commission's Green Paper on developing commercial mediation in the EU was also published and adopted in 2002 and it is anticipated by mediation providers that by the summer of 2003 the member states of the United Nations Commission on International Trade Law will have voted to adopt a model law of international commercial conciliation encouraging those countries with no mediation provision to use it as a basis for reform. The Insurance Mediation Directive of 2002 also supports this trend and seeks to ensure a high degree of professionalism and competence amongst intermediaries in insurance disputes.

Finally, in May 2002 The ADR Group and The Claim Room launched the first European-based multi-lingual online disputes resolution service which includes a virtual negotiation room and blind bidding claims settlement and the Chartered Institute of Arbitrators is currently developing the EEJ-net scheme which focuses on e-business and multiple jurisdictional or cross-border disputes. Most importantly the value of mediation at all stages of the disputants relationship is increasingly being discussed. Mediation agencies have, for instance, reported being called in to help design dispute resolution clauses and to facilitate negotiations during the life of a contract where discussions have become stuck rather than when the relationship between the parties to the contract is effectively over.

Policy makers have been keen to test the case for more extensive use of mediation in a wide range of settings. In 1996 judges in the Central London County Court (CLCC) established a pilot mediation scheme for non-family civil disputes with a value over £3,000. The scheme's objective was to offer virtually cost-free court-annexed mediation to disputing parties at an early stage in litigation, involving a three-hour session with a trained mediator assisting parties to reach a settlement, with or without legal representation. The scheme's purpose was to promote swift dispute settlement and a reduction in legal costs through an informal process that parties might prefer to court proceedings. It was also thought that mediation would achieve savings in Legal Aid. Professor Hazel Genn was asked to evaluate the scheme. In the following extract from her report on the pilot scheme she describes the aims of the evaluation study and some of the key findings which suggest that mediation has an important role to play in the litigation arena.

Hazel Genn, *The Central London County Court Pilot Mediation Scheme Evaluation Report* (*www.lcd.gov.uk/research/1998/598esfr.htm*, 1998):

"The evaluation offers an assessment of:

- the demand for mediation and causes of the prevalent rejection of mediation offers;
- the kinds of cases for which mediation is an appropriate form of dispute resolution;
- the extent to which mediation can promote settlement in civil cases;
- the extent to which mediation can reduce the time taken to settle civil cases and reduce the cost of resolving disputes;
- the extent to which mediation succeeds in achieving acceptable and lasting settlement of disputes;
- the extent to which mediation is perceived by parties and their representatives as a satisfactory method of dispute resolution . . .

Outcomes

The majority (62%) of mediated cases settled *at the mediation appointment* and this settlement rate remained constant between case types, indicating that mediation can be used across a wide spectrum of cases. Other findings on outcome were that:

- where the plaintiff had legal aid the settlement rate was lower than average;
- the settlement rate at mediation was highest (72%) when neither party had legal representation at the mediation;
- mediated cases had a *much higher settlement rate overall than non-mediated cases*, whether or not settlement occurred at the mediation appointment, supporting the contention that mediation promotes settlement after an unsettled mediation.

Plaintiffs settling at mediation appointments appear to be prepared to discount their claims heavily in order to achieve settlement, with average levels of settlement in mediated claims being about £2,000 *lower* than in non-mediated settlements.

Time and cost

Even on a very *conservative* estimate, mediated settlements occurred *several months earlier* than among non-mediated cases. Most parties whose cases settled at mediation believed that the mediation had saved time, although those whose cases did not settle often felt that the mediation had involved them in *extra* time. Solicitors felt strongly that mediation saved time. There was much more equivocation on the question of cost savings. Only half the plaintiffs settling at mediation believed they had saved costs. Solicitors tended to be more likely to think that costs had been saved. There was a common view that failure to settle at the mediation appointment led to *increased* costs.

Evaluation of mediators and mediation process

The overwhelming motivation for mediating was to save time and legal costs. Few parties or solicitors had any experience of mediation or any knowledge of the process. The vast

majority of litigants and solicitors made positive assessments of the mediation process. Confidence in mediators was generally high, although less so when cases failed to settle.
The characteristics most valued by litigants were:

- the opportunity to state their grievance and focus on the issues in the disputes;
- fully to participate in a process relatively free from legal technicality;
- the qualities of the mediators.

Solicitors particularly welcomed:

- the speed of the process;
- the opportunity to review the case with a neutral party;
- the concentration on commercial realities;
- the opportunity to repair damaged business relationships.

Most mediated settlements were perceived by litigants to have been fair although fairness was often assessed against the cost and time of continued litigation.
Negative assessments by parties centred on:

- deficiencies in mediators' knowledge of the law and issues in dispute;
- undue pressure to settle and bullying by mediators;
- mediators being *insufficiently* directive.

Mediators

Mediators in civil disputes require a wide repertoire of interpersonal and professional skills as well as sound legal knowledge. Flexibility and adaptability are crucial qualities. A 'counselling' or 'therapeutic' approach, stressing communication and reconciliation, seems less well-suited to non-family civil disputes than a more directive, interventionist approach emphasising the value of settlement. There was great variation in the skill displayed by mediators and many were very inexperienced. Some of the most successful mediators were barristers, many of whom were prepared to be explicitly evaluative during the course of mediations. Mediators exert considerable power in mediation, controlling the flow of information, the use of evidence and the architecture of settlements. There was no consistent view among mediators on the question of ethics or the nature of the mediator's responsibilities in mediation.

Conclusions

- Mediation is capable of promoting settlement in a wide range of civil cases when parties have volunteered to accept mediation.
- Personal injury cases are amenable to mediation even when both liability and quantum are in issue.

- Mediation offers a process that parties to civil disputes on the whole find satisfying.
- Conflict can be reduced and settlements reached that parties find acceptable.
- Mediation can promote and speed-up settlement.
- It is unclear to what extent mediation saves costs and unsuccessful mediation can increase costs.
- Mediation can magnify power imbalances and works best in civil disputes when there is some rough equality between the parties or in representation.
- Mediators require special personal qualities, good training and experience.
- Demand for mediation is very weak and the legal profession has a crucial role in influencing demand.

Issues requiring attention are:

- The impact on weak demand of an increase in mediation fees to an economic level.
- Mediation procedures, especially in relation to the use of documentary evidence.

- Training of mediators.
- Quality control of mediators.
- Accountability and ethics of mediators."

Mediation currently operates in the shadow of normal litigation procedures and the disadvantages of those procedures provide much of the incentive for parties to settle during mediation. Procedural changes could further strengthen the existing low-level of demand. Education of the profession and a change of litigation culture could also strengthen it. In seeking to stimulate some enthusiasm among the grass roots of the profession, it is important for mediation proponents to focus on the value that mediation adds to normal settlement negotiations between solicitors, rather than simply setting-up mediation in opposition to trial. The experience of the profession is that most cases are not, in the end, tried. Mediation can add value to the normal claims settlement process in civil disputes. It offers a cathartic pseudo "day in court" to parties; it gets cards on the table and all the parties around the table; and, with the help of a skilled mediator, it introduces some authoritative objectivity into the assessment of the strengths and weaknesses of the parties' claims.

THE PROBLEMS WITH MEDIATION

Despite the support given to mediated settlement by Professor Genn, it is important to note that demand for mediation in the pilot scheme remained low. As Professor Genn goes on to explain:

"The rate at which both parties accepted mediation offers remained at about five percent throughout the life of the scheme and despite vigorous attempts to stimulate demand. Demand was virtually non-existent among personal injury cases, although these comprised almost half of the cases offered mediation. Contract, goods/services disputes and debt cases had the highest levels of demand although the joint acceptance rate was less than ten percent. The joint demand for mediation was *lowest* when both parties had legal representation. Acceptance of mediation was highest among disputes between businesses. Interviews with solicitors rejecting mediation revealed:

- lack of experience and widespread ignorance of mediation among the legal profession;
- apprehension about showing weakness through accepting mediation within the context of traditional adversarial litigation;
- evidence of litigant resistance to the idea of compromise, particularly in the early stages of litigation."

Other evaluations of mediation schemes have also suggested that lack of demand for mediation from litigants and their representatives is a problem. Reflecting on her own evaluation of the Department of Health's Mediation pilot scheme, Mulcahy has suggested that much of the responsibility for the lack of take up lies with the legal profession rather than their clients.

Linda Mulcahy, "Can Leopards Change their Spots? An Evaluation of the Role of Lawyers in Medical Negligence Mediation" (2001) 8(3) *International Journal of the Legal Profession* 203–224:

"There have been a range of responses to this new environment. There is some evidence of resistance from the grass roots of the legal profession who see mediation as yet another new initiative in an ever changing and uncertain legal world. Globalisation, debate over rights of audience and judicial appointments, changes to legal aid, reform of complaints systems, the introduction of conditional fees have all transformed the last decade into a tumultuous period for legal practitioners. For litigators reeling from the changes to practice introduced by the Woolf reforms mediation provides a new threat, which as gatekeepers to many of the most recent pilot schemes, they still have the power to resist. Mediation is not a form of dispute resolution which is commonly used by High Street practitioners and not something which clients will automatically associate with them. This and fear of diversion of cases away from the courts has led to fears about the potential loss of fees. Firms of solicitors also have concerns that their levels of investment in litigation departments will prove to be misplaced. Some have expressed more principled objections to this open challenge to their monopoly. For this group the court room continues to be the most appropriate backdrop to settlement negotiations. In their view wholesale diversion of cases away from this forum brings with it a risk that too many cases will be decided by reference to the standards of the parties rather than the wider needs of the communities in which we live.

But whilst some members of the professional group have in Luhmanian terms remained normatively closed to such changes, others have proved cognitively open to the threat to their shared world. This suggests that either they have embraced the alternative ideology of mediation or that they are buying time whilst they renegotiate the jurisdictional boundaries of their professional world. A considerable number of lawyers have undertaken training as mediators and many of the larger city firms are renaming their litigation departments to reflect a broader approach to dispute settlement. At national level elite members of the profession appear to have embraced mediation enthusiastically. The Law Society, Bar Council and the Lord Chancellor have all pledged their support for this form of dispute resolution. For some this is seen as an acknowledgement by the elite of the profession that there are serious failings in the traditional claims management system. Others have interpreted it as reflecting a proprietorial interest in mediation as a way of maintaining lawyers' professional status and dominance. The latter argument is convincing when one considers that the support of professional bodies has been contingent on lawyers playing a central role as mediators or representatives of the parties in state sponsored schemes. The Law Society has, for example, claimed regulatory control over the conduct of solicitors when they are acting as mediators rather than advisers or adversaries. Roberts has argued that giving public support for such innovation is an attempt by some members of the legal profession to secure or colonise new areas of work and stake a claim to be the only legitimate occupants of it. Reflecting on this array of responses it would seem that the mediation pilot scheme had the potential to create inter-professional rivalries between lawyers and mediators as well as intra-professional rivalries between those lawyers willing to embrace mediation because it preserves market share, those who accept the alternative ideology of mediation and those who see no point in supporting it at all.

It is my contention that at present these developments are little more than a skirmish at the edge of the professional world of lawyers. Legal activists have minimised the challenge posed by mediation by mobilising during the planning stage of the pilot scheme. By helping to frame its parameters medical negligence specialists secured their inclusion in it. The majority came to understand and give meaning to mediation as an off-shoot of the civil justice system which could be used in the rare cases in which solicitors are not able to achieve settlement through bi-lateral negotiations. In this way mediation became an adjunct of the courts and litigation system rather than an alternative to it. But the data presented also suggest that solicitors confidence in their ability to adapt to this new forum was often misplaced. Lawyers involved in the pilot scheme were more surprised by the informality of proceedings and the effect of the presence of their clients than they had anticipated. Even more significant was the finding that participation in the scheme challenged the professional identity of lawyers in ways that they did not anticipate. By focusing on the accounts of grievances provided by clients mediators forced them to reflect upon and justify the nature of their claim to a special knowledge and expertise. . . .

A challenging agenda?

Mediation challenges the professional identity of lawyers in a number of ways which increase as ADR processes become more visible through their institutionalisation and promotion by government and court officials. The first threat is that mediation can, and often does, take place without lawyers. Community and family mediation are excellent examples of this model. They are also reminders that although law and lawyers have become inextricably linked in the popular imagination they do not have to co-exist. Some legal systems dispense with lawyers and many lawyers in the West perform tasks which involve very little formal law. Anthropologists of law constantly remind us that mediation is a folk concept which existed prior to the evolution of state law, legal system and lawyer-litigators. In a modern context, the popularity of mediation in some settings has actually been explained by a distrust of formalised law, lawyers and government agencies as tending to impose coercive, bureaucratic and 'outside' solutions on disputants. Reactions against state sanctioned dispute resolution systems have also been fuelled by the conviction that the courts and lawyers are unresponsive to the needs and interests of disadvantaged communities and a perception that legal rules are dogmatic, unpragmatic and distant. For some mediation represents a radical alternative legality fuelled by the needs of the populace and their call for greater participation in, and access to, justice. Whilst lawyers in the UK have secured a close association with law these alternative conceptualisations of law and lawyers provide us with a forceful reminder that the legal profession need to remain sensitive to the need to justify their participation in dispute resolution.

The increased popularity of state-sanctioned mediation amongst politicians and civil servants has also be construed as posing a threat to senior members of the legal profession. Commentators have argued that in the final decades of the twentieth century the judiciary has been subjected to an unprecedented array of reforms which could be seen as heralding the retreat of law from society. Mediation can be seen as a contemporary example of an increasingly bureaucratic state which constrains judicial autonomy by means of administrative case management and the regulation of funding. The creation of the NHS Litigation Authority, the adoption of the medical negligence pre-action protocol, and recent reforms of legal aid are excellent examples of the increase in the regulatory culture in a medico-legal context. The essence of this challenge is the demystification of law. In contrast to the claims to abstract, exclusive and theoretical understanding of the rules, signs and symbols of the law made by lawyers, such bureaucratisation of law has been viewed as encouraging movement towards the rationalisation and compartmentalisation of knowledge.

It is also the case that by identifying the need for an alternative form of dispute resolution, proponents of mediation are making a direct attack on the current litigation system and lawyers' ability to resolve cases efficiently and fairly. The ideology of co-operation espoused by mediators provides a justification for taking cases out of an adversarial litigation system. Mediators involved in state sanctioned and private mediation schemes compete for cases with litigators and judges. Prominent mediators and judges are often at pains to stress that their functions should be viewed as symbiotic, that forward thinking practitioners aim for a form of dispute resolution which best suits the parties and the case, rather than competing for the same cases. But empirical studies have demonstrated that competitive strategies are rife. Emphasising the horrors of adjudication has provided mediators with a powerful tool in their attempts to persuade disputants to select mediation instead of court based adjudication.

Mediation also questions the relevance of lawyers' training and skills to effective dispute resolution. It has been repeatedly argued that academic and vocational legal education places too much emphasis on the courts, and in particular the upper courts, as the main forum where citizens' disputes are resolved. Legal training imbues graduates with an inappropriate fidelity to formal legality and the judiciary. Critics have, for instance, drawn attention to the lack of training in informal and conciliatory dispute resolution processes provided for fledgling lawyers. It has been suggested that the traditional law school curriculum inappropriately privileges an adversarial approach to disputes and pays undue attention to the case based method at the expense of more holistic or contextualised understandings of grievances. As Hunt has argued:

> '"Thinking like lawyers" was a conceivable educational objective when the ideal model was that of mooting as a preparation for a career as an advocate. But this model embodies only a small part of what only a few graduates will end up doing. Once we recognise that lawyering is probably more about interviewing skills, negotiating strategies, financial and office management etc then the orthodox model is less than satisfactory.'

In short legal education pays 'endless attention to trees at the expense of forests', a situation which has led some to call for a radical rethinking of legal training and the role of lawyers.

Hunt's criticisms suggest that critics' concerns run deeper than arguments that current training programmes are incomplete. Mediation also undermines the claim of lawyers to classify disputes, to define the parameters of disputes and what constitutes successful process and outcome. Lawyers do much more than reproduce the arguments made by their clients. They play a pivotal role in the evolution of the grievances their clients present to them. They mould them and reinvent them as formal claims which are recognised by the legal system. The rhetorical accounts of common sense morality offered by disputants become generalised accounts of harm which fit into categories recognised by statute and case law. In a similar fashion, the desires of the clients are transformed into financial remedies. In the words of Felstiner and Sarat 'To fit into the system the client must reduce her conception of justice to what the law can provide'. Thus, the epistemological perspective of lawyers is a reductionist one. They place stress on the universal applicability of law and on the similarities in fact patterns rather than differences in the grievances recounted to them. The juridification of the client's account transforms the expert from the client's biographer to their autobiographer.

Within legal circles this change is considered to be an appropriate, indeed an essential, function of lawyers. The professional status of lawyers and their role in litigation is based on the contention that they are better able than the laity to interpret complex legal rules and to apply such abstract frameworks to the cases presented to them. Lawyers make a claim to represent clients because they are able to say things that their client can not because they lack eloquence or are too emotionally involved. They restrain clients from talking when they are likely to reveal too much about their case. Their distance from their clients and objectivity is a feature of their work which compares favourably with the unmanageable subjectivity of their client. Boon and Flood found this characteristic of their work to be positively celebrated by the profession. The disputant's grievance is not recognised in its entirety by the lawyer's interpretative framework leading them to routinely negate their client's understandings which are seen as sites of bias.

But the special knowledge claimed by lawyers is also a social construct. It reproduces and constitutes an order which keeps the expression of lay narratives in check. The mystery of the legal system serves to legitimate lawyers as translators but also provides incentives for them to constantly invent and recreate mystery. Viewed in this way law becomes a tool for the lawyer rather than a tool for the client. Bankowski and Mungham have argued that such control would be impossible to maintain if disputants were without fear and uncertainty. Their alienation from law is reinforced by their failure to speak for themselves. In the words of Bankowski and Mungham:

> '. . . the more the client knows, the less the lawyer is able to earn . . . a significant erosion of the monopoly of legal knowledge is not in the lawyer's interest either, for if this base begins to wither away then so does the claim of the lawyer to power and privileges in society.'

Mediation provides a direct challenge to this ordering. Mediators claim to take account of the disputant's narrative and the specificity of their grievance. They claim to privilege the client's story and encourage discussion of both legal and non-legal aspects of grievances. They place emphasise on achieving an outcome which is shaped by the disputants in accordance with their own meanings and objectives. Rather than placing grievances into existing categories commentators have suggested that the process provides important opportunities for norm creation and political debates about what constitutes a preferred standard, or at least acts as a rehearsal ground for the adaptation of norms. Mediators stress the importance of self determination and encourage the parties to mobilise their own resources in disputes resolution rather than relying on those of their lawyers or the state."

It is clear then that, a number of key issues in relation to ADR remain unresolved. In the following critique, Cappelletti hints at some of the wider concerns that academics have expressed about the process.

Mauro Cappelletti, "Alternative Dispute Resolution Processes within the Framework of the World-Wide Access-to-Justice Movement" (1993) 56 M.L.R. 282 at 283:

"[T]he search for alternatives has represented what Professor Bryant Garth and I happened to call 'the third wave' in the access-to-justice movement. Needless to say, there are here many hard questions and difficulties—perhaps contradictions, as was emphasised by Professor Abel in a well-known and often cited article ten years ago. Among the hard questions to be faced, two stand out. First, what are the best kinds of institutions to be promoted? Possibilities include arbitration, mediation, conciliation and, of course, an array of simplified procedures as well as small claims courts. Second, which are the best kinds of persons to staff such institutions? These may include lay persons and, quite often . . . persons involved with and personally aware of the same kinds of interests and problems as the parties in the case. . . . Another hard question concerns the minimum standards and guarantees to be maintained even in these alternative kinds of adjudicatory organs and procedures. The risk, of course, is that the alternative will provide only a *second class justice* because, almost inevitably, the adjudicators in these alternative courts and procedures would lack, in part at least, those safeguards of independence and training that are present in respect of ordinary judges. And the procedures themselves might often lack, in part at least, those formal guarantees of procedural fairness which are typical of ordinary litigation."

NOTES AND QUESTIONS

- What is meant by the fear that ADR will bring about "second class justice"? Do you think those fears are justified?

- Cappelletti goes on to suggest that ADR may be particularly suited to situations where the parties have an ongoing relationship which needs to be maintained? On what basis do you think he makes this argument.

In a seminal article on the topic, Fiss takes up some of these concerns.

Owen M. Fiss, "Against Settlement" (1984) 93 *Yale Law Journal* 1073 at 1075, 1076, 1078, 1085:

"In my view . . . the case for settlement rests on questionable premises. I do not believe that settlement as a generic practice is preferable to judgment or should be institutionalized on a wholesale and indiscriminate basis. It should be treated instead as a highly problematic technique for streamlining dockets. Settlement is for me the civil analogue of plea bargaining: Consent is often coerced; the bargain may be struck by someone without authority; the absence of a trial and judgment renders subsequent judicial involvement troublesome; and although dockets are trimmed, justice may not be done. Like plea bargaining, settlement is a capitulation to the conditions of mass society and should be neither encouraged nor praised.

The imbalance of power

By viewing the lawsuit as a quarrel between two neighbors, the dispute-resolution story that underlies ADR implicitly asks us to assume a rough equality between the contending parties. It treats settlement as the anticipation of the outcome of trial and assumes that the terms of settlement are simply a product of the parties' predictions of that outcome. In truth, however, settlement is also a function of the resources available to each party to finance the litigation, and those resources are frequently distributed unequally. Many lawsuits do not involve a property dispute between two neighbors, or between AT&T and the government (to update the story), but rather concern a struggle between a member of a racial minority and a municipal police department over alleged brutality, or a claim by a worker against a large corporation over work-related injuries. In these cases, the distribution of financial resources, or the ability of one party to pass along its costs, will invariably infect the bargaining process, and the settlement will be at odds with a conception of justice that seeks to make the wealth of the parties irrelevant.

The disparities in resources between the parties can influence the settlement in three ways. First, the poorer party may be less able to amass and analyze the information needed to predict the outcome of the litigation, and thus be disadvantaged in the bargaining process. Second, he may need the damages he seeks immediately and thus be induced to settle as a way of accelerating payment, even though he realizes he would get less now than he might if he awaited judgment. All plaintiffs want their damages immediately, but an indigent plaintiff may be exploited by a rich defendant because his need is so great that the defendant can force him to accept a sum that is less than the ordinary present value of the judgment. Third, the poorer party might be forced to settle because he does not have the resources to finance the litigation, to cover either his own projected expenses, such as his lawyer's time, or the expenses his opponent can impose through the manipulation of procedural mechanisms such as discovery. It might seem that settlement benefits the plaintiff by allowing him to avoid the costs of litigation, but this is not so. The defendant can anticipate the plaintiff's costs if the case were to be tried fully and decrease his offer by that amount. The indigent plaintiff is a victim of the costs of litigation even if he settles. . . .

The absence of authoritative consent

The argument for settlement presupposes that the contestants are individuals. These individuals speak for themselves and should be bound by the rules they generate. In many situations, however, individuals are ensnared in contractual relationships that impair their autonomy: Lawyers or insurance companies might, for example, agree to settlements that are in their interests but are not in the best interests of their clients, and to which their clients would not agree if the choice were still theirs. But a deeper and more intractable problem arises from the fact that many parties are not individuals but rather organizations or groups. We do not know who is entitled to speak for these entities and to give the consent upon which so much of the appeal of settlement depends.

Some organizations, such as corporations or unions, have formal procedures for identifying the persons who are authorized to speak for them. But these procedures are imperfect: They are designed to facilitate transactions between the organization and outsiders, rather than to insure that the members of the organization in fact agree with a particular decision. Nor do they eliminate conflicts of interests. The chief executive officer of a corporation may settle a suit to prevent embarrassing disclosures about his managerial policies, but such disclosures might well be in the interest of the shareholders. The president of a union may agree to a settlement as a way of preserving his power within the organization; for that very reason, he may not risk the dangers entailed in consulting the rank and file or in subjecting the settlement to ratification by the membership. . . .

Justice rather than peace

The dispute-resolution story makes settlement appear as a perfect substitute for judgment, as we just saw, by trivializing the remedial dimensions of a lawsuit, and also by reducing the social function of the lawsuit to one of resolving private disputes: In that story, settlement appears to achieve exactly the same purpose as judgment—peace between the parties —but at considerably less expense to society. The two quarreling neighbors turn to a court in order to resolve their dispute, and society makes courts available because it wants to aid in the achievement of their private ends or to secure the peace.

In my view, however, the purpose of adjudication should be understood in broader terms. Adjudication uses public resources, and employs not strangers chosen by the parties but public officials chosen by a process in which the public participates. These officials, like members of the legislative and executive branches, possess a power that has been defined and conferred by public law, not by private agreement. Their job is not to maximize the ends of private parties, nor simply to secure the peace, but to explicate and give force to the values embedded in authoritative texts such as . . . statutes: to interpret those values and to bring reality into accord with them. This duty is not discharged when the parties settle.

In our political system, courts are reactive institutions. They do not search out interpretive occasions, but instead wait for others to bring matters to their attention. They also rely for the most part on others to investigate and present the law and facts. A settlement will thereby deprive a court of the occasion, and perhaps even the ability, to render an interpretation. A court cannot proceed (or not proceed very far) in the face of a settlement. To be against settlement is not to urge that parties be 'forced' to litigate, since that would interfere with their autonomy and distort the adjudicative process; the parties will be inclined to make the court believe that their bargain is justice. To be against settlement is only to suggest that when the parties settle, society gets less than what appears, and for a price it does not know it is paying. Parties might settle while leaving justice undone."

Armstrong explains the tension which Fiss describes, as stemming from two competing models of the civil justice process.

Nick Armstrong, "Making Tracks" in *Reform of Civil Procedure: Essays on "Access to Justice"* (A.A.S. Zuckerman and Ross Cranston, eds., Clarendon Press, Oxford, 1995), p.97:

"The debate over the function of a civil justice system revolves around a tension between two different models of civil process: the 'dispute resolution' model and the 'policy implementation' model. Under the former, adjudication is understood simply as a method for peacefully resolving a conflict between private parties. The private interests are sovereign, and the state or public interest is limited to maximising the satisfaction of those interests in order to avoid forcible self-help. In other words, the interests of the parties must be realised, and the civil justice system must preserve its reputation of being capable of realising those interests, in order to create the incentives for disputants to use the court system: 'the rules of procedure should contain some carrots as well as sticks.' The provision of courts and legal services, or 'access to justice', may therefore be explained as 'civilisation's substitute for vengeance'.

The policy implementation model, by contrast, recognises a wider public interest. As well as observing the need to resolve the immediate dispute, this model also takes account of its potential effect on the future conduct of others. The existence of the private conflict becomes an opportunity to clarify and determine the standards by which society governs itself. Those standards include the Rule of Law, the maintenance of which transcends the interests of the private parties in order to achieve justice for those who are never involved in actual proceedings.

The difference between the two models, therefore, is one of emphasis between private and public interests. Under the dispute resolution model, the private interests of the parties take precedence; under the policy implementation model, they must sometimes yield to the wider public interest."

NOTES AND QUESTIONS

- Can you think of examples of types of cases which support Fiss' views against the virtues of settlement?

- In response to the critics of ADR, Menkel-Meadow has replied: "[M]ost of these critiques ignore the fact that ours is a party-initiated system—one in which the parties may choose to remove their disputes from the formal legal system at any time should they choose to negotiate privately. Thus, the key to understanding the appropriateness of any negotiation process is whether justice is ill-served by the processes the parties choose, be they public litigation or private negotiation. Difficulties abound here—what are the appropriate baseline measures of what is a good settlement or fair process? Can the parties or their lawyers make an intelligent choice of process? Do they understand enough about the differences between and among processes? Are the lawyers sufficiently skilled at either negotiation or advocative activities or both to choose the process that will work most effectively for their clients? Most significantly, which processes will produce the 'best' solution?"[1]

Menkel-Meadow's point is that it will require a more sophisticated analysis of particular cases to determine the merits (or not) of ADR as opposed to litigation. She suggests that there are no simple answers. This point is one to bear in mind as you examine the various perspectives on ADR which are the focus of this section.

---

[1] Carrie Menkel-Meadow, "Lawyer Negotiations: theories and Realities—What We Learn from Mediation" (1993) 56 M.L.R., 361 at 369–370.

FEMINIST PERSPECTIVES ON MEDIATION

Feminist lawyers and legal scholars have long considered the promise and perils of ADR. In particular, mediation has been the subject of considerable debate, especially in a family law context. The following two excerpts underscore both the possibilities and also the pitfalls of mediation; in terms of advancing an alternative approach to law and dispute resolution. We start with the case *for* mediation.

Janet Rifkin, "Mediation from a Feminist Perspective: Promise and Problems" (1984) 2 *Law and Inequality* 21 at 21, 25:

"The interest in alternative dispute resolution is intensifying in this country and others as well. Programs offering mediation, arbitration, negotiation and conciliation services are proliferating throughout the United States, Canada, Australia and Western Europe. These programs may be court-related or community-based. In either case, the overt justifications for mediation programs are similar. Mediating conflict as a substitute for litigating disputes has been justified by two basic rationales: First, the formal court system is not suited to handle the range and number of disputes being brought to it. Second, the adversary process itself is not suited to resolve interpersonal disputes.

While mediation is flourishing, concern about the theory and practice of 'informal' justice is also increasing. Most of the criticisms focus on the manipulative potential of informal systems such as mediation. For example, critics suggest the bureaucratic logic that supports state legality is as much a part of the process in informal and non-bureaucratic settings as it is in the formal court of law. Critics also suggest that the state, faced with fiscal crisis, achieves spending cuts by resorting to informalization, accompanied by appeals to popular participation, consensual social life, and the struggle against bureaucracy. Others argue that mediation fosters the privatization of life—the cult of the personal—and denies the existence of irreconcilable structural conflicts between classes or between citizen and state. Finally, critics claim that mediation is detrimental to the interests of women, who, being less empowered, need both the formal legal system and aggressive legal representation to protect existing rights and pursue new legal safeguards.

Although these criticisms remain, the debate about mediation lacks a careful questioning of law and alternative dispute programs from a feminist perspective. For the most part, mediation's critics predicate their questions on the traditional view of law that litigation leads to social change and that the 'lawsuit' is the appropriate and most effective vehicle for challenging unfair social practices, for protecting individuals, and for delineating new areas of guaranteed 'rights.'

This dominant view leaves unchallenged the patriarchal paradigm of law as hierarchy, combat, and adversarialness; and, therefore, generates only a certain kind of questioning of mediation. This viewpoint has not asked whether and in what way alternative dispute resolution reflects a feminist analysis of law and conflict resolution, and whether in theory and practice mediation challenges or reinforces gender inequality in contemporary society.

My intention in this discussion is to articulate some of the questions basic to an understanding of the relationship between law, mediation and feminist inquiry. . . . What is not yet clearly developed is how mediation in theory reflects 'a new jurisprudence, a new relation between life and law.' Further, what is not yet known is whether in practice, mediating disputes reflects feminist jurisprudential differences from the male ideology of law or whether mediating simply reinforces the 'objective epistemology' of law. . . .

Mediation in practice operates as a process of discussion, clarification, and compromise aided by third party facilitators. It is a process in which the third party has no state-enforced power. A third party's power lies in the ability to persuade the parties to reach a voluntary settlement. It involves the creation of consensus between the parties in which the parties are brought together in an atmosphere of confidentiality to discover shared social and moral values as a means of coming to an agreement.

In mediation, the focus is not on formal and substantive rights. The emphasis is on the process by which the individual parties are encouraged to work out their own solution in a spirit of compromise. The intervention of a mediator turns the initial dyad of a dispute into a triadic interaction of some kind. However, the disputing parties retain their ability to decide whether or not to agree and accept proposals for an outcome irrespective of the source of the proposals.

The following chart highlights some of the main contrasts between adjudication and the practice of mediation.

Adjudication	Mediation
public	private
formal	informal
strict evidentiary rules	no formal parameters—conversationalist
coercive	voluntary
emphasis on conflict of interest, value dissensus	emphasis on areas of agreement, points in common
win/lose—combative	compromise—conciliatory
decision oriented	agreement oriented
rule oriented	person oriented
professional decision maker	community lay volunteers
representation by lawyer	direct participation

Although the mediator is a neutral intervenor with no self-interest, a mediator does become a negotiator. In that role the mediator inevitably brings to the process, deliberately or not, certain ideas, knowledge and assumptions. What a mediator can do is also affected by the particular context and the parties' expectations of mediation. . . .

The rhetoric of mediation rejects the 'objectivist epistemology' of the law. Theoretically, in mediation precedents, rules, and a legalized conception of facts are not only irrelevant but constrain the mediator's job of helping the parties to reorient their perception of the problem to the extent that an agreement can be reached. The legal rights of the parties are not central to the discussion which takes place in mediation. Again, in theory, the lack of focus in mediation on abstract legal rights contrasts with the emphasis on them in legal proceedings.

These differences, however, are clearer in theory than in practice. The following two case studies reflect this. . . .

Case study 1: separation and divorce

The participants in this study were a man and a woman who wanted to separate after fifteen years of marriage. They had three children aged six, eight, and ten. They had each retained separate counsel but after legal negotiations had broken down they decided to try mediation.

The woman came to the office first. The couple had agreed to separate ten months before but still occupied the same house. Relations were hostile and communication strained. The woman said that her children were not speaking to her and she felt that her husband was turning them against her. At the initial interview the woman said that the atmosphere among them—the lawyers, the children, and she and her husband—was so hostile that resolution of their marital dispute appeared impossible. She also indicated that she thought he needed 'help.'

The husband's interview verified her description. His anger and frustration were compounded because he had lost his job and was moving out of town within a month. He wanted to resolve the dispute before he moved. He also commented that she needed 'help.'

The following is a *summary* of their concerns:

Custody: *He* wanted custody of the children.

                   She supported his having custody, but feared that she might never see them again. During the mediation she agreed to give him full custody of the children once assured of ample visitation rights.

Child Support: *He* would 'take care of his kids.'

                   She was not in a position to support the children.

Alimony: *He* wasn't willing to give her alimony.

                   She was uncertain of her financial needs but said that she wanted some financial help while looking for a job. She agreed to no alimony.

Property: The financial settlement involved an extensive and complex division of property. The main asset was their house. She agreed to accept a lump sum of money and twenty-five per cent of the net sale of the house over £80,000 in lieu of alimony.

Their attitudes and relationship with their lawyers became one of the most difficult and perhaps interesting aspects of this case. Both of their attorneys initially agreed that mediation might be useful. The man stated that he planned to drop his lawyer and represent himself in court if the mediation went well. His lawyer offered to put any final mediation agreement into legal language for presentation to the court. In the end, the man represented himself with his attorney's approval.

The woman came to the project with conflicting feelings about her lawyer. Although aware that she might gain financially with a formal, contested divorce, she feared the process could irreparably damage her relationship with her children. The case coordinator initially advised her to talk with her attorney about using mediation. She did so and her attorney agreed, with some reservations about her ability to protect her own interests. As the mediation proceeded, she was advised several times to consult with her attorney but the case coordinator suspected that she was not doing so.

In the end, her attorney rejected the final mediation agreement and told her it was impossible for him to represent her if she insisted on keeping the agreement as the divorce settlement. She chose to discontinue the relationship with her attorney and she, like her husband, represented herself in court proceedings. Her attorney was very upset and told the judge in her presence that he objected to her mediated settlement. The judge accepted the agreement after speaking with her at length.

Case study 2: sexual harassment

A twenty-five year old undergraduate woman was very troubled about what she described as sexual harassment by one of her professors. She claimed that he had made many inappropriate inquiries in class about the backgrounds of the women students, wanting to know about their boyfriends, their parties, and other similar matters. During a conversation with him regarding a research assistantship, he offered to drive her home. She consented to this and on the way, they stopped for a drink. During their conversation she learned the position would involve working closely with him. The conversation led to a discussion of personal matters and he told her of his unhappy marriage. Later on he mentioned that he was very attracted to her and would like to go to bed with her. She felt extremely uneasy and said that she would have to think about it.

The next day she went to his office and rejected his sexual proposal. He said that he was disappointed. Two weeks passed without any mention of the job. When she finally approached him, he told her the position was no longer available. She was upset and went to the department chair, who recommended that she consider mediation. She also spoke to the school's dean, who initially reacted with disbelief, but later believed the student after speaking to the professor. The dean told them both that he wanted the dispute worked out in mediation, but indicated that if he received another complaint he would dismiss the faculty member.

In a lengthy meeting with the mediation staff, the student learned that she could arrange for a more formal, potentially punitive process by requesting the administration to form an ad hoc hearing committee. She considered this alternative but requested mediation, claiming she did not want the professor fired. The professor also agreed to mediation.

During a four hour mediation session with the two parties, the student explained why the incident was so upsetting. The professor responded with tears and an apology. At the end of the mediation, they shook hands and both expressed satisfaction to the mediator. She said she mostly wanted the opportunity to make him hear her point of view. He said he understood and expressed appreciation at being spared the humiliation of a more public proceeding. She also expressed her relief at being able to avoid the pain of a public and more formalized hearing where her credibility might be subject to review and cross-examination. At the end of the mediation he apologized and offered her a job, which she rejected. He also promised not to penalize her by lowering her grade.

Summary

Although critics of mediation charge that it may keep the less powerful party from achieving equality and equal bargaining power, it is not so clear from these case studies how this operates in practice. These objections to mediation are inextricably tied to the view that the formal legal system offers both a better alternative and a greater possibility of achieving a fair and just resolution to the conflict. The general assumption that the lawyer can 'help' the client more meaningfully than a mediator is part of the problem with this view. In many instances, although new substantive rights or legal protections are realized, patterns of domination are reinforced by the lawyer-client relationship, in which the client is a passive recipient of the lawyer's expertise. This is particularly true for women clients, for whom patterns of domination are at the heart of the problem.

In both case studies, it can be argued that the pattern of *dominance* was affected. 'Dominance produces hierarchical arrangement of the partners, which is reflected in differences in such aspects of the relationship as freedom of movement, the utilization of resources, and rights and responsibilities.' In these situations, the women felt that the relationship of dominance had been altered and the hierarchy in the relationship had to some extent been altered. A transformation of the pattern of dominance will affect the power relationships as well.

Although mediation programs are proliferating, many questions remain. Why is the interest in alternatives intensifying? What kinds of disputes are best suited to mediation?

Who should be mediators—lay persons, lawyers, or other professionals? What kind of training should mediators receive? Can mediation in practice alter the patterns of gender inequality in our society more effectively than formal law? Can the teaching of mediation begin to change and challenge the traditional approach to legal study? The answers to these questions may remain unclear, but if these issues are not addressed, mediation will simply become another popular 'technique' marketed as a panacea for a range of complex social problems."

NOTES AND QUESTIONS

• According to Rifkin, in what ways does mediation exemplify a "new way of thinking about law"? In other words, how does the process of mediation differ from more formal and legalised methods of resolving disputes?

• Consider the two case studies discussed in the extract. Did you find the outcomes to be satisfactory or problematic? Was the mediation process able to cope adequately with the power relationships that existed as between the parties?

• Do you think that mediation *necessarily* provides a preferable way of resolving disputes, as opposed to a more formal and binding legal process, in cases involving domestic violence or abusive relationships? Are there advantages in these (and other) cases provided by the legal system and the "rule of law"? For further reading on the subject, see Hilary Astor, "The Weight of Silence; Talking About Violence in Family Mediation", in *Public and Private: Feminist Legal Debates* (Margaret Thornton, ed., Oxford University Press, Melbourne, 1995).

As a contrast to Rifkin's advocacy of mediation, examine Grillo's concerns below. Although she is particularly concerned about *mandatory* mediation processes, which we have already considered, she has reservations about mediation in general, and the dangers for women in dispute situations.

Trina Grillo, "The Mediation Alternative: Process Dangers for Women" (1991) 100 *Yale Law Journal* 1545 at 1547, 1601, 1607:

"The western concept of law is based on a patriarchal paradigm characterized by hierarchy, linear reasoning, the resolution of disputes through the application of abstract principles, and the idea of the reasonable person. Its fundamental aspiration is objectivity, and to that end it separates public from private, form from substance, and process from policy. This objectivist paradigm is problematic in many circumstances, but never more so than in connection with a marital dissolution in which the custody of children is at issue, where the essential question for the court is what is to happen next in the family. The family court system, aspiring to the idea of objectivity and operating as an adversary system, can be relied on neither to produce just results nor to treat those subject to it respectfully and humanely.

There is little doubt that divorce procedure needs to be reformed, but reformed how? Presumably, any alternative should be at least as just, and at least as humane, as the current system, particularly for those who are least powerful in society. Mediation has been put

forward, with much fanfare, as such an alternative. The impetus of the mediation movement has been so strong that in some states couples disputing custody are required by
statute or local rule to undergo a mandatory mediation process if they are unable to reach
an agreement on their own. Mediation has been embraced for a number of reasons. First,
it rejects an objectivist approach to conflict resolution, and promises to consider disputes
in terms of relationships and responsibility. Second, the mediation process is, at least in
theory, cooperative and voluntary, not coercive. The mediator does not make a decision;
rather, each party speaks for himself. Together they reach an agreement that meets the
parties' mutual needs. In this manner, the process is said to enable the parties to exercise
self-determination and eliminate the hierarchy of dominance that characterizes the
judge/litigant and lawyer/client relationships. Third, since in mediation there are no rules
of evidence or legalistic notions of relevancy, decisions supposedly may be informed by
context rather than by abstract principle. Finally, in theory at least, emotions are recognized and incorporated into the mediation process. This conception of mediation has led
some commentators to characterize it as a feminist alternative to the patriarchally inspired
adversary system.

Whether mandatory mediation, required as part of court proceedings, fulfills these aspirations, or instead substitutes another objectivist, patriarchal, and even more damaging
form of conflict resolution for its adversarial counterpart, is the subject of this Article.
Many divorcing couples seem pleased with their mediation experiences. Indeed, studies
have shown that mediation clients are more satisfied with their divorce outcomes than
persons using the adversary system. Although there are significant methodological problems with each of these studies, the existence of substantial client satisfaction with some
models of mediation cannot be completely discounted.

Nonetheless, I conclude that mandatory mediation provides neither a more just nor a
more humane alternative to the adversarial system of adjudication of custody, and, therefore, does not fulfill its promises. In particular, quite apart from whether an acceptable
result is reached, mandatory mediation can be destructive to many women and some men
because it requires them to speak in a setting they have not chosen and often imposes a
rigid orthodoxy as to how they should speak, make decisions, and be. This orthodoxy is
imposed through subtle and not-so-subtle messages about appropriate conduct and about
what may be said in mediation. It is an orthodoxy that often excludes the possibility of the
parties' speaking with their authentic voices.

Moreover, people vary greatly in the extent to which their sense of self is 'relational'—
that is, defined in terms of connection to others. If two parties are forced to engage with
one another, and one has a more relational sense of self than the other, that party may feel
compelled to maintain her connection with the other, even to her own detriment. For this
reason, the party with the more relational sense of self will be at a disadvantage in a mediated negotiation. Several prominent researchers have suggested that, as a general rule,
women have a more relational sense of self than do men, although there is little agreement
on what the origin of this difference might be. Thus, rather than being a feminist alternative to the adversary system, mediation has the potential actively to harm women.

Some of the dangers of mandatory mediation apply to voluntary mediation as well.
Voluntary mediation should not be abandoned, but should be recognized as a powerful
process which should be used carefully and thoughtfully. Entering into such a process with
one who has known you intimately and who now seems to threaten your whole life and
being has great creative, but also enormous destructive, power. Nonetheless, it should be
recognized that when two people themselves decide to mediate and then physically appear
at the mediation sessions, that decision and their continued presence serve as a rough indication that it is not too painful or too dangerous for one or both of them to go on. . . .

As discussed earlier, several feminist scholars have suggested that women have a more
'relational' sense of self than do men. The most influential of these researchers, Carol
Gilligan, describes two different, gendered modes of thought. The female mode is characterized by an 'ethic of care' which emphasizes nurturance, connection with others, and contextual thinking. The male mode is characterized by an 'ethic of justice' which emphasizes
individualism, the use of rules to resolve moral dilemmas, and equality. Under Gilligan's

view, the male mode leads one to strive for individualism and autonomy, while the female mode leads one to strive for connection with and caring for others. Some writers, seeing a positive virtue in the ethic of care, have applied Gilligan's work to the legal system. But her work has been criticized by others for its methodology, its conflation of biological sex with gender, and its failure to include race and class differences in its analysis. (Indeed, it is not likely that the male/female differences Gilligan notes are consistent across racial and class lines.) The 'ethic of care' has also been viewed as the manifestation of a system of gender domination. Nevertheless, it is clear that those who operate in a 'female mode'—whether biologically male or female—will respond more 'selflessly' to the demands of mediation.

Whether the ethic of care is to be enshrined as a positive virtue, or criticized as a characteristic not belonging to all women and contributing to their oppression, one truth emerges: many women see themselves, and judge their own worth, primarily in terms of relationships. This perspective on themselves has consequences for how they function in mediation.

Carrie Menkel-Meadow has suggested that the ethic of care can and should be brought into the practice of law—that the world of lawyering would look very different from the perspective of that ethic. Some commentators have identified mediation as a way to incorporate the ethic of care into the legal system and thereby modify the harshness of the adversary process. And, indeed, at first glance, mediation in the context of divorce might be seen as a way of bringing the woman-identified values of intimacy, nurturance, and care into a legal system that is concerned with the most fundamental aspects of women's and men's lives.

If mediation does not successfully introduce an ethic of care, however, but instead merely sells itself on that promise while delivering something coercive in its place, the consequences will be disastrous for a woman who embraces a relational sense of self. If she is easily persuaded to be cooperative, but her partner is not, she can only lose. If it is indeed her disposition to be caring and focused on relationships, and she has been rewarded for that focus and characterized as 'unfeminine' when she departs from it, the language of relationship, caring, and cooperation will be appealing to her and make her vulnerable. Moreover, the intimation that she is not being cooperative and caring or that she is thinking of herself instead of thinking selflessly of the children can shatter her self-esteem and make her lose faith in herself. In short, in mediation, such a woman may be encouraged to repeat exactly those behaviors that have proven hazardous to her in the past. . . .

It has been said that '[d]isputes are cultural events, evolving within a framework of rules about what is worth fighting for, what is the normal or moral way to fight, what kinds of wrongs warrant action, and what kinds of remedies are acceptable.' The process by which a society resolves conflict is closely related to its social structure. Implicit in this choice is a message about what is respectable to do or want or say, what the obligations are of being a member of the society or of a particular group within it, and what it takes to be thought of as a good person leading a virtuous life. In the adversary system, it is acceptable to want to win. It is not only acceptable, but expected, that one will rely on a lawyer and advocate for oneself without looking out for the adversary. The judge, a third party obligated to be neutral and bound by certain formalities, bears the ultimate responsibility for deciding the outcome. To the extent that women are more likely than men to believe in communication as a mode of conflict resolution and to appreciate the importance of an adversary's interests, this system does not always suit their needs.

On the other hand, under a scheme of mediation, the standards of acceptable behavior and desires change fundamentally. Parties are to meet with each other, generally without their lawyers. They are encouraged to look at each other's needs and to reach a cooperative resolution based on compromise. Although there are few restrictions on her role in the process, the mediator bears no ultimate, formal responsibility for the outcome of the mediation. In sum, when mediation is the prototype for dispute resolution, the societal message is that a good person—a person following the rules—cooperates, communicates, and compromises.

The glories of cooperation, however, are easily exaggerated. If one party appreciates cooperation more than the other, the parties might compromise unequally. Moreover, the self-disclosure that cooperation requires, when imposed and not sought by the parties, may feel and be invasive. Thus, rather than representing a change in the system to accommodate the 'feminine voice,' cooperation might, at least for the time being, be detrimental to their lives and the lives of their children. Under a system of forced mediation, women are made to feel selfish for wanting to assert their own interests based on their need to survive."

NOTES AND QUESTIONS

- Explain the difference between an "ethic of care" and an "ethic of justice". To what extent do you think those ethics are gendered? Are there political dangers to women implicit in the ascription of an "ethic of care" and to men?

- Grillo's article raises a point which we have already considered: is compromise always a good thing? Can you think of circumstances where it clearly is not? In those cases, is mediation a poor substitute for more formalised legal proceedings?

- Which argument do you find more convincing—Rifkin's or Grillo's? Does it all depend upon the particular context of the dispute? Should we avoid "grand theories" about the promise and dangers of mediation in favour of context-specific analysis?

INDEX